Visual C++.NET:
The Complete Reference

Visual C++.NET: The Complete Reference

William H. Murray III
and Chris H. Pappas

McGraw-Hill/Osborne

New York Chicago San Francisco Lisbon
London Madrid Mexico City Milan New Delhi
San Juan Seoul Singapore Sydney Toronto

McGraw-Hill/Osborne
2600 Tenth Street
Berkeley, California 94710
U.S.A.

To arrange bulk purchase discounts for sales promotions, premiums, or fund-raisers, please contact **McGraw-Hill/**Osborne at the above address. For information on translations or book distributors outside the U.S.A., please see the International Contact Information page immediately following the index of this book.

Visual C++.NET: The Complete Reference

1234567890 DOC DOC 01987654321

ISBN 0-07-212958-1

Publisher
   Brandon A. Nordin

**Vice President &
Associate Publisher**
   Scott Rogers

Acquisitions Editor
   Ann Sellers

Acquisitions Coordinator
   Tim Madrid

Technical Editor
   Paul Garland

Project Manager
   Deidre Dolce

Freelance Project Manager
   Laurie Stewart

Copy Editors
   Sarah Kaminker and
   Sachi Guzman

Proofreader
   Kelly Marshall

Indexers
   William Murray and
   Chris Pappas

Computer Designers
   Maureen Forys and
   Kate Kaminski,
   Happenstance
   Type-O-Rama

Illustrator
   Brian Wells

Series Design
   Peter Hancik

This book was composed with QuarkXPress 4.11 on a Macintosh G4.

To our friend, Emma Scearce

Contents at a Glance

Contents

Part III

Foundations for Object-Oriented Programming

Part IV

Windows and Wizards

Part V

Advanced Programming Concepts

Part VI

Appendices

Introduction

This book was written with two main goals: to help you become more familiar with the Microsoft Visual C++/C# compiler component of Visual Studio.NET, and to help people with different programming backgrounds become more proficient in C++, C#, and 32-bit Windows programming. This is quite a task, even for a book containing hundreds of pages, but it was written with you in mind.

Our two major goals encompass a number of specific aims.

- This book introduces you to the powerful programming tools provided in your Microsoft Visual Studio.NET C++ and C# compiler package. These include the compiler, debugger, and various Windows ME, 2000, and XP development tools. This book complements your Microsoft reference manuals and on-line help to provide a quick start with each of the components in the compiler package.

- Programmers need a thorough understanding of each programming language they intend to use. You will find that this book covers all the important programming concepts in the C++ and Windows languages, including the Microsoft Foundation Class Library (MFC), and provides a great introduction to the new C# language. If you are a novice programmer, early chapters will help you build the solid foundation you need to write more sophisticated programs. For advanced programmers, early chapters will serve as a reference and will introduce you to exciting C++ and C# concepts.

- You will learn how to debug program code and write programs that are free of syntax and logical programming errors.

- You will gain an understanding of how procedural programming differs from object-oriented programming and how to develop simple OOPs programs.

- You will explore the exciting world of Microsoft Windows programming. Chapters are devoted to helping you understand Windows concepts and how to write simple to intermediate programs in both C++ and C#.

We believe in teaching by example. We have made every effort to make each example in this book simple, complete, and bug-free. You can study these examples, alter them, and expand them into programs tailored to fit your needs.

This book will serve as a lasting reference to the Microsoft Visual Studio.NET C++ and C# compiler and the tools it supports.

How this Book Is Organized

Chapters 1 through 4 introduce you to the programming tools contained in the Microsoft Visual Studio.NET C++ and C# compiler package.

Chapters 5 through 14 teach the foundational programming concepts needed for the C++ language. These are procedure-oriented chapters that teach traditional C++ programming concepts.

Chapters 15 through 19 give you a complete introduction to object-oriented programming with C++. Here you will find terminology, definitions, and complete programming examples to help you with your development of object-oriented programs. Chapter 19 discusses in detail the use of the Standard Template Library (STL).

Chapters 20 and 21 introduce you to Microsoft Windows ME, 2000, and XP programming concepts and show you how to use the Microsoft Visual Studio.NET C++ compiler to develop applications that include GDI primitives, cursors, icons, menus, and dialog boxes. The applications in these chapters are traditional message-based programs.

Chapters 22 and 23 are devoted to programming with the Microsoft Foundation Class Library (MFC). By using the power of C++ classes, the MFC will shorten both your Windows application development cycle and your program length.

Chapter 24 teaches you how to build Windows applications, not with the MFC of earlier chapters, but with the new and exciting graphical interface of C#. You'll learn how to integrate C# concepts into usable Windows code and see plenty of examples in this chapter.

Chapter 25 takes us back to the Standard Template Library (STL) but with a new twist—using the STL in Windows applications. Complete code is provided for the applications in this chapter.

Chapter 26 explains the concepts of Object Linking and Embedding (OLE) and provides example code that you can expand into additional projects.

The MFC and Wizard discussion continues with Chapter 27 where you'll be introduced to the concepts of ActiveX control design. Again, complete project code is provided in this chapter.

In Chapters 28 and 29 you'll learn the fundamentals of Dynamic Link Libraries (DLLs) and investigate problems that they can bring to the NET.

How the Material Was Developed

The material in this book was developed and tested on a variety of computers. The primary development took place on two HP 1.5 GHz computers with 386 MB of RAM. The applications were tested, at various stages, under Windows ME, 2000, and XP.

The entire manuscript was prepared with Microsoft Office XP. All screen shots were taken with FullShot 6.0, a Windows screen capture utility.

The
Complete
Reference

Visual C++.NET

Part I

A Quick Overview of C++

Visual C++.NET

Chapter 1

The Visual Studio.NET C++ Compiler (Version 7)

The new Microsoft Visual Studio.NET C++ compiler provides you with a comprehensive, up-to-the-minute production-level development environment for creating all Windows ME, Windows 2000, and XP applications. Visual Studio is the complete suite of tools for rapidly building Enterprise Web applications, in addition to its ability to build classic, high-performing desktop applications. This suite includes powerful component-based development tools, such as the new Microsoft developed language C# (pronounced see-sharp), Visual Basic, Visual C++, and Visual FoxPro, as well as a number of additional technologies to simplify team-based design, development, and deployment of your solutions. Also included is the MSDN Library, which contains all the documentation for these development tools. Microsoft's Visual Studio.NET C++ (version 7.0) ships in three different configurations: the Standard, the Professional, and the Enterprise Editions.

What's New for Visual C++ Version 7.0?

The most exciting addition to Visual Studio.NET C++ is the incorporation of Microsoft's new premier programming language C#. Microsoft Visual C++ version 7.0 provides many other new features such as AutoCompletion to facilitate coding, and Edit and Continue to optimize your debugging sessions. C#, Visual Basic, Visual C++, and Microsoft Developer Network (MSDN) make up the Visual Studio Integrated Development Environment (IDE). Sharing a single IDE provides many benefits, including consolidating similar tools from the various products into a set of shared tools used throughout Visual Studio.

The Visual Studio Start Page provides a quick way to set your user preferences for how the IDE behaves, including the active keyboard mapping scheme, window layout, and help filter, as well as the ability to access recent, existing, or new projects. You can also view links to the latest articles, events, and topics on MSDN Online. The Visual Studio Start Page appears by default each time you launch Visual Studio and is the default Web browser home page for the IDE.

You can display Web pages directly within the IDE. To display a Web browser window in the IDE, choose View | Web Browser. The first time you open a Web browser window, the Visual Studio Start Page appears by default. When a Web browser window is open, the Web toolbar appears, which allows you to enter URLs, move backward and forward within the navigation history, and return to the Web browser home page. You can also now access your Web browser favorites as well as add links to the favorites list from within Visual Studio.

The Command window is a union of a command line and Visual Basic's Immediate window. You can enter IDE command names into the window by typing an angle bracket (>), as well as entering a number of Immediate window commands. You can create aliases, or short names, for commands. Auto-completion works for command names, aliases, and file names. In Immediate mode, you can execute code statements, set or assign variables, evaluate expressions, and more.

Microsoft provides two versions of Visual C++ 7.0. The following discussion presents the purpose and special features of each edition. This text was prepared using the Enterprise Edition, however all of the material covered (except where noted in the text) is portable to all three editions.

Professional Edition

The Professional Edition of Microsoft Visual C++ version 7.0 provides features that let you develop and distribute commercial-quality software products. The Professional Edition includes the following features:

Programming Features

- C# programming language
- Microsoft Foundation Classes
- Active Template Library (ATL)
- ATL server
- Component Object Model (COM)
- Compiler COM support
- OLE DB Provider and Consumer templates
- C/C++ run-time libraries
- Standard C++ library
- Support for common controls in Internet Explorer
- Active document containment
- Samples

Internet Features

- Internet Server API (ISAPI) extensions
- CHttpConnection (and other CHttp* MFC classes)
- CInternetConnection (and other CInternet* MFC classes)

ActiveX Controls

- Composite control fundamentals
- Developing MFC ActiveX controls
- Developing ATL ActiveX controls
- Adding an ActiveX control to a project

Project Features

- Wizard support for creating applications
- Integrated Development Environment and more IDE topics
- Debugging your application
- Component and Object Gallery
- InstallShield

Optimizations

- Inline optimizing of your code
- Compiler optimization options
- Linker Optimizations (/OPT)
- C++ Exception Handling

Database Support

- ActiveX controls for Databinding
- ADO
- Read-only versions of Microsoft Visual Database Tools (Enterprise Edition has full-feature Visual Database Tools)

Enterprise Edition (Used for This Book)

The Enterprise Edition of Microsoft Visual C++ 7.0 provides many tools and components for building and validating enterprise-level distributed Component Object Model (COM) applications. Visual C++ Enterprise Edition is best suited for developers building distributed database applications in a team environment. For these developers, SQL debugging and MTS are integrated into the development environment making development of distributed-transaction-oriented applications faster and easier. (SQL Server and MTS come with the Enterprise Edition of Visual C++.) The Enterprise Edition also includes Microsoft Visual Source Safe, a tool that allows a team of developers to share and mutually update a common repository of source code.

The Visual C++ Enterprise Edition includes all the features in the Professional Edition, plus the following features:

- Microsoft Transaction Server
- Visual database tools
- SQL Editor
- SQL Debugger
- MFC Database Classes

- ADO Databinding
- AppWizard and Data Sources
- Remote automation components
- MFC Databinding
- Visual SourceSafe
- Remote Automation

The following samples are also included with the Visual C++ Enterprise Edition:

- OLE DB templates samples index
- Visual C++ Samples home page

Note   *Unless specifically mentioned, the applications in this book can be compiled with any version of the compiler. For example, the applications in Chapters 1 through 20 are standard command-line C or C++ applications that can be run under MS_DOS or in a compatibility box under Windows ME, Windows 2000, or XP. Likewise, the Windows applications developed in Chapter 25 will run under Windows ME, Windows 2000, or XP.*

Recommended Hardware and Software

Minimal hardware and software requirements are not always the optimal choice for ease of use, performance, and overall product enjoyment. We recommend the following system profile to optimize the development cycle of Visual Studio.NET projects:

- A Pentium III–based PC, running at 733 MHz (or higher)
- 256 MB of RAM
- A 20 GB hard disk
- A Super-VGA monitor
- 30x CD-ROM drive (for online documentation)
- Microsoft IntelliPoint mouse
- Cable or DSL Internet connection

You will want a fast microprocessor that can handle the size and complexity of advanced Windows applications. Having a lot of RAM memory maximizes the overall performance of both Microsoft Visual Studio.NET and the Windows environment. (You can also obtain many of these performance enhancements by having a large amount of free disk space.)

Two operating systems are emerging as the new standard for 32-bit PC-based computers: Windows ME, and its more robust cousin Windows 2000. If you have not upgraded to either Windows ME or Windows 2000, you should do so before installing your Microsoft Visual Studio.NET package.

The improvements made to Windows ME and Windows 2000 provide you with the features and performance necessary to create state-of-the-art Windows applications. As you develop these applications in a graphical environment, your eyes will appreciate Super-VGA resolution monitors. Buy a monitor with as large a screen as possible.

A cable or DSL Internet connection will enhance your upload and download capabilities. You'll find this critical, if for nothing else than product updates.

A Typical Windows Installation

The Microsoft Visual C++ compiler package installs almost automatically. However, there are some questions that you will need immediate answers for. In this section we'll take a look at a typical installation for the 32-bit version of the compiler.

1. Run the setup.exe program on your first Visual C++ diskette or CD-ROM, while operating under Windows ME, Windows 2000, or XP.

2. You will be given a choice of install options such as Typical, Custom, Minimum, or CD_ROM. The amount of hard disk space you must have depends upon the option you choose. We recommend a Typical installation. It is also possible to set which hard drive and/or subdirectory the installation will take place under.

3. You will be prompted for your Name, Organization, and Product ID. Enter this information carefully.

4. At this point, files will be copied from your diskettes or CD-ROM to your hard disk. You can view the progress by watching the File Copy Process dialog box.

5. With the installation complete, reboot your entire system to allow all changes to take effect.

Directories

The following table shows a subset of the more frequently accessed subdirectories for the Visual C++ compiler installation made in the Vc7 (Visual Studio version 70) subdirectory:

Location	Purpose
Atlmfc	Atlmfc include, lib, and source folder
Bin	Executable files and build tools needed to build 32-bit applications

Location	Purpose
Crt	C run-time library folder
Include	C++ run-time and header files
Lib	C++ run-time and Win32 SDK libraries
Vcprojects	Subdirectory used to organize your development projects
VCResourseTemplates	Subdirectory used to organize object templates

You will also find several readme files located in the Microsoft Visual Studio.NET subdirectory. These files are used to provide the latest release (and bug) information for the compiler.

Documentation

Visual C++ online documentation consists of Books Online and the new Dynamic Help. Books Online is the documentation set for Visual C++ in online format. Dynamic Help (accessed by selecting Help | Dynamic Help) allows you to quickly look up context-sensitive information while you program. The hierarchical display within the Dynamic Help pane automatically tracks your every keystroke, matching its contents to Visual Studio features, language features, and compiler options as you change input focus. Every Dynamic Help topic has a link to Books Online, where complete information is available.

Depending on which install option you choose, Visual C++ will set up Quick Reference files on your hard disk, while Books Online files may remain on the CD-ROM.

Note

Choose this install configuration if you need to conserve hard disk space.

You can customize where to set up files or where to get information, or go directly to Books Online for context-sensitive (F1) help. Topics covered include:

- How to use Books Online
- User's guides
- Microsoft Foundation Classes (MFCs)
- Programming with the Microsoft Foundation Class library
- Class library reference
- Shared Classes
- Standard C++ library
- Old iostream library

- MFC samples
- MFC technical notes
- C/C++
- Programming techniques
- C language reference
- C++ language reference
- Run-time library reference
- iostream reference (changes from iostream.h to iostream)
- Preprocessor reference
- C/C++ samples
- Win32 Software Development Kit (SDK)
- API 32 functions
- Win32s programmer's reference
- Windows sockets
- OLE Software Development Kit (SDK)

The Development System

The Microsoft 32-bit Visual C++ compiler for Windows ME, Windows 2000, and XP incorporates new, fully integrated Windows development tools and a visual interface. For example, the debugging capabilities of Microsoft's original CodeView are now directly accessible from within the compiler's integrated debugger. The following sections list those stand-alone utilities that are now incorporated directly into the Microsoft Visual C++ compiler.

Solution Explorer

The Visual Studio 7.0 Solution Explorer is an enhancement to the Workspace View found in its predecessor. Solution Explorer integrates into one view resource lists, class lists, file views, and any combination of Help views, such as content or index.

The Integrated Debugger

Microsoft pulls the horsepower of its original CodeView debugger directly into the Visual C++ platform with its integrated debugger. The debugger is accessed by selecting Debug | Start Debugging. The integrated debugger allows you to execute programs in single steps, view and change variable contents, and even back out of code sections. You will find it to be a big help when programs compile but don't seem to perform as expected.

The Integrated Resource Editors

These editors are accessed from the Resource menu. The resource editors allow you to design and create Windows resources such as bitmaps, cursors, icons, menus, and dialog boxes. Resources allow you to create visually appealing user interfaces to your applications. In the next sections, we'll look at some specific information on four of the most popular resource editors.

The Dialog Box Editor

The Dialog Box editor is a slick, graphical development tool that allows you to easily and quickly create professional-looking dialog boxes. The Dialog Box editor allows you to customize a dialog box's labels, framing, option and check box selections, text windows, and scroll bars.

   The Dialog Box editor allows you to combine numerous controls into your custom dialog boxes. Controls combine a visual graphical representation of some feature with a predefined set of properties that you can customize. For example, check boxes, radio buttons, and list boxes are all forms of Windows controls.

The Image Editors

The graphical image editors allow you to easily create custom bitmaps, icons, and cursors. A bitmap is a picture of something, for example, an exclamation point used in a warning message. An icon is a small color image used to represent an application when it has been minimized. Visual C++ even allows you to use an image editor to create custom cursors. For example, you could design a financial package with a cursor that looks like a dollar sign. Custom icons, cursors, and bitmaps can be saved with an .rc file extension and used in resource script files. You'll learn how these resources are used in Chapters 20 through 23.

The Binary Editor

The Binary editor allows you to edit a resource at the binary level in either hexadecimal or ASCII format. You can also use the Find command to search for either ASCII strings or hexadecimal bytes, and use regular expressions with the Find command to match a pattern. You should use the Binary editor only when you need to view or make minor changes to custom resources or resource types not supported by the Microsoft Developer Studio environment.

The String Editor

The String editor allows you to create and edit string tables. A string table is a Windows resource that contains a list of IDs, values, and captions for all the strings of your application. For example, the status bar prompts are located in the string table. An application can have only one string table. String tables make it easy to localize your application into different languages. If all strings are in a string table, you can localize the application by translating the strings (and other resources) without changing source code.

Tools and Utilities

The Developer Studio has many improved features to make it easier than ever to develop world-class applications. Additions include improved support for hosting Visual J++ and Visual InterDev, as well as Microsoft's new C# programming language.

Automation and Macros

Customizable scripts allow you to automate routine or repetitive tasks. Macro recording allows for quick and easy authoring. The Developer Studio allows you to manipulate Studio components as objects, allowing you to automate tasks that include opening, editing, and closing documents, or sizing windows. You can also create integrated add-ins using Developer Studio's object model.

ClassView

ClassView now not only works with Java classes as well as C++ classes, but also with CLS (Common Language Specification) class definitions. You can create new classes using MFC, or your own classes. ClassView can also view and edit interfaces for COM objects implemented in MFC. You can also use folders to organize classes the way you want.

Invariably, within the life cycle of a project you will want to change or add to that project's functionality. Very often this involves creating new classes, adding new member functions and variables, and adding automation methods and properties. In addition to ClassView, Microsoft Visual Studio.NET code Wizards streamline a project's evolution.

Customizable Toolbars and Menus

Developer Studio makes it easy to customize toolbars and menus to fit the way you work. For example, you can:

- Add a menu to a toolbar.
- Add or delete menu commands or toolbar buttons.
- Change a toolbar button into a menu command.
- Clone a menu or toolbar button from one toolbar to another so it is always accessible.
- Design new toolbars or menus.
- Personalize an existing toolbar or menu.
- Reassign a menu command, making it a toolbar button.

Internet Connectivity

Viewing Microsoft on the Web pages in Developer Studio is a snap with the all-new What's New, Online Community, or Search Online Start Page links and your own registered Web browser. This feature allows Visual Studio users assurance of the latest breaking news, documentation, fixes, and/or upgrades as they become available.

Project Solutions and Files

The new Developer Studio's flexible solution system makes it easy to have a workspace with different project types. For example, you can create a solution containing a Visual InterDev project, J++ applet, and now the new C# assembly code. Microsoft Visual C++ solution files have an .sln file extension to distinguish them from workspace files. Note: workspace files now have the extension .dsw (formerly .mdp). Project files (primary builds) now have the extension .vcproj (which were .dsp in VC6 and formerly .mak in VC5). All vcproj files are created when you create a new project within the Developer Studio environment or when you convert a project from a previous version. Projects can now include active documents, such as spreadsheets and Word document files. You can even edit them without leaving Visual Studio's Integrated Development Environment.

When you start a new workspace, the Developer Studio creates a file by the name, yourWorkspaceName.sln, with the new extension .sln. Workspace files no longer include data specific to your local computer. At this point you may:

- Add the workspace file to a previously defined source control project
- Copy a workspace from another computer or a network directory and open the workspace copy directly, without creating a new workspace file for your local computer
- Use resource editors
- Use the Wizard Bar with dialog boxes to hook up code to the visual elements of your program

Wizards

The new Microsoft Developer Studio incorporates many new Wizards, including Wizards for the new integrated C#, Visual Basic.NET, and Visual InterDev packages (available if you have these packages installed). You can use these Wizards to create files, controls, and new types of projects.

Important Compiler Features

The Visual C++ compiler package contains many useful enhancements, new features, and options. The following sections introduce you to these improvements and briefly explain their uses.

Precompiled Headers and Types

Visual C++ places generic types, function prototypes, external references, and member function declarations in special files called header files. These header files contain many of the critical definitions needed by the multiple source files that are pulled together to create the executable version of your program. Portions of these header files are typically recompiled for every module that includes the header. Unfortunately, repeatedly compiling portions of code can cause the compiler to slow down.

Visual C++ speeds up the compile process by allowing you to precompile your header files. While the concept of precompiled headers isn't new, the way that Microsoft has implemented the feature certainly is. Precompilation saves the state of an application's compilation to a certain point and represents the relationship that is set up between the source file and the precompiled header. It is possible to create more than one precompiled header file per source file.

One of the best applications of this technology involves the development cycle of an application that has frequent code changes but not frequent base class definitions. If the header file is precompiled, the compiler can concentrate its time on the changes in the source code. Precompiled headers also provide a compile time boost for applications with headers that comprise large portions of code for a given module, as often happens with C++ programs.

The Visual C++ compiler assumes that the current state of the compiler environment is the same as when any precompiled headers were compiled. The compiler will issue a warning if it detects any inconsistencies. Such inconsistencies could arise from a change in memory models, a change in the state of defined constants, or the selection of different debugging or code generation options.

Unlike many popular C++ compilers, the Microsoft C++ compiler does not restrict precompilation to header files. Since the process allows you to precompile a program up to a specified point, you can even precompile source code. This is extremely significant for C++ programs which contain most of their member function definitions in header files. In general, precompilation is reserved for those portions of your program that are considered stable; it is designed to minimize the time needed to compile the parts of your program under development.

The Microsoft Foundation Class Library

Windows applications are easy to use, however, they are not as easy to develop. Many programmers get waylaid by having to master the use of hundreds of Windows API functions required to write Windows applications.

Microsoft's solution to this steep learning curve is the object-oriented Foundation Classes library. The reusable C++ classes are much easier to master and use. The Microsoft Foundation Class (MFC) library takes full advantage of the data abstraction offered by C++, and its use simplifies Windows programming. Beginning programmers can use the classes in a "cookbook" fashion, and experienced C++ programmers can extend the classes or integrate them into their own class hierarchy.

The MFC library features classes for managing Windows objects and offers a number of general-purpose classes than can be used in both MS-DOS and Windows applications. For example, there are classes for creating and managing files, strings, time, persistent storage, and exception handling.

In effect, the Microsoft Foundation Class library represents virtually every Windows API feature and includes sophisticated code that streamlines message processing, diagnostics, and other details that are a normal part of all Windows applications. This logical combination and enhancement of Windows API functions has nine key advantages:

MFC Library   The MFC library provides support for all of the frequently used Windows API functions including windowing functions, messages, controls, menus, dialog boxes, GDI (graphics device interface), objects (fonts, brushes, pens, and bitmaps), object linking, and the multiple document interface (MDI).

Simple to use MFC Definitions   Microsoft has attempted to match the names of the MFC functions and associated parameters to their Windows API parent classes. This cloning of syntax and definitions minimizes the confusion for experienced Windows programmers rolling their code over to the simplified MFC platform. This common set of definitions and code styling makes it very easy for a beginning Windows programmer to experiment with additional Windows API functions when the need arises.

Optimized C++ Compiler Output   The C++ compiler has been optimized to generate executables that are only slightly larger when using MFC library routines. Execution speeds of an MFC application are similar to that of the same application written in C++ using the standard Windows API.

The MFC Library Offers Automatic Message Handling   The Microsoft Foundation Class library eliminates one frequent source of programming errors, the Windows API message loop. The MFC classes are designed to automatically handle every one of the Windows messages. Instead of using the standard **switch-case** statements, each Window message is mapped directly to a member function, which takes the appropriate action.

The MFC Library Allows Self-Diagnostics   Incorporated into the MFC library is the ability to perform self-diagnostics. This means that you can dump information about various objects into a file and validate an object's member variables, all in an easily understood format.

The MFC Library Incorporates a Robust Architecture   Anticipating the much-needed ANSI C/C++ throw/catch standard, the Microsoft Foundation Class library already incorporates an extensive exception-handling architecture. This allows an MFC object to eloquently recover from standard error conditions such as "out of memory" errors, invalid option selection, and file or resource loading problems. Every component of the architecture is upward compatible with the proposed ANSI C recommendations.

The MFC Library Offers Dynamic Object Typing   This extremely powerful feature postpones the typing of a dynamically allocated object until run time. This allows you to manipulate an object without having to worry about its underlying datatype.

The MFC Library Can Harmoniously Co-Exist with C-based Windows Applications   The most important feature of the Microsoft Foundation Class library is its ability to co-exist with C++-based Windows applications that use the Windows API. Programmers can use a combination of MFC classes and Windows API calls within the same program. This allows an MFC application to easily evolve into true C++ object-oriented code as experience or demand requires. This transparent environment is possible because of the common naming conventions between the two architectures. This means that MFC headers, types, and global definitions do not conflict with Windows API names.

Function Inlining

The Microsoft Visual C++ compiler supports complete function inlining. This means that functions of any type or combination of instructions can be expanded in line. Many popular C++ compilers restrict inlining to certain types of statements or expressions. For example, the inline option would be ignored by any function that contains a **switch**, **while**, or **for** statement. The Visual C++ compiler allows you to inline your most speed-critical routines (including seldom-used class member functions or constructors) without restricting their content. This option is set by selecting Project | Properties, then choosing the C/C++ folder, and selecting Optimizations from the left pane.

Compiler Options

Microsoft Visual C++ compilers discussed in this book are global optimizing compilers that allow you to take advantage of several speed or code size options for every type of program development.

The following compiler options allow you to optimize your code for executable size, speed, or build time. If you do not see an appreciable performance boost, it is possible that your test application does not contain enough code. To access a solution's project settings, click the solution's name, or the source file's name in the Solution Explorer. Make certain you have the Properties pane open, and the Properties pane will display the solution's or the source file's properties. By clicking the Property Page icon at the top of the Property pane you gain instant access to most of the tabs and settings described next, listed by logical category.

General

From the General selection under the Configurations folder, you can specify the use, or non-use, of the Microsoft Foundation Class library. Output directories can also be given for intermediate and final C/C++ compiled files in the C/C++ folder.

Debug

From the Debugging tab, the location of the executable file can be specified along with the working directory, optional program arguments, and a remote executable path and file name. Additionally, by using the Category list, additional Dynamic Link Libraries (DLLs) can be specified.

C/C++

The C/C++ tab allows you to select from the following categories: General, C++ Language, Code Generation, Customization, Listing Files, Optimizations, Precompiled Headers, and Preprocessor.

General

The General category permits the warning error level to be set, debug information to be specified, compiler optimizations to be set, preprocessor definitions to be given, and project options to be listed.

C++ Language

The C++ Language category allows the representation method to be specified, exception handling to be set, run-time type information to be set, construction displacements to be set, and project options to be listed.

Code Generation

The Code Generation category allows the microprocessor to be targeted (80386 to Pentium), calling convention to be given, run-time library to be specified, and structure member alignment to be noted. Project options are, again, listed.

Customization

The Customization category allows the following items to be enabled or disabled:

- Language extensions
- Function-level linking
- Duplicate strings
- Minimal rebuild
- Incremental compilation
- Banner and information message suppression

Browse Information

The Listing Files category allows the generation of browse information. Additionally, the browse file destination can be set. Local variables can be allowed in the browse file. The file types can also be optionally set. Project Options are listed.

Optimization

The Optimizations category allows various code optimizations to be set, such as speed, size, and so on. Inline function expansion can also be given. Project Options are listed.

Precompiled Headers

The Precompiled Headers category allows the use of precompiled header files. These are files with .pch extensions. Precompiled header files speed the compile and link process, but should be eliminated from your directory upon project completion because of their large size. Project Options are listed.

Preprocessor

The Preprocessor category allows preprocessor definitions to be given. It is also possible to add additional include directories and ignore standard paths. Project Options are listed.

Link

The Link tab allows you to select from the following categories: General, Customization, Debug, Input, and Output.

General

From the General category the name of the file and extension can be specified. Most frequently the extension will be an .exe file extension. Object/library modules can also be entered. These are very important for multimedia applications, where specific libraries are not assumed. The following items can also be included:

- Debug information
- Incremental linking
- Profiling
- Ignoring default libraries
- Map file generation

Customization

The Customization category allows the following items to be included:

- Incremental linking
- Program database

- Output file name
- Process message printing
- Startup banner

Debug

The Debug category allows the generation of a map file and debug information in various formats.

Input

The Input category allows the specification of object/library modules. Additionally, symbol references and MS-DOS stub file names are given.

Output

The Output category allows the base address, entry-point, stack allocation, and version information for the project to be set.

Resource

The Resource tab permits the resource file (usually a file with an .rc file extension) to be given. Additional features include the Language, resource include directories, and preprocessor definitions.

Browse Info

The Browse Info tab allows the Browse info file name to be specified. Additionally, the browse info file and startup banner can be checked.

What's Coming?

In this chapter you explored the new Microsoft Visual Studio.NET C++ compiler with its comprehensive, up-to-the-minute production-level development environment for creating all Windows ME, Windows 2000, and XP applications. In the next chapter you will take a high-level overview of the main menu options, familiarizing yourself with the tools provided and their locations.

Visual C++.NET

Chapter 2

A Quick Start
Using the MDE

21

The Visual C++.NET MDE (Microsoft Development Environment), sometimes referred to as the IDE (Integrated Development Environment), is an integrated development environment that allows you to easily create, open, view, edit, save, compile, and debug all of your C and C++ applications. As an integral part of the Microsoft Visual Studio.NET, the C/C++ environment operates as a cohesive component within the entire Microsoft family of languages, including Microsoft's new C#, Visual Basic, and Visual J++.

The advantage to this language development suite is the ease of learning and use provided by such a cohesive set of development features and tools. To a very large degree, except for each specific language's syntax, once you have learned one environment's features, for example Visual C++, you automatically know how to use the others! With Microsoft Visual Studio 's language integration, you can easily develop and combine multi-language source files into one program.

As do all of the Development Studio components, Visual C++ contains options for fine-tuning your work environment according to your personal preferences and to comply with application-specific hardware requirements. Many of the features discussed in the next sections are demonstrated in Chapter 3.

Starting the Visual C++ MDE

Launching the Visual C++ MDE is easy. If you are using a mouse, you can double-click the Visual C++ icon, which is found in the Microsoft Visual C++ group. Figure 2-1 shows the initial screen for the Visual C++ MDE.

At the time of this writing, only the Beta version of Visual C++ 7.0 was available.

The Visual Studio Start Page provides a quick way to set your user preferences for how the MDE behaves, including the active keyboard mapping scheme, window layout, and help filter, as well as the ability to access recent, existing, or new projects. You can also view links to the latest articles, events, and topics on MSDN Online. The Visual Studio Start Page appears by default each time you launch Visual Studio and is the default Web browser home page for the MDE.

Accessing Context-Sensitive Help

Help for each Visual C++ MDE feature is easily accessed because all of the compiler's documentation is online. Tapping into this valuable resource is as simple as placing the cursor on the feature in question and pressing F1.

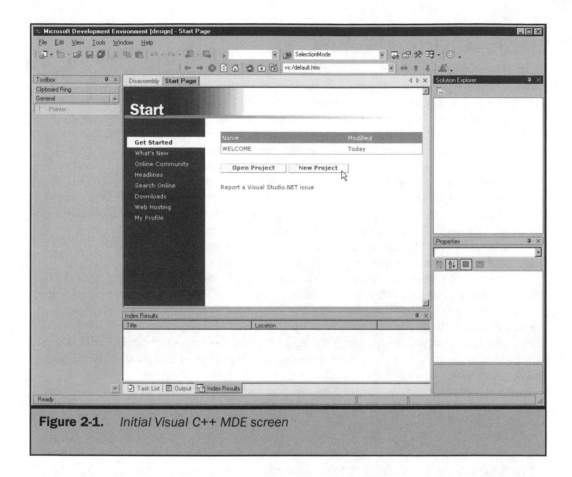

Figure 2-1. *Initial Visual C++ MDE screen*

However, context-sensitive help is not restricted to Visual C++ MDE features. If you place the cursor on a C/C++ language construct and press F1, the help utility will automatically display a description of the construct's syntax, an explanation of its use, and often a clarifying, executable example.

This chapter is designed to give you a broad overview of each Visual C++ MDE option. Do not become discouraged by the number of features and options available. You can use the default settings of many of the Visual C++ MDE's capabilities, which make it easy to get an application up and running.

As your experience grows and your application requirements increase in complexity, you will gradually gain hands-on experience with the more sophisticated capabilities of this powerful environment. While you are reading this chapter, take a pencil and check those Visual C++ MDE features that sound interesting to you. When the need arises to use one of these features, you can easily refer back to this section for an explanation of how to use the option.

Understanding Menus

Before beginning a discussion of each Visual C++ MDE feature, let us examine a few traits that all menu items have in common. For example, there are two ways to access menu items. The most common approach is to place the mouse pointer over the preferred option and click the left mouse button. The second approach is to use the underscored hot key. For instance, you can access the File menu directly from the keyboard by simultaneously pressing the ALT key and the letter F.

Menu items can be selected using the same sequences described previously, and there is often one additional way to select them. You can directly activate some menu items from anywhere within the integrated environment by using their specific hot key combinations. If a menu item has this capability, the option's specific hot key combination is displayed to the right of the menu item on the menu. For example, the first option listed on the File menu is New. This option can be invoked immediately, avoiding the necessity of first selecting the File menu, simply by pressing CTRL-N.

Here are some additional comments concerning menus. First, if a menu item is grayed, the integrated environment is alerting you to the fact that that particular option is currently unavailable. This means that the integrated environment is lacking some necessary prerequisite for that particular option to be valid. For example, the File menu's Save option will be grayed if the edit window is empty. The option knows that you cannot save something that does not exist, and it indicates this by deactivating and graying the Save command.

Second, any menu item followed by three periods, ..., indicates an option that, when selected, will automatically display a dialog box or a submenu. For example, the File menu's Open command, when selected, causes the Open dialog box to appear.

Finally, you can activate some menu items by clicking their associated buttons on the toolbars, which are below the main menu bar.

Let's look at the interesting MDE features that are usually available via a menu choice.

Docking or Floating a Toolbar

You can make the Standard toolbar (found just under the Visual C++ title bar), or any other toolbar docked or floating. In docked mode, a toolbar is fixed to any of the four borders of the application window. You cannot modify the size of a toolbar when it is docked.

In floating mode, a toolbar has a thin title bar and can appear anywhere on your screen. A floating toolbar is always on top of all other windows. You can modify the size or position of a toolbar when it is floating.

When you want to change a docked toolbar into a floating toolbar you first click (keep left mouse button depressed) on the title bar or on a blank area in the toolbar. Next, you drag the toolbar away from the dock to any position you desire.

When you want to dock a floating toolbar, first you click (hold down the left mouse button) on the title bar or on a blank area in the toolbar. You follow this by dragging the toolbar to any of the four borders in the application window.

Positioning a floating toolbar over a docked toolbar is as simple as clicking (hold down the left mouse button) on the title bar or on a blank area in the toolbar, then pressing the CTRL key, and dragging the toolbar over any docking area within the application window.

Auto Hide

Auto Hide allows you to minimize tool windows, such as the Solution Explorer and Toolbox, along the edges of the IDE so that the windows do not occupy valuable space. By minimizing tool windows, you can increase the viewable space of the editor.

Navigate Backward and Navigate Forward

Navigate Backward and Navigate Forward allow you to navigate through the open windows in the environment as well as the selection and cursor history within files in much the same way that back and forward work in Web browsers. For example, if you edit code on line 37 and then move to line 215, you can use the Navigate Backward button to quickly return to the exact same location in line 37. Both the Navigate Backward and Navigate Forward buttons have a drop-down list that displays the navigation history. The Navigate Backward and Navigate Forward buttons are located on the Standard toolbar. You can also use CTRL-(-) and CTRL-SHIFT-(-), respectively.

The File Menu

The Visual C++ MDE File menu localizes the standard set of file manipulation commands common to many Windows applications. Figure 2-2 shows the command options available from the File menu.

Grayed menu options indicate a feature that is unavailable for the current input focus, project type and/or settings, or language being used.

New

You choose the File | New option, followed by Project to begin a new project, or File | New | File menu item to open a new edit dialog box window. You usually begin any new application at this point. The MDE automatically titles and numbers each window you open. Numbering begins at 1, so your first window title will always be *xxx*1, your second window title *xxx*2, and so on. The *xxx* is a label identifying the type of file you are working with (code, project, resource, bitmap, binary, icon, or cursor).

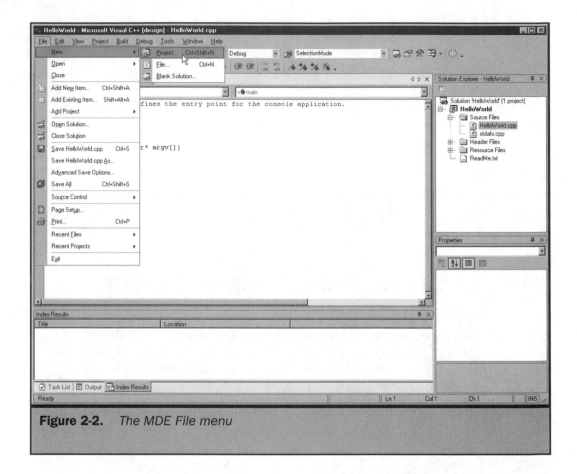

Figure 2-2.   *The MDE File menu*

If you have windows titled *xxx*1 through *xxx*6 open and then decide to close the window titled *xxx*2, the next time you invoke the New option, that title (in this case, *xxx*2) will not be reused. Windows automatically supplies the next higher number (for this example, *xxx*7).

The quickest way to open a new edit dialog box is to click the leftmost button on the toolbar. This button has a picture of a file on it. You can invoke the New option directly by clicking this control.

Open

Unlike New, which opens an edit dialog box window for a previously nonexistent file, the Open menu item opens a dialog box that requests information on a previously saved file. This dialog box is the standard Open File dialog box, which displays the default drive, path, and file search parameters, and allows you to select your own.

The dialog box has a time-saving feature that automatically remembers your preferences, using these as defaults each time you use the Open command. Attempting to open an already opened file automatically invokes an audible alert and warning message. This useful reminder prevents you from accidentally opening two or more copies of the same file, editing only one of them, and then re-saving the non-updated version!

The second button from the left on the toolbar, which has a picture of a folder with an open arrow on it, can be used to invoke the Open option directly.

Close

The Close menu item is used to close an open file. If you have multiple files opened, this command will close the *active* or *selected* window. You can tell which window is active by looking at the window's border. Active or selected windows have the keyboard and mouse focus and are displayed with your system's selected color preferences. These preferences usually include colored title bars and darker window borders. Inactive windows usually have grayed title bars and window borders.

If you accidentally attempt to close an unsaved file, do not worry. The integrated environment automatically protects you from this potentially devastating scenario by warning you that the file has not been previously saved, and it asks you if you want to save the file at this point.

Add New Item/Existing Item/Project

The File | Add New Item/Existing Item menu option adds a new/existing project to the current solution or adds a new/existing solution item, such as an .htm, .css, .txt, or frameset to the current solution and opens it.

Open/Close Solution

These menu options are available to open an existing solution or close an active solution.

Save Selected Item(s)

The Save menu items save the contents of the currently selected or active window(s) to the file specified. You can distinguish the previously saved contents of a window from the unsaved contents of a window by simply checking the window's title bar. If you see a default title, such as *xxx*1, you will know that the window's contents have never been given a valid filename and saved. Saving a previously unsaved file will automatically invoke the Save As dialog box.

You can also use the Save button on the toolbar. The third from the left, this button has the image of a floppy disk on it. If a file was opened in read-only mode (see the description of the View | Properties command), the control's image will be grayed, indicating that the option is currently unavailable.

Save Selected Item(s) As

The Save As menu item allows you to save a copy of the active window's contents under a new name. If you are wondering why you might choose this option, here's a possible scenario. You have just finished a project. You have a working program. However, you would like to try a few changes. For the sake of security, you do not want to tweak the current version. By choosing the Save As option, you can copy the file's contents under a new name, and then you can tweak the duplicate. Should disaster ensue, you can always go back to your original file.

Save All

If you have never written a C, C++, Windows ME, Windows 2000, or XP application, you will be stunned at the actual number of files involved in creating a project's executable file. The problem with the Save option is that it only saves the active window's contents. The Save All menu item saves every window's contents. If any window contains previously unsaved text, the Save All command will automatically invoke the Save As dialog box, prompting you for a valid filename for each window.

Source Control

The Diff-Merge option compares file properties and combines unique components. The Connection Manager moderates database connection, access, and update parameters.

Page Setup

The most frequent use for the Page Setup menu item is to document and format your hard copies. The Page Setup dialog box allows you to select a header for each printed page, and you can use it to set the top, bottom, left, and right print margins.

Print

Obtaining a hard copy of the active window's contents is as simple as selecting the Print menu item. The Print dialog box provides you with several options. First, you can choose between printing the entire window's contents, or printing only selected text by clicking the appropriate radio button. You can also select which printer to use and configure the selected printer by choosing the Setup option.

If you wish to print only a portion of a window's contents, you must first select the desired text. Selecting text is as simple as placing the mouse pointer on the first character in the text you want to print and holding the left mouse button down while you drag the mouse to the right and/or down through the text. This causes the selected text to be displayed in reverse video. When text is selected, the Print dialog box will show the Print Range Selection radio button in normal type (not grayed), indicating the option's availability.

Recent Files

Right below the Print menu item is a list of the most recently edited files. The nice feature about such lists (often called *history lists*) is that they are context sensitive. History lists save you time by remembering the last several items you have selected for a particular option. For this menu, the items remembered are previously opened files. The first time you use the Visual C++ MDE, this portion of the File menu is empty, because there is no history of opened files.

Recent Projects

The recent project list is immediately below the recent file list on the menu. This history list is similar to the recent file list, except that the recent project list contains only project files. To open any file, in either list, double-click the left mouse button on the selected item.

Exit

The Exit menu item allows you to quit the Visual C++ MDE. Do not worry if you have forgotten to save a window's contents before selecting Exit. The MDE will automatically display a warning message for each window containing unsaved text, allowing you to save the information before exiting.

The Edit Menu

Edit menu items allow you to quickly edit or search through an active window's contents in much the same way you would with any standard word processor (see Figure 2-3).

Figure 2-3 shows the Visual C++ MDE Edit menu. The following discussion highlights the most frequently used Edit menu options.

Undo

The Undo menu item allows you to reverse the most recent editing change you made. You can also use the Undo option from the toolbar. The Undo option is the left-pointing arrow on the toolbar. This is the seventh icon from the left on our system.

Redo

The Redo menu item allows you to reverse the action of the last Undo. Use this option to reinstate a valid editing change that you thought was an incorrect change. The Redo option can also be used from the toolbar. On the toolbar, the Redo option is the right-pointing arrow. This is the eighth icon from the left on our system.

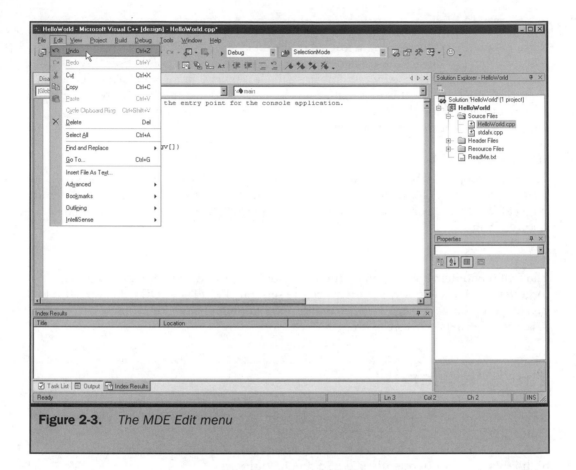

Figure 2-3.   *The MDE Edit menu*

Cut

The Cut menu item copies the selected text in the active window to the Clipboard and then deletes the text from the active window. Selecting text is as simple as placing the mouse pointer on the first character in the text you want to cut and holding the left mouse button down while you drag the mouse to the right and/or down through the text. This causes the selected text to be displayed in reverse video.

The Cut command is often used in conjunction with the Paste command to move text from one location to another. When the cut text is placed on the Clipboard, all previous Clipboard contents are destroyed.

The Cut option can also be used from the toolbar. On the toolbar, the Cut option is the scissors icon. This is the fourth icon from the left on our system.

Copy

Like Cut, the Copy menu item places the selected text on the Clipboard. However, unlike Cut, Copy leaves the original selected text in place. A good use for this option would be to reproduce intricate code sequences or clarify comments needed in multiple source files.

The Copy command is often used in conjunction with the Paste command to copy text from one location to another. When the copied text is placed on the Clipboard, all previous Clipboard contents are destroyed.

The Copy option can also be used from the toolbar. On the toolbar, the Copy option is the dual page icon. This is the fifth icon from the left on our system.

Paste

The Paste menu item is used to insert the contents of the Clipboard at the current cursor location. The Clipboard can only paste information that has been previously placed on the Clipboard by the Cut or Copy command.

The Paste option can also be used from the toolbar. On the toolbar, the Paste option is the clipboard-page icon. This is the sixth icon from the left on our system.

Cycle Clipboard Ring

When text is cut or copied, the fragments are stored in an environment clipboard known as the Clipboard Ring where you can pick and choose among them and paste back into your code.

Delete

Works like a word processor delete option in the Edit pane.

Select All

The Select All menu item is used to select the entire contents of the active window for cutting, copying, or deleting.

Find and Replace

The Find and Replace menu item works very much like a standard word processor's search option. However, since the C/C++ language is case sensitive, the Find command can be tailored to search for case-sensitive, case-insensitive, and whole-word-only matches. The Find dialog box also allows you to set the direction for the search (up or down) from the current cursor location.

One very useful and sophisticated Find option that is not usually associated with any word processor's search capabilities is the Regular Expression option. Table 2-1 lists and describes the Regular Expression search pattern symbols that can be used in the Find What window.

Pattern	Meaning
*	Substitutes for any number of characters Example: Data*1 Finds: Data1, DataIn1, DataOut1
.	Substitutes for a single character Example: Data. Finds: Data1, Data2 but not DataIn1
^	Starts a search at the beginning of a line for the string Example: ^do Finds: each line beginning with "do"
+	Substitutes for any number of characters preceding the string Example: +value Finds: i_value, fvalue, lng_value
$	Starts a search at the end of each line for the string Example: some_var_n);$ Finds: each line ending with "some_var_n);"
[]	Starts a search of the given character subset Example: Data[A..Z] Finds: DataA not Data1 Example: Data[1248] Finds: Data2 not Data3
\	Starts a search for strings where the preceding character must be exactly matched Example: Data[A..Zi\0..9] Finds: DataAi1 not DataDo3
\{\}	Starts a search for any sequence of characters placed between the braces Example: \{no\}*_answer Finds: answer, no_answer, nono_answer, nonono_answer

Table 2-1. *Regular Expression Search String Patterns*

Replace

The Replace menu item invokes the Replace dialog box, which allows you to replace text. Simply type in the string to search for, then type in the replacement string, and finally select from several matching criteria. Matching options include whole words only, case-sensitive or case-insensitive matches, and Regular Expressions (see the previous "Find and Replace" section).

Be careful when selecting the Replace All option, because this can have disastrous results. There are two things to remember when doing a replace: first, save the file *before* you invoke the command; second, if something goes wrong with the replace, remember that you can always use the Undo option.

Find in Files/Replace in Files

Find in Files, is one of the most valuable tools you'll ever use once you understand its capabilities. Find/Replace in Files, while identical in horsepower to Find/Replace, adds one special advantage: the search has multiple-file scope! You may ask yourself, "Why would I ever need such a feature?" Here is why. If you are learning a new C/C++ language feature, use this option to scan for all programs containing it. If you are modifying a program, use Find/Replace in Files to make certain you have caught all occurrences of the older syntax. If you are working on a large project, use Find in Files to locate all of the code authored by a particular group or programmer. And remember, Find/Replace in Files isn't just capable of searching one subdirectory, or one hard drive. Find in Files/Replace can scan an entire network, intranet, or the Internet, tracking down any name, string, keyword, method, and much more.

Find Symbol

Similar to Find, Find Symbol adds several search options, including substring and prefix matching.

Go To

You can quickly move the cursor to a specified location within an active edit window with the Go To menu item. Choosing this option invokes a Line dialog box that allows you to enter the line number for the line of code you wish to jump to. Entering a line number greater than the actual number of source code lines available causes the command to place the cursor at the bottom of the window's text file.

Insert File As Text

Selecting the Insert File As Text option activates the File Manager window allowing you to select a text file to be copied into the active document.

Advanced

The Advanced option allows you to control edit window tabbing, columnizing, white-space viewing/deleting, word wrap, and blank line removal.

Bookmarks

The Bookmarks option allows you to set bookmarks to mark frequently accessed lines in your source file. Once a bookmark is set, you can use menu or keyboard commands to move to it. You can remove a bookmark when you no longer need it. You can use both named and unnamed bookmarks. Unnamed bookmarks are saved between editing sessions. Once you create a named bookmark, you can jump to that location whether or not the file is open. Named bookmarks store both the line number and the column number of the location of the cursor when the bookmark was created. This location is adjusted whenever you edit the file. Even if you delete the characters around the bookmark, the bookmark remains in the correct location.

Outlining

Visual Studio 7.0 Code Editor offers you the option of expanding or contracting all code segments, allowing you to see or hide details of an algorithm. You can select a block of text and hide it so that it appears under a + symbol. You can then expand or hide the region by clicking the plus sign symbol next to the collapsed code. When you are through outlining, you can remove the outline information without disturbing your underlying code. The outlined code is not deleted, it is merely hidden from view.

There are always five different commands available. You may Hide Selected code, which was explained previously. You can Toggle Current, which reverses the current hidden or expanded state of the procedure in which the cursor lies. The Toggle All option sets all procedures to the same hidden or expanded state. To remove all outlining from an algorithm, choose the Stop Outlining option. However, to remove outlining from selected text only, first highlight the code and choose the Hiding Current option.

IntelliSense

When a function or statement is entered into the Code Editor, its complete syntax and arguments are shown in a ToolTip. In addition, languages that support early binding display available functions, statements, constants, and other values in a list that you can choose from.

View Menu

The View menu contains commands that enable you to change your view of the current solution, project(s), classes, code, templates and much more (see Figure 2-4).

The View menu accesses a high-level list of windows and view panes that display everything from your solution's source files (Solution Explorer), to the properties for any solution component.

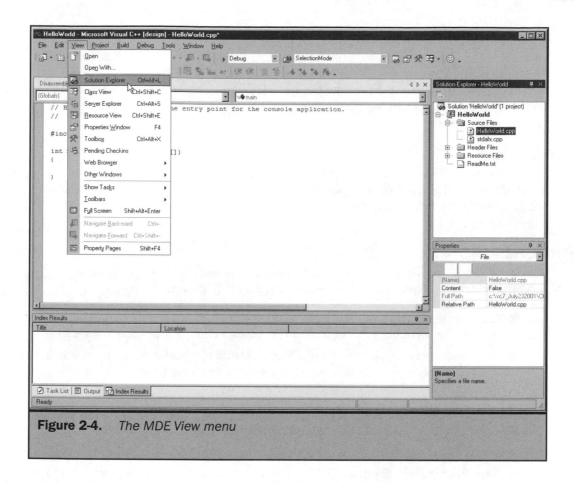

Figure 2-4. *The MDE View menu*

Open/Open With

The Open command opens a file in the selected editor, such as the Binary or Resource editor. To open the file with a particular encoding, select an editor with encoding support, such as Source Code (Text) with Encoding or HTML/XML Editor with Encoding.

Solution Explorer

The Solution Explorer allows you to view the content of your solution and to perform various solution-related tasks. For example, you can drag-and-drop files from one project to another, display file and project properties, and add new or existing files and projects.

Using Solution Explorer

Opening a file is straightforward with the Solution Explorer—you simply double-click the selected file. You can move a file from one project to another by simply clicking the file's name and dragging it to the new location. The same procedure can make a duplicate copy however, by simply beginning the drag-and-drop process while pressing the CTRL key.

Class View

The right pane in WMI CIM Studio is the Class Viewer, which displays details on a selected class. Using the tabs, you can display the properties, methods, and associations defined for a class. Selecting a class in the Class Explorer automatically updates the Class Viewer display.

Server Explorer

The Server Explorer window allows you to view and manipulate resources on any server to which you have network access. Using Server Explorer, you can

- Connect to servers and view their resources, including their message queues, performance counters, services and processes, event logs, and database objects.

- Reference server resources in your Visual Studio applications, either by adding a component to your project that references the resource or by creating components that monitor the resource's activity.

- Make data connections to SQL Server or other types of databases.

- Configure and integrate Exchange 2000 Servers into your application.

- Find out information about processes, services, and DLLs loaded on a server.

- View information about available Web services and the methods and schemas they make available.

Resource View

The Resource view displays a list of all active application resources.

Properties Window

The Properties window details properties ordered by category, alphabet, individual properties, or the property pages.

Toolbox

The Toolbox window displays a variety of items, such as design-time controls, ActiveX controls, NGWS (Next Generation Windows Services) components, HTML fragments, objects, and text based on the designer or editor you are using. These Toolbox items are made available only when the associated designer or editor is active. The Toolbox displays two tabs, General and Clipboard, by default. As an editor or designer becomes active, more tabs and tools may become available. You can also add custom tabs and tools to the Toolbox.

Pending Checkins

Visual Studio.NET makes it possible for you to share updated source code with other users. To do this, however, you must make your changes available to other users by checking in the file. When you check in a file, the version you have created is copied to the source control provider. It becomes the latest version of the file, and is generally available to users who have the appropriate permissions. To view the list of modified files, select View | Pending Checkins to display a list of the checked-out files in the current solution and to check in these files with a single button click.

Web Browser

You can display Web pages directly within the IDE. The first time you open a Web browser window, the Visual Studio Start Page appears by default. When a Web browser window is open, the Web toolbar appears, which allows you to enter URLs, move backward and forward within the navigation history, and return to the Web browser home page. You can also now access your Web browser favorites as well as add links to the favorites list from within Visual Studio.

Other Windows

The Other Windows menu item references additional views of macros, objects, document outlines, task lists, and find and search results, including a new Command window. The Command window is an amalgamation of a command line and Visual Basic's Immediate window. You can enter IDE command names into the window by typing an angle bracket (>), as well as enter a number of Immediate window commands. You can create aliases, or short names, for commands. Auto-completion works for command names, aliases, and file names. In Immediate mode, you can execute code statements, set or assign variables, evaluate expressions, and more.

Show Tasks

Choose this option to display all registered task lists by category: All, Comment, Compile/Build/Deploy, User, Shortcut, Policy, Current File, Checked, and Unchecked.

Toolbars

This option activates the same pop-up Toolbar List window as the single right-mouse button click on the Visual Studio main menu bar. The option allows you to easily activate or deactivate all available toolbars.

Full Screen

View Full Screen instantly zooms your code page to full screen dimensions for easy viewing and editing.

Navigate Backward/Forward

Navigate Backward and Navigate Forward allow you to navigate through the open windows in the environment as well as the selection and cursor history within files in much the same way that back and forward work in Web browsers. For example, if you edit code on line 44 and then moved to line 312, you can use the Navigate Backward button to quickly return to the exact same location in line 44. Both the Navigate Backward and Navigate Forward buttons have a drop-down list that displays the navigation history. The Navigate Backward and Navigate Forward buttons are located on the Standard toolbar. You can also use CTRL-(-) and CTRL-SHIFT-(-), respectively.

Property Pages

The Properties window details properties ordered by category, alphabet, individual properties, or the property pages. You can select View | Property Pages as an optional approach to accessing the fourth option of the Properties window menu item.

Project Menu

The Project menu commands enable you to manage all of your open projects (see Figure 2-5).

The good news about the Project menu options is that all of the programs illustrated in this text use a single solution and project hierarchy. However, the following section is included to cleanly present an overview of all Visual Studio.NET capabilities.

Add Class/Resource/New-Existing Item

The first four Project menu options (Add Class, Resource, New-Existing) add their designated components, respectively, to the current Project. The New Folder option creates a new project-related subdirectory for localization of project resources.

Add Web Reference

This new feature of Visual Studio.NET opens up an Add Web Reference browser that allows you to locate online Web services, adding them to your application.

Set As StartUp Project

In advanced program development there comes a time where it is best to break a large project down into subprojects. A subproject establishes a dependency of one project on another in a hierarchical fashion. Subprojects are used in Visual C++ projects, for example, when a project builds an executable program that depends on a static library. If the static library is a subproject of the project that builds the executable program, then the library will be updated before the executable program is built. The Set As StartUp Project option determines which project, or subproject, is currently active.

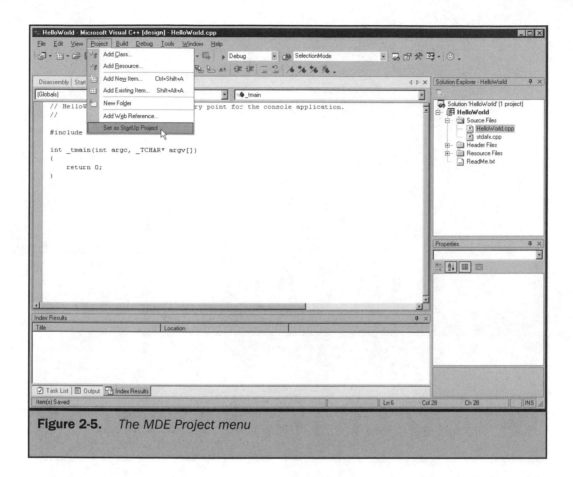

Figure 2-5. *The MDE Project menu*

Build Menu

The options in the Build menu provide access to the MDE features that are involved in actual code generation, debugging, and running your program (see Figure 2-6).

Of all the Build options, the most important menu option you will need to clearly understand is Rebuild All. The other Build options trail off into advanced customizable build settings unnecessary for this text.

Build

Typical C/C++ programs are comprised of many files. Some of these files may be supplied by the compiler, the operating system, the programmer, or even third-party vendors. It can get even more complicated if the project's files are created by several

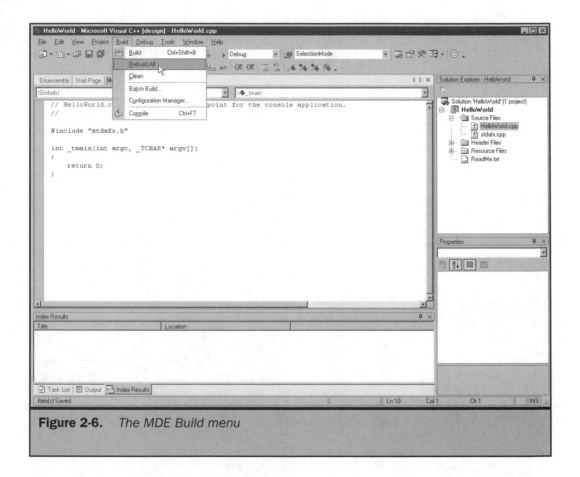

Figure 2-6.   *The MDE Build menu*

programming teams. Because there can be so many files, and because the compile process can take a very long time, the Build menu item becomes an extremely useful tool. Build examines all of the files in the project and then compiles and links only those dependent files displaying dates and times more recent than the project's executable file.

One decision you must make when selecting Build is whether the resulting file is to include debugging information (Debug Mode) or not (Release Mode). These modes are activated by selecting Project | Settings. Once you have a program up and running, you should usually choose a Build without the debug option, since inclusion of the information makes the resulting executable file unnecessarily large.

If the Build process detects any syntax errors—either non-fatal warnings or fatal errors—these are displayed in the Output window. Use the Next Error or Previous Error menu items to search forward or backward through this list.

If you have the toolbar visible, you can use the sixth button from the right to invoke Build. This button has a picture that looks like a bucket with two dark-colored, downward-pointing arrows on it.

Rebuild All

The only difference between Build and Rebuild All is that Rebuild All ignores the dates of all of a project's files and painstakingly compiles and links all of them.

Imagine the following scenario. Your company, for the sake of economy, has decided to go without any systems maintenance personnel. This decision, coupled with the seasonal time change, system down time, and so on, results in your discovery that the systems on your network all have different system clock settings. Because of this, newly created files are being stamped with the previous day's date! Choosing the Build option in this case could leave these current, updated files out of the final executable file. However, by choosing Rebuild All, you avoid any date/time stamp checks, creating an executable file that truly reflects the current state of all included files.

If the Rebuild All process detects any syntax errors—either non-fatal warnings or fatal errors—these are displayed in the Output window. Use the Next Error or Previous Error menu items to search forward or backward through this list.

If you have the toolbar visible, you can use the fifth button from the right to invoke Rebuild All. This button has a picture that looks like a bucket with three light-colored, downward-pointing arrows on it.

Clean

With the Clean command you can easily remove all files from the intermediate directories in any project configuration in your project workspace. Removing the files forces the development environment to build these files if you subsequently click the Build command.

Batch Build

This option is similar to the Build menu item except that it builds multiple project targets.

Configuration Manager

During deployment, an administrator can add configuration details to an assembly. While the assembly manifest describes the assembly at the time it was built, certain types of information cannot be supplied until the application is deployed. For example, information regarding physical deployment locations and remoting information is not known when the application is built. In addition, the administrator may want to override information kept in the manifest. For instance, an administrator may want to apply specific version policies to control which version of a given assembly is loaded by the NGWS run time. Configuration information is supplied in XML configuration files that are either associated directly with the application, with a specific user, or with the entire machine.

Compile

Choosing this option instructs the MDE to compile the active window's contents. Compiling in this sense is asking the environment to check the syntax of the active file, for example C/C++ or C# source code.

Debug Menu

You use the Debug menu, seen in Figure 2-7, to activate and customize all Debugger options. Integrated Debuggers are invaluable tools enabling a programmer to efficiently locate, analyze, and repair code breaks.

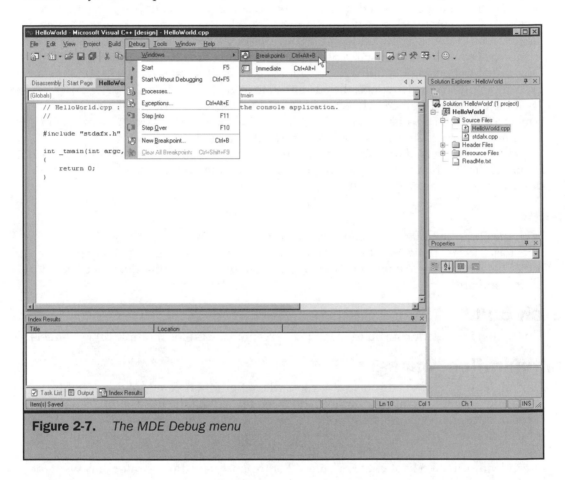

Figure 2-7.   *The MDE Debug menu*

With debugging such a vital phase in application development, knowing what the Debugger is capable of doing, and how to quickly access its features is a must. Initially accessing Debugger options is easiest with mouse clicks. However, you will quickly evolve to using the few hot-key strokes necessary to access the day-to-day features such as F5 (Start Debugging), CTRL-F5 for execution without debugging, and F10 and F11 for single-step modes.

Windows

Select Debug | Windows to access Breakpoints, Exceptions, and Immediate windows. The Breakpoints and Exceptions windows allow you to easily select and view flagged breakpoints and exceptions.

Choose Debug | Windows | Immediate to open the Command window. The Command window has two modes of operation: command mode and immediate mode. Use the command mode to quickly execute Visual Studio Commands. Use immediate mode to change the value of variables when you debug applications.

Start

Unlike a full-speed program execution, this option instructs the MDE to begin executing your program line-by-line, or up to any set breakpoint.

Start Without Debugging

Start Without Debugging, unlike Start, instructs the MDE to full-speed execute your algorithm, bypassing any debugging tools.

Processes

Choosing the Debug | Processes option opens up the Processes dialog box. From here you can view and manipulate programs in a Visual Studio solution. The dialog box selections allow you to debug multiple programs at the same time.

Exceptions

The Debug | Exceptions option opens up the Exceptions dialog box containing a hierarchical view of categorized exceptions. With a simple click you can select entire exception categories and then instruct Visual Studio.NET how to handle them. The dialog box contains several radio buttons. You can click any exception or category to select it, then change its handling using the radio buttons in the option categories titled When The Exception Is Thrown and If The Exception Is Not Handled Groups.

Step Into/Step Over

The Debug Step Into and Step Over options are identical single-step modes of operation. The only time the two commands differ is when the Debugger is about to single-step execute a function or method call. When you want to debug *into* a subroutine, line-by-line, you choose the appropriately named Step Into option. However, if you know the subroutine the Debugger is about to invoke needs no special debug attention, choose the Step Over option. Step Over full-speed executes the called subroutine, returning to the line immediately below the invoking statement.

New Breakpoint

This option sets a breakpoint in your source code allowing you to full-speed execute solid code in an application up to and stopping on the breakpoint.

Clear All Breakpoints

Since an application may have more than one breakpoint, it would be too time-consuming to manually locate each one in order to remove them. The Clear All Breakpoints option simultaneously removes all set breakpoints.

Tools Menu

The Tools menu (see Figure 2-8) localizes many of the Visual Studio.NET advanced utilities necessary for managing extremely advanced C++ applications. While the utilities are unnecessary for developing this text's applications, a discussion of their individual use provides a broad overview of just what you can do in a Microsoft Visual Studio.NET environment.

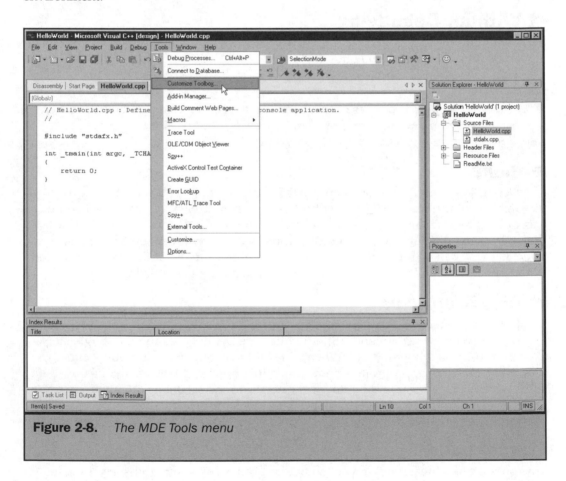

Figure 2-8. *The MDE Tools menu*

Debug Processes

This is similar to the Debug | Processes menu option, which opens the Processes dialog box allowing you to select the processes for debugging. The option allows you to debug multiple programs at the same time.

Connect to Database

This option instructs Visual Studio.NET on how it should connect to Microsoft SQL Server data.

Customize Toolbox

Use this dialog box to add or remove controls, objects, and other items in the Toolbox window. This dialog box is available by choosing Tools | Customize. The Customize Toolbox dialog box replaces the Components dialog box used in previous versions of Visual Basic and the Customize dialog box for controls used in previous versions of Visual C++.

Add-In Manager

An Addin object provides information about an add-in to other add-ins. Only registered add-ins are represented by an Addin object. The Add-In Manager displays an add-ins list.

Build Comment Web Pages

The Build Comment Web Pages dialog box allows you to create a series of .htm pages that display the code structure within files that are in projects and solutions, as well as display information you have included in your code using the code comment syntax.

Macros

The Macros menu option provides complete control over Visual C++ MDE environment macros. When you record a macro, the environment tracks the environment elements you alter and the keys that you enter and generates macro code based on that input. Not every UI (user interface) element or event, however, can be recorded. For the PDC Tech Preview, the recording is limited to

- Text/Code editors, such as the Code Editor window.
- Commands, such as menu items. By default, Visual Studio records command invocations by name if the commands themselves do not emit code against an automation model particular to the UI feature.
- Common tree view tool windows, such as the Project Explorer.
- The Add Item dialog box.
- The Find and Replace dialog boxes.
- Windows and their events in general, such as activating and closing.

If you are recording a macro and you happen to manipulate an element of the environment that does not generate macrocode, and did not go through a standard environment command—such as editing in an edit control in a dialog box—you will have a gap in your macro, and thus, the macro won't work as expected.

External Tools

You use the External Tools dialog box to add custom commands to the Tools menu that launch external tools, such as Spy++ or Notepad, from within the development environment. You can specify arguments as well as a working directory when launching the tool. In addition, the outputs from some tools can be displayed in the Output window of the development environment or even added to the Task List.

Customize

This standard option allows you to easily customize all MDE toolbars by adding or removing user-selected command buttons and behaviors.

Options

Use this page of the Options dialog box to change default settings for the MDE.

Window Menu

With the possible exception of the Docking View command, you will see that the remaining Window menu options are similar to those found in all standard Windows products (see Figure 2-9).

The Window menu differs from the View menu's options in that it defines how a pane with the input focus is displayed, not *which* pane is opened.

New Window

The New Window command provides one of the many ways to begin entering and editing a new file.

Split

The Split option places a four quadrant pane over the Edit view allowing you to determine both a horizontal and vertical split point.

Dockable, Hide, Floating, Auto Hide/All

A dockable toolbar can be attached, or docked, to any side of its parent window, or it can be detached, or floated, in its own mini-frame window. Not all views are dockable, but if the active window is—for example the Workspace view—this is one method for docking and undocking the pane.

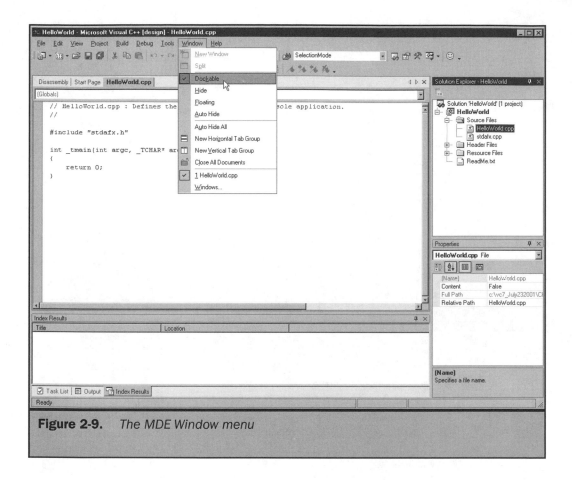

Figure 2-9.   *The MDE Window menu*

History List

This is a dynamic list of open windows, by name, allowing you to make the highlighted window active.

Windows

Opens a list of all currently active windows, allowing you to switch view focus with a single mouse click.

Help Menu

The Help menu begins with the standard Online documentation Contents and Search options and then diverges into several new Help features, for example the Documentation Home Page (see Figure 2-10).

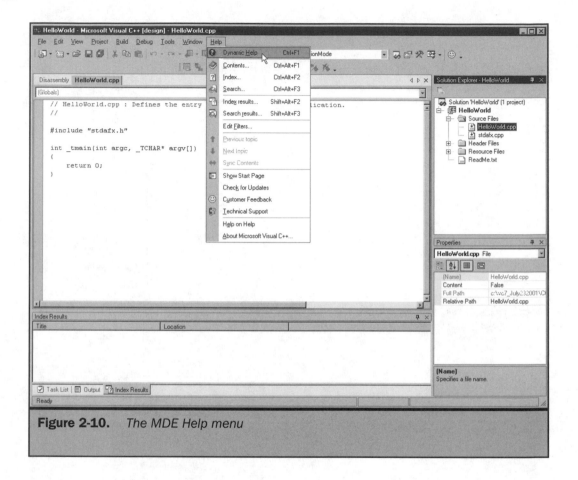

Figure 2-10.   *The MDE Help menu*

While not receiving five thousand pages of documentation with your new Visual Studio.NET is both a financial and storage space blessing, it does create a set of problems all its own, namely, how do you find the information you need? The Visual Studio.NET Help facilities have been reorganized, restructured, and improved with new menu options. The most significant of these new options is Dynamic Help.

Dynamic Help

The Microsoft Visual C++ MDE provides a range of methods for you to quickly find and view product documentation. The Dynamic Help window allows you to view a list of samples, wizards, topics, and other information based on the current operation you are performing. For example, if you have an .htm file open in HTML view and the cursor is on the element TITLE, a link to the HTML reference topic for that element appears in the Dynamic Help window.

You can search for topics in the product documentation directly from the MDE using the Search dialog box available from the Help menu. Multiple topic matches for index and search operations are displayed in the Index Results window and Search Results window, respectively. You can customize your view of help topics directly in the MDE or in a separate window.

Contents, Index, Search

These standard Online Documentation navigation controls provide the expected access to Microsoft's extensive online documentation.

Previous/Next Topic and Sync Contents

These grayed options (refer to Figure 2-10) are available when the Edit window's focus contains Help topic information.

Show Start Page

The Show Start Page instantly reverts the Edit window's contents to the initial Visual Studio.NET startup page allowing you quick and easy access to the latest news involving Visual Studio.NET, Online Communities, and to view your personal Profile.

Check for Updates

Microsoft has made it as simple as possible to keep your Visual Studio.NET state-of-the-art via the Check for Updates Help menu option.

Customer Feedback, Technical Support

Your interaction with Microsoft, as it relates to Visual Studio, is accessed through either the Customer Feedback or Technical Support structures available through the Help menu.

Help on Help

Help on Help is the all-inclusive source for understanding how to use the sophisticated, context-sensitive help options available in Visual Studio.NET and how to fine-tune the utilities output contents.

About Microsoft Visual C++

A standard About box displays the version, Product ID, and installed component ID numbers.

What's Coming?

In Chapter 2 you have examined the Visual C++.NET MDE (Microsoft Development Environment), sometimes referred to as the IDE (Integrated Development Environment), and how to easily create, open, view, edit, save, compile, and debug all of your C and C++ applications. Chapter 3 adds to this knowledge a sample debug cycle where you encounter the most frequently used debugger tools available in the MDE.

Visual C++.NET

Chapter 3

Writing, Compiling, and Debugging Simple Programs

The Visual C++ component of the Visual Studio.NET development environment, just like any new state-of-the-art development environment, can on first encounter, be a very intimidating product. While the initial window seems straightforward, as soon as you begin peeking and poking around submenus and their related dialog windows, you can become easily overwhelmed by the options and apparent complexity of this new world.

You see, developing a multi-tasking, object-oriented, GUI (graphical user interface), multi-media, Internet-aware application, really is no easy task. That is, if you had to do all of this from ground zero. However, today's language development environments automate the code generation for the majority of these goals. This text is designed to give you a thorough understanding of the C and C++ languages, along with experience in today's number one development environment, i.e., Microsoft's Visual C++.NET, while learning the logic, constructs, and tools necessary to develop state-of-the-art programs.

This chapter is designed to give you hands-on experience with the commands needed to create, edit, save, compile, and debug simple programs. At this point, if you haven't done so already, you may want to take out a highlighting pen. Since the integrated environment offers so many ways to initiate each operation, you might want to highlight the text where you see the method that you prefer. For example, some people prefer to use keyboard commands, while others like the point-'n'-click mouse/menu interaction.

Starting the Developer Studio

In Chapter 2, you learned that starting the Visual C++ MDE (Microsoft Development Environment) is easy. If you are using a mouse, you can double-click the Visual C++ icon, which is found in the Microsoft Visual Studio.NET 7.0 group. Alternatively, you can access the Windows menu system by performing the following steps:

1. While simultaneously pressing CTRL-ESC, enter **P** for Programs Group, followed by repeated presses of the CURSOR-DOWN key until the Microsoft Visual Studio.NET 7.0 Group is highlighted.

2. Press the right-arrow cursor key, until the Microsoft Visual Studio.NET 7.0 program is highlighted.

3. Press the ENTER key!

(Here's the first opportunity to highlight your personal preference!) Use the method you prefer, and start Microsoft Visual Studio.NET 7.0 now.

Creating Your First Program

The first thing you need to do before you enter a program is to tell the MDE what type of application you are developing. You can use the MDE to develop Visual Basic, Visual FoxPro, C, C++, dynamic link libraries (.DLLs), and now—C# applications. The quickest way to get started, however, is to simply click the New Project hot-link shown in Figure 3-1.

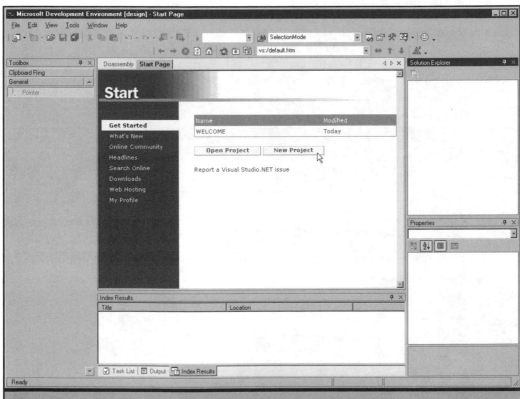

Figure 3-1. *The New Project hot-link allows the programmer to start a new program.*

The New Project dialog box opens, listing all available project types and their related templates. This dialog box is used to select the type of file you wish to create. Before leaving this dialog box by clicking the OK button, you will want to make sure you

- Select Visual C++ Projects
- Click the Win32 Projects folder
- Click the Win32 Projects icon within the Templates pane
- Choose a project file Location
- Give the project a Name

Double-check all your entries in the dialog box (see Figure 3-2) before clicking the OK button. Accidentally selecting the wrong configuration option(s) at this point will drastically affect how the MDE auto-generates code templates. As soon as you click the OK button, the MDE presents you with the Win32 Application Wizard, as shown in Figure 3-3.

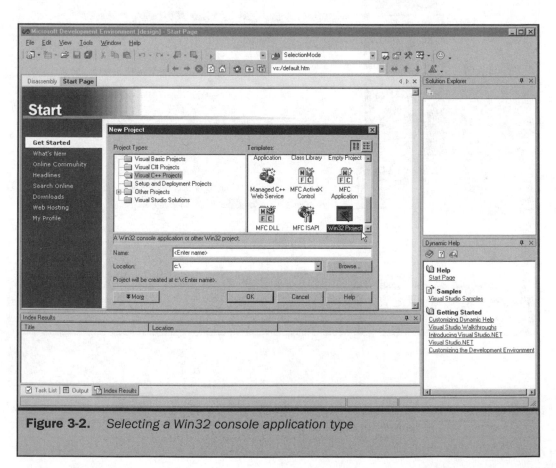

Figure 3-2.   *Selecting a Win32 console application type*

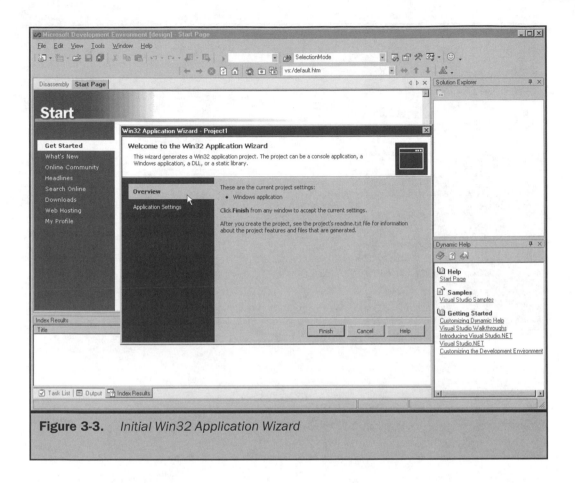

Figure 3-3. *Initial Win32 Application Wizard*

LOOK OUT! If you make a mistake on selections at this point, you'll send yourself off into auto-generated code chaos. The default settings in Figure 3-3 are *not* what you want. To create a simple command line Windows application, you must first click the Application Settings tab right below the default selection of Overview.

Figure 3-4 displays a correctly configured Application Settings check box. Make certain you have clicked the Console Application radio-button at the top of the Application Type section.

You *do not* want to create a Windows application, DLL, or Static library. You do *not* need to click the Empty Project check box in the Additional Options category. Finally, you do *not* want to click either the ATL or MFC Add Support For check boxes.

Once again, take a moment to double-check your selections before clicking the Finish button.

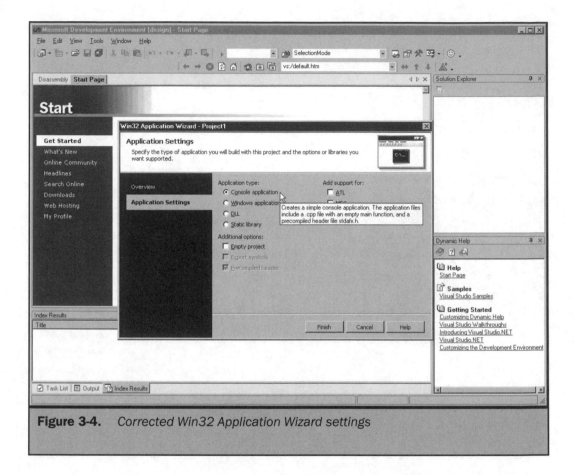

Figure 3-4.   *Corrected Win32 Application Wizard settings*

Figure 3-5 shows the automatically generated default tmain() function (_tmain meets the MBCSmultibyte character set—if you have no need for Unicode compliant algorithms, main() is preferred). You get this view by first moving to the Solution Explorer pane (right-edge) of the MDE window and clicking the Project1 folder. This expands the hierarchy tree, allowing you to view the four categories: Source Files, Header Files, Resource Files, and ReadMe.txt. Next, you will need to click the Source Files folder. Nested underneath are the stdafx.cpp and Project1.cpp filenames. When you double-click the Project1.cpp filename, your MDE window should resemble Figure 3-5.

The following code segment contains a simple C program, with several intentionally entered syntax and logic errors. You will use this algorithm to practice entering, editing, saving, debugging, and executing C/C++ source code.

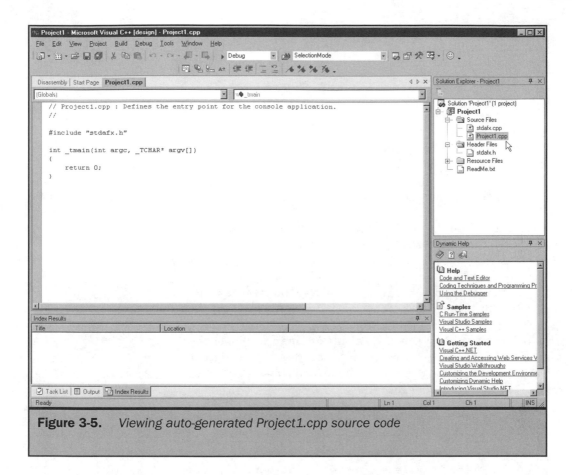

Figure 3-5.   *Viewing auto-generated Project1.cpp source code*

Enter the program exactly as you see it. If you are familiar with the C language, you will notice that there are errors in the program. Do not correct them. The errors were placed there specifically to give you hands-on experience with various features of the integrated environment.

```
// Project1.cpp : Defines the entry point for the console application.
//
/* NOTE: This program contains errors      */
/* entered for the purpose of teaching      */
/* you how to use the Integrated Debugger! */

#include "stdafx.h"
```

```cpp
#include <cstdio>
using namespace std;

/* The following symbolic constant is used to
   dimension the array */
#define SIZE 5

/* Function Prototype   */
void print_them(int offset,char continue,int iarray[SIZE]);

int _tmain(int argc, _TCHAR* argv[]) // sample meeting MBCS standard!
{
  int offset;        /* array element selector    */
  int iarray[SIZE];  /* integer array             */
  char continue = 0; /* used to hold user's response */

/* First function call prints variable's "as is"  */
  print_them(offset,continue,iarray);

/* Welcome message and input of user's response    */
  Printf(\n\nWelcome to a trace demonstration!");
  printf("\nWould you like to continue (Y/N) ");
  scanf("%c",continue);

/* User-input of new integer array data            */
  if(continue == 'Y')
    for(offset=0; offset < SIZE; offset++) {
      printf("\nPlease enter an integer: ");
      scanf("%d",&iarray[offset]);
    }

/* Second function call prints user-entered data   */
  print_them(offset,continue,iarray);

  return 0;
}
/* Function outputs the contents of all variables  */
void print_them(int offset, char continue, int iarray[SIZE])
{
  printf("\n\n%d",offset);
  printf("\n\n%d",continue);
  for(offset=0; offset < SIZE, offset++)
    printf("\n%d",iarray[offset]);
}
```

The section titled Debugging Programs, found later in this chapter, will only make sense *if* you have not altered and/or corrected any of the preceding code. Check your screen version against the listing to ensure the two are clones of one another.

Editing Source Code

One of the main reasons for the success of Microsoft Windows is the graphical user interface. A consistent GUI means that when a particular feature appears in two different applications—for example, a Windows word processor and the Visual C++ MDE editor—that feature usually has the same menu and keyboard commands in the same locations in both applications.

This means that even if you have never used the Visual C++ MDE editor, you should find that correcting mistakes or moving to the end of a line, the beginning of a line, or the bottom of the Edit window is just as easy and familiar as it is in your favorite Windows word processor.

Here are some helpful tips for working with the Visual C++ MDE editor: To move quickly through a line, hold down the CTRL key while pressing the left or right cursor key. This causes the edit cursor to move to the right or the left (depending on the cursor key pressed), one whole word at a time. (A word is defined as anything delimited by a blank space or punctuation.)

To delete an entire word instead of a single character, place the cursor on the space before or after the word to be deleted and press either CTRL-DELETE (to delete the word to the right) or CTRL-BACKSPACE (to delete the word to the left).

To allow for the maximum amount of editing workspace, the horizontal and vertical scroll bars can be turned off (see Tools | Options). If you chose this option, the mouse cannot be used to scroll the window either horizontally or vertically. For this reason, you need to know two key combinations: CTRL-PAGE UP, which moves you to the top of a program, and CTRL-END, which moves you to the bottom of a program. How are you doing with that highlighter?

Perhaps you are wondering why we have made no mention of the horizontal movement keyboard equivalents. There is a reason: Most professionally written code fits within the standard monitor's 80-column width. This makes for easy reading and code debugging—since each line of code is completely visible, there can be no hidden bugs in column 95.

Saving Files

There is usually a major conflict between you and the compiler. You think that you write flawless code, while the compiler believes otherwise. If that insult is not bad enough, there's the linker's impression of your algorithmic genius. However, the final blow to your ego comes from the microprocessor itself, which, after being passed an executable file filtered by both the compiler and the linker, chokes on your digital instructions.

Although disagreements between you and the compiler or the linker are not catastrophic, disagreements between you and the microprocessor are. So here's the moral to this story: Save your file before you compile, before you link, and definitely before you try to run a program. Many a sad story has been told of a programmer who runs an unsaved file, crashes the application or the system, and then has to reenter the entire program.

If you have not already done so, save the example program you are working with. You can do so by either clicking the fourth button from the left on the toolbar (the picture on this button looks like a 3½-inch floppy disk), using the File | Save command, or pressing CTRL-S.

Figure 3-6 shows the Edit window as it looks just before the file is saved. Note the MDE will, by default, save your files when you execute a Build or Rebuild All (see Figure 3-7). Additional help comes when you try to exit the MDE and have forgotten to save any open files. Once again, the MDE will protect you by prompting you to save the file(s) before exiting.

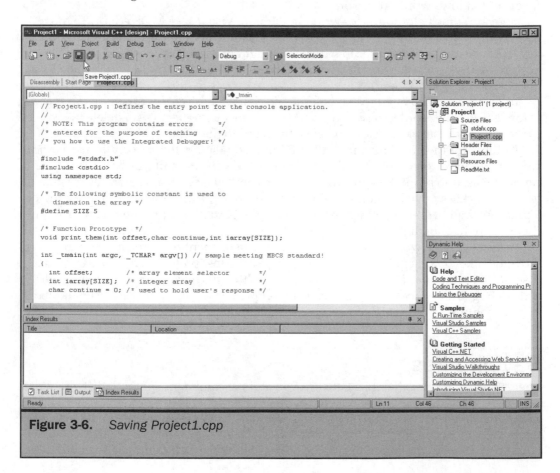

Figure 3-6.   *Saving Project1.cpp*

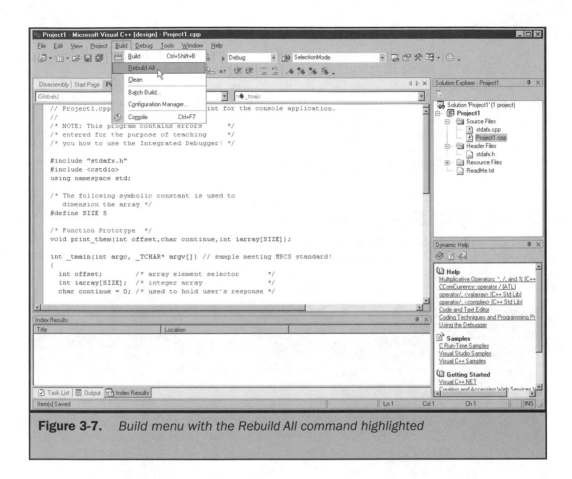

Figure 3-7.   *Build menu with the Rebuild All command highlighted*

Creating the Executable File

A full-blown Windows 2000/ME/98/95 or Windows NT program contains many files. Initially, however, simple C/C++ programs start with just one file, the main() C/C++ file. As you become a more experienced programmer, this introductory approach will prove to be inefficient. As your understanding of C/C++ and Windows application development increases, you will begin to break your solutions into multiple, logically related C/C++ files. To these you will add your own header files (header files have an h file extension). By the time you reach the end of this book, you will be creating applications with source code files, header files, resource files, and so on. So, even though the sample program contains just a single file (Project1.cpp), the following sections explain the steps necessary to build a fully formed C/C++ application under Windows.

Choosing Build or Rebuild All

Now that the project file has been created, you are ready to instruct the MDE to create the executable file. Remember, under Visual C++ this process is called a *build*.

In Chapter 2, you learned that the only difference between the Build and Rebuild All commands is that Rebuild All does not check the dates of any of the files used by the project. This command always recompiles and links every file in the project. Because a poorly maintained system can have inaccurate internal clock settings, it is always safest to choose the Rebuild All option for small applications. Now, activate the build process by clicking the Rebuild All command or pressing ENTER when the command is highlighted.

Debugging Programs

If your program contains syntax errors, executing a Build or Rebuild All command automatically opens the compiler output message window, as seen at the bottom of the screen in Figure 3-8.

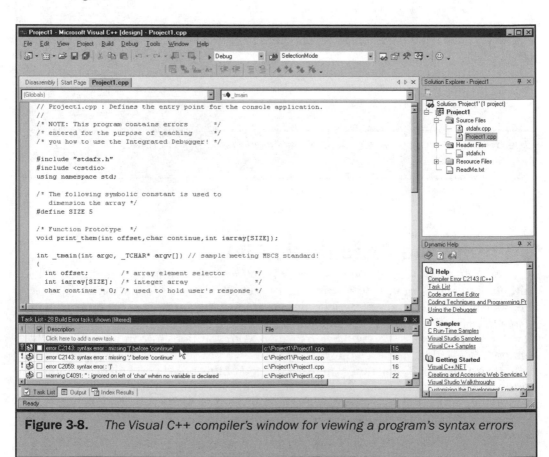

Figure 3-8.   *The Visual C++ compiler's window for viewing a program's syntax errors*

Each message begins with an error number, category (warning or error), brief description, and flagged statement's source filename, which for this example is C:\VC7Book\BC7chp03\ \MyProjects\Error\Project1.cpp. This filename is important because the typical Windows application contains many source files.

> **Note**   *You will probably need to have your monitor's screen resolution set high enough to actually view the entire error or warning messages described in the following text.*

Immediately to the right of the source file's name is the line number in which the warning or error was detected. Programs can run with warning messages, but not with error messages. Warnings do not necessarily mean there is something wrong with your source code. Warnings can mean that you are using a feature of C or C++, which can get you into run-time trouble—and the warning is just a reminder to you to double-check the particular statement.

Differences Between Warning and Error Messages

Sometimes warning messages flag the use of a standard C/C++ automatic rule. For example, an automatic rule might be invoked when having a **float** value automatically truncated as it is assigned to an integer variable. This does not mean that the code was written incorrectly, only that the statement is using some sort of behind-the-scenes feature of C/C++.

Another example of valid warnings comes from the functions prototyped in cmath (new name for math.h), which have formal arguments of the type *double* and return the type *double*. If your program passes to one of these functions an argument of the type *float*, the compiler will generate a warning. This warning will inform you that a conversion is taking place from the type *float* to the type *double* as the argument is pushed onto the call stack.

You can remove many warning messages by overriding automatic language defaults. You do this by placing, in the foreground, those operators or functions designed to perform the behind-the-scenes operation. The example-warning message described in the preceding paragraph would be removed by doing an explicit cast of the argument from the type *float* to the type *double*.

Your First Unexpected Bug

The first error message, shown earlier in Figure 3-8, shows what might happen when you are using a new language for the first time. Here the programmer tried to give a variable the name of a reserved, or language, keyword. If you are using a programming language that you are familiar with, you will probably not have this problem.

In C/C++, the word *continue* is a reserved, or language, keyword. In the sample program, the variable's name was chosen for self-documenting, readability reasons; however, it bumped into a language restriction. Chapter 6 contains a table (Table 6-1) of these reserved words for you to refer to when initially creating your source code.

Viewing Output and Source Windows

Once you have viewed your list of warning and error messages, you will want to switch back to the Edit window to make the necessary code changes. You can select the Edit window by either clicking the mouse inside the Edit window itself or by going to the Window menu and clicking the filename, Project1.cpp. Using whichever approach you prefer (has the highlighter dried out yet?), make the Edit window the active window.

Using Find and Replace

There will be times when you will want to quickly locate something within your program. You can do this by bringing down the Edit | Replace dialog box, but the Visual C++ MDE provides a quicker option. If you look closely at the toolbar in Figure 3-9, you will see the word *continue* in the Quick Find list box.

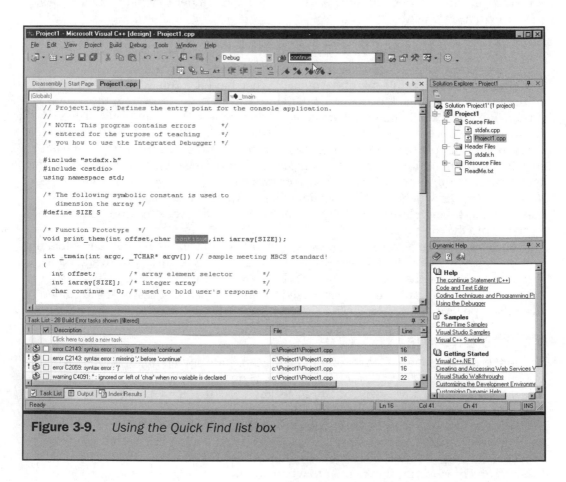

Figure 3-9.   *Using the Quick Find list box*

To use Quick Find, simply click the left mouse button anywhere within the control's interior and type the label you want to find. Quick Find can now be activated by pressing ENTER. Figure 3-9 shows the results of this action. The first occurrence of the *continue* variable is highlighted.

This approach is fine for locating first occurrences, but in our case it is inefficient because we need to locate all occurrences of the *continue* variable. For this reason, the Edit | Replace dialog box, shown in Figure 3-10, is a better choice.

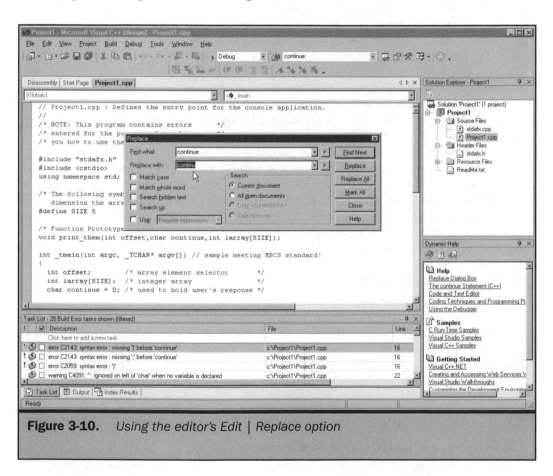

Figure 3-10.   *Using the editor's Edit | Replace option*

The easiest way to use Replace is to first place the cursor on the word to search for *before* you invoke the Edit | Replace option. If you follow this sequence, the word being searched for will be automatically entered into the Find What list when you invoke the command.

In Figure 3-10, you saw this approach used by first placing the cursor on the variable *continue*, which was highlighted in the previous figure. Practice this sequence and see if you can get your screen to appear like the one in Figure 3-10.

For our sample program, we want the variable that is currently named *continue* to still be readable, but it needs to be spelled differently from the reserved word. At this point, you need to manually enter the word *continu* into the Replace dialog box's Replace With list.

Notice that this dialog box contains many of the standard word processor search-and-replace options, such as the ability to match whole words and designate case sensitivity. If you are new to the C/C++ language, you will be surprised to find that C/C++ is case sensitive. For this reason, variables named *TOTAL* and *total* are treated as different variables.

One word of advice: Before you perform any search-and-replace operation, save the file. This will allow you to easily recover from a disastrous pattern match. Another approach is to use the Edit | Undo command. However, if your Undo buffer is not sufficiently large enough to hold all the changes the search-and-replace operation made, Undo might not be able to restore your whole program.

Now that you have entered the proper information into the Replace dialog box, you are ready to execute the replacement. However, there is one problem. The program contains the output statement "\nWould you like to continue (Y/N)". If you were to choose the Replace dialog box option of Replace All, your output statement would have a spelling error in it, because a Replace All would misspell the word *continue* in the program's run-time output. For this reason, click the Find Next button.

Using Replace Options

The Replace dialog box presents you with several search options. Find Next searches for the search string's next occurrence. Replace inserts the substitute string. The Replace All option races through your code without interruption, finding and replacing the targeted text.

In this example, you need to repeatedly choose Replace, followed by Find Next, until you have replaced every use of the variable *continue* with the new spelling, *continu*. Remember, do not change the spelling of the word *continue* in the **printf()** statement.

Shortcuts to Switching Views

Earlier you saw that switching between the Output message window and the Edit window required some keyboard or mouse gymnastics. There is an easier way to get these two windows to interact. But first, if you are following the example development cycle, you need to stop and rebuild your program. If you made all of the necessary *continu* substitutions described previously, your output message window should look like the one in Figure 3-11.

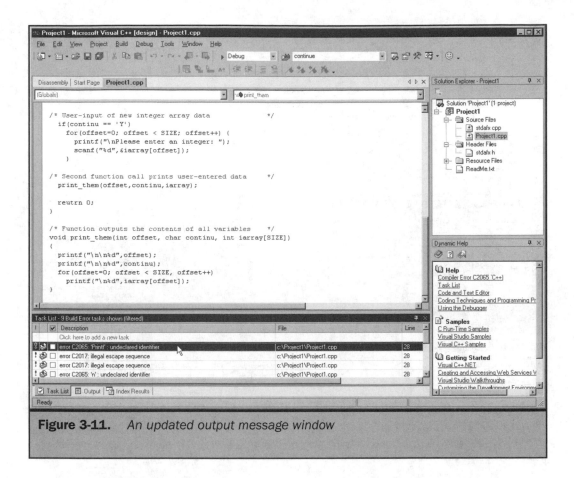

Figure 3-11.   *An updated output message window*

The improved way to interact with these two windows is very straightforward. First, place the cursor on the warning or error message of interest. For our example, pick the first message in the new Output message window:

```
error C2065: 'Printf' : undeclared identifier
```

Now press ENTER. Voilà! The integrated environment automatically switches to the Edit window and highlights the suspicious code segment (with an arrow), as shown in Figure 3-12.

You can obtain the same auto-window switching by double-clicking a warning or error message. The MDE will automatically locate the offending statement in any of the project's source files.

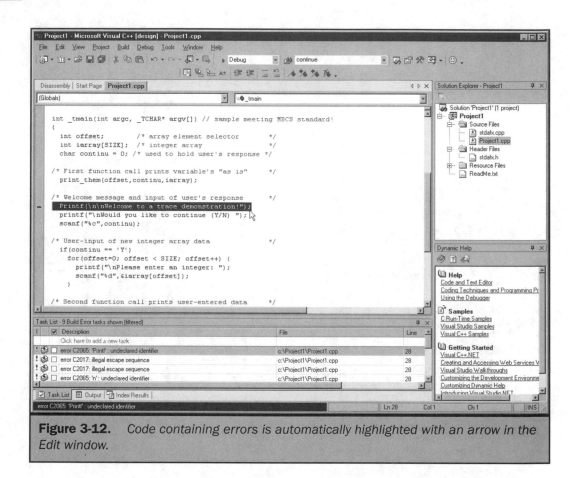

Figure 3-12. Code containing errors is automatically highlighted with an arrow in the Edit window.

Useful Warning and Error Messages

When you learn a new language, you actually encounter two major learning curves. First, there's the time it takes to learn the syntax and nuances of the new language itself. But the second, subtler learning curve involves understanding this new environment's help, warning, and error messages. In other words, you have to learn how this new compiler processes source code.

The good news is that the Visual C++ compiler produces some of the most accurate messages ever produced by any language environment. In our example, the compiler adroitly detected the misuse of a language keyword, *continue*.

As you now know, C/C++ is case sensitive. Once again, the compiler correctly detected an error. The function printf(), supplied with your compiler, was defined in all lowercase letters. Because this function was accidentally entered with an uppercase

"P," the compiler was unable to locate a matching library function Printf(). With this word highlighted in the Edit window, make the edit change by replacing the uppercase "P" with its lowercase equivalent. Don't forget to save your file.

More Work with the Debugger

At this point the program is ready for another attempt at building an executable file. Return to the Build menu and select the Rebuild All menu item. Figure 3-13 shows the updated output messages.

Do you remember how to easily switch to the Edit window and automatically locate the illegal escape sequence identified in the error message? (All you need to do is place the cursor on the error message and press ENTER.)

As it turns out, the same statement that contained the misspelled printf() function has a second error. In C/C++, all format strings must begin with a double quote. Edit the line by placing a double quote (") after the opening parenthesis in the printf() function—that is, after printf().

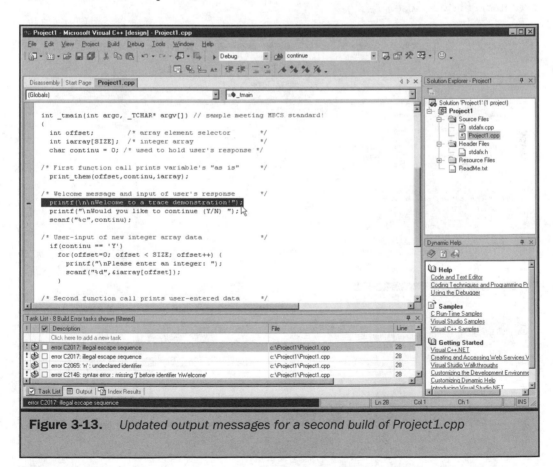

Figure 3-13.   *Updated output messages for a second build of Project1.cpp*

Make sure that your first **printf()** statement matches the one in Figure 3-14. Now, save the file, and attempt another rebuild. Figure 3-14 shows the third updated output message window.

Our last error message was

```
error C2143: syntax error : missing ';' before ')'
```

Place the cursor on the message and press ENTER. In the C/C++ language, unlike in Pascal, a semicolon is considered to be a statement terminator, not a statement separator. For this reason, the second statement within the **for** loop expression needs a terminating semicolon, not a comma. Change the comma after the constant *SIZE* to a semicolon, save the file, and execute a Rebuild All once again.

Success? According to the output message window, you should now have no warnings and no errors, and the Rebuild All command has successfully generated the executable file, error.exe.

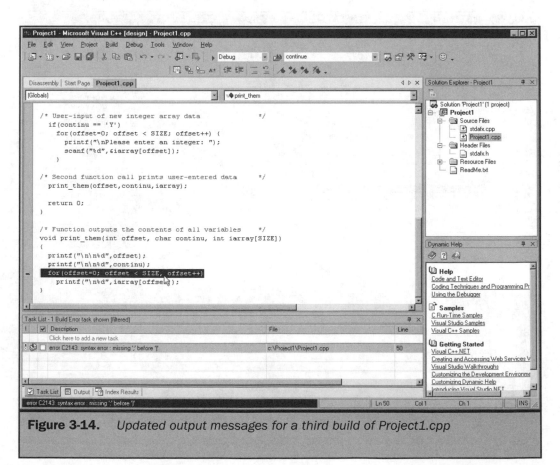

Figure 3-14.   *Updated output messages for a third build of Project1.cpp*

Note   *At this point if your compiler's errors and warnings message window does* not *show 0 errors and 1 warning (you have inadvertently added a few typos of your own), simply retrace your steps and edit the necessary code statements.*

Running Your First Program

To run a program after you have completed a successful Build or Rebuild All operation, simply click the Debug menu's Start Without Debugging command.

Figure 3-15 highlights just one of the many new features built into Visual Studio 7.0. The warning message is flagging the use of the variable *offset* in the print_them() function call. The MDE recognizes that the variable has been declared but never given a valid value. (This logical error was intentionally inserted into Project1.cpp to demonstrate this feature—you can leave the variable's initial value undefined to see how the Debugger addresses this issue, or assign it a value of 0 now.)

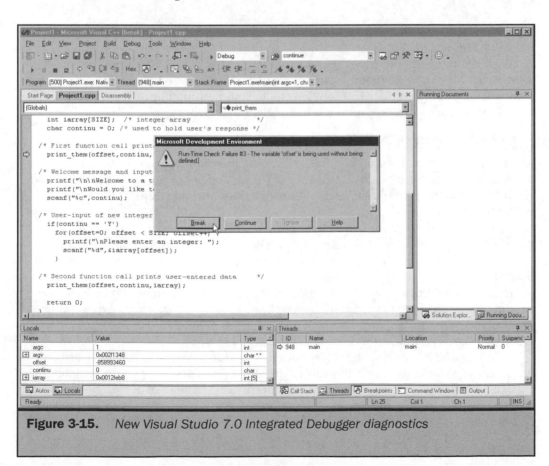

Figure 3-15.   *New Visual Studio 7.0 Integrated Debugger diagnostics*

Normally, you would click the Abort button to correct any flagged code errors. However, for this demonstration, resume program execution by clicking the Ignore button. You should see something like the following:

```
-858993460

0
-858993460
-858993460
-858993460
-858993460
-858993460

Welcome to a trace demonstration!
Would you like to continue (Y/N) y
```

Enter a **Y** when asked if you would like to continue. Your screen should now resemble Figure 3-16.

While it is true the program compiled without any errors or warnings, the run-time scenario looked quite different. From the flagged mis-use of an uninitialized variable, to a fatal break in the execution, it is obvious there is something logically incorrect with the algorithm. Your only recourse—use the Integrated Debugger.

Using the Integrated Debugger

The sample program's output begins by dumping the uninitialized contents of the array. It then asks if you want to continue. A *Y* (yes) answer logically indicates that you would now like to fill the array with your own values and then reprint the array's contents to the screen.

In this sample execution, you responded with a *Y*. However, if you examine the program's output, you can easily see that you were never prompted for input. In addition, the array's contents have not been changed, as evidenced by the duplicated output.

In other words, although you have a program that appears to be syntactically correct—there are no syntax errors—the application fails to perform as expected. These types of errors are called *logical* errors. Fortunately, the Visual C++ MDE Integrated Debugger has several features ready to come to your rescue.

Although the Integrated Debugger has many features, you will regularly use only a small subset of the commands. Basically, a debugger provides two powerful capabilities. First, it allows you to execute your program line by line instead of at full speed. Second, it allows you to examine the contents of any variable at any point in your program.

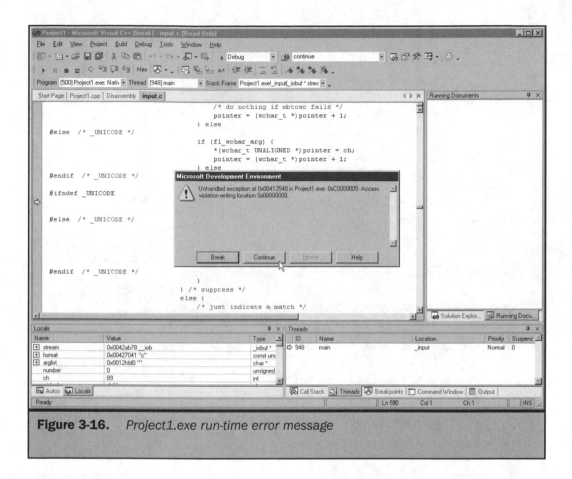

Figure 3-16.   *Project1.exe run-time error message*

When used correctly, these capabilities allow you to quickly locate an offending line of code. Unfortunately, the debugger does not automatically correct the code. (So, for the moment, your job security as a programmer is still not threatened!)

The Subtle Differences Between Step Into and Step Over

Figure 3-17 shows the Debug menu. When you start the debugger, usually by pressing F11, an optional Debug Toolbar may appear when you select the View | Toolbars | Debugger menu option (not shown in this text). Two of the more frequently used buttons represent the options Step Into (fifth button from the left on the Debug Toolbar) and Step Over (the sixth button). Both commands execute your program line by line.

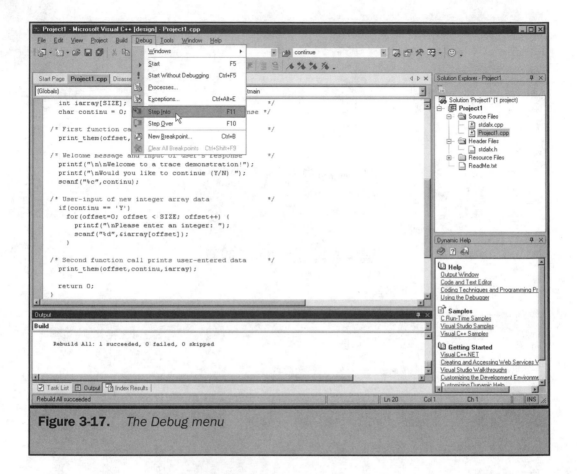

Figure 3-17.   *The Debug menu*

The appearance of the Edit window is different if you are using either the Step Into or Step Over commands. When you are debugging a program using one of these commands, the Integrated Debugger highlights the line of code *about* to be executed.

The only difference between Step Into and Step Over occurs when the statement about to be executed is a function call. If you select Step Into on a function call, the debugger jumps to the function header and continues debugging the code inside the function. If you select Step Over on a function call, the debugger executes the associated function at full speed and then returns to the statement following the function call. You should use this command whenever you are debugging a program that incorporates previously tested subroutines.

Using either Step command, invoke the command three times. Figure 3-18 shows the sample program as it will appear after you have invoked Step Into or Step Over three times.

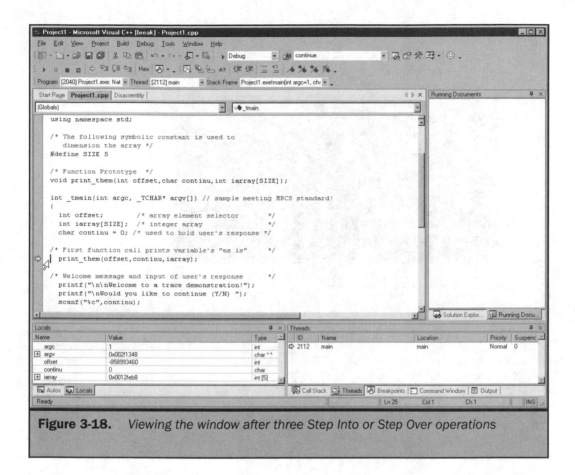

Figure 3-18. *Viewing the window after three Step Into or Step Over operations*

As you can see from Figure 3-18, the single-step arrow (also called a trace arrow) is positioned next to the call for the print_them() function.

For now, we want to execute the function at full speed. To do this, choose the Step Over command now. If you watch closely, you will notice that the function executes and the trace arrow stops on the first **printf()** statement. So far, so good. Now press F10 three times until the trace arrow stops on the **scanf()** statement. (Remember, for this exercise, ignore the fatal error message window by clicking the Continue button.)

At this point, you need to switch to the program's execution window. You can do this by pressing the ALT-TAB key combination. (You may need to use this key combination several times, depending on the number of tasks you have loaded.) When you are in ERROR's window, as shown in Figure 3-19, answer the question "Would you like to continue (Y/N)?" with a **Y**, and press ENTER.

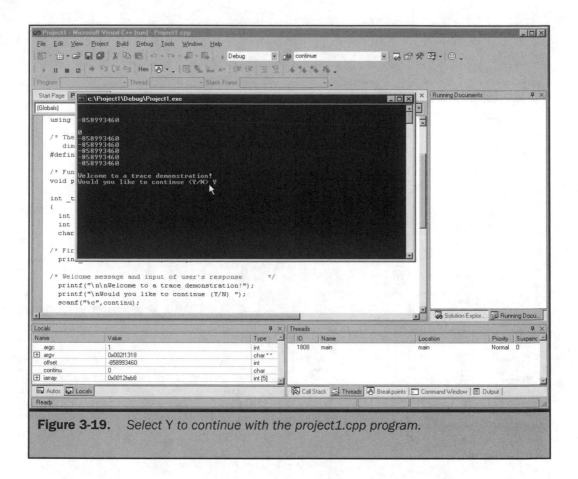

Figure 3-19. *Select* Y *to continue with the project1.cpp program.*

The Integrated Debugger immediately responds with the error message shown in Figure 3-20.

This message relates to the **scanf()** statement just executed. See if you understand enough of the C language to figure out what the problem is. The problem relates to the incorrect use of the scanf() function. The scanf() function expects to receive the address of a memory location to fill. Examine this statement:

```
scanf("%c",continu);
```

As you can see, this statement does not provide an address. The solution is to place the address operator (&) in front of the variable *continu*. Correct the statement so that it looks like this statement:

```
scanf("%c",&continu);
```

Save the change and execute a Rebuild All.

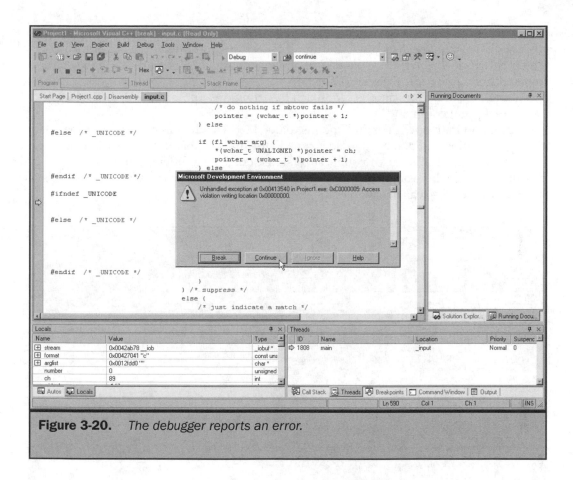

Figure 3-20.   *The debugger reports an error.*

Advanced Debugging Techniques

You can think of a breakpoint as a stop sign for the Integrated Debugger. Logically, breakpoints tell the debugger that all statements prior to the breakpoint are okay, so the debugger shouldn't waste time single-stepping through them.

The easiest way to set a breakpoint is to click the breakpoint control, which you can do if the toolbar is visible. This button is the second from the right on the toolbar. The picture on it resembles a hand signaling "stop." Or, since Microsoft has added the VB method of setting breakpoints, the easiest way now is to click the bar at the left of the line of code.

The breakpoint button is a toggle. If the line that the cursor is on when you click the button does not contain a breakpoint, the command sets one. If the line that the cursor is on already has a breakpoint set, the command removes it. You can set as many breakpoints as you need by repeating this sequence. The Go command, when selected, will always run your program from the current line up to the next breakpoint.

For the sample program, you know that all statements prior to the scanf() function call are okay. You have just edited this line and are now interested in seeing if the new statement works properly. For the sake of efficient debugging, you are going to set a breakpoint on line 30, at the scanf() function.

Figure 3-21 illustrates another approach to setting breakpoints: using the Debug | New Breakpoint command.

This menu item opens the Breakpoints dialog box. The default breakpoint type is Break at Location. All you need to do is type in the line number in the Location box. For our example, this is line 30. (If your **scanf()** statement is on a different line number, possibly because there are extra blank lines in the source code, enter your source file's line number for the **scanf()** statement.) Now choose the OK button.

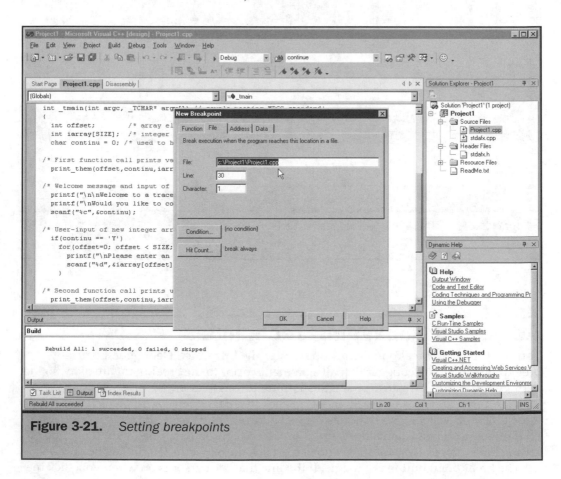

Figure 3-21. *Setting breakpoints*

Using Breakpoints

To debug a program at full speed up to, but not including, the breakpoint, you can use the Debug | Start menu item, as shown in Figure 3-22.

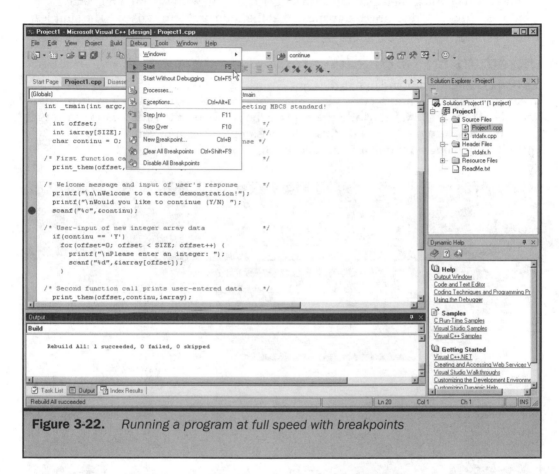

Figure 3-22. *Running a program at full speed with breakpoints*

Assuming that you have the previously described breakpoint set, invoke the Start command. (Either select the command with the mouse, use the keyboard to access the command via the menus, or press F5.) Notice that the trace arrow speeds quickly to the statement containing the scanf() function call and then stops.

Once the debugger stops at a breakpoint, you can return to single-stepping through the program or even pause to examine a variable's contents. For now, we are interested in seeing if the syntax change made to the **scanf()** statement works. Choose the Step Over option, switch to the program's execution window, type an uppercase **Y**, and press ENTER. (You want Step Over so debugger doesn't attempt to step into scanf() function. Stepping in will prompt for the location of scanf.c file. If you cancel this then you're in disassembly and the window won't be ready to accept input, etc.)

Success! The Integrated Debugger no longer flags you with warning message windows. However, does this really mean that the code problem is fixed? The simplest way to answer this question is to examine the current contents of the variable *continu*.

An Introduction to QuickWatch

The QuickWatch command opens the QuickWatch dialog box, which allows you to instantaneously view and modify the contents of a variable. The fastest way to put a variable in the QuickWatch window is to place the cursor on the variable in your source code and press SHIFT-F9. If you do this with the sample program, you will see a QuickWatch dialog box similar to the one in Figure 3-23.

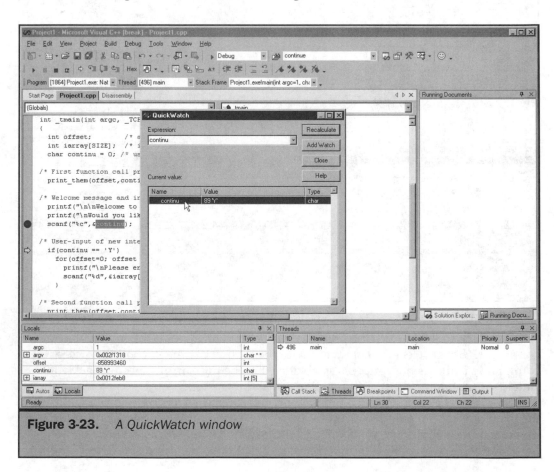

Figure 3-23.   *A QuickWatch window*

Now that you know the contents of *continu* are correct (see Figure 3-24), you can run the program at full speed to the end, using the Debug | Start command.

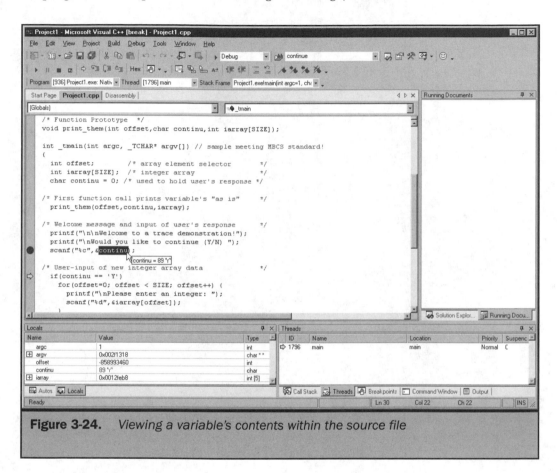

Figure 3-24.   *Viewing a variable's contents within the source file*

What's Coming?

In this chapter, you rehearsed the day-to-day commands necessary to create, edit, save, build, and debug a simple C program. In Chapter 4, you will learn about programming issues specific to more sophisticated C++ applications using STL (the Standard Template Library).

Chapter 4

Advanced Visual C++
Features

There are two very significant enhancements to Microsoft's Visual Studio.NET, the Standard Template Library, or STL, and even more notably Microsoft's brand new programming language named C#. Microsoft bundles these powerful programming language evolutions into Visual Studio.NET. Although each topic is beyond the scope of a single chapter, this chapter provides a high-level overview of the advantages of C++ programming with STL, and explains why C# could easily end up the de facto standard for Windows program development for the next half decade.

What Is the Standard Template Library?

From a programming point-of-view, today's development environment is a hundred times more complex than a decade ago. Instead of PC application development targeting a standalone DOS text-mode environment, it must now deal with hundreds of PC clones and other popular competing platforms.

The Complexity of Multiplatform Target Environments

These new architectures have their own evolving operating systems and multitasking, multimedia capabilities. Add to this the typical Internet presence. In other words, today's programming environment, programmed by a single developer, was once the domain of systems, communications, security, networking, and utility specialists all working as a team to keep the "mother ship," or mainframe, up and running!

Something had to come along to enable application developers to keep pace with this ever-increasing resource management nightmare. Voilá, enter C and C++. These new languages incorporated brand new programming capabilities to melt through this hidden iceberg of programming demands.

Unintentional Misuse or Ignorance of C/C++ Features

The biggest stumbling block to accessing these incredibly powerful C/C++ features is ignorance of their existence. In the real world, most experienced FORTRAN, COBOL, Pascal, PL/I, and Assembly Language programmers, when asked by their bosses to use a new language, taught themselves the new language! Why? Because of course, the company wouldn't give them training. They diligently studied nights and weekends, on their own, and mapped their understanding of whatever language they knew well, to the new language's syntax.

This approach worked for decades as long as a programmer went from one "older, high-level language" to the next. Unfortunately, this approach, when it comes to C/C++, leaves the diligent, self-motivated, learn-on-one's-own employee, fired and wondering what went wrong this time?

Here's a very small example to illustrate the point. In COBOL, for instance, to increment a variable by 1, you would write

```
accumulator = accumulator + 1;
```

Then one day the boss says you need to write the program in FORTRAN. You learn FORTRAN and rewrite the statement:

```
accumulator = accumulator + 1;
```

No problem. Then your company migrates to Pascal and once again you teach yourself the new syntax:

```
accumulator := accumulator + 1;
```

Tada! Then your boss says that your million-dollar code needs to be ported over to Microsoft Windows in C/C++. After a heart attack and alcohol addiction you emerge feeling you have mastered Microsoft Windows C/C++ logic and syntax and finally rewrite the statement:

```
iaccumulator = iaccumulator + 1; //i for integer in Hungarian notation
```

and you get fired! The senior programmer, hired from a local two-year college, looks at your code and scoffs at your inept translation. Oh sure, you got the idea behind Hungarian Notation (a C/C++ naming convention that precedes every variable's name with an abbreviation of its data type), but you created a literal statement *translation* instead of incorporating the efficiency alternatives available in C/C++.

Your senior programmer, green, 20 years younger than you, only knowing Microsoft Windows C/C++ syntax, knew the statement should have been written like this:

```
iaccumulator++;
```

This statement, using the C/C++ increment operator, efficiently instructs the compiler to delete the double fetch/decode of the incorrectly written *translation*, and to treat the variable *iaccumulator*, as its name implies, as an accumulator within a register—a much more efficient machine language encoding.

This extremely simple code example is only the beginning of hundreds of C/C++ language features waiting, like quicksand, to catch the unwary programmer.

Data Structures: The Course to Separate the Hackers from the Pros!

In a programmer's formal educational path, there stands a course typically called Data Structures, which statistically has an attrition rate of 50%. Why? Because it deals with two extremely efficient concepts, pointers, and dynamic memory allocation/de-allocation, which when combined, generate a geometric complexity in program development and debugging requirements. These concepts typically present such a steep learning curve that many programmers either avoid the course altogether or just get by, and then *never* use the concepts in the real world.

This is unfortunate since pointers and dynamic memory allocation present some of the most powerful and efficient algorithms available to a programmer. Enter the Standard Template Library!

So, Just What Is the Standard Template Library?

In a nutshell, STL (the Standard Template Library) encapsulates the pure raw horsepower of the C/C++ languages, plus the advanced efficient algorithms engendered within a good Data Structures course, all bundled into a simple-to-use form! It is similar in a way to having struggled with years of pre-calc and calculus courses, only to be given an advanced portable calculator that does all the work for you.

You may view STL as an extensible framework that contains components for language support, diagnostics, general utilities, strings, locales, a standard template library (containers, iterators, algorithms, numerics) and input/output.

The Origins of STL

With the ever increasing popularity of C/C++ and Microsoft Windows-controlled environments, many third-party vendors evolved into extremely profitable commodities by providing libraries of routines designed to handle the storage and processing of data. In an ever-ongoing attempt to maintain C/C++'s viability as a programming language of choice, and to keep the ball rolling by maintaining a strict control of the languages' formal definition, the ANSI/ISO C++ added a new approach to defining these libraries, called the STL.

STL is expected to become the standard approach to storing and processing data. Major compiler vendors are beginning to incorporate the STL into their products. The Standard Template Library is more than just a minor addition to the world's most popular programming language—it represents a revolutionary new capability. The STL brings a surprisingly mature set of generic containers and algorithms to the C++ programming language, adding a dimension to the language that simply did not exist before.

What Do I Need to Know to Take Advantage of STL?

You have all you need to know, simply by picking up this book. Unlike many other STL books that simply enumerate endless lists of STL template names, functions, constants, and so on, this book will begin by first teaching you the advanced C/C++ language fundamentals that make the Standard Template Library syntactically possible.

Along the way, this instructional section will show you the syntax that allows an algorithm to be generic. In other words, how C/C++ syntactically separate *what* a program does from the *data type(s)* it uses. You will learn about generic **void** * pointer's strengths and weaknesses, "a better way" with generic types, "an even better way" using templates, and finally, the "best way" with cross-platform, portable Standard Templates!

The section on template development begins with simple C/C++ structures used syntactically to create *objects*. (Yes, you can create an object with this keyword. However it is a very bad idea—you'll have to wait 'til the next chapter to see why!) The **struct** object definition is then evolved over, logically and syntactically, into the C++ **class**. Finally, the **class** object is mutated into a generic **template**. This progressive approach allows you to easily assimilate the new features of C/C++ and paves the way to technically correct use of the STL. With this under your belt, you will both logically and syntactically understand how the STL works and begin to immediately incorporate this technology into your application development.

Generic programming is going to provide you with the power and expressiveness of languages like SmallTalk while retaining the efficiency and compatibility of C++. STL is guaranteed to increase the productivity of any programmer who uses it.

A High-Level View of STL

Although the STL is large and its syntax can be initially intimidating, it is actually quite easy to use once you understand how it is constructed and what elements it employs. At the core of the STL are three foundational items called *containers, algorithms*, and *iterators*. The libraries work together allowing you to generate, in a portable format, frequently employed algorithmic solutions, such as array creation, element insertion/deletion, sorting, and element output. But the STL goes even further by providing internally clean, seamless, and efficient integration of iostreams and exception handling.

Kudos to the ANSI/ISO C and C++ Committee

Multi-vendor implementations of C/C++ compilers would have long ago died on the vine were it not for the ANSI/ISO C/C++ committee. It is this committee who is responsible for giving us portable C and C++ code by filing in the missing details for the formal language descriptions of both C and C++ as presented by their authors, Dennis Ritchie and Bjarne Stroustrup, respectively. And to this day, it is the ANSI/ISO C++ committee that continues to guarantee C++'s portability into the next millennium.

While on the subject of language authorship, it is Alexander Stepanov and Meng Lee of Hewlett Packard who developed the concept and coding behind the Standard Template Library. As mentioned, the industry anticipates that STL will become *the* standard approach to storing and processing data.

The ANSI/ISO C++ committee's current standards exceed its past recommendations, which historically decided only to codify existing practices and resolve ambiguities and contradictions among existing translator implementations. The C++ committee's changes are innovative. In most cases, the changes implement features that committee members admired in other languages, features that they viewed as deficiencies in traditional C++, or features they'd always wanted in a programming language. A great deal of thought and discussion have been invested in each change, and consequently, the committee feels that the new C++ definition, along with the evolutionary definition of STL, is the best definition of C++ possible today.

Most of these recommended changes consist of language additions that should not affect existing code. Old programs should still compile with newer compilers as long as the old codes do not coincidentally use any of the new keywords as identifiers. However, even experienced C++ programmers may be surprised at how much of C++ has evolved even without discussing STL, e.g., the use of namespaces, new-style-type casting, and runtime-type information (discussed in detail in Chapter 2).

STL's Tri-Component Nature

Conceptually, STL encompasses three separate algorithmic problem solvers. The three most important are containers, algorithms, and iterators. A container is a way that stored data is organized in memory, e.g., an array, stack, queue, linked list, or binary-tree. However, there are many other kinds of containers, and the STL includes the most useful. The STL containers are implemented by template classes so they can be easily customized to hold different data types.

All the containers have common management member functions defined in their template definitions: insert(), erase(), begin(), end(), size(), capacity(), and so on. Individual containers have member functions that support their unique requirements.

Algorithms are behaviors or functionality applied to containers to process their contents in various ways. For example, there are algorithms to sort, copy, search, and merge container contents. In the STL, algorithms are represented by template functions. These functions are not member functions of the container classes. Instead, they are standalone functions. Indeed, one of the surprising characteristics of the STL is that its algorithms are so general. You can use them not only on STL containers, but also on ordinary C++ arrays or any other application-specific container.

A standard suite of algorithms provides for searching, copying, reordering, transforming, and performing numeric operations on the objects in the containers. The same algorithm is used to perform a particular operation for all containers of all object types!

Once you have decided on a container type and data behaviors, the only thing left is to interact the two with iterators. You can think of an iterator as a generalized pointer that points to elements within a container. You can increment an iterator, as you can a pointer, so it points in turn to each successive element in the container. Iterators are a key part of the STL because they connect algorithms with containers.

Containers

All STL library syntax incorporates the full use of C++ templates (data-type independent syntax). As we discuss the container types, remember that they are implemented as templates; the types of objects they contain are determined by the template arguments given when the program instantiates the containers. There are six major types of containers: vectors (or dynamic arrays), deques (or double-ended queues), linear lists, bitset, map, and multimap.

Sequence containers store finite sets of objects of the same type in a linear organization. An array of names is a sequence. You use one of the sequence containers—vector, list, deque, linear list, bitset, map, or multimap—for a particular application depending on its retrieval requirements.

vector Class   Vector sequences allow random data access. A vector is an array of contiguous homogeneous objects with an instance counter or pointer to indicate the end of the vector sequence. Random access is facilitated through the use of a subscript operation. Vector sequences allow you to append entries to and remove entries from the end of the dynamic structure without undue overhead. Inserts and deletes from the middle, however, naturally take longer due to the time involved in shifting the remaining entries to make room for the new or deleted item.

list Class   A list sequence provides bidirectional access; it allows you to perform inserts and deletes anywhere without undue performance penalties. Random access is simulated by forward or backward iteration to the target object. A list consists of noncontiguous objects linked with forward and backward pointers.

deque Class   A deque sequence is similar to a vector sequence except that a deque sequence allows fast inserts and deletes at the beginning as well as the end of the container. Random inserts and deletes are less efficient.

bitset Class   The **bitset** class supports operations on a set of bits, such as **flip()**, **reset()**, **set()**, **size()**, **to_string**, etc.

map Class   The **map** class provides associative containers with unique keys mapped to specific values.

multimap Class   The **multimap** class is very similar to the map class in raw horsepower except for one minor difference, the availability of a non-unique key mapped to specific values.

Container Adapters

STL supports three adapter containers, which you can combine with one of the sequence containers listed above. The scenario goes like this: First you select the appropriate application-specific container; next, you instantiate a container adapter class by naming the existing container in the declaration.

```
queue< list< bank_customer_struct > >TellerOneQueue;
```

The example instantiates a queue container—one of the three adapter containers supported by STL—by using the list container as the underlying data structure built around a hypothetical bank customer waiting for an available teller.

Container adapters hide the public interface of the underlying container and implements its own. A queue data structure, for example, resembles a list but has its own requirements for its user interface. STL incorporates three standard adapter containers: stack, queue, and priority_queue.

stack Class   The stack adapter provides the logical operations of **push()** and **pop()**, enabling the standard Last In First Out, or LIFO, solution. Stacks are great for certain types of problem solutions like evaluating an Infix arithmetic expression that has been translated into Postfix for the purposes of unambiguous evaluation.

queue Class   Regardless of whether the storage sequence container is a vector or linked list, the queue adapter uses this underlying scheme to add items to the end of the list, using the **push()** method, and to delete or remove items from the front of the list, **using pop()**. The acronym for a queue algorithm is First In First Out, or FIFO.

priority_queue Class   A priority_queue is similar to a queue adapter in that all items added to the queue are at the end of the list. However, unlike a queue adapter, which only removes items from the front of the list, a priority_queue adapter removes the highest priority item within the list first!

Algorithms

Similar to container adapters, algorithms also act on containers. Algorithms provide for container initializations, sorting, searching, and data transformations. Interestingly, algorithms are not implemented as class methods, but instead, standalone template functions. For this reason they not only work on STL containers, but also work on standard C++ arrays or with container classes you create yourself.

Typical algorithmic behaviors include **find()**, to locate a specific item, **count()**, letting you know how many items are in the list, **equal()**, for comparisons, and **search()**, **copy()**, **swap()**, **fill()**, **sort()**, and so on.

Iterators

Whenever an application needs to move through the elements of a container, it uses an iterator. Iterators are similar to pointers used to access individual data items. In the STL, an iterator is represented by an object of an iterator class. You can increment an iterator with the C/C++ increment operator ++, moving it to the address of the next element. You can also use the dereference operator * to access individual members within the selected item. Special iterators are capable of remembering the location of specific container elements.

There are different classes of iterators that must be used with specific container types. The three major classes of iterators are forward, bidirectional, and random access.

- Forward iterators can only advance forward through the container one item at a time. It cannot move backward, nor can it be updated to point to any location in the middle of the container.

- Backward iterators work like the forward iterator counterparts, except backward.

- Bidirectional iterators can move forward as well as backward, and cannot be assigned or updated to point to any element in the middle of the container.

- Random-access iterators go one step further than bidirectional iterators in that they do allow the application to perform arbitrary location jumps within the container.

In addition, STL defines two specialized categories known as input and output iterators. Input and output iterators can point to specific devices (e.g., an input iterator may point to a user-defined input file, or cin, and is used to perform sequential reads into the container; likewise, an output iterator may point to a user-defined output file or count, performing the logical inverse operation of sequentially outputting container elements).

Unlike forward, backward, bidirectional, and random-access iterators, input and output iterators cannot store their current values. The first four iterators must hold their values in order for them to know where they are within the container. The last two, input and output, (pointers to devices) do not structurally represent the same type of information and therefore have no memory capabilities.

Additional Elements

Beyond containers, algorithms, and iterators, STL defines

- *Allocators,* for managing memory allocation for an individual container.

- *Predicates,* which are unary or binary in nature, meaning they work on either one operand or two, and always return either true or false.

- *Comparison function,* a unique binary predicate comparing two elements and returning true only if the first argument is less than the second.

- *Function objects,* including plus, minus, multiply, divide, modulus, negate, equal_to, not_equal_to, greater, greater_equal, less, less_equal, logical_and, logical_or, logical_not, and so on.

STL Review

The following review is included to help you formalize the structural components of the Standard Template Library. You can logically divide the STL into the following categories:

STL headers that can be grouped into three major organizing concepts

- Containers are template classes that support common ways to organize data: <deque>, <list>, <map>, <multimap>, <queue>, <set>, <stack>, and <vector>.

- Algorithms are template functions for performing common operations on sequences of objects including <algorithm>, <functional>, and <numeric>.

- Iterators are the glue that pastes together algorithms and containers and include <iterator>, <memory>, and <utility>.

Input Output, which includes components for

- Forward declarations of iostreams: <iosfwd>
- Predefined iostreams objects: <iostream>
- Base iostreams classes: <ios>
- Stream buffering: <streambuf>
- Stream formatting and manipulators: <iosmanip>, <istream>, and <ostream>
- String streams: <sstream>
- File streams: <fstream>

Other Standard C++ headers include

Language Support

- Components for common-type definitions used throughout the library: <cstddef>
- Characteristics of the predefined types: <limits>, <cfloat>, and <climits>
- Functions supporting start and termination of a C++ program: <cstdlib>
- Support for dynamic memory management: <new>
- Support for dynamic-type identification: <typeinfo>
- Support for exception processing: <exception>
- Other run-time support: <cstdarg>, <ctime>, <csetlmp>, and <csignal>

Diagnostics

- Reporting several kinds of exceptional conditions: <stdexcept>

- Documenting program assertions: <cassert>
- A global variable for error number codes: <cerrno>

Strings

- String classes: <string>
- Null-terminated sequence utilities: <cctype>, <cwctype>, and <cwchar>

Cultural Language

- Internationalization support for character classification and string collation: numeric, monetary, date/time formatting and parsing, and message retrieval using <locale>and <clocale>

Microsoft's New Language: C#

Microsoft states that "C# is a simple, modern, object-oriented, and type-safe programming language derived from C and C++." The first thing you will notice when using C# (C sharp) is how familiar you already are with many of the constructs of this language. Object-oriented by design, the C# language provides access to the class libraries available to Visual Basic and Visual C++ programmers. C#, however, does not provide its own class library.

C# is implemented by Microsoft in the latest version of the Microsoft Visual Studio and provides access to the Next Generation Windows Services (NGWS). These services include a common execution engine for code development.

Your First C# Console Application

Most programmers learn best by coded example. The following simple C# application demonstrates the similarities and differences between a C/C++ algorithm and C#. If you are already familiar with Visual Basic, you will even recognize a few syntax similarities nested in the C# example!

```
namespace HelloWorld
{
using System;

/// <summary>
///     Summary description for Class1.
/// </summary>
public class Class1
{
    public Class1()
```

```
    {
        //
        // TODO: Add Constructor Logic here
        //
    }

    public static int Main(string[] args)
    {
        //
        // TODO: Add code to start application here
        //

        Console.WriteLine("Hello, C# world");

        return 0;
    }
}
}
```

When you examine this simple portion of code, you will notice many of the elements that you are already familiar with when writing C or C++ console applications.

Let's briefly examine the familiar elements and the new additions. First, the application uses the using System directive. The System namespace, provided by the NGWS at runtime, permits access to the Console class used in the Main method. The use of **Console.WriteLine()** is actually an abbreviated form of **System.Console.WriteLine()** where **System** represents the **namespace**, **Console**, a class defined within the namespace, and **WriteLine()** as a static method defined within the Console class.

C# Program Structure Details

In C# programs, functions and variables are always contained within class and structure definitions and are never global.

You will probably notice the use of "." as a separator in compound names. C# uses this separator in place of "::" and "->". Also, C# does not need forward declarations because the order is not important. The lack of **#include** statements is an indicator that the C# language handles dependencies symbolically. Another feature of C# is automatic memory management. Automatic memory management frees developers from dealing with this complicated problem.

Value and Reference Types

C# supports two main categories of types: value and reference. You are already familiar with value types.

Value types include **char, enum, float, int, struct**, and so on. The key feature of the value type is that the variable actually contains the data.

Reference types, on the other hand, include class, array, delegate, and interface types. It is possible that an assignment to a reference type can affect other reference types derived from that reference type.

Predefined Types

In addition to the value and reference types discussed in the previous section, C# provides several predefined types.

For example, predefined value types include **bool, byte, char, decimal, double, float, int, long, sbyte, short, uint, ulong,** and **ushort**. Table 4-1 lists and describes these types.

Type	Description
bool	Boolean type, true or false, 1 or 0
byte	Unsigned 8-bit integer
char	Unicode char
decimal	28-digit decimal type
double	Double-precision real
float	Single-precision real
int	Signed 32-bit integer
long	Signed 64-bit integer
object	Base type for all other C# types
sbyte	Signed 8-bit integer
short	Signed 16-bit integer
string	A sequence of unicode characters
uint	Unsigned 32-bit integer
ulong	Unsigned 64-bit integer
ushort	Unsigned 16-bit integer

Table 4-1.   *C# Predefined Value Types*

The types listed in Table 4-1 are abbreviated versions of a longer structure name, but ones preferred in C#.

Arrays

C# supports the same variety of arrays as C and C++, including both single and multi-dimensional arrays. This type of array is often referred to as a rectangular array, as opposed to a jagged array.

To declare a single dimension integer array named *myarray*, the following C# syntax could be used:

```
int[] myarray = new int[12];
```

The array could then be initialized with twelve values using a **for** loop in the following manner:

```
for (int i = 0; i < myarray.Length; i++)
    myarray[i] = 2 * i;
```

The contents of the array, could be written to the screen with a **for** loop and **WriteLine()** statement:

```
for (int i = 0; i < myarray.Length; i++)
    Console.WriteLine("myarray[{0}] = {1}", i, myarray[i]);
```

Note that i values will be substituted for the {0} and "myarray[I]" values for {1} in the argument list provided with the **WriteLine()** statement.

Other array dimensions can follow the same pattern. For example, the syntax used for creating a two-dimensional array would take on this form:

```
int[,] my2array = new int[12, 2];
```

The array could then be initialized with values using two **for** loops in the following manner:

```
for (int i = 0; i < 12; i++)
    for (int j = 0; j < 2; j++)
        my2array[i, j] = 2 * i;
```

The contents of the array could then be displayed on the console with the following syntax:

```
for (int i = 0; i < 12; i++)
    for (int j = 0; j < 2; j++)
        Console.WriteLine("my2array[{0}, {1}] = {2}",
                          i, j, my2array[i, j]);
```

Three-dimensional arrays can be handled with similar syntax using this form:

```
int[,,] my3array = new int[3, 6, 9];
```

In addition to handling multidimensional rectangular arrays, C# handles jagged arrays. A jagged array can be declared using the following syntax:

```
int[][] jagarray1;
int[][][] jagarray2;
```

For example, suppose a jagged array is declared as:

```
int[][] jagarray1 = new int[2][];
jagarray1[0] = new int[] {2, 4};
jagarray1[1] = new int[] {2, 4, 6, 8};
```

Here, jagarray1 represents an array of an array of *int*. The jagged appearance of the structure gives rise to the array's type name. The following line of code would print the value 6 to the screen:

```
Console.WriteLine(jagarray1[1][2]);
```

For a little practice, try to write the code necessary to print each array element to the screen.

Boxing, Unboxing, and the Unified Type System

All types in C# can be treated as objects. For example, the following line of code is acceptable in C#:

```
Console.WriteLine(12345.ToString());
```

In this case, the **ToString()** method is used on the integer 12345 by treating it as an object.

An object box can be used when a value is to be converted to a reference type. This is called *boxing*. *Unboxing* is used to convert a reference type back to a value. For example:

```
int num1 = 12345;
object myobject = num1;        // boxed
int num2 = (int) myobject;      // unboxed
```

Here the integer number 12345 is first converted to a reference type with the use of boxing, then converted from an object back to an integer value by casting the object (unboxing).

Statements

Statement syntax in C# is basically the same as that for C and C++. In the following sections you'll see several familiar coding examples.

Blocks

C# allows blocking code so that one or more statements can be written in sequence. The following portion of code shows several blocks:

```
// block 1
Console.WriteLine("This is the first block");
{
    // block 2
    Console.WriteLine("This is the second block");
    {
        // block 3
        Console.WriteLine("This is the third block");
    }
}
```

Any number of blocks can be created using this format.

Miscellaneous Statements

C# provides a number of miscellaneous statements that are listed and briefly explained in Table 4-2.

Statement	Use
break	For exiting an enclosing—**do**, **for**, **foreach**, **switch**, or **while** statement
checked	To control the overflow checking context for arithmetic operations—all expressions are evaluated in a checked context
continue	For starting a new iteration of a **do**, **for**, **foreach**, **switch**, or **while** statement
lock	To obtain a mutual-exclusive lock for an object—with the lock in place, the statement will be executed, then the lock will be released
return	To return control to the caller of the statement in which it appears
throw	To throw an exception
try	For catching exceptions while a block is executing
unchecked	To control the overflow checking context for arithmetic operations—all expressions are evaluated in an unchecked context

Table 4-2. *Miscellaneous C# Statements*

You are already familiar with a number of these statements from your work with C and C++.

The do Statement

A **do** statement continues to execute a statement until the Boolean test is false. Here is a small portion of code:

```
int num1 = 0;
do {
    Console.WriteLine(num1);
    num1 += 2;
}
while (num1 != 20);
```

The output from this code will be the numbers 0 to 18. Every **do** statement will be executed at least one time with the Boolean test being made after the statement.

The Expression Statement

An expression statement evaluates a given expression and discards any value calculated in the process. Expressions such as (x + s), (y * 3), (t ==2), and so on are not allowed as statements. The following is an example of an expression statement:

```
static int HereWeGo() {
    Console.WriteLine("We made it to HereWeGo");
    return 0;
}
public static int Main(string[] args)
{
    //
    // TODO: Add code to start application here
    //
    HereWeGo();
    return 0;
}
```

Once again, the value returned by **HereWeGo()** is discarded.

The for Statement

The **for** statement, like its C and C++ counterparts, initializes the expression, then executes an expression while the Boolean test is true. For example:

```
for (int i  = 0; i < 10; i++) {
    Console.Write("the value of i is: ");
    Console.WriteLine(i);
}
```

This portion of code will report the value of i to the screen. The value of i increments from 0 to 9 before the Boolean condition is false.

The foreach Statement

The **foreach** statement is used to enumerate the contents of a collection. For example:

```
int[] myint = new int[] {1,2,3,4,5};
foreach (object o in myint) {
```

```
        Console.Write("the value of myint is: ");
        Console.WriteLine(o);
}
```

In this collection, each integer element will be reported to the screen. The collection, in general, can be any type.

The if and if-else Statements

The **if** statement executes based on a Boolean decision. If the statement is true, the expression will execute. If false, the statement will not execute. When used in conjunction with an **else**, the **if-else** combination will pass operation to the **else** when the **if** statement is false.

For example:

```
int i = 2 * 23 / 12;

if ( i >= 5)
    Console.WriteLine("This is a big number");
else
    Console.WriteLine("This is a reasonable number");
```

This portion writes one message or another based on the calculated value of the integer result.

The Label and goto Statements

The **goto** statement is used in conjunction with a label to transfer program control. For example:

```
goto C;

A: Console.WriteLine("This should be printed last");
return 0;

B: Console.WriteLine("This should be printed second");
goto A;

C: Console.WriteLine("This should be printed first");
goto B;
```

This concept is fairly straightforward. We recommend, however, a limited use of **goto** statements.

The switch (case-break) Statement

C# **switch** statements, like those of C and C++, execute statements that are associated with the value of a particular expression. When no match occurs, a default condition is executed:

```
string str = "Top";

switch (str.Length) {
    case 0:
        Console.WriteLine("No characters in the string.");
        break;
    case 1:
        Console.WriteLine("One character in the string.");
        break;
    case 2:
        Console.WriteLine("Two characters in the string.");
        break;
    case 3:
        Console.WriteLine("Three characters in the string.");
        break;
    default:
        Console.WriteLine("A lot of characters in the string.");
        break;
}
```

A default option should always be provided in **switch** statements.

The while Statement

A **while** statement continues to execute while the Boolean result is true. For example:

```
int i = 5;

while (i <= 300) {
    i += 5;
    Console.WriteLine("Not there yet!");
}
```

The value of i is initialized to 5. When the final increment is made, the value in i will be 305, and thus the loop will stop executing. The **while** statement continues to execute until the value of i exceeds 300.

Classes, Structures, and Enum

C# provides simple, but unique, implementations to these common object-oriented features.

Classes

C# classes allow only single inheritance. Members of a class can include constants, constructors, destructors, events, indexers, methods, properties, and operators. Each member can, in turn, have a public, protected, internal, protected internal, or private access.

The makeup of a class is similar to that used in C and C++. For example:

```
public class Form1 : System.WinForms.Form
{
    // variable declaration
    public double radius = 7.5;

    /// <summary>
    ///     Required designer variable
    /// </summary>
    private System.ComponentModel.Container components;
    private System.WinForms.Label label1;
    private System.WinForms.Button button1;
    private System.WinForms.TextBox textBox1;
     .
     .
     .
```

In this example, the class itself is public and contains a variable with public access. The designer variables, however, use a private qualifier to limit access. Classes use a pass by reference scheme as compared to a structures pass by value. For this reason, they tend to be faster than the equivalent structure.

Structures

Structures, as in C and C++, are very similar to classes. As a matter of fact, they can be created with members similar to those described for classes. Structures differ from classes in that they are value types with values being stored on the stack. This tends to make structures slower than an equivalent class because passing by value is slower than passing by reference.

Point is typically used and implemented in C, C++, and C# as a structure:

```
struct Point
{
    public int x, y;
    public Point(int x, int y) {
        this.x = x;
        this.y = y;
    }
}
```

This example illustrates the typical syntax for creating a structure.

Enum

The **enum** type declaration is used to provide a type name for a group of symbolic constants. These constants are usually related to one another. For example:

```
enum vehicle {
    Chrysler,
    Ford,
    GM
}
```

Use vehicle.GM to access the GM element, and so on.

Namespaces

C# uses namespaces as an organization system applied both internally and externally.

As a convention, developers usually name namespaces after the company they are developing code for.

The Visual C# AppWizard uses the following convention when creating a C# console code template:

```
namespace tester
{
using System;

public class Class1
{
    public Class1()
    {
    }
```

```
    public static int Main(string[] args)
    {
        int[] myint = new int[] {1,2,3,4,5};

        foreach (object o in myint) {
            Console.Write("the value of myint is: ");
            Console.WriteLine(o);
        }

        return 0;
    }
}
}
```

We can modify that code to take on the following appearance:

```
namespace Nineveh_National_Research.CSharp.Tester
{
using System;

public class ForEachDemo
{
    public ForEachDemo()
    {
    }

    public static int Main(string[] args)
    {
        int[] myint = new int[] {1,2,3,4,5};

        foreach (object o in myint) {
            Console.Write("the value of myint is: ");
            Console.WriteLine(o);
        }

        return 0;
    }
}
}
```

The namespace Nineveh_National_Research.CSharp.Tester is hierarchical. It really means that there is a namespace Nineveh_National_Reaearch that contains a namespace named CSharp that itself contains a namespace named Tester.

The *using* directive can be used as a shorthand notation, instead of writing out the whole namespace name. In the previous listing, the using directive allows all of the types in System to be used without qualification.

Attributes, Events, Indexers, Properties, and Versioning

Many of the terms in this section are employed when developing applications for Windows. If you have worked with Visual Basic or MFC and C++, you are familiar with the terms, attributes, events, and properties as they apply to controls. In the following sections, we'll generalize those definitions even more.

Attributes

C# attributes allow programmers to identify and program new kinds of declarative information. For example, attributes that identify the accessibility of a method are public, private, and protected.

An element's attribute information can be returned at run-time using the NGWS runtime's reflection support.

Events

Events are used to allow classes to provide notifications as to which clients can provide executable code. This code is in the form of event handlers. Again, if you have developed MFC C++ Windows code, you are already familiar with event handlers.

Here is code for a button click event handler, extracted from a project developed later in this book:

```
protected void button1_Click(object sender, System.EventArgs e)
{
    radius = Convert.ToDouble(textBox1.Text);
    textBox2.Text = (radius * radius * 22 / 7).ToString();
    textBox3.Text = (radius * 2.0 * 22 / 7).ToString();
}
```

The event handler contains code that will be executed when a button click event occurs. The button is a pushbutton that resides on a form in a C# Windows application.

Indexers

Indexers are used by C# to expose array-like data structures, such as an array of strings. This data structure might be used by a C# Windows control, such as a **CheckedListBox** control.

```
public class CheckedListBox: Control
{
    private string[] items;
```

```
    public string this[int index] {
        get {
            return items[index];
        }
        set {
            items[index] = value;
            Repaint();
        }
    }
}
```

The **CheckedListBox** class can then be altered with the following code:

```
CheckedListBox MyListBox;
MyListBox[0] = "List box title";
Console.Write(MyListBox[0]);
```

The array-like access provided by indexers is similar to the field-like access provided by properties.

Properties

A property is an attribute that is associated with a class or object. Windows controls offer a wide variety of changeable properties, including caption name, ID value, color, font, location, size, text, and so on.

Here is a small portion of a C# Windows program that modifies the properties of a button control:

```
button1.Location = new System.Drawing.Point(152, 192);
button1.Size = new System.Drawing.Size(176, 24);
button1.TabIndex = 6;
button1.Text = "Push to Calculate";
button1.AddOnClick(new System.EventHandler(button1_Click));
```

Properties can be read or written to, as the need arises.

Versioning

C# supports versioning by addressing two levels of compatibility. The first is source compatibility. Source compatibility occurs when code developed on an early version can be simply recompiled to work on a later version.

The second type of compatibility is binary compatibility. Binary compatibility occurs when code developed under an earlier version works under a newer version without recompiling.

Whichever direction you choose—enhanced portable C++ programming with STL, or Web-enabled, language-independent C#—you are certain to find Microsoft's Visual Studio.NET the most exciting development environment to come along in years.

What's Coming?

In this chapter you learned that there are two very significant enhancements to Microsoft's Visual Studio.NET: the Standard Template Library, or STL, and even more notably Microsoft's brand new programming language named C#. In the next chapter you will learn just how programming languages have evolved from C to today's state-of-the-art C#.

The
Complete
Reference

Visual C++.NET

Part II

Programming Foundations

The Complete Reference

Visual C++.NET

Chapter 5

C++ Foundations

First, There Was C

Beginning with this chapter, you will explore the origins, syntax, and usage of the C++ language. However, since C++ is a superset of C, the discussion of C++'s history begins with a discussion of C because it reveals the languages' successful design philosophies and helps you understand why C and C++ will be the language of choice for years to come. Before you proceed, you should be comfortable with the Microsoft Visual C++ development environment (see Chapters 1 through 4). By now you should have installed the package, configured it to your personal requirements, and practiced using the compiler and the integrated debugger.

 For several examples you might receive a warning message during compile. The message warns that data may be truncated in a conversion from double to float. It is safe to ignore this message in this chapter.

C Archives

Our archeological dig for the origins of the C language begins with a discussion of the UNIX operating system, since both the system and most of the programs that run on it are written in C. However, this does not mean that C is tied to UNIX or any other operating system or machine. The UNIX/C co-development environment has given C a reputation for being a system programming language because it is useful for writing compilers and operating systems. C is also very useful for writing major programs in many different domains.

The UNIX OS was originally developed in 1969 on what would now be considered a small DEC PDP-7 at Bell Laboratories in Murray Hill, New Jersey. UNIX was written entirely in PDP-7 assembly language. By design, this operating system was intended to be "programmer friendly," providing useful development tools, lean commands, and a relatively open environment. Soon after the development of UNIX, Ken Thompson implemented a compiler for a new language called B.

At this point it is helpful to examine the origins and history behind Ken Thompson's B language, a direct predecessor to C. Following is a comprehensive C lineage:

Language	Origins/Inventor
Algol 60	Designed by an international committee in early 1960
CPL (Combined Programming Language)	Developed at both Cambridge and the University of London in 1963
BCPL (Basic Combined Programming Language)	Developed at Cambridge by Martin Richards in 1967
B	Developed by Ken Thompson, Bell Labs, in 1970
C	Developed by Dennis Ritchie, Bell Labs, in 1972

Then in 1983, the American National Standards Institute (ANSI) committee was formed for the purpose of creating ANSI C—a standardization of the C language.

Algol 60 was a language that appeared only a few years after FORTRAN was introduced. This new language was more sophisticated and had a strong influence on the design of future programming languages. Its authors paid a great deal of attention to the regularity of syntax, modular structure, and other features usually associated with high-level structured languages. Unfortunately, Algol 60 never really caught on in the United States. Many say this was due to the language's abstractness and generality.

The inventors of CPL (Combined Programming Language) intended to bring Algol 60's lofty intent down to the realities of an actual computer. However, just as Algol 60 was hard to learn and difficult to implement, so was CPL. This led to its eventual downfall. Still clinging to the best of what CPL had to offer, the creators of BCPL (Basic Combined Programming Language) wanted to boil CPL down to its basic good features.

When Ken Thompson designed the B language for an early implementation of UNIX, he was trying to further simplify CPL. He succeeded in creating a very sparse language that was well suited for use on the hardware available to him. However, both BCPL and B may have carried their streamlining attempts a bit too far; they became limited languages, useful only for dealing with certain kinds of problems.

For example, no sooner had Ken Thompson implemented the B language than a new machine, called the PDP-11, was introduced. UNIX and the B compiler were immediately transferred to this new machine. While the PDP-11 was a larger machine than its PDP-7 predecessor, it was still quite small by today's standards. It had only 24K of memory, of which the system used 16K, and one 512K fixed disk. Some thought was given to rewriting UNIX in B, but the B language was slow because of its interpretive design. There was another problem as well: B was word oriented, but the PDP-11 was byte oriented. For these reasons, work was begun in 1971 on a successor to B, appropriately named C.

Dennis Ritchie is credited with creating C, which restored some of the generality lost in BCPL and B. He accomplished this through a shrewd use of data types, while maintaining the simplicity and direct access to the hardware that were the original design goals of CPL.

Many languages developed by a single individual (C, Pascal, Lisp, and APL) contain a cohesiveness that is missing from those created by large programming teams (Ada, PL/I, and Algol 60). It is also typical for a language written by one person to reflect the author's field of expertise. Dennis Ritchie was noted for his work in systems software—computer languages, operating systems, and program generators.

Given Ritchie's areas of expertise, it is easy to understand why C is a language of choice for systems software design. C is a relatively low-level language that allows you to specify every detail in an algorithm's logic to achieve maximum computer efficiency. But C is also a high-level language that can hide the details of the computer's architecture, thereby increasing programming efficiency.

C Versus Older High-Level Languages

At this point, you may be asking, "How does C compare to other programming languages?" A possible continuum is shown in Figure 5-1. If you start at the bottom of the continuum and move upward, you go from the tangible and empirical to the elusive and theoretical. The dots represent major advancements, with many steps left out. Early ancestors of the computer, like the Jacquard loom (1805) and Charles Babbage's "analytical engine" (1834), were programmed in hardware. The day may well come when we will program a machine by plugging a neural path communicator into a socket implanted in the temporal lobe (language memory) or Broca's area (language motor area) of the brain's cortex.

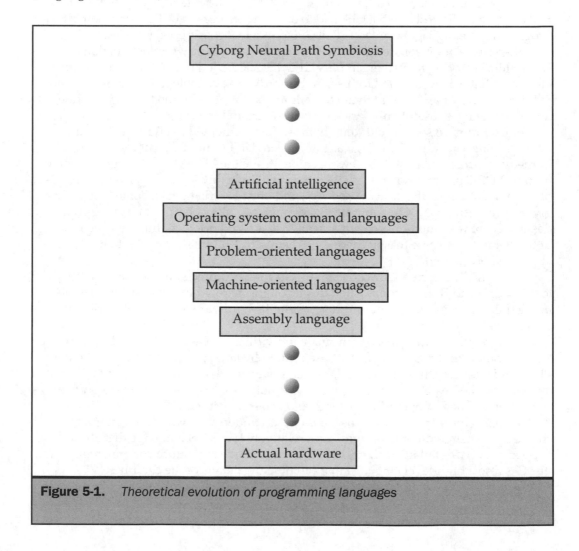

Figure 5-1.   *Theoretical evolution of programming languages*

The first assembly languages, which go back to the original introduction of electronic computers, provide a way of working directly with a computer's built-in instruction set, and are fairly easy to learn. Because assembly languages force you to think in terms of hardware, you have to specify every operation in the machine's terms. Therefore, you were always moving bits into or out of registers, adding them, shifting register contents from one register to another, and finally storing the results in memory. This was a tedious and error-prone endeavor.

The first high-level languages, such as FORTRAN, were created as alternatives to assembly languages. High-level languages were much more general and abstract, and they allowed you to think in terms of the problem at hand rather than in terms of the computer's hardware.

Unfortunately, the creators of high-level languages made the fallacious assumption that everyone who had been driving a standard, so to speak, would prefer driving an automatic. Excited about providing ease in programming, they left out some necessary options. FORTRAN and Algol are too abstract for systems-level work; they are problem-oriented languages, the kind used for solving problems in engineering, science, or business. Programmers who wanted to write systems software still had to rely on their machine's assembler.

In reaction to this situation, a few systems software developers took a step backward—or lower, in terms of the continuum—and created the category of machine-oriented languages. As you saw in C's genealogy, BCPL and B fit into this class of very low-level software tools. These languages were excellent for a specific machine but not much use for anything else; they were too closely related to a particular architecture. The C language is one step above machine-oriented languages but still a step below most problem-solving languages. C is close enough to the computer to give you great control over the details of an application's implementation, yet far enough away to ignore the details of the hardware. This is why the C language is considered at once a high- and a low-level language.

Advantages of C

Every computer language you use has a definite look to its source code. APL has its hieroglyphic appearance, assembly language its columns of mnemonics, and Pascal its easily read syntax. And then there's C. Many programmers encountering C for the first time will find its syntax cryptic and perhaps intimidating. C contains very few of the friendly English-like syntax structures found in many other programming languages. Instead, C presents the software engineer with unusual-looking operators and a plethora of pointers. New C programmers will soon discover a variety of language characteristics whose roots go back to C's original hardware/software progenitor. The following sections highlight the strengths of the C language.

Optimal Code Size

There are fewer syntax rules in C than in many other languages, and it is possible to write a top-quality C compiler that will operate in only 256K of total memory. There are actually more operators and combinations of operators in C than there are keywords.

Terse Set of Keywords

The original C language, as developed by Dennis Ritchie, contained a mere 27 keywords. The ANSI C standard (discussed later in this chapter) has added several reserved words. Microsoft C/C++ further enhances the instruction set and brings the total Microsoft C/C++ keyword count to over 70.

Many of the functions commonly defined as part of other programming languages are not included in C. For example, C does not contain any built-in input and output capabilities, nor does it contain any arithmetic operations (beyond those of basic addition and subtraction) or string-handling functions. Since any language missing these capabilities is of little use, C provides a rich set of library functions for input/output, arithmetic operations, and string manipulation. This agreed-upon library set is so commonly used that it can almost be seen as part of the language itself. One of the strengths of C, however, is its loose structure, which enables you to recode these functions easily.

Lightning-Fast Executables

The C code produced by most compilers tends to be very efficient. The combination of a small language, a small run-time system, and the fact that the language is close to the hardware makes many C programs run at speeds close to their assembly language equivalents.

Limited Type Checking

Unlike Pascal, which is a strongly typed language, C treats data types somewhat more loosely. This is a carryover from the B language, which was also a loosely typed language. This looseness allows you to view data in different ways. For example, at one point in a program, the application may need to see a variable as a character, and yet, for purposes of uppercasing (by subtracting 32), it may want to see the same memory cell as the ASCII equivalent of the character.

Top-Down Design Implementations

C contains all of the control structures you would expect of a modern-day language. This is impressive when you consider C's 1971 incubation period, which predated formal structured programming. For loops, if and if-else constructs, case (switch) statements, and while loops are all incorporated into the language. C also provides for the compartmentalization of code and data by managing their scope. For example, C provides local variables for this purpose and calls-by-value for subroutine data privacy.

Modular Structure

C supports modular programming, which is the concept of separate compilation and linking. This allows you to recompile only the parts of a program that have been changed during development. This feature can be extremely important when you are developing large programs, or even medium-size programs on slow systems. Without support for modular programming, the amount of time required to compile a complete program can make the change, compile, test, and modify cycle prohibitively slowly.

Transparent Interface to Assembly Language

There is a well-defined method for calling assembly language routines from most C compilers. Combined with the separation of compilation and linking, this makes C a very strong contender in applications that require a mix of high-level and assembler routines. C routines can also be integrated into assembly language programs on most systems.

Bit Manipulation

Often in systems programming it is necessary to manipulate objects at the bit level. Naturally, with C's origins so closely tied to the UNIX operating system, the language provides a rich set of bit-manipulation operators.

Pointer Data Types

One of the features an operating system requires of a language is the ability to address specific areas of memory. This capability also enhances the execution speed of a program. The C language meets these design requirements by using pointers (discussed in Chapter 10). While it is true that other languages implement pointers, C is noted for its ability to perform pointer arithmetic. For example, if the variable *student_record_ptr* points to the first element of an array *student_records*, then *student_record_ptr + 1* will be the address of the second element of *student_records*.

Extensible Structures

All arrays in C are one-dimensional. Multidimensional arrangements are built from combinations of these one-dimensional arrays. Arrays and structures (records) can be joined in any manner desired, creating database organizations that are limited only by the programmer's ability. Arrays are discussed in more detail in Chapter 9.

Memory Efficient

For many of the same reasons that C programs tend to be fast, they tend to be very memory efficient. The lack of built-in functions saves programs from having to carry around support for functions that are not needed by that application.

Cross-Platform Portability

Portability is a measure of the ease of converting a program running on one computer or operating system to another computer or operating system. Programs written in C are among the most portable in the modern computer world. This is especially true in the mini- and microcomputer worlds.

PROGRAMMING
FOUNDATIONS

Powerful Library Routines

There are many commercial function libraries available for all popular C compilers. Libraries are available for graphics, file handling, database support, screen windowing, data entry, communications, and general support functions. By using these libraries, you can save a great deal of development time.

Disadvantages of C

There are no perfect programming languages. Different programming problems require different solutions. It is the software engineer's task to choose the best language for a project. On any project, this is one of the first decisions you need to make, and it is nearly irrevocable once you start coding. The choice of a programming language can also make the difference between a project's success and failure. The following sections cover some of the weaknesses of the C language to give you a better idea of when to use and when not to use C for a particular application.

Limited Type Checking!

The fact that C is not strongly typed is one of its strengths, but it is also one of its weaknesses. Technically, typing is a measure of how closely a language enforces the use of variable types. (For example, integer and floating-point are two different types of numbers.) In some languages it is illegal to assign one data type to another without invoking a conversion function. This protects the data from being compromised by unexpected roundoffs.

As discussed earlier, C will allow an integer to be assigned to a character variable, and vice versa. What this means to you is that you are going to have to properly manage your variables. For experienced programmers this will present no problem. However, novice program developers may want to remind themselves that this can be the source of side effects.

A side effect in a language is an unexpected change to a variable or other item. Because C is not a strongly typed language, it gives you great flexibility to manipulate data. For example, the assignment operator (=) can appear more than once in the same expression. This flexibility, which you can use to your advantage, means that expressions can be written that have no clear and definite value. Restricting the use of the assignment and similar operators, or eliminating all side effects and unpredictable results, would have seriously lessened much of C's power and appeal as a high-level assembly language.

Limited Run-Time Monitors

C's lack of checking in the run-time system can cause many mysterious and transient problems to go undetected. For example, the run-time system would not warn you if your application exceeded an array's bounds. This is one of the costs of streamlining a compiler for the sake of speed and efficiency.

C Is Not for Children!

C's tremendous range of features—from bit manipulation to high-level formatted I/O—and its relative consistency from machine to machine have led to its acceptance in science, engineering, and business applications. It has directly contributed to the wide availability of the UNIX operating system on computers of all types and sizes.

Like any other powerful tool, however, C imposes a heavy responsibility on its users. C programmers need to acquire a discipline very quickly, adopting various rules and conventions in order to make their programs understandable both to themselves, long after the programs are written, and to others trying to analyze the code for the first time. In C, programming discipline is essential. The good news is that it comes almost automatically with practice.

American National Standards Institute: ANSI C

The ANSI (American National Standards Institute) committee has developed standards for the C language. This section describes some of the significant changes suggested and implemented by the committee. Some of these changes are intended to increase the flexibility of the language, others to standardize features previously left to the discretion of the compiler implementer.

Previously, the only standard available was the book *The C Programming Language* by B. Kernighan and D. Ritchie (Prentice-Hall, 1988). This book was not specific on some language details, which led to a divergence among compilers. The ANSI standard strives to remove these ambiguities. Although a few of the proposed changes could cause problems for some previously written programs, they should not affect most.

The ANSI C standard provides an even better opportunity than before to write portable C code. The standard has not corrected all areas of confusion in the language, however, and because C interfaces efficiently with machine hardware, many programs will always require some revision when they are moved to a different environment. The ANSI committee that developed the standard adopted as guidelines some phrases that collectively have been called the "spirit of C." Some of those phrases are:

- Trust the programmer.
- Don't prevent the programmer from doing what needs to be done.
- Keep the language small and simple.

Additionally, the international community was consulted to ensure that ANSI (American) standard C would be identical to the ISO (International Standards Organization) standard version. Because of these efforts, C is the only language that effectively deals with alternate collating sequences, enormous character sets, and multiple user cultures. Table 5-1 highlights just some of the areas the ANSI committee addressed.

Feature	Standardized
Data Types	(four): character, integer, float point, and enumeration
Comments	(/*) opening, (*/) closing, proposed(//)—anything to symbol's right is ignored by the compiler
Identifier Length	31 characters to distinguish uniqueness
Standard Identifiers and Header Files	An agreed-upon minimum set of identifiers and header files necessary to perform basic operations such as I/O
Preprocessor Statements	The # in preprocessor directives can have leading white space (any combination of spaces and tabs), permitting indented preprocessor directives for clarity—some earlier compilers insisted that all preprocessor directives begin in column one
New Preprocessor Directives	#if defined (expression); #elif (expression)
Adjacent Strings	The committee decided that adjacent literal strings should be concatenated—for example, this would allow a #define directive to extend beyond a single line
Standard Libraries	The proposed ANSI standard specifies a basic set of system-level and external routines, such as read() and write()
Output Control	An agreed-upon set of escape codes representing formatting control codes such as newline, new page, and tabs
Keywords	An agreed-upon minimum set of verbs used to construct valid C statements
sizeof()	The committee agreed that the sizeof function should return the type size_t, instead of a possibe system-limiting variable of size integer
Prototyping	The committee agreed that all C compilers should handle programs that do/do not employ prototyping

Table 5-1.   *ANSI C Recommendations*

Feature	Standardized
Command Line Arguments	In order for the C compiler to properly handle command line arguments, an agreed-upon syntax was defined
Void Pointer Type	The **void** keyword can be applied to functions that do not return a value—a function that does return a value can have its return value cast to void to indicate to the compiler that the value is being deliberately ignored
Structure Handling	Structure handling has been greatly improved—the member names in structure and union definitions need not be unique; structures can be passed as arguments to functions, returned by functions, and assigned to structures of the same type
Function Declarations	Function declarations can include argument-type lists (function prototyping) to notify the compiler of the number and types of arguments
Hexadecimal Character Constants	Hexadecimal character constants can be expressed using an introductory \x followed by from one to three hexadecimal digits (0–9, a–f, A–F)—for example, 16 decimal = \x10, which can be written as 0x10 using the current notation
Trigraphs	Trigraphs define standard symbol sequences that represent those characters that may not be readily available on all keyboards—for example, (??<) can be substituted for the more elaborate ({) symbol

Table 5-1. *ANSI C Recommendations (continued)*

From C to C++ and Object-Oriented Programming

Simply stated, C++ is a superset of the C language. C++ retains all of C's strengths, including its power and flexibility in dealing with the hardware/software interface, its low-level system programming, and its efficiency, economy, and powerful expressions. However, C++ brings the C language into the dynamic world of object-oriented programming and makes it a platform for high-level problem abstraction, going beyond even Ada in this respect. C++ accomplishes all of this with a simplicity and support for modularity similar to Modula-2, while maintaining the compactness and execution efficiency of C.

This new hybrid language combines the standard procedural language constructs familiar to so many programmers and the object-oriented model, which you can exploit fully to produce a purely object-oriented solution to a problem. In practice, a C++ application can reflect this duality by incorporating both the procedural programming model and the newer object-oriented model. This biformity in C++ presents a special challenge to the beginning C++ programmer; there is not only a new language to learn, but also a new way of thinking and problem solving.

C++ Archives

Not surprisingly, C++ has an origin similar to C's. While C++ is somewhat like BCPL and Algol 60, it also contains components of Simula 67. C++'s ability to overload operators and its flexibility to include declarations close to their first point of application are features found in Algol 60. The concept of subclasses (or derived classes) and virtual functions is taken from Simula 67. Like many other popular programming languages, C++ represents an evolution and refinement of some of the best features of previous languages. Of course, it is closest to C.

Bjarne Stroustrup of Bell Labs is credited with developing the C++ language in the early 1980s. (Dr. Stroustrup credits Rick Mascitti with the naming of this new language.) C++ was originally developed to solve some very rigorous event-driven simulations for which considerations of efficiency precluded the use of other languages. C++ was first used outside Dr. Stroustrup's language group in 1983, and by the summer of 1987, the language was still going through a natural refinement and evolution.

One key design goal of C++ was to maintain compatibility with C. The idea was to preserve the integrity of millions of lines of previously written and debugged C code, the integrity of many existing C libraries, and the usefulness of previously developed C tools. Because of the high degree of success in achieving this goal, many programmers find the transition to C++ much simpler than when they first went from some other language, such as FORTRAN to C.

C++ supports large-scale software development. Because it includes increased type checking, many of the side effects experienced when writing loosely typed C applications are no longer possible.

The most significant enhancement of the C++ language is its support for object-oriented programming (OOP). You will have to modify your approach to problem solving to derive all of the benefits of C++. For example, objects and their associated operations must be identified and all necessary classes and subclasses must be constructed.

Object Code Efficiency

What follows is an example of how an abstract data object in C++ can improve upon an older language's limited built-in constructs and features. For example, a FORTRAN software engineer may want to keep records on students. You could accomplish this with multiple arrays of scalar data that represent each set of data. All of the arrays are necessarily tied together by a common index. Should there be ten fields of information on each student, ten array accesses would have to be made using the same index location in order to represent the array of records.

In C++, the solution involves the declaration of a simple object, student_database, that can receive messages to add_student, delete_student, access_student, or display_student information contained within the object. The manipulation of the student_database object can then be performed in a natural manner. Inserting a new record into the student_database object becomes as simple as this:

```
student_database.add_student(new_recruit)
```

Assuming the student_database object has been appropriately declared, the **add_student()** function is a method suitably defined in the class that supports student_database objects, and the new_recruit parameter is the specific information to be added. Note that the class of objects called student_database is not a part of the underlying language itself. Instead, the programmer extends the language to suit the problem. By defining a new class of objects or by modifying existing classes (creating a subclass), a more natural mapping from the problem space to the program space (or solution space) occurs. The biggest challenge comes in truly mastering this powerful enhancement.

Subtle Differences Between C and C++

The following sections detail the minor (non-object-oriented) enhancements to the C language.

Comment Syntax

C++ introduces the comment to end-of-line delimiter //. However, the comment brackets /* and */ can still be used.

Enumerated Variables

The name of an enumeration is a type name. This streamlines the notation by not requiring the qualifier enum to be placed in front of the enumeration type name.

Structure Versus Classes

The name of a structure or class is a type name. This class construct does not exist in C. In C++ it is not necessary to use the qualifier struct or class in front of a structure or class name.

Block Scope

C++ permits declarations within blocks and after code statements. This feature allows you to declare an identifier closer to its first point of application. It even permits the loop control variable to be declared within the formal definition of the control structure, as shown here:

```
// C++ point-of-use variable declaration
   for(int index = 0; index < MAX_ROWS; index++)
```

Scope Resolution Operator

You use the new scope qualifier operator :: to resolve name conflicts. For example, if a function has a local declaration for a variable *vector_location* and there exists a global variable *vector_location*, the qualifier ::vector_location allows the global variable to be accessed within the scope of the local function. The reverse is not possible.

The const Specifier

You can use the const specifier to lock the value of an entity within its scope. You can also use it to lock the data pointed to by a pointer variable, the value of the pointer address, or the values of both the pointer address and the data pointed to.

Anonymous Unions

Unions without a name can be defined anywhere a variable or field can be defined. You can use this ability for the economy of memory storage by allowing the sharing of memory among two or more fields of a structure.

Explicit Type Conversions

You can use the name of a predefined type or user-defined type as a function to convert data from one type to another. Under certain circumstances, such an explicit type conversion can be used as an alternative to a cast conversion.

Unique Function Capabilities

C++ will please many a Pascal, Modula-2, and Ada programmer because it permits the specification by name and type for each function parameter inside the parentheses next to the function name. For example:

```
void * dupmem(void *dest, int c, unsigned count)
{
   .
   .
   .
}
```

The equivalent C interface under the ANSI standard would look exactly the same. In this case, C++ influenced the ANSI standards committee.

The C++ translator will perform type checking to ensure that the number and type of values sent into a function when it is invoked match the number and type of the formal arguments defined for the function. A check is also made to ensure that the function's return type matches the variable used in the expression invoking the function. This type of parameter checking is missing in most C systems.

Overloading Functions

In C++, functions can use the same names if you use the specifier overload, and each of the overloaded functions can be distinguished on the basis of the number and type of its parameters.

Default Parameter Values

You can assign default values to trailing sets of C++ function parameters. In this case, the function can be invoked using fewer than the total number of parameters. Any missing trailing parameters assume their default values:

```
void function_with_default_argument_values( char cValue,
    int iValue = 0)...
```

The **function_with_default_argument_Values()** can be called two ways:

```
function_with_default_argument_values('A'); // or
function_with_default_argument_values(cVariable); // or
function_with_default_argument_values('A', 10); // or
function_with_default_argument_values(cVariable,iVariable);
```

The first two function calls use the default value of 0 for the dummy argument *iValue*, while the last two function calls used the supplied actual argument values for *iValue*. Properly used, default dummy argument value assignments can guarantee that a subroutine does not crash should there be critical logical components to the called routine.

Varying-Length Argument Lists

You can define C++ functions with an unknown number and type of parameters by employing the ellipsis (...). When you use this feature, parameter type checking is suppressed to allow flexibility in the interface to the function.

Reference Argument Types

Through the use of the ampersand operator (&), a formal function parameter can be declared as a reference parameter. For example:

```
int i;
increment(i);
  .
  .
  .
void increment(int &variable_reference)
{
  variable_reference++;
}
```

Because &variable_reference is defined as a reference parameter, its address is assigned to the address of i when increment() is invoked. The value of i that is sent in is incremented within function increment() and returned to variable i outside of function increment(). It is not necessary for the address of i to be explicitly passed into function increment(), as it is in C.

Inline Functions!

You can use the inline specifier to instruct the compiler to perform inline substitution of a given function at the location where the function is invoked.

The new and delete Keywords

The new and delete operators that are introduced by C++ allow for programmer-controlled allocation and deallocation of heap storage.

void Pointers

In C++, the type void is used to indicate that a function returns nothing. Pointer variables can be declared to point to void. They can then be assigned to any other pointer that points to an arbitrary base type.

Major Differences Between C and C++

The most significant major enhancement to C involves the concept of object-oriented programming. The following sections briefly explain all of the C++ enhancements that make object-oriented programming possible.

Class Constructs and Data Encapsulation

The class construct is the fundamental vehicle for object-oriented programming. A class definition can encapsulate all of the data declarations, the initial values, and the set of operations (called *methods*) for data abstraction. Objects can be declared to be of a given class, and messages can be sent to objects. Additionally, each object of a specified class can contain its own private and public sets of data representative of that class.

The struct Class

A structure in C++ is a subset of a class definition and has no private or protected sections. This subclass can contain both data (as is expected in ANSI C) and functions.

Constructors and Destructors

Constructor and destructor methods are used to guarantee the initialization of the data defined within an object of a specified class. When an object is declared, the specified initialization constructor is activated. Destructors automatically deallocate storage for the associated object when the scope in which the object is declared is exited.

Messages

As you have seen, the object is the basic fabric of object-oriented programming. You manipulate objects by sending them messages. You send messages to objects (variables declared to be of a given class) by using a mechanism similar to invoking a function. The set of possible messages that can be sent to an object is specified in the class description for the object. Each object responds to a message by determining an appropriate action to take based on the nature of the message. For example, if Palette_Colors represents an object, and SetNumColors_Method represents a method with a single-integer parameter, sending a message to the object would be accomplished by using the following statement:

```
Palette_Colors.SetNumColors_Method(16);
```

Friends

The concept of data hiding and data encapsulation implies a denied access to the inner structures that make up an object. The class's private section is normally totally off-limits to any function outside the class. C++ does allow other functions outside methods or classes to be declared to be a friend to a specified class. Friendship breaks down a normally impenetrable wall and permits access to the class's private data and methods.

Operator Overloading

With C++, the programmer can take the set of predefined operators and functions supplied with the compiler, or user-defined operators and functions, and give them multiple meanings. For example, different functions typically have different names, but for functions performing similar tasks on different types of objects, it is sometimes better to let these functions have the same name. When their argument types are different, the compiler can distinguish them and choose the right function to call. What follows is a coded example; you could have one function called total() that was overloaded for an array of integers, of floating points, and of double values.

```
int total(int isize, int iarray[]);
float total(int isize, float farray[]);
double total(int isize, double darray[]);
      .
      .
      .
```

Since you have declared the three different functions by the same name, the compiler can look at the invoking statement and automatically decide which function is appropriate for the formal parameter list's arguments:

```
    total(isize,iarray);
     total(isize,farray);
....total(isize,darray);
```

Derived Classes

A derived class can be seen as a subclass of a specified class, thereby forming a hierarchy of abstractions. Derived class objects typically inherit all or some of the methods of the parent class. It is also common for a derived class to then incorporate these inherited methods with new methods specific to the subclass. All subclass objects contain the fields of data from the parent class as well as any of their own private data.

Polymorphism Using Virtual Functions

Polymorphism involves a tree structure of parent classes and their subclasses. Each subclass within this tree can receive one or more messages with the same name. When an object of a class within this tree receives a message, the object determines the particular application of the message that is appropriate for an object of the specified subclass.

Stream Libraries

An additional library stream is included with the C++ language. The three classes **cin**, **cout**, and **cerr** are provided for terminal and file input and output. All of the operators within these three classes can be overloaded within a user-defined class. This capability allows the input and output operations to be easily tailored to an application's needs.

Fundamental Components for a C/C++ Program

You may have heard that C is a difficult language to master. However, while it is true that a brief encounter with C code may leave you scratching your head, this is only due to C's foreign syntax, structure, and indentation schemes. By the end of this chapter, you should have enough information to have developed a working knowledge of the C/C++ languages enabling you to write short but meaningful code. In the next section you will learn about the five fundamental components of a "good" program.

Five Elements of a Good C/C++ Program Design

You may be familiar with a problem-solution format called an IPO diagram. IPO diagrams were a stylized approach to the age-old programming problem of input/process/output. The following list elaborates on these three fundamentals and encapsulates the entire application development cycle. All programs must address the following five components:

- Programs must obtain information from some input source.

- Programs must decide how this input is to be arranged and stored.

- Programs use a set of instructions to manipulate the input. These instructions can be broken down into four major categories: single statements, conditional statements, loops, and subroutines.

- Programs must report the results of the data manipulation.

- A well-written application incorporates all of the fundamentals just listed, expressed by using good modular design, self-documenting code (meaningful variable names), and a good indentation scheme.

 Note   *All C programs discussed in this chapter are for comparison purposes only. Their code style is used to contrast the C language syntax with C++, along with the old-style programming requirements against today's up-to-date ANSI/ISO C++ guidelines.*

A Simple C Program

The following C program illustrates the basic components of a C application using the old-style coding practices:

```
/*
 *   simple.c
 *   Your first example C program.
 *   Copyright (c) Chris H. Pappas and William H. Murray, 2001
 */
```

PROGRAMMING
FOUNDATIONS

```
#include <stdio.h>

int main( )()
{
  printf(" HELLO World! ");

  return(0);
}
```

There is a lot happening in this short piece of code. Let's begin with the comment block:

```
/*
*    simple.c
*    Your first example C program.
*    Copyright (c) Chris H. Pappas and William H. Murray, 2001
*/
```

All well-written source code includes meaningful comments. A meaningful comment is one that neither insults the intelligence of the programmer nor assumes too much. In C, comments begin with /* and are terminated with */. Anything between these unique symbol pairs is ignored by the compiler.

The next statement represents one of C's unique features, known as a preprocessor statement:

```
#include <stdio.h>
```

A preprocessor statement is like a precompile instruction. In this case the statement instructs the compiler to retrieve the code stored in the predefined stdio.h file into the source code on the line requested. (The stdio.h file is called a header file. Header files can include symbolic constants, identifiers, and function prototypes and have these declarations pulled out of the main program for purposes of modularity.)

Following the #include statement is the main function declaration:

```
int main( )()
{

  .

  .

  .

  return(0);  /*   or return 0;  */
}
```

All C programs are made up of function calls. Every C program must have one called main(). The main() function is usually where program execution begins, and it ends with a return() from the main(). The int to the left of main() defines the function's return type, in this case integer, and explains why the return statement contains a number inside the parentheses. A value of 0 is interpreted as meaning a successful program termination. It is also legal to use **return()** statements without the parentheses.

Following the main() function header is the body of the function itself. Notice the { and } symbol pairs. These are called *braces.* You use braces to encapsulate multiple statements. These braces may define the body for a function, or they may bundle together statements that are dependent on the same logic control statement, as is the case when several statements are executed based on the validity of an **if** statement. In this example, the braces define the body of the main program.

The next line is the only statement in the body of the main() function and is the simplest example of an output statement:

```
printf(" HELLO World! ");
```

The printf() function was previously prototyped in stdio.h. Because no other parameters are specified, the sentence will be printed to the display monitor.

A Simple C++ Program

The example that follows performs the same function as the C program just discussed, but it takes advantage of those features unique to C++:

```
//
// simple2.cpp : Defines the entry point for the console application.
// Your first C++ example program.
// Copyright (c) Chris H. Pappas and William H. Murray, 2001
//

#include "stdafx.h"
#include <iostream>

using namespace std;

int main(int argc, char* argv[])
{
    cout << " HELLO World! ";

    return 0;
}
```

There are five major differences between this example and the last. First, the comment designator has been changed from the /* */ pair to //. C-style comments can encapsulate multiple statements between their matching paired symbols. However, all C++ comments are automatically terminated at the end of each line of code. This explains why the C++ program example duplicates the double-slash symbols before each comment line.

The second change involves the inclusion of the stdafx.h header file. This file is used to build a precompiled header file projname.pch and a precompiled types file stdafx.obj. The file stdafx.h is an include file for standard system include files and for project-specific include files that are used frequently but are changed infrequently. Stdafx.cpp contains the preprocessor directive `include "stdafx.h"` and adds include files for precompiled types. Precompiled files of any type, including header files, support faster compilation times by restricting compilation only to those files that require it. Once your project is built the first time, you will notice much faster build times on subsequent builds due to the presence of the precompiled header files.

Next, the second #include filename has been changed from stdio.h to iostream. The C header, stdio.h, contained C-specific definitions necessary to enable the C language to perform standard I/O-type operations. The period h, (.h) syntax flags the algorithm as using the old-style program syntax. The switch from stdio.h to iostream pulls in object-oriented C++-specific definitions necessary to teach C++ how to perform simple I/O operations. The filename without the period h, (.h) extension flags this algorithm as meeting the latest ANSI/ISO C++ code requirements.

The third difference involves the inclusion of a new statement, using namespace std. This is also a new ANSI/ISO C++ code requirement (discussed next). In simple terms, this new C++ keyword deals with identifier scope. In order to prevent variable name collisions within large programs, namespaces allow a programmer to encapsulate definitions. All that is considered to be standard C++ is now protected by this layer and given the standardized namespace name std. The using statement logically functions like an #include statement by pulling in these definitions and legalizing their use within the program.

The fourth change is to the main() function argument list. The main() arguments *argc* and *argv[]* enable a program to capture load-time or command-line arguments.

The fifth change involves a different output operator call, cout. Many of the examples in the book will highlight the sometimes subtle and dazzling differences between C and C++.

From main to _tmain and char* to _TCHAR

Starting with Visual Studio.NET 7.0, Microsoft has introduced what is called generic-text routine mappings. Defined in TCHAR.H are macros or inline functions mapping to the MBCS (Multibyte Character Set), SBCS (Singlebyte Character Set), and Unicode models. These mappings deal with character data being represented as single byte ANSI ASCII values or double byte Unicode encryption. Should you be writing Unicode compliant algorithms, make certain you change all main() function calls to _tmain(), and switch character pointers from char* to _TCHAR*.

Latest C++ ANSI/ISO Language Updates

While the ANSI/ISO committee was busy incorporating STL, it took the opportunity to introduce modifications to the C++ language definition. These modifications, in most cases, implement features that the committee members admired in other languages, features that they viewed as deficiencies in traditional C++. These new changes, which consist of language additions, should not affect any previously written code.

Using namespace

We'll look at the definition for namespace from a bottom-up point of view. Namespaces control scope or identifier visibility (constants, variables, functions, classes, etc.). The tightest scope is local—those identifiers declared within a function. Associated at this level would be member function or method declarations. Higher up on the scale would be class scope.

There are visibility issues associated with file scope, such as when 1.cpp, 2.cpp, and 3.cpp are combined to generate 123.exe. Identifiers declared in 1.cpp, for example, are not visible (by default) in 2.cpp and 3.cpp.

At the highest level is program or workspace scope. Historically, this worked fine until the advent of today's complex programming environment where source files are coming at you from all directions. Today's programs are a combination of source files you write, those supplied by the compiler(s), some from the operating system itself, and from third-party vendors. Under these circumstances, program scope is not sufficient to prevent identifier collisions between categories. Namespaces allow you to lock down all program identifiers, successfully preventing these types of collisions.

Collisions usually fell under the category of external global identifiers used throughout a program. They are visible to all object modules in the application program, in third-party class and function libraries, and in the compiler's system libraries. When two variables in global scope have the same identifier, the linker generates an error.

Many compiler manufacturers initially solved this problem by assigning unique identifiers to each variable. For example, under Standard C, the compiler system prefixes its internal global identifiers with underscore characters, and programmers are told to avoid that usage to avoid conflicts.

Third-party vendors prepended unique mnemonic prefixes to global identifiers in an attempt to prevent collisions. However, even this failed whenever two developers chose the same prefix. The problem is that the language had no built-in mechanism with which a library publisher could stake out a so-called namespace of its own—one that would insulate its global identifiers from those of other libraries being linked into the same application.

Traditionally programmers had three choices to eliminating the collisions: They could get the source code, modify it, and rebuild-all; have the authors of the offending code change their declarations; or select an alternate code source containing the same functionality. Not a very pleasant set of alternatives!

The C++ namespace keyword limits an identifier's scope to the namespace identifier. All references from outside the block to the global identifiers declared in the block must, in one way or another, qualify the global identifier's reference with the namespace identifier. In actuality, this is logically similar to prepending prefixes. However, namespace identifers tend to be longer than the typical two- or three-character prefixes and stand a better chance of working.

namespace Syntax

To define a namespace, you encapsulate your declarations within a namespace block, as in:

```
namespace your_namespace_name {
  int ivalue;
  class my_class {/*....*/};
  // more declarations;
}
```

In the above example, any code statements within the your_namespace_name have direct access to the namespace's declarations. However, any code statements outside of the your_namespace_name must use a qualifying syntax. For example, from the main() function, accessing ivalue would look like:

```
void main ( void )
{
  your_namespace_name::ivalue++;
}
```

The using namespace Statement

If you do not like the idea of always having to qualify an identifier with its namespace every time you access it, you can use the using statement, as in:

```
using namespace your_namespace_name;
void main ( void )
{
  ivalue++;
}
```

This approach can, however, be like giving a hotel guest the key to the entire hotel instead of a single room—inviting trouble! The using namespace syntax provides access to all of the namespace's declarations. Each application will benefit from the best selection of these two approaches.

The Selective using Statement

Somewhere between a fully qualified namespace identifier (your_namespace_name::ivaluel++;) and the using namespace your_namespace_name syntax, there's the simpler using statement. The using directive tells the compiler that you intend to use specific identifiers within a namespace. Using the previous examples, this would look like:

```
using your_namespace_name::ivalue;
void main ( void )
{
  ivalue++;
}
```

Just as a programmer would not choose to always use **for** loops, when there are **while** and **do-while** alternatives, so too a programmer should carefully select the best application-specific approach to namespace identifier access.

Renaming namespaces

Sometimes third-party namespace names can get in your way because of their length. For example, your_namespace_name is quite long. For this reason the namespace feature allows a programmer to associate a new name with the namespace identifier, as in:

```
namespace YNN = your_namespace_name;
void main ( void )
{
  YNN::ivalue++;
}
```

static File Scope Versus Unnamed namespaces

One way to enforce file scope is with the keyword **static**. For example, if 1.cpp, 2.cpp, and 3.cpp all have the external variable declaration *int ivalue;*, and you do not want internal linkage (meaning all three identifiers share the same storage location), you precede all three declarations with the keyword **static**:

```
// 1.cpp              // 2.cpp                 // 3.cpp
static int ivalue;    static int ivalue;       static int ivalue;
void main ( void )    void some_funcs( void ); void more_funcs( void );
```

Unnamed namespaces provide the same capability, just a slightly different syntax:

```
// 1.cpp
namespace {
   int ivalue;
}
void main ( void )
{
   ivalue++;
}
```

To create an unnamed namespace, you simply omit a namespace identifier. The compiler then generates an internal identifier that is unique throughout the program. All identifiers declared within an unnamed namespace are available only within the defining file. Functions in other files, within the program's workspace, cannot reference the declarations.

Adding a User Interface to a C Program

The following old-style C program is a slightly more meaningful example. It is a little more complete in that it not only outputs information, but also prompts the user for input. Many of the components of this program will be elaborated on throughout the remainder of the book.

```
/*
 *   uic.c
 *   This C program prompts the user for a specified length,
 *   in feet, and then outputs the value converted to
 *   meters and centimeters
 *   Copyright (c) Chris H. Pappas and William H. Murray, 2001
 */

#include <stdio.h>
```

```
int main( )()
{
  float feet, meters, centimeters;

  printf("Enter the number of feet to be converted: ");
  scanf("%f",&feet);

  while(feet > 0 ) {
    centimeters = feet * 12 * 2.54;
    meters = centimeters/100;
    printf("%8.2f feet equals\n", feet);
    printf("%8.2f meters \n",meters);
    printf("%8.2f centimeters \n",centimeters);
    printf("\nEnter another value to be \n");
    printf("converted (0 ends the program): ");
    scanf("%f",&feet);
  }
  printf(">>> Have a nice day! <<<");

  return(0);
}
```

Declaring Variables

The first thing you will notice that's new in the program is the declaration of three variables:

```
float feet, meters, centimeters;
```

All C variables must be declared before they are used. One of the standard data types supplied by the C language is **float**. The syntax for declaring variables in C requires the definition of the variable's type before the name of the variable. In this example, the float type is represented by the keyword **float**, and the three variables *feet*, *meters*, and *centimeters* are defined.

User Interaction

The next unconventional-looking statement is used to input information from the keyboard:

```
printf("Enter the number of feet to be converted: ");
scanf("%f",&feet);
```

The scanf() function has a requirement that is called a format string. Format strings define how the input data is to be interpreted and represented internally. The "%f " function parameter instructs the compiler to interpret the input as **float** data. In Microsoft C and C++, a float occupies four bytes. (Chapter 6 contains a detailed explanation of all the C and C++ language data types.)

An Introduction to the Address Operator

In the previous statement you may have noticed that the float variable *feet* was preceded by an ampersand symbol (&). The & is known as an address operator. Whenever a variable is preceded by this symbol, the compiler uses the address of the specified variable instead of the value stored in the variable. The scanf() function has been written to expect the address of the variable to be filled.

A Simple while Loop

One of the simplest loop structures to code in C is the **while** loop:

```
while(feet > 0) {
    .
    .
    .
}
```

This **pretest** loop starts with the reserved word **while**, followed by a Boolean expression that returns either a TRUE or a FALSE. The opening brace ({) and closing brace (}) are optional; they are needed only when more than one executable statement is to be associated with the loop repetition. Braced statements are sometimes referred to as compound statements, compound blocks, or code blocks.

If you are using compound blocks, make certain you use the agreed-upon brace style. While it doesn't matter to the compiler where the braces are placed (in terms of skipped spaces or lines), programmers reading your code will certainly appreciate the style and effort. An opening loop brace is placed at the end of the test condition, and the closing brace is placed in the same column as the first character in the test condition.

Screen Output

In analyzing the second program, you will notice more complex printf() function calls:

```
printf("%8.2f feet equals\n", feet);
printf("%8.2f meters \n",meters);
printf("%8.2f centimeters \n",centimeters);
printf("\nEnter another value to be \n");
printf("converted (0 ends the program): ");
```

If you are familiar with the PL/I language developed by IBM, you will be right at home with the concept of a format or control string. Whenever a printf() function is invoked to print not only literal strings (any set of characters between double quote marks), but also values, a format string is required. The format string represents two things: a picture of how the output string is to look, combined with the format interpretation for each of the values printed. Format strings are always between double quote marks.

Let's break down the first printf() format string ("%8.2f feet equals\n", feet) into its separate components:

Control	Action
%8.2f	Take the value of feet, interpret it as a float, and print it in a field of eight spaces with two decimal places.
feet equals	After printing the float feet, skip one space and then print the literal string "feet equals."
\n	Once the line is complete, execute a new line feed.
,	The comma separates the format string from the variable name(s) used to satisfy all format descriptors. (In this case, there is only one %8.2f.)

The next two **printf()** statements are similar in execution. Each statement prints a formatted float value, followed by a literal string, and ending with a new line feed. If you were to run the program, your output would look similar to this:

```
Enter the number of feet to be converted: 10
   10.00 feet equals
    3.05 meters
  304.80 centimeters

Enter another value to be
converted (0 stops program): 0
```

The C/C++ escape sequences, or output control characters, allow you to use a sequence of characters to represent special characters. Table 5-2 lists all of the output control symbols and a description of how they can be used in format strings. All leading zeros are ignored by the compiler for characters notated in hexadecimal. The compiler determines the end of a hex-specified escape character when it encounters either a non-hex character or more than two hex characters, excluding leading zeros.

Seq.	Name	Seq.	Name
\a	Alert (bell)	\?	Literal quotation mark
\b	Backspace	\'	Single quotation mark
\f	Form feed	\"	Double quotation mark
\n	New line	\\	Backslash
\r	Carriage return	\ddd	ASCII character in octal notation
\t	Horizontal tab	\xdd	ASCII character in hex notation
\v	Vertical tab		

Table 5-2. *Output Control Symbols*

Also on the subject of format strings—though this is a bit advanced—are the **scanf()** formatting controls. Table 5-3 describes the **scanf()** formatting controls and their meanings. If you wish to input a string without automatically appending a terminating null character (\0), use %nc, where *n* is a decimal integer. In this case, the c format symbol indicates that the argument is a pointer to a character array. The next *n* characters are read from the input stream into the specified location, and no null character (\0) is appended. If *n* is not specified, the default character array length is 1.

As you learn more about the various C data types, you will be able to refer back to Tables 5-2 and 5-3 for a reminder of how the different controls affect input and output.

Character	Input Type Expected	Argument Type
d	Decimal integer	Pointer to int
o	Octal integer	Pointer to int
x, X	Hexadecimal integer	Pointer to int
I	Decimal, hexadecimal	Pointer to int or octal integer
u	Unsigned decimal integer	Pointer to unsigned int
e, E	Floating-point value	Pointer to float

Table 5-3. *Format Control Symbols*

Character	Input Type Expected	Argument Type
f g, G	Consisting of an optional sign (+ or -), a series of one or more decimal digits possibly containing a decimal point, and an optional exponent ("e" or "E") followed by an optionally signed integer value	
c	Character—white-space characters that are ordinarily skipped are read when c is specified; to read the next non-white-space character, use %1s	Pointer to char
s	String	Pointer to character array auto create NULL string
n	No input read from stream or buffer	Pointer to int, into which is stored the number of characters read from the stream or buffer up to that point in call to scanf
p	In the form xxxx:yyyy, where x digits and y digits are uppercase hexadecimal digits	Pointer to far; pointer to void

Table 5-3. *Format Control Symbols (continued)*

PROGRAMMING FOUNDATIONS

Using the Integrated Debugger

To examine the actual operation of the C code presented in this section, you can use the integrated debugger. When you compile your program, make certain you have turned on debug information. This is done in conjunction with the Project utility. Once your application is compiled and linked, use the debugger to keep an eye on the variables yard, feet, and inch.

Adding a User Interface to a C++ Program

The following C++ example is identical in function to the previous C example except for some minor variations in the syntax used.

```cpp
//
// uicp.cpp : Defines the entry point for the console application.
// This C++ program prompts the user for a specified length,
// feet, and then outputs the value converted to
// meters and centimeters.
// Copyright (c) Chris H. Pappas and William H. Murray, 2001
//

#include "stdafx.h"
#include <iostream>
#include <iomanip>

using namespace std;

int main(int argc, char* argv[])
{
  float feet,meters,centimeters;

  cout << "Enter the number of feet to be converted: ";
  cin  >> feet;

  while(feet > 0 ) {
    centimeters = feet * 12 * 2.54;
    meters = centimeters/100;
    cout << setw(8) << setprecision(2)
         << setiosflags(ios::fixed) << feet << " feet equals \n";
    cout << setw(8) << meters << " meters \n";
    cout << setw(8) << centimeters << " centimeters \n";
    cout << "\nEnter another value to be \n";
    cout << "converted (0 ends the program): ";
    cin >>  feet;
  }
  cout << ">>> Have a nice day! <<<";

  return(0);
}
```

There are six major differences between the C++ example and its C counterpart. The first two changes involve the use of **cin** and **cout** for I/O. These statements use the << ("put to," or insertion) and >> ("get from," or extraction) iostream operators. Both operators have been overloaded to handle the output/input of all the predefined types. They can also be overloaded to handle user-defined types such as rational numbers.

The last four changes are all related to formatting C++ output. To gain the same output precision easily afforded by C's "%8.2f" format string, the program requires four additional statements. The file iomanip is included in the program to give access to three specific class-member inline functions: setw(), setprecision(), and setiosflags(). As you look at the code, you will notice that the calls to setw() and setprecision() are repeated. This is because their effect is only for the next output value, unlike setiosflags(), which makes a global change to fixed output.

C++ programmers who like the power and flexibility of the C output function printf() can use printf() directly from library stdio.h. The next two statements show the C and C++ equivalents:

```
printf("%8.2f feet equals\n", feet);
cout << setw(8) << setprecision(2)
     << setiosflags(ios::fixed) << feet << " feet equals \n";
```

Adding File I/O

Of course, there will be times when a C application wants its input or output, rather than the keyboard and display monitor, to deal directly with files. This brief introduction serves as an example of how to declare and use simple data files:

```
/*
 *    file1.cpp
 *    This C++ program demonstrates how to declare and use both
 *    input and output files. The example program
 *    takes the order_price from customer.dat and generates
 *    a billing_price that is printed to billing.dat.
 *    Copyright (c) Chris H. Pappas and William H. Murray, 2001
 */

#include <stdio.h>
#define MIN_DISCOUNT .97
#define MAX_DISCOUNT .95

int main( )()
{
```

```
    float forder_price, fbilling_price;
    FILE *fin,*fout;

    fin=fopen("a:\\customer.dat","r");
    fout=fopen("a:\\billing.dat","w");

    while (fscanf(fin,"%f",&forder_price) != EOF) {
      fprintf(fout,"Your order of \t\t$%8.2f\n", forder_price);
      if (forder_price < 10000)
         fbilling_price = forder_price * MIN_DISCOUNT;
      else fbilling_price = forder_price * MAX_DISCOUNT;
      fprintf(fout,"is discounted to \t$%8.2f.\n\n",
              fbilling_price);
    }
    return(0);
}
```

Each file in a C program must be associated with a file pointer, which points to information that defines various things about a file, including the path to the file, its name, and its status. A file pointer is a pointer variable of type FILE and is defined in stdio.h. The following statement from the example program declares two files, *fin and *fout:

```
, FILE *fin,*fout;
```

The next two statements in the program open two separate streams and associate each file with its respective stream:

```
fin=fopen("a:\\customer.dat","r");
fout=fopen("a:\\billing.dat","w");
```

The statements also return the file pointer for each file. Since these are pointers to files, your application should never alter their values.

The second parameter to the fopen() function is the file mode. Files may be opened in either text or binary mode. When in text mode, most C compilers translate carriage return/linefeed sequences into newline characters on input. During output, the opposite occurs. However, binary files do not go through such translations. Table 5-4 lists all of the valid file modes.

Access Type	Description
a	Opens in append mode. It creates the file if it does not already exist. All write operations occur at the end of the file.
a+	Same as above, but also allows reading.
r	Opens for reading. If the file does not exist or cannot be found, the open call will fail.
r+	Opens for both reading and writing. If the file does not exist or cannot be found, the open call will fail.
w	Opens an empty file for writing. If the file exists, all contents are destroyed.
w+	Opens an empty file for both reading and writing. If the file exists, all contents are destroyed.

Table 5-4.   *Valid C File Modes*

The r+, w+, and a+ file modes select both reading and writing. (The file is open for update.) When switching between reading and writing, you must remember to reposition the file pointer, using either fsetpos(), fseek(), or rewind().

C does perform its own file closing automatically whenever the application closes. However, there may be times when you want direct control over when a file is closed. The following listing shows the same program modified to include the necessary closing function calls (in **bold**):

```
/*
 *    file1.c
 *    This C program demonstrates how to declare and use both
 *    input and output files. The example program
 *    takes the order_price from customer.dat and generates
 *    a billing_price that is printed to billing.dat
 *    Copyright (c) Chris H. Pappas and William H. Murray, 2001
 */

#include <stdio.h>
#define MIN_DISCOUNT .97
```

```
#define MAX_DISCOUNT .95

int main( )()
{
  float forder_price, fbilling_price;
  FILE *fin,*fout;

  fin=fopen("a:\\customer.dat","r");
  fout=fopen("a:\\billing.dat","w");

  while (fscanf(fin,"%f",&forder_price) != EOF) {
    fprintf(fout,"Your order of \t\t$%8.2f\n", forder_price);
    if (forder_price < 10000)
       fbilling_price = forder_price * MIN_DISCOUNT;
    else fbilling_price = forder_price * MAX_DISCOUNT;
    fprintf(fout,"is discounted to \t$%8.2f.\n\n",
                        fbilling_price);
  }

  fclose(fin);
  fclose(fout);

  return(0);
}
```

The following program performs the same function as the one just examined, but is coded in C++:

```
//
// file2.cpp : Defines the entry point for the console application.
// This C++ program demonstrates how to declare and use both
// input and output files. The example program
// takes the order_price from customer.dat and generates
// a billing_price that is printed to billing.dat.
// Copyright (c) Chris H. Pappas and William H. Murray, 2001
//

#include "stdafx.h"
#include <fstream>
```

```
#include <iomanip>

#define MIN_DISCOUNT .97
#define MAX_DISCOUNT .95

using namespace std;

int main(int argc, char* argv[])
{
  float forder_price, fbilling_price;
  ifstream fin("a:\\customer.dat"); // user created file
  ofstream fout("a:\\billing.dat"); // containing float values
  fin >> forder_price;
  while (!fin.eof( )()) {
    fout << setiosflags(ios::fixed);
    fout << "Your order of \t\t$" << setprecision(2)
         << setw(8) << forder_price << "\n";
    if (forder_price < 10000)
       fbilling_price = forder_price * MIN_DISCOUNT;
    else fbilling_price = forder_price * MAX_DISCOUNT;
    fout << "is discounted to \t$" << setw(8)
         << fbilling_price << ".\n\n";
    fin >> forder_price;
  }

  fin.close( )();
  fout.close( )();

  return(0);
}
```

Disk file input and output are slightly different in C++ than in C. C++ has a two-part design in its stream library—a streambuf object and a stream. This same model performs I/O for keyboard and terminal as well as disk I/O. The same operators and operations perform in precisely the same way. This greatly simplifies a programming task that has always been difficult and confusing. To facilitate disk file I/O, the stream library defines a filebuf object, which is a derivative of the standard streambuf type. Like its progenitor type, filebuf manages a buffer, but in this case, the buffer is attached to a disk file. You will learn more about files in Chapter 11.

What's Coming?

In this chapter you were introduced to the origins of C++, namely the C language. All professional programmers know that there is no one computer language that is perfect for all circumstances. Knowing some of the similarities and differences between C and C++ help you use both more efficiently.

This chapter also pointed out the similarities in overall program syntax between C and C++ applications, while highlighting the necessary syntax updates required by moving from the old-style program layout to the new ANSI/ISO C++ definitions. And no doubt, C, C++, and now C# will continue to evolve with today's programmer needs.

In the next chapter, you will bootstrap your understanding of the common C/C++ data types. The close-up view will guarantee you pick the right data type to maximize code efficiency and minimize code size.

The Complete Reference

Visual C++.NET

Chapter 6

Working with Data

Here is a true statement: "You will never truly be a C/C++ programmer until you stop thinking in some other language and *translating* into C/C++!" You may have formally learned either COBOL, FORTRAN, Pascal, or PL/I, and then, with brute force, taught yourself one or more of the other languages listed, and been quite successful at it.

The same approach will *not* work with C and C++. The reason for this is that these new state-of-the-art languages have unique features, constructs, and ways of doing things that *have no equivalent* in the listed, older, high-level languages. If you attempt to do a mental translation, you will end up not taking advantage of all that C and C++ have to offer. Even worse, in the presence of a truly experienced C/C++ programmer, you will look like an obvious novice. Technically and philosophically correct C/C++ source code design has many nuances that quickly expose fraudulent claims of expertise!

Fully appreciating all that C and C++ have to offer takes time and practice. In Chapter 6, you begin your exploration of their underlying structures. The great stability of these languages begins with the standard C and C++ data types and the modifiers and operators that can be used with them.

Identifiers

Identifiers are the names you use to represent variables, constants, types, functions, and labels in your program. You create an identifier by specifying it in the declaration of a variable, type, or function. You can then use the identifier in later program statements to refer to the associated item.

An identifier is a sequence of one or more letters, digits, or underscores that begins with a letter or underscore. Identifiers can contain any number of characters, but only the first 31 are significant to the compiler. (However, other programs that read the compiler output, such as the linker, may recognize even fewer characters.)

C and C++ are *case sensitive*. This means that the C compiler considers uppercase and lowercase letters to be distinct characters. For example, the compiler sees the variables *NAME_LENGTH* and *Name_Length* as two unique identifiers representing different memory cells. This feature enables you to create distinct identifiers that have the same spelling but different cases for one or more of the letters.

The selection of case can also help you understand your code. For example, identifiers declared in **#include** header files are often created using only uppercase letters. Because of this, whenever you encounter an uppercase identifier in the source file, you have a visual clue as to where that particular identifier's definition can be found.

While it is syntactically legal, you should not use leading underscores in identifiers you create. Identifiers beginning with an underscore can cause conflicts with the names of system routines or variables and produce errors. As a result, programs containing names beginning with leading underscores are not guaranteed to be portable. Use of two sequential underscore characters (__) in an identifier is reserved for C++ implementations and standard libraries.

One stylistic convention adopted by many C programmers is to precede all identifiers with an abbreviation of the identifier's data type. For example, all integer identifiers would begin with an "i," floats would begin with an "f," null-terminated strings would begin with "sz," pointer variables would begin with a "p," and so on. With this naming convention, you can easily look at a piece of code and see not only which identifiers are being used, but also their data type. This makes it easier to learn how a particular section of code operates and to do line-by-line source debugging. The programs throughout this book use both variable naming conventions since many of the programs you encounter in real life will use one format or another.

The following are examples of identifiers:

```
i
itotal
frange1
szfirst_name
lfrequency
imax
iMax
iMAX
NULL
EOF
```

See if you can determine why the following identifiers are illegal:

```
1st_year
#social_security
Not_Done!
```

The first identifier is illegal because it begins with a decimal number. The second begins with a # symbol, and the last ends with an illegal character.

Take a look at the following identifiers. Are they legal or not?

```
O
OO
OOO
_____
```

Actually, all four identifiers are legal. The first three use the uppercase letter "O." Since each has a different number of Os, they are all unique. The fourth identifier is composed of five underscore (_) characters. Is it meaningful? Definitely not. Is it legal?

Yes. While these identifiers meet the letter of the law, they greatly miss its spirit. The point is that all identifiers, functions, constants, and variables should have meaningful names.

Since uppercase and lowercase letters are considered distinct characters, each of the following identifiers is unique:

```
MAX_RATIO
max_ratio
Max_Ratio
```

The C compiler's case sensitivity can create tremendous headaches for the novice C programmer. For example, trying to reference the printf() function when it was typed PRINTF() will invoke "unknown identifier" complaints from the compiler. In Pascal, however, a writeln is a WRITELN is a WriteLn.

With experience, you would probably detect the preceding printf() error, but can you see what's wrong with this next statement?

```
printf("%D",integer_value);
```

Assuming that *integer_value* was defined properly, you might think that nothing was wrong. Remember, however, that C is case sensitive—the %*D* print format has never been defined, only %*d* has.

For more advanced applications, some linkers may further restrict the number and type of characters for globally visible symbols. Also, the linker, unlike the compiler, may not distinguish between uppercase and lowercase letters. By default, the Visual C/C++ LINK sees all public and external symbols, such as *MYVARIABLE*, *MyVariable*, and *myvariable*, as the same. You can, however, make LINK case sensitive by using the /NOI option. This would then force LINK to see the preceding three example variables as unique. One last word on identifiers: an identifier cannot have the same spelling and case as a keyword of the language. The next section lists C and C++ keywords.

Keywords

Keywords are predefined identifiers that have special meanings to the C/C++ compiler. You can use them only as defined. Remember, the name of a program identifier cannot have the same spelling and case as a C/C++ keyword. The C/C++ language keywords are listed in Table 6-1. Keywords with leading underscores are Microsoft specific.

__alignof	__unaligned	extern	selectany [1]
__asm	__uuidof	FALSE	short
__assume	__virtual_inheritance	Float	signed
__based	Align [1]	for	Sizeof
__cdecl	allocate [1]	Friend	static
__declspec	auto	Goto	static_cast
__except	Bool	If	Struct
__fastcall	Break	inline	Switch
__finally	Case	Int	template
__forceinline	catch	Long	this
__inline	Char	mutable	thread [1]
__int16	Class	naked [1]	Throw
__int32	const	namespace	TRUE
__int64	const_cast	New	try
__int8	continue	noinline [1]	typedef
__interface	default	noreturn [1]	Typeid
__leave	Delete	nothrow [1]	typename
__multiple_ inheritance	deprecated [1]	Novtable [1]	Union
__noop	dllexport [1]	operator	Unsigned
__pragma	dllimport [1]	private	using declaration
__ptr64	Do	property [1]	using directive
__sealed	double	protected	uuid [1]
__single_ inheritance	dynamic_cast	Public	virtual
			Void
__stdcall	Else	register	volatile
__super	Enum	reinterpret_cast	wchar_t
__try/__except	explicit	Return	While
__try/__finally			

[1] Extended attributes for the __declspec keyword.

Table 6-1.   *C/C++ Keywords (Those with Leading Underscores Are Microsoft Specific)*

You cannot redefine keywords. However, you can specify text to be substituted for keywords before compilation by using C preprocessor directives.

Microsoft Specific

In Microsoft C++, identifiers with two leading underscores are reserved for compiler implementations. Therefore, the Microsoft convention is to precede Microsoft-specific keywords with double underscores. These words cannot be used as identifier names.

Microsoft extensions are enabled by default. To ensure that your programs are fully portable, you can disable Microsoft extensions by specifying the ANSI-compatible /Za command-line option (compile for ANSI compatibility) during compilation. When you do this, Microsoft-specific keywords are disabled.

When Microsoft extensions are enabled, you can use the Microsoft-specific keywords in your programs. For ANSI compliance, these keywords are prefaced by a double underscore. For backward compatibility, single-underscore versions of all the double-underscored keywords except **__except**, **__finally**, **__leave**, and **__try** are supported. In addition, **__cdecl** is available with no leading underscore. The **__asm** keyword replaces C++ **asm** syntax. **asm** is reserved for compatibility with other C++ implementations, but not implemented. Use **__asm**. The **__based** keyword has limited uses for 32-bit target compilations.

Standard C and C++ Data Types

All programs deal with some kind of information that you can usually represent by using one of the eight basic C and C++ types: text or **char**, integer values or **int**, floating-point values or **float**, double floating-point values or **double** (**long double**), enumerated or **enum**, valueless or **void**, pointers, and **bool**. Following is an explanation of the types:

- *Text* (data type **char**) is made up of single characters, such as a, Z, ?, and 3; and strings, such as "There is more to life than increasing its speed." (Usually, 8 bits, or 1 byte per character, with the range of 0 to 255.)

- *Integer values* are those numbers you learned to count with (1, 2, 7, -45, and 1,345). (Usually, 16 bits wide, 2 bytes, or 1 word, with the range of -32,768 to 32,767. Under Windows ME, 2000, and XP, integers are now 32 bits wide with a range from -2147483648 to 2147483647.)

- *Floating-point values* are numbers that have a fractional portion, such as pi (3.14159), and exponents (7.563^{1021}). These are also known as real numbers. (Usually, 32 bits, 4 bytes, or 2 words, with the range of +/- 3.4E-38 to 3.4E+38.)

- *Double floating-point values* have an extended range (usually, 64 bits, 8 bytes, or 4 words, with the range of 1.7E-308 to 1.7E+308). **Long double** floating-point values are even more precise (usually, 80 bytes, or 5 words, with the range of +/- 1.18E-4932 to 1.18E+4932).

- *Enumerated* data types allow for user-defined types.

- The type **void** is used to signify values that occupy zero bits and have no value. (This type can also be used for the creation of generic pointers, as discussed in Chapter 10.)

- The *pointer* data type doesn't hold information in the normal sense of the other data types; instead, each pointer contains the address of the memory location holding the actual data. (This is also discussed in Chapter 10.)

- The new **bool** data type, which can be assigned the two constants, **true**, and **false**.

Characters

Every language uses a set of characters to construct meaningful statements. For instance, all books written in English use combinations of 26 letters of the alphabet, the ten digits, and the punctuation marks. Similarly, C and C++ programs are written using a set of characters consisting of the 26 lowercase letters of the alphabet:

abcdefghijklmnopqrstuvwxyz

the 26 uppercase letters of the alphabet:

ABCDEFGHIJKLMNOPQRSTUVWXYZ

the ten digits:

0 1 2 3 4 5 6 7 8 9

and the following symbols:

+ - * / = , . _ : ; ? \ " ' ~ | ! # % $ & () [ ] { } ^ @

C and C++ also use the blank space, sometimes referred to as white space. Combinations of symbols, with no blank space between them, are also valid C and C++ characters. In fact, the following is a mixture of valid C and C++ symbols:

++ -- == && | | << >> >= <= += -= *= /= ?: :: /* */ //

The following C program illustrates how to declare and use **char** data types. The C version is included here because it illustrates one of the few places where a C++ programmer can get into serious trouble when using C.

The issue deals with C++'s automated input mechanisms versus C's *manual* code approach. When viewing the algorithm, pay particularly close attention to the use of the address operator &:

```
/*
*    char.c
*    A C program demonstrating the char data type and showing
```

PROGRAMMING
FOUNDATIONS

```
*   how a char variable can be interpreted as an integer.
*   Copyright (c) Chris H. Pappas and William H. Murray, 2001
*/

#include <stdio.h>
#include <ctype.h>

int main( )()
{
  char csinglechar, cuppercase, clowercase;

  printf("\nPlease enter a single character: ");
  scanf("%c",&csinglechar);

  cuppercase = toupper(csinglechar);
  clowercase = tolower(csinglechar);

  printf("The UPPERcase character \'%c\' has a decimal ASCII"
         " value of %d\n",cuppercase,cuppercase);
  printf("The ASCII value represented in hexadecimal"
         " is %X\n",cuppercase);

  printf("If you add sixteen you will get \'%c\'\n",
         (cuppercase+16));
  printf("The calculated ASCII value in hexadecimal"
         " is %X\n",(cuppercase+16));
  printf("The LOWERcase character \'%c\' has a decimal ASCII"
         " value of %d\n",clowercase,clowercase);

  return(0);
}
```

The output from the program looks like this:

```
Please enter a single character: d
The UPPERcase character 'D' has a decimal ASCII value of 68
The ASCII value represented in hexadecimal is 44
If you add sixteen you will get 'T'
The calculated ASCII value in hexadecimal is 54
The LOWERcase character 'd' has a decimal ASCII value of 100
```

The *%X* format control instructs the compiler to interpret the value as an uppercase hexadecimal number.

The C statement:

```
scanf("%c",&csinglechar);
```

when written in C++ takes on a much simpler syntax:

```
cin >> csinglechar;
```

C's scanf() function expects the address of the memory location to fill. This means YOU must remember to place the address operator in front of the variable. Omitting the address operator causes the compiler to use the garbage contents of the variable as the *address* of the memory location being filled—disaster awaits!

Three Integers

Microsoft Visual C/C++ supports three types of integers. Along with the standard type **int**, the compiler supports **short int** and **long int**. These are most often abbreviated to just **short** and **long**. While the C language is not hardware dependent (syntax, etc.), data types used by the C language are. Thus, the actual sizes of **short**, **int**, and **long** depend upon the implementation. Across all C compilers, the only guarantee is that a variable of type **short** will not be larger than one of type **long**. Microsoft Visual C/C++ allocates 2 bytes for both **short** and **int**. (Under Windows ME, 2000, and XP, integers are now 32 bits.) The type **long** occupies 4 bytes of storage.

Unsigned Modifier

All C and C++ compilers allow you to declare certain types to be **unsigned**. Currently, you can apply the **unsigned** modifier to four types: **char**, **short int**, **int**, and **long int**. When one of these data types is modified to be **unsigned**, you can think of the range of values it holds as representing the numbers displayed on a car odometer. An automobile odometer starts at 000..., increases to a maximum of 999..., and then recycles back to 000.... It also displays only positive whole numbers. In a similar way, an **unsigned** data type can hold only positive values in the range of zero to the maximum number that can be represented.

For example, suppose you are designing a new data type called *my_octal* and have decided that *my_octal* variables can hold only 3 bits. You have also decided that the data type *my_octal* is signed by default. Since a variable of type *my_octal* can only contain the bit patterns 000 through 111 (or zero to 7 decimal), and you want to represent both positive and negative values, you have a problem. You can't have both positive and negative numbers in the range zero to 7 because you need one of the 3 bits to represent the sign of the number. Therefore, *my_octal*'s range is a subset. When the most significant bit is zero, the value is positive. When the most significant bit is 1, the value is negative. This gives a *my_octal* variable the range of -4 to +3.

However, applying the **unsigned** data type modifier to a *my_octal* variable would yield a range of zero to 7, since the most significant bit can be combined with the lower 2 bits to represent a broader range of positive values instead of identifying the sign of the number. This simple analogy holds true for any of the valid C data types defined to be of type **unsigned**. The storage and range for the fundamental C/C++ data types are summarized in Table 6-2.

Type Name	Bytes	Other Names	Range of Values
Int	*	signed, signed int	System dependent
Unsigned int	*	Unsigned	System dependent
__int8	1	char, signed char	-128 to 127
__int16	2	short, short int, signed short int	-32,768 to 32,767
__int32	4	signed, signed int	-2,147,483,648 to 2,147,483,647
__int64	8	None	-9,223,372,036,854,775,808 to 9,223,372,036,854,775,807
Char	1	signed char	-128 to 127
Unsigned char	1	None	0 to 255
Short	2	short int, signed short int	-32,768 to 32,767
Unsigned short	2	unsigned short int	0 to 65,535
Long	4	long int, signed long int	-2,147,483,648 to 2,147,483,647
Unsigned long	4	unsigned long int	0 to 4,294,967,295
Enum	*	None	Same as **int**
Float	4	None	3.4E +/- 38 (7 digits)
Double	8	None	1.7E +/- 308 (15 digits)
long double	10	None	1.2E +/- 4932 (19 digits)

Table 6-2.   *ANSI C/C++ Standard Data Types and Sizes*

The **long double** data type (80-bit, 10-byte precision) is mapped directly to **double** (64-bit, 8-byte precision) in Windows Me, 2000, and XP. **Signed** and **unsigned** are modifiers that can be used with any integral type. The **char** type is signed by default, but you can specify /J to make it **unsigned** by default. The **int** and **unsigned int** types have the size of the system word. This is 2 bytes (the same as **short** and **unsigned short**) in MS-DOS and 16-bit versions of Windows, and 4 bytes in 32-bit operating systems. However, portable code should not depend on the size of **int**. Microsoft C/C++ also features support for sized integer types. Table 6-3 lists the valid data type modifiers in all of the various legal and abbreviated combinations.

Type Specifier	Equivalent(s)
signed char	Char
signed int	signed, int
signed short int	Short, signed short
signed long int	long, signed long
Unsigned char	None
Unsigned int	unsigned
unsigned short int	unsigned short
unsigned long int	unsigned long
Float	None
long double	None

Table 6-3.   *Valid Data Type Modifier Abbreviations*

Floating Point

Visual C/C++ uses the three floating-point types: **float**, **double**, and **long double**. While the ANSI C standard does not specifically define the values and storage that are to be allocated for each of these types, the standard did require each type to hold a minimum of any value in the range 1E-37 to 1E+37. As you saw in Table 6-2, the Microsoft Visual C/C++ environment has greatly expanded upon this minimum requirement. Historically, most C compilers have always had the types **float** and

double. The ANSI C committee added the third type, **long double**. Here are some examples of floating-point numbers:

```
float altitude = 47000;
double joules;
long double budget_deficit;
```

You can use the third type, **long double**, on any computer, even those that have only two types of floating-point numbers. However, if the computer does not have a specific data type of **long double**, then the data item will have the same size and storage capacity as a **double**.

The following C++ program illustrates how to declare and use floating-point variables:

```
//
// float.cpp : Defines the entry point for the console application.
// A C++ program demonstrating using the float data type.
// Copyright (c) Chris H. Pappas and William H. Murray, 2001
//

#include "stdafx.h"
#include <iostream>
#include <iomanip>

#include "stdafx.h"
#include <iostream>
#include <iomanip>

using namespace std;

int main(int argc, char* argv[])
{
  long loriginal_flags=cin.flags( )( );
  float fvalue;

  cout << "Please enter a float value to be formatted: ";
  cin >> fvalue;

  cout << "Standard Formatting:   " << fvalue << "\n";
  cout.setf(ios::scientific);
  cout << "Scientific Formatting: " << fvalue << "\n";
```

```
    cout.setf(ios::fixed);
    cout << "Fixed Formatting:      " << setprecision(2)
        << fvalue;

    cout.flags(loriginal_flags);

    return(0);
}
```

The output looks like this:

```
Please enter a float value to be formatted: 1234.5678
Standard Formatting:    1234.57
Scientific Formatting: 1.234568e+003
Fixed Formatting:       1.2e+003
```

Notice the different value printed depending on the print format specification standard, scientific or fixed.

Enumerated

When an enumerated variable is defined, it is associated with a set of named integer constants called the *enumeration set*. (These are discussed in Chapter 12.) The variable can contain any one of the constants at any time, and the constants can be referred to by name. For example, the following definition creates the enumerated type *air_supply*; the enumerated constants EMPTY, USEABLE, and FULL; and the enumerated variable *instructor_tank*:

```
enum air_supply { EMPTY,
                  USEABLE,
                  FULL=5 } instructor_tank;
```

All the constants and variables are type **int**, and each constant is automatically provided a **default** initial value unless another value is specified. In the preceding example, the constant name EMPTY has the integer value zero by default since it is the first in the list and was not specifically overridden. The value of USEABLE is 1 since it occurs immediately after a constant with the value of zero. The constant FULL was specifically initialized to the value 5, and if another constant were included in the list after FULL, the new constant would have the integer value of 6.

Having created *air_supply*, you can later define another variable, *student_tank*, as follows:

```
enum air_supply student_tank;
```

After this statement it is legal to say:

```
instructor_tank = FULL;
student_tank    = EMPTY;
```

This places the value 5 into the variable *instructor_tank* and the value of zero into the variable *student_tank*.

Note   *When defining additional enumerated variables in C++, it is not necessary to repeat the* **enum** *keyword. However, both syntaxes are accepted by the C++ compiler.*

One common mistake is to think that *air_supply* is a variable. It is a "type" of data that can be used later to create additional enumerated variables like *instructor_tank* or *student_tank*.

Since the name *instructor_tank* is an enumerated variable of type *air_supply*, *instructor_tank* can be used on the left of an assignment operator and can receive a value. This occurred when the enumerated constant FULL was explicitly assigned to it. EMPTY, USEABLE, and FULL are names of constants; they are not variables and their values cannot be changed.

Tests can be performed on the variables in conjunction with the constants. The following is a complete C++ program that uses the preceding definitions:

```
//
// enum.cpp : Defines the entry point for the console application.
// A C++ program demonstrating the use of enumeration variables
// Copyright (c) Chris H. Pappas and William H. Murray, 2001
//

#include "stdafx.h"
#include <iostream>

using namespace std;

int main(int argc, char* argv[])
{
```

```
enum air_supply { EMPTY,
                  USEABLE,
                  FULL=5 }  instructor_tank;
enum air_supply student_tank;

instructor_tank = FULL;
student_tank = EMPTY;

cout << "The value of instructor_tank is "
     << instructor_tank << endl;

if (student_tank < USEABLE) {
  cout << "Refill this tank.\n";
  cout << "Class is cancelled.\n";
  exit(1);
}
if (instructor_tank >= student_tank)
  cout << "Proceed with lesson\n";
else
  cout << "Class is cancelled!\n";

return(0);
}
```

In C, an **enum** type is equivalent to the type **int**. This technically allows a program to assign integer values directly to enumerated variables. C++ enforces a stronger type check and does not allow this mixed-mode operation. The output from the program looks like this:

The value of instructor_tank is 5

Refill this tank.

Class is cancelled.

The New C++ Type: bool

This keyword is an integral type. A variable of this type can have values true and false. All conditional expressions now return a value of type **bool**. For example, myvar! = 0 now returns **true** or **false** depending on the value of *myvar*.

The values true and false have the following relationship:

!false == true

!true == false

Look at the following statement:

```
if (myexpression)
   statement1;
```

If *myexpression* evaluates to true, *statement1* is always executed; if *myexpression* evaluates to false, *statement1* is never executed. An important fundamental to keep in mind when writing test expressions is this: Both C and C++ view *any* nonzero (!0) value as true, and *any* expression evaluating to zero (0) as false.

*When a postfix or prefix ++ operator is applied to a variable of type **bool**, the variable is set to true. The postfix or prefix -- operator cannot be applied to a variable of this type. Also, the **bool** type participates in integral promotions. An r-value of type **bool** can be converted to an r-value of type **int**, with false becoming zero and true becoming 1.*

Access Modifiers

The **const** and **volatile** modifiers are new to C and C++. They were added by the ANSI C standard to help identify which variables will never change (**const**) and which can change unexpectedly (**volatile**).

const Modifier

At certain times you will need to use a value that does not change throughout the program. Such a quantity is called a *constant*. For example, if a program deals with the area and circumference of a circle, the constant value pi=3.14159 would be used frequently. In a financial program, an interest rate might be a constant. In such cases, you can improve the readability of the program by giving the constant a descriptive name.

Using descriptive names can also help prevent errors. Suppose that a constant value (not a constant variable) is used at many points throughout the program. A typographical error might result in the wrong value being typed at one or more of these points. However, if the constant is given a name, a typographical error would then be detected by the compiler because the incorrectly spelled identifier would probably not have been declared.

Suppose you are writing a program that repeatedly uses the value pi. It might seem as though a *variable* called *pi* should be declared with an initial value of 3.14159. However, the program should not be able to change the value of a constant. For instance, if you inadvertently wrote "pi" to the left of an equal sign, the value of pi would be changed, causing all subsequent calculations to be in error. C and C++ provide mechanisms that prevent such an error from occurring—you can establish constants, the values of which cannot be changed.

In C and C++, you declare a constant by writing "**const**" before the keyword (such as **int**, **float**, or **double**) in the declaration. For example:

```
const int iMIN=1,iSALE_PERCENTAGE=25;
const float fbase_change=32.157;
int irow_index=1,itotal=100,iobject;
double ddistance=0,dvelocity;
```

Because a constant cannot be changed, it must be initialized in its declaration. The integer constants iMIN and iSALE_PERCENTAGE are declared with values 1 and 25, respectively; the constant *fbase_change* is of type **float** and has been initialized to 32.157. In addition, the integer (nonconstant) variables *irow_index*, *itotal*, and *iobject* have been declared. Initial values of 1 and 100 have been established for *irow_index* and *itotal*, respectively. Finally, *ddistance* and *dvelocity* have been declared to be (nonconstant) variables of type **double**. An initial value of zero has been set up for *ddistance*.

Constants and variables are used in the same way in a program. The only difference is that the initial values assigned to the constants cannot be changed. That is, the constants are not *lvalues*; they cannot appear to the left of an equal sign. (Expressions that refer to memory locations are called *lvalue expressions*. Expressions referring to modifiable locations are *modifiable lvalues*. One example of a modifiable *lvalue* expression is a variable name declared without the **const** specifier.)

Normally, the assignment operation assigns the value of the right-hand operand to the storage location named by the left-hand operand. Therefore, the left-hand operand of an assignment operation (or the single operand of a unary assignment expression) must be an expression that refers to a modifiable memory location.

#define Constants

C and C++ provide another method for establishing constants: the **#define** compiler directive. Let's look at an example. Suppose that at the beginning of a program you have the statement:

```
#define SALES_TEAM 10
```

The form of this statement is **#define** followed by two strings of characters separated by blanks. When the program is compiled, there are several passes made through it. The first step is accomplished by the *compiler preprocessor*, which does such things as carry out the **#include** and **#define** directives. When the preprocessor encounters the **#define** directive, it replaces every occurrence of SALES_TEAM in the source file(s) with the number 10.

In general, when the preprocessor encounters a **#define** directive, it replaces every occurrence of the first string of characters, "SALES_TEAM," in the program with the second string of characters, "10". Additionally, no value can be assigned to SALES_TEAM because it has never been declared to be a variable. As a result of the syntax, SALES_TEAM has all the attributes of a constant. Note that the **#define** statement is *not* terminated by a semicolon. If a semicolon followed the value 10, then every occurrence of SALES_TEAM would be replaced with "10;". The directive's action is to replace the first string with *everything* in the second string.

All of the programs that have been discussed so far are short, and would usually be stored in a single file. If a statement such as the **#define** for SALES_TEAM appeared at the beginning of the file, the substitution of "10" for "SALES_TEAM" would take place throughout the program. (Chapter 13 of this book discusses breaking a program down into many subprograms, with each subprogram being broken down into separate files.) Under these circumstances, the compiler directive would be effective only for the single file in which it is written.

The preceding discussion explored two methods for defining constants—the keyword **const** and the **#define** compiler directive. In many programs, the action of each of these two methods is essentially the same. On the other hand, the use of the modifier keyword **const** results in a "variable" whose value cannot be changed. Later in this chapter, in the section "Storage Classes," you will see how variables can be declared in such a way that they exist only over certain regions of a program. The same can be said for constants declared with the keyword **const**. Thus, the **const** declaration is somewhat more versatile than the **#define** directive. Also, the **#define** directive is found in standard C and is therefore already familiar to C programmers.

volatile Modifier

The **volatile** keyword signifies that a variable can unexpectedly change because of events outside the control of the program. For example, the following definition indicates that the variable *event_time* can have its value changed without the knowledge of the program:

```
volatile int event_time;
```

A definition like this is needed, for example, if *event_time* is updated by hardware that maintains the current clock time. The program that contains the variable *event_time* could be interrupted by the timekeeping hardware and the variable *event_time* changed.

A data object should be declared **volatile** if it is a memory-mapped device register or a data object shared by separate processes, as would be the case in a multitasking operating environment.

const and volatile Used Together

You can use the **const** and **volatile** modifiers with any other data types (for example, **char** and **float**) and also with each other. The following definition specifies that the program does not intend to change the value in the variable *constant_event_time*:

```
const volatile constant_event_time;
```

However, the compiler is also instructed, because of the **volatile** modifier, to make no assumptions about the variable's value from one moment to the next. Therefore, two things happen. First, an error message will be issued by the compiler for any line of source code that attempts to change the value of the variable *constant_event_time*. Second, the compiler will not remove the variable *constant_event_time* from inside loops since an external process can also be updating the variable while the program is executing.

pascal, cdecl, near, far, and huge Modifiers

The first two modifiers, **pascal** and **cdecl**, are used most frequently in advanced applications. Microsoft Visual C/C++ allows you to write programs that can easily call other routines written in different languages. The opposite of this also holds true. For example, you can write a Pascal program that calls a C++ routine. When you mix languages this way, you have to take two very important issues into consideration: identifier names and the way parameters are passed.

When Microsoft Visual C/C++ compiles your program, it places all of the program's global identifiers (functions and variables) into the resulting object code file for linking purposes. By default, the compiler saves those identifiers using the same case in which they were defined (uppercase, lowercase, or mixed). Additionally, the compiler appends an underscore (_) to the front of the identifier. Since Microsoft Visual C/C++'s integrated linking (by default) is case sensitive, any external identifiers you declare in your program are also assumed to be in the same form with a prepended underscore and the same spelling and case as defined.

pascal

The Pascal language uses a different calling sequence than C and C++. Pascal (along with FORTRAN) passes function arguments from left to right and does not allow variable-length argument lists. In Pascal, it is also the called function's responsibility to remove the arguments from the stack, rather than having the invoking function do so when control returns from the invoked function.

A C and C++ program can generate this calling sequence in one of two ways. First, it can use the compile-time switch /Gc, which makes the Pascal calling sequence the **default** for all enclosed calls and function definitions. Second, the C program can override the **default** C calling sequence explicitly by using the **pascal** keyword in the function definition.

As mentioned earlier, when C generates a function call, by default it appends an underscore to the function name and declares the function as external. It also preserves the casing of the name. However, when the **pascal** keyword is used, the underscore is not prepended and the identifier (function or variable) is converted to all uppercase.

The following code segment demonstrates how to use the **pascal** keyword on a function. (The same keyword can be used to ensure FORTRAN code compatibility.)

```
float pascal pfcalculate(int iscore, int iweight)
{
    .
    .
    .
}
```

Of course, variables can also be given a Pascal convention, as seen in this next example:

```
#define TABLESIZE 30

float pascal pfcalculate(int iscore, int iweight)
{
    .
    .
    .
}

float pascal pfscore_table[TABLESIZE];

int main( )()
{
    int iscore 95, iweight = 10;

    pfscore_table[0] = pfcalculate(iscore,iweight);

    return(0);
}
```

In this example, *pfscore_table* has been globally defined with the **pascal** modifier. Function main() also shows how to make an external reference to a **pascal** function type. Since both functions, main() and pfcalculate(), are in the same source file, the function pfcalculate() is global to main().

cdecl

If the /Gz compile-time switch was used to compile your C or C++ program, all function and variable references were generated matching the Pascal calling convention. However, there may be occasions when you want to guarantee that certain identifiers you are using in your program remain case sensitive and keep the underscore at the front. This is most often the case for identifiers being used in another C file.

To maintain this C compatibility (preserving the case and having a leading underscore prepended), you can use the **cdecl** keyword. When the **cdecl** keyword is used in front of a function, it also affects how the parameters are passed.

Note that all C and C++ functions prototyped in the header files of Microsoft Visual C/C++—for example, stdio.h—are of type **cdecl**. This ensures that you can link with the library routines, even when you are compiling using the /Gz option. The following example was compiled using the /Gz option and shows how you would rewrite the previous example to maintain C compatibility:

```
#define TABLESIZE 30

float cdecl cfcalculate(int iscore, int iweight)
{
    .
    .
    .
}

float cdecl cfscore_table[TABLESIZE];

int main( )()
{
  int iscore 95, iweight = 10;

  cfscore_table[0] = cfcalculate(iscore,iweight);

  return(0);
}
```

near, far, and huge

This is an appropriate time to caution you. C and C++ are continuing to evolve, even as you read this text. Therefore, any time you peruse other C/C++ literature, beware: there are Historic C, C, ANSI C, Historic C++, C++, ANSI C++, and the flavor-of-the-month languages out there! Case in point: the old-style keywords **near**, **far**, and **huge**.

Note *These old-style C/C++ keywords are only mentioned here in case you run across them in an older text or program. They are 16-bit C/C++ compiler specific and are no longer needed by today's state-of-the-art 32-bit C/C++ compilers.*

You use the three modifiers—**near**, **far**, and **huge**—to affect the action of the indirection operator (*); in other words, they modify pointer sizes to data objects. A **near** pointer is only 2 bytes long, a **far** pointer is 4 bytes long, and a **huge** pointer is also 4 bytes long. The difference between the **far** pointer and the **huge** pointer is that the latter has to deal with the form of the address.

Data Type Conversions

In the programs so far, the variables and numbers used in any particular statement were all of the same type, for example, **int** or **float**. You can write statements that perform operations involving variables of different types. These operations are called *mixed-mode operations.* In contrast to some other programming languages, C and C++ perform automatic conversions from one type to another. As you progress through the book, additional types will be introduced, and mixing of those types will be discussed.

Data of different types is stored differently in memory. Suppose that the number 10 is being stored. Its representation will depend upon its type. That is, the pattern of zeros and ones in memory will be different when 10 is stored as an integer than when it is stored as a floating-point number.

Suppose that the following operation is executed, where both *fresult* and *fvalue* are of type **float**, and the variable *ivalue* is of type **int**:

```
fresult = fvalue * ivalue;
```

The statement is therefore a mixed-mode operation. When the statement is executed, the value of *ivalue* will be converted into a floating-point number before the multiplication takes place. The compiler recognizes that a mixed-mode operation is occurring, and therefore generates code to perform the following operations. The integer value assigned to *ivalue* is read from memory. This value is then converted to the corresponding floating-point value, which is multiplied by the real value assigned to *fvalue,* and the resulting floating-point value is assigned to *fresult.* In other words, the compiler performs the conversion automatically. Note that the value assigned to *ivalue* is unchanged by this process and remains of type **int**.

You have seen that in mixed-mode operations involving a value of type **int** and another value of type **float**, the value of type **int** is converted into a value of type **float** for calculation. This is done without changing the stored integral value during the conversion process. Now let's consider mixed-mode operations between two different types of variables.

Before doing this, you need to know that there is in fact a *hierarchy of conversions*, in that the object of lower priority is temporarily converted to the type of higher priority for the performance of the calculation. The hierarchy of conversions takes the following structure, from highest priority to lowest:

double

float

long

int

short

For example, the type **double** has a higher priority than the type **int**. When a type is converted to one that has more significant digits, the value of the number and its accuracy are unchanged.

Look at what happens when a conversion from type **float** to type **int** takes place. Suppose that the variables *ivalue1* and *ivalue2* have been defined to be of type **int**, while *fvalue* and *fresult* have been defined to be of type **float**. Consider the following sequence of statements:

```
ivalue1 = 3;
ivalue2 = 4;
fvalue = 7.0;
fresult = fvalue + ivalue1/ivalue2;
```

The statement *ivalue1/ivalue2* is *not* a mixed-mode operation; instead, it represents the division of two integers, and its result is zero since the fractional part (0.75, in this case) is *discarded* when integer division is performed. Therefore, the value stored in *fresult* is 7.0.

What if *ivalue2* had been defined to be of type **float**? In this case, *fresult* would have been assigned the floating-point value 7.75, since the statement *ivalue1/ivalue2* would be a mixed-mode operation. Under these circumstances, the value of *ivalue1* is temporarily converted to the floating-point value 3.0, and the result of the division is 0.75. When that is added to *fvalue*, the result is 7.75.

It is important to know that the type of the value to the left of the assignment statement determines the type of the result of the operation. For example, suppose that *fx* and *fy* have been declared to be of type **float** and *iresult* has been declared to be of type **int**. Consider the following statements:

```
fx = 7.0;
fy = 2.0;
iresult = 4.0 + fx/fy
```

The result of executing the statement fx/fy is 3.5; when this is added to 4.0, the floating-point value generated is 7.5. However, this value cannot be assigned to *iresult* because *iresult* is of type **int**. The number 7.5 is therefore converted into an integer. When this is done, the fraction part is truncated. The resulting whole number is converted from a floating-point representation to an integer representation, and the value assigned to *iresult* is the integer number 7.

Explicit Type Conversions Using the Cast Operator

You have seen that the C and C++ compiler automatically changes the format of a variable in mixed-mode operations using different data types. However, there are circumstances where, although automatic conversion is *not* performed, type conversion would be desirable. For those occasions, you must specifically designate that a change of type is to be made. These explicit specifications also clarify to other programmers the statements involved. The C language provides several procedures that allow you to designate that type conversion must occur.

One of these procedures is called the *cast operator*. Whenever you want to temporarily change the format of a variable, you simply precede the variable's identifier with the parenthesized type you want it converted to. For example, if *ivalue1* and *ivalue2* were defined to be of type **int** and *fvalue* and *fresult* have been defined to be of type **float**, the following three statements would perform the same operation:

```
fresult = fvalue + (float)ivalue1/ivalue2;
fresult = fvalue + ivalue1/(float)ivalue2;
fresult = fvalue + (float)ivalue1/(float)ivalue2;
```

All three statements perform a floating-point conversion and division of the variables *ivalue1* and *ivalue2*. Because of the usual rules of mixed-mode arithmetic discussed earlier, if either variable is cast to type **float**, a floating-point division occurs. The third statement explicitly highlights the operation to be performed.

New Casting Operations!

The previous discussion on casting is included for two reasons. First, you could easily view C/C++ source files using this syntax; second, it's to prove the point that C and C++ are evolving languages. You will always need to use extra care when writing C/C++ code to ensure that the syntax meets the latest ANSI/ISO C/C++ standards.

As it turns out, traditional style casting proved to be unsafe, error-prone, difficult to spot when reading programs, and even more challenging when searched for in large bodies of source code. The newer style cast is a huge improvement. There are four new types of casts and the general syntax looks like:

```
cast_operator <castType> (objectToCast)
```

Dynamic Cast

You use a *dynamic_cast* whenever you need to convert a base class pointer or reference to a derived class pointer or reference. The one restriction is that the base, parent, or root class must have at least one **virtual** function. The syntax for a *dynamic_cast* looks like:

```
dynamic_cast < castType > ( objectToCast );
```

This type of cast allows a program, at run time, to determine whether a base class pointer or reference points to an object of a specific derived class or to an object of a class derived from the specified class.

You also use a *dynamic_cast* to upcast a pointer or reference to a derived class to a pointer or reference to one of the base, parent, or root, classes in the same hierarchy. Upcasting allows a program to determine, at run time, whether a pointer to a derived class really contains the address of an object of that class and, at the same time, you want to force the address into a pointer of one of the object's ancestor classes.

Static Cast

A *static_cast* implicitly converts between types that are not in the same class hierarchy. The type checking is static, where the compiler checks to ensure that the conversion is valid, as opposed to the dynamic run time type checking that is used with *dynamic_cast*s. The syntax for a *static_cast* looks like:

```
static_cast < castType > ( objectToCast );
```

The *static_cast* operator can be used for operations such as converting a pointer to a base class to a pointer to a derived class. Such conversions are not always safe. For example:

```
class typeA { ... };

class typeB : public typeA { ... };

void someFunction(typeA* ptypeA, typeB* ptypeB)
{
    typeB* ptypeB2 = static_cast<typeB*>(ptypeA);  // not safe, ptypeB may
                                                   // point to just typeB

    typeA* ptypeA2 = static_cast<typeA*>(ptypeB);  // BETTER - this is a
                                                   // safe conversion

    ...
}
```

In this code segment, the object pointed to by *ptypeA* may not be an object of type *typeB*, in which case the use of **ptypeB2* could be disastrous. For instance, calling a function that is a member of the *typeB* class, but not the *typeA* class, could result in an access violation.

Newer C-type Cast

The *reinterpret_cast* operator replaces many of the older C-type casts except those removing an identifier **const** restriction. The *reinterpret_cast* is capable of converting one pointer type into another, numbers into pointers, and vice-versa, pointers into numbers. The syntax looks like:

```
reinterpret_cast < castType > ( objectToCast );
```

The *reinterpret_cast* operator can be used for conversions such as **char*** to **int***, or **Base_class*** to **anyOtherNONrelated_class***, which are inherently unsafe.

The result of a *reinterpret_cast* cannot safely be used for anything other than being cast back to its original type. Other uses are, at best, nonportable. The following code segment demonstrates a pointer type cast in C, C++, and C# using the *reinterpret_cast* syntax:

```
void main ( void )
{
  int * pointer_to_int;
  /* in C */
  pointer_to_int = malloc(100); /* implicit void * cast to int *,
                          with warning */
  pointer_to_int = (int *) new int[100]; // C++ required cast of void *
                                      to int *
  pointer_to_int = reinterpret_cast<int *>( new int[100]); // new style
                                                    cast
}
```

Constant Cast

The *const_cast* operator can be used to remove the **const**, **volatile**, and **__unaligned** attribute(s) from a class. The general syntax looks like:

```
const_cast < castType > ( objectToCast )
```

With a *const_cast*, your program can cast a pointer to any object type or to a data member with a type that is identical except for the **const**, **volatile**, and **__unaligned** qualifiers. For pointers and references, the result will refer to the original object. For pointers to data members, the result will refer to the same member as the original (uncast) pointer to data member.

Storage Classes

Visual C/C++ supports four storage-class specifiers. They are

auto

register

static

extern

The storage class precedes the variable's declaration and instructs the compiler how the variable should be stored. Items declared with the **auto** or **register** specifier have local lifetimes; items declared with the **static** or **extern** specifier have global lifetimes.

The four storage-class specifiers affect the visibility of a variable or function, as well as its storage class. *Visibility* (sometimes defined as *scope*) refers to that portion of the source program in which the variable or function can be referenced by name. An item with a global lifetime exists throughout the execution of the source program.

The placement of a variable or a function declaration within a source file also affects storage class and visibility. Declarations outside all function definitions are said to appear at the *external level*, while declarations within function definitions appear at the *internal level*.

The exact meaning of each storage-class specifier depends on two factors: whether the declaration appears at the external or internal level and whether the item being declared is a variable or a function.

Variable Declarations at the External Level

Variable declarations at the external level may only use the **static** or **extern** storage class, not **auto** or **register**. They are either definitions of variables or references to variables defined elsewhere. An external variable declaration that also initializes the variable (implicitly or explicitly) is a defining declaration:

```
static int ivalue1;        // implicit 0 by default
static int ivalue1 = 10    // explicit

int ivalue2 = 20;          // explicit
```

Once a variable is defined at the external level, it is visible throughout the rest of the source file in which it appears. The variable is not visible prior to its definition in the same source file. Also, it is not visible in other source files of the program unless a referencing declaration makes it visible, as described shortly.

You can define a variable at the external level only once within a source file. If you give the **static** storage-class specifier, you can define another variable with the same name and the **static** storage-class specifier in a different source file. Since each static definition is visible only within its own source file, no conflict occurs.

The **extern** storage-class specifier declares a reference to a variable defined elsewhere. You can use an external declaration to make a definition in another source file visible or to make a variable visible above its definition in the same source file. The variable is visible throughout the remainder of the source file in which the declared reference occurs.

For an external reference to be valid, the variable it refers to must be defined once, and only once, at the external level. The definition can be in any of the source files that form the program. The following C++ program demonstrates the use of the **extern** keyword:

```
//
//      Source File A - incomplete file do not compile.
//
#include <iostream.h>

extern int ivalue;                  // makes ivalue visible
                                    // above its declaration

int main( )()
{
  ivalue++;                         // uses the above extern
                                    // reference
  cout << ivalue << "\n";           // prints 11
  function_a( )();

  return(0);
}

int ivalue = 10;                    // actual definition of
                                    // ivalue

void function_a(void)
{
  ivalue++;                         // references ivalue
```

```
    cout << ivalue << "\n";              // prints 12
    function_b( )( );
}


----------------------------------------


//
//     Source File B
//

#include <iostream.h>

extern int ivalue;                       // references ivalue
                                         // declared in Source A

void function_b(void)
{
  ivalue++;
  cout <<("%d\n", ivalue);               // prints 13
}
```

Variable Declarations at the Internal Level

You can use any of the four storage-class specifiers for variable declarations at the internal level. (The default is **auto**.) The **auto** storage-class specifier declares a variable with a local lifetime. It is visible only in the block in which it is declared and can include initializers.

The **register** storage-class specifier tells the compiler to give the variable storage in a register, if possible. This specifier speeds access time and reduces code size. It has the same visibility as an **auto** variable. If no registers are available when the compiler encounters a **register** declaration, the variable is given the **auto** storage class and stored in memory.

ANSI C does not allow for taking the address of a **register** object. However, this restriction does not apply to C++. Applying the address operator (&) to a C++ register variable forces the compiler to store the object in memory, since the compiler must put the object in a location for which an address can be represented.

A variable declared at the internal level with the **static** storage-class specifier has a global lifetime but is visible only within the block in which it is declared. Unlike **auto** variables, **static** variables keep their values when the block is exited. You can initialize a **static** variable with a constant expression. It is initialized to zero by default.

A variable declared with the **extern** storage-class specifier is a reference to a variable with the same name defined at the external level in any of the source files of the program. The internal **extern** declaration is used to make the external-level variable definition visible within the block. The next program demonstrates these concepts:

```
int ivalue1=1; // incomplete file do not compile.

void main( )()
{ // references the ivalue1 defined above
    extern int ivalue1;

  // default initialization of 0, ivalue2 only visible
  // in main( )()
    static int ivalue2;

  // stored in a register (if available), initialized
  // to 0
    register int rvalue = 0;

  // default auto storage class, int_value3 initialized
  // to 0
    int int_value3 = 0;

  // values printed are 1, 0, 0, 0:
    cout << ivalue1 << rvalue \
        <<ivalue2 << int_value3;
    function_a( )();
}

void function_a(void)
{
  // stores the address of the global variable ivalue1
    static int *pivalue1= &ivalue1;

  // creates a new local variable ivalue1 making the
  // global ivalue1 unreachable
    int ivalue1 = 32;

  // new local variable ivalue2
  // only visible within function_a
    static int ivalue2 = 2;

    ivalue2 += 2;
```

```
// the values printed are 32, 4, and 1:
    cout << ivalue1 << ivalue2 \
    << *pivalue1);
}
```

Since *ivalue1* is redefined in **function_a()**, access to the global *ivalue1* is denied. However, by using the data pointer *pivalue1* (discussed in Chapter 10), the address of the global *ivalue1* was used to print the value stored there.

Variable Scope Review

To review, there are four rules for variable visibility, also called *scope rules*. The four scopes for a variable are the block, function, file, and program. A variable declared within a block or function is known only within the block or function. A variable declared external to a function is known within the file in which it appears, from the point of its appearance to the end of the file. A variable declared as external in one source file and declared as external in other files has program scope.

Function Declarations at the External Level

When declaring a function at the external or internal level, you can use either the **static** or the **extern** storage-class specifier. Functions, unlike variables, always have a global lifetime. The visibility rules for functions vary slightly from the rules for variables.

Functions declared to be **static** are visible only within the source file in which they are defined. Functions in the same source file can call the **static** function, but functions in *other* source files cannot. Also, you can declare another **static** function with the same name in a different source file without conflict.

Functions declared as external are visible throughout *all* source files that make up the program (unless you later redeclare such a function as **static**). Any function can call an external function. Function declarations that omit the storage-class specifier are external by default.

Operators

C and C++ have many operators not found in other languages. These include bitwise operators, increment and decrement operators, conditional operators, the comma operator, and assignment and compound assignment operators.

Bitwise Operators

Bitwise operators treat variables as combinations of bits rather than as numbers. They are useful in accessing the individual bits in memory, such as the screen memory for a graphics display. Bitwise operators can operate only on integral data types, not on floating-point numbers. Three bitwise operators act just like the logical operators, but on each bit in an integer. These are AND (&), OR (|), and XOR (^). An additional operator is the one's complement (~), which simply inverts each bit.

AND

The bitwise AND operation compares two bits; if both bits are a 1, the result is a 1, as shown here:

Bit 0	Bit 1	Result
0	0	0
0	1	0
1	0	0
1	1	1

Note that this is different from binary addition, where the comparison of two 1 bits would result in a sum flag set to zero and the carry flag set to 1. Very often, the AND operation is used to select out, or *mask,* certain bit positions.

OR

The bitwise OR operation compares two bits and generates a 1 result if either or both bits are a 1, as shown here:

Bit 0	Bit 1	Result
0	0	0
0	1	1
1	0	1
1	1	1

The OR operation is useful for setting specified bit positions.

XOR

The EXCLUSIVE OR operation compares two bits and returns a result of 1 when, and only when, the two bits are complementary, as shown here:

Bit 0	Bit 1	Result
0	0	0
0	1	1
1	0	1
1	1	0

This logical operation can be very useful when it is necessary to complement specified bit positions, as in the case of computer graphics applications.

Following is an example of using these operators with the hexadecimal and octal representation of constants. The bit values are shown for comparison.

```
0xF1       &   0x35              yields 0x31 (hexadecimal)
0361       &   0065              yields 061 (octal)
11110011   &   00110101          yields 00110001 (bitwise)


0xF1       |   0x35              yields 0xF5 (hexadecimal)
0361       |   0065              yields 0365 (octal)
11110011   |   00110101          yields 11110111 (bitwise)


0xF1       ^   0x35              yields 0xC4 (hexadecimal)
0361       ^   0065              yields 0304 (octal)
11110011   ^   00110101          yields 00000000 11000110 (bitwise)


~0xF1                            yields 0xFF0E (hexadecimal)
~0361                            yields 0177416 (octal)
~11110011                        yields 11111111 00001100 (bitwise)
```

PROGRAMMING
FOUNDATIONS

Left Shift and Right Shift

C incorporates two shift operators, the left shift (<<) and the right shift (>>). The left shift moves the bits to the left and sets the rightmost (least significant) bit to zero. The leftmost (most significant) bit shifted out is thrown away.

In terms of unsigned integers, shifting the number one position to the left and filling the LSB with a zero doubles the number's value. The following C++ code segment demonstrates how this would be coded:

```
unsigned int value1 = 65;
value1 <<= 1;
cout << value1;
```

If you were to examine *value1*'s lower byte, you would see the following bit changes performed:

```
<< 0100 0001 ( 65 decimal)
-------------------------
   1000 0010 (130 decimal)
```

The right shift operator moves bits to the right. The lower-order bits shifted out are thrown away. Halving an unsigned integer is as simple as shifting the bits one position to the right, filling the MSB position with a zero. A C-coded example would look very similar to the preceding example except for the compound operator assignment statement (discussed later in the chapter in the "Compound Assignment Operator" section) and the output statement:

```
unsigned int value1 = 10;
value1 >>= 1;
printf("%d",value1);
```

Examining just the lower byte of the variable *value1* would reveal the following bit changes:

```
>> 0000 1010 (10 decimal)
------------------------
   0000 0101 ( 5 decimal)
```

Increment and Decrement

Adding 1 to or subtracting 1 from a number is so common in programs that C has a special set of operators to do this. They are the *increment* (++) and *decrement* (−−) *operators*. The two characters must be placed next to each other without any white space. They can be applied only to variables, not to constants. Instead of coding as follows:

```
value1 + 1;
```

you can write

```
value1++;
```

or

```
++value1;
```

When these two operators are the sole operators in an expression, you will not have to worry about the difference between the different syntaxes. A **for** loop very often uses this type of increment for the loop control variable:

```
sum = 0;
for(i = 1; i <= 20; i++)
  sum = sum + i;
```

A decrement loop would be coded as:

```
sum = 0;
for(i = 20; i >= 1; i--)
  sum = sum + i;
```

If you use these operators in complex expressions, you have to consider *when* the increment or decrement actually takes place.

The postfix increment, for example *i*++, uses the value of the variable in the expression first and then increments its value. However, the prefix increment, for example, ++*i*, increments the value of the variable first and then uses the value in the expression. Assume the following data declarations:

```
int i=3,j,k=0;
```

See if you can figure out what happens in each of the following statements. For simplicity, for each statement assume the original initialized values of the variables:

```
k = ++i;            // i = 4, k = 4
k = i++;            // i = 4, k = 3
k = --i;            // i = 2, k = 2
k = i--;            // i = 2, k = 3
i = j = k--;        // i = 0, j = 0, k = -1
```

While the subtleties of these two different operations may currently elude you, they are included in the C language because of specific situations that cannot be eloquently handled in any other way. In Chapter 10, you will look at a program that uses array indexes that need to be manipulated by using the initially confusing prefix syntax.

Arithmetic Operators

The C language naturally incorporates the standard set of arithmetic operators for addition (+), subtraction (-), multiplication (*), division (/), and modulus (%). The first four are straightforward and need no amplification. However, an example of the modulus operator will help you understand its usage and syntax:

```
int a=3,b=8,c=0,d;

d = b % a;              // returns 2
d = a % b;              // returns 3

d = b % c;              // returns an error message
```

The modulus operator returns the remainder of integer division. The last assignment statement attempts to divide 8 by 0, resulting in an error message.

Assignment Operator

The assignment operator in C is different than the assignment statement in other languages. Assignment is performed by an assignment operator rather than an assignment statement. Like other C operators, the result of an assignment operator is a value that is assigned. An expression with an assignment operator can be used in a large expression such as this:

```
8 * (value2 = 5);
```

Here, *value2* is first assigned the value 5. This is multiplied by the 8, with *value1* receiving a final value of 40.

Overuse of the assignment operator can rapidly lead to unmanageable expressions. There are two places in which this feature is normally applied. First, it can be used to set several variables to a particular value, as in the following:

```
value1 = value2 = value3 = 0;
```

The second use is most often seen in the condition of a **while** loop, such as the following:

```
while ((c = getchar( )()) != EOF) {
   .
```

```
          .
          .
  }
```

This assigns the value that **getchar()** returned to *c* and then tests the value against EOF. If it is EOF, the loop is not executed. The parentheses are necessary because the assignment operator has a lower precedence than the nonequality operator. Otherwise, the line would be interpreted as:

```
  c = (getchar( )() != EOF)
```

The variable *c* would be assigned a value of 1 (TRUE) each time **getchar()** returned EOF.

Compound Assignment Operators

The C language also incorporates an enhancement to the assignment statement used by other languages. This additional set of assignment operators allows for a more concise way of expressing certain computations. The following code segment shows the standard assignment syntax applicable in many high-level languages:

```
  irow_index = irow_index + irow_increment;
  ddepth = ddepth - d1_fathom;
  fcalculate_tax = fcalculate_tax * 1.07;
  fyards = fyards / ifeet_convert;
```

C's compound assignment statements would look like this:

```
  irow_index += irow_increment;
  ddepth -= d1_fathom;
  fcalculate_tax *= 1.07;
  fyards /= ifeet_convert;
```

If you look closely at these two code segments, you will quickly see the required syntax. Using a C compound assignment operator requires you to remove the redundant variable reference from the right-hand side of the assignment operator and place the operation to be performed immediately before the =. The bottom of Table 6-4 lists all of the compound assignment operators. Other parts of this table are discussed in the section "Understanding Operator Precedence Levels" later in this chapter.

Symbol	Name or Meaning	Associates from
++	Postincrement	Left to right
−−	Postdecrement	
( )( )	Function call	
[ ]	Array element	
->	Pointer to structure member	
.	Structure or union member	
++	Preincrement	Right to left
−−	Predecrement	
!	Logical NOT	
~	Bitwise NOT	
-	Unary minus	
+	Unary plus	
&	Address	
*	Indirection	
Sizeof	Size in bytes	
New	Allocate program memory	
Delete	Deallocate program memory	
(type)	type cast [for example, (**int**) i]	
.*	Pointer to member (objects)	Left to right
->*	Pointer to member (pointers)	
*	Multiply	Left to right
/	Divide	
%	Remainder	
+	Add	Left to right

Table 6-4. *C/C++ Operator Precedence Levels (from Highest to Lowest)*

Symbol	Name or Meaning	Associates from
-	Subtract	
<<	Left shift	Left to right
>>	Right shift	
<	Less than	Left to right
<=	Less than or equal to	
>	Greater than	
>=	Greater than or equal to	
==	Equal	Left to right
!=	Not equal	
&	Bitwise AND	Left to right
^	Bitwise EXCLUSIVE OR	Left to right
|	Bitwise OR	Left to right
&&	Logical AND	Left to right
||	Logical OR	Left to right
? :	Conditional	Right to left
=	Assignment	Right to left
*=, /=, %=, +=, -=, <<=, >>=, &=, ^=, |=	Compound assignment	
,	Comma	Left to right

Table 6-4.   *C/C++ Operator Precedence Levels (from Highest to Lowest) (continued)*

Relational and Logical Operators

All relational operators are used to establish a relationship between the values of the operands. They always produce a value of !0 if the relationship evaluates to TRUE or a

0 value if the relationship evaluates to FALSE. Following is a list of the C and C++ relational operators:

Operator	Meaning
==	Equality (not assignment)
!=	Not equal
>	Greater than
<	Greater than or equal
<=	Less than or equal

The logical operators AND (&&), OR (||), and NOT (!) produce a TRUE (!0) or FALSE (zero) based on the logical relationship of their arguments. The simplest way to remember how the logical AND && works is to say that an ANDed expression will only return a TRUE (!0) when both arguments are TRUE (!0). The logical OR || operation in turn will only return a FALSE (zero) when both arguments are FALSE (zero). The logical NOT ! simply inverts the value. Following is a list of the C and C++ logical operators:

Operator	Meaning
!	NOT
&&	AND
||	OR

Have some fun with the following C++ program as you test the various combinations of relational and logical operators. See if you can predict the results ahead of time. You may be surprised at some of the results obtained for some of the logical comparisons. Remember, there is a very strict comparison that occurs for both data types **float** and **double** when values of these types are compared with zero. A number that is only slightly different from another number is still not equal. Also, a number that is just slightly above or below zero is still TRUE (!0).

```
//
// opers.cpp : Defines the entry point for the console application.
// A C++ program demonstrating some of the subtleties of
// logical and relational operators.
// Copyright (c) William H. Murray and Chris H. Pappas, 2001
//

#include "stdafx.h"
#include <iostream>

using namespace std;
```

```
int main(int argc, char* argv[])
{
  float foperand1, foperand2;

  cout << "\nEnter foperand1 and foperand2: ";
  cin >> foperand1 >> foperand2;
  cout << "\n";
  cout << "  foperand1  > foperand2 is "
       <<   (foperand1  > foperand2) << "\n";
  cout << "  foperand1  < foperand2 is "
       <<   (foperand1  < foperand2) << "\n";
  cout << "  foperand1 >= foperand2 is "
       <<   (foperand1 >= foperand2) << "\n";
  cout << "  foperand1 <= foperand2 is "
       <<   (foperand1 <= foperand2) << "\n";
  cout << "  foperand1 == foperand2 is "
       <<   (foperand1 == foperand2) << "\n";
  cout << "  foperand1 != foperand2 is "
       <<   (foperand1 != foperand2) << "\n";
  cout << "  foperand1 && foperand1 is "
       <<   (foperand1 && foperand2) << "\n";
  cout << "  foperand1 || foperand2 is "
       <<   (foperand1 || foperand2) << "\n";

  return(0);
}
```

Conditional Operator

You can use the conditional operator (?:) in normal coding, but its main use is for creating macros. The operator has the syntax:

```
condition ? true_expression : false-expression
```

If the *condition* is TRUE, the value of the conditional expression is *true-expression*. Otherwise, it is the value of *false-expression*. For example, look at the following statement:

```
if('A' <= c && c <= 'Z')
  printf("%c",'a' + c - 'A');
else
  printf("%c",c);
```

You could rewrite the statement using the conditional operator:

```
printf("%c",('A' <= c && c <= 'Z') ? ('a' + c - 'A') : c );
```

Both statements will make certain that the character printed, "c", is always lowercase (the second is a duplicate statement found in ctype.h).

Comma Operator

The comma operator (,) evaluates two expressions where the syntax allows only one. The value of the comma operator is the value of the right-hand expression. The format for the expression is:

```
left-expression, right-expression
```

One place where the comma operator commonly appears is in a **for** loop, where more than one variable is being iterated. For example:

```
for(min=0,max=length-1; min < max; min++,max--) {
  .
  .
  .
}
```

Understanding Operator Precedence Levels

The order of evaluation of an expression in C is determined by the compiler. This normally does not alter the value of the expression, unless you have written one with side effects. Side effects are those operations that change the value of a variable while yielding a value that is used in the expression, as seen with the increment and decrement operators. The other operators that have side effects are the assignment and compound assignment operators.

Calls to functions that change values of external variables also are subject to side effects. For example:

```
inum1 = 3;
ianswer = (inum1 = 4) + inum1;
```

This could be evaluated in one of two ways: either *inum1* is assigned 4 and *ianswer* is assigned 8 (4+4); or the value of 3 is retrieved from *inum1* and 4 is then assigned to *inum1*, with the result being assigned a 7.

There are, however, four operators for which the order of evaluation is guaranteed to be left to right: logical AND (&&), logical OR (| |), the comma operator (,), and the conditional operator (?:). Because of this default order of evaluation, you can specify a typical test as follows:

```
while((c=getchar( )()) != EOF) && (C!='\n'))
```

The second part of the logical AND (&&) is performed after the character value is assigned to *c*.

Table 6-4 lists all of the C and C++ operators from highest precedence to lowest and describes how each operator is associated (left to right or right to left). All operators between lines have the same precedence level. Throughout the book you will be introduced to the various operators and how their precedence level affects their performance.

Standard C and C++ Libraries

Certain calculations are routinely performed in many programs and are written by almost all programmers. Taking the square root of a number is an example of such a calculation. Mathematical procedures for calculating square roots make use of combinations of the basic arithmetic operations of addition, subtraction, multiplication, and division.

It would be a waste of effort if every programmer had to design and code a routine to calculate the square root and then to incorporate that routine into the program. C and C++ resolve difficulties like this by providing you with *libraries* of functions that perform particular common calculations. With the libraries, you need only a single statement to invoke such a function.

This section discusses functions that are commonly provided with the C and C++ compiler. These library functions are usually not provided in source form but in compiled form. When linking is performed, the code for the library functions is combined with the compiled programmer's code to form the complete program.

Library functions not only perform mathematical operations, they also deal with many other commonly encountered operations. For example, there are library functions that deal with reading and writing disk files, managing memory, input/output, and a variety of other operations. Library functions are not part of standard C or C++, but virtually every system provides certain library functions.

Most library functions are designed to use information contained in particular files that are supplied with the system. These files, therefore, must be included when the library functions are used, and are provided with the Visual C/C++ compiler. They usually have the extension .H and are called *header files*. To see the most up-to-date list of header files supplied with your Microsoft Visual C++ Development Studio, route your File Manager over to the \include subdirectory, found nested within the Development Studio subdirectory.

In general, different header files are required by different library functions. The header files a function needs will be listed in the description for that function. For example, the sqrt() function needs the declarations found in the math.h header file. Your *Microsoft Visual C/C++ Run-Time Library Reference* lists all of the library functions and their associated header files.

The following list briefly summarizes the library categories provided by the Visual C/C++ compiler:

- Classification routines
- Conversion routines
- Directory control routines
- Diagnostic routines
- Graphics routines
- Input/output routines
- Interface routines (DOS, 8086, BIOS)
- Manipulation routines
- Math routines
- Memory allocation routines
- Process control routines
- Standard routines
- Text window display routines
- Time and date routines

Check your reference manual for a detailed explanation of the individual functions provided by each library.

After reading this chapter, you should understand C/C++'s basic data types and operators, so it's time to move on to the topic of logic control. Chapter 7 introduces you to C/C++'s decision, selection, and iteration control statements.

What's Coming?

Phew! What a chapter. Whether you know it or not, Chapter 6 has detailed many C/C++ language fundamentals. These are the building blocks to robust, successful, accurate algorithm design. Get one of these steps wrong, and look out—you could have easily introduced run-time errors, *not* compile-time errors, which are hard to detect and fix. You are also vicariously discovering just how similar C++ is to C. Actually, C is 70 to

80 percent C++. The only area in which they differ is object-oriented syntax. For this reason you'll get a freebie—while learning C++ you'll simultaneously learn C!

Your design starting point begins with selecting the appropriate data type(s) to accurately represent your data. Next, there are the operators that are new to many programmers and previously unseen in older, high-level languages, such as increment, ++ and decrement −−, with their confusing prefix and postfix forms. Add to this the parsing complexity generated by combining operators in the same statement.

Storage classes and access modifiers, when used properly make for a knock-down-drag-out robust program solution. When misused, or omitted altogether, the potential side effects generated remain a continual nuisance.

Chapter 6 is well worth re-reading several times until you have fully absorbed the syntax and principles discussed. In the next chapter you will learn about program logic control statements, some of which are unique in performance and syntax to pre-C/C++ languages.

PROGRAMMING
FOUNDATIONS

Chapter 7

Program Controls

You will need a few more tools in your tool kit in order to begin writing simple C++ programs. This chapter discusses C++'s control statements. Remember, C++ is 70 to 80 percent C so as you learn about C++'s control statements you will simultaneously learn about C's. Many of these control statements are similar to other high-level language controls, such as **if**, **if-else**, and **switch** statements and **for**, **while**, and **do-while** loops. However, there are several new control statements unique to C/C++, such as the **?:** (conditional), **break**, and **continue** statements.

The *new* controls, introduced here, typically have no equivalent in the traditional older, high-level languages such as FORTRAN, COBOL, and Pascal. Therefore, beginner C/C++ programmers leave them out of their problem solutions. That is unfortunate for two reasons. First, it means you are not taking advantage of the coding efficiencies provided by these new controls. Second, it flags you immediately as a beginner.

Conditional Controls

The C/C++ language supports four basic conditional statements: **if**, **if-else**, conditional **?:**, and **switch**. Before a discussion of the individual conditional statements, however, one general rule needs to be highlighted.

Most of the conditional statements can be used to selectively execute either a single line of code or multiple lines of related code (called a *block*). Whenever a conditional statement is associated with only one line of executable code, braces ({}) are *not* required around the executable statement. However, if the conditional statement is associated with multiple executable statements, braces are required to relate the block of executable statements with the conditional test. For this reason, **switch** statements are required to have an opening and a closing brace.

if

The **if** statement can be used to conditionally execute a segment of code. The simplest form of the **if** statement is:

```
if (expression)
  true_action;
```

You will notice that the expression must be enclosed in parentheses. To execute an **if** statement, the expression must evaluate to either TRUE or FALSE. If *expression* is TRUE, *true_action* will be performed and execution will continue on to the next statement following the action. However, if *expression* evaluates to FALSE, *true_action* will *not* be executed, and the statement following *action* will be executed. For example, the following code segment will print the message "Have a great day!" whenever the variable *ioutside_temp* is greater than or equal to 72:

```
if(ioutside_temp >= 72)
  printf("Have a great day!");
```

The syntax for an **if** statement associated with a block of executable statements looks like this:

```
if ( expression ) {
  true_action1;
  true_action2;
  true_action3;
  true_action4;
}
```

The syntax requires that all of the associated statements be enclosed by a pair of braces ({}) and that each statement within the block must also end with a semicolon (;). Here is an example of a compound **if** statement:

```
//
// if.cpp : Defines the entry point for the console application.
// A C++ program demonstrating an if statement
// Copyright (c) Chris H. Pappas and William H. Murray, 2001
//

#include "stdafx.h"
#include <iostream>
#include <iomanip>

using namespace std;

int main(int argc, char* argv[])
{
  int inum_As, inum_Bs, inum_Cs;
  float fGPA;

  cout << "\nEnter number of courses receiving a grade of A: ";
  cin >> inum_As;
  cout << "\nEnter number of courses receiving a grade of B: ";
```

PROGRAMMING FOUNDATIONS

```
cin >> inum_Bs;
cout << "\nEnter number of courses receiving a grade of C: ";
cin >> inum_Cs;
fGPA = (inum_As * 4 + inum_Bs * 3 + inum_Cs * 2)/
       (float) (inum_As + inum_Bs + inum_Cs);
cout << "\nYour overall GPA is: " << fGPA << endl;
if(fGPA >= 3.5) {
  cout << "\nC O N G R A T U L A T I O N S !\n";
  cout << "You are on the President's list.";
}
return(0);
}
```

If *fGPA* is greater than or equal to 3.5, in this example, a congratulatory message is added to the calculated *fGPA*. Regardless of whether the **if** block was entered, the calculated *fGPA* is printed.

if-else

The **if-else** statement allows a program to take two separate actions based on the validity of a particular expression. The simplest syntax for an **if-else** statement looks like this:

```
if (expression)
  true_action;

else
  false_action;
```

In this case, if *expression* evaluates to TRUE, *true_action* will be taken; otherwise, when *expression* evaluates to FALSE, *false_action* will be executed. Here is a coded example:

```
if(ckeypressed == UP)
  iy_pixel_coord++;

else
  iy_pixel_coord--;
```

This example takes care of either incrementing or decrementing the current horizontal coordinate location based on the current value stored in the character variable *ckeypressed*.

Of course, either *true_action*, *false_action*, or both could be compound statements, or blocks, requiring braces. The syntax for these three combinations is straightforward:

```
if (expression) {
  true_action1;
  true_action2;
  true_action3;
}
else
  false_action;


if (expression)
  true_action;
else {
  false_action1;
  false_action2;
  false_action3;
}


if (expression) {
  true_action1;
  true_action2;
  true_action3;
}
else {
  false_action1;
  false_action2;
  false_action3;
}
```

Remember, whenever a block action is being taken, you do not follow the closing brace (}) with a semicolon.

The C++ program that follows uses an **if-else** statement with the **if** part being a compound block:

```
//
// cmpif.cpp : Defines the entry point for the console application.
// A C program demonstrating the use of a compound
// if-else statement.
```

```
// Copyright (c) Chris H. Pappas and William H. Murray, 2001
//

#include "stdafx.h"
#include <iostream>

using namespace std;

int main(int argc, char* argv[])
{
  char c;
  int ihow_many, imore;

  imore=1;

  while(imore == 1) {
    cout << "Please enter the product name: ";
    if( (c = cin.get()) != EOF) {
      while(c != '\n') {
        cout << c;
        c = cin.get();
      }
      cout << "s purchased? ";
      cin >> ihow_many;

      for(int i = 1;i <= ihow_many; i++)
        cout << "*";
      cout << endl;
    }
    else
      imore=0;
  }
  return(0);
}
```

This program prompts the user for a product name, and if the user does not enter a
^Z (EOF), the program inputs the product name character by character, echo printing
the information to the next line. The "s purchased" string is appended to the product,
requesting the number of items sold. Finally, a **for** loop prints out the appropriate number
of asterisks (*). Had the user entered a ^Z, the **if** portion of the **if-else** statement would
have been ignored and program execution would have picked up with the **else** setting
the *imore* flag to zero, thereby terminating the program.

Nested if-elses

When **if** statements are nested, care must be taken to ensure that you know which **else** action will be matched up with which **if**. Look at an example and see if you can figure out what will happen:

```
if(iout_side_temp < 50)
if(iout_side_temp < 30) printf("Wear the down jacket!");
else printf("Parka will do.");
```

The listing was purposely misaligned so as not to give you any visual clues as to which statement went with which **if**. The question becomes, what happens if *iout_side_temp* is 55? Does the "Parka will do." message get printed? The answer is no. In this example, the **else** action is associated with the second **if** expression. This is because C matches each **else** with the first unmatched **if**.

To make debugging as simple as possible under such circumstances, the C compiler has been written to associate each **else** with the closest **if** that does not already have an **else** associated with it.

Of course, proper indentation will always help clarify the situation:

```
if(iout_side_temp < 50)
  if(iout_side_temp < 30) printf("Wear the down jacket!");
  else printf("Parka will do.");
```

The same logic can also be represented by the alternate listing that follows:

```
if(iout_side_temp < 50)
  if(iout_side_temp < 30)
    printf("Wear the down jacket!");
  else
    printf("Parka will do.");
```

Each particular application you write will benefit most by one of the two styles, as long as you are consistent throughout the source code.

See if you can figure out this next example:

```
if(test1_expression)
  if(test2_expression)
    test2_true_action;
```

```
else
  test1_false_action;
```

You may be thinking this is just another example of what has already been discussed. That's true, but what if you really did want *test1_false_action* to be associated with *test1* and not *test2*? The examples so far have all associated the **else** action with the second, or closest, **if**. (By the way, many a programmer has spent needless time debugging programs of this nature. They're indented to work the way you are logically thinking, as was the preceding example, but unfortunately, the compiler doesn't care about your "pretty printing.")

Correcting this situation requires the use of braces:

```
if(test1_expression) {
  if(test2_expression)
    test2_true_action;
}
else
  test1_false_action;
```

The problem is solved by making *test2_expression* and its associated *test2_true_action* a block associated with a TRUE evaluation of *test1_expression*. This makes it clear that *test1_false_action* will be associated with the **else** clause of *test1_expression*.

if-else-if

The **if-else-if** statement combination is often used to perform multiple successive comparisons. The general form of this statement looks like this:

```
if(expression1)
  test1_true_action;

else if(expression2)
  test2_true_action;

else if(expression3)
  test3_true_action;
```

Each action, of course, could be a compound block requiring its own set of braces (with the closing brace *not* followed by a semicolon). This type of logical control flow evaluates each expression until it finds one that is TRUE. When this occurs, all remaining test conditions are bypassed. In the preceding example, if none of the expressions evaluated to TRUE, no action would be taken.

Consider the next example and see if you can guess the result:

```
if(expression1)
   test1_true_action;

else if(expression2)
   test2_true_action;

else if(expression3)
   test3_true_action;

else
   default_action;
```

This differs from the previous example. This **if-else-if** statement combination will always perform some action. If none of the **if** expressions evaluate to TRUE, the **else** *default_action* will be executed. For example, the following program checks the value assigned to *econvert_to* to decide which type of conversion to perform. If the requested *econvert_to* is not one of the ones provided, the code segment prints an appropriate message:

```
if(econvert_to == YARDS)
   fconverted_value = length / 3;

else if(econvert_to == INCHES)
   fconverted_value = length * 12;

else if(econvert_to == CENTIMETERS)
   fconverted_value = length * 12 * 2.54;

else if(econvert_to == METERS)
   fconverted_value = (length * 12 * 2.54)/100;

else
   printf("No conversion required");
```

The ? Conditional Operator

The conditional statement **?** provides a quick way to write a test condition. Associated actions are performed depending on whether *test_expression* evaluates to TRUE or

FALSE. The operator can be used to replace an equivalent **if-else** statement. The syntax for a conditional statement is:

```
test_expression ? true_action : false_action;
```

The **?** operator is also sometimes referred to as the ternary operator because it requires three operands. Examine this statement:

```
if(fvalue >= 0.0)
  fvalue = fvalue;
else
  fvalue = -fvalue;
```

You can rewrite the statement using the conditional operator:

```
fvalue=(fvalue >= 0.0) ? fvalue : -fvalue;
```

In this situation, both statements yield the absolute value of *fvalue*. The precedence of the conditional operator is less than that of any of the other operators used in the expression; therefore, no parentheses are required in the example. Nevertheless, parentheses are frequently used to enhance readability.

```
The following C++ program uses the ?: operator to cleverly format the
program's output://
// condit.cpp : Defines the entry point for the console application.
// A C++ program using the CONDITIONAL OPERATOR
// Copyright (c) Chris H. Pappas and William H. Murray, 2001
//

#include "stdafx.h"
#include <cmath>                    // for abs macro def.
#include <iostream>

using namespace std;

int main(int argc, char* argv[])
{
  float fbalance, fpayment;
```

```
cout << "Enter your loan balance: ";
cin  >> fbalance;

cout << "\nEnter your loan payment amount: ";
cin  >> fpayment;

cout << "\n\nYou have ";
cout << ((fpayment > fbalance) ? "overpaid by $" : "paid $");
cout << ((fpayment > fbalance) ? fabs(fbalance - fpayment) :
     fpayment);
cout << " on your loan of $" << fbalance << ".";

return(0);
}
```

The program uses the first conditional statement inside a **cout** statement to decide which string—"overpaid by $" or "paid $"—is to be printed. The following conditional statement calculates and prints the appropriate dollar value.

switch-case

It is often the case that you will want to test a variable or an expression against several values. You could use nested **if-else-if** statements to do this, or you could use a **switch** statement. Be very careful, though, the C **switch** statement has a few peculiarities. The syntax for a **switch** statement is:

```
switch (integral_expression) {
 case constant1:
   statements1;
   break;
 case constant2:
   statements2;
   break;
   .
   .
   .
 case constantn:
   statementsn;
   break;
 default: statements;
}
```

The redundant statement you need to pay particular attention to is the **break** statement. In the preceding syntax, if the **break** statement had been removed from *constant1*'s section of code, a match similar to the one used in the preceding paragraph would have left *statements2* as the next statement to be executed. It is the **break** statement that causes the remaining portion of the **switch** statements to be skipped. Let's look at a few examples. Examine the following **if-else-if** code segment:

```
if(emove == SMALL_CHANGE_UP)
  fycoord =    5;

else if(emove == SMALL_CHANGE_DOWN)
  fycoord =   -5;

else if(emove == LARGE_CHANGE_UP)
  fycoord =   10;

else
  fycoord = -10;
```

This code can be rewritten using a **switch** statement:

```
switch(emove) {
  case  SMALL_CHANGE_UP:
    fycoord =    5;
    break;
  case  SMALL_CHANGE_DOWN:
    fycoord =   -5;
    break;
  case  LARGE_CHANGE_UP:
    fycoord =   10;
    break;
  default:
    fycoord = -10;
}
```

The value of *emove*, in this example, is consecutively compared to each **case** value looking for a match. When one is found, *fycoord* is assigned the appropriate value. Then the **break** statement is executed, skipping over the remainder of the **switch** statements. However, if no match is found, the **default** assignment is performed (*fycoord = -10*). Since this is the last option in the **switch** statement, there is no need to include a **break**. A **switch** default is optional.

Proper placement of the **break** statement within a **switch** statement can be very useful. Look at the following example:

```
//
// switch.cpp : Defines the entry point for the console application.
// A C program demonstrating the
// drop-through capabilities of the switch statement.
// Copyright (c) Chris H. Pappas and William H. Murray, 1998
//

#include "stdafx.h"

int main(int argc, char* argv[])
{
  char c='a';
  int ivowelct=0, iconstantct=0;

  switch(c) {
    case 'a':
    case 'A':
    case 'e':
    case 'E':
    case 'i':
    case 'I':
    case 'o':
    case 'O':
    case 'u':
    case 'U': ivowelct++;
              break;
    default : iconstantct++;
  }
  return(0);
}
```

This program actually illustrates two characteristics of the **switch** statement: the enumeration of several test values that all execute the same code section and the drop-through characteristic.

Other high-level languages have their own form of selection (the **case** statement in Pascal and the **select** statement in PL/I), which allows for several test values, all producing the same result, to be included on the same selection line. C and C++, however, require a separate **case** for each. But notice in this example how the same effect has been created by not inserting a **break** statement until all possible vowels have been checked. Should *c* contain a constant, all of the vowel case tests will be checked and skipped until the **default** statement is reached.

The next example shows a C++ program that uses a **switch** statement to invoke the appropriate function:

```
//
// fnswth.cpp : Defines the entry point for the console application.
// A C program demonstrating the switch statement
// Copyright (c) Chris H. Pappas and William H. Murray, 2001
//

#include "stdafx.h"
#include <iostream>

using namespace std;

#define QUIT 0
#define BLANK ' '

double fadd(float fx,float fy);
double fsub(float fx,float fy);
double fmul(float fx,float fy);
double fdiv(float fx,float fy);

int main(int argc, char* argv[])
{
  float fx,fy;
  char coperator = BLANK;

  while (coperator != QUIT) {
    cout << "\nPlease enter an expression (a (operator) b): ";
    cin >> fx >> coperator >> fy;

    switch (coperator) {
      case '+': cout << "answer = " << fadd(fx,fy) << endl;
                break;
      case '-': cout << "answer = " << fsub(fx,fy) << endl;
                break;
      case '*': cout << "answer = " << fmul(fx,fy) << endl;
                break;
      case '/': cout << "answer = " << fdiv(fx,fy) << endl;
```

```
            break;
      case 'x': coperator = QUIT;
                break;
      default : cout << "\nOperator not implemented";
    }
  }
  return(0);
}

double fadd(float fx,float fy)
  {return(fx + fy);}

double fsub(float fx,float fy)
  {return(fx - fy);}

double fmul(float fx,float fy)
  {return(fx * fy);}

double fdiv(float fx,float fy)
  {return(fx / fy);}
```

While the use of functions in this example is a bit advanced (functions are discussed in detail in Chapter 8), the use of the **switch** statement is very effective. After the user has entered an expression such as 10 + 10 or 23 * 15, the *coperator* is compared in the body of the **switch** statement to determine which function to invoke. Of particular interest is the last set of statements, where the *coperator* equals *x*, and the **default** statement outputs a warning message.

When the user enters an expression with an *x* operator, the *coperator* variable is assigned a QUIT value, and the **break** statement is executed, skipping over the **default** **cout** statement. However, if the user enters an unrecognized operator, for example %, only the **default** statement is executed, printing the message that the *coperator* has not been implemented.

```
The following C++ program illustrates the similarity in syntax
between a C switch statement and its C++ counterpart://
// calndr.cpp : Defines the entry point for the console application.
//  A C++ program using a switch statement
//  to print a yearly calendar.
//  Copyright (c) Chris H. Pappas and William H. Murray, 2001
//
```

```cpp
#include "stdafx.h"
#include <iostream>

using namespace std;

int main(int argc, char* argv[])
{
  int jan_1_start_day,num_days_per_month,
      month,date,leap_year_flag;

  cout << "Please enter January 1's starting day;\n";
  cout << "\nA 0 indicates January 1 is on a Monday,";
  cout << "\nA 1 indicates January 1 is on a Tuesday, etc: ";
  cin >> jan_1_start_day;
  cout << "\nEnter the year you want the calendar generated: ";
  cin >> leap_year_flag;
  cout << "\n\n The calendar for the year " << leap_year_flag;

  leap_year_flag=leap_year_flag % 4;
  cout.width(20);

  for (month = 1;month <= 12;month++) {
    switch(month) {
     case 1:
       cout << "\n\n\n" << " January" << "\n";
       num_days_per_month = 31;
       break;
     case 2:
       cout << "\n\n\n" << " February" << "\n";
       num_days_per_month = leap_year_flag ? 28 : 29;
       break;
     case 3:
       cout << "\n\n\n" << "  March " << "\n";
       num_days_per_month = 31;
       break;
     case 4:
       cout << "\n\n\n" << "  April " << "\n";
       num_days_per_month = 30;
       break;
     case 5:
       cout << "\n\n\n" << "   May  " << "\n";
       num_days_per_month = 31;
```

```
        break;
    case 6:
      cout << "\n\n\n" << "  June  " << "\n";
      num_days_per_month = 30;
      break;
    case 7:
      cout << "\n\n\n" << "  July  " << "\n";
      num_days_per_month = 31;
      break;
    case 8:
      cout << "\n\n\n" << " August " << "\n";
      num_days_per_month = 31;
      break;
    case 9:
      cout << "\n\n\n" << "September" << "\n";
      num_days_per_month = 30;
      break;
    case 10:
      cout << "\n\n\n" << " October " << "\n";
      num_days_per_month = 31;
      break;
    case 11:
      cout << "\n\n\n" << "November " << "\n";
      num_days_per_month = 30;
      break;
    case 12:
      cout << "\n\n\n" << "December " << "\n";
      num_days_per_month = 31;
      break;
  }

  cout.width(0);
  cout << "\nSun  Mon  Tue  Wed  Thu  Fri  Sat\n";
  cout << "---  ---  ---  ---  ---  ---  ---\n";

  for ( date = 1; date <= 1 + jan_1_start_day * 5; date++ )
    cout <<  "  ";

  for ( date = 1; date <= num_days_per_month; date++ ) {
    cout.width(2);
    cout << date;
    if ( ( date + jan_1_start_day ) % 7 > 0 )
```

```
        cout <<  "    ";
      else
        cout <<  "\n ";
    }
    jan_1_start_day=(jan_1_start_day + num_days_per_month) % 7;
  }
  return(0);
}
```

This application starts by asking the user to enter an integer code representing the day of the week on which January 1st occurs (zero for Monday, 1 for Tuesday, and so on). The second prompt asks for the year for the calendar. The program can now print the calendar heading, and use the year entered to generate a *leap_year_flag*. Using the modulus operator (%) with a value of 4 generates a remainder of zero whenever it is leap year and a nonzero value whenever it is not leap year.

Next, a 12-iteration loop is entered, printing the current month's name and assigning *num_days_per_month* the correct number of days for that particular month. All of this is accomplished by using a **switch** statement to test the current *month* integer value.

Outside the **switch** statement, after the month's name has been printed, day-of-the-week headings are printed, and an appropriate number of blank columns is skipped, depending on when the first day of the month is.

The last **for** loop actually generates and prints the dates for each month. The last statement in the program prepares the *day_code* for the next month to be printed.

Combining if-else-if and switch

The next example application uses an enumerated type (**enum**) to perform the requested length conversions:

```
//
// ifelsw.cpp : Defines the entry point for the console application.
// A C++ program demonstrating the if-else-if statement
// used in a meaningful way with several switch statements.
// Copyright (c) Chris H. Pappas and William H. Murray, 2001
//

#include "stdafx.h"
#include <iostream>

using namespace std;
```

```
typedef enum conversion_type {YARDS, INCHES, CENTIMETERS, METERS}
C_TYPE;

int main(int argc, char* argv[])
{
  int iuser_response;
  C_TYPE C_Tconversion;
  int ilength;
  float fmeasurement;

  cout << "\nPlease enter the foot measurement to be converted : ";
  cin >> ilength;

  //The following is one long line . . . remove the \s
  cout << "\nPlease enter :              \
          \n\t\t 0 for YARDS          \
          \n\t\t 1 for INCHES         \
          \n\t\t 2 for CENTIMETERS    \
          \n\t\t 3 for METERS         \
          \n\n\t\tYour response >> ";

  cin >> iuser_response;

  switch(iuser_response) {
    case 0  :  C_Tconversion = YARDS;
               break;
    case 1  :  C_Tconversion = INCHES;
               break;
    case 2  :  C_Tconversion = CENTIMETERS;
               break;
    default :  C_Tconversion = METERS;
  }


  if(C_Tconversion == YARDS)
    fmeasurement = ilength / 3;

  else if(C_Tconversion == INCHES)
    fmeasurement = ilength * 12;

  else if(C_Tconversion == CENTIMETERS)
    fmeasurement = ilength * 12 * 2.54;
```

```
else if(C_Tconversion == METERS)
  fmeasurement = (ilength * 12 * 2.54)/100;

else
  cout << "No conversion required";


switch(C_Tconversion) {
  case YARDS        : cout << "\n\t\t" << fmeasurement
                             << " yards";
                      break;
  case INCHES       : cout << "\n\t\t" << fmeasurement
                             << " inches";
                      break;
  case CENTIMETERS  : cout << "\n\t\t" << fmeasurement
                             << " centimeters";
                      break;
  default           : cout << "\n\t\t" << fmeasurement
                             << " meters";
}

return(0);
}
```

This application uses an enumerated type to perform the specified length conversion. In standard C, enumerated types exist only within the code itself (for reasons of readability) and cannot be input or output directly. The program uses the first **switch** statement to convert the input code to its appropriate *C_Tconversion* type. The nested **if-else-if** statements perform the proper conversion. The last **switch** statement prints the converted value with its appropriate "literal" type. Of course, the nested **if-else-if** statements could have been implemented by using a **switch** statement. (A further discussion of enumerated types can be found in Chapter 12.)

Loop Controls

The C and C++ languages include the standard set of repetition control statements: **for** loops, **while** loops, and **do-while** loops (called repeat-until loops in several other high-level languages). You may be surprised, however, by the ways a program can leave a repetition loop. C and C++ provide four methods for altering the repetitions in a loop. All repetition loops can naturally terminate based on the expressed test condition. In C and C++, however, a repetition loop can also terminate because of an anticipated error condition by using either a **break** or **exit** statement. Repetition loops can also have their logic control flow altered by a **break** statement or a **continue** statement.

The basic difference between a **for** loop and a **while** or **do-while** loop has to do with the "known" number of repetitions. Typically, **for** loops are used whenever there is a definite predefined required number of repetitions, and **while** and **do-while** loops are reserved for an "unknown" number of repetitions.

for

The syntax for a **for** loop is:

```
for(initialization_exp; test_exp; increment_exp)
  statement;
```

When the **for** loop statement is encountered, the *initialization_exp* is executed first. This is done at the start of the loop, and it is never executed again. Usually this statement involves the initialization of the loop control variable. Following this, *test_exp*, which is called the *loop terminating condition*, is tested. Whenever *test_exp* evaluates to TRUE, the statement or statements within the loop are executed. If the loop was entered, then after all of the statements within the loop are executed, *increment_exp* is executed. However, if *test_exp* evaluates to FALSE, the statement or statements within the loop are ignored, along with *increment_exp*, and execution continues with the statement following the end of the loop. The indentation scheme applied to **for** loops with several statements to be repeated looks like this:

```
for(initialization_exp; test_exp; increment_exp) {
  statement_a;
  statement_b;
  statement_c;
  statement_n;
}
```

In the case where several statements need to be executed, a pair of braces is required to tie their execution to the loop control structure. Let's examine a few examples of **for** loops.

The following example sums up the first five integers. It assumes that *isum* and *ivalue* have been predefined as integers:

```
isum = 0;
for(ivalue=1; ivalue <= 5; ivalue++)
  isum += ivalue;
```

After *isum* has been initialized to zero, the **for** loop is encountered. First, *ivalue* is initialized to 1 (this is done only once); second, *ivalue*'s value is checked against the loop terminating condition, <= 5. Since this is TRUE, a 1 is added to *isum*. Once the statement is executed, the loop control variable (*ivalue*) is incremented by 1. This process continues four more times until *ivalue* is incremented to 6 and the loop terminates.

In C++, the same code segment could be written as follows. See if you can detect the subtle difference:

```
for(int ivalue=1; ivalue <= 5; ivalue++)
   isum += ivalue;
```

C++ allows the loop control variable to be declared and initialized within the **for** loop. This brings up a very sensitive issue among structured programmers, which is the proper placement of variable declarations. In C++, you can declare variables right before the statement that actually uses them. In the preceding example, since *ivalue* is used only to generate an *isum*, with *isum* having a larger scope than *ivalue*, the local declaration for *ivalue* is harmless. However, look at the following code segment:

```
int isum = 0;
for(int ivalue=1; ivalue <= 5; ivalue++)
   isum += ivalue;
```

This would obscure the visual "desk check" of the variable *isum* because it was not declared below the function head. For the sake of structured design and debugging, it is best to localize all variable declarations. It is the rare code segment that can justify the usefulness of moving a variable declaration to a nonstandard place, in sacrifice of easily read, easily checked, and easily modified code.

The value used to increment **for** loop control variables does not always have to be 1 or ++. The following example sums all the odd numbers up to 9:

```
iodd_sum = 0;
for(iodd_value = 1; iodd_value <= 9; iodd_value += 2);
   iodd_sum += iodd_value;
```

In this example, the loop control variable *iodd_value* is initialized to 1 and is incremented by 2.

Another unique feature is that **for** loops don't always have to go from a smaller value to a larger one. The following example uses a **for** loop to read into an array of characters and then print the character string backward:

```
//
// forlp.cpp : Defines the entry point for the console application.
// A C++ program that uses a for loop to input a character array
// Copyright (c) Chris H. Pappas and William H. Murray, 2001
//


#include "stdafx.h"
#include <iostream>

using namespace std;

#define CARRAY_SIZE 10

int main(int argc, char* argv[])
{
  int ioffset;
  char carray[CARRAY_SIZE];

  for(ioffset = 0; ioffset < CARRAY_SIZE; ioffset++)
    carray[ioffset] = cin.get();
  for(ioffset = CARRAY_SIZE - 1; ioffset >= 0; ioffset++)
    cout.put(carray[ioffset]);

  return(0);
}
```

In this application, the first **for** loop initialized *ioffset* to zero (necessary since all array indexes are offsets from the starting address of the first array element), and while there is room in *carray*, reads characters in one at a time. The second **for** loop initializes the loop control variable *ioffset* to the offset of the last element in the array and, while *ioffset* contains a valid offset, prints the characters in reverse order. This process could be used to parse an infix expression that was being converted to prefix notation.

When combining or nesting **for** loops, as in the next example, take care to include the appropriate braces to make certain the statements execute properly:

```
//
// nslop1.cpp : Defines the entry point for the console application.
// A C++ program demonstrating
// the need for caution when nesting for loops.
// Copyright (c) Chris H. Pappas and William H. Murray, 2001
```

```
//

#include "stdafx.h"
#include <iostream>
#include <iomanip>

using namespace std;

int main(int argc, char* argv[])
{
  int iouter_val, iinner_val;

  for(iouter_val = 1; iouter_val <= 4; iouter_val++) {
    cout << "\n" << setw(3) << iouter_val << " -- ";
    for(iinner_val = 1; iinner_val <= 5; iinner_val++ )
      cout << setw(3) << iouter_val * iinner_val;
  }

  return(0);
}
```

The output produced by this program looks like this:

```
1 --   1   2   3   4   5
2 --   2   4   6   8  10
3 --   3   6   9  12  15
4 --   4   8  12  16  20
```

However, suppose the outer **for** loop had been written without the braces, like this:

```
//
// nslop2.cpp : Defines the entry point for the console application.
// A C++ program demonstrating what happens when you nest
// for loops without the logically required braces {}.
// Copyright (c) Chris H. Pappas and William H. Murray, 2001
//

#include "stdafx.h"
#include <iostream>
#include <iomanip>

using namespace std;
```

```
int main(int argc, char* argv[])
{
  int iouter_val, iinner_val;

 for(iouter_val = 1; iouter_val <= 4; iouter_val++)
   cout << "\n" << setw(3) << " -- " << iouter_val;
   for(iinner_val = 1; iinner_val <= 5; iinner_val++ )
     cout << setw(3) << iouter_val * iinner_val;

  return(0);
}
```

The output would have looked quite different:

```
1 --
2 --
3 --
4 --   5 10 15 20 25
```

Without the braces surrounding the first **for** loop, only the first **cout** statement is associated with the loop. Once the **cout** statement is executed four times, the second **for** loop is entered. The inner loop uses the last value stored in *iouter_val*, or 5, to generate the values printed by its **cout** statement.

The need to include or not include braces can be a tricky matter at best that needs to be approached with some thought to readability. Look at the next two examples and see if you can figure out if they would produce the same output.

Here is the first application:

```
//
// lpdmo1.cpp : Defines the entry point for the console application.
// Another C++ program demonstrating the need
// for caution when nesting for loops.
// Copyright (c) Chris H. Pappas and William H. Murray, 2001
//

#include "stdafx.h"
#include <iostream>
#include <iomanip>

using namespace std;
```

```
int main(int argc, char* argv[])
{
  int iouter_val, iinner_val;

  for(iouter_val = 1; iouter_val <= 4; iouter_val++) {
    for(iinner_val = 1; iinner_val <= 5; iinner_val++ )
      cout << setw(3) << iouter_val * iinner_val;
  }

  return(0);
}
```

Compare the preceding program with the following example:

```
//
// lpdmo2.cpp : Defines the entry point for the console application.
// A comparison C++ program demonstrating the need
// for caution when nesting for loops.
// Copyright (c) Chris H. Pappas and William H. Murray, 2001
//

#include "stdafx.h"
#include <iostream>
#include <iomanip>

using namespace std;

int main(int argc, char* argv[])
{
  int iouter_val, iinner_val;

  for(iouter_val = 1; iouter_val <= 4; iouter_val++)
    for(iinner_val = 1; iinner_val <= 5; iinner_val++ )
      cout << setw(3) << iouter_val * iinner_val;

  return(0);
}
```

Both programs produce the identical output:

```
1 2 3 4 5 2 4 6 8 10 3 6 9 12 15 4 8 12 16 20
```

In these last two examples, the only statement associated with the outer **for** loop is the inner **for** loop. The inner **for** loop is considered a single statement. This would still be the case even if the inner **for** loop had multiple statements to execute. Since braces are needed only around code blocks or multiple statements, the outer **for** loop does not need braces to execute the program properly.

while

The C and C++ **while** loop is a *pretest loop* just like the **for** loop. This means that the program evaluates *test_exp* before entering the statement or statements within the body of the loop. Because of this, pretest loops may be executed from zero to many times. The syntax for a C **while** loop is:

```
while(test_exp)
  statement;
```

For **while** loops with several statements, braces are needed:

```
while(test_exp) {
  statement1;
  statement2;
  statement3;
  statementn;
}
```

Typically, **while** loop control structures are used whenever an indefinite number of repetitions is expected. The following C++ program uses a **while** loop to control the number of times *ivalue* is shifted to the right. The program prints the binary representation of a signed integer.

```
//
// while1.cpp : Defines the entry point for the console application.
// A C++ program using a pretest while loop with flag
// Copyright (c) Chris H. Pappas and William H. Murray, 2001
//

#include "stdafx.h"
#include <iostream>

using namespace std;
```

```
#define WORD 16
#define ONE_BYTE 8

int main(int argc, char* argv[])
{
  int ivalue = 256, ibit_position=1;
  unsigned int umask = 1;

  cout << "The following value " << ivalue
       << " in binary form looks like: ";

  while(ibit_position <= WORD) {
    if((ivalue >> (WORD - ibit_position)) & umask) /*shift each*/
      cout << "1";                                 /*bit to 0th*/
    else                                           /*position &*/
      cout << "0";                                 /*compare to*/
    if(ibit_position == ONE_BYTE)                  /*umask     */
      cout << " ";
    ibit_position++;
  }

  return(0);
}
```

This application begins by defining two constants, *WORD* and *ONE_BYTE*, that can be easily modified for different architectures. *WORD* will be used as a flag to determine when the **while** loop will terminate. Within the **while** loop, *ivalue* is shifted, compared to *umask*, and printed from most significant bit to least. This allows the algorithm to use a simple **cout** statement to output the results.

In the next example the application prompts the user for an input filename and an output filename. The program then uses a **while** loop to read in and echo print the input file of unknown size.

```
//
// while2.cpp : Defines the entry point for the console application.
// A C++ program using a while loop to echo print a file
// The program demonstrates additional file I/O techniques
// Copyright (c) Chris H. Pappas and William H. Murray, 2001
//

#include "stdafx.h"
#include <fstream>
```

```cpp
#include <iostream>

using namespace std;

#define sz_TERMINATOR 1        /* sz, null-string designator */
#define MAX_CHARS 30

int main(int argc, char* argv[])
{
  int c;

  char sziDOS_file_name[MAX_CHARS + sz_TERMINATOR],
       szoDOS_file_name[MAX_CHARS + sz_TERMINATOR];

  cout << "Enter the input file's name: ";
  cin.getline(sziDOS_file_name,MAX_CHARS + sz_TERMINATOR);

  ifstream ifile(sziDOS_file_name);

  if(!ifile) {
    cout << "\nFile: " << sziDOS_file_name << " cannot be opened";
    exit(1);
  }

  cout << "Enter the output file's name: ";
  cin.getline(szoDOS_file_name,MAX_CHARS + sz_TERMINATOR);

  ofstream ofile(szoDOS_file_name);

  if(!ofile) {
    cout << "\nFile: " << sziDOS_file_name << " cannot be opened";
    exit(1);
  }

  c = ifile.get();
  while(!ifile.eof()) {
    ofile.put(c);
    c = ifile.get();
  }

  return(0);
}
```

Here, the **while** loop contains two executable statements, so the brace pair is required. The program also illustrates the use of several file I/O statements like **get()** and **put()**, along with **eof()** (discussed in Chapter 11).

do-while

The **do-while** loop differs from the **for** and **while** loops. The **do-while** loop is a *post-test loop*. In other words, the loop is always entered at least once, with the loop condition being tested at the end of the first iteration. In contrast, **for** loops and **while** loops may execute from zero to many times, depending on the loop control variable. Since **do-while** loops always execute at least one time, they are best used whenever there is no doubt you want the particular loop entered. For example, if your program needs to present a menu to the user, even if all the user wants to do is immediately quit the program, he or she needs to see the menu to know which key terminates the application.

The syntax for a **do-while** loop is:

```
do
 action;
while(test_condition);
```

Braces are required for **do-while** statements that have compound actions:

```
do {
 action1;
 action2;
 action3;
 actionn;
} while(test_condition);
```

The following application uses a **do-while** loop to calculate some statistics for a user-entered sentence:

```
//
// dowhile.cpp : Defines the entry point for the console application.
// A C++ program demonstrating the usefulness of a
// do-while loop to process user-defined sentence.
// Copyright (c) Chris H. Pappas and William H. Murray, 2001
//
```

```
#include "stdafx.h"
#include <iostream>

using namespace std;

#define NULL_TERM 1
#define LENGTH 80

int main(int argc, char* argv[])
{
  char cSentence[LENGTH + NULL_TERM];
  int iNumChars = 0, iNumWords = 1;

  do {
    cout << "Please enter your sentence : ";
    cin.getline(cSentence,LENGTH + NULL_TERM);
  } while (cSentence[0] == '\0');

  while (cSentence[iNumChars] != '\0') {
    if (cSentence[iNumChars] == ' ')
      iNumWords++;
    iNumChars++;
  }

  cout << "You entered " << iNumChars << " characters\n";
  cout << "You entered " << iNumWords << " words";

  return (0);
}
```

The **do-while** loop in this program repeats the prompt and input statements for the user-requested sentence until the user enters at least one character. Simply pressing the ENTER key causes the getline() function to store the null character in the first array element position, repeating the loop. Once the user enters the sentence, the program jumps out of the **do-while** loop printing the calculated statistics.

break

The **break** statement can be used to exit a loop before the test condition becomes FALSE. The **break** statement is similar in many ways to a **goto** statement, only the point jumped to is not known directly. When breaking out of a loop, program execution continues with the next statement following the loop itself. Look at this simple application:

```
//
// break.cpp : Defines the entry point for the console application.
// A C program demonstrating the use of the break statement.
// Copyright (c) Chris H. Pappas and William H. Murray, 2001
//

#include "stdafx.h"

int main(int argc, char *argv[])
{
  int itimes = 1, isum = 0;

  while(itimes < 10){
    isum += isum + itimes;
    if(isum > 20)
      break;
    itimes++;
  }

  return(0);
}
```

Use the integrated debugger to trace through the program. Trace the variables *isum* and *itimes*. Pay particular attention to which statements are executed after *isum* reaches the value 21.

What you should have noticed is that when *isum* reached the value 21, the **break** statement was executed. This caused the increment of *itimes* to be jumped over, *itimes++*, with program execution continuing on the line of code below the loop. In this example, the next statement executed was the return.

continue

There is a subtle difference between the **break** statement and the **continue** statement. As you have already seen from the last example program, **break** causes the loop to terminate execution altogether. In contrast, the **continue** statement causes all of the statements following the **continue** statement to be ignored but does *not* circumvent incrementing the loop control variable or the loop control test condition. In other words, if the loop control variable still satisfies the loop test condition, the loop will continue to iterate.

The following program demonstrates this concept, using a number guessing game:

```cpp
//
// continu.cpp : Defines the entry point for the console application.
// A C++ program demonstrating the use of the continue
// statement.
// Copyright (c) Chris H. Pappas and William H. Murray, 2001
//

#include "stdafx.h"
#include <iostream>

using namespace std;

#define TRUE 1
#define FALSE 0

int main(int argc, char* argv[])
{
  int ilucky_number=77,
      iinput_val,
      inumber_of_tries=0,
      iam_lucky=FALSE;

  while(!iam_lucky){
    cout << "Please enter your lucky guess: ";
    cin >> iinput_val;
    inumber_of_tries++;
    if(iinput_val == ilucky_number)
      iam_lucky=TRUE;
    else
      continue;
    cout << "It only took you " << inumber_of_tries
         << " tries to get lucky!";
  }

  return(0);
}
```

As an exercise, enter the preceding program and trace the variables *iinput_val,* *inumber_of_tries,* and *iam_lucky.* Pay particular attention to which statements are executed after *iinput_val* is compared to *ilucky_number.*

The program uses a **while** loop to prompt the user for a value, increments the
inumber_of_tries for each guess entered, and then determines the appropriate action to
take based on the success of the match. If no match was found, the **else** statement is
executed. This is the **continue** statement. Whenever the **continue** statement is executed,
the **cout** statement is ignored. Note, however, that the loop continues to execute. When
iinput_val matches *ilucky_number*, the *iam_lucky* flag is set to TRUE and the **continue**
statement is ignored, allowing the **cout** statement to execute.

Combining break and continue

The **break** and **continue** statements can be combined to solve some interesting program
problems. Look at the following C++ example:

```
//
// bracntg.cpp : Defines the entry point for the console application.
// A C++ program demonstrating the usefulness of combining
// the break and continue statements.
// Copyright (c) Chris H. Pappas and William H. Murray, 2001
//

#include "stdafx.h"
#include <iostream>
#include <cctype>

using namespace std;

#define NEWLINE '\n'

int main(int argc, char* argv[])
{
  int c;

  while((c=getchar()) != EOF)
  {
    if(isascii(c) == 0) {
      cout << "Not an ASCII character; ";
      cout << "not going to continue/n";
      break;
    }

    if(ispunct(c) || isspace(c)) {
      putchar(NEWLINE);
      continue;
```

```
    }

    if(isprint(c) == 0) {
      c = getchar();
      continue;
    }

    putchar(c);
  }

  return(0);
}
```

Before seeing how the program functions, take a look at the input to the program:

```
word control ^B exclamation! apostrophe' period.
^Z
```

Also examine the output produced:

```
word
control
B
exclamation

apostrophe

period
```

This application continues to read character input until the EOF character ^Z is typed. It then examines the input, removing any nonprintable characters, and places each "word" on its own line. It accomplishes all of this by using some very interesting functions defined in cctype.h, including isascii(), ispunct(), isspace(), and isprint(). Each of the functions is passed a character parameter and returns either a zero or some other value indicating the result of the comparison.

The function isascii() indicates whether the character passed falls into the acceptable ASCII value range, ispunct() indicates whether the character is a punctuation mark, isspace() indicates whether the character is a space, and function isprint() reports whether the character parameter is a printable character.

By using these functions, the application determines whether to continue the program at all and, if it is to continue, what it should do with each of the character's input.

The first test within the **while** loop evaluates whether the file is even in readable form. For example, the input data could have been saved in binary format, rendering the program useless. If this is the case, the associated **if** statements are executed, printing a warning message and breaking out of the **while** loop permanently.

If no errors are encountered, the second **if** statement is encountered; it checks whether the character input is either a punctuation mark or a blank space. If either of these conditions is TRUE, the associated **if** statements are executed. This causes a blank line to be skipped in the output and executes the **continue** statement. The **continue** statement efficiently jumps over the remaining test condition and output statement but does not terminate the loop. It merely indicates that the character's form has been diagnosed properly and that it is time to obtain a new character.

The third **if** statement asks whether the character is printable or not, but only if the file is in an acceptable format and the character input is not punctuation or a blank. This test takes care of any control codes. Notice that the example input to the program included a control ^B. Since ^B is not printable, this **if** statement immediately obtains a new character and then executes a **continue** statement. In a like manner, this **continue** statement indicates that the character in question has been diagnosed, the proper action has been taken, and it is time to get another character. The **continue** statement also causes the **putchar()** statement to be ignored while *not* terminating the **while** loop.

exit()

Under some circumstances, it is possible for a program to terminate long before all of the statements in the program have been examined and/or executed. For these specific circumstances, C incorporates the exit() library function. The function exit() expects one integer argument, called a *status value*. The UNIX and MS-DOS operating systems interpret a status value of zero as signaling a normal program termination, while any nonzero status values signify different kinds of errors.

The particular status value passed to exit() can be used by the process that invoked the program to take some action. For example, if the program were invoked from the command line and the status value indicated some type of error, the operating system might display a message. In addition to terminating the program, exit() writes all output waiting to be written and closes all open files.

The following application averages a list of up to 30 grades. The program will exit if the user requests to average more than *LIMIT* number of integers.

```
//
// exit1.cpp : Defines the entry point for the console application.
// A C++ program demonstrating the use of the exit function
// Copyright (c) Chris H. Pappas and William H. Murray, 2001
//

#include "stdafx.h"
```

```cpp
#include <iostream>
#include <cstdlib>

using namespace std;

#define LIMIT 30

int main(int argc, char* argv[])
{
  int irow,irequested_qty;
  float fscores[LIMIT],
        fsum=0,fmax_score=0,fmin_score=100,faverage;

  cout << "\nEnter the number of scores to be averaged: ";
  cin >>  irequested_qty;
  if(irequested_qty > LIMIT) {
    cout << "\nYou can only enter up to " << LIMIT << \
            " scores" << " to be averaged.\n";
    cout << "\n          >>> Program was exited. <<<\n";
    exit(1);
  }

  for(irow = 0; irow < irequested_qty; irow++) {
    cout << "\nPlease enter a grade " << irow+1 << ":   ";
    cin >> fscores[irow];
  }

  for(irow = 0; irow < irequested_qty; irow++)
    fsum = fsum + fscores[irow];

  faverage = fsum/(float)irequested_qty;

  for(irow = 0; irow < irequested_qty; irow++) {
    if(fscores[irow] > fmax_score)
      fmax_score = fscores[irow];
    if(fscores[irow] < fmin_score)
      fmin_score = fscores[irow];
  }

  cout << "\nThe maximum grade is " << fmax_score;
  cout << "\nThe minimum grade is " << fmin_score;
  cout << "\nThe average grade is " << faverage;

  return(0);
}
```

The application starts by including the cstdlib header file. Either cstdlib or iostream can be included to prototype the function exit(). The constant LIMIT is declared to be 30 and is used to dimension the array of integers, *iscores*. After the remaining variables are declared, the program prompts the user for the number of *iscores* to be entered. For this program, the user's response is to be typed next to the prompt.

The application inputs the requested value into the variable *irequested_qty* and uses this for the **if** comparison. When the user wants to average more numbers than will fit in *iscores*, the two warning messages are printed and then the **exit()** statement is executed. This terminates the program altogether.

Examine the following listing and see if you can detect the two subtle differences between the preceding program and this one:

```
//
// exit2.cpp : Defines the entry point for the console application.
// A C++ program demonstrating the use of the exit function
// Copyright (c) Chris H. Pappas and William H. Murray, 2001
//

#include "stdafx.h"
#include <iostream>
#include <cstdlib>

using namespace std;

#define LIMIT 30

int main(int argc, char* argv[])
{
  int irow,irequested_qty;
  float fscores[LIMIT],
        fsum=0,fmax_score=0,fmin_score=100,faverage;

  cout << "\nEnter the number of scores to be averaged: ";
  cin >>  irequested_qty;
  if(irequested_qty > LIMIT) {
    cout << "\nYou can only enter up to " << LIMIT << \
            " scores" << " to be averaged.\n";
    cout << "\n        >>> Program was exited. <<<\n";
    exit(EXIT_FAILURE);
  }
```

```
for(irow = 0; irow < irequested_qty; irow++) {
  cout << "\nPlease enter a grade " << irow+1 << ":   ";
  cin >> fscores[irow];
}

for(irow = 0; irow < irequested_qty; irow++)
  fsum = fsum + fscores[irow];

faverage = fsum/(float)irequested_qty;

for(irow = 0; irow < irequested_qty; irow++) {
  if(fscores[irow] > fmax_score)
    fmax_score = fscores[irow];
  if(fscores[irow] < fmin_score)
    fmin_score = fscores[irow];
}

cout << "\nThe maximum grade is " << fmax_score;
cout << "\nThe minimum grade is " << fmin_score;
cout << "\nThe average grade is " << faverage;

return(EXIT_SUCCESS);
}
```

A close examination of cstdlib yields two additional definitions: EXIT_SUCCESS (which returns a value of zero) and EXIT_FAILURE (which returns an unsuccessful value). This program used the EXIT_SUCCESS definition for a *more readable* parameter to the function exit().

atexit()

Whenever a program invokes the **exit()** function or performs a normal program termination, it can also call any registered "exit functions" posted with atexit(). The following C++ program demonstrates this capability:

```
//
// atexit.cpp : Defines the entry point for the console application.
// A C++ program demonstrating the relationship between the
// function atexit and the order in which the functions
// declared are executed.
// Copyright (c) Chris H. Pappas and William H. Murray, 2001
```

```cpp
//

#include "stdafx.h"
#include <iostream>
#include <cstdlib>

using namespace std;

void atexit_fn1(void);
void atexit_fn2(void);
void atexit_fn3(void);

int main(int argc, char *argv[])
{

  atexit(atexit_fn1);
  atexit(atexit_fn2);
  atexit(atexit_fn3);

  cout << "Atexit program entered.\n";
  cout << "Atexit program exited.\n\n";
  cout << ">>>>>>>>>> <<<<<<<<<<\n\n";

  return(0);
}

void atexit_fn1(void)
{
  cout << "atexit_fn1 entered.\n";
}

void atexit_fn2(void)
{
  cout << "atexit_fn2 entered.\n";
}

void atexit_fn3(void)
{
  cout << "atexit_fn3 entered.\n";
}
```

The output from the program looks like this:

```
Atexit program entered.
Atexit program exited.

>>>>>>>>>> <<<<<<<<<<

atexit_fn3 entered.
atexit_fn2 entered.
atexit_fn1 entered.
```

The atexit() function uses the name of a function as its only parameter and registers the specified function as an exit function. Whenever the program terminates normally, as in the preceding example, or invokes the exit() function, all atexit() declared functions are executed.

Technically, each time the **atexit()** statement is encountered in the source code, the specified function is added to a list of functions to execute when the program terminates. When the program terminates, any functions that have been passed to atexit() are executed, with the *last* function added being the *first* one executed. This explains why the *atexit_fn3* output statement was printed before the similar statement in *atexit_fn1*. atexit() functions are normally used as cleanup routines for dynamically allocated objects. Since one object (B) can be built upon another (A), atexit() functions execute in reverse order. This would delete object B before deleting object A.

What's Coming?

In this chapter you examined the C/C++ logic control statements. Many were similar to older high-level languages, but a significant portion of these control statements either required additional syntax or performed in a less-automatic manner, such as the **switch-case** statement. However, C and C++ contain several important control structures that have no equivalent in other programming languages, such as the conditional operator. These new logic control options require special attention. First, they are easy for you to omit because of their unfamiliarity. Secondly, they are easily misused both logically and syntactically. The authors of C and C++ included these control options to enable you to write cleaner code that in many cases executes more efficiently. Before moving on to the next chapter, make certain you understand the intricacies of the **switch-case**, **break**, **continue**, **exit()**, and **atexit()** statements.

PROGRAMMING
FOUNDATIONS

Visual C++.NET

Chapter 8

Writing and Using Functions

The cornerstone of C++ programming can be described in one word—functions. This chapter introduces the concept of a function and how it is prototyped under the latest ANSI C++ standard. Many example programs will be used to examine the different types of functions and how arguments are passed. You will also learn how to use the standard C/C++ variables *argc* and *argv* to pass command-line arguments to the main() function. Additionally, the chapter explores several unique features available in C++.

Functions form the main building blocks of most C and C++ programs. Functions allow you to separate and code parts of your program in separate modules. Thus, functions allow your program can take on a modular appearance. Modular programming allows a program to be separated into workable parts that contribute to a final program form. For example, one function might be used to capture input data, another to print information, and yet another to write data to the disk. As a matter of fact, all C and C++ programming is done within a function. The one function every C or C++ program has is main().

You will find that C and C++ functions are similar to programming modules in other languages. For example, Pascal uses functions and procedures, while FORTRAN uses just functions. The proper development of functions determines, to a great extent, the efficiency, readability, and portability of your program code.

This chapter contains many programming examples that will show you how to create and implement a wide range of functions. Many of the example programs also use built-in C++ library functions that give your program extended power.

What Is Function Prototyping?

When the ANSI C standard was implemented for C, it was the C functions that underwent the greatest change. The ANSI C standard for functions is based on the function prototype that has already been extensively used in C++.

The Syntax for Prototypes

If you are not familiar with writing C functions, you probably have a few questions. What does a function look like? Where do functions go in a program? How are functions declared? What constitutes a function? Where is type checking performed?

With the new ANSI C standard, all functions must be prototyped. The prototyping can take place in the C or C++ program itself or in a header file. For the programs in this book, most function prototyping is contained within the program itself. Function declarations begin with the C and C++ function prototype. The function prototype is simple, and it is usually included at the start of program code to notify the compiler of the type and number of arguments that a function will use. Prototyping enforces stronger type checking than was previously possible when C standards were not as strictly enforced.

Although other prototyping style variations are legal, this book recommends the function prototype form that is a replication of the function's declaration line, with the addition of a semicolon at the end, whenever possible. For example:

```
return_type function_name(argument_type optional_argument_name [,...]);
```

The function can be of type **void, int, float,** and so on. The *return_type* gives this specification. The *function_name()* is any meaningful name you choose to describe the function. If any information is passed to the function, an *argument_type* followed by an *optional*_argument_name should also be given. Argument types can also be of type **void, int, float,** and so on. You can pass many values to a function by repeating the argument type and name separated by a comma. It is also correct to list just the argument type, but that prototype form is used specifically for library routine prototypes.

The function itself is actually an encapsulated piece of C or C++ program code that usually follows the main() function definition. A function can take the following form:

```
return_type function_name(argument_types and names)
{
   .

   .

   (data declarations and body of function)

   .

   .

   return();
}
```

Notice that the first line of the actual function header is identical to the prototype that is listed at the beginning of a program, with one important exception: it does *not* end with a semicolon. A function prototype and function used in a program are shown in the following application:

```
//
// proto.cpp : Defines the entry point for the console application.
// A C++ program to illustrate function prototyping.
// Function adds two integers
// and returns an integer result.
// Copyright (c) Chris H. Pappas and William H. Murray, 2001
//

#include "stdafx.h"
```

```
#include <iostream>

using namespace std;

int iadder(int ix,int iy);            /* function prototype  */

int main(int argc, char* argv[])
{
  int ia = 23;
  int ib = 13;
  int ic;

  ic = iadder(ia,ib);
  cout << "The sum is: " << ic << endl;

  cout << "ia = " << ia;

  return (0);
}

int iadder(int ix,int iy)             /* function declaration */
{
  int iz;

  iz = ix + iy;
  return(iz);                         /* function return      */
}
```

The function is called iadder(). The prototype states that the function will accept two integer arguments and return an integer type. Actually, the ANSI C++ standard suggests that all functions be prototyped in a separate header file. This, as you might guess, is how header files are associated with their appropriate C++ libraries. For simple programs, as already mentioned, including the function prototype within the body of the program is acceptable.

Ways to Pass Actual Arguments

In the previous two examples, arguments have been *passed by value* to the functions. When variables are passed by value, a copy of the variable's actual contents is passed to the function. Since a copy of the variable is passed, the variable in the calling function itself is not altered. Calling a function by value is the most popular means of passing information to a function, and it is the default method in C and C++. The major restriction to the call-by-value method is that the function typically returns only one value.

When you use a *call-by-reference*, the address of the argument, rather than the actual value, is passed to the function. This approach also requires less program memory than a call-by-value. When you use call-by-reference, the variables in the calling function can be altered. Another advantage to a call-by-reference is that more than one value can be returned by the function.

The next example uses the iadder() function from the previous section. The arguments are now passed by a call-by-reference. In C, you accomplish a call-by-reference by using a pointer as an argument, as shown here. This same method can be used with C++.

```cpp
//
// cbref.cpp : Defines the entry point for the console application.
// A C++ program to illustrate call by reference.
// Copyright (c) Chris H. Pappas and William H. Murray, 2001
//

#include "stdafx.h"
#include <iostream>

using namespace std;

int iadder(int *pix,int *piy);

int main(int argc, char* argv[])
{
  int ia = 23;
  int ib = 13;
  int ic;

  ic = iadder(&ia,&ib);
  cout << "The sum is: " << ic << endl;

  cout << "ia = " << ia;

  return (0);
}

int iadder(int *pix,int *piy)
{
  int iz;

  *pix = 33;
```

```
  iz=*pix+*piy;
  return(iz);
}
```

You have learned in C that you can use variables and pointers as arguments in function declarations. C++ uses variables and pointers as arguments in function declarations and adds a third type. In C++, the third argument type is called a *reference type*. The reference type specifies a location but does not require a dereferencing operator. Many advanced C++ programs use this syntax to simplify the use of pointer variables within called subroutines. Examine the following syntax carefully and compare it with the previous example:

```cpp
//
// referenc.cpp : Defines the entry point for the console application.
// C++ program to illustrate an equivalent
// call-by-reference, using the C++ reference type.
// Copyright (c) Chris H. Pappas and William H. Murray, 2001
//

#include "stdafx.h"
#include <iostream>

using namespace std;

int iadder(int &rix,int &riy);

int main(int argc, char* argv[])
{
  int ia = 23;
  int ib = 13;
  int ic;

  ic = iadder(ia,ib);
  cout << "The sum is: " << ic << endl;

  cout << "ia = " << ia;

  return (0);
}

int iadder(int &rix,int &riy)
```

```
{
  int iz;

  rix = 33;

  iz = rix + riy;
  return(iz);
}
```

Did you notice the lack of pointers in the previous C++ program code? The reference types in this example are *rix* and *riy*. In C++, references to references, references to bit-fields, arrays of references, and pointers to references are not allowed. Regardless of whether you use call-by-reference or a reference type, C++ always uses the address of the argument.

Default Argument Lists

You can also define a function that will automatically supply default data values. Look at the three function calls that follow:

```
function_with_default_arguments("start");
function_with_default_arguments("middle", 5);
function_with_default_arguments("end, n-1, 0);
```

Notice that the three function calls all use the same function name, yet have different numbers of actual arguments. Now, take a look at the prototyped function:

```
function_with_default_arguments(char *direction,
                                int start_pt = 0,
                                int end_pt = 100);
```

The first example function call:

```
function_with_default_arguments("start");
```

uses the default values of 0, and 100 for the *start_pt* and *end_pt* dummy arguments. The second call:

```
function_with_default_arguments("middle", 5);
```

supplies an actual argument value of 5 for the second parameter, overriding the default 0 assignment to *start_pt*, but uses the default value for *end_pt*. The final call supplies all three actual values:

```
function_with_default_arguments("end, n-1, 0);
```

This syntax of supplying default values to dummy arguments makes for some very interesting algorithms—always guaranteeing that the variables have values, that the subroutine performs a minimum, predefined task when not otherwise directed, and yet allowing the subroutine to adjust its performance on demand.

There is only one syntax requirement when using default dummy argument assignments. Once you begin specifying default dummy argument values, you cannot go back to undefined dummy argument definitions. The following example is illegal:

```
illegal_function_definition(int start_pt = 0,
                            char *direction,
                            int end_pt = 100);
```

Since the first dummy argument, *start_pt* has a default argument assignment value, all successive dummy arguments must have assigned default values, and *direction* does not meet this syntax requirement.

Storage Classes

Storage classes can be affixed to data type declarations, as you saw earlier in Chapter 6. A variable might, for example, be declared as:

```
static float fyourvariable;
```

Functions can also use **extern** and **static** storage class types. A function is declared with an **extern** storage class when it has been defined in another file, external to the present program. A function can be declared static when external access, apart from the present program, is not permitted.

Identifier Visibility Rules

The *scope* of a variable, when used in a function, refers to the range of effect that the variable has. The scope rules are similar for C and C++ variables used with functions. Variables can have a local, file, or class scope.

It is possible to use a *local variable* completely within a function definition. Its scope is then limited to the function itself. The variable is said to be accessible, or visible, within the function only and has a local scope.

Variables with a *file scope* are declared outside of individual functions or classes. These variables have visibility or accessibility throughout the file in which they are declared and are global in range.

A variable may be used with a file scope and later within a function definition with a *local scope*. When this is done, the local scope takes precedence over the file scope. C++ offers a new programming feature called the scope resolution operator (::). When the C++ resolution operator is used, a variable with local scope is changed to one with file scope. In this situation, the variable would possess the value of the "global" variable. The syntax for referencing the global variable is:

```
::yourvariable
```

The scope rules allow unique programming errors to occur. Various scope rule errors are discussed at the end of this chapter.

Recursion

Recursion takes place in a program when a function calls itself. Initially, this might seem like an endless loop, but it is not. Both C and C++ support recursion. Recursive algorithms allow for creative, readable, and terse problem solutions. For example, the next program uses recursion to generate the factorial of a number. The *factorial* of a number is defined as the number multiplied by all successively lower integers. For example:

```
8 * 7 * 6 * 5 * 4 * 3 * 2 * 1
  = 40320
```

Care must be taken when choosing data types since the product increases very rapidly. The factorial of 15 is 1307674368000.

```
//
// factr.cpp : Defines the entry point for the console application.
// A C++ program illustrating recursive function calls.
// Calculation of the factorial of a number.
// Example:  7! = 7 x 6 x 5 x 4 x 3 x 2 x 1 = 5040
// Copyright (c) Chris H. Pappas and William H. Murray, 2001
//

#include "stdafx.h"
#include <iostream>
```

```
using namespace std;

int dfactorial(int danswer);

int main(int argc, char* argv[])
{
  int dnumber = 15;
  int dresult;

  dresult = dfactorial(dnumber);

  cout << "The factorial of " << dnumber
       << " is: " << dresult;

  return (0);
}

int dfactorial(int danswer)
{
  if (danswer <= 1)
    return(1);
  else
    return(danswer*dfactorial(danswer - 1));
}
```

Recursion occurs because the function, dfactorial(), has a call to itself within the function. Recursive algorithms use the internal call stack mechanism encoded into the executable file by the compiler. They are usually very terse subroutines, packed with a lot of horsepower, and if you are unfamiliar with their internal workings, difficult to debug.

Function Arguments

This section discusses how to pass function arguments to a function. These arguments go by many different names. Some programmers call them arguments, while others refer to them as parameters or dummy variables.

Function arguments are optional. Some functions you design may receive no arguments, while others may receive many. Function argument types can be mixed; that is, you can use any of the standard data types as a function argument. Many of the following examples illustrate passing various data types to functions. Furthermore, these programs employ functions from the various C and C++ libraries. Additional details on these library functions and their prototypes can be found in the Visual C/C++ reference manuals.

Actual Versus Formal Parameters

Each function definition contains an argument list called the *formal argument list*. Items in the list are optional, so the actual list may be empty or it may contain any combination of data types, such as **integer**, **float**, and **character**.

When the function is called by the program, an argument list is also passed to the function. This list is called the *actual argument list*. In general, there is usually a 1:1 match, when writing ANSI C code, between the formal and actual argument lists, although in reality no strong enforcement is used.

Examine the following line of C code:

```
printf("This is hexadecimal %x and octal %o",ians);
```

In this situation, only one argument is being passed to printf(), although two are expected. When fewer arguments are supplied, the missing arguments are initialized to meaningless values. C++ overcomes this problem, to a degree, by permitting a default value to be supplied with the formal argument list. When an argument is missing in the actual argument list, the default argument is automatically substituted. For example, in C++, the function prototype might appear as:

```
int iyourfunction(int it,float fu=4.2,int iv=10)
```

Notice, if either *fu* or *iv* is not specified in the call to the function iyourfunction(), the values shown (4.2 or 10) will be used. C++ requires that all formal arguments using default values be listed at the end of the formal argument list. In other words, iyourfunction(10) and iyourfunction(10,15.2) are valid. If *fu* is not supplied, *iv* cannot be supplied either.

void Parameters

In ANSI C **void** should be used to explicitly state the absence of function arguments. In C++, the use of **void** is not yet required, but its use is considered wise. The following program has a simple function named voutput() that receives no arguments and does not return a value. The main() function calls the function voutput(). When the voutput() function is finished, control is returned to the main() function. This is one of the simplest types of functions you can write:

```
//
// fvoid.cpp : Defines the entry point for the console application.
// A C++ program that will print a message with a function.
// Function uses a type void argument and sqrt function
```

```
// from the standard C library.
// Copyright (c) Chris H. Pappas and William H. Murray, 2001
//

#include "stdafx.h"
#include <iostream>
#include <cmath>

using namespace std;

void voutput(void);

int main(int argc, char* argv[])
{
  cout << "This program will find the square root. \n\n";
  voutput();

  return (0);
}

void voutput(void)
{
  double dt = 12345.0;
  double du;

  du = sqrt(dt);
  cout << "The square root of " << dt
       << " is " << du;
}
```

As you study the example, notice that the voutput() function calls a C library function named sqrt(). The prototype for the sqrt() library function is contained in cmath. It accepts a double as an argument and returns the square root as a double value.

char Parameters

Character information can also be passed to a function. In the next example, a single character is intercepted from the keyboard, in the function main(), and passed to the function voutput(). The get() function reads the character. There are other functions that are closely related to get() in the standard C library: getc(), getchar(), and getche(). These functions can also be used in C++, but in many cases a better choice will probably be cin. Additional details for using get() are contained in your Visual C/C++ reference manuals and are available as online help. The get() function intercepts a character from the standard input device (keyboard) and returns a character value, without echo to the screen, as shown here:

```
//
// fchar.cpp : Defines the entry point for the console application.
// C++ program will accept a character from keyboard,
// pass it to a function and print a message using
// the character.
// Copyright (c) Chris H. Pappas and William H. Murray, 2001
//

#include "stdafx.h"
#include <iostream>

using namespace std;

void voutput(char c);

int main(int argc, char* argv[])
{
  char cyourchar;

  cout << "Enter one character from the keyboard -> ";
  cyourchar = cin.get();
  voutput(cyourchar);

  return (0);
}

void voutput(char c)
{
  cout << "\nThe character entered is: " << c << endl;
  cout << "\nThe next five characters are:";
  for( int j = 0; j < 5; j++ )
    cout << " " << ++c;
}
```

Notice, in the previous listing, that a single character is passed to the function. The function then prints a message and the next 5 successive characters.

PROGRAMMING
FOUNDATIONS

int Parameters

In the following application, a single integer will be read from the keyboard with C++'s cin function. That integer will be passed to the function vside(). The vside() function uses the supplied length to calculate and print the area of a square, the volume of a cube, and the surface area of a cube.

```cpp
//
// finit.cpp : Defines the entry point for the console application.
// C++ program will calculate values given a length.
// Function uses a type int argument, accepts length
// from keyboard with scanf function.
// Copyright (c) Chris H. Pappas and William H. Murray, 2001
//

#include "stdafx.h"
#include <iostream>

using namespace std;

void vside(int is);

int main(int argc, char* argv[])
{
  int iyourlength;

  cout << "Enter the length, as an integer,\n";
  cout << "from the keyboard -> ";
  cin >> iyourlength;
  vside(iyourlength);

  return (0);
}

void vside(int is)
{
  int iarea,ivolume,isarea;

  iarea = is * is;
  ivolume = is * is * is;
  isarea = 6 * iarea;
```

```
    cout << "\nThe length of a side is " << is << endl;
    cout << "A square would have an area of " << iarea << endl;
    cout << "A cube would have a volume of " << ivolume << endl;
    cout << "The surface area of the cube is " << isarea;
}
```

Note that the variable, *is*, and all calculated values are integers. What would happen if *is* represented the radius of a circle and sphere to the calculated types? Try rewriting the algorithm to see the differences.

float Parameters

Floats can also be passed as arguments to a function. In the following example, two floating-point values are passed to a function called vhypotenuse(). The cin function is used to intercept both float values from the keyboard.

```
//
// ffloat.cpp : Defines the entry point for the console application.
// C++ program will find hypotenuse of a right triangle.
// Function uses a type float argument and accepts
// input from the keyboard with the scanf function.
// Copyright (c) Chris H. Pappas and William H. Murray, 2001
//

#include "stdafx.h"
#include <iostream>
#include <cmath>

using namespace std;

void vhypotenuse(float fx, float fy);

int main(int argc, char* argv[])
{
   float fxlen,fylen;

   cout << "Enter the base of the right triangle -> ";
   cin >> fxlen;

   cout << "\nEnter the height of the right triangle -> ";
   cin >> fylen;
```

```
   vhypotenuse(fxlen,fylen);

   return (0);
}

void vhypotenuse(float ft,float fu)
{
  double dresult;

  dresult = hypot((double) ft,(double) fu);
  cout << "\nThe hypotenuse of the right triangle is "
       << dresult;
}
```

Observe that both arguments received by vhypotenuse() are cast to doubles when used by the hypot() function from math.h. All math.h functions accept and return **double** types. Your programs can use the additional math functions listed in Table 8-1. You can also display the contents of your cmath header file for additional details.

double _cabs(struct _complex);	double atan2(double, double);
double _hypot(double, double);	double atof(const char *);
double _j0(double);	double cabs(struct _complex);
double _j1(double);	double ceil(double);
double _jn(int, double);	double cos(double);
double _y0(double);	double cosh(double);
double _y1(double);	double exp(double);
double _yn(int, double);	double fabs(double);
double abs(double _X)	double floor(double);
double acos(double);	double fmod(double, double);
double asin(double);	double frexp(double, int *);
double atan(double);	double hypot(double, double);

Table 8-1.   *Macro and Function Prototypes Provided by cmath*

```
double j0(double);              Float atan(float _X)
double j1(double);              float atan2(float _Y, float _X)
double jn(int, double);         Float atan2f( float , float );
double ldexp(double, int);      float atan2f(float _X, float _Y)
double log(double);             float atanf( float );
double log10(double);           Float atanf(float _X)
double modf(double, double *);  Float ceil(float _X)
double pow(double _X, int _Y)   Float ceilf( float );
double pow(double, double);     float ceilf(float _X)
double pow(int _X, int _Y)      float cos(float _X)
double sin(double);             float cosf( float );
double sinh(double);            Float cosf(float _X)
double sqrt(double);            Float cosh(float _X)
double tan(double);             Float coshf( float );
double tanh(double);            float coshf(float _X)
double y0(double);              float exp(float _X)
double y1(double);              float expf( float );
double yn(int, double);         Float expf(float _X)
float abs(float _X)             Float fabs(float _X)
Float acos(float _X)            Float fabsf( float );
Float acosf( float );           float fabsf(float _X)
float acosf(float _X)           float floor(float _X)
float asin(float _X)            float floorf( float );
float asinf( float );           Float floorf(float _X)
Float asinf(float _X)           Float fmod(float _X, float _Y)
```

Table 8-1.   *Macro and Function Prototypes Provided by cmath (continued)*

```
Float fmodf( float , float );          float sinhf(float _X)

float fmodf(float _X, float _Y)        Float sqrt(float _X)

float frexp(float _X, int * _Y)        Float sqrtf( float );

Float frexpf(float _X, int *_Y)        Float sqrtf(float _X)

float hypotf(float, float);            float tan(float _X)

Float ldexp(float _X, int _Y)          float tanf( float );

float ldexpf(float _X, int _Y)         float tanf(float _X)

float log(float _X)                    Float tanh(float _X)

Float log10(float _X)                  Float tanhf( float );

Float log10f( float );                 Float tanhf(float _X)

Float log10f(float _X)                 long abs(long _X)

float logf( float );                   long double _atold(const char *);

float logf(float _X)                   long double _cabsl(struct
                                       _complexl);
float modf(float _X, float * _Y)
                                       long double _hypotl(long double,
Float modff( float , float* );         long double);

Float modff(float _X, float *_Y)       long double _j0l(long double);

Float pow(float _X, float _Y)          long double _j1l(long double);

float pow(float _X, int _Y)            long double _jnl(int, long
                                       double);
float powf( float , float );
                                       long double _y0l(long double);
float powf(float _X, float _Y)
                                       long double _y1l(long double);
Float sin(float _X)
                                       long double _ynl(int, long
Float sinf( float );                   double);

Float sinf(float _X)                   long double abs(long double _X)

float sinh(float _X)                   long double acos(long double _X)

float sinhf( float );                  long double acosl(long double _X)
```

Table 8-1.   *Macro and Function Prototypes Provided by cmath (continued)*

```
long double acosl(long double);

long double asin(long double _X)

long double asinl(long double _X)

long double asinl(long double);

long double atan(long double _X)

long double atan2(long double _Y,
long double _X)

long double atan2l(long double
_X, long double _Y)

long double atan2l(long double,
long double);

long double atanl(long double _X)

long double atanl(long double);

long double ceil(long double _X)

long double ceill(long double _X)

long double ceill(long double);

long double cos(long double _X)

long double cosh(long double _X)

long double coshl(long double _X)

long double coshl(long double);

long double cosl(long double _X)

long double cosl(long double);

long double exp(long double _X)

long double expl(long double _X)

long double expl(long double);

long double fabs(long double _X)
```

```
long double fabsl(long double _X)

long double fabsl(long double);

long double floor(long double _X)

long double floorl(long
double _X)

long double floorl(long double);

long double fmod(long double _X,
long double _Y)

long double fmodl(long double _X,
long double _Y)

long double fmodl(long double,
long double);

long double frexp(long double
_X, int * _Y)

long double frexpl(long double
_X, int *_Y)

long double frexpl(long double,
int *);

long double ldexp(long double _X,
int _Y)

long double ldexpl(long
double _X, int _Y)

long double ldexpl(long double,
int);

long double log(long double _X)

long double log10(long double _X)

long double log10l(long
double _X)

long double log10l(long double);
```

Table 8-1.   *Macro and Function Prototypes Provided by cmath (continued)*

```
long double logl(long double _X)        long double sinh(long double _X)

long double logl(long double);          long double sinhl(long double _X)

long double modf(long double _X,        long double sinhl(long double);
long double * _Y)
                                        long double sinl(long double _X)
long double modfl(long double _X,
long double *_Y)                        long double sinl(long double);

long double modfl(long double,          long double sqrt(long double _X)
long double *);
                                        long double sqrtl(long double _X)
long double pow(long double _X,
int _Y)                                 long double sqrtl(long double);

long double pow(long double _X,         long double tan(long double _X)
long double _Y)
                                        long double tanh(long double _X)
long double powl(long double _X,
long double _Y)                         long double tanhl(long double _X)

long double powl(long double,           long double tanhl(long double);
long double);
                                        long double tanl(long double _X)
long double sin(long double _X)
                                        long double tanl(long double);
```

Table 8-1.   *Macro and Function Prototypes Provided by cmath (continued)*

double Parameters

The **double** type is a very precise float value. All cmath functions accept and return **double** types. The next program accepts two double values from the keyboard. The function named vpower() will raise the first number to the power specified by the second number. Since both values are of type **double**, you can calculate 45.7 raised to the power of 5.2 and find that it equals 428118741.757.

```
//
// fdouble.cpp : Defines the entry point for the console application.
// C++ program will raise a number to a power.
// Function uses a type double argument and the pow function.
// Copyright (c) Chris H. Pappas and William H. Murray, 2001
//
```

```
#include "stdafx.h"
#include <iostream>
#include <cmath>

using namespace std;

void vpower(double dt, double du);

int main(int argc, char* argv[])
{
  double dtnum,dunum;

  cout << "Enter the base number -> ";
  cin >> dtnum;
  cout << "\nEnter the power -> ";
  cin >> dunum;
  vpower(dtnum,dunum);

  return (0);
}

void vpower(double dt,double du)
{
  double danswer;

  danswer = pow(dt,du);
  cout.setf(ios::fixed);
  cout << "\nThe result is " << setprecision(3) << danswer;
}
```

This function uses the library function pow() to raise one number to a power, prototyped in cmath.

Array Parameters

The next application shows how the contents of an array are passed to a function as a call-by-reference. In this example the address of the first array element is passed via a pointer:

```
//
// fpntr.cpp : Defines the entry point for the console application.
// C++ program will call a function with an array.
```

```
// Function uses a pointer to pass array information.
// Copyright (c) Chris H. Pappas and William H. Murray, 2001
//

#include "stdafx.h"
#include <iostream>

using namespace std;

void voutput(int *pinums);

int main(int argc, char* argv[])
{
  int iyourarray[7] = {2,7,15,32,45,3,1};

  cout << "Send array information to function." << endl;
  voutput(iyourarray);

  return (0);
}

void voutput(int *pinums)
{
    cout << "The array's contents are:";
    for(int t = 0; t < 7; t++)
    cout << " " << pinums[t];
}
```

When the function is called, only the name *iyourarray* is specified. In Chapter 9 you will learn more details concerning arrays. In this example, by specifying the name of the array, you are providing the address of the first element in the array. Since *iyourarray* is an array of integers, it is possible to pass the array by specifying a pointer of the element type.

It is also permissible to pass the address information by using an unsized array. The next example shows how you can do this in C++. (The same approach can be used in C.) The information in *iyourarray* is transferred by passing the address of the first element.

```
//
// farray.cpp : Defines the entry point for the console application.
//  C++ program will call a function with an array.
//  Function passes array information, and calculates
```

```
//   the average of the numbers.
//   Copyright (c) Chris H. Pappas and William H. Murray, 2001
//

#include "stdafx.h"
#include <iostream>

using namespace std;

void avg(float fnums[]);

int main(int argc, char* argv[])
{
  float iyourarray[8] = {12.3,25.7,82.1,6.0,7.01,
                         0.25,4.2,6.28};

  cout << "Send information to averaging function. \n";
  avg(iyourarray);

  return (0);
}

void avg(float fnums[])
{
  float fsum=0.0;
  float faverage;

  for(int iv = 0; iv < 8; iv++) {
    fsum += fnums[iv];
    cout << "number " << iv+1 << " is " << fnums[iv] << endl;
  }
  faverage = fsum/iv;
  cout << "\nThe average is " << faverage << endl;
}
```

The average is determined by summing each of the terms together and dividing by the total number of terms. The **cout** stream is used to format the output to the screen.

Function Return Types

In this section you will find an example for each of the important return types for functions possible in C and C++ programming. Function types specify the type of value returned by the function. None of the examples in the last section returned information from the function and thus were of type **void**.

void Return Type

Since **void** was used in all of the previous examples, the example for this section is a little more involved. You have learned that both C and C++ permit numeric information to be formatted in hexadecimal, decimal, and octal formats—but not binary. Specifying data in a binary format is useful for doing binary arithmetic or developing bit masks. The function vbinary() will convert a decimal number entered from the keyboard to a binary representation on the screen. The binary digits are not packed together as a single binary number but are stored individually in an array. Thus, to examine the binary number, the contents of the array must be printed out:

```cpp
//
// voidf.cpp : Defines the entry point for the console application.
// C++ program illustrates the void function type.
// Program will print the binary equivalent of a number.
// Copyright (c) Chris H. Pappas and William H. Murray, 2001
//

#include "stdafx.h"
#include <iostream>

using namespace std;

void vbinary(int ivalue);

int main(int argc, char* argv[])
{
  int ivalue;

  cout << "Enter a number (base 10) for conversion to "
       << "binary -> ";
  cin >> ivalue;
  vbinary(ivalue);

  return (0);
}

void vbinary(int idata)
{
  int t = 0;
  int iyourarray[50];
```

```
while (idata !=0) {
  iyourarray[t] = (idata % 2);
  idata /= 2;
  t++;
}

for(--t; t >= 0; t--)
  cout << iyourarray[t];
cout << endl;
}
```

The conversion process from higher order to lower order bases is a rather simple mathematical algorithm. For example, base 10 numbers can be converted to another base by dividing the number by the new base a successive number of times. If conversion is from base 10 to base 2, a 2 is repeatedly divided into the base 10 number. This produces a quotient and a remainder. The quotient becomes the dividend for each subsequent division. The remainder becomes a digit in the converted number. In the case of binary conversion, the remainder is either a one or a zero.

In the function vbinary(), a **while** loop is used to perform the arithmetic as long as *idata* has not reached zero. The modulus operator determines the remainder and saves the bit in the array. Division is then performed on *idata*, saving only the integer result. This process is repeated until the quotient (also *data* in this case) is reduced to zero.

The individual array bits, which form the binary result, must be unloaded from the array in reverse order. You can observe this in the program listing. Examine the **for** loop used in the function. Can you think of a way to perform this conversion and save the binary representation in a variable instead of an array?

char Return Type

Let's examine an example that is a minor variation of an earlier application. The C++ function clowercase() accepts a character argument and returns the same character type. For this example, an uppercase letter received from the keyboard is passed to the function. The function uses the library function tolower() (from the standard library and prototyped in cctype) to convert the character to a lowercase letter. Related functions to tolower() include toascii() and toupper().

```
//
// charf.cpp : Defines the entry point for the console application.
// C++ program illustrates the character function type.
// Function receives uppercase character and
// converts it to lowercase.
// Copyright (c) Chris H. Pappas and William H. Murray, 2001
//
```

```
#include "stdafx.h"
#include <iostream>
#include <cctype>

using namespace std;

char clowercase(char c);

int main(int argc, char* argv[])
{
  char clowchar, chichar;

  cout << "Enter an uppercase character -> ";
  chichar = cin.get();

  clowchar = clowercase(chichar);
  cout << "The character in lowercase is: " << clowchar;

  return (0);
}

char clowercase(char c)
{
  return(tolower(c));
}
```

bool Return Type

The use of the new **bool** data type is illustrated in the following application by defining two functions is_upper() and is_lower() that return this new ANSI C type:

```
//
// bool.cpp : Defines the entry point for the console application.
// C++ program illustrating the use
// of the new ANSI C/C++ type bool
// Copyright (c) Chris H. Pappas and William H. Murray, 2001
//

#include "stdafx.h"
#include <iostream>
```

```
using namespace std;

bool is_upper(char);
bool is_lower(char);

int main(int argc, char* argv[])
{
  char cTestChar = 'T';
  bool bIsUppercase, bIsLowercase;

  bIsUppercase = is_upper(cTestChar);
  bIsLowercase = is_lower(cTestChar);

  cout << "The letter T"
       << (bIsUppercase ? "is" : "isn't") << " upper case.\n";
  cout << "The letter T"
       << (bIsLowercase ? "is" : "isn't") << " lower case.";

  return(0);
}

bool is_upper(char ch)
{
  return ( ch >= 'A' && ch <= 'Z' );
}

bool is_lower(char ch)
{
  return ( ch >= 'a' && ch <= 'z' );
}
```

Here the use of the conditional operator **?:** is used to reduce each printf() statement to a single line, instead of the more verbose **if-else** alternative.

int Return Type

The following function accepts and returns integers. The function icube() accepts a number generated in main() (0, 2, 4, 6, 8, 10, and so on), cubes the number, and returns the integer value to main(). The original number and its cube are printed to the screen:

```
//
// intf.cpp : Defines the entry point for the console application.
```

```
// C++ program illustrates the integer function type.
// Function receives integers, one at a time, and
// returns the cube of each, one at a time.
// Copyright (c) Chris H. Pappas and William H. Murray, 2001
//

#include "stdafx.h"
#include <iostream>

using namespace std;

int icube(int ivalue);

int main(int argc, char* argv[])
{
  int inumbercube;

  for (int k = 0; k < 20; k+=2) {
    inumbercube = icube(k);
    cout << "The cube of the number " << k
         << " is " << inumbercube << endl;
  }

  return (0);
}

int icube(int ivalue)
{
  return (ivalue * ivalue * ivalue);
}
```

long Return Type

In the following C++ application you'll see how a program accepts an integer value as an argument and returns a type **long**. The **long** type, used by Visual C/C++ and other popular compilers, is not recognized as a standard ANSI C type. The function will raise the number 2 to an integer power.

```
//
// longf.cpp : Defines the entry point for the console application.
// C++ program illustrates the long integer function type.
// Function receives integers, one at a time, and
```

```
// returns 2 raised to that integer power.
// Copyright (c) Chris H. Pappas and William H. Murray, 2001
//

#include "stdafx.h"
#include <iostream>

using namespace std;

long lpower(int ivalue);

int main(int argc, char* argv[])
{
  long lanswer;

  for (int k = 0; k < 31; k++) {
    lanswer = lpower(k);
    cout << "2 raised to the " << k << " power is "
         << lanswer << endl;
  }

  return (0);
}

long lpower(int ivalue)
{
  int t;
  long lseed=1;

  for (t=0;t<ivalue;t++)
    lseed*=2;
  return (lseed);
}
```

In this application, the function simply multiplies the original number by the number of times it is to be raised to the specified power. For example, if you wanted to raise 2 to the 6th power, the program will perform the following multiplication:

```
2 * 2 * 2 * 2 * 2 * 2  = 64
```

Can you think of a function described in cmath that could achieve the same results? See Table 8-1 (earlier in this chapter) for some ideas.

PROGRAMMING
FOUNDATIONS

float Return Type

The following application illustrates how a float array argument will be passed to a function and a float will be returned. This C++ example will find the product of all the elements in an array:

```cpp
//
// floatf.cpp : Defines the entry point for the console application.
// C++ program illustrates the float function type.
// Function receives an array of floats and returns
// their product as a float.
// Copyright (c) Chris H. Pappas and William H. Murray, 2001
//

#include "stdafx.h"
#include <iostream>

using namespace std;

float fproduct(float farray[]);

int main(int argc, char* argv[])
{
  float fmyarray[7] = {4.3,1.8,6.12,3.19,0.01234,0.1,9876.2};
  float fmultiplied;

  fmultiplied = fproduct(fmyarray);
  cout << "The product of all array entries is: "
       << fmultiplied << endl;

  return (0);
}

float fproduct(float farray[])
{
  float fpartial;

  fpartial = farray[0];
  for (int i = 1; i < 7; i++)
    fpartial *= farray[i];
  return (fpartial);
}
```

Since the elements are multiplied together, the first element of the array must be loaded into *fpartial* before the **for** loop is entered. Observe that the loop in the function fproduct() starts at 1 instead of the normal zero value.

double Return Type

The next application shows how a program accepts and returns a **double** type. The function dtrigcosine() will convert an angle, expressed in degrees, to its cosine value:

```cpp
//
// double.cpp : Defines the entry point for the console application.
// C++ program illustrates the double function type.
// Function receives integers from 0 to 90, one at a
// time, and returns the cosine of each, one at a time.
// Copyright (c) Chris H. Pappas and William H. Murray, 2001
//

#include "stdafx.h"
#include <iostream>
#include <cmath>

using namespace std;

const double dPi = 3.14159265359;
double dtrigcosine(double dangle);

int main(int argc, char* argv[])
{
  double dcosine;

  for (int j = 0; j < 91; j++) {
    dcosine = dtrigcosine((double) j);
    cout << "The cosine of " << j
         << " degrees is " << dcosine << endl;
  }

  return (0);
}

double dtrigcosine(double dangle)
{
  double dpartial;
  dpartial = cos((dPi/180.0)*dangle);
  return (dpartial);
}
```

Note that the cos() function found in math.h is used by dtrigcosine() for obtaining the results. Angles must be converted from degrees to radians for all trigonometric functions. Recall that pi radians equals 180 degrees.

Command Line Arguments

Both C and C++ share the ability to accept command-line arguments. *Command-line arguments* are those arguments entered along with the program name when called from the operating system's command line. This gives you the ability to pass arguments directly to your program without additional program prompts. For example, a program might pass four arguments from the command line:

```
YOURPROGRAM  Tia, ThinkingDog, Tango, BigDog
```

In this example, four values are passed from the command line to YOURPROGRAM. Actually, it is main() that is given specific information. One argument received by main(), *argc*, is an integer giving the number of command-line terms plus 1. The program title is counted as the first term passed from the command line. The second argument is a pointer to an array of string pointers called *argv*. All arguments are strings of characters, so *argv* is of type **char** *[*argc*]. Since all programs have a name, *argc* is always one greater than the number of command-line arguments. In the following examples, you will learn different techniques for retrieving various data types from the command line. The argument names *argc* and *argv* are the commonly agreed upon variable names used in all C/C++ programs.

Alphanumeric

Arguments are passed from the command line as strings of characters, and thus they are the easiest to work with. In the next example, the C++ program expects that the user will enter several names on the command line. To ensure that the user enters several names, if *argc* isn't greater than 2, the user will be returned to the command line with a reminder to try again.

```
//
// sargv.cpp : Defines the entry point for the console application.
// C++ program illustrates how to read string data
// into the program with a command-line argument.
// Copyright (c) Chris H. Pappas and William H. Murray, 2001
//

#include "stdafx.h"
#include <iostream>
```

```
#include <cstdlib>

using namespace std;

int main(int argc, char* argv[])
{
  if( argc < 2 ) {
    cout << "Enter several names on the command line\n";
    cout << "when executing this program!\n";
    cout << "Please try again.\n";
    exit(1);
  }

  for (int t= 1; t < argc; t++)
    cout << "Entry #" << t << " is " << argv[t]<< endl;

  return (0);
}
```

You might have noticed that this program is completely contained in main() and does not use additional functions. The names entered on the command line are printed to the screen in the same order. If numeric values are entered on the command line, they will be interpreted as an ASCII string of individual characters and must be printed as such.

Integral

It is often desirable to be able to enter integer numbers on the command line, perhaps in a program that would find the average of a student's test scores. In such a case, the ASCII character information must be converted to an integer value. The C++ example in this section will accept a single integer number on the command line. Since the number is actually a character string, it will be converted to an integer with the atoi() library function. The command-line value *ivalue* is passed to a function used earlier, called vbinary(). The function will convert the number in *ivalue* to a string of binary digits and print them to the screen. When control is returned to main(), the *ivalue* will be printed in octal and hexadecimal formats:

```
//
// iargv.cpp : Defines the entry point for the console application.
// C++ program illustrates how to read an integer
// into the program with a command-line argument.
// Copyright (c) Chris H. Pappas and William H. Murray, 2001
//
```

```cpp
#include "stdafx.h"
#include <iostream>
#include <cstdlib>

using namespace std;

void vbinary(int idigits);

int main(int argc, char* argv[])
{
  int ivalue;

  if( argc != 2 ) {
    cout << "Enter a decimal number on the command line.\n";
    cout << "It will be converted to binary, octal and\n";
    cout << "hexadecimal.\n";
    exit(1);
  }

  ivalue = atoi(argv[1]);
  vbinary(ivalue);
  cout << "The octal value is: " << oct
       << ivalue << endl;
  cout << "The hexadecimal value is: "
       << hex << ivalue << endl;

  return (0);
}

void vbinary(int idigits)
{
  int t = 0;
  int iyourarray[50];

  while (idigits != 0) {
    iyourarray[t]=(idigits % 2);
    idigits /= 2;
    t++;
  }

  cout << "The binary value is: ";
  for(--t; t >= 0; t--)
```

```
        cout << dec << iyourarray[t];
        cout << endl;
}
```

You might be interested in the formatting of the various numbers. You learned earlier that the binary number is saved in the array and printed one digit at a time, using decimal formatting, by unloading the array *iyourarray* in reverse order:

```
cout << dec << myarray[i];
```

To print the number in octal format, the statement is:

```
cout << "The octal value is: "
    << oct << ivalue << endl;
```

It is also possible to print the hexadecimal equivalent by substituting *hex* for *oct*, as shown here:

```
cout << "The hexadecimal value is: "
    << hex << ivalue << endl;
```

Without additional formatting, the hexadecimal values a, b, c, d, e, and f are printed in lowercase. You'll learn many formatting techniques for C++ in Chapter 11, including how to print those characters in uppercase.

Real

You will find that floats are just as easy as integers to intercept from the command line. The following C++ example will allow several angles to be entered on the command line. The cosine of the angles will be extracted and printed to the screen. Since the angles are of type **float**, they can take on values such as 12.0, 45.78, 0.12345, or 15.

```
//
// fargv.cpp : Defines the entry point for the console application.
// C++ program illustrates how to read float data types
// into the program with a command-line argument.
// Copyright (c) Chris H. Pappas and William H. Murray, 2001
//
```

```
#include "stdafx.h"
#include <iostream>
#include <cmath>
#include <cstdlib>

using namespace std;

const double dPi=3.14159265359;

int main(int argc, char* argv[])
{
  double ddegree;

  if( argc < 2 ) {
    cout << "Type several angles on the command line.\n";
    cout << "Program will calculate and print\n";
    cout << "the cosine of the angles entered.\n";
    exit(1);
  }

  for (int t = 1; t < argc; t++) {
    ddegree = (double) atof(argv[t]);
    cout << "The cosine of " << ddegree
         << "is " << cos((dPi/180.0)*ddegree) << endl;
  }

  return (0);
}
```

The atof() function converts the command-line string argument to a **float** type. The program uses the cos() function within the printf() function to retrieve the cosine information.

Functions in C Versus C++

C++ allows the use of several special features when writing functions. The ability to write inline functions is one such advantage. The code for an inline function is reproduced at the spot where the function is called in the main program. Since the compiler places the code at the point of the function call, execution time is saved when using short, frequently called functions.

C++ also allows function overloading. *Overloading* permits several function prototypes to be given the same function name. The numerous prototypes are then recognized by their type and argument list, not just by their name. Overloading is very useful when a function is required to work with different data types.

When Is a Function a Macro?

Think of the **inline** keyword as a directive or, better yet, a suggestion to the C++ compiler to insert the function inline, similar to a macro, but better—read on. The compiler may ignore this suggestion for any of several reasons. For example, the function might be too long. Inline functions are used primarily to save time when short functions are called many times within a program.

```
//
// inline.cpp : Defines the entry point for the console application.
// C++ program illustrates the use of an inline function.
// Inline functions work best on short functions that are
// used repeatedly. This example calculates the square
// of an integer.
// Copyright (c) Chris H. Pappas and William H. Murray, 2001
//

#include "stdafx.h"
#include <iostream>

using namespace std;

inline long squareit(int iValue) {return iValue * iValue;}

int main(int argc, char* argv[])
{
  int iValue = 5;

  cout << squareit(iValue)
       << endl;

 return (0);
}
```

The function squareit() is declared **inline**, which returns the square of the formal integer argument *iValue*. When the function main() calls function squareit(), the compiler substitutes the function call with the expression *iValue * iValue*. In other words, the compiler replaces the function call with the function's statement and also replaces the function's parameters with the function's arguments.

One advantage of **inline** functions versus macros is error checking. Invoking a macro with the wrong data type goes unchecked by the compiler. However, since an **inline** function has a prototype, the compiler performs type matching between the formal argument type(s) in the prototype and the actual argument(s) in the function call.

Prototyping Multiple Functions with the Same Name

The next example illustrates function overloading. Notice that two functions with the same name are prototyped within the same scope. The correct function will be selected based on the arguments provided. A function call to adder() will process integer or float data correctly:

```cpp
//
// ovrlod.cpp : Defines the entry point for the console application.
// C++ program illustrates function overloading.
// Overloaded function receives an array of integers or
// floats and returns either an integer or float product.
// Copyright (c) Chris H. Pappas and William H. Murray, 2001
//

#include "stdafx.h"
#include <iostream>

using namespace std;

int adder(int iarray[]);
float adder(float farray[]);

int main(int argc, char* argv[])
{
  int iarray[7] = {5,1,6,20,15,0,12};
  float farray[7] = {3.3,5.2,0.05,1.49,3.12345,31.0,2.007};
  int isum;
  float fsum;

  isum = adder(iarray);
  fsum = adder(farray);
  cout << "The sum of the integer numbers is: "
       << isum << endl;
  cout << "The sum of the float numbers is: "
       << fsum << endl;
```

```
   return (0);
}

int adder(int iarray[])
{
  int ipartial;

  ipartial = iarray[0];
  for (int i = 1; i < 7; i++)
    ipartial += iarray[i];
  return (ipartial);
}

float adder(float farray[])
{
  float fpartial;

  fpartial = farray[0];
  for (int i = 1; i < 7; i++)
    fpartial += farray[i];
  return (fpartial);
}
```

There are a few programming snags to function overloading that must be avoided. For example, if a function differs only in the function type and not in the arguments, the function cannot be overloaded. Also, the following attempt at overloading is not permitted:

```
int yourfunction(int number)
int yourfunction(int &value)    //not allowed
```

This syntax is not allowed because each prototype would accept the same type of arguments. Despite these limitations, overloading is a very important topic in C++ and is fully explored starting with Chapter 14.

Functions with Varying Length Formal Argument Lists

For functions with varying length formal argument lists, you'll use the ellipsis. The ellipsis is used when the number of arguments is not known. As such, they can be specified within the function's formal argument statement. For example:

```
void yourfunction(int t,float u,...);
```

This syntax tells the C++ compiler that other arguments may or may not follow *t* and *u*, which are required. Naturally, type checking is suspended with the ellipsis.

The following C++ program demonstrates how to use the ellipsis. You may want to delay an in-depth study of the algorithm, however, until you have a thorough understanding of C++ string pointer types (see Chapters 9 and 10).

```cpp
//
// elip.cpp : Defines the entry point for the console application.
// A C++ program demonstrating the use of ... and its support
// macros va_arg, va_start, and va_end
// Copyright (c) Chris H. Pappas and William H. Murray, 2001
//

#include "stdafx.h"
#include <iostream>
#include <cstdarg>

using namespace std;

void vsmallest(char *szmessage, ...);

int main(int argc, char* argv[])
{
  //sample C printf() syntax
  vsmallest("Print %d integers, %d %d %d",10,4,1);

  return(0);
}

void vsmallest(char *szmessage, ...)
{
  int inumber_of_percent_ds = 0;
  va_list type_for_ellipsis;
  int ipercent_d_format = 'd';
  char *pchar;
  pchar = strchr(szmessage,ipercent_d_format);

  while(*++pchar != '\0') {
    pchar++;
    pchar = strchr(pchar,ipercent_d_format);
    inumber_of_percent_ds++;
  }
```

```
    cout << "Print " << inumber_of_percent_ds << " integers,";

    va_start(type_for_ellipsis,szmessage);

    while(inumber_of_percent_ds--)
      cout << " " << va_arg(type_for_ellipsis,int);

    va_end(type_for_ellipsis);
}
```

The function vsmallest() has been prototyped to expect two arguments, a string pointer, and an argument of type ..., or a varying length argument list. Naturally, functions using a varying length argument list are not omniscient. Something within the argument list must give the function enough information to process the varying part. In elip.cpp, this information comes from the string argument.

In a very crude approach, attempts to mimic the printf() function. The vsmallest() subroutine scans the *szmessage* format string to see how many %ds it finds. It then uses this information to make a calculated fetching and printing of the information in the variable argument. While this sounds straightforward, the algorithm requires a sophisticated sequence of events.

The strchr() function returns the address of the location containing the "d" in %d. The first %d can be ignored since this is required by the output message. The **while** loop continues processing the remainder of the *szmessage* string looking for the variable number of %ds and counting them (*inumber_of_percent_ds*). With this accomplished, the beginning of the output message is printed.

The va_start() macro sets the *type_for_ellipsis* pointer to the beginning of the variable argument list. The va_arg() support macro retrieves the next argument in the variable list. The macro uses its second parameter to know what data type to retrieve; for the example program, this is type **int**. The function vsmallest() terminates with a call to va_end(). The last of the three standard C ellipsis support macros, va_end(), resets the pointer to null.

Things Not to Do with Functions

When variables are used with different scope levels, it is possible to run into completely unexpected programming results, called *side effects*. For example, it is possible to use a variable of the same name with both file and local scopes. The scope rules state that the variable with a local scope (called a *local variable*) will take precedence over the variable with a file scope (called a *global variable*). That all seems easy enough, but let's now consider some problem areas you might encounter in programming that are not so obvious.

Attempting to Access Out of Scope Identifiers

In the following example, four variables are given a local scope within the function main(). Copies of the variables *il* and *im* are passed to the function iproduct(). This does not violate scope rules. However, when the iproduct() function attempts to use the variable *in*, it cannot find the variable. Why? Because the scope of the variable was local to main() only.

```
//
// scopep.cpp : Defines the entry point for the console application.
// C++ program to illustrate problems with scope rules.
// Function is supposed to form a product of three numbers.
// Compiler signals problems since variable n isn't known
// to the function multiplier.
// Copyright (c) Chris H. Pappas and William H. Murray, 2001
//

#include "stdafx.h"
#include <iostream>

using namespace std;

int iproduct(int iw, int ix);

int main(int argc, char* argv[])
{
  int il = 3;
  int im = 7;
  int in = 10;
  int io;

  io = iproduct(il,im);
  cout << "The product of the numbers is: " <<  io;

  return (0);
}

int iproduct(int iw,int ix)
{
  int iy;
```

```
        iy = iw * ix * in;
        return(iy);
}
```

The C++ compiler issues a warning and an error message. It first reports a warning that the *in* variable is never used within the function and then the error message that *in* has never been declared in the function iproduct(). One way around this problem is to give the variable *in* a file scope.

Note   *The Default Warnings setting doesn't give a warning for variables not used in the function (Level 3). Setting to Level 4 gives that warning (and ones about argv, argc as well).*

External Versus Internal Identifier Access

In the following application, the variable *in* is given a file scope. Making *in* global to the whole file allows both main() and iproduct() to use it. Also note that both main() and iproduct() can change the value of the variable. It is good programming practice not to allow functions to change global program variables if they are created to be truly portable.

```
//
// fscope.cpp : Defines the entry point for the console application.
// C++ program to illustrate problems with scope rules.
// Function is supposed to form a product of three numbers.
// Previous problem is solved, c variable is given file
// scope.
// Copyright (c) Chris H. Pappas and William H. Murray, 2001
//

#include "stdafx.h"
#include <iostream>

using namespace std;

int iproduct(int iw, int ix);

int in = 10;

int main(int argc, char* argv[])
{
```

```
  int il = 3;
  int im = 7;
  int io;

  io = iproduct(il,im);
  cout << "The product is: " << io;

  return (0);
}

int iproduct(int iw,int ix)
{
  int iy;

  iy = iw * ix * in;
  return(iy);
}
```

This program will compile correctly and print the product 210 to the screen.

Internal Versus External Identifier Access

The scope rules state that a variable with both file and local scope will use the local variable value over the global value. Here is a small program that illustrates this point:

```
//
// lscope.cpp : Defines the entry point for the console application.
// C++ program to illustrate problems with scope rules.
// Function forms a product of three numbers, but which
// three?  Two are passed as function arguments. The
// variable c has both a file and local scope.
// Copyright (c) Chris H. Pappas and William H. Murray, 2001
//

#include "stdafx.h"
#include <iostream>

using namespace std;

int iproduct(int iw, int ix);

int in = 10;
```

```
int main(int argc, char* argv[])
{
  int il = 3;
  int im = 7;
  int io;

  io = iproduct(il,im);
  cout << "The product of the numbers is: " << io;

  return (0);
}

int iproduct(int iw,int ix)
{
  int iy;
  int in = 2;

  iy = iw * ix * in;
  return(iy);
}
```

In this example, the variable *in* has both file and local scope. When *in* is used within the function iproduct(), the local scope takes precedence and the product of 3 * 7 * 2 = 42 is returned.

It's Legal, but Don't Ever Do It!

In the next C++ example, everything works fine up to the point of printing the information to the screen. The **cout** statement prints the values for *il* and *im* correctly. When selecting the *in* value, it chooses the global variable with file scope. The program reports that the product of 3 * 7 * 10 = 42, which is clearly a mistake. You know that in this case the iproduct() function used the local value of *in*.

```
//
// scoper.cpp : Defines the entry point for the console application.
// C++ program to illustrate problems with scope rules.
// Function forms a product of three numbers. The n
// variable is of local scope and used by function
// product. However, main function reports that
// the n value used is 10. What is wrong here?
// Copyright (c) Chris H. Pappas and William H. Murray, 2001
//
```

```cpp
#include "stdafx.h"
#include <iostream>

using namespace std;

int iproduct(int iw, int ix);

int in = 10;

int main(int argc, char* argv[])
{
  int il = 3;
  int im = 7;
  int io;

  io = iproduct(il,im);
  cout << "The product of " << il <<" * " << im
       << " * " << in << " is: " << io << endl;

  return (0);
}

int iproduct(int iw,int ix)
{
  int iy;
  int in = 2;

  iy = iw * ix * in;
  return(iy);
}
```

If you actually wanted to form the product with the global value of *in*, how could this conflict be resolved? C++ would permit you to use the scope resolution operator mentioned earlier in the chapter, as shown here:

```cpp
iy = iw * ix * ::in;
```

Overriding Internal Precedence

In this example, the scope resolution operator (::) is used to avoid conflicts between a variable with both file and local scope. The last program reported an incorrect product since the local value was used in the calculation. Notice in the following listing that the iproduct() function uses the scope resolution operator:

```cpp
//
// gscope.cpp : Defines the entry point for the console application.
// C++ program to illustrate problems with scope rules,
// and how to use the scope resolution operator.
// Function product uses resolution operator to "override"
// local scope and utilize variable with file scope.
// Copyright (c) Chris H. Pappas and William H. Murray, 2001
//

#include "stdafx.h"
#include <iostream>

using namespace std;

int iproduct(int iw, int ix);

int in = 10;

int main(int argc, char* argv[])
{
  int il = 3;
  int im = 7;
  int io;

  io = iproduct(il,im);
  cout << "The product of " << il <<" * " << im
       << " * " << in << " is: " << io;

  return (0);
}

int iproduct(int iw,int ix)
{
  int iy;
  int in = 2;

  iy = iw * ix * ::in;
  return(iy);
}
```

The scope resolution operator need not be enclosed in parentheses, as they were used for emphasis in this example. Now, the value of the global variable, with file scope, will be used in the calculation. When the results are printed to the screen, you will see that 3 * 7 * 10 = 210.

The scope resolution operator is very important in C++. Additional examples illustrating the resolution operator are given starting with Chapter 16.

What's Coming?

In this chapter, you learned the fundamental principles and syntax necessary to define C/C++ functions. Along the way you examined some of the more frequently used cmath library routines and the nuances of the main() arguments *argc* and *argv[]*. The good news is that most of this learning maps over directly to C++ class methods! In the next chapter, you will combine your new understanding of function syntax with the interesting way arrays are passed and processed in subroutines.

Chapter 9

Working with Arrays

I n C and C++, the topics of arrays, pointers, and strings are all related. In this chapter you learn how to define and use arrays. Many C/C++ books combine the topics of arrays and pointers into one discussion. This is unfortunate because there are many uses for arrays in C and C++ that are not dependent on a detailed understanding of pointers. Also, since there is a great deal of material to cover about arrays in general, it is best not to confuse the topic with a discussion of pointers. Pointers, however, allow you to fully comprehend just how an array is processed. Chapter 10 examines the topic of pointers and completes this chapter's discussion of arrays.

What Are Arrays?

Think of *arrays* as variables containing several homogeneous data types. Each individual data item can be accessed by using a subscript, or index, into the variable. In the C and C++ languages, an array is not a standard data type; instead, it is an aggregate type made up of any other type of data. It is possible to have an array of anything: characters, integers, floats, doubles, arrays, pointers, structures, and so on. The concept of arrays and their use is basically the same in both C and C++.

Array Properties

There are four basic properties to an array:

- The individual data items in the array are called *elements*.
- All elements must be of the same data type.
- All elements are stored contiguously in the computer's memory, and the subscript (or index) of the first element is zero.
- The name of the array is a constant value that represents the address of the first element in the array.

Since all elements of an array are assumed to be the same size, arrays cannot be defined by using mixed data types. Without this assumption, it would be very difficult to determine where any given element was stored. Since the elements are all the same size and because that fact is used to help determine how to locate a given element, it follows that the elements are stored contiguously in the computer's memory (with the lowest address corresponding to the first element, the highest address to the last element). This means that there is no filler space between elements and that they are physically adjacent in the computer.

It is possible to have arrays within arrays, that is, multidimensional arrays. Actually, if an array element is a structure (which will be covered in Chapter 13), then mixed data types can exist in the array by existing inside the structure member.

The name of an array represents a constant value that cannot change during the execution of the program. For this reason, arrays can never be used as *lvalues*. *lvalues* represent storage locations that can have their contents altered by the program; they frequently appear to the left of assignment statements. If array names were legal *lvalues*, your program could change their contents. The effect would be to change the starting address of the array itself. This may seem like a small thing, but some forms of expressions that might appear valid on the surface are not allowed. All programmers eventually learn these subtleties, but it helps if you understand why these differences exist.

Array Declarations

The following are examples of array declarations:

```
int  iarray[12];  // an array of twelve integers
char carray[20];  // an array of twenty characters
```

As is true with all data declarations, an array's declaration begins with its data type, followed by a valid array name and a pair of matching square brackets enclosing a constant expression. The constant expression defines the size of the array. It is illegal to use a variable name inside the square brackets. For this reason it is not possible to avoid specifying the array size until the program executes. The expression must reduce to a constant value so that the compiler knows exactly how much storage space to reserve for the array.

It is best to use defined constants to specify the size of the array:

```
#define iARRAY_MAX 20
#define fARRAY_MAX 15

int iarray[iARRAY_MAX];
float farray[fARRAY_MAX];
```

Use of defined constants guarantees that subsequent references to the array will not exceed the defined array size. For example, it is very common to use a **for** loop to access array elements:

```
#include <iostream>
using namespace std;

#define iARRAY_MAX 20
```

```
int iarray[iARRAY_MAX];

int main(int argc, char* argv[])
{
  int i;
  for(i = 0; i < iARRAY_MAX; i++) {
  .
  .
  .
  }
  return(0);
}
```

Initializing Arrays

There are three techniques for initializing arrays:

- By default when they are created. This applies only to global and static arrays.
- Explicitly when they are created, by supplying constant initializing data.
- During program execution when you assign or copy data into the array.

You can only use constant data to initialize an array when it is created. If the array elements must receive their values from variables, you must initialize the array by writing explicit statements as part of the program code.

Default Initialization

The ANSI C++ standard specifies that arrays are either global (defined outside of main() and any other function) or static automatic (static, but defined after any opening brace) and will always be initialized to binary zero if no other initialization data is supplied. C/C++ initializes numeric arrays to zero. Pointer arrays are initialized to null. You can run the following program to make certain that a compiler meets this standard:

```
//
// initar.cpp : Defines the entry point for the console application.
// A C++ program verifying array initialization
// Copyright (c) Chris H. Pappas and William H. Murray, 2001
//

#include "stdafx.h"
#include <iostream>
using namespace std;
```

```
#define iGLOBAL_ARRAY_SIZE 10
#define iSTATIC_ARRAY_SIZE 20

int iglobal_array[iGLOBAL_ARRAY_SIZE];            // a global array

int main(int argc, char* argv[])
{
  static int istatic_array[iSTATIC_ARRAY_SIZE]; // a static array
  cout << "iglobal_array[0]: " << iglobal_array[0] << endl;
  cout << "istatic_array[0]: " << istatic_array[0] << endl;

  return 0;
}
```

When the program is run, you should see zeros printed verifying that both array types are automatically initialized. This program also highlights another very important point: the first subscript for all arrays in C++ is zero. Unlike other languages, there is no way to make a C++ program think that the first subscript is 1. If you are wondering why, remember that one of C++'s strengths is its close link to assembly language. In assembly language, the first element in a table is always at the zeroth offset.

Explicit Initialization

Just as you can define and initialize variables of type **int**, **char**, **float**, **double**, and so on, you can also initialize arrays. The ANSI C++ standard lets you supply initialization values for any array, global or otherwise, defined anywhere in a program. The following code segment illustrates how to define and initialize four arrays:

```
int iarray[3] = {-1,0,1};
static float fpercent[4] = {1.141579,0.75,55E0,-.33E1};
static int idecimal[3] = {0,1,2,3,4,5,6,7,8,9};
char cvowels[] = {'A','a','E','e','I','i','O','o','U','u'};
```

The first line of code declares the *iarray* array to be three integers and provides the values of the elements in curly braces, separated by commas. As usual, a semicolon ends the statement. The effect of this is that after the compiled program loads into the memory of the computer, the reserved space for the *iarray* array will already contain the initial values, so they won't need assignments when the program executes. It is important to realize that this is more than just a convenience—it happens at a different time. If the program goes on to change the values of the *iarray* array, they stay changed. Many compilers permit you to initialize arrays only if they are global or static, as in the second line of code. This statement initializes the array *fpercent* when the entire program loads.

The third line of code illustrates putting the wrong count in the array declaration. Many compilers consider this an error, while others reserve enough space to hold whichever is greater—the number of values you ask for or the number of values you provide. This example will draw complaints from the Visual C/C++ compiler by way of an error message indicating too many initializers. In the opposite case, when you ask for more space than you provide values for, the values go into the beginning of the array and the extra elements become zeros. This also means that you do not need to count the values when you provide all of them. If the count is empty, as in the fourth line of code, the number of values determines the size of the array.

Unsized Initialization

You can provide the size of the array or the list of actual array values. It usually doesn't matter for most compilers, as long as you provide at least one of them. For example, a program will frequently want to define its own set of error messages. This can be done two ways. Here is the first method:

```
char szInput_Error[37] = "Please enter a value between 0 - 9:\n";
char szDevice_Error[16] = "Disk not ready\n";
char szMonitor_Error[32] = "Program needs a color monitor.\n";
char szWarning[44] = "This operation will erase the active file!\n";
```

This method requires you to count the number of characters in the string, remembering to add 1 to the count for the unseen null-string terminator \0. This can become a very tedious approach at best, straining the eyes as you count the number of characters, and very error prone. The second method allows C++ to automatically dimension the arrays through the use of unsized arrays, as shown here:

```
char szInput_Error[] = "Please enter a value between 0 - 9:\n";
char szDevice_Error[] = "Disk not ready\n";
char szMonitor_Error[] = "Program needs a color monitor.\n";
char szWarning[] = "This operation will erase the active file!\n";
```

When an array initialization statement is encountered and the array size is not specified, the compiler automatically creates an array big enough to hold all of the specified data.

There are a few major pitfalls that await the inexperienced programmer when initializing arrays. For example, an array with an empty size declaration and no list of values has a null length. If there are any data declarations after the array, then the name of the null array refers to the same address, and storing values in the null array puts them in addresses allocated to other variables.

Unsized array initializations are not restricted to one-dimensional arrays. For multidimensional arrays, you must specify all but the leftmost dimension for C++ to properly index the array. With this approach you can build tables of varying lengths, with the compiler automatically allocating enough storage.

Accessing Array Elements

A variable declaration usually reserves one or more cells in internal memory and, through a lookup table, associates a name with the cell or cells that you can use to access the cells. For example, the following definition reserves only one integer-sized cell in internal memory and associates the name *ivideo_tapes* with that cell. See the top of Figure 9-1.

```
int ivideo_tapes;
```

On the other hand, the next definition reserves seven contiguous cells in internal memory and associates the name *ivideo_library* with the seven cells. See the bottom of Figure 9-1.

```
int ivideo_library[7];
```

Since all array elements must be of the same data type, each of the seven cells in the array *ivideo_library* can hold one integer.

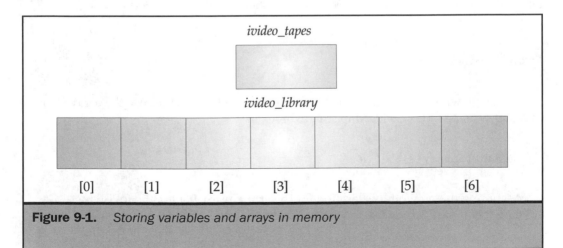

Figure 9-1.   *Storing variables and arrays in memory*

Consider the difference between accessing the single cell associated with the variable *ivideo_tapes* and the seven cells associated with the array *ivideo_library*. To access the cell associated with the variable *ivideo_tapes*, you simply use the name *ivideo_tapes*. For the array *ivideo_library*, you must specify an *index* to indicate exactly which cell among the seven you wish to access. The following statements designate the first cell, the second cell, the third cell, and so on, up to the last cell of the array:

```
ivideo_library[0];
ivideo_library[1];
ivideo_library[2];
ivideo_library[3];
           .
           .
           .
ivideo_library[6];
```

When accessing an array element, the integer enclosed in the square brackets is the index, which indicates the *offset*, or the distance between the cell to be accessed and the first cell.

One of the principal mistakes novice programmers make has to do with the index value used to reference an array's first element. The first element is not at index position [1]; instead, it is [0] since there is zero distance between the first element and itself. The third cell has an index value of 2 because its distance from the first cell is 2.

When working with arrays, you can use the square brackets in two very different ways. When you are defining an array, the number of cells is specified in square brackets:

```
int ivideo_library[7];
```

However, when you are accessing a specific array element, you use the array's name together with an index enclosed in square brackets:

```
ivideo_library[3];
```

Assuming the previous declaration for the array *ivideo_library*, the following statement is logically incorrect:

```
ivideo_library[7] = 53219;
```

It is not a legal reference to a cell under the name *ivideo_library*. The statement attempts to reference a cell that is a distance of 7 from the first cell, that is, the eighth cell. Because there are only seven cells, this is an error. It is up to you to ensure that index expressions remain within the array's bounds.

Examine the following declarations:

```
#define iDAYS_OF_WEEK 7

int ivideo_library[iDAYS_OF_WEEK];
int iweekend = 1;
int iweekday = 2;
```

Take a look at what happens with this set of executable statements:

```
ivideo_library[2];
ivideo_library[iweekday];
ivideo_library[iweekend + iweekday];
ivideo_library[iweekday - iweekend];
ivideo_library[iweekend - iweekday];
```

The first two statements both reference the third element of the array. The first statement accomplishes this with a constant value expression, while the second statement uses a variable. The last three statements demonstrate that you can use expressions as subscripts, as long as they evaluate to a valid integer index. Statement three has an index value of 3 and references the fourth element of the array. The fourth statement, with an index value of 1, accesses the second element of the array. The last statement is illegal because the index value -1 is invalid.

It is also possible to access any element in an array without knowing how big each element is. For example, suppose you want to access the third element in *ivideo_library*, an array of integers. Remember from Chapter 6 that different systems allocate different size cells to the same data type. On one computer system, an integer might occupy 2 bytes of storage, whereas on another system, an integer might occupy 8 bytes of storage. On either system, you can access the third element as *ivideo_library[2]*. The index value indicates the number of elements to move, regardless of the number of bits allocated.

This offset addressing holds true for other array types. On one system, integer variables might require twice as many bits of storage as does a **char** type; on another system, integer variables might require four times as many bits as do character variables. Yet to access the fourth element in either an array of integers or an array of characters, you would use an index value of 3.

Calculating Array Dimensions

You have already learned that the sizeof() operator returns the physical size, in bytes, of the data object to which it is applied. You can use it with any type of data object except bit-fields. A frequent use of sizeof() is to determine the physical size of a variable when the size of the variable's data type can vary from machine to machine. You have already seen how an integer can be either 2 or 4 bytes, depending on the machine being used. If an additional amount of memory to hold seven integers will be requested from the operating system, some way is needed to determine whether 14 bytes (7x2 bytes/integer) or 28 bytes (7x4 bytes/integer) are needed. The following program automatically takes this into consideration (and prints a value of 28 for systems allocating 4 bytes per integer cell):

```
//
// sizeof.cpp : Defines the entry point for the console application.
// A C++ program applying sizeof() to determine an array's size
// Copyright (c) Chris H. Pappas and William H. Murray, 2001
//

#include "stdafx.h"
#include <iostream>
using namespace std;

#define iDAYS_OF_WEEK 7

int main(int argc, char* argv[])
{
  int ivideo_library[iDAYS_OF_WEEK]={1,2,3,4,5,6,7};

  cout << "There are " << (int)sizeof(ivideo_library)
       << " number of bytes in the array" << endl;

  return 0;
}
```

This concept becomes essential when the program must be portable and independent of any particular hardware. If you are wondering why there is an **int** type cast on the result returned by sizeof(), in the ANSI C++ standard sizeof() does not return an **int** type. Instead, sizeof() returns a data type, **size_t**, that is large enough to hold the return value. The ANSI C+ standard added this to C++ because on certain computers an integer is not big enough to represent the size of all data items. Had the example program been written in C, casting the return value to an integer would allow the value to match a %d

C format specifier for the printf() function. By changing *iarray*'s data type in the following program, you can explore how various data types are stored internally:

```
//
// array.cpp : Defines the entry point for the console application.
// A C++ program illustrating contiguous array storage
// Copyright (c) Chris H. Pappas and William H. Murray, 2001
//

#include "stdafx.h"
#include <iostream>
using namespace std;

#define iMAX 10

int main(int argc, char* argv[])
{
  int index, iarray[iMAX];

  cout << "sizeof(int) is " << (int)sizeof(int) << "\n\n";

  for(index = 0; index < iMAX; index++)
    cout << "&iarray[" << index << "] = " << index
         << &iarray[index] << endl;

    return 0;
}
```

If the program is run on a machine with a word length of 4 bytes, the output will look similar to the following:

```
sizeof(int) is 4

&iarray[0] = 00012FEA8
&iarray[1] = 10012FEAC
&iarray[2] = 20012FEB0
&iarray[3] = 30012FEB4
&iarray[4] = 40012FEB8
&iarray[5] = 50012FEBC
&iarray[6] = 60012FEC0
&iarray[7] = 70012FEC4
&iarray[8] = 80012FEC8
&iarray[9] = 90012FECC
```

PROGRAMMING
FOUNDATIONS

Notice how the & (address) operator can be applied to any variable, including an array element. An array element can be treated like any other variable; its value can form an expression, it can be assigned a value, and it can be passed as an argument (or parameter) to a function. In this example you can see how the array elements' addresses are exactly 4 bytes apart. You will see the importance of this contiguous storage when you use arrays in conjunction with pointer variables.

Array Index Out of Bounds

There is a popular saying that states, "You don't get something for nothing." This holds true with array types. The "something" you get is faster executing code at the expense of the "nothing," which is zero boundary checking. Remember, since C and C++ were designed to replace assembly language code, error checking was left out of the compiler to keep the code lean. Without any compiler error checking, you must be very careful when dealing with array boundaries. For example, the following program elicits no complaints from the compiler, yet it can change the contents of other variables or even crash the program by writing beyond the array's boundary:

```cpp
//
// norun.cpp
// Do NOT run this C++ program
// Copyright (c) Chris H. Pappas and William H. Murray, 2001
//

#include "stdafx.h"
#include <iostream>
using namespace std;

#define iMAX 10
#define iOUT_OF_RANGE 50

int main(int argc, char* argv[])
{
  int inot_enough_room[iMAX], index;

  for(index=0; index < iOUT_OF_RANGE; index++)
    inot_enough_room[index]=index;

  return(0);
}
```

Output and Input of Strings

While C and C++ do supply the data type **char**, they do not have a data type for character strings. Instead, the programmer must represent a string as an array of characters. The array uses one cell for each character in the string, with the final cell holding the null character \0.

The next example, written in C, shows how you can represent the three major types of transportation as a character string. The array *szmode1* is initialized character by character by use of the assignment operator, the array *szmode2* is initialized by use of the function scanf(), and the array *szmode3* is initialized in the following definition. The coded C example is presented here to contrast the subtle syntax changes necessary when performing string I/O in C versus C++:

```c
/*
 * string.c
 * This C program demonstrates the use of strings.
 * Implemented using "old-style" C syntax.
 * Copyright (c) Chris H. Pappas and William H. Murray, 2001
 */

#include <stdio.h>

int main()
{
  char        szmode1[4],              /* car   */
              szmode2[6];              /* plane */
  static char szmode3[5] = "ship";     /* ship  */

  szmode1[0] = 'c';
  szmode1[1] = 'a';
  szmode1[2] = 'r';
  szmode1[3] = '\0';

  printf("\n\n\tPlease enter the mode --> plane ");
  scanf("%s",szmode2);

  printf("%s\n",szmode1);
  printf("%s\n",szmode2);
  printf("%s\n",szmode3);

  return(0);
}
```

The next definitions show how C and C++ treat character strings as arrays of characters:

```
char    szmode1[4],                     /* car    */
        szmode2[6];                     /* plane */
static char szmode3[5] = "ship";        /* ship   */
```

Even though the *szmode1* "car" has three characters, the array *szmode1* has four cells—one cell for each letter in the mode "car" and one for the null character. Remember, \0 counts as one character. Similarly, the mode "plane" has five characters ("ship" has four) but requires six storage cells (five for *szmode3*), including the null character. Remember, you could also have initialized the *szmode3[5]* array of characters by using braces:

```
static char szmode3[5] = {'s','h','i','p','\0'};
```

When you use double quotes to list the initial values of the character array, the system will automatically add the null terminator \0. Also, remember that the same line could have been written like this:

```
static char szmode3[] = "ship";
```

This uses an unsized array. Of course, you could have chosen the tedious approach to initializing an array of characters that was done with *szmode1*. A more common approach is to use the scanf() function to read the string directly into the array as was done with *szmode2*. The scanf() function uses a *%s* conversion specification. This causes the function to skip white space (blanks, tabs, and carriage returns) and then to read into the character array *szmode2* all characters up to the next white space. The system will then automatically add a null terminator. Remember, the array's dimension must be large enough to hold the string along with a null terminator. Look at this statement one more time:

```
scanf("%s",szmode2);
```

Are you bothered by the fact that *szmode2* was not preceded by the address operator &? While it is true that scanf() was written to expect the address of a variable, as it turns out, an array's name, unlike simple variable names, is an address expression—the address of the first element in the array.

When you use the printf() function in conjunction with a *%s*, the function is expecting the corresponding argument to be the address of some character string. The string is printed up to, but not including, the null character.

The following listing illustrates these principles by using an equivalent C++ algorithm:

```cpp
//
// string.cpp : Defines the entry point for the console application.
// This C++ program demonstrates the use of strings
// Copyright (c) Chris H. Pappas and William H. Murray, 2001
//

#include "stdafx.h"
#include <iostream>
using namespace std;

int main(int argc, char* argv[])
{
  char          szmode1[4],              // car
                szmode2[6];              // plane
  static char szmode3[5] = "ship";       // ship

  szmode1[0] = 'c';
  szmode1[1] = 'a';
  szmode1[2] = 'r';
  szmode1[3] = '\0';

  cout << "\n\n\tPlease enter the mode -->> plane ";
  cin >> szmode2;

  cout << szmode1 << "\n";
  cout << szmode2 << "\n";
  cout << szmode3 << "\n";

  return(0);
}
```

The output from the program looks like this:

```
car
plane
ship
```

Multidimensional Arrays

The term *dimension* represents the number of indexes used to reference a particular element in an array. All of the arrays discussed so far have been one-dimensional and require only one index to access an element. By looking at an array's declaration, you can tell how many dimensions it has. If there is only one set of brackets ([ ]), the array is one-dimensional; two sets of brackets ([ ][ ]) indicate a two-dimensional array, and so on. Arrays of more than one dimension are called *multidimensional arrays*. For real-world modeling, the working maximum number of dimensions is usually three.

The following declarations set up a two-dimensional array that is initialized while the program executes:

```
//
// 2darray.cpp : Defines the entry point for the console application.
// A C++ program demonstrating the use of a two-dimensional array
// Copyright (c) Chris H. Pappas and William H. Murray, 2001
//

#include "stdafx.h"
#include <iostream>
using namespace std;

#define iROWS 4
#define iCOLUMNS 5

int main(int argc, char* argv[])
{
  int irow;
  int icolumn;
  int istatus[iROWS][iCOLUMNS];
  int iadd;
  int imultiple;

  for(irow=0; irow < iROWS; irow++)
    for(icolumn=0; icolumn < iCOLUMNS; icolumn++) {
      iadd = iCOLUMNS - icolumn;
      imultiple = irow;
      istatus[irow][icolumn] = (irow+1) *
        icolumn + iadd * imultiple;
    }
```

```
for(irow=0; irow<iROWS; irow++) {
  cout << "CURRENT ROW: " << irow << endl;
  cout << "RELATIVE DISTANCE FROM BASE: " << endl;
  for(icolumn=0; icolumn<iCOLUMNS; icolumn++)
    cout << " " << istatus[irow][icolumn];
  cout << "\n\n";
}

return(0);
}
```

The program uses two **for** loops to calculate and initialize each of the array elements to its respective "offset from the first element." The created array has 4 rows (*iROWS*) and 5 columns (*iCOLUMNS*) per row, for a total of 20 integer elements. Multidimensional arrays are stored in linear fashion in the computer's memory. Elements in multi-dimensional arrays are grouped from the rightmost index inward. In the preceding example, row 1, column 1 would be element three of the storage array. Although the calculation of the offset appears a little tricky, note how easily each array element itself is referenced:

```
istatus[irow][icolumn] = . . .
```

The output from the program looks like this:

```
CURRENT ROW: 0
RELATIVE DISTANCE FROM BASE:
 0  1  2  3  4

CURRENT ROW: 1
RELATIVE DISTANCE FROM BASE:
 5  6  7  8  9

CURRENT ROW: 2
RELATIVE DISTANCE FROM BASE:
 10  11  12  13  14

CURRENT ROW: 3
RELATIVE DISTANCE FROM BASE:
 15  16  17  18  19
```

PROGRAMMING FOUNDATIONS

Multidimensional arrays can also be initialized in the same way as one-dimensional arrays. For example, the following program defines a two-dimensional array *dpowers* and initializes the array when it is defined. The function pow() returns the value of *x* raised to the *y* power:

```
//
// 2dadbl.cpp : Defines the entry point for the console application.
// A C++ program using a 2-dimensional array of doubles
// Copyright (c) Chris H. Pappas and William H. Murray, 2001
//

#include "stdafx.h"
#include <cmath>
#include <iostream>
using namespace std;

#define iBASES 6
#define iEXPONENTS 3
#define iBASE 0
#define iRAISED_TO 1
#define iRESULT 2

int main(int argc, char *argv[])
{
  double dpowers[iBASES][iEXPONENTS]={
    1.1, 1, 0,
    2.2, 2, 0,
    3.3, 3, 0,
    4.4, 4, 0,
    5.5, 5, 0,
    6.6, 6, 0
  };

  int irow_index;

  for(irow_index=0; irow_index < iBASES; irow_index++)
    dpowers[irow_index][iRESULT] =
      pow(dpowers[irow_index][iBASE],
      dpowers[irow_index][iRAISED_TO]);

  for(irow_index=0; irow_index < iBASES; irow_index++) {
```

```
    cout << "    " << (int)dpowers[irow_index][iRAISED_TO]
        << endl;
    cout << " " << dpowers[irow_index][iBASE]
        << " = " << dpowers[irow_index][iRESULT]
        << "\n\n";
}

return(0);
}
```

The array *dpowers* was declared to be of type **double** because the function pow() expects two double variables and returns a double. Of course, you must take care when initializing two-dimensional arrays; you must make certain you know which dimension is increasing the fastest. Remember, this is always the rightmost dimension.

The output from the program looks like this:

```
    1
1.1 = 1.1

    2
2.2 = 4.84

    3
3.3 = 35.937

    4
4.4 = 374.81

    5
5.5 = 5032.84

    6
6.6 = 82654
```

Arrays as Function Arguments

Just like other variables, arrays can be passed from one function to another. Because arrays as function arguments can be discussed in full only after an introduction to pointers, this chapter begins the topic and Chapter 10 expands upon this base.

Passing Arrays to C++ Functions

Consider a function isum() that computes the sum of the array elements *inumeric_values[0], inumeric_values[1],..., numeric_values[n]*. Two parameters are required—an array parameter called *iarray_address_received* to hold a copy of the array's address and a parameter called *imax_size* to hold the index of the last item in the array to be summed. Assuming that the array is an array of integers and that the index is also of type **int**, the parameters in isum() can be described as:

```
int isum(int iarray_address_received[], int imax_size)
```

The parameter declaration for the array includes square brackets to signal the function isum() that *iarray_address_received* is an array name and not the name of an ordinary parameter. Note that the number of cells is not enclosed in the square brackets. Of course, the simple parameter *imax_size* is declared as previously described. Invoking the function is as simple as this:

```
isum(inumeric_values,iactual_index);
```

Passing the array *inumeric_values* is a simple process of entering its name as the argument. When passing an array's name to a function, you are actually passing the *address* of the array's first element. Look at the following expression:

```
inumeric_values
is really shorthand for
&inumeric_values[0]
```

Technically, you can invoke the function isum() with either of the following two valid statements:

```
isum(inumeric_values,iactual_index);
itotal = isum(&inumeric_values[0],iactual_index);
```

In either case, within the function isum() you can access every cell in the array.

When a function is going to process an array, the calling function includes the name of the array in the function's argument list. This means that the function receives and carries out its processing on the actual elements of the array, not on a local copy as in single-value variables where functions pass only their values.

By default all arrays are passed call-by-variable or call-by-reference. This prevents the frequent "stack overruns heap" error message many Pascal programmers encounter if they have forgotten to include the **var** modifier for formal array argument declarations. In contrast, the Pascal language passes all array arguments call-by-value. A call-by-value forces the compiler to duplicate the array's contents. For large arrays, this is time consuming and wastes memory.

When a function is to receive an array name as an argument, there are two ways to declare the argument locally: as an array or as a pointer. Which one you use depends on how the function processes the set of values. If the function steps through the elements with an index, the declaration should be an array with square brackets following the name. The size can be empty since the declaration does not reserve space for the entire array, just for the address where it begins. Having seen the array declaration at the beginning of the function, the compiler then permits brackets with an index to appear after the array name anywhere in the function.

The following example declares an array of five elements, and after printing its values, calls in a function to determine what the smallest value in the array is. To do this, it passes the array name and its size to the function iminimum(), which declares them as an array called *iarray[]* and an integer called *isize*. The function then passes through the array, comparing each element against the smallest value it has seen so far, and every time it encounters a smaller value, it stores that new value in the variable *icurrent_minimum*. At the end, it returns the smallest value it has seen for the main() to print.

```
//
// fncarray.cpp : Defines the entry point for the console application.
// A C++ program demonstrating how to use arrays with functions
// Copyright (c) Chris H. Pappas and William H. Murray, 2001
//

#include "stdafx.h"
#include <iostream>
using namespace std;

#define iSIZE 5
void vadd_1(int iarray[]);

int main(int argc, char* argv[])
{
  int iarray[iSIZE]={0,1,2,3,4};
  int i;

  cout << "iarray before calling add_1:\n\n";
  for(i=0; i < iSIZE; i++)
    cout << "  " << iarray[i];
```

PROGRAMMING
FOUNDATIONS

```
   vadd_1(iarray);

  cout << "\n\niarray after calling add_1:\n\n";
  for(i=0; i < iSIZE; i++)
    cout << "   " << iarray[i];

  return(0);
}


void vadd_1(int iarray[])
{
  int i;

  for(i=0; i < iSIZE; i++)
    iarray[i]++;
}
```

The output from the program looks like this:

```
iarray before calling add_1:

  0  1  2  3  4

iarray after calling add_1:

  1  2  3  4  5
```

Here is a question you should be able to answer. What do the values in the output tell you about the array argument? Is the array passed call-by-value or call-by-reference? The function vadd_1() simply adds 1 to each array element. Since this incremented change is reflected back in main() *iarray,* it would appear that the parameter was passed call-by-reference. Previous discussions about what an array name really is indicate that this is true. Remember, array names are addresses to the first array cell.

The following C++ program incorporates many of the array features discussed so far, including multidimensional array initialization, referencing, and arguments:

```
//
// 2darray2.cpp : Defines the entry point for the console application.
// A C++ program that demonstrates how to define, pass,
```

```
// and walk through the different dimensions of an array
// Copyright (c) Chris H. Pappas and William H. Murray, 2001
//

#include <stdafx.h>
#include <iostream>
using namespace std;

void vdisplay_results(char carray[][3][4]);

char cglobal_cube[5][4][5]= {
                {
                  {'P','L','A','N','E'},
                  {'Z','E','R','O',' '},
                  {' ',' ',' ',' ',' '},
                  {'R','O','W',' ','3'},
                },
                {
                  {'P','L','A','N','E'},
                  {'O','N','E',' ',' '},
                  {'R','O','W',' ','2'}
                },
                {
                  {'P','L','A','N','E'},
                  {'T','W','O',' ',' '}
                },
                {
                  {'P','L','A','N','E'},
                  {'T','H','R','E','E'},
                  {'R','O','W',' ','2'},
                  {'R','O','W',' ','3'}
                },
                {
                  {'P','L','A','N','E'},
                  {'F','O','U','R',' '},
                  {'r','o','w',' ','2'},
                  {'a','b','c','d','e'}
                }
};

int imatrix[4][3]={ {1},{2},{3},{4} };
```

```cpp
main()
{
  int irow_index, icolumn_index;
  char clocal_cube[2][3][4];

  cout << "sizeof clocal_cube        = "<< sizeof(clocal_cube)
                                        << "\n";
  cout << "sizeof clocal_cube[0]     = "<< sizeof(clocal_cube[0])
                                        << "\n";
  cout << "sizeof clocal_cube[0][0]  = "<<
          sizeof(clocal_cube[0][0])     << "\n";
  cout << "sizeof clocal_cube[0][0][0] = "<<
          sizeof(clocal_cube[0][0][0])  << "\n";

  vdisplay_results(clocal_cube);

  cout << "cglobal_cube[0][1][2] is   = "
       << cglobal_cube[0][1][2] << "\n";
  cout << "cglobal_cube[1][0][2] is   = "
       << cglobal_cube[1][0][2] << "\n";

  cout << "\nprint part of the cglobal_cube's plane 0\n";
  for(irow_index=0; irow_index < 4; irow_index++) {
    for(icolumn_index=0; icolumn_index < 5; icolumn_index++)
      cout << cglobal_cube[0][irow_index][icolumn_index];
    cout << "\n";
  }

  cout << "\nprint part of the cglobal_cube's plane 4\n";
  for(irow_index=0; irow_index < 4; irow_index++) {
    for(icolumn_index=0; icolumn_index < 5; icolumn_index++)
      cout << cglobal_cube[4][irow_index][icolumn_index];
    cout << "\n";
  }

  cout << "\nprint all of imatrix\n";
  for(irow_index=0; irow_index < 4; irow_index++) {
    for(icolumn_index=0; icolumn_index < 3; icolumn_index++)
      cout << imatrix[irow_index][icolumn_index];
    cout << "\n";
  }
```

```
   return (0);
}

void vdisplay_results(char carray[][3][4])
{
cout << "sizeof carray              = " << sizeof(carray) << "\n";
cout << "sizeof carray[0]           = " << sizeof(carray[0]) << "\n";
cout << "sizeof cglobal_cube        = " << sizeof(cglobal_cube) << "\n";
cout << "sizeof cglobal_cube[0]     = " << sizeof(cglobal_cube[0])
                                        << "\n";

}
```

Notice, first, how *cglobal_cube* is defined and initialized. Braces are used to group the characters together so that they have a form similar to the dimensions of the array. This helps in visualizing the form of the array. The braces are not required in this case since you are not leaving any gaps in the array with the initializing data. If you were initializing only a portion of any dimension, various sets of the inner braces would be required to designate which initializing values should apply to which part of the array. The easiest way to visualize the three-dimensional array is to imagine five layers, each having a two-dimensional, four-row by five-column array (see Figure 9-2).

The first four lines of the program output show the size of the *clocal_cube* array, various dimensions, and an individual element. The output illustrates how the total size of the multidimensional array is the product of all the dimensions times the size of the array data type, that is, 2 * 3 * 4 * *sizeof(char)*, or 24.

Observe how the array element *clocal_cube[0]* is in itself an array that contains a two-dimensional array of [3][4], thereby giving *clocal_cube[0]* the size of 12. The size of *clocal_cube[0][0]* is 4, which is the number of elements in the final dimension since each element has a size of 1, as the *sizeof(clocal_cube[0][0][0])* shows.

To fully understand multidimensional arrays, it is very important to realize that *clocal_cube[0]* is both an array name and a pointer constant. Because the program did not subscript the last dimension, the expression does not have the same type as the data type of each fundamental array element. Because *clocal_cube[0]* does not refer to an individual element, but rather to another array, it does not have the type of **char**. Since *clocal_cube[0]* has the type of pointer constant, it is not a legal *lvalue* and cannot appear to the left of an assignment operator in an assignment expression.

Something very interesting happens when you use an array name in a function argument list, as was done when the function *vdisplay_results()* was invoked with *clocal_cube*. While inside the function, if you perform a sizeof() operation against the formal parameter that represents the array name, you do not correctly compute the actual size of *carray*. What the function sees is only a copy of the address of the first element in the array. Therefore, the function sizeof() will return the size of the address, not the item to which it refers.

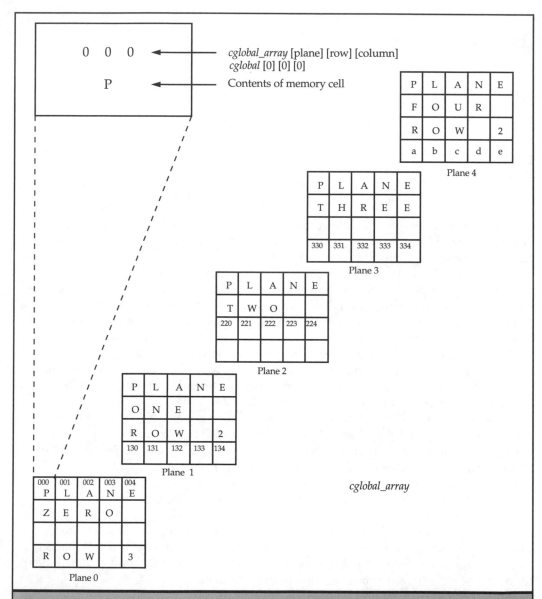

Figure 9-2.   *Conceptual view of the array* cglobal_cube

The sizeof() *carray[0]* in function *vdisplay_results()* is 12 because it was declared in the function that the formal parameter was an array whose last two dimensions were [3] and [4]. You could not have used any values when you declared the size of these last two dimensions because the function prototype defined them to be [3] and [4]. Without a prototype, the compiler would not be able to detect the difference in the way the array was dimensioned. This would let you redefine the way in which you viewed the array's organization. The function *vdisplay_results()* also outputs the size of the global *cglobal_cube*. This points out that while a function may have access to global data directly, it has access only to the address of an array that is passed to a function as an argument.

With regard to the main() function, the next two statements demonstrate how to reference specific elements in *cglobal_cube* when they are executed. *cglobal_cube[0][1][2]* references the zeroth layer, second row, third column, or "R." *cglobal_cube[1][0][2]* references the second layer, row zero, third column, or "A."

The next block of code in main() contains two nested **for** loops demonstrating that the arrays are stored in plane-row-column order. As already seen, the rightmost subscript (column) of the array varies the fastest when you view the array in a linear fashion. The first **for** loop pair hardwires the output to the zeroth layer and selects a row, with the inner loop traversing each column in *cglobal_cube*. The program continues by duplicating the same loop structures but printing only the fifth layer (plane [4]), of the *cglobal_cube*.

The last **for** loop pair displays the elements of *imatrix* in the form of a rectangle, similar to the way many people visualize a two-dimensional array.

The output from the program looks like this:

```
sizeof clocal_cube          = 24
sizeof clocal_cube[0]       = 12
sizeof clocal_cube[0][0]    = 4
sizeof clocal_cube[0][0][0] = 1
sizeof carray               = 4
sizeof carray[0]            = 12
sizeof cglobal_cube         = 100
sizeof cglobal_cube[0]      = 20
cglobal_cube[0][1][2] is    = R
cglobal_cube[1][0][2] is    = A

print part of the cglobal_cube's plane 0
PLANE
ZERO

ROW 3
```

```
print part of the cglobal_cube's plane 4
PLANE
FOUR
row 2
abcde

print all of imatrix
100
200
300
400
```

Does the output catch your attention? Look at the initialization of *imatrix*. Because each inner set of braces corresponds to one row of the array and enough values were not supplied inside the inner braces, the system padded the remaining elements with zeros. Remember, C and C++ automatically initialize all undefined static automatic numeric array elements to zero.

String Functions and Character Arrays

Because of the way string data types are handled, many of the functions that use character arrays as function arguments were not discussed. Specifically, these functions are gets(), puts(), fgets(), fputs(), sprintf(), stpcpy(), strcat(), strncmp(), and strlen(). Understanding how these functions operate will be much easier now that you are familiar with the concepts of character arrays and null-terminated strings. One of the easiest ways to explain these functions is to show a few program examples.

gets(), puts(), fgets(), fputs(), and sprintf()

The following C program demonstrates how you can use gets(), puts(), fgets(), fputs(), and sprintf() to format I/O:

```
/*
 *  strio.cpp : Defines the entry point for the console application.
 *  A C program using several string I/O functions
 *  Copyright (c) Chris H. Pappas and William H. Murray, 2001
 */

#include <stdafx.h>
#include <cstdio>
```

```
#define iSIZE 20

int main(int argc, char* argv[])
{
  char sztest_array[iSIZE];

  fputs("Please enter the first string  : ",stdout);
  gets(sztest_array);
  fputs("The first string entered is    : ",stdout);
  puts(sztest_array);

  fputs("Please enter the second string : ",stdout);
  fgets(sztest_array,iSIZE,stdin);
  fputs("The second string entered is   : ",stdout);
  fputs(sztest_array,stdout);

  sprintf(sztest_array,"This was %s a test","just");
  fputs("sprintf() created              : ",stdout);
  fputs(sztest_array,stdout);

  return(0);
}
```

Here is the output from the first run of the program:

```
Please enter the first string  : string one
The first string entered is    : string one
Please enter the second string : string two
The second string entered is   : string two
sprintf() created               : This was just a test
```

Since the strings that were entered were less than the size of *sztest_array*, the program works fine. However, when you enter a string longer than *sztest_array*, something similar to the following can occur when the program is run:

```
Please enter the first string  : one two three four five
The first string entered is    : one two three four five
Please enter the second string : six seven eight nine ten
The second string entered is   : six seven eight ninsprintf() created
  : This was just a test
```

Take care when running the program. The gets() function receives characters from standard input (**stdin**, the keyboard by default for most computers) and places them into the array whose name is passed to the function. When you press the ENTER key to terminate the string, a newline character is transmitted. When the gets() function receives this newline character, it changes it into a null character, thereby ensuring that the character array contains a string. No checking occurs to ensure that the array is big enough to hold all the characters entered.

The puts() function echoes to the terminal just what was entered with gets(). It also adds a newline character on the end of the string in the place where the null character appeared. The null character, remember, was automatically inserted into the string by the gets() function. Therefore, strings that are properly entered with gets() can be displayed with puts().

When you use the fgets() function, you can guarantee a maximum number of input characters. This function stops reading the designated file stream when *one fewer* character is read than the second argument specifies. Since *sztest_array size* is 20, only 19 characters will be read by fgets() from **stdin**. A null character is automatically placed into the string in the last position; and if a newline were entered from the keyboard, it would be retained in the string. (It would appear before the null debug example.) The fgets() function does not eliminate the newline character like gets() does; it merely adds the null character at the end so that a valid string is stored. In much the same way as gets() and puts() are symmetrical, so too are fgets() and fputs(). fgets() does not eliminate the newline, nor does fputs() add one.

To understand how important the newline character is to these functions, look closely at the second run output given. Notice the phrase "sprintf() created..."; it follows immediately after the numbers six, seven, eight, and nine that had just been entered. The second input string actually had five more characters than the fgets() function read in (one fewer than *iSIZE* of 19 characters). The others were left in the input buffer. Also dropped was the newline that terminated the input from the keyboard. (It is left in the input stream because it occurs after the 19th character.) Therefore, no newline character was stored in the string. Since fputs() does not add 1 back, the next fputs() output begins on the line where the previous output ended. Reliance was on the newline character read by fgets() and printed by fputs() to help control the display formatting.

The function sprintf() stands for "string printf()." It uses a control string with conversion characters in exactly the same way as does printf(). The additional feature is that sprintf() places the resulting formatted data in a string rather than immediately sending the result to standard output. This can be beneficial if the exact same output must be created twice, for example, when the same string must be output to both the display monitor and the printer.

To review:

- gets() converts newline to a null.
- puts() converts null to a newline.
- fgets() retains newline and appends a null.
- fputs() drops the null and does not add a newline; instead, it uses the retained newline (if one was entered).

strcpy(), strcat(), strncmp(), and strlen()

All of the functions discussed in this section are predefined in the string.h header file. When using these functions, make certain to include the header file in your program. Remember, all of the string functions prototyped in string.h expect null-terminated string parameters. The following program demonstrates how to use the strcpy() function:

```cpp
//
// strcpy.cpp : Defines the entry point for the console application.
// A C++ program using the strcpy function
// Copyright (c) Chris H. Pappas and William H. Murray, 2001
//

#include <stdafx.h>
#include <iostream>
#include <string.h>
using namespace std;

#define iSIZE 20

int main(int argc, char* argv[])
{
  char szsource_string[iSIZE]="Initialized String!",
       szdestination_string[iSIZE];

  strcpy(szdestination_string,"String Constant");
  cout << szdestination_string << endl;

  strcpy(szdestination_string,szsource_string);
  cout << szdestination_string;

  return(0);

}
```

The function strcpy() copies the contents of one string, *szsource_string,* into a second string, *szdestination_string.* The preceding program initializes *szsource_string* with the message, "Initialized String!" The first strcpy() function call actually copies "String Constant" into the *szdestination_string,* while the second call to the strcpy() function copies *szsource_string* into the *szdestination_string* variable. The program outputs this message:

```
String Constant
Initialized String!
```

The strcat() function appends two separate strings. Both strings must be null-terminated and the result itself is null-terminated. The following program builds on your understanding of the strcpy() function and introduces strcat():

```
//
// strcat.cpp : Defines the entry point for the console application.
// A C++ program demonstrating how to use the strcat function
// Copyright (c) Chris H. Pappas and William H. Murray, 2001
//

#include <stdafx.h>
#include <iostream>
#include <string.h>
using namespace std;

#define iSTRING_SIZE 35

int main(int argc, char* argv[])
{
  char szgreeting[] = "Good morning",
       szname[] =" Carolyn, ",
       szmessage[iSTRING_SIZE];

  strcpy(szmessage,szgreeting);
  strcat(szmessage,szname);
  strcat(szmessage,"how are you?");
  cout << "\n" << szmessage;

  return(0);
}
```

In this example, both *szgreeting* and *szname* are initialized, while *szmessage* is not. The first thing the program does is to use the function strcpy() to copy the *szgreeting* into *szmessage*. Next, the strcat() function is used to concatenate *szname* (" *Carolyn,* ") to "*Good morning*", which is stored in *szmessage*. The last strcat() function call demonstrates how a string constant can be concatenated to a string. Here, "how are you?" is concatenated to the now current contents of *szmessage* ("Good morning Carolyn, "). The program outputs the following:

```
Good morning Carolyn, how are you?
```

The next program demonstrates how to use strncmp() to decide if two strings are identical:

```
//
// strncmp.cpp : Defines the entry point for the console application.
// A C++ program that uses strncmp to compare two strings with
// the aid of the strlen function
// Copyright (c) Chris H. Pappas and William H. Murray, 2001
//

#include <stdafx.h>
#include <iostream>
#include <string.h>
using namespace std;

int main(int argc, char* argv[])
{
  char szstringA[]="Adam", szstringB[]="Abel";
  int istringA_length,iresult=0;

  istringA_length=strlen(szstringA);
  if (strlen(szstringB) >= strlen(szstringA))
    iresult = strncmp(szstringA,szstringB,istringA_length);
  cout << "The string "
       << (iresult == 0 ? "was" : "wasn't") << " found";

  return(0);
}
```

The strlen() function is very useful; it returns the number of characters, not including the null-terminator, in the string pointed to. In the preceding program it is used in two different forms just to give you additional exposure to its use. The first call to the function assigns the length of *szstringA* to the variable *istringA_length*. The second invocation of the function is actually encountered within the **if** condition. Remember, all test conditions must evaluate to a TRUE (not 0 or !0) or FALSE (0). The **if** test takes the results returned from the two calls to strlen() and then asks the relational question >=. If the length of *szstringB* is >= to that of *szstringA*, the strncmp() function is invoked.

Why is the program using a >= test instead of an = =? To know the answer you need a further explanation of how strncmp() works. The function strncmp() compares two strings, starting with the first character in each string. If both strings are identical, the function returns a value of zero. However, if the two strings aren't identical, strncmp()

will return a value less than zero if *szstringA* is less than *szstringB,* or a value greater than zero when *szstringA* is greater than *szstringB.* The relational test >= was used in case you wanted to modify the code to include a report of equality, greater than, or less than for the compared strings.

The program terminates by using the value returned by *iresult,* along with the conditional operator (?:), to determine which string message is printed. For this example, the program output is:

```
The string wasn't found
```

Before moving on to the next chapter, remind yourself that two of the most frequent causes for irregular program behavior deal with exceeding array boundaries and forgetting that character arrays, used as strings, must end with \0, a null-string terminator. Both errors can sit dormant for months until that one user enters a response one character too long.

What's Coming?

In this chapter you have reviewed, in many cases, the fundamentals of all arrays as used in any high-level programming language. You have also been cautioned on those areas of C/C++ array usage that are unique to these two new languages. This information has covered array declarations, default initializations and dimensioning, along with the unique offset values applied to each array element. Remember that the sizeof() operator can logically report back the incorrect size of an array-argument-type from within a called routine. Finally, you learned that all arrays, no matter what their element type (strings included), are passed to subroutines, call-by-reference. And since strings are special cases of arrays-of-characters with a last element of null \0, you explored the unique functions used to manipulate string contents. Chapter 10 will elaborate on many of the concepts discussed here as you move on to this most efficient level of code design.

The Complete Reference

Visual C++.NET

Chapter 10

Using Pointers

U
nless you have taken a formal course in data structures, you have probably never encountered pointer variables. Pointer variables take the normally invisible memory address of a variable and bring it into the foreground. This can make for extremely efficient algorithms and definitely adds some complexity to your coding. It's similar to the difference between an automobile with an automatic transmission (or static variables—see definition below) and a manual transmission (or dynamic variables—see definition that follows). So, while you have the ability to select just the right gear at the right time, you also need to know how to clutch! And if you remember back to the first time you attempted to drive a stick shift, you know there were a few bumps and grinds until you perfected your skill.

In C/C++, the topics of pointers, arrays, and strings are closely related. Consequently, you can consider Chapter 10 to be an extension of Chapter 9. Learning about pointers— what they are and how to use them—can be a challenging experience to the novice programmer. However, by mastering the concept of pointers, you will be able to author extremely efficient, powerful, and flexible C/C++ applications.

It is very common practice for most introductory-level programs to use only the class of variables known as static. *Static variables,* in this sense, are variables declared in the variable declaration block of the source code. While the program is executing, the application can neither obtain more of these variables nor deallocate storage for a variable. In addition, you have no way of knowing the address in memory for each variable or constant. Accessing an actual cell is a straightforward process—you simply use the variable's name. For example, in C/C++, if you want to increment the **int** variable *idecade* by 10, you access *idecade* by name:

```
idecade += 10;
```

Pointer Variables

Another, often more convenient and efficient way to access a variable is through a second variable that holds the address of the variable you want to access. Chapter 8 introduced the concept of pointer variables, which are covered in more detail in this chapter. For example, suppose you have an **int** variable called *imemorycell_contents* and another variable called *pimemorycell_address* (admittedly verbose, but highly symbolic) that can hold the *address* of a variable of type **int**. In C/C++, you have already seen that preceding a variable with the & address operator returns the address of the variable instead of its contents. Therefore, the syntax for assigning the address of a variable to another variable of the type that holds addresses should not surprise you:

```
pimemorycell_address = &imemorycell_contents;
```

A variable that holds an address, such as *pimemorycell_address*, is called a *pointer variable*, or simply a *pointer*. Figure 10-1 illustrates this relationship. The variable *imemorycell_contents* has been placed in memory at address 7751. After the preceding statement is executed, the address of *imemorycell_contents* will be assigned to the pointer variable *pimemorycell_address*. This relationship is expressed in English by saying that *pimemorycell_address* points to *imemorycell_contents*. Figure 10-2 illustrates this relationship. The arrow is drawn from the cell that stores the address to the cell whose address is stored.

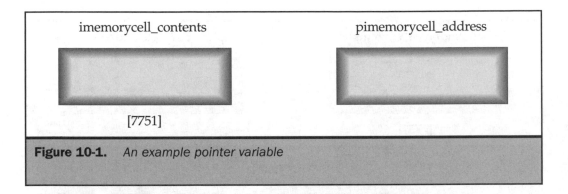

Figure 10-1. *An example pointer variable*

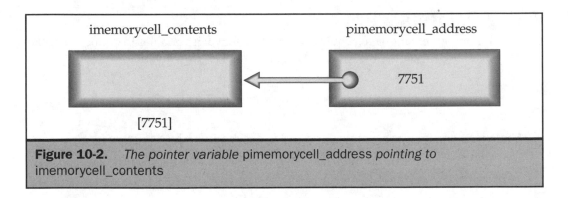

Figure 10-2. *The pointer variable* pimemorycell_address *pointing to* imemorycell_contents

Accessing the contents of the cell whose address is stored in *pimemorycell_address* is as simple as preceding the pointer variable with an asterisk: **pimemorycell_address*. What you have done is to *dereference* the pointer *pimemorycell_address*. For example, if you execute the following two statements, the value of the cell named *imemorycell_contents* will be 20 (see Figure 10-3):

```
pimemorycell_address = &imemorycell_contents;
*pimemorycell_address = 20;
```

You can think of the * as a directive to follow the arrow (see Figure 10-3) to find the cell referenced. Notice that if *pimemorycell_address* holds the address of *imemorycell_contents*, then both of the following statements will have the same effect; that is, both will store the value of 20 in *imemorycell_contents*:

```
imemorycell_contents = 20;
*pimemorycell_address = 20;
```

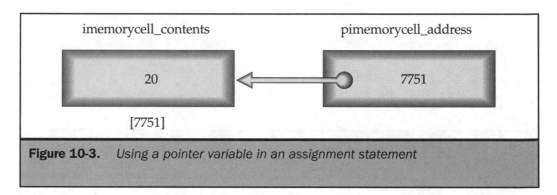

Figure 10-3.   *Using a pointer variable in an assignment statement*

Declaring Pointers

C/C++, like any other language, requires a definition for each variable. To define a pointer variable *pimemorycell_address* that can hold the address of an **int** variable, you write:

```
int *pimemorycell_address;
```

Actually, there are two separate parts to this declaration. The data type of *pimemorycell_address* is:

```
int *
```

and the identifier for the variable is:

```
pimemorycell_address
```

The asterisk following **int** means "pointer to." That is, the following data type is a pointer variable that can hold an address to an **int**:

```
int *
```

This is a very important concept to remember. In C/C++, unlike many other languages, a pointer variable holds the address of a *particular* data type.

Let's look at an example:

```
char *pcaddress;
int *piaddress;
```

The data type of **pcaddress** is distinctly different from the data type of the pointer variable *piaddress*. Run-time errors and compile-time warnings may occur in a program that defines a pointer to one data type and then uses it to point to some other data type. It would be poor programming practice to define a pointer in one way and then use it in some other way. For example, look at the following code segment:

```
int *pi;
float real_value = 98.26;
pi = &real_value;
```

Here *pi* is defined to be of type **int ***, meaning it can hold the address of a memory cell of type **int**. The third statement attempts to assign *pi* the address, *&real_value*, of a declared float variable.

Using Pointer Variables

The following code segment exchanges the contents of the variables *iresult_a* and *iresult_b* but uses the address and dereferencing operators to do so:

```
int iresult_a = 15, iresult_b = 37, itemporary;
int *piresult;

piresult = &iresult_a;
itemporary = *piresult;
*piresult = iresult_b;
iresult_b = itemporary;
```

The first line of the program contains standard definitions and initializations. The statement allocates three cells to hold a single integer, gives each cell a name, and initializes two of them (see Figure 10-4). For discussion purposes, assume that the cell named *iresult_a* is located at address 5328, the cell named *iresult_b* is located at address 7916, and the cell named *itemporary* is located at address 2385.

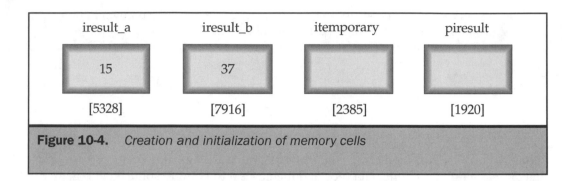

Figure 10-4.   *Creation and initialization of memory cells*

The second statement in the program defines *piresult* to be a pointer to an **int** data type. The statement allocates the cell and gives it a name (placed at address 1920). Remember, when the * is combined with the data type (in this case, **int**), the variable contains the *address* of a cell of the same data type. Because *piresult* has not been initialized, it does not point to any particular **int** variable. If your program were to try to use *piresult*, the compiler would not give you any warning and would try to use the variable's garbage contents to point with. The fourth statement assigns *piresult* the address of *iresult_a* (see Figure 10-5).

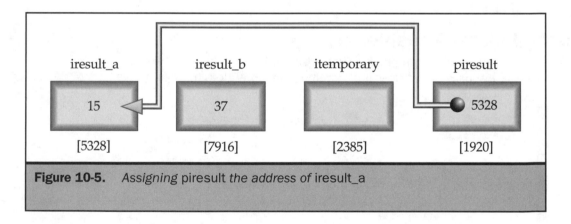

Figure 10-5.   *Assigning* piresult *the address of* iresult_a

The next statement in the program uses the expression **piresult* to access the contents of the cell to which *piresult* points—*iresult_a*:

```
itemporary = *piresult;
```

Therefore, the integer value 15 is stored in the variable *itemporary* (see Figure 10-6). If you left off the * in front of *piresult*, the assignment statement would illegally store the contents of *piresult*—the address 5328—in the cell named *itemporary*, but *itemporary* is supposed to hold an integer, not an address. This can be a very annoying bug to locate since many compilers will not issue any warnings or errors. (The Visual C/C++ compiler issues the warning "different levels of indirection.")

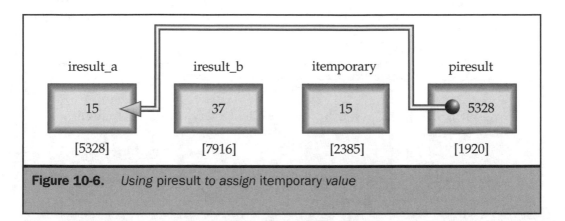

Figure 10-6.   *Using* piresult *to assign* itemporary *value*

To make matters worse, most pointers are near, meaning they occupy 2 bytes, the same data size as a PC-based integer. The fifth statement in the program copies the contents of the variable *iresult_b* into the cell pointed to by the address stored in *piresult* (see Figure 10-7):

```
*piresult = iresult_b;
```

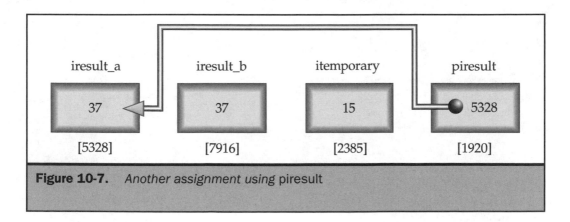

Figure 10-7.   *Another assignment using* piresult

The last statement in the program simply copies the contents of one integer variable, *itemporary*, into another integer variable, *iresult_b* (see Figure 10-8). Make certain you understand the difference between what is being referenced when a pointer variable is preceded (**piresult*) and when it is not preceded (*piresult*) by the dereference operator *. For this example, the first syntax is a pointer to a cell that can contain an integer value. The second syntax references the cell that holds the address to another cell that can hold an integer.

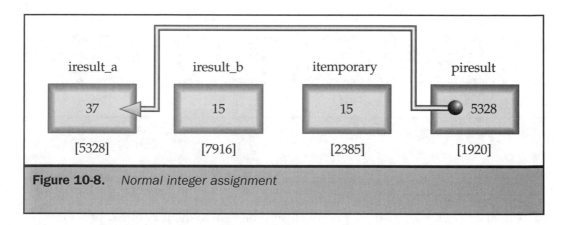

Figure 10-8.   *Normal integer assignment*

The following short program illustrates how to manipulate the addresses in pointer variables. Unlike the previous example, which swapped the program's data within the variables, this program swaps the addresses to where the data resides:

```
char cswitch1 = 'S', cswitch2 = 'T';
char *pcswitch1, *pcswitch2, *pctemporary;

pcswitch1   = &cswitch1;
pcswitch2   = &cswitch2;
pctemporary = pcswitch1;
pcswitch1   = pcswitch2;
pcswitch2   = pctemporary;
printf( "%c%c", *pcswitch1, *pcswitch2);
```

Figure 10-9 shows the cell configuration and values after the execution of the first four statements of the program. When the fifth statement is executed, the contents of *pcswitch1* are copied into *pctemporary* so that both *pcswitch1* and *pctemporary* point to *cswitch1* (see Figure 10-10).

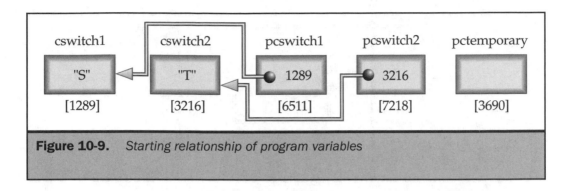

Figure 10-9.   *Starting relationship of program variables*

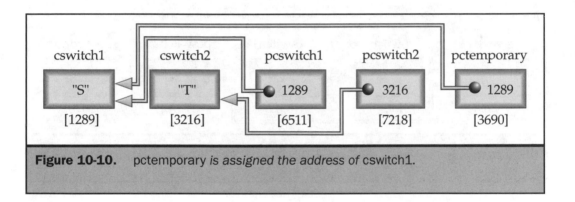

Figure 10-10.   pctemporary *is assigned the address of* cswitch1.

Executing the following statement copies the contents of *pcswitch2* into *pcswitch1* so that both pointers point to *cswitch2* (see Figure 10-11):

```
pcswitch1 = pcswitch2;
```

Notice that if the code had not preserved the address to *cswitch1* in a temporary location, *pctemporary,* there would be no pointer access to *cswitch1*. The next-to-last statement copies the address stored in *pitemporary* into *pcswitch2* (see Figure 10-12). When the *printf* statement is executed, since the value of **pcswitch1* is "T" and the value of **pcswitch2* is "S", you will see:

```
TS
```

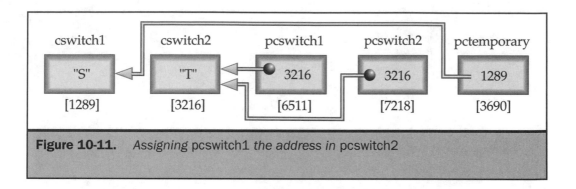

Figure 10-11.   *Assigning* pcswitch1 *the address in* pcswitch2

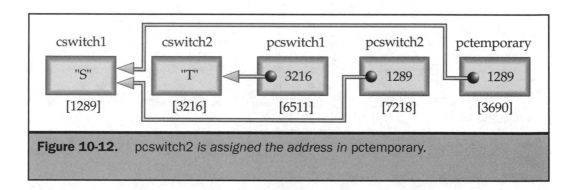

Figure 10-12.   pcswitch2 *is assigned the address in* pctemporary.

Notice how the actual values stored in the variables *cswitch1* and *cswitch2* haven't changed from their original initializations. However, since you have swapped the contents of their respective pointers, **pcswitch1* and **pcswitch2*, it *appears* that their order has been reversed. This is an important concept to grasp. Depending on the size of a data object, moving a pointer to the object can be much more efficient than copying the entire contents of the object.

Initializing Pointers

Pointer variables can be initialized in their definitions, just like many other variables in C/C++. For example, the following two statements allocate storage for the two cells *iresult* and *piresult*:

```
int iresult;
int *piresult = &iresult;
```

The variable *iresult* is an ordinary integer variable, and *piresult* is a pointer to an integer. Additionally, the code initializes the pointer variable *piresult* to the address of *iresult*. Be careful: the syntax is somewhat misleading; you are *not* initializing **piresult* (which would have to be an integer value) but *piresult* (which must be an address to an integer). The second statement in the preceding listing can be translated into the following two equivalent statements:

```
int *piresult;
piresult = &iresult;
```

The following code segment shows how to declare a string pointer and then initialize it:

```
//
// psz.cpp : Defines the entry point for the console application.
// A C program that initializes a string pointer and
// then prints the palindrome backwards then forwards
// Copyright (c) Chris H. Pappas and William H. Murray, 2001
//

#include <stdafx.h>
#include <iostream>
#include <string.h>
using namespace std;

int main(int argc, char* argv[])
{
  char *pszpalindrome = "MADAM I'M ADAM";

  for (int i = strlen(pszpalindrome)-1; i >= 0; i--)
    cout << pszpalindrome[i];
    cout << endl << pszpalindrome;

  return 0;
}
```

Technically, the C/C++ compiler stores the address of the first character of the string "MADAM I'M ADAM" in the variable *pszpalindrome*. While the program is running, it can use *pszpalindrome* like any other string. This is because all C/C++ compilers create a *string table,* which is used internally by the compiler to store the string constants a program is using.

The strlen() function prototyped in string.h calculates the length of a string. The function expects a pointer to a null-terminated string and counts all of the characters up to, but not including, the null character itself. The index variable *i* is initialized to one less than the value returned by strlen() since the **for** loop treats the string *psz* like an array of characters. The palindrome has 14 letters. If *psz* is treated as an array of characters, each element is indexed from 0 to 13. This example program highlights the somewhat confusing relationship between pointers to character strings and arrays of characters. However, if you remember that an array's name is actually the address of the first element, you should understand why the compiler issues no complaints.

What Not to Do with the Address Operator

You cannot use the address operator on every C/C++ expression. The following examples demonstrate those situations where the & address operator cannot be applied:

```
/*
   not with CONSTANTS
*/

pivariable = &48;


/*
   not with expressions involving operators such as + and /
   given the definition int iresult = 5;
*/

pivariable = &(iresult + 15);


/*
   not preceding register variables
   given the definition register register1;
*/

pivariable = &register1;
```

The first statement tries to illegally obtain the address of a hardwired constant value. Since the 48 has no memory cell associated with it, the statement is meaningless.

The second assignment statement attempts to return the address of the expression *iresult + 15*. Since the expression itself is actually a stack manipulation process, there is no address associated with the expression.

Normally, the last example honors the programmer's request to define *register1* as a register rather than as a storage cell in internal memory. Therefore, no memory cell address could be returned and stored. Microsoft Visual C/C++ gives the variable memory, not register storage.

Pointers to Arrays

As mentioned, pointers and arrays are closely related topics. Remember from Chapter 9 that an array's name is a constant whose value represents the address of the array's first element. For this reason, the value of an array's name cannot be changed by an assignment statement or by any other statement. Given the following data declarations, the array's name, *ftemperatures,* is a constant whose value is the address of the first element of the array of 20 floats:

```
#define IMAXREADINGS 20

float ftemperatures[IMAXREADINGS];
float *pftemp;
```

The following statement assigns the address of the first element of the array to the pointer variable *pftemp*:

```
pftemp = ftemperatures;
```

An equivalent statement looks like this:

```
pftemp = &ftemperatures[0];
```

However, if *pftemp* holds the address of a float, the following statements are illegal:

```
ftemperatures = pftemp;
&ftemperatures[0] = pftemp;
```

These statements attempt to assign a value to the constant *ftemperatures* or its equivalent *&ftemperatures[0]*, which makes about as much sense as:

```
10 = pftemp;
```

Pointers to Pointers

In C/C++, it is possible to define pointer variables that point to other pointer variables, which in turn point to the data, such as an integer. Figure 10-13 illustrates this relationship; *ppi* is a pointer variable that points to another pointer variable whose contents can be used to point to 10.

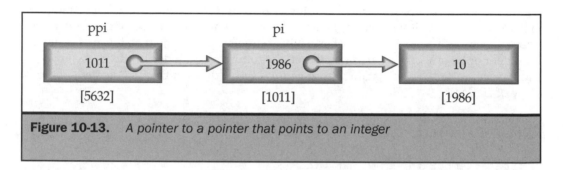

Figure 10-13.   *A pointer to a pointer that points to an integer*

You may be wondering why this is necessary. The arrival of Windows and the Windows NT programming environment signals the development of multitasking operating environments designed to maximize the use of memory. To compact the use of memory, the operating system has to be able to move objects in memory. If your program points directly to the physical memory cell where the object is stored and the operating system moves it, disaster will strike. Instead of pointing directly to a data object, your application points to a memory cell address that will not change while your program is running (for example, let's call this a *virtual_address*), and the *virtual_address* memory cell holds the *current_physical_address* of the data object. Now, whenever the operating environment wants to move the data object, all the operating system has to do is update the *current_physical_address* pointed to by the *virtual_address*. As far as your application is concerned, it still uses the unchanged address of the *virtual_address* to point to the updated address of the *current_physical_address*.

To define a pointer to a pointer in C/C++, you simply increase the number of asterisks preceding the identifier:

```
int **ppi;
```

In this example, the variable *ppi* is defined to be a pointer to a pointer that points to an **int** data type. *ppi*'s data type is:

```
int **
```

Each asterisk is read "pointer to." The number of pointers that must be followed to access the data item or, equivalently, the number of asterisks that must be attached to the variable to reference the value to which it points, is called the *level of indirection* of the pointer variable. A pointer's level of indirection determines how much dereferencing must be done to access the data type given in the definition. Figure 10-14 illustrates several variables with different levels of indirection.

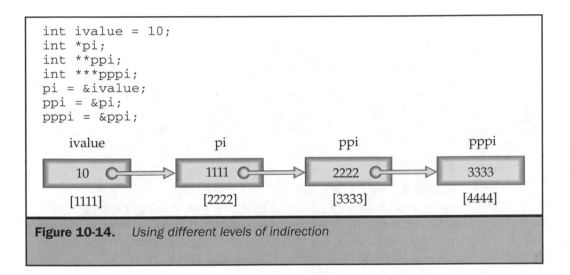

Figure 10-14.   *Using different levels of indirection*

The first four lines of code in Figure 10-14 define four variables: the integer variable *ivalue,* the *pi* pointer variable that points to an integer (one level of indirection), the *ppi* variable that points to a pointer that points to an integer (two levels of indirection), and *pppi*, illustrating that this process can be extended beyond two levels of indirection. The fifth line of code is:

```
pi = &ivalue;
```

This is an assignment statement that uses the address operator. The expression assigns the address of *&ivalue* to *pi*. Therefore, *pi*'s contents contain 1111. Notice that there is only one arrow from *pi* to *ivalue*. This indicates that *ivalue*, or 10, can be accessed by dereferencing *pi* just once. The next statement, along with its accompanying picture, illustrates double indirection:

```
ppi = &pi;
```

Because *ppi*'s data type is **int ****, to access an integer you need to dereference the variable twice. After the preceding assignment statement, *ppi* holds the address (not the contents) of *pi*, so *ppi* points to *pi*, which in turn points to *ivalue*. Notice that you must follow two arrows to get from *ppi* to *ivalue*.

The last statement demonstrates three levels of indirection:

```
pppi = &ppi;
```

It also assigns the address (not the contents) of *ppi* to *pppi*. Notice that the accompanying illustration shows that three arrows are now necessary to reference *ivalue*.

To review, *pppi* is assigned the address of a pointer variable that indirectly points to an integer, as in the preceding statement. However, ***pppi (the cell pointed to) can only be assigned an integer value, not an address, since ***pppi is an integer:

```
***pppi = 10;
```

C/C++ allows pointers to be initialized like any other variable. For example, *pppi* could have been defined and initialized using the following single statement:

```
int ***pppi = &ppi;
```

Pointers to Strings

A string constant such as "File not ready" is actually stored as an array of characters with a null-terminator added as the last character (see Figure 10-15). Because a **char** pointer can hold the address of a character, it is possible to define and initialize it. For example:

```
char *psz = "File not ready";
```

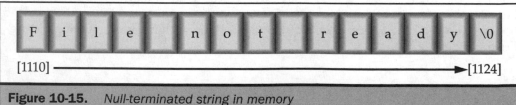

Figure 10-15.   *Null-terminated string in memory*

This statement defines the **char** pointer *psz* and initializes it to the address of the first character in the string (see Figure 10-16). Additionally, the storage is allocated for the string itself. The same statement could have been written as follows:

```
char *psz;
psz = "File not ready";
```

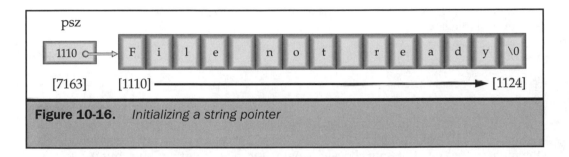

Figure 10-16.   *Initializing a string pointer*

Again, care must be taken to realize that *psz* was assigned the address, not **psz*, which points to the "F." The second example given helps to clarify this by using two separate statements to define and initialize the pointer variable.

The following example highlights a common misconception when dealing with pointers to strings and pointers to arrays of characters:

```
char *psz = "File not ready";
char pszarray[] = "Drive not ready";
```

The main difference between these two statements is that the value of *psz* can be changed (since it is a pointer variable), but the value of *pszarray* cannot be changed (since it is a pointer constant). Along the same line of thinking, the following assignment statement is illegal:

```
/* NOT LEGAL */
char pszarray[16];
pszarray = "Drive not ready";
```

While the syntax looks similar to the correct code in the preceding example, the assignment statement attempts to copy the *address* of the first cell of the storage for the string "Drive not ready" into *pszarray*. Because *pszarray* is a pointer constant, not a pointer variable, an error results.

The following input statement is incorrect because the pointer *psz* has not been initialized:

```
/* NOT LEGAL */
char *psz;
cin >> psz;
```

Correcting the problem is as simple as reserving storage for and initializing the pointer variable *psz*:

```
char sztring[10];
char *psz = sztring;
cin.get(psz,10);
```

Since the value of *sztring* is the address of the first cell of the array, the second statement in the code not only allocates storage for the pointer variable, but it also initializes it to the address of the first cell of the array *sztring*. At this point, the **cin.get** statement is satisfied since it is passed the valid address of the character array storage.

Pointer Arithmetic

If you are familiar with assembly language programming, then you are already comfortable with using actual physical addresses to reference information stored in tables. For those of you who are only used to using subscript indexing into arrays, believe it or not, you have been effectively using the same assembly language equivalent. The only difference is that in the latter case you were allowing the compiler to manipulate the addresses for you.

Remember that one of C/C++'s strengths is their closeness to the hardware. In C/C++, you can actually manipulate pointer variables. Many of the example programs seen so far have demonstrated how one pointer variable's address, or address contents, can be assigned to another pointer variable of the same data type. C/C++ allows you to perform only two arithmetic operations on a pointer address—namely, addition and subtraction. Let's look at two different pointer variable types and perform some simple pointer arithmetic:

```
//
// ptarth.cpp : Defines the entry point for the console application.
// A C++ program demonstrating pointer arithmetic
// Copyright (c) Chris H. Pappas and William H. Murray, 2001
//
```

```
#include <stdafx.h>
#include <iostream>
using namespace std;

int main(int argc, char* argv[] )
{
  int *pi;
  float *pf;

  int an_integer;
  float a_real;

  pi = &an_integer;
  pf = &a_real;

  cout << "original values:    " << pi << '\t' << pf << endl;

  pi++;
  pf++;

  cout << "incremented values: " << pi << '\t' << pf << endl;

  return 0;
}
```

Let's also assume that an integer is 4 bytes and a float is 8 bytes (for 32-bit C/C++ environments; 2 and 4 respectively for a 16-bit environment). Also, *an_integer* is stored at memory cell address 2000, and *a_real* is stored at memory cell address 4000. When the last two lines of the program are executed, *pi* will contain the address 2004 and *pf* will contain the address 4008. But wait a minute—didn't you think that the increment operator ++ incremented by 1? This is true for character variables but not always for pointer variables.

The output from the program looks similar to:

```
original values:    0012FEC0    0012FEB4
incremented values: 0012FEC4    0012FEB8
```

In Chapter 6, you were introduced to the concept of operator overloading. Increment (++) and decrement (−−) are examples of this C/C++ construct. For the immediate example, since *pi* was defined to point to integers (which for the system in this example are 4 bytes), when the increment operation is invoked, it checks the variable's type and then chooses an appropriate increment value. For integers, this value is 4; for floats, the value is 8 (on the example system). This same principle holds true for whatever data type the pointer is pointing to. Should the pointer variable point to a structure of 20 bytes, the increment or decrement operator would add or subtract 20 from the current pointer's address.

You can also modify a pointer's address by using integer addition and subtraction, not just the ++ and -- operators. For example, moving 4 float values over from the one currently pointed to can be accomplished with the following statement:

```
pf = pf + 4;
```

Look at the following program carefully and see if you can predict the results. Does the program move the float pointer *pf* one number over?

```
//
//   sizept.cpp
//   A C++ program using sizeof and pointer arithmetic
//   Copyright (c) Chris H. Pappas and William H. Murray, 2001
//

#include <stdafx.h>
#include <iostream>
#include <cstddef>
using namespace std;

int main(int argc, char* argv[])
{
  float fvalues[] = {15.38,12.34,91.88,11.11,
                     22.22,55.99,63.21,88.27};
  float *pf;
  size_t fwidth;

  pf = &fvalues[0];

  fwidth = sizeof(float);

  pf = pf + fwidth;

  return 0;
}
```

Try using the integrated debugger to single-step through the program. Use the Trace window to keep an eye on the variables *pf* and *fwidth*.

Assume that the debugger has assigned *pf* the address of *fvalues* and that *pf* contains C000. The variable *fwidth* is assigned the sizeof(float) that returns an 8. When you executed the final statement in the program, what happened? The variable *pf* changed to C040, not C008. Why? You forgot that pointer arithmetic takes into consideration the size of the object pointed to (8 * (8-byte floats) = 64). The program actually moves the *pf* pointer over 8 floats, right off the end of the vector!

Actually, you were intentionally misled by the naming of the variable *fwidth*. To make logical sense, the program should have been written as:

```cpp
//
// ptsize.cpp : Defines the entry point for the console application.
// The same C++ program using meaningful variable names
// Copyright (c) Chris H. Pappas and William H. Murray, 2001
//

#include <stdafx.h>
#include <iostream>
using namespace std;

int main(int argc, char* argv[])
{
  float fvalues[] = {15.38,12.34,91.88,11.11,22.22};
  float *pf;
  int inumber_of_elements_to_skip;

  pf = fvalues;

  inumber_of_elements_to_skip = 1;

  pf = pf + inumber_of_elements_to_skip;

  return 0;
}
```

Pointer Arithmetic and Arrays

The following two programs index into a ten-character array. Both programs read in ten characters and then print out the same ten characters in reverse order. The first program uses the more conventional high-level language approach of indexing with subscripts.

The second program is identical except that the array elements are referenced by address, using pointer arithmetic. Here is the first program:

```
//
// araysub.cpp : Defines the entry point for the console application.
// A C++ program using normal array subscripting
// Copyright (c) Chris H. Pappas and William H. Murray, 2001
//

#include <stdafx.h>
#include <iostream>
using namespace std;

#define ISIZE 10

int main(int argc, char* argv[])
{
  char string10[ISIZE];
  int i;

  for(i = 0; i < ISIZE; i++)
    string10[i] = cin.get();

  for(i = ISIZE - 1; i >= 0; i--)
    cout.put(string10[i]);

  return 0;
}
```

Here is the second example:

```
//
// aryptr.cpp : Defines the entry point for the console application.
// A C program using pointer arithmetic to access elements
// Copyright (c) Chris H. Pappas and William H. Murray, 2001
//

#include <stdafx.h>
#include <iostream>
using namespace std;
```

```
#define ISIZE 10

int main(int argc, char* argv[])
{
  char string10[ISIZE];
  char *pc;
  int icount;

  pc = string10;

  for(icount = 0; icount < ISIZE; icount++) {
    *pc = cin.get();
    pc++;
  }

  pc = string10 + (ISIZE - 1);

  for(icount = 0; icount < ISIZE; icount++) {
    cout.put(*pc);
    pc--;
  }

  return 0;
}
```

Since the first example is straightforward, the discussion will center on the second program, which uses pointer arithmetic. *pc* has been defined to be of type **char ***, which means it is a pointer to a character. Because each cell in the array *string10* holds a character, *pc* is suitable for pointing to each. The following statement stores the address of the first cell of *string10* in the variable *pc*:

```
pc = string10;
```

The **for** loop reads *ISIZE* characters and stores them in the array *string10*. The following statement uses the dereference operator * to ensure that the target, the left-hand side of this assignment (another example of an *lvalue*), will be the cell to which *pc* points, not *pc* (which itself contains just an address):

```
*pc = cin.get();
```

The idea is to store a character in each cell of *string10*, not to store it in *pc*.

To start printing the array backward, the program first initializes the *pc* to the last element in the array:

```
pc = string10 + (ISIZE - 1);
```

By adding 9 (*ISIZE - 1*) to the initial address of *string10, pc* points to the *tenth* element. Remember, these are offsets. The first element in the array is at offset zero. Within the **for** loop, *pc* is decremented to move backward through the array elements. Make certain you use the integrated debugger to trace through this example if you are unsure of how *pc* is modified.

Problems with the Operators ++ and −−

Just as a reminder, the following two statements do *not* perform the same cell reference:

```
*pc++ = cin.get();
*++pc = cin.get();
```

The first statement assigns the character returned by *cin.get()* to the *current* cell pointed to by *pc* and then increments *pc*. The second statement increments the address in *pc* first and then assigns the character returned by the function to the cell pointed to by the updated address. Later in this chapter you will use these two different types of pointer assignments to reference the elements of *argv*.

Using const with Pointers

Just when you think you are getting the hang of it, C/C++ throws you a subtle potential curveball. Look at the following two pointer variable declarations and see if you can detect the subtle differences:

```
const MYTYPE *pmytype_1;
MYTYPE * const pmytype_2 = &mytype;
```

The first pointer declaration defines *pmytype_1* as a pointer variable that may be assigned any address to a memory location of type *MYTYPE*. The second declaration defines *pmytype_2* as a pointer constant to *mytype*. Was that enough of a hint?

Okay, let's try that one more time. The identifier *pmytype_1* is a pointer variable. Variables can be assigned *any* value appropriate to their defined type—in this case, *pmytype_1* can be assigned any address to a previously defined location of type *MYTYPE*.

Well then, you might ask, what does the **const** keyword do in the declaration? What that **const** tells the compiler is this: While *pmytype_1* may be assigned any address to a memory cell of type *MYTYPE*, when you use *pmytype_1* to actually point to a memory location, what you point to cannot be changed. The following sample statements highlight these subtleties:

```
pmytype_1 = &mytype1; // legal
pmytype_1 = &mytype2; // legal
*pmytype_1 = (MYTYPE)some_legal_value; // illegal
```

Now, compare *pmytype_1* with *pmytype_2*, which is declared as a pointer constant. In other words, *pmytype_2* can hold the address to a memory location of type *MYTYPE*. However, it is a locked address. Therefore, *pmytype_2* must be initialized to hold a valid address when the pointer constant is declared (= *&mytype;*). On the other hand, the contents of the memory location pointed to by *pmytype_2* are not locked. Look at the following statements, which highlight these subtleties:

```
pmytype_2 = &mytype_n; // illegal
*pmytype_2 = (MYTYPE) some_legal_value_1; // legal
*pmytype_2 = (MYTYPE) some_legal_value_n; // legal
```

Now, of the two uses for the **const** keyword with pointer declarations, which do you think is closest to an array declaration? Answer: the second use of **const**, as in *pmytype_2*'s declaration. Remember, the name of an array is a locked address to the array's first element:

```
int iarray[ SIZE ];
```

For this reason, the compiler views the identifier *iarray* as if you had actually declared it as:

```
int * const iarray = &array[0];
```

Comparing Pointers

You have already seen examples demonstrating the effect of incrementing and decrementing pointers using the ++ and −− operators and the effect of adding an integer to a pointer. There are other operations that may be performed on pointers. These include:

- Subtracting an integer from a pointer
- Subtracting two pointers (usually pointing to the same object)
- Comparing pointers using a relational operator such as <=, =, or >=

Since (pointer - integer) subtraction is so similar to (pointer + integer) addition (these have already been discussed by example), it should be no surprise that the resultant pointer value points to a storage location for integer elements before the original pointer.

Subtracting two pointers yields a constant value that is the number of array elements between the two pointers. This assumes that both pointers are of the same type and initially point into the same array. Subtracting pointers that are not of the same type or that initially point to different arrays will yield unpredictable results.

Note *No matter which pointer arithmetic operation you choose, there is no check to see if the pointer value calculated is outside the defined boundaries of the array.*

Pointers of like type (that is, pointers that reference the same kind of data, like **int** and **float**) can also be compared to each other. The resulting TRUE (!0) or FALSE (0) can either be tested or assigned to an integer, just like the result of any logical expression. Comparing two pointers tests whether they are equal, not equal, greater than, or less than each other. One pointer is less than another pointer if the first pointer refers to an array element with a lower number subscript. (Remember that pointers and subscripts are virtually identical.) This operation also assumes that the pointers reference the same array. Finally, pointers can be compared to zero, the null value. In this case, only the test for equal or not equal is valid since testing for negative pointers makes no sense. The null value in a pointer means that the pointer has no value, or does not point to anything. Null, or zero, is the only numeric value that can be directly assigned into a pointer without a type cast.

It should be noted that pointer conversions are performed on pointer operands. This means that any pointer may be compared to a constant expression evaluating to zero and any pointer may be compared to a pointer of type **void ***. (In this last case, the pointer is first converted to **void ***.)

Pointer Portability

The examples in this section have represented addresses as integers. This may suggest to you that a C/C++ pointer is of type **int**. It is not. A pointer holds the address of a particular type of variable, but a pointer itself is not one of the primitive data types **int**, **float**, and the like. A particular C/C++ system may allow a pointer to be copied into an **int** variable and an **int** variable to be copied into a pointer; however, C/C++ does not guarantee that pointers can be stored in **int** variables. To guarantee code portability, this practice should be avoided.

Also, not all arithmetic operations on pointers are allowed. For example, it is illegal to add two pointers, to multiply two pointers, or to divide one pointer by another.

Using sizeof( ) with Pointers under 16-Bit DOS Environments

Note

The following section describes old, outdated keywords. These pointer size modifiers are no longer needed under the newer 32-bit C/C++ compilers and operating systems. Under a 32-bit operating system and C/C++ compiler, all addresses are a full 32 bits (equivalent to the _ _far and _ _huge modifiers described below). However, as many readers already know, you often encounter code, for purposes of reference or modification, that is written in Historic C/C++, ANSI C/C++, and so forth. For this reason the discussion of these old-style keywords is presented here.

The actual size of a pointer variable depends on one of two things: the size of the memory model you have chosen for the application or the use of the nonportable, implementation-specific _ _near, _ _far, and _ _huge keywords.

The 80486 to 8088 microprocessors use a *segmented addressing* scheme that breaks an address into two pieces: a *segment* and an *offset*. Many local post offices have several walls of post office boxes, with each box having its own unique number. Segment:offset addressing is similar to this design. To get to your post office box, you first need to know which bank of boxes, or wall, yours is on (the segment), and then the actual box number (the offset).

When you know that all of your application's code and data will fit within a single 64K of memory, you choose the small memory model. Applying this to the post office box metaphor, this means that all of your code and data will be in the same location, or wall (segment), with the application's code and data having a unique box number (offset) on the wall.

For those applications where this compactness is not feasible, possibly because of the size and the amount of data that must be stored and referenced, you would choose a large memory model. Using the analogy, this could mean that all of your application's code would be located on one wall, while all the data would be on a completely separate wall.

When an application shares the same memory segment for code and data, calculating an object's memory location merely involves finding out the object's offset within the segment. This is a very simple calculation.

When an application has separate segments for code and data, calculating an object's location is a bit more complicated. First, the code or data's segment must be calculated, and then it's offset within the respective segment. Naturally, this requires more processor time.

C++ also allows you to override the default pointer size for a specific variable by using the keywords _ _**near**, _ _**far**, and _ _**huge**. Note, however, that by including these in your application, you make your code less portable since the keywords produce different results on different compilers. The _ _**near** keyword forces an offset-only pointer when the pointers would normally default to segment:offset. The _ _**far** keyword forces a segment:offset pointer when the pointers would normally default to offset-only. The _ _**huge** keyword also forces a segment:offset pointer that has been normalized. The _ _**near** keyword is generally used to increase execution speed, while the _ _**far** keyword forces a pointer to do the right thing regardless of the memory model chosen.

For many applications, you can simply ignore this problem and allow the compiler to choose a default memory model. But eventually you will run into problems with this approach, for example, when you try to address an absolute location (some piece of hardware, perhaps, or a special area in memory) outside your program's segment area.

On the other hand, you may be wondering why you can't just use the largest memory model available for your application. You can, but you pay a price in efficiency. If all of your data is in one segment, the pointer is the size of the offset. However, if your data and code range all over memory, your pointer is the size of the segment *and* the offset, and both must be calculated every time you change the pointer. The following program uses the function sizeof() to print out the smallest pointer size and largest pointer size available.

This C++ program prints the default pointer sizes, their _ _**far** sizes, and their _ _**near** sizes. The program also uses the *stringize* preprocessor directive (#) with the *A_POINTER* argument, so the name as well as the size of the pointer will be printed.

```cpp
//   PROGRAM WILL NOT EXECUTE PROPERLY ON A 32-BIT C/C++ COMPILER!
//   strize.cpp
//   A C++ program illustrating the sizeof(pointers).
//   The program is only valid under 16-bit C/C++ environments.
//   Copyright (c) Chris H. Pappas and William H. Murray, 2001
//

#include <stdio.h>

#define PRINT_SIZEOF(A_POINTER) \
  printf("sizeof\t("#A_POINTER")\t= %d\n", \
  sizeof(A_POINTER))

void main()
{
  char *reg_pc;
  long double *reg_pldbl;
  char _ _far *far_pc;
  long double _ _far *far_pldbl;
  char _ _near *near_pc;
  long double _ _near *near_pldbl;

  PRINT_SIZEOF(reg_pc);
```

```
    PRINT_SIZEOF(reg_pldbl);
    PRINT_SIZEOF(far_pc);
    PRINT_SIZEOF(far_pldbl);
    PRINT_SIZEOF(near_pc);
    PRINT_SIZEOF(near_pldbl);
}
```

The output from the program looks like this:

```
sizeof   (reg_pc)     = 2
sizeof   (reg_pldbl)  = 2
sizeof   (far_pc)     = 4
sizeof   (far_pldbl)  = 4
sizeof   (near_pc)    = 2
sizeof   (near_pldbl) = 2
```

Pointers to Functions

All the examples so far have shown you how various items of data can be referenced by a pointer. As it turns out, you can also access *portions of code* by using a pointer to a function. Pointers to functions serve the same purpose as do pointers to data; that is, they allow the function to be referenced indirectly, just as a pointer to a data item allows the data item to be referenced indirectly.

A pointer to a function can have a number of important uses. For example, consider the qsort() function. The qsort() function has as one of its parameters a pointer to a function. The referenced function contains the necessary comparison that is to be performed between the array elements being sorted. qsort() has been written to require a function pointer because the comparison process between two elements can be a complex process beyond the scope of a single control flag. It is not possible to pass a function by value, that is, pass the code itself. C/C++, however, does support passing a pointer to the code, or a pointer to the function.

The concept of function pointers is frequently illustrated by using the qsort() function supplied with the compiler. Unfortunately, in many cases, the function pointer is declared to be of a type that points to other built-in functions. The following C and C++ programs demonstrate how to define a pointer to a function and how to "roll your own" function to be passed to the cstdlib function qsort(). Here is the program:

```
//
// qsort.cpp : Defines the entry point for the console application.
// A C++ program illustrating how to declare your own
// function and function pointer to be used with qsort()
```

```
// Copyright (c) Chris H. Pappas and William H. Murray, 2001
//

#include <stdafx.h>
#include <iostream>
#include <cstdlib>
using namespace std;

#define IMAXVALUES 10

int icompare_funct(const void *iresult_a, const void *iresult_b);
int (*ifunct_ptr)(const void *,const void *);

int main(int argc, char* argv[])
{
  int i;
  int iarray[IMAXVALUES]={0,5,3,2,8,7,9,1,4,6};

  ifunct_ptr=icompare_funct;
  qsort(iarray,IMAXVALUES,sizeof(int),ifunct_ptr);
  for(i = 0; i < IMAXVALUES; i++)
    cout << '[' << i << "] " << iarray[i] << endl;

  return 0;
}

int icompare_funct(const void *iresult_a, const void *iresult_b)
{
  return((*(int *)iresult_a) - (*(int *)iresult_b));
}
```

The function icompare_funct() (which will be called the *reference function*) was prototyped to match the requirements for the fourth parameter to the function qsort() (which will be called the *invoking function*).

To digress slightly, the fourth parameter to the function qsort() must be a function pointer. This reference function must be passed two **const void *** parameters and it must return a type **int**.

Note *Remember that the position of the **const** keyword, in the formal parameter list, locks the data pointed to, not the address used to point. This means that even if you write your compare routine so that it does not sort properly, it can in no way destroy the contents of your array!*

This is because qsort() uses the reference function for the sort comparison algorithm. Now that you understand the prototype of the reference function icompare_funct(), take a minute to study the body of the reference function.

If the reference function returns a value < 0, then the reference function's first parameter value is less than the second parameter's value. A return value of zero indicates parameter value equality, with a return value > 0 indicating that the second parameter's value was greater than the first's. All of this is accomplished by the single statement in icompare_funct():

```
return((*(int *)iresult_a) - (*(int *) iresult_b));
```

Since both of the pointers were passed as type **void ***, they were cast to their appropriate pointer type **int *** and then **dereferenced (*)**. The result of the subtraction of the two values pointed to returns an appropriate value to satisfy qsort()'s comparison criterion.

While the prototype requirements for icompare_funct() are interesting, the meat of the program begins with the pointer function declaration below the icompare_funct() function prototype:

```
int icompare_funct(const void *iresult_a, const void *iresult_b);
int (*ifunct_ptr)(const void *, const void *);
```

A function's type is determined by its return value and argument list signature. A pointer to icompare_funct() must specify the same signature and return type. You might therefore think the following statement would accomplish this:

```
int *ifunct_ptr(const void *, const void *);
```

That is almost correct. The problem is that the compiler interprets the statement as the definition of a function ifunct_ptr() taking two arguments and returning a pointer of type **int ***. The dereference operator unfortunately is associated with the type specifier, not ifunct_ptr(). Parentheses are necessary to associate the dereference operator with ifunct_ptr().

The corrected statement declares ifunct_ptr() to be a pointer to a function taking two arguments and with a return type **int**; that is, a pointer of the same type required by the fourth parameter to qsort().In the body of main(), the only thing left to do is to initialize ifunct_ptr() to the address of the function icompare_funct(). The parameters to qsort() are the address to the base or zeroth element of the table to be sorted (*iarray*), the number of entries in the table (*IMAXVALUES*), the size of each table element (sizeof(int)), and a function pointer to the comparison function (ifunct_ptr()).

Learning to understand the syntax of a function pointer can be challenging. Let's look at just a few examples. Here is the first one:

```
int *(*(*ifunct_ptr)(int))[5];
float (*(*ffunct_ptr)(int,int))(float);
typedef double (*(*(*dfunct_ptr)())[5])();
  dfunct_ptr A_dfunct_ptr;
(*(*function_ary_ptrs())[5])();
```

The first statement defines ifunct_ptr() to be a function pointer to a function that is passed an integer argument and returns a pointer to an array of five **int** pointers.

The second statement defines ffunct_ptr() to be a function pointer to a function that takes two integer arguments and returns a pointer to a function taking a float argument and returning a float.

By using the typedef declaration, you can avoid the unnecessary repetition of complicated declarations. The typedef declaration (discussed in greater detail in Chapter 13) is read as follows: dfunct_ptr() is defined as a pointer to a function that is passed nothing and returns a pointer to an array of five pointers that point to functions that is passed nothing and returns a double.

The last statement is a function declaration, not a variable declaration. The statement defines function_ary_ptrs() to be a function taking no arguments and returning a pointer to an array of five pointers that point to functions taking no arguments and returning integers. The outer functions return the default C and C++ type **int**.

The good news is that you will rarely encounter complicated declarations and definitions like these. However, by making certain you understand these declarations, you will be able to confidently parse the everyday variety.

Dynamic Memory

When a C/C++ program is compiled, the computer's memory is broken down into three zones that contain the program's code, all global data, the stack, and the heap. The *heap* is an area of free memory (sometimes referred to as the *free store*) that is manipulated by using the dynamic allocation functions malloc() and free().

When malloc() is invoked, it allocates a contiguous block of storage for the object specified and then returns a pointer to the start of the block. The function free() returns previously allocated memory to the heap, permitting that portion of memory to be reallocated.

The argument passed to malloc() is an integer that represents the number of bytes of storage that is needed. If the storage is available, malloc() will return a **void ***, which can be cast into whatever type pointer is desired. The concept of *void pointers* was introduced in the ANSI C standard and means a pointer of unknown type, or a generic pointer. A void pointer cannot itself be used to reference anything (since it doesn't point to any specific type of data), but it can contain a pointer of any other type. Therefore, any pointer can be converted into a void pointer and back without any loss of information.

The following code segment allocates enough storage for 300 float values:

```
float *pf;
int inum_floats = 300;

pf = (float *) malloc(inum_floats * sizeof(float));
```

The malloc() function has been instructed to obtain enough storage for 300 * the current size of a float. The cast operator (float *) is used to return a float pointer type. Each block of storage requested is entirely separate and distinct from all other blocks of storage. Absolutely no assumption can be made about where the blocks are located. Blocks are typically "tagged" with some sort of information that allows the operating system to manage the location and size of the block. When the block is no longer needed, it can be returned to the operating system by using the following statement:

```
free((void *) pf);
```

Just as in C, C++ allocates available memory in two ways. When variables are declared, they are created on the stack by pushing the stack pointer down. When these variables go out of scope (for instance, when a local variable is no longer needed), the space for that variable is freed automatically by moving the stack pointer up. The size of stack-allocated memory must always be known at compilation.

Your application may also have to use variables with an unknown size at compilation. Under these circumstances, you must allocate the memory yourself, on the free store. The free store can be thought of as occupying the bottom of the program's memory space and growing *upward*, while the stack occupies the top and grows *downward*.

Your C and C++ programs can allocate and release free store memory at any point. It is important to realize that free-store-allocated memory variables are not subject to scoping rules, as other variables are. These variables never go out of scope, so once you allocate memory on the heap, you are responsible for freeing it. If you continue to allocate free store space without freeing it, your program could eventually crash.

Most C compilers use the library functions malloc() and free(), just discussed, to provide dynamic memory allocation, but in C++ these capabilities were considered so important they were made a part of the core language. C++ uses new and delete to allocate and free free store memory. The argument to new is an expression that returns the number of bytes to be allocated; the value returned is a pointer to the beginning of this memory block. The argument to delete is the starting address of the memory block to be freed. The following two programs illustrate the similarities and differences between a C and C++ application using dynamic memory allocation. Here is the C example:

```
//
// malloc.cpp : Defines the entry point for the console application.
// A simple C program using malloc(), free()
// Copyright (c) Chris H. Pappas and William H. Murray, 2001
//

#include <stdafx.h>
#include <iostream>
#include <cstdlib>
using namespace std;

#define ISIZE 512

int main(int argc, char* argv[])
{
  int *pimemory_buffer;

  pimemory_buffer = (int *)malloc(ISIZE * sizeof(int));

  if(pimemory_buffer == NULL)
    cout << "Insufficient memory" << endl;
  else
    cout << "Memory allocated" << endl;
  free(pimemory_buffer);
}
```

The first point of interest in the program begins with the second **#include** statement that brings in the cstdlib header file, containing the definitions for both functions, malloc() and free(). After the program defines the **int *** pointer variable *pimemory_buffer*, the malloc() function is invoked to return the address to a memory block that is ISIZE * sizeof(int) big. A robust algorithm will always check for the success or failure of the memory allocation, and it explains the purpose behind the **if-else** statement. The function malloc() returns a null whenever not enough memory is available to allocate the block. This simple program ends by returning the allocated memory to the free store by using the function free() and passing it the beginning address of the allocated block.

The C++ program does not look significantly different:

```
//
// newdel.cpp : Defines the entry point for the console application.
// A simple C++ program using new and delete
```

```
// Copyright (c) Chris H. Pappas and William H. Murray, 2001
//

#include <stdafx.h>
#include <iostream>
// #include <stdlib.h> not needed for malloc(), free()
using namespace std;

#define NULL 0
#define ISIZE 512

int main(int argc, char* argv[])
{
  int *pimemory_buffer;

  pimemory_buffer=new int[ISIZE];
  if(pimemory_buffer == NULL)
    cout << "Insufficient memory\n";
  else
    cout << "Memory allocated\n";
  delete(pimemory_buffer);

  return 0;
}
```

The only major difference between the two programs is the syntax used with the function free() and the operator new. Whereas the function free() requires the sizeof operator to ensure proper memory allocation, the operator new has been written to automatically perform the sizeof() function on the declared data type it is passed. Both programs will allocate 512 4-byte blocks of consecutive memory (on systems that allocate 4 bytes per integer).

Using void Pointers

Now that you have a detailed understanding of the nature of pointer variables, you can begin to appreciate the need for the pointer type void. To review, the concept of a pointer is that it is a variable that contains the address of another variable. If you always knew how big a pointer was, you wouldn't have to determine the pointer type at compile time. You would therefore also be able to pass an address of any type to a function. The function could then cast the address to a pointer of the proper type (based on some other piece of information) and perform operations on the result. This process would enable you to create functions that operate on a number of different data types.

That is precisely the reason C++ introduced the void pointer type. When void is applied to a pointer, its meaning is different from its use to describe function argument lists and return values (which mean "nothing"). A void pointer means a pointer to any type of data. The following C++ program demonstrates this use of void pointers:

```
//
// voidptr.cpp : Defines the entry point for the console application.
// A C++ program using void pointers
// Copyright (c) Chris H. Pappas and William H. Murray, 2001
//

#include <stdafx.h>
#include <iostream>
using namespace std;

#define ISTRING_MAX 50

void voutput(void *pobject, char cflag);

int main(int argc, char* argv[])
{
  int *pi;
  char *psz;
  float *pf;
  char cresponse,cnewline;

  cout << "Please enter the dynamic data type\n";
  cout << "    you would like to create.\n\n";
  cout << "Use (s)tring, (i)nt, or (f)loat ";
  cin >> cresponse;
    cin.get(cnewline);
      switch(cresponse) {
        case 's':
          psz = new char[ISTRING_MAX];
          cout << "\nPlease enter a string: ";
          cin.get(psz,ISTRING_MAX);
          voutput(psz,cresponse);
          break;
        case 'i':
          pi = new int;
          cout << "\nPlease enter an integer: ";
          cin >> *pi;
```

```
              voutput(pi,cresponse);
              break;
          case 'f':
            pf = new float;
            cout << "\nPlease enter a float: ";
            cin >> *pf; voutput(pf,cresponse);
            break;
          default:
            cout << "\n\n  Object type not implemented!";
      }

   return 0;
}
void voutput(void *pobject, char cflag)
{
   switch(cflag) {
     case 's':
       cout << "\nThe string read in:  " << (char *) pobject;
       delete pobject;
       break;
     case 'i':
       cout << "\nThe integer read in: "
            << *((int *) pobject);
       delete pobject;
       break;
     case 'f':
       cout << "\nThe float value read in: "
            << *((float *) pobject);
       delete pobject;
       break;
     }
}
```

The first statement of interest in the program is the voutput() function prototype. Notice that the function's first formal parameter, *pobject*, is of type **void ***, or a generic pointer. Moving down to the data declarations, you will find three pointer variable types: **int ***, **char ***, and **float ***. These will eventually be assigned valid pointer addresses to their respective memory cell types.

The action in the program begins with a prompt asking the user to enter the data type he or she would like to dynamically create. You may be wondering why the two separate input statements are used to handle the user's response. The first **cin** statement reads in the single-character response but leaves the \n linefeed hanging around. The second input statement, **cin.get(cnewline)**, remedies this situation.

The **switch** statement takes the user's response and invokes the appropriate prompt and pointer initialization. The pointer initialization takes one of three forms:

```
psz = new char;
pi = new int;
pf = new float;
```

The following statement is used to input the character string, and in this example it limits the length of the string to ISTRING_MAX 50 characters.

```
cin.get(psz,ISTRING_MAX 50);
```

Since the **cin.get()** input statement expects a string pointer as its first parameter, there is no need to dereference the variable when the voutput() function is invoked:

```
voutput(psz,cresponse);
```

Things get a little quieter if the user wants to input an integer or a float. The last two case options are the same except for the prompt and the reference variable's type.

Notice how the three invocations of the function voutput() have different pointer types:

```
voutput(psz,cresponse);
voutput(pi,cresponse);
voutput(pf,cresponse);
```

Function voutput() accepts these parameters only because the matching formal parameter's type is **void ***. Remember, in order to use these pointers, you must first cast them to their appropriate pointer type. When using a string pointer with **cout**, you must first cast the pointer to type **char ***. Just as creating integer and float dynamic variables was similar, printing their values is also similar. The only difference between the last two case statements is the string and the cast operator used.

While it is true that all dynamic variables pass into bit oblivion whenever a program terminates, each of the case options takes care of explicitly deleting the pointer variable. When and where your program creates and deletes dynamic storage is application dependent.

Pointers and Arrays: A Closer Look

The following sections include many example programs that deal with the topic of arrays and how they relate to pointers. This symbiotic relationship can throw the initial

C/C++ programmer. Take your time reviewing the examples to make certain you understand how C/C++ interrelate the topics of pointers and arrays.

Strings (Arrays of Type char)

Many string operations in C/C++ are generally performed by using pointers and pointer arithmetic to reference character array elements. This is because character arrays or strings tend to be accessed in a strictly sequential manner. Remember, all strings in C/C++ are terminated by a null (\0). The following C++ program is a modification of a program used earlier in this chapter to print palindromes and illustrates the use of pointers with character arrays:

```
//
// chrary.cpp : Defines the entry point for the console application.
// A C++ program that prints a character array backwards
// using a character pointer and the decrement operator
// Copyright (c) Chris H. Pappas and William H. Murray, 2001
//

#include <stdafx.h>
#include <iostream>
#include <string.h>
using namespace std;

int main(int argc, char* argv[])
{
  char pszpalindrome[]="POOR DAN IN A DROOP";
  char *pc;

  pc = pszpalindrome + (strlen(pszpalindrome)-1);
  do {
    cout << *pc ;
    pc--;
  } while (pc >= pszpalindrome);

  return 0;
}
```

After the program declares and initializes the *pszpalindrome* palindrome, it creates a *pc* of type **char ***. Remember that the name of an array is in itself an address variable. The body of the program begins by setting the *pc* to the address of the last character in the array. This requires a call to the function strlen(), which calculates the length of the character array.

Note   *The* strlen() *function counts just the number of characters, excluding the null terminator* \0.

You were probably thinking that was the reason for subtracting the 1 from the function's returned value. This is not exactly true; the program has to take into consideration the fact that the first array character's address is at offset zero. Therefore, you want to increment the pointer variable's offset address to one less than the number of valid characters.

Once the pointer for the last valid array character has been calculated, the **do-while** loop is entered. The loop simply uses the pointer variable to point to the memory location of the character to be printed and prints it. It then calculates the next character's memory location and compares this value with the starting address of *pszpalindrome.* As long as the calculated value is >=, the loop iterates.

Arrays of Pointers

In C and C++, you are not restricted to making simple arrays and simple pointers. You can combine the two into a very useful construct—arrays of pointers. An *array of pointers* is an array whose elements are pointers to other objects. Those objects can themselves be pointers. This means you can have an array of pointers that point to other pointers.

The concept of an array of pointers to pointers is used extensively in the *argc* and *argv* command-line arguments for main() that you were introduced to in Chapter 8. The following program finds the largest or smallest value entered on the command line. Command-line arguments can include numbers only, or they may be prefaced by a command selecting a choice for the smallest value entered (-s,-S) or the largest (-l,-L).

```
//
// argcgv.cpp : Defines the entry point for the console application.
// A C++ program using an array of pointers to process
// the command-line arguments argc, argv
// Copyright (c) Chris H. Pappas and William H. Murray, 2001
//

#include <stdafx.h>
#include <iostream>
#include <cstdlib>        // exit(), atoi()
using namespace std;

#define IFIND_LARGEST 1
#define IFIND_SMALLEST 0

int main(int argc, char *argv[])
```

```
{
  char *psz;
  int ihow_many;
  int iwhich_extreme = 0;
  int irange_boundary = 32767;

  if(argc < 2) {
    cout << "\nYou need to enter an -S,-s,-L,-l"
         << " and at least one integer value";
    exit(1);
  }

  while(--argc > 0 && (*++argv)[0] == '-') {
    for(psz = argv[0]+1; *psz != '\0'; psz++) {
      switch(*psz) {
        case 's':
        case 'S':
          iwhich_extreme = IFIND_SMALLEST;
          irange_boundary = 32767;
          break;
        case 'l':
        case 'L':
          iwhich_extreme = IFIND_LARGEST;
          irange_boundary = 0;
          break;
        default:
          cout << "unknown argument "<< *psz << endl;
          exit(1);
      }
    }
  }

  if(argc==0) {
    cout << "Please enter at least one number\n";
    exit(1);
  }

  ihow_many=argc;

  while(argc--) {
    int present_value;
    present_value = atoi(*(argv++));
```

```
    if(iwhich_extreme == IFIND_LARGEST && present_value >
       irange_boundary)
     irange_boundary=present_value;
    if(iwhich_extreme == IFIND_SMALLEST && present_value <
       irange_boundary)
     irange_boundary=present_value;
  }

  cout << "The ";
  cout << ((iwhich_extreme) ? "largest" : "smallest");
  cout << " of the " << ihow_many << " value(s) input is " <<
         irange_boundary << endl;

  return(0);
}
```

Before looking at the source code, take a moment to familiarize yourself with the possible command combinations that can be used to invoke the program. The following list illustrates the possible command combinations:

```
10argcgv
10argcgv 98
10argcgv 98 21
10argcgv -s 98
10argcgv -S 98 21
10argcgv -l 14
10argcgv -L 14 67
```

Looking at the main() program, you will see the formal parameters *argc* and *argv* that you were introduced to in Chapter 8. To review, *argc* is an integer value containing the number of separate items, or arguments, that appeared on the command line. The variable *argv* refers to an array of pointers to character strings.

Note argv *is not a constant. It is a variable whose value can be altered, a key point to remember when viewing how* argv *is used below. The first element of the array,* argv[0], *is a pointer to a string of characters that contains the program name.*

Moving down the code to the first **if** statement, you find a test to determine if the value of *argc* is less than 2. If this test evaluates to TRUE, it means that the user has typed just the name of the program *extremes* without any switches. Since this action would indicate that the user does not know the switch and value options, the program will prompt the user at this point with the valid options and then exit().

The **while** loop test condition evaluates from left to right, beginning with the decrement of *argc*. If *argc* is still greater than zero, the right side of the logical expression will be examined.

The right side of the logical expression first increments the array pointer *argv* past the first pointer entry *(++argv)*, skipping the program's name, so that it now points to the second array entry. Once the pointer has been incremented, it is then used to point *(*++argv)* to the zeroth offset *((*++argv)[0])* of the first character of the string pointed to. Obtaining this character, if it is a - symbol, the program diagnoses that the second program command was a possible switch, for example, -s or -L.

The **for** loop initialization begins by taking the current pointer address of *argv*, which was just incremented in the line previously to point to the second pointer in the array. Since *argv*'s second element is a pointer to a character string, the pointer can be subscripted *(argv[0])*. The complete expression, *argv[0]+1*, points to the second character of the second string pointed to by the current address stored in *argv*. This second character is the one past the command switch symbol -. Once the program calculates this character's address, it stores it in the variable *psz*. The **for** loop repeats while the character pointed to by **psz* is not the null terminator \0.

The program continues by analyzing the switch to see if the user wants to obtain the smallest or largest of the values entered. Based on the switch, the appropriate constant is assigned to the *iwhich_extreme*. Each case statement also takes care of initializing the variable *irange_boundary* to an appropriate value for the comparisons that follow. Should the user enter an unrecognized switch—for example, -d—the default case will take care of printing an appropriate message.

The second **if** statement now checks to see if *argc* has been decremented to zero. An appropriate message is printed if the switches have been examined on the command line and there are no values left to process. If so, the program terminates with an exit code of decimal 1.

A successful skipping of this test means there are now values from the command line that need to be examined. Since the program will now decrement *argc*, the variable *ihow_many* is assigned *argc*'s current value.

The **while** loop continues while there are at least two values to compare. The **while** loop needs to be entered only if there is more than one value to be compared, since the **cout** statement following the **while** loop is capable of handling a command line with a single value.

The function atoi() converts each of the remaining arguments into an integer and stores the result in the variable *present_value*. Remember, *argv++* needed to be incremented first so that it points to the first value to be compared. Also, the **while** loop test condition had already decremented the pointer to make certain the loop wasn't entered with only a single command value.

The last two **if** statements take care of updating the variable *irange_boundary* based on the user's desire to find either the smallest or largest of all values entered. Finally, the results of the program are printed by using an interesting combination of string literals and the conditional operator.

More on Pointers to Pointers

The next program demonstrates the use of pointer variables that point to other pointers. It is included at this point in the chapter instead of in the section "Pointers to Pointers" because the program uses dynamic memory allocation. You may want to refer back to the general discussion of pointers to pointers before looking at the program.

```cpp
//
// dblptr.cpp : Defines the entry point for the console application.
// A C++ program using pointer variables with double indirection
//  Copyright (c) Chris H. Pappas and William H. Murray, 2001
//

#include <stdafx.h>
#include <iostream>
#include <cstdlib>
using namespace std;

#define IMAXELEMENTS 3

void voutput(int **ppiresult_a, int **ppiresult_b,
             int **ppiresult_c);
void vassign(int *pivirtual_array[],int *pinewblock);

int main(int argc, char* argv[])
{
  int **ppiresult_a, **ppiresult_b, **ppiresult_c;
  int *pivirtual_array[IMAXELEMENTS];
  int *pinewblock, *pioldblock;

  ppiresult_a = &pivirtual_array[0];
  ppiresult_b = &pivirtual_array[1];
  ppiresult_c = &pivirtual_array[2];

  pinewblock = new int[IMAXELEMENTS];
  pioldblock = pinewblock;

  vassign(pivirtual_array,pinewblock);

  **ppiresult_a = 7;
  **ppiresult_b = 10;
  **ppiresult_c = 15;
```

```
      voutput(ppiresult_a,ppiresult_b,ppiresult_c);

      pinewblock = new int[IMAXELEMENTS];

      *pinewblock = **ppiresult_a;
      *(pinewblock+1) = **ppiresult_b;
      *(pinewblock+2) = **ppiresult_c;

      free(pioldblock);

      vassign(pivirtual_array,pinewblock);

      voutput(ppiresult_a,ppiresult_b,ppiresult_c);

      return 0;
}
void vassign(int *pivirtual_array[],int *pinewblock)
{
  pivirtual_array[0] = pinewblock;
  pivirtual_array[1] = pinewblock+1;
  pivirtual_array[2] = pinewblock+2;
}

void voutput(int **ppiresult_a, int **ppiresult_b, int **ppiresult_c)
{
  cout << **ppiresult_a << endl;
  cout << **ppiresult_b << endl;
  cout << **ppiresult_c << endl;
}
```

The program is designed so that it highlights the concept of a pointer variable (*ppiresult_a*, *ppiresult_b*, and *ppiresult_c*), pointing to a constant address (*&pivirtual_array[0]*, *&pivirtual_array[1]*, and *&pivirtual_array[2]*), whose pointer address contents can dynamically change.

Look at the data declarations in main(). *ppiresult_a*, *ppiresult_b*, and *ppiresult_c* have been defined as pointers to pointers that point to integers. Let's take this slowly, looking at the various syntax combinations:

```
ppiresult_a
*ppiresult_a
**ppiresult_a
```

The first syntax references the address stored in the pointer variable *ppiresult_a*. The second syntax references the pointer address pointed to by the address in *ppiresult_a*. The last syntax references the integer that is pointed to by the pointer address pointed to by *ppiresult_a*. Make certain you do not proceed any further until you understand these three different references.

The three variables *ppiresult_a*, *ppiresult_b*, and *ppiresult_c* have all been defined as pointers to pointers that point to integers **int ****. The variable *pivirtual_array* has been defined to be an array of integer pointers **int ***, of size IMAXELEMENTS. The last two variables, *pinewblock* and *pioldblock,* are similar to the variable *pivitrual_array*, except they are single variables that point to integers **int ***. Figure 10-17 shows what these seven variables look like after their storage has been allocated and, in particular, after *ppiresult_a*, *ppiresult_b,* and *ppiresult_c* have been assigned the address of their respective elements in the *pivirtual_array*.

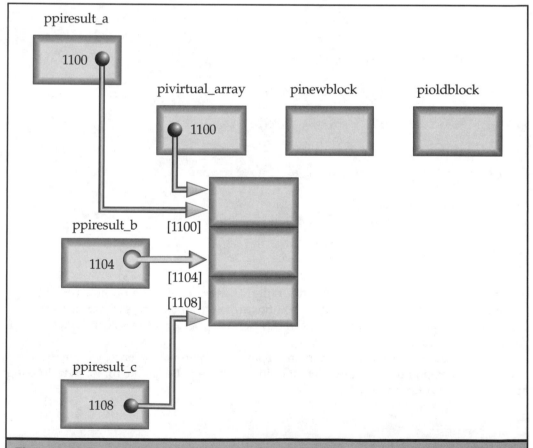

Figure 10-17.   *The variables after* ppiresult_a, ppiresult_b, *and* ppiresult_c *get their initial addresses*

It is this array that is going to hold the addresses of the dynamically changing memory cell addresses. Something similar actually happens in a true multitasking environment. Your program thinks it has the actual physical address of a variable stored in memory, when what it really has is a fixed address to an array of pointers that in turn point to the current physical address of the data item in memory. When the multitasking environment needs to conserve memory by moving your data objects, it simply moves their storage locations and updates the array of pointers. The variables in your program, however, are still pointing to the same physical address, albeit not the physical address of the data but of the array of pointers.

To understand how this operates, pay particular attention to the fact that the physical addresses stored in the pointer variables *ppiresult_a*, *ppiresult_b*, and *ppiresult_c* never change once they are assigned.

Figure 10-18 illustrates what has happened to the variables after the dynamic array *pinewblock* has been allocated and *pioldblock* has been initialized to the same address of the new array. Most importantly, notice how the physical addresses of *pinewblock*'s individual elements have been assigned to their respective counterparts in *pivirtual_array*.

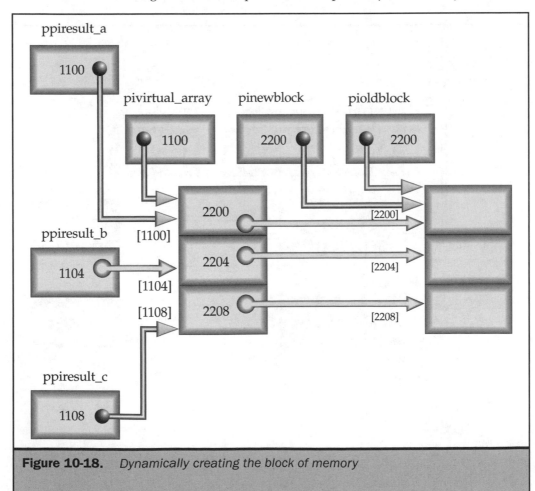

Figure 10-18.   *Dynamically creating the block of memory*

The pointer assignments were all accomplished by the vassign() function. vassign() was passed the *pivirtual_array* (call-by-value) and the address of the recently allocated dynamic memory block in the variable *pinewblock*. The function takes care of assigning the addresses of the dynamically allocated memory cells to each element of the *pivirtual_array*. Since the array was passed call-by-value, the changes are effective in the main().

At this point, if you were to use the debugger to print out *ppiresult_a*, you would see ACC8 (the address of *pivirtual_array*'s first element), and **ppiresult_a* would print 1630 (or the contents of the address pointed to). You would encounter a similar dump for the other two pointer variables, *ppiresult_b* and *ppiresult_c*.

Figure 10-19 shows the assignment of three integer values to the physical memory locations. Notice the syntax to accomplish this:

```
**ppiresult_a = 7;
**ppiresult_b = 10;
**ppiresult_c = 15;
```

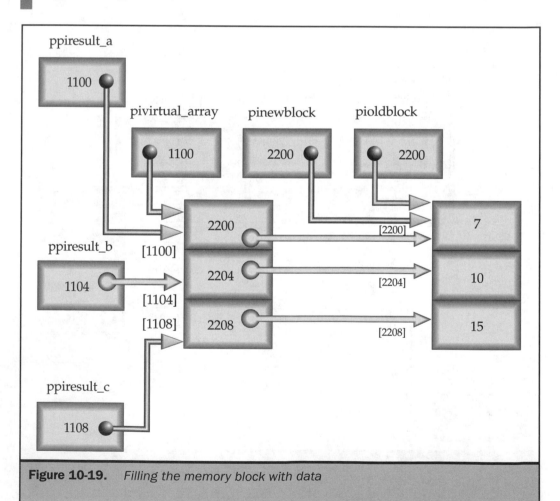

Figure 10-19.   *Filling the memory block with data*

At this point, the program prints out the values 7, 10, and 15 by calling the function voutput(). Notice that the function has been defined as receiving three **int** ** variables. Notice that the actual parameter list does *not* need to precede the variables with the double indirection operator ** since that is their type by declaration.

As shown in Figure 10-20, the situation has become very interesting. A new block of dynamic memory has been allocated with the new function, with its new physical memory address stored in the pointer variable *pinewblock*. *pioldblock* still points to the previously allocated block of dynamic memory. Using the incomplete analogy to a multitasking environment, the figure would illustrate the operating system's desire to physically move the data objects' memory locations.

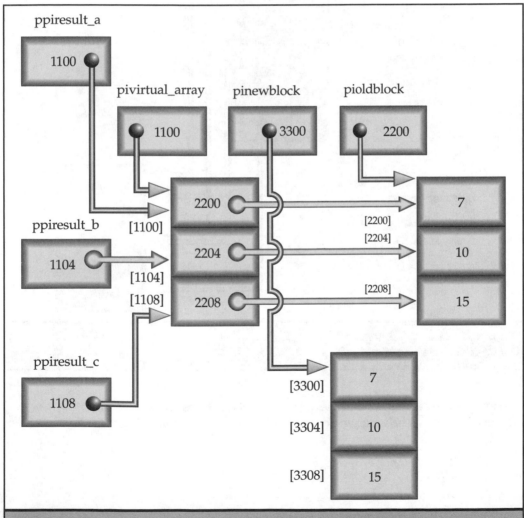

Figure 10-20.   *Dynamically allocating and filling the second block of memory*

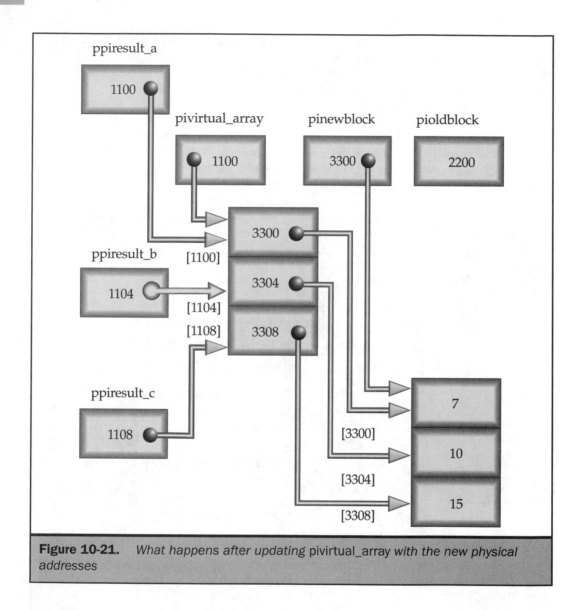

Figure 10-21. *What happens after updating* pivirtual_array *with the new physical addresses*

Figure 10-20 also shows that the data objects themselves were copied into the new memory locations. The program accomplished this with the following three lines of code:

```
*pinewblock = **ppiresult_a;
*(pinewblock+1) = **ppiresult_b;
*(pinewblock+2) = **ppiresult_c;
```

Since the pointer variable *pinewblock* holds the address to the first element of the dynamic block, its address is dereferenced (*), pointing to the memory cell itself, and the 7 is stored there. Using a little pointer arithmetic, the other two memory cells are accessed by incrementing the pointer. The parentheses were necessary so that the pointer address was incremented *before* the dereference operator * was applied.

Figure 10-21 shows what happens when the function free() is called and the function vassign() is called to link the new physical address of the dynamically allocated memory block to the *pivirtual_array* pointer address elements.

The most important fact to notice in this last figure is that the actual physical address of the three pointer variables *ppiresult_a, ppiresult_b,* and *ppiresult_c* has not changed. Therefore, when the program prints the values pointed to **ppiresult_a* and so on, you still see the values 7, 10, and 15, even though their *physical* location in memory has changed.

Arrays of String Pointers

One of the easiest ways to keep track of an array of strings is to define an array of pointers to strings. This is much simpler than defining a two-dimensional array of characters. The following program uses an array of string pointers to keep track of three function error messages:

```
//
// aofptr.cpp : Defines the entry point for the console application.
// A C++ program that demonstrates how to define and use
// arrays of pointers.
// Copyright Chris H. Pappas and William H. Murray, 2001
//

#include <stdafx.h>
#include <cctype>
#include <fstream>
#include <iostream>
using namespace std;

#define INUMBER_OF_ERRORS 3

char *pszarray[INUMBER_OF_ERRORS] =
        {
           "\nFile not available.\n",
           "\nNot an alpha character.\n",
           "\nValue not between 1 and 10.\n"
        };
```

```cpp
void fopen_a_file(char *psz);
char cget_a_char(void);
int iget_an_integer(void);

ifstream pfa_file;

int main(int argc, char* argv[])
{
  char cvalue;
  int ivalue;

  fopen_a_file("input.dat");
  cvalue = cget_a_char();
  ivalue = iget_an_integer();

  return 0;
}

void fopen_a_file(char *psz)
{
  const ifopen_a_file_error = 0;

  pfa_file.open(psz);
  if(!pfa_file)
    cout << pszarray[ifopen_a_file_error];
}

char cget_a_char(void)
{
  char cvalue;
  const icget_a_char_error = 1;

  cout << "\nEnter a character: ";
  cin >> cvalue;
  if(!isalpha(cvalue))
    cout << pszarray[icget_a_char_error];
  return(cvalue);
}

int iget_an_integer(void)
{
  int ivalue;
  const iiget_an_integer = 2;
  cout << "\nEnter an integer between 1 and 10: ";
```

```
   cin >> ivalue;
   if( (ivalue < 1) || (ivalue > 10) )
     cout << pszarray[iiget_an_integer];
   return(ivalue);
}
```

The *pszarray* is initialized outside all function declarations. This gives it a global lifetime. For large programs, an array of this nature could be saved in a separate source file dedicated to maintaining all error message control. Notice that each function, fopen_a_file(), cget_a_char(), and iget_an_integer(), takes care of defining its own constant index into the array. This combination of an error message array and unique function index makes for a very modular solution to error-exception handling. If a project requires the creation of a new function, the new piece of code selects a vacant index value and adds one error condition to *pszarray*. The efficiency of this approach allows each code segment to quickly update the entire application to its peculiar I/O requirements without having to worry about an elaborate error detection or alert mechanism.

The C++ Reference Type

C++ provides a form of call-by-reference that is even easier to use than pointers. First, let's examine the use of reference variables in C++. As with C, C++ enables you to declare regular variables or pointer variables. In the first case, memory is actually allocated for the data object; in the second case, a memory location is set aside to hold an address for an object that will be allocated at another time. C++ has a third kind of declaration, the reference type. Like a pointer variable, a *reference variable* refers to another variable location, but like a regular variable, it requires no special dereferencing operators. The syntax for a reference variable is straightforward:

```
int iresult_a = 5;
int& riresult_a = iresult_a; // valid
int& riresult_b;             // invalid: uninitialized
```

This example sets up the reference variable *riresult_a* and assigns it to the existing variable *iresult_a*. At this point, the referenced location has two names associated with it—*iresult_a* and *riresult_a*. Because both variables point to the same location in memory, they are, in fact, the same variable. Any assignment made to *riresult_a* is reflected through *iresult_a*; the inverse is also true, and changes to *iresult_a* occur through any access to *riresult_a*. Therefore, with the reference data type, you can create what is sometimes referred to as an *alias* for a variable.

The reference type has a restriction that serves to distinguish it from pointer variables, which, after all, do something very similar. The value of the reference type must be set at declaration, and it cannot be changed during the run of the program. After you initialize this type in the declaration, it always refers to the same memory location. Therefore, any assignments you make to a reference variable change only the data in memory, not the address of the variable itself. In other words, you can think of a reference variable as a pointer to a constant location.

For example, using the preceding declarations, the following statement doubles the contents of *iresult_a* by multiplying 5 * 2:

```
riresult_a *= 2;
```

The next statement assigns *icopy_value* (assuming it is of type **int**) a copy of the value associated with *riresult_a*:

```
icopy_value = riresult_a;
```

The next statement is also legal when using reference types:

```
int *piresult_a = &riresult_a;
```

This statement assigns the address of *riresult_a* to the **int** * variable *piresult_a*.

The primary use of a reference type is as an argument or a return type of a function, especially when applied to user-defined class types (see Chapter 15).

Functions Returning Addresses

When you return an address from a function using either a pointer variable or a reference type, you are giving the user a memory address. The user can read the value at the address, and if you haven't declared the pointer type to be **const**, the user can always write the value. By returning an address, you are giving the user permission to read and, for non-**const** pointer types, write to private data. This is a significant design decision. See if you can anticipate what will happen in this next program:

```
//
// refvar.cpp : Defines the entry point for the console application.
// A C++ program showing what NOT to do with address variables
// Copyright (c) Chris H. Pappas and William H. Murray, 2001
//

#include <stdafx.h>
```

```
#include <iostream>
using namespace std;

int *ifirst_function(void);
int *isecond_function(void);

int main(int argc, char* argv[])
{
  int *pi = ifirst_function();
  isecond_function();
  cout << "Correct value? " << *pi;

  return 0;
}

int *ifirst_function(void)
{
  int ilocal_to_first = 11;
  return &ilocal_to_first;
}

int *isecond_function(void)
{
  int ilocal_to_second = 44;
  return &ilocal_to_second;
}
```

To examine the operation of this C++ code while it is actually working, you can use the integrated debugger. Use the Trace window to keep an eye on the variable *pi*.

What has happened? When the ifirst_function() is called, local space is allocated on the stack for the variable *ilocal_to_first*, and the value 11 is stored in it. At this point the ifirst_function() returns the address of this *local* variable (very bad news). The second statement in the main program invokes the isecond_function(). isecond_function() in turn allocates local space for *ilocal_to_second* and assigns it a value of 44. So how does the **printf** statement print a value of 44 when it was passed the address of *ilocal_to_first* when ifirst_function() was invoked?

What happened was this: When the address of the *itemporary* local variable *ilocal_to_first* was assigned to *pi* by ifirst_function(), the address to the *itemporary* location was retained even after *ilocal_to_first* went out of scope. When *b* was invoked, it also needed local storage. Since *ilocal_to_first* was gone, *ilocal_to_second* was given the same storage location as its predecessor. With *pi* hanging on to this same busy memory cell, you can see why printing the value it now points to yields a 44. Extreme care must be taken not to return the addresses of local variables.

When Should You Use Reference Types?

To review, there are four main reasons for using C++ reference types:

- They lend themselves to more readable code by allowing you to ignore details of how a parameter is passed.

- They put the responsibility for argument passing on the programmer who writes the functions, not on the individual who uses them.

- They are a necessary counterpart to operator overloading.

- They are also used with passing classes to functions so constructors and destructors are not called.

These concepts are described in greater detail in Chapter 16.

What's Coming?

Data structures is typically a fifteen-week second or third semester course that revolves around two fundamentals: pointers and dynamic memory allocation. Chapter 10 has thoroughly introduced you to the logic and syntax of these most powerful C/C++ language features. However, the interaction of these two cornerstones to efficient programming generates some of the most difficult bugs to detect and repair. Many of the following chapters build upon these basics. It is well worth your while to review Chapter 10 until you are comfortable with using pointers.

The Complete Reference

Visual C++.NET

Chapter 11

An Introduction to I/O in C++

W hile it is technically true that C++ is a superset of the C language, this does not mean that by simply taking a C statement and translating it into a C++ equivalent form, you have written a C++ program! In many cases C++ has a better way of solving a programming problem. Often the C++ equivalent of a C program streamlines the way your program inputs and outputs data. However, this is not always true. Chapter 11 introduces you to C++ I/O.

The topic of advanced C++ input and output is continued in Chapter 17. The division of the topic is necessary because of the diverse I/O capabilities available to C++ programmers. Chapters 15 and 16 teach the fundamentals of object-oriented programming. Once you understand how objects are created, it will be much easier to understand advanced object-oriented C++ I/O. Chapter 17 picks up with C++'s ability to effortlessly manipulate objects.

Streamlining I/O with C++

The software supplied with the Microsoft Visual C++ compiler includes a standard library that contains functions commonly used by the C++ community. The standard I/O library for C, described by the header file cstdio (old-style stdio.h), is still available in C++. However, C++ introduces its own header file, called iostream (old-style iostream.h), which implements its own collection of I/O functions.

The C++ stream I/O is described as a set of classes in iostream. These classes overload the "put to" and "get from" operators, << and >>. To better understand why the stream library in C++ is more convenient than its C counterpart, let's first review how C handles input and output.

First, recall that C has no built-in input or output statements; functions such as printf() are part of the standard library but not part of the language itself. Similarly, C++ has no built-in I/O facilities. The absence of built-in I/O gives you greater flexibility to produce the most efficient user interface for the data pattern of the application at hand.

The problem with the C solution to input and output lies with its implementation of these I/O functions. There is little consistency among them in terms of return values and parameter sequences. Because of this, programmers tend to rely on the formatted I/O functions printf(), scanf(), and so on, especially when the objects being manipulated are numbers or other noncharacter values. These formatted I/O functions are convenient and, for the most part, share a consistent interface, but they are also big and unwieldy because they must manipulate many kinds of values.

In C++, the class provides modular solutions to your data manipulation needs. The standard C++ library provides three I/O classes as an alternative to C's general-purpose I/O functions. These classes contain definitions for the same pair of operators—>> and <<—that are optimized for all kinds of data. (See Chapter 16 for a discussion of classes.)

cin, cout, and cerr

The C++ stream counterparts to **stdin**, **stdout**, and **stderr**, prototyped in cstdio, are **cin**, **cout**, and **cerr**, which are prototyped in iostream. These three streams are opened automatically when your program begins execution and become the interface between the program and the user. The **cin** stream is associated with the terminal keyboard. The **cout** and **cerr** streams are associated with the video display.

The >> Extraction and << Insertion Operators

Input and output in C++ have been significantly enhanced and streamlined by the stream library operators >> ("get from" or *extraction*) and << ("put to" or *insertion*). One of the major enhancements that C++ added to C was operator overloading. Operator overloading allows the compiler to determine which like-named function or operator is to be executed based on the associated variables' data types. The extraction and insertion operators are good examples of this new C++ capability. Each operator has been overloaded so it can handle all of the standard C++ data types, including classes. The following two code segments illustrate the greater ease of use for basic I/O operations in C++. First, take a quick look at a C output statement using printf():

```
printf("Integer value: %d, Float value: %f",ivalue,fvalue);
```

Here is the C++ equivalent:

```
cout << "Integer value: " << ivalue << ", Float value: "
    << fvalue;
```

A careful examination of the C++ equivalent will reveal how the insertion operator has been overloaded to handle the three separate data types: string, integer, and float. If you are like many C programmers, you are not going to miss having to hunt down the % symbol needed for your printf() and scanf() format specifications. As a result of operator overloading, the insertion operator will examine the data type you have passed to it and determine an appropriate format.

An identical situation exists with the extraction operator, which performs data input. Look at the following C example and its equivalent C++ counterpart:

```
/* C code */
scanf("%d%f%c",&ivalue,&fvalue,&c);

// C++ code
cin >> ivalue >> fvalue >> c;
```

No longer is it necessary to precede your input variables with the & address operator. In C++, the extraction operator takes care of calculating the storage variable's address, storage requirements, and formatting.

Having looked at two examples of the C++ operators << and >>, you might be slightly confused as to why they are named the way they are. The simplest way to remember which operator performs output and which performs input is to think of these two operators as they relate to the stream I/O files. When you want to input information, you extract it (>>) from the input stream, **cin**, and put the information into a variable, for example, *ivalue*. To output information, you take a copy of the information from the variable *fvalue* and insert it (<<) into the output stream, **cout**.

As a direct result of operator overloading, C++ will allow a program to expand upon the insertion and extraction operators. The following code segment illustrates how the insertion operator can be overloaded to print the new type **stclient**:

```
ostream& operator << (ostream& osout, stclient staclient)
{
  osout << " " << staclient.pszname;
  osout << " " << staclient.pszaddress;
  osout << " " << staclient.pszphone;

  return osout;
}
```

Assuming the structure variable *staclient* has been initialized, printing the information becomes a simple one-line statement:

```
cout << staclient;
```

Last but not least, the insertion and extraction operators have an additional advantage—their final code size. The general-purpose I/O functions printf() and scanf() carry along code segments into the final executable version of a program that are often unused. In C, even if you are dealing only with integer data, you still pull along all of the conversion code for the additional standard data types. In contrast, the C++ compiler incorporates only those routines actually needed.

The following program demonstrates how to use the input, or extraction, operator >> to read different types of data:

```
//
// insrt1.cpp : Defines the entry point for the console application.
// A C++ program demonstrating how to use the
// extraction >> operator to input a char,
// integer, float, double, and string.
// Copyright (c) Chris H. Pappas and William H. Murray, 2001
//
```

```
#include "stdafx.h"
#include <iostream>

using namespace std;

#define INUMCHARS 45
#define INULL_CHAR 1

int main(int argc, char* argv[])
{
  char canswer;
  int ivalue;
  float fvalue;
  double dvalue;
  char pszname[INUMCHARS + INULL_CHAR];

  cout << "This program allows you to enter various data types." << endl;
  cout << "Would you like to try it? " << endl;
  cout << "Please type a Y for yes and an N for no: ";

  cin  >> canswer;

  if(canswer == 'Y') {

    cout << "\n" << "Enter an integer value: ";
    cin >> ivalue;
    cout << "\n\n";

    cout << "Enter a float value: ";
    cin >> fvalue;
    cout << "\n\n";

    cout << "Enter a double value: ";
    cin >> dvalue;
    cout << "\n\n";

    cout << "Enter your first name: ";
    cin >> pszname;
    cout << "\n\n";
  }

  return 0;
}
```

In this example, the insertion operator << is used in its simplest form to output literal string prompts. Notice that the program uses four different data types and yet each input statement, **cin >>**, looks identical except for the variable's name. For those of you who are fast typists but are tired of trying to find the infrequently used %, ", and & symbols (required by scanf()), you can give your fingers and eyes a rest. The C++ extraction operator makes code entry much simpler and less error prone.

Because of the rapid evolutionary development of C++, you have to be careful when using C or C++ code found in older manuscripts. For example, if you had run the previous program under a C++ compiler, Release 1.2, the program execution would look like the following example:

```
This program allows you to enter various data types
Would you like to try it?

Please type a Y for yes and an N for no: Y

Enter an integer value:
                10
```

This is because the C++ Release 1.2 input stream is processing the newline character you entered after typing the letter *Y*. The extraction operator >> reads up to, but does not get rid of, the newline. The following program solves this problem by adding an additional input statement:

```
//
// insrt2.cpp : Defines the entry point for the console application.
// A C++ program demonstrating how to use the
// extraction >> operator to input a char,
// integer, float, double, and string.
// Copyright (c) Chris H. Pappas and William H. Murray, 2001
//

#include "stdafx.h"
#include <iostream>

using namespace std;

#define INUMCHARS 45
#define INULL_CHAR 1
```

```
int main(int argc, char* argv[])
{
  char canswer,cAnewline;
  int ivalue;
  float fvalue;
  double dvalue;
  char pszname[INUMCHARS + INULL_CHAR];

  cout << "This program allows you to enter various data types." << endl;
  cout << "Would you like to try it? " << endl;
  cout << "Please type a Y for yes and an N for no: ";

  cin  >> canswer;
  cin.get(cAnewline);

  if(canswer == 'Y') {

    cout << "\n" << "Enter an integer value: ";
    cin >> ivalue;
    cout << "\n\n";

    cout << "Enter a float value: ";
    cin >> fvalue;
    cout << "\n\n";

    cout << "Enter a double value: ";
    cin >> dvalue;
    cout << "\n\n";

    cout << "Enter your first name: ";
    cin >> pszname;
    cout << "\n\n";
  }

  return 0;
}
```

Did you notice the change? After *canswer* is read in, the program executes:

```
cin.get(cAnewline);
```

This processes the newline character so that when the program runs, it now looks like this:

```
This program allows you to enter various data types
Would you like to try it?

Please type a Y for yes and an N for no:

Enter an integer value: 10
```

Both algorithms work properly since the introduction of C++ Release 2.0. However, it is worth mentioning that you must take care when modeling your code from older texts. Mixing what is known as historic C and C++ with current compilers can cause you to spend many hours trying to figure out why your I/O doesn't perform as expected.

This next example demonstrates how to use the output, or insertion, operator << in its various forms:

```cpp
//
// extrct.cpp : Defines the entry point for the console application.
// A C++ program demonstrating how to use the
// insertion << operator to input a char,
// integer, float, double, and string.
// Copyright (c) Chris H. Pappas and William H. Murray, 2001
//

#include "stdafx.h"
#include <iostream>

using namespace std;

int main(int argc, char* argv[])
{
  char c='A';
  int ivalue=10;
  float fvalue=45.67;
  double dvalue=2.3e32;
  char fact[]="For all have...";

  cout << "Once upon a time there were ";
  cout << ivalue << " people." << endl;
  cout << "Some of them earned " << fvalue;
  cout << " dollars per hour." << "\n";
```

```
    cout << "While others earned " << dvalue << " per year!";
    cout << "\n\n" << "But you know what they say: ";
    cout << fact << "\n\n";
    cout << "So, none of them get an ";
    cout << c;
    cout << "!";

    return 0;
}
```

The output from the program looks like this:

```
Once upon a time there were 10 people.
Some of them earned 45.67 dollars per hour.
While others earned 2.3e+32 per year!

But you know what they say: "For all have..."

So, none of them get an A!
```

When comparing the C++ source code with the output from the program, one thing you should immediately notice is that the insertion operator << does not automatically generate a newline. You still have complete control over when this occurs by including the newline symbol \n or **endl** when necessary.

endl is very useful for outputting data in an interactive program because it not only inserts a newline into the stream but also flushes the output buffer. You can also use **flush**; however, this does not insert a newline. Notice too that the placement of the newline symbol can be included after its own << insertion operator or as part of a literal string, as is contrasted in the second and fourth << statements in the program.

Also notice that while the insertion operator very nicely handles the formatting of integers and floats, it isn't very helpful with doubles. Another interesting facet of the insertion operator has to do with C++ Release 1.2 character information. Look at the following line of code:

```
cout << c;
```

This would have given you the following output in Release 1.2:

```
So, none of them get an 65!
```

This is because the character is translated into its ASCII equivalent. The Release 1.2 solution is to use the put() function for outputting character data. This would require you to rewrite the statement in the following form:

```
cout.put(c);
```

Try running this next example:

```
//
// string.cpp : Defines the entry point for the console application.
// A C++ program demonstrating what happens when you use
// the extraction operator >> with string data.
// Copyright (c) Chris H. Pappas and William H. Murray, 2001
//

#include "stdafx.h"
#include <iostream>

using namespace std;

#define INUMCHARS 45
#define INULL_CHARACTER 1

int main(int argc, char* argv[])
{
  char pszname[INUMCHARS + INULL_CHARACTER];

  cout << "Please enter your first and last name: ";
  cin >> pszname;
  cout << "\n\nThank you, " << pszname;

  return 0;
}
```

A sample execution of the program looks like this:

```
Please enter your first and last name: Kirsten Tuttle

Thank you, Kirsten
```

There is one more fact you need to know when inputting string information. The extraction operator >> is written to stop reading in information as soon as it encounters white space. *White space* can be a blank, tab, or newline. Therefore, when *pszname* is printed, only the first name entered is output. You can solve this problem by rewriting the program and using the cin.get() function:

```
//
// cinget.cpp : Defines the entry point for the console application.
// A C++ program demonstrating what happens when you use
// the extraction operator >> with cin.get() to process an
// entire string.
// Copyright (c) Chris H. Pappas and William H. Murray, 2001
//

#include "stdafx.h"
#include <iostream>

using namespace std;

#define INUMCHARS 45
#define INULL_CHARACTER 1

int main(int argc, char* argv[])
{
  char pszname[INUMCHARS + INULL_CHARACTER];

  cout << "Please enter your first and last name: ";
  cin.get(pszname,INUMCHARS);
  cout << "\n\nThank you, " << pszname;

  return 0;
}
```

The output from the program now looks like this:

```
Please enter your first and last name: Kirsten Tuttle

Thank you, Kirsten Tuttle
```

The cin.get() function has two additional parameters. Only one of these, the number of characters to input, was used in the previous example. The function cin.get() will read everything, including white space, until the maximum number of characters specified has been read in, or up to the next newline, whichever comes first. The optional third parameter, not shown, identifies a terminating symbol. For example, the following line would read into *pszname INUMCHARS* characters, all of the characters up to but not including a * symbol, or a newline, whichever comes first:

```
cin.get(pszname,INUMCHARS,'*');
```

From stream.h to iostream

One of the most exciting enhancements to the compiler is the new C++ I/O library, referred to as the iostream library. By not including input/output facilities within the C++ language itself, but rather implementing them in C++ and providing them as a component of a C++ standard library, I/O can evolve as needed.

At its lowest level, C++ interprets a file as a sequence, or *stream*, of bytes. At this level, the concept of a data type is missing. One component of the I/O library is involved in the transfer of these bytes. From the user's perspective, however, a file is composed of a series of intermixed alphanumerics, numeric values, or possibly, class objects. A second component of the I/O library takes care of the interface between these two viewpoints. The iostream library predefines a set of operations for handling reading and writing of the built-in data types. The library also provides for user-definable extensions to handle class types.

Basic input operations are supported by the **istream** class and basic output via the **ostream** class. Bidirectional I/O is supported via the **iostream** class, which is derived from both **istream** and **ostream**. There are four stream objects predefined for the user:

cin   An istream class object linked to standard input.

cout   An ostream class object linked to standard output.

cerr   An unbuffered output ostream class object linked to standard error.

clog   A buffered output ostream class object linked to standard error.

Any program using the iostream library must include the header file iostream. Since iostream treats stream as an alias, programs written using stream may or may not need alterations, depending on the particular structures used.

You can also use the new I/O library to perform input and output operations on files. You can tie a file to your program by defining an instance of one of the following three class types:

Fstream   Derived from iostream and links a file to your application for both input and output.

Ifstream   Derived from istream and links a file to your application for input only.

Ofstream   Derived from ostream and links a file to your application for output only.

Operators and Member Functions

The extraction operator and the << insertion operator have been modified to accept arguments of any of the built-in data types, including **char** *. They can also be extended to accept class argument types.

Probably the first upgrade incompatibility you will experience when converting a C++ program using the older I/O library will be the demised **cout << form** extension. Under the new release, each iostream library class object maintains a *format state* that controls the details of formatting operations, such as the conversion base for integral numeric notation or the precision of a floating-point value.

You can manipulate the format state flags by using the setf() and unsetf() functions. The setf() member function sets a specified format state flag. There are two overloaded instances:

```
setf(long);
setf(long,long);
```

The first argument can be either a format bit *flag* or a format bit *field*. Table 11-1 lists some of the format bit fields you can use with the **setf(long,long)** instance (using a format flag and format bit field).

Bit Field	Meaning	Flags
ios::basefield	Integral base	ios::hex,
		ios::oct,
		ios::dec
ios::floatfield	Floating-point	ios::fixed,
		ios::scientific

Table 11-1.   *Format Flags*

There are certain predefined defaults. For example, integers are written and read in decimal notation. You can change the base to octal, hexadecimal, or back to decimal. By default, a floating-point value is output with six digits of precision. You can modify this by using the precision member function. The following C++ program uses these new member functions:

```
//
// advio.cpp : Defines the entry point for the console application.
// A C++ program demonstrating advanced conversions and
```

```
// formatting member functions.
// Copyright (c) Chris H. Pappas and William H. Murray, 2001
//

#include "stdafx.h"
#include <string.h>
#include <iostream>
#include <strstream>

using namespace std;

#define INULL_TERMINATOR 1

void row(void);

int main(int argc, char* argv[])
{
  char   c        =    'A',
         psz1[]   =    "In making a living today many no ",
         psz2[]   =    "longer leave any room for life.";
  int    iln      =    0,
         ivalue   =    1234;
  double dPi       =    3.14159265;

  char psz_padstring5[5+INULL_TERMINATOR],
  psz_padstring38[38+INULL_TERMINATOR];

  // conversions

  // print the c
  row(); // [ 1]
  cout << c;

  // print the ASCII code for c
  row(); // [ 2]
  cout << (int)c;

  // print character with ASCII 90
  row(); // [ 3]
  cout << (char)90;

  // print ivalue as octal value
  row(); // [ 4]
  cout << oct << ivalue;
```

```
// print lower-case hexadecimal
row(); // [ 5]
cout << hex << ivalue;

// print upper-case hexadecimal
row(); // [ 6] cout.setf(ios::uppercase);
cout << hex << ivalue;
cout.unsetf(ios::uppercase);    // turn uppercase off
cout << dec;                    // return to decimal base

// conversions and format options

// minimum width 1
row(); // [ 7]
cout << c;

// minimum width 5, right-justify
row(); // [ 8]
ostrstream(psz_padstring5,sizeof(psz_padstring5))
<< "    " << c << ends;
cout << psz_padstring5;

// minimum width 5, left-justify
row(); // [ 9]
ostrstream(psz_padstring5,sizeof(psz_padstring5))
<< c << "    " << ends;
cout << psz_padstring5;

// 33 automatically
row(); // [10]
cout << psz1;

// 31 automatically
row(); // [11]
cout << psz2;

// minimum 5 overriden, auto
// notice that the width of 5 cannot be overridden!
row(); // [12]
cout.write(psz1,5);

// minimum width 38, right-justify
// notice how the width of 38 ends with garbage data
row(); // [13]
```

```
   cout.write(psz1,38);

   // the following is the correct approach
   cout << "\n\nCorrected approach:\n";
   ostrstream(psz_padstring38,sizeof(psz_padstring38)) << "      "
     << psz1 << ends;
   row(); // [14]
   cout << psz_padstring38;

   // minimum width 38, left-justify
   ostrstream(psz_padstring38,sizeof(psz_padstring38))
     << psz2 << "          " << ends;
   row(); // [15]
   cout << psz_padstring38;

   // default ivalue width
   row(); // [16]
   cout << ivalue;

   // printf ivalue with + sign
   row(); // [17]
   cout.setf(ios::showpos);      // don't want row number with +
   cout << ivalue;
   cout.unsetf(ios::showpos);

   // minimum 3 overridden, auto
   row(); // [18]
   cout.width(3); // don't want row number padded to width of 3
   cout << ivalue;

   // minimum width 10, right-justify
   row(); // [19]
   cout.width(10);     // only in effect for first value printed
   cout << ivalue;

   // minimum width 10, left-justify
   row(); // [20]
   cout.width(10);
   cout.setf(ios::left);
   cout << ivalue;
   cout.unsetf(ios::left);

   // right-justify with leading 0's
   row(); // [21]
```

```
cout.width(10);
cout.fill('0');
cout << ivalue;
cout.fill(' ');

// using default number of digits
row(); // [22]
cout << dPi;

// minimum width 20, right-justify
row(); // [23]
cout.width(20);
cout << dPi;

// right-justify with leading 0's
row(); // [24]
cout.width(20);
cout.fill('0');
cout << dPi;
cout.fill(' ');

// minimum width 20, left-justify
row(); // [25]
cout.width(20);
cout.setf(ios::left);
cout << dPi;

// left-justify with trailing 0's
row(); // [26]
cout.width(20);
cout.fill('0');
cout << dPi;
cout.unsetf(ios::left);
cout.fill(' ');

// additional formatting precision

// minimum width 19, print all 17
row(); // [27]
cout << psz1;

// prints first 2 chars
row(); // [28]
cout.write(psz1,2);
```

```cpp
  // prints 2 chars, right-justify
  row(); // [29]
  cout << "                    "; cout.write(psz1,2);

  // prints 2 chars, left-justify
  row(); // [30]
  cout.write(psz1,2);

  // using printf arguments
  row(); // [31]
  cout << "                "; cout.write(psz1,6);

  // width 10, 8 to right of '.'
  row(); // [32]
  cout.precision(9);
  cout << dPi;

  // width 20, 2 to right-justify
  row(); // [33]
  cout.width(20);
  cout.precision(2);
  cout << dPi;

  // 4 decimal places, left-justify
  row(); // [34]
  cout.precision(4);
  cout << dPi;

  // 4 decimal places, right-justify
  row(); // [35]
  cout.width(20);
  cout << dPi;

  // width 20, scientific notation
  row(); // [36] cout.setf(ios::scientific); cout.width(20);
  cout << dPi; cout.unsetf(ios::scientific);

  return(0);
}

void row (void)
{
  static int ln=0;
```

```
    cout << "\n[";
    cout.width(2);
    cout << ++ln << "] ";
}
```

You can use the output from the program to help write advanced output statements of your own:

```
[ 1] A
[ 2] 65
[ 3] Z
[ 4] 2322
[ 5] 4d2
[ 6] 4d2
[ 7] A
[ 8]     A
[ 9] A
[10] In making a living today many no
[11] longer leave any room for life.
[12] In ma
[13] In making a living today many no   ????

Corrected approach:

[14]      In making a living today many no
[15] longer leave any room for life.
[16] 1234
[17] +1234
[18] 1234
[19]      1234
[20] 1234
[21] 0000001234
[22] 3.14159
[23]               3.14159
[24] 00000000000003.14159
[25] 3.14159
[26] 3.141590000000000000
[27] In making a living today many no
[28] In
[29]              In
[30] In
[31]             In mak
```

```
[32] 3.14159265
[33]                     3.1
[34] 3.142
[35]                 3.142
[36] 3.142
```

The following section highlights those output statements used in the preceding program that need special clarification. One point needs to be made: iostream is automatically included by strstream. The latter file is needed to perform string output formatting. If your application needs to output numeric data or simple character and string output, you will need to include only **iostream#**.

C++ Character Output

In the I/O library, the insertion operator << has been overloaded to handle character data. With the earlier release, the following statement would have output the ASCII value of *c*:

```
cout << c;
```

In the older style I/O library, the letter itself is output. For those programs needing the ASCII value, a case is required:

```
cout << (int)C;
```

C++ Base Conversions

There are two approaches to outputting a value using a different base:

```
cout << hex << ivalue;
```

and

```
cout.setf(ios::hex,ios::basefield);
cout << ivalue;
```

Both approaches cause the base to be permanently changed from the statement forward (not always the effect you want). Each value output will now be formatted as a hexadecimal value. Returning to some other base is accomplished with the unsetf() function:

```
cout.unsetf(ios::hex,ios::basefield);
```

If you are interested in uppercase hexadecimal output, use the following statement:

```
cout.setf(ios::uppercase);
```

When it is no longer needed, you will have to turn this option off:

```
cout.unsetf(ios::uppercase);
```

C++ String Formatting

Printing an entire string is easy in C++. One approach to string formatting is to declare an array of characters and then select the desired output format, printing the string buffer:

```
pszpadstring38[38+INULL_TERMINATOR];
.
.
.
ostrstream(pszpadstring38,sizeof(pszpadstring38))
    << "       "   << psz1;
```

The ostrstream() member function is part of strstream and has three parameters: a pointer to an array of characters, the size of the array, and the information to be inserted. This statement appends leading blanks to right-justify *psz1*. Portions of the string can be output using the **write** form of **cout**:

```
cout.write(psz1,5);
```

This statement will output the first five characters of *psz1*.

C++ Numeric Formatting

You can easily format numeric data with right or left justification, varying precisions, varying formats (floating-point or scientific), leading or trailing fill patterns, and signs. There are certain defaults. For example, the default for justification is right and for floating-point precision is six. The following code segment outputs *dPi* left-justified in a field width of 20, with trailing zeros:

```
cout.width(20);
cout.setf(ios::left);
cout.fill('0');
cout << dPi;
```

Had the following statement been included, *dPi* would have been printed with a precision of two:

```
cout.precision(2);
```

With many of the output flags such as left justification, selecting uppercase hexadecimal output, base changes, and many others, it is necessary to unset these flags when they are no longer needed. The following statement turns left justification off:

```
cout.unsetf(ios::left);
```

Selecting scientific format is a matter of flipping the correct bit flag:

```
cout.setf(ios::scientific);
```

You can print values with a leading + sign by setting the *showpos* flag:

```
cout.setf(ios::showpos);
```

There are many minor details of the I/O library functions that will initially cause some confusion. This has to do with the fact that certain operations, once executed, make a permanent change until turned off, while others take effect only for the next output statement. For example, an output width change, as in *cout.width(20);*, affects only the next value printed. That is why the function row() has to repeatedly change the width to get the output row numbers formatted within two spaces, as in [1]. However, other formatting operations like base changes, uppercase, precision, and floating-point/scientific remain active until specifically turned off.

C++ File Input and Output

All of the examples so far have used the predefined streams **cin** and **cout**. It is possible that your program will need to create its own streams for I/O. If an application needs to create a file for input or output, it must include the fstream header file (fstream includes iostream). The classes **ifstream** and **ofstream** are derived from **istream** and **ostream** and inherit the extraction and insertion operations, respectively. The following C++ program demonstrates how to declare a file for reading and writing using **ifstream** and **ofstream**, respectively:

```
//
// fstrm.cpp : Defines the entry point for the console application.
// A C++ program demonstrating how to declare an
// ifstream and ofstream for file input and output.
// Copyright (c) Chris H. Pappas and William H. Murray, 2001
//

#include "stdafx.h"
#include <fstream>
#include <iostream> // access to cerr

using namespace std;

int main(int argc, char* argv[])
{
  char c;

  ifstream ifsin("a:\\text.in",ios::in);
  if( !ifsin )
    cerr << "\nUnable to open 'text.in' for input.";

  ofstream ofsout("a:\\text.out",ios::out);
  if( !ofsout )
    cerr << "\nUnable to open 'text.out' for output.";

  while( ofsout && ifsin.get(c) )
    ofsout.put(c);

  ifsin.close();
  ofsout.close();

  return(0);
}
```

The program declares *ifsin* to be of class **ifstream** and is associated with the file text.in stored in the A drive. It is always a good idea for any program dealing with files to verify the existence or creation of the specified file in the designated mode. By using the handle to the file *ifsin*, a simple **if** test can be generated to check the condition of the file. A similar process is applied to *ofsout*, with the exception that the file is derived from the **ostream** class.

The **while** loop continues inputting and outputting single characters while the *ifsin* exists and the character read in is not *EOF*. The program terminates by closing the two files. Closing an output file can be essential to dumping all internally buffered data.

There may be circumstances when a program will want to delay a file specification or when an application may want to associate several file streams with the same file descriptor. The following code segment demonstrates this concept:

```
ifstream ifsin;
.
.
.
ifsin.open("week1.in");
.
.
.
ifsin.close();
ifsin.open("week2.in");
.
.
.
ifsin.close();
```

Whenever an application wishes to modify the way in which a file is opened or used, it can apply a second argument to the file stream constructors. For example:

```
ofstream ofsout("week1.out",ios::app|ios::noreplace);
```

This statement declares *ofsout* and attempts to append it to the file named "week1.out". Because **ios::noreplace** is specified, the file will not be created if week1.out doesn't already exist. The **ios::app** parameter appends all writes to an existing file. The following table lists the second argument flags to the file stream constructors that can be logically ORed together:

Mode Bit	Action
ios::in	Opens for reading
ios::out	Opens for writing
ios::ate	Seeks to *EOF 0after file is created*
ios::app	All writes added to end of file
ios::trunc	If file already exists, truncates
ios::nocreate	(NOT used under the new iostream library— unsuccessful open if file does not exist)

Mode Bit	Action
ios::noreplace	(NOT used under the new iostream library—unsuccessful open if file does exist)
ios::binary	Opens file in binary mode (default text)

An **fstream** class object can also be used to open a file for both input and output. For example, the following definition opens the file update.dat in both input and append mode:

```
fstream io("update.dat",ios::in|ios::app);
```

You can reposition all **iostream** class types by using either the seekg() or seekp() member function, which can move to an absolute address within the file or move a byte offset from a particular position. Both seekg() (sets or reads the get pointer's position) and seekp() (sets or reads the put pointer's position) can take one or two arguments. When used with one parameter, the **iostream** is repositioned to the specified pointer position. When it is used with two parameters, a relative position is calculated. The following listing highlights these differences, assuming the preceding declaration for *io*:

```
streampos current_position = io.tellp();
io << obj1 << obj2 << obj3;
io.seekp(current_position);
io.seekp(sizeof(MY_OBJ),ios::cur);
io << objnewobj2;
```

The pointer *current_position* is first derived from **streampos** and initialized to the current position of the put-file pointer by the function tellp(). With this information stored, three objects are written to *io*. Using seekp(), the put-file pointer is repositioned to the beginning of the file. The second seekp() statement uses the sizeof() operator to calculate the number of bytes necessary to move one object's width into the file. This effectively skips over *obj1*'s position, permitting an *objnewobj2* to be written.

If a second argument is passed to seekg() or seekp(), it defines the direction to move: **ios::beg** (from the beginning), **ios::cur** (from the current position), and **ios::end** (from the end of the file). For example, this line will move into the *get_file* pointer file 5 bytes from the current position:

```
io.seekg(5,ios::cur);
```

The next line will move the *get_file* pointer 7 bytes backward from the end of the file:

```
io.seekg(-7,ios::end);
```

PROGRAMMING FOUNDATIONS

C++ File Condition States

Associated with every stream is an error state. When an error occurs, bits are set in the state according to the general category of the error. By convention, inserters ignore attempts to insert things into an ostream with error bits set, and such attempts do not change the stream's state. The iostream library object contains a set of predefined condition flags, which monitor the ongoing state of the stream. The following table lists the six member functions that can be invoked:

Member Function	Action
eof()	Returns a nonzero value on end-of-file
fail()	Returns a nonzero value if an operation failed
bad()	Returns a nonzero value if an error occurred
good()	Returns a nonzero value if no state bits are set
rdstate()	Returns the current stream state
clear()	Sets the stream state (int=0)

You can use these member functions in various algorithms to solve unique I/O conditions and to make the code more readable:

```
ifstream pfsinfile("sample.dat",ios::in);
if(pfsinfile.eof())
  pfsinfile.clear(); // sets the state of pfsinfile to 0

if(pfsinfile.fail())
  cerr << ">>> sample.dat creation error <<<";

if(pfsinfile.good())
  cin >> my_object;

if(!pfsinfile) // shortcut
  cout << ">>> sample.dat creation error <<<";
```

What's Coming?

This chapter has served as an introduction to C++ I/O concepts. To really understand various formatting capabilities, you'll need to learn about C++ classes and various overloading techniques. Chapters 15 and 16 teach object-oriented programming concepts. With this information, you'll be introduced to additional C++ I/O techniques in Chapter 17.

Visual C++.NET

Chapter 12

Structures, Unions, and Miscellaneous Items

his chapter investigates several advanced C and C++ types, such as structures, unions, and bit-fields, along with other miscellaneous topics. You will learn how to create and use structures in programs. The chapter also covers how to pass structure information to functions, use pointers with structures, create and use unions in programs, and use other important features, such as **typedef** and enumerated types (**enum**).

The bulk of the chapter concentrates on two important features common to C and C++, the structure and the union. The C or C++ structure is conceptually an array or vector of closely related items. Unlike an array or vector, however, a structure permits the contained items to be of assorted data types.

The structure is very important to C and C++. Structures serve as the flagship of a more advanced C++ type, called the *class*. If you become comfortable with structures, it will be much easier for you to understand C++ classes. This is because C++ classes share, and expand upon, many of the features of a structure. Chapters 16 and 18 are devoted to the C++ class.

Unions are another advanced type. Unions allow you to store different data types at the same place in your system's memory. These advanced data types serve as the foundation of most spreadsheet and database programs.

In the section that follows, you will learn how to build simple structures, create arrays of structures, pass structures and arrays of structures to functions, and access structure elements with pointers.

Structures

The notion of a data structure is a very familiar idea in everyday life. A card file containing friends' addresses, telephone numbers, and so on, is a structure of related items. A file of favorite CDs or LP records is a structure. A computer's directory listing is a structure. These are examples that use a structure, but what is a structure? Literally, a *structure* can be thought of as a group of variables, which can be of different types, held together in a single unit. The single unit is the structure.

Syntax and Rules

A structure is formed in C or C++ by using the keyword **struct**, followed by an optional tag field, and then a list of members within the structure. The optional tag field is used to create other variables of the particular structure's type. The syntax for a structure with the optional tag field looks like this:

```
struct tag_field {
  member_type member1;
  member_type member2;
  member_type member3;
```

```
       .
       .
       .
   member_type member n;
};
```

A semicolon terminates the structure definition because it is actually a C and C++ statement. Several of the example programs in this chapter use a structure similar to the following:

```
struct stboat {
   char sztype [iSTRING15 + iNULL_CHAR];
   char szmodel[iSTRING15 + iNULL_CHAR];
   char sztitle[iSTRING20 + iNULL_CHAR];
   int iyear;
   long int lmotor_hours;
   float fsaleprice;
};
```

The structure is created with the keyword **struct** followed by the tag field or type for the structure. In this example, *stboat* is the tag field for the structure.

This structure declaration contains several members; *sztype*, *szmodel*, and *sztitle* are null-terminated strings of the specified length. These strings are followed by an integer, *iyear*, a long integer, *lmotor_hours*, and a float, *fsaleprice*. The structure will be used to save sales information for a boat.

So far, all that has been defined is a new hypothetical structure type called **stboat**. However, no variable has been associated with the structure at this point. In a program, you can associate a variable with a structure by using a statement similar to the following:

```
struct stboat stused_boat;
```

The statement defines *stused_boat* to be of the type **struct stboat**. Notice that the declaration required the use of the structure's tag field. If this statement is contained within a function, then the structure, named *stused_boat*, is local in scope to that function. If the statement is contained outside of all program functions, the structure will be global in scope. It is also possible to declare a structure variable using this syntax:

```
struct stboat {
   char sztype [iSTRING15 + iNULL_CHAR];
   char szmodel[iSTRING15 + iNULL_CHAR];
```

```
    char sztitle[iSTRING20 + iNULL_CHAR];
    int iyear;
    long int lmotor_hours;
    float fsaleprice;
} stused_boat;
```

Here, the variable declaration is sandwiched between the structure's closing brace (}) and the required semicolon (;). In both examples, *stused_boat* is declared as structure type **stboat**. Actually, when only one variable is associated with a structure type, the tag field can be eliminated, so it would also be possible to write:

```
struct {
    char sztype [iSTRING15 + iNULL_CHAR];
    char szmodel[iSTRING15 + iNULL_CHAR];
    char sztitle[iSTRING20 + iNULL_CHAR];
    int iyear;
    long int lmotor_hours;
    float fsaleprice;
} stused_boat;
```

Notice that this structure declaration does not include a tag field and creates what is called an *anonymous structure type*. While the statement does define a single variable, *stused_boat*, there is no way the application can create another variable of the same type somewhere else in the application. Without the structure's tag field, there is no syntactically legal way to refer to the new type. However, it is possible to associate several variables with the same structure type, without specifying a tag field, as shown in the following listing:

```
struct {
    char sztype [iSTRING15 + iNULL_CHAR];
    char szmodel[iSTRING15 + iNULL_CHAR];
    char sztitle[iSTRING20 + iNULL_CHAR];
    int iyear;
    long int lmotor_hours;
    float fsaleprice;
} stboat1,stboat2,stboat3;
```

The compiler allocates all necessary memory for the structure members, as it does for any other variable. To decide if your structure declarations need a tag field, ask yourself the following questions: "Will I need to create other variables of this structure type somewhere else in the program?" and "Will I be passing the structure type to functions?" If the answer to either of these questions is yes, you need a tag field.

C++ Structures: Additional Syntax and Rule Extensions

C++, in many cases, can be described as a superset of C. In general, this means that what works in C should work in C++.

> **Note**   *Using C design philosophies in a C++ program often ignores C++'s streamlining enhancements.*

The structure declaration syntax styles just described all work with both the C and C++ compilers. However, C++ has one additional method for declaring variables of a particular structure type. This exclusive C++ shorthand notation eliminates the need to repeat the keyword **struct**. The following example highlights this subtle difference:

```
/* legal C and C++ structure declaration syntax */
struct stboat stused_boat;

// exclusive C++ structure declaration syntax
stboat stused_boat;
```

Accessing Structure Members

Individual members can be referenced within a structure by using the *dot* or *member operator* (.). The syntax is:

```
stname.mname
```

Here, *stname* is the variable associated with the structure type and *mname* is the name of any member variable in the structure.

In C, for example, information can be placed in the *szmodel* member with a statement such as:

```
gets(stused_boat.szmodel);
```

Here, *stused_boat* is the name associated with the structure and *szmodel* is a member variable of the structure. In a similar manner, you can use a printf() function to print information for a structure member:

```
printf("%ld",stused_boat.lmotor_hours);
```

The syntax for accessing structure members is basically the same in C++:

```
cin >> stused_boat.sztype;
```

This statement will read the make of the *stused_boat* into the character array, while the next statement will print the *stused_boat* selling price to the screen:

```
cout << stused_boat.fsaleprice;
```

Structure members are handled like any other C or C++ variable with the exception that the dot operator must always be used with them.

Constructing a Simple Structure

In the following example, you will see a structure similar to the *stboat* structure given earlier in this chapter. Examine the listing to see if you understand how the various structure elements are accessed by the program:

```
//
// struct_c.cpp : Defines the entry point for the console application.
/*
 *    C program illustrates how to construct a structure.
 *    Program stores data about your boat in a C structure.
 *    Copyright (c) Chris H. Pappas and William H. Murray, 2000
 */

#include "stdafx.h"
#include <cstdio>

#define iSTRING15 15
#define iSTRING20 20
#define iNULL_CHAR 1

struct stboat {
  char sztype [iSTRING15 + iNULL_CHAR];
  char szmodel[iSTRING15 + iNULL_CHAR];
  char sztitle[iSTRING20 + iNULL_CHAR];
  int iyear;
  long int lmotor_hours;
  float fsaleprice;
} stused_boat;
```

```
int main(int argc, char* argv[])
{
  printf("\nPlease enter the make of the boat: ");
  gets(stused_boat.sztype);

  printf("\nPlease enter the model of the boat: ");
  gets(stused_boat.szmodel);

  printf("\nPlease enter the title number for the boat: ");
  gets(stused_boat.sztitle);

  printf("\nPlease enter the model year for the boat: ");
  scanf("%d",&stused_boat.iyear);

  printf("\nPlease enter the current hours on ");
  printf("the motor for the boat: ");
  scanf("%ld",&stused_boat.lmotor_hours);

  printf("\nPlease enter the purchase price of the boat: ");
  scanf("%f",&stused_boat.fsaleprice);

  printf("\n\n\n");
  printf("A %d %s %s with title number #%s\n",
     stused_boat.iyear,stused_boat.sztype,
     stused_boat.szmodel,stused_boat.sztitle);
  printf("currently has %ld motor hours",
     stused_boat.lmotor_hours);
  printf(" and was purchased for $%8.2f\n",
     stused_boat.fsaleprice);

  return (0);
}
```

The output from the preceding example shows how information can be manipulated with a structure:

```
A 1952 Chris Craft with title number #CC1011771018C
currently has 34187 motor hours and was purchased for $68132.98
```

You might notice, at this point, that *stused_boat* has a global file scope since it was declared outside of any function.

Passing Structures to Functions

It is often necessary to pass structure information to functions. When a structure is passed to a function, the information is passed call-by-value. Since only a copy of the information is being passed in, it is impossible for the function to alter the contents of the original structure. You can pass a structure to a function by using the following syntax:

```
fname(stvariable);
```

If *stused_boat* was made local in scope to main(), if you move its declaration inside the function, it could be passed to a function named vprint_data() with the statement:

```
vprint_data(stused_boat);
```

The vprint_data() prototype must declare the structure type it is about to receive, as you might suspect:

```
/* legal C and C++ structure declaration syntax */
void vprint_data(struct stboat stany_boat);

// exclusive C++ structure declaration syntax
void vprint_data(stboat stany_boat);
```

Passing entire copies of structures to functions is not always the most efficient way of programming. Where time is a factor, the use of pointers might be a better choice. If saving memory is a consideration, the malloc() function for dynamically allocating structure memory in C when using linked lists is often used instead of statically allocated memory. You'll see how this is done in Chapter 13.

The next example shows how to pass a complete structure to a function. Notice that it is a simple modification of the last example. The next four example programs use the same basic approach. Each program modifies only that portion of the algorithm necessary to explain the current subject. This approach will allow you to easily view the code and syntax changes necessary to implement a particular language feature. Study the listing and see how the structure, *stused_boat*, is passed to the function vprint_data().

```
//
// passst_c.cpp : Defines the entry point for the console application.
/*
*    C program shows how to pass a structure to a function.
*    Copyright (c) Chris H. Pappas and William H. Murray, 2000
```

```
*/

#include "stdafx.h"
#include <cstdio>

#define iSTRING15 15
#define iSTRING20 20
#define iNULL_CHAR 1

struct stboat {
  char sztype [iSTRING15 + iNULL_CHAR];
  char szmodel[iSTRING15 + iNULL_CHAR];
  char sztitle[iSTRING20 + iNULL_CHAR];
  int iyear;
  long int lmotor_hours;
  float fsaleprice;
};

void vprint_data(struct stboat stany_boat);

int main(int argc, char* argv[])
{
  struct stboat stused_boat;

  printf("\nPlease enter the make of the boat: ");
  gets(stused_boat.sztype);

  printf("\nPlease enter the model of the boat: ");
  gets(stused_boat.szmodel);

  printf("\nPlease enter the title number for the boat: ");
  gets(stused_boat.sztitle);

  printf("\nPlease enter the model year for the boat: ");
  scanf("%d",&stused_boat.iyear);

  printf("\nPlease enter the current hours on ");
  printf("the motor for the boat: ");
  scanf("%ld",&stused_boat.lmotor_hours);

  printf("\nPlease enter the purchase price of the boat: ");
  scanf("%f",&stused_boat.fsaleprice);
```

```
   vprint_data(stused_boat);

   return (0);
}

void vprint_data(struct stboat stany_boat)
{
  printf("\n\n");
  printf("A %d %s %s with title number #%s\n",stany_boat.iyear,
      stany_boat.sztype,stany_boat.szmodel,stany_boat.sztitle);
  printf("currently has %ld motor hours",stany_boat.lmotor_hours);
  printf(" and was purchased for $%8.2f",
        stany_boat.fsaleprice);
}
```

In this example, an entire structure was passed by value to the function. The calling procedure simply invokes the function by passing the structure variable, *stused_boat*. Notice that the structure's tag field, *stboat*, was needed in the vprint_data() function prototype and declaration. As you will see later in this chapter in the "Using Pointers to Structures" section, it is also possible to pass individual structure members by value to a function. The output from this program is similar to the previous example.

Constructing an Array of Structures

A structure can be thought of as similar to a single card from a card file. The real power in using structures comes about when a collection of structures, called an *array of structures,* is used. An array of structures is similar to a whole card file containing a great number of individual cards. If you maintain an array of structures, a database of information can be manipulated for a wide range of items.

This array of structures might include information on all of the boats at a local marina. It would be practical for a boat dealer to maintain such a file and be able to pull out of a database all boats on the lot selling for less than $45,000 or all boats with a minimum of one stateroom. Study the following example and note how the code has been changed from earlier examples:

```
//
// starray_c.cpp : Defines the entry point for the console application.
/*
 *   C program uses an array of structures.
 *   This example creates a "used boat inventory" for
 *   Nineveh Boat Sales.
 *   Copyright (c) Chris H. Pappas and William H. Murray, 2000
 */
```

```
#include "stdafx.h"
#include <cstdio>

#define iSTRING15 15
#define iSTRING20 20
#define iNULL_CHAR 1
#define iMAX_BOATS 50

struct stboat {
  char sztype [iSTRING15 + iNULL_CHAR];
  char szmodel[iSTRING15 + iNULL_CHAR];
  char sztitle[iSTRING20 + iNULL_CHAR];
  char szcomment[80];
  int iyear;
  long int lmotor_hours;
  float fretail;
  float fwholesale;
};

int main(int argc, char* argv[])
{
  int i,iinstock;
  struct stboat astNineveh[iMAX_BOATS];

  printf("How many boats in inventory? ");
  scanf("%d",&iinstock);

  for (i=0; i<iinstock; i++) {

    flushall();      /* flush keyboard buffer */
    printf("\nPlease enter the make of the boat: ");
    gets(astNineveh[i].sztype);

    printf("\nPlease enter the model of the boat: ");
    gets(astNineveh[i].szmodel);

    printf("\nPlease enter the title number for the boat: ");
    gets(astNineveh[i].sztitle);

    printf("\nPlease enter a one line comment about the boat: ");
    gets(astNineveh[i].szcomment);

    printf("\nPlease enter the model year for the boat: ");
    scanf("%d",&astNineveh[i].iyear);
```

```
        printf("\nPlease enter the current hours on ");
        printf("the motor for the boat: ");
        scanf("%ld",&astNineveh[i].lmotor_hours);

        printf("\nPlease enter the retail price of the boat :");
        scanf("%f",&astNineveh[i].fretail);

        printf("\nPlease enter the wholesale price of the boat :");
        scanf("%f",&astNineveh[i].fwholesale);
    }

    printf("\n\n\n");

    for (i=0; i<iinstock; i++) {
      printf("A %d %s %s beauty with %ld low hours.\n",
             astNineveh[i].iyear,astNineveh[i].sztype,
             astNineveh[i].szmodel,astNineveh[i].lmotor_hours);
      printf("%s\n",astNineveh[i].szcomment);
      printf(
         "Grab the deal by asking your Nineveh salesperson for");
      printf(" #%s ONLY! $%8.2f.\n",astNineveh[i].sztitle,
             astNineveh[i].fretail);
      printf("\n\n");
    }

    return (0);
}
```

Here, Nineveh Boat Sales has an array of structures set up to hold information about the boats in the marina.

The variable *astNineveh[iMAX_BOATS]* associated with the structure, **struct stboat**, is actually an array. In this case, *iMAX_BOATS* sets the maximum array size to 50. This simply means that data on 50 boats can be maintained in the array of structures. It will be necessary to know which of the boats in the file you wish to view. The first array element is zero. Therefore, information on the first boat in the array of structures can be accessed with a statement such as:

```
gets(astNineveh[0].sztitle);
```

As you study the program, notice that the array elements are accessed with the help of a loop. In this manner, element members are obtained with code, such as:

```
gets(astNineveh[i].sztitle);
```

The **flushall()** statement inside the **for** loop is necessary to remove the newline left in the input stream from the previous **scanf()** statements (the one before the loop is entered and the last **scanf()** statement within the loop). Without the call to **flushall()**, the **gets()** statement would be skipped over. Remember, **gets()** reads everything up to, and including, the newline. Both **scanf()** statements leave the newline in the input stream. Without the call to **flushall()**, the **gets()** statement would simply grab the newline from the input stream and move on to the next executable statement.

The previous program's output serves to illustrate the small stock of boats on hand at Nineveh Boat Sales. It also shows how structure information can be rearranged in output statements:

```
A 1957 Chris Craft Dayliner 124876 low hours.
A great riding boat owned by a salesperson.
Grab the deal by asking your Nineveh salesperson for
#BS12345BFD ONLY! $36234.00.

A 1988 Starcraft Weekender a beauty with 27657 low hours.
Runs and looks great. Owned by successful painter.
Grab the deal by asking your Nineveh salesperson for
#BG7774545AFD ONLY! $18533.99.

A 1991 Scarab a wower with 1000 low hours.
A cheap means of transportation. Owned by grandfather.
Grab the deal by asking your Nineveh salesperson for
#156AFG4476 ONLY! $56999.99.
```

When you are working with arrays of structures, be aware of the memory limitations of the system you are programming on; statically allocated memory for arrays of structures can require large amounts of system memory.

Using Pointers to Structures

In the following example, an array of structures is created in a similar manner to the last program. The *arrow operator* is used in this example to access individual structure members. The arrow operator can be used *only* when a pointer to a structure has been created.

```
//
// ptrst_c.cpp : Defines the entry point for the console application.
/*
 *  C program uses pointers to an array of structures.
 *  The Nineveh boat inventory example is used again.
 *  Copyright (c) Chris H. Pappas and William H. Murray, 2000
 */
```

```
#include "stdafx.h"
#include <cstdio>

#define iSTRING15 15
#define iSTRING20 20
#define iNULL_CHAR 1
#define iMAX_BOATS 50

struct stboat {
  char sztype [iSTRING15 + iNULL_CHAR];
  char szmodel[iSTRING15 + iNULL_CHAR];
  char sztitle[iSTRING20 + iNULL_CHAR];
  char szcomment[80];
  int iyear;
  long int lmotor_hours;
  float fretail;
  float fwholesale;
};

int main(int argc, char* argv[])
{
  int i,iinstock;
  struct stboat astNineveh[iMAX_BOATS],*pastNineveh;
  pastNineveh=&astNineveh[0];

  printf("How many boats in inventory? ");
  scanf("%d",&iinstock);


    for (i=0; i<iinstock; i++) {
       flushall();      /*  flush keyboard buffer */
       printf("\nPlease enter the make of the boat: ");
       gets(pastNineveh->sztype);

       printf("\nPlease enter the model of the boat: ");
       gets(pastNineveh->szmodel);

       printf("\nPlease enter the title number for the boat: ");
       gets(pastNineveh->sztitle);

       printf(
          "\nPlease enter a one line comment about the boat: ");
       gets(pastNineveh->szcomment);
```

```
      printf("\nPlease enter the model year for the boat: ");
      scanf("%d",&pastNineveh->iyear);

      printf("\nPlease enter the current hours on ");
      printf("the motor for the boat: ");
      scanf("%ld",&pastNineveh->lmotor_hours);

      printf("\nPlease enter the retail price of the boat: ");
      scanf("%f",&pastNineveh->fretail);

      printf(
         "\nPlease enter the wholesale price of the boat: ");
      scanf("%f",&pastNineveh->fwholesale);

      pastNineveh++;
   }

pastNineveh=&astNineveh[0];
printf("\n\n\n");

for (i=0; i<iinstock; i++) {
  printf("A %d %s %s beauty with %ld low hours.\n",
            pastNineveh->iyear,pastNineveh->sztype,
            pastNineveh->szmodel,pastNineveh->lmotor_hours);
  printf("%s\n",pastNineveh->szcomment);
  printf(
     "Grab the deal by asking your Nineveh salesperson for:");
  printf("\n#%s ONLY! $%8.2f.\n",pastNineveh->sztitle,
        pastNineveh->fretail);
        printf("\n\n");
        pastNineveh++;
  }

  return (0);
}
```

The array variable, *astNineveh[iMAX_BOATS]*, and the pointer, **pastNineveh*, are associated with the structure by using the following statement:

```
struct stboat astNineveh[iMAX_BOATS],*pastNineveh;
```

The address of the array, *astNineveh*, is copied into the pointer variable, *pastNineveh*, with the following code:

```
pastNineveh=&astNineveh[0];
```

While it is syntactically legal to reference array elements with the syntax that follows, it is not the preferred method:

```
gets((*pastNineveh).sztype);
```

Because of operator precedence, the extra parentheses are necessary to prevent the dot (.) member operator from binding before the pointer, *pastNineveh*, is dereferenced. It is better to use the arrow operator, which makes the overall operation much cleaner:

```
gets(pastNineveh->sztype);
```

While this is not a complex example, it does illustrate the use of the arrow operator. The example also prepares you for the real advantage in using pointers—passing an array of structures to a function.

Passing an Array of Structures to a Function

You learned earlier in the chapter that passing a pointer to a structure could have a speed advantage over simply passing a copy of a structure to a function. This fact becomes more evident when a program makes heavy use of structures. The next program shows how an array of structures can be accessed by a function with the use of a pointer:

```
//
// ptast_c.cpp : Defines the entry point for the console application.
/*
 *   C program shows how a function can access an array
 *   of structures with the use of a pointer.
 *   The Nineveh boat inventory is used again!
 *   Copyright (c) Chris H. Pappas and William H. Murray, 2000
 */

#include "stdafx.h"
#include <cstdio>

#define iSTRING15 15
#define iSTRING20 20
#define iNULL_CHAR 1
```

```
#define iMAX_BOATS 50

int iinstock;

struct stboat {
  char sztype [iSTRING15 + iNULL_CHAR];
  char szmodel[iSTRING15 + iNULL_CHAR];
  char sztitle[iSTRING20 + iNULL_CHAR];
  char szcomment[80];
  int iyear;
  long int lmotor_hours;
  float fretail;
  float fwholesale;
};

void vprint_data(struct stboat *stany_boatptr);

int main(int argc, char* argv[])
{
  int i;
  struct stboat   astNineveh[iMAX_BOATS],*pastNineveh;
  pastNineveh=&astNineveh[0];

  printf("How many boats in inventory?\n");
  scanf("%d",&iinstock);

  for (i=0; i<iinstock; i++) {

    flushall();       /*  flush keyboard buffer */
    printf("\nPlease enter the make of the boat: ");
    gets(pastNineveh->sztype);

    printf("\nPlease enter the model of the boat: ");
    gets(pastNineveh->szmodel);

    printf("\nPlease enter the title number for the boat: ");
    gets(pastNineveh->sztitle);

    printf("\nPlease enter a one line comment about the boat: ");
    gets(pastNineveh->szcomment);

    printf("\nPlease enter the model year for the boat: ");
    scanf("%d",&pastNineveh->iyear);

    printf("\nPlease enter the current hours on ");
```

```
        printf("the motor for the boat: ");
        scanf("%ld",&pastNineveh->lmotor_hours);

        printf("\nPlease enter the retail price of the boat: ");
        scanf("%f",&pastNineveh->fretail);

        printf("\nPlease enter the wholesale price of the boat: ");
        scanf("%f",&pastNineveh->fwholesale);

        pastNineveh++;
    }

    pastNineveh=&astNineveh[0];

    vprint_data(pastNineveh);

    return (0);
}

void vprint_data(struct stboat *stany_boatptr)
{
    int i;
    printf("\n\n\n");
    for (i=0; i<iinstock; i++) {
        printf("A %d %s %s beauty with %ld low hours.\n",
                stany_boatptr->iyear,stany_boatptr->sztype,
                stany_boatptr->szmodel,stany_boatptr->lmotor_hours);
        printf("%s\n",stany_boatptr->szcomment);
        printf(
            "Grab the deal by asking your Nineveh salesperson for");
        printf(" #%s ONLY! $%8.2f.\n",stany_boatptr->sztitle,
                stany_boatptr->fretail);
        printf("\n\n");
        stany_boatptr++;
    }
}
```

The first indication that this program will operate differently from the last program comes from the vprint_data() function prototype:

```
void vprint_data(struct stboat *stany_boatptr);
```

This function expects to receive a pointer to the structure mentioned. In the function, main(), the array *astNineveh[iMAX_BOATS]*, and the pointer *pastNineveh* are associated with the structure with the following code:

```
struct stboat astNineveh[iMAX_BOATS],*pastNineveh;
```

Once the information has been collected for Nineveh Boat Sales, it is passed to the vprint_data() function by passing the pointer:

```
vprint_data(pastNineveh);
```

One major advantage of passing an array of structures to a function using pointers is that the array is now passed call-by-variable or call-by-reference. This means that the function can now access the original array structure, not just a copy. With this calling convention, any change made to the array of structures within the function is global in scope. The output from this program is the same as for the previous examples.

Structure Use in C++

The following C++ program is similar to the previous C program. In terms of syntax, both languages can handle structures in an identical manner. However, the example program takes advantage of C++'s shorthand structure syntax:

```
//
// struct.cpp : Defines the entry point for the console application.
// C++ program shows the use of pointers when
// accessing structure information from a function.
// Note:  Comment line terminates with a period (.)
// Copyright (c) Chris H. Pappas and William H. Murray, 2000
//

#include "stdafx.h"
#include <iostream>

using namespace std;

#define iSTRING15 15
#define iSTRING20 20
#define iNULL_CHAR 1
#define iMAX_BOATS 50

int iinstock;
```

```cpp
struct stboat {
  char sztype [iSTRING15 + iNULL_CHAR];
  char szmodel[iSTRING15 + iNULL_CHAR];
  char sztitle[iSTRING20 + iNULL_CHAR];
  char szcomment[80];
  int iyear;
  long int lmotor_hours;
  float fretail;
  float fwholesale;
};

void vprint_data(stboat *stany_boatptr);

int main(int argc, char* argv[])
{
  int i;
  char newline;
  stboat astNineveh[iMAX_BOATS],*pastNineveh;
  pastNineveh=&astNineveh[0];

  cout << "How many boats in inventory? ";
  cin >> iinstock;

  for (i=0; i<iinstock; i++) {
    cout << "\nPlease enter the make of the boat: ";
    cin >> pastNineveh->sztype;

    cout << "\nPlease enter the model of the boat: ";
    cin >> pastNineveh->szmodel;

    cout << "\nPlease enter the title number for the boat: ";
    cin >> pastNineveh->sztitle;

    cout << "\nPlease enter the model year for the boat: ";
    cin >> pastNineveh->iyear;

    cout << "\nPlease enter the current hours on "
         << "the motor for the boat: ";
    cin >> pastNineveh->lmotor_hours;

    cout << "\nPlease enter the retail price of the boat: ";
    cin >> pastNineveh->fretail;

    cout << "\nPlease enter the wholesale price of the boat: ";
```

```
      cin >> pastNineveh->fwholesale;

      cout << "\nPlease enter a one line comment about the boat: ";
      cin.get(newline);    // process carriage return
      cin.get(pastNineveh->szcomment,80,'.');
      cin.get(newline);    // process carriage return

      pastNineveh++;
    }

  pastNineveh=&astNineveh[0];
  vprint_data(pastNineveh);

  return (0);
}

void vprint_data(stboat *stany_boatptr)
{
  int i;
  cout << "\n\n\n";
  for (i=0; i<iinstock; i++) {
    cout << "A " << stany_boatptr->iyear << " "
         << stany_boatptr->sztype << " "
         << stany_boatptr->szmodel << " beauty with "
         << stany_boatptr->lmotor_hours << " low hours.\n";
    cout << stany_boatptr->szcomment << endl;
    cout << "Grab the deal by asking your Nineveh "
         << "salesperson for #";
    cout << stany_boatptr->sztitle << "ONLY! $"
         << stany_boatptr->fretail << "\n\n";
    stany_boatptr++;
  }
}
```

One of the real differences between the C++ and C programs is how stream I/O is handled. Usually, simple C++ **cout** and **cin** streams can be used to replace the standard C printf() and gets() functions. For example:

```
cout << "\nPlease enter the wholesale price of the boat: ";
cin >> pastNineveh->fwholesale;
```

One of the program statements requests that the user enter a comment about each boat. The C++ input statement needed to read in the comment line uses a different approach for

I/O. Recall that **cin** will read character information until the first white space. In this case, a space between words in a comment serves as white space. If **cin** were used, only the first word from the comment line would be saved in the *szcomment* member of the structure. Instead, a variation of **cin** is used so that a whole line of text can be entered:

```
cout << "\nPlease enter a one line comment about the boat: ";
cin.get(newline);   // process carriage return
cin.get(pastNineveh->szcomment,80,'.');
cin.get(newline);   // process carriage return
```

First, **cin.get(newline)** is used in a manner similar to the flushall() function of earlier C programs. In a buffered keyboard system, it is often necessary to strip the newline character from the input buffer. There are, of course, other ways to accomplish this, but they are not more eloquent. The statement **cin.get(newline)** receives the newline character and saves it in *newline*. The variable *newline* is just a collector for the information and is not actually used by the program. The comment line is accepted with the following code:

```
cin.get(pastNineveh->szcomment,80,'.');
```

Here, **cin.get()** uses a pointer to the structure member, followed by the maximum length of the *szcomment*, 80, followed by a termination character (.). In this case, the comment line will be terminated when (*n*-1) or 80-1 characters are entered or a period is typed (the *n*th space is reserved for the null-string terminator, \0). The period is not saved as part of the comment, so the period is added back when the comment is printed. Locate the code that performs this action.

Additional Manipulations with Structures

There are a few points regarding structures that the previous examples have not illustrated. For example, it is also possible to pass individual structure members to a function. Another property allows the nesting of structures.

Passing Structure Members to a Function

Passing individual structure members is an easy and efficient means of limiting access to structure information within a function. For example, a function might be used to print a list of wholesale boat prices available on the lot. In that case, only the *fwholesale* price, which is a member of the structure, would be passed to the function. If this is the case, the call to the function would take the form:

```
vprint_price(astNineveh.fwholesale);
```

In this case, vprint_price() is the function name and *astNineveh.fwholesale* is the structure name and member.

Nesting Structures Within Structures

Structure declarations can be nested. That is, one structure contains a member or members that are structure types. Consider that the following structure could be included in yet another structure:

```
struct strepair {
  int ioilchange;
  int iplugs;
  int iairfilter;
  int ibarnacle_cleaning;
};
```

In the main structure, the **strepair** structure could be included as follows:

```
struct stboat {
  char sztype [iSTRING15 + iNULL_CHAR];
  char szmodel[iSTRING15 + iNULL_CHAR];
  char sztitle[iSTRING20 + iNULL_CHAR];
  char szcomment[80];
  struct strepair strepair_record;
  int iyear;
  long int lmotor_hours;
  float fretail;
  float fwholesale;
} astNineveh[iMAX_BOATS];
```

If a particular member from *strepair_record* is desired, it can be reached by using the following code:

```
printf("%d\n",astNineveh[0].strepair_record.ibarnacle_cleaning);
```

Structures and Bit-Fields

Both C and C++ give you the ability to access individual bits within a larger data type, such as a byte. This is useful, for example, in altering data masks used for system information and graphics. The capability to access bits is built around the C and C++ structure.

For example, it might be desirable to alter the keyboard status register in a computer. The keyboard status register on a computer contains the following information:

```
                                        register bits
Keyboard Status:          76543210
Port(417h)
```

where

bit 0 = RIGHT SHIFT depressed (1)

bit 1 = LEFT SHIFT depressed (1)

bit 2 = CTRL depressed (1)

bit 3 = ALT depressed (1)

bit 4 = SCROLL LOCK active (1)

bit 5 = NUM LOCK active (1)

bit 6 = CAPS LOCK active (1)

bit 7 = INS active (1)

In order to access and control this data, a structure could be constructed that uses the following form:

```
struct stkeybits {
  unsigned char
    ucrshift  : 1,        /* lsb */
    uclshift  : 1,
    ucctrl    : 1,
    ucalt     : 1,
    ucscroll  : 1,
    ucnumlock : 1,
    uccaplock : 1,
    ucinsert  : 1;        /* msb */
} stkey_register;
```

The bits are specified in the structure starting with the least significant bit (lsb) and progressing toward the most significant bit (msb). It is feasible to specify more than one bit by just typing the quantity (in place of the 1). Only integer data types can be used for bit-fields.

The members of the bit-field structure are accessed in the normal fashion.

Unions

A *union* is another data type that can be used in many distinctive ways. A specific union, for example, could be construed as an integer in one operation and a float or double in another operation. Unions have an appearance similar to structures. However, they are not alike at all. Like a structure, a union can contain a group of many data types. In a union, however, those data types all share the same location in memory! Thus, a union can contain information on only one data type at a time. Many other high-level languages refer to this capability as a "variant record."

Syntax and Rules

A union is constructed by using the keyword **union** and the syntax that follows:

```
union tag_field {
  type field1;
  type field2;
  type field3;

       .
       .
       .

  type fieldn;
};
```

A semicolon is used for termination because the structure definition is actually a C and C++ statement.

Notice the declaration syntax similarities between structures and unions in the following example declaration:

```
union unmany_types {
  char c;
  int ivalue;
  float fvalue;
  double dvalue;
} unmy_union
```

The union is defined with the keyword **union** followed by the optional tag field, *unmany_types*. The union's optional tag field operates exactly the way its structure counterpart does. This union contains several members: a character, integer, float, and double. The union will allow *unmany_types* to save information on any one data type at a time.

The variable associated with the union is *unmy_union*. If this statement is contained in a function, the union is local in scope to that function. If the statement is contained outside of all functions, the union will be global in scope.

As with structures, it is also possible to associate several variables with the same union. Also like a structure, members of a union are referenced by using the dot (.) operator. The syntax is simply:

```
unname.mname
```

In this case, *unname* is the variable associated with the union type and *mname* is the name of any member of the union.

Constructing a Simple Union

In order to illustrate some concepts about unions, the following C++ program creates a union of the type just discussed. The purpose of this example is to show that a union can contain the definitions for many data types but can hold the value for only one type at a time.

```cpp
//
// unions.cpp : Defines the entry point for the console application.
// C++ program demonstrates the use of a union.
// A union is created with several data types.
// Copyright (c) Chris H. Pappas and William H. Murray, 2000
//

#include "stdafx.h"
#include <iostream>

using namespace std;

union unmany_types {
  char c;
  int ivalue;
  float fvalue;
  double dvalue;
} unmy_union;

int main(int argc, char* argv[])
{
  // valid I/O
```

```
    unmy_union.c='b';
    cout << unmy_union.c << "\n";

    unmy_union.ivalue=1990;
    cout << unmy_union.ivalue << "\n";

    unmy_union.fvalue=19.90;
    cout << unmy_union.fvalue << "\n";

    unmy_union.dvalue=987654.32E+13;
    cout << unmy_union.dvalue << "\n";

    // invalid I/O

    cout << unmy_union.c << "\n";
    cout << unmy_union.ivalue << "\n";
    cout << unmy_union.fvalue << "\n";
    cout << unmy_union.dvalue << "\n";

    // union size
    cout << "The size of this union is: "
         << sizeof(unmany_types) << " bytes." << "\n";

    return (0);
}
```

The first part of this program (valid I/O) simply loads and unloads information from the union. The program works because the union is called upon to store only one data type at a time. In the second part of the program (invalud I/O), however, an attempt is made to output each data type from the union. The only valid value is the double, since it was the last value loaded in the previous portion of code.

```
b
1990
19.9
9.876543e+018
ÿ
-154494568
-2.05461e+033
9.87654e+018
The size of this union is: 8 bytes.
```

Unions set aside storage room for the largest data type contained in the union. All other data types in the union share part, or all, of this memory location.

By using the integrated debugger, you can get an idea of what is happening with storage within a union.

Miscellaneous Items

There are two additional topics that should be mentioned at this point: **typedef** declarations and enumerated types using **enum**. Both typedef and **enum** have the capability to clarify program code when used appropriately.

Using typedef

New data types can be associated with existing data types by using **typedef**. In a mathematically intense program, for example, it might be necessary to use the data type **fixed**, **whole**, **real**, or **complex**. These new types can be associated with standard C++ types with **typedef**. In the next program, two novel data types are created:

```
//
// typedef.cpp : Defines the entry point for the console application.
// C++ program shows the use of typedef.
// Two new types are created, "whole" and "real",
// which can be used in place of "int" and "double".
// Copyright (c) Chris H. Pappas and William H. Murray, 2000
//

#include "stdafx.h"
#include <iostream>

using namespace std;

typedef int whole;
typedef double real;

int main(int argc, char* argv[])
{
  whole wvalue=123;
  real  rvalue=5.6789;

  cout << "The whole number is " << wvalue << endl;
  cout << "The real number is  " << rvalue << endl;

  return (0);
}
```

Be aware that using too many newly created types can have a reverse effect on program readability and clarity. Use **typedef** carefully.

You can use a **typedef** declaration to simplify declarations. Look at the next two coded examples and see if you can detect the subtle code difference introduced by the **typedef** keyword:

```
struct stboat {
  char sztype [iSTRING15 + iNULL_CHAR];
  char szmodel[iSTRING15 + iNULL_CHAR];
  char sztitle[iSTRING20 + iNULL_CHAR];
  int iyear;
  long int lmotor_hours;
  float fsaleprice;
} stused_boat;
typedef struct {
  char sztype [iSTRING15 + iNULL_CHAR];
  char szmodel[iSTRING15 + iNULL_CHAR];
  char sztitle[iSTRING20 + iNULL_CHAR];
  int iyear;
  long int lmotor_hours;
  float fsaleprice;
} STBOAT;
```

Three major changes have taken place:

- The optional tag field has been deleted. (However, when using **typedef** you can still use a tag field, although it is redundant in meaning.)

- The tag field, *stboat*, has now become the new type STBOAT and is placed where structure variables have been defined traditionally.

- There now is no variable declaration for *stused_boat*.

The advantage of **typedef** lies in its usage. For the remainder of the application, the program can now define variables of the type STBOAT using the simpler syntax:

```
STBOAT STused_boat;
```

The use of uppercase letters is not syntactically required by the compiler; however, it does illustrate an important coding convention. With all of the possible sources for an identifier's declaration, C programmers have settled on using uppercase to indicate the definition of a new type, constant, enumerated value, and macro, usually defined in a header file. The visual contrast between lowercase keywords and uppercase user-defined identifiers makes for more easily understood code since all uppercase usually means, "Look for this declaration in another file."

Using enum

The enumerated data type, **enum**, exists for one reason only, to make your code more readable. In other computer languages, this data type is referred to as a user-defined type. The general syntax for enumerated declarations looks like this:

```
enum op_tag_field { val1,. . .valn } op_var_dec ;
```

As you may have already guessed, the optional tag field operates exactly as it does in structure declarations. If you leave the tag field off, you must list the variable or variables after the closing brace. Including the tag field allows your application to declare other variables of the tag type. When declaring additional variables of the tag type in C++, it is not necessary to repeat the keyword **enum**.

Enumerated data types allow you to associate a set of easily understood human symbols, for example, Monday, Tuesday, Wednesday, and so on, with an integral data type. They also help you create self-documenting code. For example, instead of having a loop that goes from 0 to 4, it can now read from Monday to Friday:

```
enum eweekdays { Monday, Tuesday, Wednesday, Thursday, Friday };

/* C enum variable declaration    */
enum eweekdays ewToday;

/* Same declaration in C++        */
eweekdays ewToday;

/* Not using the enumerated type */
for(i = 0; i <= 4; i++)

     .

     .

     .

/* Using the enumerated type     */
for(ewToday = Monday; ewToday <= Friday; ewToday++)
```

C compilers, historically speaking, have seen no difference between the data types **int** and **enum**. This meant that a program could assign an integer value to an enumerated type. In C++ the two types generate a warning message from the compiler without an explicit type cast:

```
/* legal in C not C++ */
ewToday = 1;
```

```
/* correcting the problem in C++ */
ewToday = (eweekdays)1;
```

The use of **enum** is popular in programming when information can be represented by a list of integer values such as the number of months in a year or the number of days in a week. This type of list lends itself to enumeration.

The following example contains a list of the number of months in a year. These are in an enumeration list with a tag name *emonths*. The variable associated with the list is *emcompleted*. Enumerated lists will always start with zero unless forced to a different integer value. In this case, January is the first month of the year.

```cpp
//
// enum.cpp : Defines the entry point for the console application.
// C++ program shows the use of enum types.
// Program calculates elapsed months in year, and
// remaining months using enum type.
// Copyright (c) Chris H. Pappas and William H. Murray, 2000
//

#include "stdafx.h"
#include <iostream>

using namespace std;

enum emonths {
  January=1,
  February,
  March,
  April,
  May,
  June,
  July,
  August,
  September,
  October,
  November,
  December
} emcompleted;

int main(int argc, char* argv[])
{
```

```
int ipresent_month;
int isum,idiff;

cout << "Please enter the present month (1 to 12): ";
cin >> ipresent_month;

emcompleted = December;
isum = ipresent_month;
idiff = (int)emcompleted - ipresent_month;

cout << "\n" << isum << " month(s) past, "
     << idiff << " months to go.";

return (0);
}
```

The enumerated list is actually a list of integer values, from 1 to 12, in this program. Since the names are equivalent to consecutive integer values, integer arithmetic can be performed with them. The enumerated variable *emcompleted*, when set equal to December, is actually set to 12.

This short program will just perform some simple arithmetic and report the result to the screen:

```
Please enter the current month (1 to 12): 4
4 month(s) past, 8 months to go.
```

What's Coming?

In this chapter you learned all about structures, unions, **typedef**s, and enumerated types. Remember to use caution when dealing with a structure's, union's, or **typedef**'s optional tag field. Also, look out for the subtle changes between a simple structure's syntax versus a **typedef** structure's syntax.

The next two chapters complete the coverage of C and C++ programming features. In Chapter 13 we will look at advanced C and C++ features, and Chapter 14 will address useful libraries. After completing Chapter 14, you will be ready to investigate the fundamentals of object-oriented programming, which are presented in Chapter 15.

Chapter 13

Advanced
Programming Topics

433

T his chapter deals with advanced programming concepts common to both C and
C++. Many of the topics discussed, such as type compatibility and macros, will
illustrate those areas of the language where caution must be used when designing
an algorithm. Other topics discussed, such as compiler-supplied macros and conditional
preprocessor statements, will help you create more streamlined applications. The chapter
ends by examining the concepts and syntax necessary to create dynamic linked lists.

Once you have completed Chapters 5 through 14, you will have enough knowledge
of C and C++ to make a jump to the world of object-oriented programming. That topic
occupies the bulk of the remainder of this book.

Type Compatibility

You have learned that C is not a strongly typed language. C++ is only slightly more
strongly typed (for example, enumerated types). You have also learned how C can
perform automatic type conversions and explicit type conversions using the cast
operator. The following section highlights the sometimes confusing way the compiler
interprets compatible types.

ANSI C Definition for Type Compatibility

The ANSI C committee is chiefly responsible for the discussion and solution to compatible
types. Many of the committee's recommendations added features to C that made the
language more readily maintained, such as function prototyping. The committee tried to
define a set of rules or coded syntax that nailed down the language's automatic behind-
the-scenes behavior.

The ANSI C committee decided that for two types to be compatible, they either
must be the same type, or must be pointers, functions, or arrays with certain properties
as described in the following sections.

What Is an Identical Type?

The term composite type is associated with the subject of compatibility. The composite
type is the common type that is produced by two compatible types. Any two types that
are the same are compatible and their composite type is the same type.

Two arithmetic types are identical if they are the same type. Abbreviated declarations
for the same type are also identical. In the following example, both *shivalue1* and
shivalue2 are identical types:

```
short shivalue1;
short int shivalue2;
```

Similarly, the type **int** is the same as **signed int** in this next example:

```
int sivalue1;
signed int sivalue2;
```

However, the types **int**, **short**, and **unsigned** are all different. When dealing with character data, the types **char**, **signed char**, and **unsigned char** are always different.

The ANSI C/C++ committee stated that any type preceded by an access modifier generates incompatible types. For example, the next two declarations are not compatible types:

```
int ivalue1;
const int ivalue2;
```

In this next set of declarations, see if you can guess which types are compatible:

```
char *pc1, * pc2;
struct {int ix, iy;} stanonymous_coord1, stanonymous_coord2;
struct stxy {int ix, iy;} stanycoords;
typedef struct stxy STXY;
STXY stmorecoords;
```

Both *pc1* and *pc2* are compatible character pointers since the additional space between the * symbol and *pc2* in the declaration is superfluous.

You are probably not surprised that the compiler sees *stanonymous_coord1* and *stanonymous_coord2* as the same type. However, the compiler does not see *stanycoords* as being the identical type to the previous pair of variables. Even though all three variables seem to have the same two integer fields, *stanonymous_coord1* and *stanonymous_coord2* are of an anonymous structure type, while *stanycoords* is of tag type, *stxy*.

Because of the **typedef** declaration, the compiler does see *struct stxy* as being identical type to *STXY*. For this reason *stanycoords* is identical to *stmorecoords*.

It is important to remember that the compiler sees **typedef** declarations as being synonymous for types, not totally new types. The following code segment defines a new type called MYFLOAT that is the same type as **float**:

```
typedef float MYFLOAT;
```

Enumerated Types

The ANSI C committee initially stated that each enumerated type be compatible with the implementation-specific integral type; this is not the case with C++. In C++, enumeration types are not compatible with integral types. In both C and C++, no two enumerated type definitions in the same source file are compatible. This rule is analogous to the tagged and untagged (anonymous) structures. This explains why *ebflag1* and *ebflag2* are compatible types, while *eflag1* is not a compatible type:

```
enum boolean {0,1} ebflag1;
enum {0,1} eflag1;
enum boolean ebflag2;
```

Array Types

If two arrays have compatible array elements, the arrays are considered compatible. If only one array specifies a size, or neither does, the types are still compatible. However, if both arrays specify a size, both sizes must be identical for the arrays to be compatible. See if you can find all of the compatible arrays in the following declarations:

```
int imax20[20];
const int cimax20[20];
int imax10[10];
int iundefined[];
```

The undimensioned integer array *iundefined* is compatible with both *imax20* and *imax10*. However, this last pair is incompatible because they use different array bounds. The arrays *imax20* (element type **int**) and *cimax20* (element type **const int**) are incompatible because their elements are not compatible. If either array specifies an array bound, the composite type of the compatible arrays has that size also. Using the previous code segment, the composite type of *iundefined* and *imax20* is **int[20]**.

Function Types

There are three conditions that must be met in order for two prototyped functions to be considered compatible. The two functions must have the same return types and number of parameters, and the corresponding parameters must be compatible types. However, parameter names do not have to agree.

Structure and Union Types

Each new structure or union type a program declares introduces a new type that is not the same as, nor compatible with, any other type in the same source file. For this reason, the variables *stanonymous1*, *stanonymous2*, and *stfloat1* in the following code segment are all different.

However, a reference to a type specifier that is a structure, union, or enumerated type is the same type. You use the tag field to associate the reference with the type declaration. For this reason, the tag field can be thought of as the name of the type. This rule explains why *stfloat1* and *stfloat2* are compatible types.

```
struct {float fvalue1, fvalue2;} stanonymous1;
struct {float fvalue1, fvalue2;} stanonymous2;
struct sttwofloats {float fvalue1, fvalue2} stfloat1;
struct sttwofloats stfloat2;
```

Pointer Types

Two pointer types are considered compatible if they both point to compatible types. The composite type of the two compatible pointers is the same as the pointed-to composite type.

Multiple Source File Compatibility

The compiler views each declaration of a structure, union, or enumerated type as being a new noncompatible type. This might raise the question, "What happens when you want to reference these types across files within the same program?"

Multiple structure, union, and enumerated declarations are compatible across source files if they declare the same members, in the same order, with compatible member types. However, with enumerated types, the enumeration constants do not have to be declared in the same order, although each constant must have the same enumeration value.

Macros

In Chapter 6 you learned how to use the **#define** preprocessor to declare symbolic constants. You can use the same preprocessor to define macros. A macro is a piece of code that can look and act just like a function.

The advantage of a properly written macro is in its execution speed. A macro is expanded (replaced by its **#define** definition) during preprocessing, creating inline code. For this reason, macros do not have the overhead normally associated with function calls. However, each substitution lengthens the overall code size.

Conversely, function definitions expand only once no matter how many times they are called. The trade-off between execution speed and overall code size can help you decide which way to write a particular routine.

There are other subtle differences between macros and functions that are based on when the code is expanded. These differences fall into three categories:

■ In C, a function name evaluates to the address of where to find the subroutine. Because macros sit inline and can be expanded many times, there is no one address associated with a macro. For this reason, a macro cannot be used in a context requiring a function pointer. Also, you can declare pointers to functions, but you cannot declare a pointer to a macro.

■ The compiler sees a function declaration differently from a **#define** macro. Because of this, the compiler does not do any type checking on macros. The result is that the compiler will not flag you if you pass the wrong number or wrong type of argument to a macro.

■ Because macros are expanded before the program is actually compiled, some macros treat arguments incorrectly when the macro evaluates an argument more than once.

What Is a Macro?

Macros are defined the same way you define symbolic constants. The only difference is that the *substitution_string* usually contains more than a single value:

```
#define search_string substitution_string
```

The following example uses the preprocessor statement to define both a symbolic constant and a macro to highlight the similarities:

```
/* #define symbolic constant */
#define iMAX_ROWS 100

/* #define macro              */
#define NL putchar('\n')
```

The **NL** macro causes the preprocessor to search through the source code looking for every occurrence of **NL** and substituting it with **putchar**('\n'). Notice that the macro did not end with a semicolon. The reason for this has to do with how you invoke a macro in your source code:

```
int main(void)
{
    .
    .
    .
  NL;
```

The compiler requires that the macro call end with a semicolon if the *substitution_string* of the macro ends with a semicolon:

```
#define NL putchar('\n');
```

After the macro expansion has taken place, the compiler would see the following code:

```
int main(void)
{
    .
    .
    .
  putchar('\n');;
```

Macros and Parameters

Both C and C++ support macros that take arguments. These macros must be defined with parameters, which serve a purpose similar to that of a function's parameters. The parameters act as placeholders for the actual arguments. The following example demonstrates how to define and use a parameterized macro:

```
/* macro definition */
#define READ_RESPONSE(c) scanf("%c",(&c))
#define MULTIPLY(x,y) ((x)*(y))

int main(void)
{
  char cresponse;
  int a = 10, b = 20;
    .
    .
    .
  READ_RESPONSE(cresponse); /* macro expansions */

 printf("%d",MULTIPLY(a,b));
```

In this example *x*, *y*, and *c* serve as placeholders for *a*, *b*, and *cresponse*, respectively. The two macros, **READ_RESPONSE** and **MULTIPLY**, demonstrate the different ways you can invoke macros in your program. For example, **MULTIPLY** is substituted within a **printf()** statement, while **READ_RESPONSE** is standalone.

Problems with Macro Expansions

Macros operate purely by substituting one set of characters, or tokens, with another. The actual parsing of the declaration, expression, or statement invoking the macro occurs after the macro expansion process. This can lead to some surprising results if you're not careful. For example, the following macro definition appears to be perfectly legal:

```
#define SQUAREIT(x) x * x
```

If the statement is invoked with a value of 5, as in:

```
iresult = SQUAREIT(5);
```

the compiler sees the following statement:

```
iresult = 5 * 5;
```

On the surface everything still looks okay. However, the same macro invoked with this next statement:

```
iresult = SQUAREIT(x + 1);
```

is seen by the compiler as:

```
iresult = x + (1 * x) + 1;
```

instead of:

```
iresult = (x + 1) * (x + 1);
```

As a general rule, it is safest to always parenthesize each parameter appearing in the body of the macro, as seen in the previous **READ_RESPONSE** and **MULTIPLY** macro definitions. And under those circumstances where the macro expansion may appear in a cast expression, for example:

```
dresult = (double)SQUAREIT(x + 1);
```

it is best to parameterize the entire body of the macro:

```
#define SQUAREIT(x) ((x) * (x))
```

Most of the time the compiler is insensitive to additional spacing within standard C and C++ statements. This is not the case with macro definitions. Look closely at this next example and see if you can detect the error:

```
/* incorrect macro definition */
#define BAD_MACRO (ans) scanf("%d",(&ans))
```

Remember that the **#define** preprocessor searches for the *search_string* and substitutes it with the *substitution_string*. These two strings are delineated by one or more blanks. The definition above, when expanded, will appear to the compiler as:

```
(ans) scanf("%d",(&ans));
```

This creates an illegal statement. The problem has to do with the space between the macro name **BAD_MACRO** and *(ans)*. That extra space made the parameter list part of the *substitution_string* instead of its proper place in the *search_string*. To fix the **BAD_MACRO** definition, remove the extra space:

```
#define BAD_MACRO(ans) scanf("%d",(&ans))
```

To see if you really understand the hidden problems that you can encounter when using macros, see if you can determine what the following statement evaluates to:

```
int x = 5;
iresult = SQUAREIT(x++);
```

The situation gets worse when using certain C and C++ operators like increment, ++, and decrement, −−. The result of this expression may be 30, instead of the expected 25, because various compilers may evaluate the expression in several different ways. For example, the macro could be expanded syntactically to read:

```
/* iresult = x * x; */
iresult = 5 * 5;
```

or

```
/* iresult = x * (x+1); */
iresult = 5 * 6;
```

How to Create and Use Your Own Macros

Macros can include other macros in their definitions. This feature can be used to streamline your source code. For example, look at the following progressive macro definitions:

```
#define NL putchar('\n')
#define TAB putchar('\t')
#define FORMAT1 NL, NL, TAB
#define FORMAT2 NL, TAB, TAB
#define BEGIN_PROMPT FORMAT1, printf("Want to begin?"); \
                                printf("\nType 1 for yes, 0 for no")
#define READ_RESPONSE FORMAT2,scanf("%d",(&c))
#define FORMAT_PRINT(ccontrol,ivalue,fvalue) \
        printf("\n%c\t%d\t%8.2f",(ccontrol),(ivalue),(fvalue))
```

Now, instead of seeing all of the code defined in the macro, your program code takes on the following appearance:

```
int main(void)
{
  char cresponse;
  int ivalue = 23;
  float fvalue = 56.78;

      .

      .

      .

  BEGIN_PROMPT;
  READ_RESPONSE(cresponse);
  FORMAT_PRINT(cresponse,ivalue,fvalue);
```

Remember, however, that you trade automatic compiler type checking for source code readability, along with possible side effects generated by invoking the statement's syntax.

Macros Shipped with the Compiler

The ANSI C/C++ committee has recommended that all C/C++ compilers define five special macros that take no arguments. Each macro name begins and ends with two underscore characters as listed in Table 13-1.

Macro Name	Meaning
__LINE__	A decimal integer constant representing the line number of the current source program line
__FILE__	A string constant representing the name of the current source file
__DATE__	A string constant representing the calendar date of the translation in the form "Mmm dd yyyy"
__TIMESTAMP__	A string constant representing the date and time of the last modification of the source file, in the form "Ddd Mmm hh:mm:ss yyyy"
__STDC__	Represents a decimal 1 if the compiler is ANSI C compatible

Table 13-1.   *Predefined Macros*

Predefined macros are invoked the same way user-defined macros are invoked. For example, print your program's name, date, and current line number to the screen with the following statement:

```
printf("%s | %s | Line number: %d",__FILE__,__DATE__,__LINE__);
```

Advanced Preprocessor Statements

There are actually 14 standard preprocessor statements, sometimes referred to as directives, shown in the following listing:

```
#define
#else
```

```
#elif
#endif
#error
#if
#ifdef
#ifndef
#import
#include
#line
#pragma
#undef
#using
```

You are already familiar with two of them, **#include**, and **#define**. Recall that the preprocessor processes a source file before the compiler translates the program into object code. By carefully selecting the correct directives, you can create more efficient header files, solve unique programming problems, and prevent combined files from crashing in on your declarations.

The following sections explain the unique function of each of the ten new preprocessor directives not previously discussed. Some of the examples will use the code found in cstdio to illustrate the construction of header files.

#ifdef and #endif Directives

The **#ifdef** and **#endif** directives are two of several conditional preprocessor statements. They can be used to selectively include certain statements in your program. The **#endif** directive is used with all of the conditional preprocessor statements to signify the end of the conditional block. For example, if the name LARGE_CLASSES has been previously defined, the following code segment will define a new name called MAX_SEATS:

```
#ifdef LARGE_CLASSES
#define MAX_SEATS 100
#endif
```

Whenever a C++ program uses standard C functions, use the **#ifdef** directive to modify the function declarations so that they have the required **extern** "C" linkage, which inhibits the encoding of the function name. This usually calls for the following pair of directive code segments to encapsulate the translated code:

```
/*  used in GRAPH.H  */
#ifdef __cplusplus
extern "C" {           /* allow use with C++ */
```

```
#endif

/* translation units */

#ifdef __cplusplus
}
#endif
```

#undef Directive

The **#undef** directive tells the preprocessor to cancel any previous definition of the specified identifier. This next example combines your understanding of **#ifdef** with the use of **#undef** to change the dimension of MAX_SEATS:

```
#ifdef LARGE_CLASSES
#undef MAX_SEATS 30
#define MAX_SEATS 100
#endif
```

The compiler will not complain if you try to undefine a name not previously defined. Notice that once a name has been undefined, it may be given a completely new definition with another **#define** directive.

#ifndef Directive

Undoubtedly, you are beginning to understand how the conditional directives operate. The **#ifndef** preprocessor checks to see if the specified identifier does not exist, and then performs some action. The code segment that follows is taken directly from cstdio:

```
#ifndef _SIZE_T_DEFINED
typedef unsigned int size_t;
#define _SIZE_T_DEFINED
#endif
```

In this case the conditionally executed statements include both a **typedef** and **#define** preprocessor. This code takes care of defining the type *size_t*, specified by the ANSI C/C++ committee as the return type for the operator sizeof(). Make sure that you read the section titled "Proper Use of Header Files" later in this chapter to understand what types of statements can be placed in header files.

#if Directive

The **#if** preprocessor also recognizes the term **defined**:

```
#if defined(LARGE_CLASSES) && !defined (PRIVATE_LESSONS)
#define MAX_SEATS 30
#endif
```

This next code shows how the **#if** directive, together with the **defined** construct, accomplishes what would otherwise require an **#ifndef** nested in an **#ifdef**:

```
#ifdef LARGE_CLASSES
#ifndef PRIVATE_LESSONS
#define MAX_SEATS 30
#endif
```

The two examples produce the same result, but the first is more immediately discerned. Both **#ifdef** and **b** directives are restricted to a single test expression. However, the **#if** combined with **defined** allows compound expressions.

#else Directive

The **#else** directive has the expected use. Suppose a program is going to be run on a VAX computer and a PC operating under DOS. The VAX may allocate 4 bytes, or 32 bits, to the type **integer**, while the PC may allocate only 2 bytes, or 16 bits. The following code segment uses the **#else** directive to make certain that an integer is seen the same on both systems:

```
#ifdef VAX_SYSTEM
#define INTEGER short int
#else
#define INTEGER int
#endif
```

Of course the program will have to take care of defining the identifier VAX_SYSTEM when you run it on the VAX. As you can readily see, combinations of preprocessor directives make for interesting solutions.

This type of directive played a major role in the development of Windows applications that were to be source code-compatible among Windows 3.x, Windows 95, Windows 98, and Windows NT. Windows 3.2 applications were 16-bit, while Windows 95, Windows 98, ME, NT, and 2000 applications were essentially 32-bit.

#elif Directive

The **#elif** directive is an abbreviation for "else if" and provides an alternate approach to nested **#if** statements. The following code segment checks to see which class size is defined and uniquely defines the **BILL** macro:

```
#if defined (LARGE_CLASSES)
    #define BILL printf("\nCost per student $100.00.\n")
  #elif defined (PRIVATE_LESSONS)
    #define BILL printf("\nYour tuition is $1000.00.\n")
   #else
    #define BILL printf("\nCost per student $150.00.\n")
#endif
```

Notice that the preprocessors don't have to start in column 1. The ability to indent preprocessor statements for readability is only one of the many useful recommendations made by the ANSI C committee and adopted by Visual C++.

#line Directive

The **#line** directive overrides the compiler's automatic line numbering. You can use it to help in debugging your program. Suppose that you have just merged a 50-line routine into a file of over 400 statements. All you care about are any errors that could be generated within the merged code.

Normally, the compiler starts line numbering from the beginning of the file. If your routine had an error, the compiler would print a message with a line number of, say, 289. Where is that in relation to your merged file?

However, if you include a **#line** directive in the beginning of your freshly merged subroutine, the compiler would give you a line error number relative to the beginning of the function:

```
#line 1
int imy_mergefunction(void)
{
    .
    .
    .
}
```

#error Directive

The **#error** directive instructs the compiler to generate a user-defined error message. It can be used to extend the compiler's own error-detection and message capabilities.

After the compiler encounters an **#error** directive, it scans the rest of the program for syntax errors but does not produce an object file. For example:

```
#if !defined( _CHAR_UNSIGNED )
#error /J option required.
#endif
```

This code prints a warning message if _CHAR_UNSIGNED is undefined.

#pragma Directive

The **#pragma** directive gives the compiler implementation-specific instructions. The Visual C++ compiler supports the pragma directives shown in the following list:

```
alloc_text
auto_inline
check_pointer
check_stack
code_seg
comment
data_seg
function
hdrstop
init_seg
inline_depth
inline_recursion
intrinsic
linesize
loop_opt
message
native_caller
optimize
pack
pagesize
skip
subtitle
title
warning
```

Conditional Compilation

Preprocessor statements aren't always found in header files. Preprocessor directives can be used in a program's source code to generate efficient compilations. Look at this next code segment and see if you can detect the subtle difference (hint: executable code size):

```
// compiled if statement
if(DEBUG_ON) {
  cout << "Entering Example Function";
  cout << "First argument passed has a value of " << ifirst_arg;
}

// comparison statement
#if defined(DEBUG_ON)
  cout << "Entering Example Function";
  cout << "First argument passed has a value of " << ifirst_arg;
#endif
```

The first **if** statement is always compiled. This means that the debugging information is perpetually reflected in the executable size of your program. But what if you don't want to ship a product with your intermediate development cycle code? The solution is to conditionally compile these types of statements.

The second portion of the code demonstrates how to selectively compile code with the **#if**-defined directive. To debug your program, you simply define DEBUG_ON. This makes the nested **#if...#endif** statements visible to the compiler. However, when you are ready to ship the final product, you remove the DEBUG_ON definition. This makes the statements invisible to the compiler, reducing the size of the executable file.

Try the following simple test to prove to yourself how invisible the **#if...#endif** directives make the **cout** statement pair. Copy the previous code segment into a simple C program that does nothing else. Include all necessary overhead (**#include**, **main()**, {, and so on). Do not define DEBUG_ON. Make certain that when you compile the program, there are no error messages. Now, remove the **#include** <iostream>, and using namespace std; statements from the program and recompile.

At this point the compiler stops at the first **cout** statement nested within the **if...cout** block statement. The message printed is "Function 'cout' should have a prototype." You would expect this since the **cout** statement within the **if** statement is always visible to the compiler. Now, simply remove or comment out the **if...cout** block statement and recompile.

The compiler does not complain about the **cout** statements nested within the **#if...#endif** preprocessors. It never saw them. They would only become visible to the compilation phase of the compiler if DEBUG_ON is defined. You can use this selective visibility for more than executable statements. Look at this next code streamlining option:

```
#if defined(DEBUG_ON)
  /*****************************************/
  /* The following code segment performs   */
```

```
/* a sophisticated enough solution step  */
/* to require a comment and debug output */
/*****************************************/
cout << "    debug code goes here        ";
#endif
```

This example not only has a conditional output debug statement, but it also provides room for an explanatory comment. The little extra time it takes to write conditionally compiled code has its trade-off in easily debugged code and small executable code size.

Preprocessor Operators

There are three operators that are only available to preprocessor directives. These are the stringize, #, concatenation, ##, and charizing, #@, operators.

Stringize Operator

Placing a single # in front of a macro parameter causes the compiler to insert the name of the argument instead of its value. This has the overall effect of converting the argument name into a string. The operator is necessary because parameters are not replaced if they occur inside string literals that are explicitly coded in a macro. The following example demonstrates the syntax for the stringize operator:

```
#define STRINGIZE(ivalue) printf(#ivalue " is: %d",ivalue)
    .
    .
    .
int ivalue = 2;
  STRINGIZE(ivalue);
```

The output from the macro will appear as:

```
ivalue is: 2
```

Concatenation Operator

The concatenation operator is useful when building variable and macro names dynamically. The operator concatenates the items, removing any white space on either side, forming a new token. When ## is used in a macro, it is processed after the macro parameters are substituted and before the macro is examined for any additional macro processing. For example, the following code shows how to create preprocessed variable names:

```
#define IVALUE_NAMES(icurrent_number) ivalue ## icurrent_number;
    .
    .
    .
int IVALUE_NAMES(1);
```

The compiler sees the previous listing as the following declaration:

```
int ivalue1;
```

Notice that the preprocessor removed the blanks so that the compiler didn't see *ivalue1* as *ivalue 1*. The operator can be combined with other preprocessor directives to form complex definitions. The following example uses the concatenation operator to generate a macro name, which causes the preprocessor to invoke the appropriate macro:

```
#define MACRO1 printf("MACRO1 invoked.")
#define MACRO2 printf("MACRO2 invoked.")

#define MAKE_MACRO(n) MACRO ## n
    .
    .
    .
MAKE_MACRO(1);
```

The output from the example will appear as:

```
MACRO1 invoked.
```

#@ Charizing Operator

The charizing preprocessor precedes formal parameters in a macro definition. This causes the actual argument to be treated as a single character with single quotation marks around it. For example:

```
#define CHARIZEIT(cvalue) #@cvalue
    .
    .
```

```
cletter = CHARIZEIT(z);
```

The compiler sees the previous code as:

```
cletter = 'z';
```

Proper Use of Header Files

Since header files are made up of syntactically correct C and C++ ASCII text, and are included in other files at the point of the **#include** directive, many beginning programmers misuse them. Sometimes they are incorrectly used to define entire functions, or collections of functions. While this approach does not invoke any complaints from the compiler, it is a logical misuse of the structure.

Header files are used to define and share common declarations with several source files. They provide a centralized location for the declaration of all external variables, function prototypes, class definitions, and inline functions. Files that must declare a variable, function, or class include (**#include**) header files.

This provides two safeguards. First, all files are guaranteed to contain the same declarations. Second, should a declaration require updating, only one change to the header file needs to be made. The possibility of failing to update the declaration in a particular file is removed. Header files are frequently made up of:

- **const** declarations
- Enumerated types
- Function prototypes
- Preprocessor directives
- References to **extern**s
- Structure definitions
- **typedef**s

Caution should be exercised when designing header files. The declarations provided should logically belong together. A header file takes time to compile. If it is too large or filled with too many disparate elements, programmers will be reluctant to incur the compile-time cost of including them.

A second consideration is that a header file should never contain a nonstatic definition. If two files in the same program include a header file with an external definition, most link editors will reject the program because of multiply defined symbols. Because constant values are often required in header files, the default linkage of a **const** identifier is static. For this reason constants can be defined inside header files.

More Efficient Header Files

The compiling of header files is made more efficient by using combinations of preprocessor directives. The best way to learn how to construct an efficient header file is to look at an example:

```
#ifndef _INC_IOSTREAM
#define _INC_IOSTREAM

#if !defined(_INC_DEFS )
#include <_defs.h>
#endif

#if !defined(_INC_MEM )
#include <mem.h>     // to get memcpy and NULL
#endif
#endif  /* !_INC_IOSTREAM */
```

Before looking at the individual statements in the example, you need to know that pass one of the compiler builds a symbol table. One of the entry types in a symbol table is the mangled names of header files. *Mangling* is something that the compiler does to distinguish one symbol from another. The C compiler prepends an underscore to these symbols.

The easiest way to control the compiled visibility of a header file is to surround the code within the header file with a tri-statement combination in the form:

```
#ifndef _INC_MYHEADER
#define _INC_MYHEADER    // begin _INC_MYHEADER visibility
     .
     .
     .
#endif // end of conditional _INC_MYHEADER visibility
```

This is exactly what was done with the previous coded example where _INC_IOSTREAM was substituted for _INC_MYHEADER. The first time the compiler includes this header file, _INC_IOSTREAM is undefined. The code segment is included, making all of the nested statements visible. From this point forward, any additional **#include** <iostream> statements found in any of the other files used to create the executable bypass the nested code.

Precompiled Header Files

Writing efficient header files is one method of speeding up the compiling of a program. Another technique is to use precompiled header files. Precompilation is most useful for compiling a stable body of code for use with another body of code that is under development.

Creating Precompiled Headers

When working in the development environment, the compiler is set, by default, to automatically use precompiled header files. To create such files, select Project | Settings. Click on the C/C++ tab and select Precompiled Headers in the Category box. You will then be able to set the Create precompiled header file (.pch) option from this folder.

A similar action can be achieved from the command line. The compiler's command-line option, /Yc, instructs the compiler to create a precompiled header (.pch) file. The syntax looks like:

```
/Yc[yourfile]
```

No space is allowed between /Yc and [yourfile]. The /Yc switch causes the compiler to compile the entire source file, including any and all included header files. The precompiled file is saved with the yourfile name of the source file and a .pch extension.

 Note *Precompiled header files are often quite large. When developing multiple projects, keep an eye on how many of these files you are willing to store on your hard disk.*

Using Precompiled Headers

You must follow a certain procedure to create a project that uses precompiled headers. The use of such headers in a project makefile has certain restrictions. First, there can only be one precompiled header yourfile.pch file for each source language in the project (C and/or C++).

Second, all files for a given language must use the identical precompiled header. Additionally, each source file must include the same set of include files, in the same order, up to the include file that you specify. The same path must be specified with the include file in each source file.

The following section lists the steps necessary to ensure that a project uses precompiled headers:

1. Start by creating a normal project, making sure that you add at least one source file to the project file list. You can specify the source file from which the .pch file will be generated by selecting this file in the list of files visible in the FileView window.

2. Choose the appropriate compiler options by selecting Project | Settings, then choose the C/C++ tab.

3. Select the Precompiled Header option in the Category box. Make sure the Automatic use of precompiled headers option is selected.

climits and cfloat

The ANSI C/C++ committee requires that all C/C++ compilers document the system-dependent ranges of integer and floating-point types in order to help you write portable code. Table 13-2 contains a listing of the ANSI C/C++-required integral definitions found in the climits header file.

Defined Type	Size	Description
#define CHAR_BIT	8	number of bits in a **char**
#define CHAR_MAX	SCHAR_MAX	maximum **char** value
#define CHAR_MIN	SCHAR_MIN	minimum **char** value
#define INT_MAX	2147483647	maximum **(signed) int** value
#define INT_MIN	(-2147483647 - 1)	minimum **(signed) int** value
#define LONG_MAX	2147483647L	maximum **(signed) long** value
#define LONG_MIN	(-2147483647L - 1)	minimum **(signed) long** value
#define SCHAR_MAX	127	maximum **signed char** value
#define SCHAR_MIN	(-128)	minimum **signed char** value
#define SHRT_MAX	32767	maximum **(signed) short** value
#define SHRT_MIN	(-32768)	minimum **(signed) short** value
#define UCHAR_MAX	0xff	maximum **unsigned char** value
#define UINT_MAX	0xffffffff	maximum **unsigned int** value
#define ULONG_MAX	0xffffffffUL	maximum **unsigned long** value
#define USHRT_MAX	0xffff	maximum **unsigned short** value

Table 13-2.   *Values Defined in climits (ANSI C/C++)*

Program code can use these ranges to make certain that data will fit in the specified data type. For example, a VAX integer may be 4 bytes, while an older DOS-based integer is only 2. To solve this problem, the following code might be used:

```
if (PROGRAM_NEEDED_MAX > INT_MAX)
  pvoid = new llong_storage;
else
  pvoid = new iinteger_storage;
```

Table 13-3 shows the ANSI C/C++-required floating-point definitions.

Definition	Value	Comment
#define FLT_RADIX	2	exponent radix
#define FLT_ROUNDS	1	addition rounding: **near**
#define FLT_EPSILON	1.192092896e-07F	smallest such that 1.0+FLT_EPSILON != 1.0
#define DBL_EPSILON	2.2204460492503131e-016	smallest such that 1.0+DBL_EPSILON != 1.0
#define LDBL_EPSILON	DBL_EPSILON	smallest such that 1.0+ LDBL_EPSILON != 1.0
#define FLT_DIG	6	# of decimal digits of precision
#define DBL_DIG	15	# of decimal digits of precision
#define LDBL_DIG	DBL_DIG	# of decimal digits of precision
#define FLT_MIN	1.175494351e-38F	min positive val
#define DBL_MIN	2.2250738585072014e-308	min positive val
#define LDBL_MIN	DBL_MIN	min pos val
#define FLT_MIN_EXP	(-125)	min binary exponent

Table 13-3. *Values Defined in cfloat (ANSI C/C++)*

Definition	Value	Comment
#define DBL_MIN_EXP	(-1021)	min binary exponent
#define LDBL_MIN_EXP	DBL_MIN_EXP	min binary exponent
#define FLT_MIN_10_EXP	(-37)	min decimal exponent
#define DBL_MIN_10_EXP	(-307)	min decimal exponent
#define LDBL_MAX_10_EXP	DBL_MIN_10_EXP	max decimal exponent
#define FLT_MAX	3.402823466e+38F	max value
#define DBL_MAX	1.7976931348623158e+308	max value
#define LDBL_MAX	DBL_MAX	max value
#define FLT_MAX_EXP	128	max binary exponent
#define DBL_MAX_EXP	1024	max binary exponent
#define LDBL_MAX_EXP	DBL_MAX_EXP	max binary exponent
#define FLT_MAX_10_EXP	38	max decimal exponent
#define DBL_MAX_10_EXP	308	max decimal exponent
#define LDBL_MAX_10_EXP	DBL_MAX_10_EXP	Max decimal exponent

Table 13-3.   *Values Defined in cfloat (ANSI C/C++) (continued)*

PROGRAMMING
FOUNDATIONS

Handling Errors with perror()

One of the many interesting functions prototyped in cstdio is a function called perror().
The function prints to the **stderr** stream the system error message for the last library
routine called that generated an error. It does this by using *errno* and *_sys_errlist*
prototyped in cstdlib. The *_sys_errlist* value is an array of error message strings. The
errno value is an index into the message string array and is automatically set to the
index for the error generated. The number of entries in the array is determined by
another constant—*_sys_nerr*, also defined in cstdlib.

The function perror() has only one parameter, a character string. Normally
the argument passed is a string representing the file or function that generated the

error condition. The following example demonstrates the simplicity of the function:

```
//
// perror.cpp : Defines the entry point for the console application.
/* A C program demonstrating the function perror()
 *   prototyped in stdio.h
 *   Copyright (c) Chris H. Pappas and William H. Murray, 2000
 */

#include "stdafx.h"
#include <cstdio>

int main(int argc, char* argv[])
{
    FILE *fpinfile;
    fpinfile = fopen("input.dat", "r");

    if (!fpinfile)
      perror("Could not open input.dat in file main() ");

    return (0);
}
```

The output from the program looks like:

```
Could not open input.dat in file main() : No such file or directory
```

Linked Lists and Dynamic Memory Allocation

Linked lists are often the best choice when trying to create memory-efficient algorithms. Previous programs involving arrays of structures (see Chapter 9, for example) have all included definitions for the total number of structures used. For example, MAX_BOATS might be set to 25. This means that the program can accept data for a maximum of 25 boats. If 70 or 100 boats are brought into the marina, the program itself will have to be altered and recompiled to accommodate the increased number. This is because the structure allocation is *static* (do not confuse this with the storage class modifier static). Static used in this sense refers to a variable that is created by the compiler at compile time. These types of variables exist for their normal scope and the programmer cannot create more of them, or destroy any of them, while the program is executing. The disadvantage of static allocation should be immediately clear.

One way around the problem is to set the number of structures higher than needed. If MAX_BOATS is set to 10000, not even Nineveh Boat Sales could have a marina that large. However, 10000 means that you are requiring the computer to set aside more than 400 times more memory than before. This is not a wise or efficient way to program.

A better approach is to set aside memory dynamically as it is needed. With this approach, memory allocation for structures is requested as the inventory grows. Linked lists allow the use of dynamic memory allocation.

A linked list is a collection of structures. Each structure in the list contains an element or pointer that points to another structure in the list. This pointer serves as the link between structures. The concept is similar to an array but enables the list to grow dynamically. Figure 13-1 shows the simple linked list structure for the Nineveh Boat Sales Program.

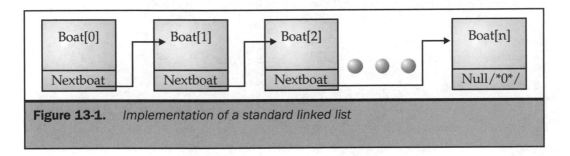

Figure 13-1.   *Implementation of a standard linked list*

The linked list for this example includes a pointer to the next boat in the inventory:

```
struct stboat {
  char sztype[15];
  char szmodel[15];
  char sztitle[20];
  char szcomment[80];
  int iyear;
  long int lmotor_hours;
  float fretail;
  float fwholesale;
  struct stboat *nextboat;
} Nineveh, *firstboat,*currentboat;
```

The user-defined structure type **stboat** is technically known as a self-referential structure because it contains a field that holds an address to another structure just like itself. The pointer, *nextboat*, contains the address of the next related structure. This allows the pointer, *nextboat*, in the first structure to point to the second structure, and so on. This is the concept of a linked list of structures.

Considerations When Using Linked Lists

To allow your program to dynamically reflect the size of your data, you need a means for allocating memory as each new item is added to the list. In C, memory allocation is accomplished with the malloc() function while in C++ new() is used. In the following section titled "A Simple Linked List," the complete program allocates memory for the first structure with the code:

```
Firstboat = new (struct stboat);
```

The following code segment demonstrates how you can use a similar statement to achieve subsequent memory allocation for each additional structure. The **while** loop continues the entire process while there is valid data to be processed:

```
while( datain(&Nineveh) == 0 ) {
  currentboat->nextboat = new (struct stboat);
  if( currentboat->nextboat == NULL ) return(1);
  currentboat=currentboat->nextboat;
  *currentboat=Nineveh;
}
```

To give you some experience with passing structures, the **while** loop begins by sending datain(), the address of the **stboat** structure, *&Nineveh*. The function datain() takes care of filling the structure with valid data or returns a value of 1 if the user has entered the letter "Q" indicating that he or she wants to quit. If datain() does not return a 1, the pointer *currentboat->nextboat* is assigned the address of a dynamically allocated **stboat** structure. The **if** statement checks to see if the function call to new() was successful or not (new() returns a NULL if unsuccessful).

Since the logical use for *currentboat* is to keep track of the address of the last valid **stboat** structure in the list, the statement after the **if** updates *currentboat* to the address of the new end of the list, namely, *currentboat*'s new *nextboat* address.

The last statement in the loop takes care of copying the contents of the **stboat** structure *Nineveh* into the new dynamically allocated structure pointed to by *currentboat*. The last structure in the list will have its pointer set to NULL. Using NULL marks the end of a linked list. See if you can tell where this is done in the complete program that follows.

A Simple Linked List

The following program shows how to implement the Nineveh Boat Sales example using linked lists. Compare this program with the one in Chapter 12 under the section titled "Constructing an Array of Structures." The example in Chapter 12 is similar except that it uses a static array implementation. Study the two listings and see which items are similar and which have changed.

```cpp
//
// simplnklst.cpp : Defines the entry point for the console application.
// C++ program is an example of a simple linked list.
// Nineveh used boat inventory example is used again
// Copyright (c) Chris H. Pappas and William H. Murray, 2000
//

#include "stdafx.h"
#include <cstdlib>
#include <iostream>

using namespace std;

struct stboat {
  char sztype[15];
  char szmodel[15];
  char sztitle[20];
  char szcomment[80];
  int iyear;
  long int lmotor_hours;
  float fretail;
  float fwholesale;
  struct stboat *nextboat;
} Nineveh, *firstboat,*currentboat;

void boatlocation(struct stboat *node);
void output_data(struct stboat *boatptr);
int datain(struct stboat *Ninevehptr);

int main(int argc, char* argv[] )
{
  firstboat = new (struct stboat);

  if( firstboat == NULL ) exit(1);

  if( datain(&Nineveh) != 0 ) exit(1);

  *firstboat = Nineveh;
  currentboat = firstboat;
```

PROGRAMMING
FOUNDATIONS

```
   while( datain(&Nineveh) == 0 ) {
   currentboat->nextboat= new (struct stboat);
   if( currentboat->nextboat == NULL ) return(1);
   currentboat = currentboat->nextboat;
   *currentboat = Nineveh;
   }

   currentboat->nextboat = NULL; // signal end of list

   boatlocation(firstboat);

   return (0);
}


void boatlocation(struct stboat *node)
{
  do{
    output_data(node);
  }while( (node = node->nextboat ) != NULL );
}

void output_data(struct stboat *boatptr)
{
  cout << "\n\n\n";
  cout << "A " << boatptr->iyear << " "
       << boatptr->sztype << boatptr->szmodel << " "
       << "beauty with " << boatptr->lmotor_hours << " "
       << "low miles.\n";
  cout << boatptr->szcomment << ".\n";
  cout << "Grab the deal by asking your Nineveh salesperson for";
  cout << " #" << boatptr->sztitle << " ONLY! $"
       << boatptr->fretail << ".\n";
}

int datain(struct stboat *Ninevehptr)
{
  char newline;

  cout << "\n[Enter new boat information - a Q quits]\n\n";
  cout << "Enter the make of the boat.\n";
  cin >> Ninevehptr->sztype;
```

```
    if (*(Ninevehptr->sztype) == 'Q') return(1);

    cout << "Enter the model of the boat.\n";
    cin >> Ninevehptr->szmodel;

    cout << "Enter the title number for the boat.\n";
    cin >> Ninevehptr->sztitle;

    cout << "Enter the model year for the boat.\n";
    cin >> Ninevehptr->iyear;

    cout << "Enter the number of hours on the boat motor.\n";
    cin >> Ninevehptr->lmotor_hours;

    cout << "Enter the retail price of the boat.\n";
    cin >> Ninevehptr->fretail;

    cout << "Enter the wholesale price of the boat.\n";
    cin >> Ninevehptr->fwholesale;

    cout << "Enter a one line comment about the boat.\n";
    cin.get(newline);     // process carriage return
    cin.get(Ninevehptr->szcomment,80,'.');

    cin.get(newline);     // process carriage return

    return(0);
}
```

Notice that the three functions are all passed pointers to a **stboat** structure:

```
int datain(struct stboat *Ninevehptr)
void boatlocation(struct stboat *node)
void output_data(struct stboat *boatptr)
```

The function boatlocation() checks the linked list for entries before calling the function output_data(). It does this with a **do...while** loop that is terminated whenever *node* pointer is assigned a NULL address. This is only true when you have tried to go beyond the last **stboat** structure in the list. The output_data() function formats the output from each linked list structure.

As you test this application, don't forget to add a period (.) at the end of the comment regarding each boat. Failure to do this will cause the program to hang.

In most high-level languages, linked lists provide the most efficient use of memory but are often the most difficult to debug. You will learn in Chapter 15 that the use of object-oriented C++ classes can improve efficiency even more.

 ## What's Coming?

In this chapter you looked at many advanced C/C++ programming language features, from type compatibility, to dynamic memory allocation and linked lists. Beginning C/C++ programmers will probably not need many of the topics discussed here. However, you cannot generate an efficiently written, easily ported, architecture-independent application without the logic and C/C++ capabilities presented in this chapter. Also, many of the topics discussed will make more logical and syntactical sense as you continue reading the next few chapters. Make a mental note of Chapter 13 as a chapter you should review as your application demands dictate.

Visual C++.NET

Chapter 14

Power Programming: Tapping Important C and C++ Libraries

P rogrammers rely heavily on functions built-in to C and C++ compiler libraries. These built-in functions save you from "reinventing the wheel" when you need a special routine. Both C and C++ offer extensive support for character, string, math, and time and date functions. Most library functions are portable from one computer to another and from one operating system to another. There are some functions, however, that are system- or compiler-dependent. Using these functions efficiently requires you to know where to locate the library functions and how to call them properly.

Many C and C++ functions have already been heavily used in earlier chapters. These include, for example, functions prototyped in the cstdio and iostream header files. It is difficult to do any serious programming without taking advantage of their power. This chapter does not repeat a study of their use; it concentrates on new functions that will enhance character, string, and math and how they work.

Important C and C++ Header Files

If you do a directory listing of your Visual C++ include subdirectory, the frequently used header files shown in Table 14-1 should be present.

There will be others, too, but these are the header files you will use repeatedly. Since these files are in ASCII format, you may want to print a copy of their contents for a reference. You will find that some header files are short while others are quite long. All contain function prototypes and many contain built-in macros.

Header File	Description
Cconio	Console and port I/O
cctype*	Character functions
Io	File handling and low-level I/O
cmath*	Math functions
Cstdio	Stream routines for C
cstdlib*	Standard library routines
Iostream	Stream routines for C++
cstring*	String functions
ctime*	Date and time utilities

Table 14-1. *Important Header Files for C and C++*

This chapter will illustrate a use for many popular functions prototyped in the header files marked with an asterisk in the preceding table. These include the system-independent functions prototyped in cstdlib, cctype, cmath, cstring, and ctime. Other functions contained in cstdio, iostream, and so on have already been used throughout the book.

Standard Library Functions (cstdlib)

The standard library macros and functions comprise a powerful group of items for data conversion, memory allocation, and other miscellaneous operations. The most frequently encountered macros and functions are shown in Table 14-2. The prototypes are found in cstdlib.

As you examine Table 14-2, notice that almost half of the functions shown perform a data conversion from one format to another.

Macro or Function	Description
_exit()	Terminates a program
_lrotl()	Rotates an **unsigned long** to the left
_lrotr()	Rotates an **unsigned long** to the right
_rotl()	Rotates an **unsigned integer** to the left
_rotr()	Rotates an **unsigned integer** to the right
abort()	Aborts program; terminates abnormally
abs()	Absolute value of an **integer**
atexit()	Registers termination function
atof()	Converts a string to a **float**
atoi()	Converts a string to an **integer**
atol()	Converts a string to a **long**
bsearch()	Binary search on an array
calloc()	Allocates main memory
div()	Divides **integer**s

Table 14-2.   *Popular Standard Library Functions*

Macro or Function	Description
_ecvt()	Converts a **float** to a string
exit()	Terminates a program
_fcvt()	Converts a **float** to a string
free()	Frees memory
_gcvt()	Converts a **float** to a string
getenv()	Gets a string from the environment
_itoa()	Converts an **integer** to a string
labs()	Absolute value of a **long**
ldiv()	Divides two **long integer**s
_ltoa()	Converts a **long** to a string
malloc()	Allocates memory
_putenv()	Puts a string in the environment
qsort()	Performs a quick sort
rand()	Random number generator
realloc()	Reallocates main memory
srand()	Initializes random number generator
strtod()	Converts a string to a **double**
strtol()	Converts a string to a **long**
strtoul()	Converts a string to an **unsigned long**
_swab()	Swaps bytes from s1 to s2
system()	Invokes DOS COMMAND.COM file
_ultoa()	Converts an **unsigned long** to a string

Table 14-2. *Popular Standard Library Functions (continued)*

You'll make use of many of these functions and macros as you develop your own C and C++ programs.

Performing Data Conversions

The first important group of functions described in cstdlib are the data converting functions. Their principal job is to convert data from one data type to another. For example, the atol() function converts string information to a **long**.

The syntax of each function is shown in the following list of function prototypes:

```
double atof(const char *s)
int atoi(const char *s)
long atol(const char *s)
char *ecvt(double value,int n,int *dec,int *sign)
char *fcvt(double value,int n,int *dec,int *sign)
char *gcvt(double value,int n,char *buf)
char *itoa(int value,char *s,int radix)
char *ltoa(long value,char *s,int radix)
double strtod(const char *s,char **endptr)
long strtol(const char *s,char **endptr,int radix)
unsigned long strtoul(const char *s,char **endptr,int radix)
char *ultoa(unsigned long value,char *s,int radix)
```

In these functions, *s points to a string, *value* is the number to be converted, *n* represents the number of digits in the string, and *dec* locates the decimal point relative to the start of the string. The variable *sign* represents the sign of the number, *buf* is a character buffer, *radix* represents the number base for the converted value, and *endptr* is usually null. If not a null value, the function sets it to the character that stops the scan.

The use of several of these functions is illustrated in the following programs.

Changing a Float to a String

The fcvt() function converts a **float** to a string. It is also possible to obtain information regarding the sign and location of the decimal point:

```
//
// fcvt.cpp : Defines the entry point for the console application.
// Demonstrating the use of the fcvt() function.
// Copyright (c) Chris H. Pappas and William H. Murray, 2000
//

#include "stdafx.h"
#include <iostream>
#include <cstdlib>

using namespace std;
```

```
int main(int argc, char* argv[] )
{
  int dec_pt,sign;
  char *ch_buffer;
  int num_char=7;

  ch_buffer = fcvt(-234.5678,num_char,&dec_pt,&sign);

  cout << "The buffer holds: " << ch_buffer << endl;
  cout << "The sign (+ = 0, - = 1) is stored as a: " << sign << endl;
  cout << "The decimal place is " << dec_pt << " characters from right\n";

  return (0);
}
```

The output from this program is shown here:

```
The buffer holds: 2345678000
The sign (+=0, -=1) is stored as a: 1
The decimal place is 3 characters from right
```

Changing a String to a Long Integer

The strtol() function converts the specified string, in the given base, to its decimal equivalent. The following example shows a string of binary characters that will be converted to a decimal number:

```
//
// strtol.cpp : Defines the entry point for the console application.
// Demonstrating the use of the strtol() function.
// Copyright (c) Chris H. Pappas and William H. Murray, 2000
//

#include "stdafx.h"
#include <cstdlib>
#include <iostream>

using namespace std;

int main(int argc, char* argv[] )
{
```

```
char *s="101101",*endptr;
long long_number;

long_number = strtol(s,&endptr,2);
cout << "The binary value " << s
     << " is equal to " << long_number
     << " decimal.\n";

return (0);
}
```

In this example, "101101" is a string that represents several binary digits. The program produces the following results:

```
The binary value 101101 is equal to 45 decimal.
```

This is an interesting function since it allows a string of digits to be specified in one base and converted to another. This function would be a good place to start if you wanted to develop a general base change program.

Performing Searches and Sorts

The bsearch() function is used to perform a binary search of an array. The qsort() function performs a quick sort. The lfind() function can be used to perform a linear search for a key in an array of sequential records. The lsearch() function performs a linear search on a sorted or unsorted table. Examine the function syntax shown in the following listing:

```
void *bsearch(const void *key,const void *base,
   size_t nelem,size_t width,int(*fcmp)(const void *,
   const void *))

void qsort(void *base,size_t nelem,size_t width,
   int(*fcmp)(const void *,const void *))

void *lfind(const void *key,const void *base,
   size_t *,size_t width,int(*fcmp)
   (const void *,const void *))

void *lsearch(const void *key, void *base,
   size_t *,size_t width,int(*fcmp)
   (const void *,const void *))
```

Here, *key* represents the search key, *base* is the array to search, *nelem* contains the number of elements in the array, *width* is the number of bytes for each table entry, *fcmp* is the comparison routine used, and *num* reports the number of records.

The next application shows the use of two of the search and sort functions just described.

Using qsort() to Sort a Group of Integers

In C and C++, as in any language, sorting data is very important. Visual C++ provides the qsort() function for sorting data. The following example is one application in which qsort() can be used:

```
//
// qsort.cpp : Defines the entry point for the console application.
// Demonstrating the use of the qsort() function.
// Copyright (c) Chris H. Pappas and William H. Murray, 2000
//

#include "stdafx.h"
#include <iostream>
#include <cstdlib>

using namespace std;

int int_comp(const void *i,const void *j);

int list[12] = {95,53,71,86,11,28,34,53,10,11,74,-44};

int main(int argc, char* argv[] )
{
  int i;

  qsort(list,12,sizeof(int),int_comp);

  cout << "The array after qsort: " << endl;

  for( i = 0; i < 12; i++ )
    cout << list[i] << endl;

  return (0);
}

int int_comp(const void *i,const void *j)
{
  return ( (*(int *)i) - (*(int *)j) );
}
```

The original numbers, in the variable *list*, are signed **integer**s. The qsort() function will arrange the original numbers in ascending order, leaving them in the variable *list*. Here, the original numbers are sorted in ascending order:

```
The array after qsort:
--44 10 11 11 28 34 53 53 71 74 86 95
```

Can qsort() be used with **float**s? Why not alter the previous program and see?

Finding an Integer in an Array of Integers

You use the bsearch() function to perform a search in an **integer** array. The search value for this example is contained in *search_number*.

```cpp
//
// bsearch.cpp : Defines the entry point for the console application.
// Demonstrating the use of the bsearch() function.
// Copyright (c) Chris H. Pappas and William H. Murray, 2000
//

#include "stdafx.h"
#include <cstdlib>
#include <iostream>

using namespace std;

int int_comp(const void *i,const void *j);

int data_array[] = {100,200,300,400,500,
                    600,700,800,900};

int main(int argc, char* argv[] )
{
  int *search_result;
  int search_number = 400;

  printf("Is 400 in the data_array? ");
  search_result = (int *)bsearch(&search_number,data_array,9,
                    sizeof(int),int_comp);
  if (search_result) printf("Yes!\n");
    else printf("No!\n");

  return (0);
```

```
}

int int_comp(const void *i,const void *j)
{
   return ((*(int *)i)-(*(int *)j));
}
```

This application sends a simple message to the screen regarding the outcome of the search, as shown here:

```
Is 400 in the data_array? Yes!
```

You can also use this function to search for a string of characters in an array.

Miscellaneous Operations

There are several miscellaneous functions, listed in Table 14-3 and described in this section, that perform a variety of diverse operations. These operations include calculating the absolute value of an **integer** and bit rotations on an **integer**.

Function	Description
Abort or End:	
void abort(void)	Returns an exit code of 3
int atexit(atexit_t func)	Calls function prior to exit
void exit(int status)	Returns zero for normal exit
int system(const char * command)	Command is a DOS command
void_exit(int status)	Terminates with no action
Math:	
div_t div(int number,int denom)	Divides and returns quotient and remainder in *div_t*
int abs(int x)	Determines absolute value of x
long labs(long x)	Determines absolute value of x

Table 14-3. *Miscellaneous Functions*

Function	Description
Math:	
ldiv_t ldiv(long numerator, long denominator)	Similar to div() with **long**s
int rand(void)	Calls random number generator
void srand(unsigned seed)	Seeds random number generator
Rotate:	
unsigned long_lrotl(unsigned long val,int count)	Rotates the **long** *val* to the left
unsigned long_l lrotr(unsigned long val,int count)	Rotates the **long** *val* to the right
unsigned _rotl(unsigned val,int count)	Rotates the **integer** *val* to the left
unsigned _rotr(unsigned val,int count)	Rotates the **integer** *val* to the right
Miscellaneous:	
char * getenv(const char * name)	Gets environment string
Int putenv(const char * name)	Puts environment string
void _swap(char * from, char * to,int nbytes)	Swaps the number of characters in nbytes

Table 14-3.   *Miscellaneous Functions (continued)*

Bit rotation functions give you the ability to perform operations that were once just in the realm of assembly language programmers.

Using the Random Number Generator

Visual C++ provides a random number function. The random number generator can be initialized or seeded with a call to srand(). The seed function accepts an **integer** argument and starts the random number generator.

```
//
// rand.cpp : Defines the entry point for the console application.
// Demonstrating the use of the srand() and rand(),
```

```
// random number functions.
// Copyright (c) Chris H. Pappas and William H. Murray, 2000
//

#include "stdafx.h"
#include <cstdlib>
#include <iostream>

using namespace std;

int main(int argc, char* argv[] )
{
  int x;

  srand(3);

  for( x = 0; x < 8; x++ )
    cout << "Trial #" << x << " random number = "
         << rand() << endl;

  return (0);
}
```

An example of random numbers generated by rand() is shown here:

```
Trial #0, random number=48
Trial #1, random number=7196
Trial #2, random number=9294
Trial #3, random number=9091
Trial #4, random number=7031
Trial #5, random number=23577
Trial #6, random number=17702
Trial #7, random number=23503
```

Random number generators are important in programming for statistical work and for applications that rely on the generation of random patterns. It is important that the numbers produced be unbiased, that is, that all numbers have an equal probability of appearing.

Rotating Data Bits

C and C++ provide a means of rotating the individual bits of **integers** and **long**s to the right and to the left. In the next example, two rotations in each direction are performed:

```cpp
//
// rotate.cpp : Defines the entry point for the console application.
// Demonstrating the use of the _rotl() and _rotr()
// bit rotate functions.
// Copyright (c) Chris H. Pappas and William H. Murray, 2000
//

#include "stdafx.h"
#include <iostream>
#include <cstdlib>

using namespace std;

int main(int argc, char* argv[] )
{
 unsigned int val = 0x2345;

 cout << "rotate bits of " << hex << val
      << " to the left 2 bits and get "
      << _rotl(val,2) << endl;

 cout << "rotate bits of " << hex << val
      << " to the right 2 bits and get "
      << _rotr(val,2) << endl;

 return(0);
}
```

Here are the results:

```
rotate bits of 2345 to the left 2 bits and get 8D14
rotate bits of 2345 to the right 2 bits and get 400008D1
```

Note that the original numbers are in hexadecimal format.

The use of the bit rotation functions and the use of logical operators such as and, or, xor, and so on, give C and C++ the ability to manipulate data bit by bit.

The Character Functions (cctype)

Characters are defined in most languages as single-byte values. Chinese is one case where 2 bytes are needed. The character macros and functions in C and C++, prototyped or contained in cctype, take **integer** arguments but utilize only the lower byte of the **integer** value. Automatic type conversion usually permits character arguments to also be passed to the macros or functions. The macros and functions shown in Table 14-4 are available.

Macro	Description
isalnum()	Checks for alphanumeric character
isalpha()	Checks for alpha character
isascii()	Checks for ASCII character
iscntrl()	Checks for control character
isdigit()	Checks for decimal digit (0–9)
isgraph()	Checks for printable character (no space)
islower()	Checks for lowercase character
isprint()	Checks for printable character
ispunct()	Checks for punctuation character
isspace()	Checks for white-space character
isupper()	Checks for uppercase character
isxdigit()	Checks for hexadecimal digit
toascii()	Translates character to ASCII equivalent
tolower()	Translates character to lowercase
toupper()	Translates character to uppercase

Table 14-4.   *Character Macros Available in C and C++*

These macros and functions allow characters to be tested for various conditions or to be converted between lowercase and uppercase.

Checking for Alphanumeric, Alpha, and ASCII Values

The macros shown in Table 14-5 allow ASCII-coded **integer** values to be checked with the use of a lookup table.

Macro	Description
int isalnum(ch)	Checks for alphanumeric values A–Z, a–z, and 0–9. ch0 is **integer**
int isalpha(ch)	Checks for alpha values A–Z and a–z. ch0 is **integer**
int isascii(ch)	Checks for ASCII values 0–127 (0–7Fh). ch0 is **integer**

Table 14-5.   *Three Important Macros*

The following program checks the ASCII integer values from zero to 127 and reports which of the preceding three functions produce a TRUE condition for each case:

```
//
// alpha.cpp : Defines the entry point for the console application.
// Demonstrating the use of the isalnum(), isalpha(),
// and isascii() library functions.
// Copyright (c) Chris H. Pappas and William H. Murray, 2000
//

#include "stdafx.h"
#include <iostream>
#include <cctype>

using namespace std;

int main(int argc, char* argv[] )
{
  int ch;

  for( ch = 0; ch <= 127; ch++ ) {
    cout << "The ASCII digit " << dec << ch << " is an: \n" << endl;
    cout << (isalnum(ch) ? "  alpha-numeric char \n" : "");
```

```
      cout << (isalpha(ch) ? "  alpha char \n" : "");
      cout << (isascii(ch) ? "  ascii char\n" : "");
      cout << endl;
   }
   return (0);
}
```

A portion of the information sent to the screen is shown here:

```
The ASCII digit 0 is an:
  ascii char

The ASCII digit 1 is an:
  ascii char
        .
        .
        .
The ASCII digit 48 is an:
  alpha-numeric char
  ascii char

The ASCII digit 49 is an:
  alpha-numeric char
  ascii char
        .
        .
        .
The ASCII digit 65 is an:
  alpha-numeric char
  alpha char
  ascii char

The ASCII digit 66 is an:
  alpha-numeric char
  alpha char
  ascii char
```

These functions are very useful in checking the contents of string characters.

Checking for Control, White Space, and Punctuation

The routines shown in Table 14-6 are implemented as both macros and functions.

Routine	Description
int iscntrl(ch)	Checks for control character
int isdigit(ch)	Checks for digit 0–9
int isgraph(ch)	Checks for printable characters (no space)
int islower(ch)	Checks for lowercase a–z
int isprint(ch)	Checks for printable character
int ispunct(ch)	Checks for punctuation
int isspace(ch)	Checks for white space
int isupper(ch)	Checks for uppercase A–Z
int isxdigit(ch)	Checks for hexadecimal value 0–9, a–f, or A–F

Table 14-6. *Routines Implemented as Both Macros and Functions*

These routines allow ASCII-coded **integer** values to be checked via a lookup table. A zero is returned for FALSE and a nonzero for TRUE. A valid ASCII character set is assumed. The value *ch* is an **integer**.

The next application checks the ASCII **integer** values from zero to 127 and reports which of the preceding nine functions give a TRUE condition for each value:

```
//
// control.cpp : Defines the entry point for the console application.
// Demonstrating several character functions such as
// isprint(), isupper(), iscntrl(), etc.
// Copyright (c) Chris H. Pappas and William H. Murray, 2000
//

#include "stdafx.h"
#include <iostream>
#include <cctype>
```

```
using namespace std;

int main(int argc, char* argv[] )
{
  int ch;

  for( ch = 0; ch <= 127; ch++ ) {

    cout << "The ASCII digit " << ch << " is a(n):\n";
    cout << (isprint(ch)  ? "  printable char\n" : "");
    cout << (islower(ch)  ? "  lowercase char\n" : "");
    cout << (isupper(ch)  ? "  uppercase char\n" : "");
    cout << (ispunct(ch)  ? "  punctuation char\n" : "");
    cout << (isspace(ch)  ? "  space char\n" : "");
    cout << (isdigit(ch)  ? "  char digit\n" : "");
    cout << (isgraph(ch)  ? "  graphics char\n" : "");
    cout << (iscntrl(ch)  ? "  control char\n" : "");
    cout << (isxdigit(ch) ? "  hexadecimal char\n" : "");
    cout << endl;
  }

  return (0);
}
```

A portion of the information sent to the screen is shown here:

```
The ASCII digit 0 is a(n):
  control char

The ASCII digit 1 is a(n):
  control char
          .
          .
          .
The ASCII digit 32 is a(n):
  printable char
  space char

The ASCII digit 33 is a(n):
  printable char
  punctuation char
  graphics char
```

```
The ASCII digit 34 is a(n):
  printable char
  punctuation char
  graphics char
          .
          .
          .
The ASCII digit 65 is a(n):
  printable char
  uppercase char
  graphics char
  hexadecimal char

The ASCII digit 66 is a(n):
  printable char
  uppercase char
  graphics char
  hexadecimal char
```

Conversions to ASCII, Lowercase, and Uppercase

The macros and functions shown in Table 14-7 allow ASCII-coded **integer** values to be translated.

Macro	Description
int toascii(ch)	Translates to ASCII character
int tolower(ch)	Translates *ch* to lowercase if uppercase
int _tolower(ch)	Translates *ch* to lowercase
int toupper(ch)	Translates *ch* to uppercase if lowercase
int _toupper(ch)	Translates *ch* to uppercase

Table 14-7.   *Functions Used to Translate ASCII-Coded Integer Values*

The macro **toascii()** converts *ch* to ASCII by retaining only the lower 7 bits. The functions tolower() and toupper() convert the character value to the format specified. The macros **_tolower()** and **_toupper()** return identical results when supplied proper ASCII values. A valid ASCII character set is assumed. The value *ch* is an **integer**.

The next example shows how the macro **toascii()** converts **integer** information to correct ASCII values:

```
//
// ascii.cpp : Defines the entry point for the console application.
// Demonstrating the use of the toascii() function.
// Copyright (c) Chris H. Pappas and William H. Murray, 2000
//

#include "stdafx.h"
#include <iostream>
#include <cctype>

using namespace std;

int ch;

int main(int argc, char* argv[] )
{
  for( ch = 0; ch <= 512; ch++ ) {
    cout << "The ASCII value for " << ch << " is "
         << toascii(ch) << endl;
  }
  return (0);
}
```

Here is a partial list of the information sent to the screen:

```
The ASCII value for 0 is 0
The ASCII value for 1 is 1
The ASCII value for 2 is 2
            .
            .
            .
The ASCII value for 128 is 0
The ASCII value for 129 is 1
The ASCII value for 130 is 2
            .
            .
            .
The ASCII value for 256 is 0
The ASCII value for 257 is 1
```

```
The ASCII value for 258 is 2
                    .
                    .
                    .
The ASCII value for 384 is 0
The ASCII value for 385 is 1
The ASCII value for 386 is 2
```

The String Functions (cstring)

Strings in C and C++ are usually considered one-dimensional character arrays terminated with a null character. The string functions, prototyped in cstring, typically use pointer arguments and return pointer or **integer** values. You can study the syntax of each command in the next section, or in more detail from the Help facility provided with the Visual C++ compiler. Additionally, buffer-manipulation functions such as memccpy() and memset() are also prototyped in cstring. The functions shown in Table 14-8 are the most popular ones in this group.

Function	Description
memccpy()	Copies from source to destination
memchr()	Searches buffer for first *ch*
memcmp()	Compares *n* characters in buf1 and bufs
memcpy()	Copies *n* characters from source to destination
memicmp()	Same as memcmp(), except case sensitive
memmove()	Moves one buffer to another
memset()	Copies ch into *n* character positions in buf
strcat()	Appends a string to another string
strchr()	Locates first occurrence of a *ch* in a string
strcmp()	Compares two strings
strcmpi()	Compares two strings (case insensitive)

Table 14-8.   *Popular String Functions*

Function	Description
strcoll()	Compares two strings (local specific)
strcpy()	Copies string to another string
strcspn()	Locates first occurrence of a character in string from a given character set
strdup()	Replicates the string
strerror()	Saves system-error message
stricmp()	Same as strcmpi()
strlen()	Length of string
strlwr()	Converts string to lowercase
strncat()	Appends characters of string
strncmp()	Compares characters of two strings
strncpy()	Copies characters of a string to another
strnicmp()	Compares characters of two strings (case insensitive)
strnset()	Sets string characters to a given character
strpbrk()	First occurrence of character from one string in another string
strrchr()	Last occurrence of character in string
strrev()	Reverses characters in a string
strset()	Sets all characters in string to given character
strspn()	Locates first substring from given character set in string
strstr()	Locates one string in another string
strtok()	Locates tokens within a string
strupr()	Converts string to uppercase
strxfrm()	Transforms local-specific string

Table 14-8.   *Popular String Functions (continued)*

The memory and string functions provide flexible programming power to C and C++ programmers.

Working with Memory Functions

The memory functions, discussed in the previous section, are accessed with the syntax shown in the following listing:

```
void *memccpy(void *dest,void *source,int ch,unsigned count)

void *memchr(void *buf,int ch,unsigned count)

int memcmp(void *buf1,void *buf2,unsigned count)

void *memcpy(void *dest,void *source,unsigned count)

int memicmp(void *buf1,void *buf2,unsigned count)

void *memmove(void *dest,void *source,unsigned count)

void *memset(void *dest,int ch,unsigned count)
```

Here, *buf, *buf1, *buf2, *dest, and *source are pointers to the appropriate string buffer. The **integer** ch points to a character value. The **unsigned** count holds the character count for the function.

The next section includes a number of examples that show the uses of many of these functions.

Finding a Character in a String

In this example, the buffer is searched for the occurrence of the lowercase character "f," using the memchr() function:

```
//
// memchr.cpp : Defines the entry point for the console application.
// Demonstrating the use of the memchr() function.
// Finding a character in a buffer.
// Copyright (c) Chris H. Pappas and William H. Murray, 2000
//

#include "stdafx.h"
#include <cstring>
```

```
#include <iostream>

using namespace std;

char buf[35];
char *ptr;

int main(int argc, char* argv[] )
{
  strcpy(buf,"This is a fine day for a search." );
  ptr = (char *)memchr(buf,'f',35);
  if( ptr != NULL )
    cout << "character found at location: "
          << ptr-buf + 1 << endl;
  else
    cout << "character not found." << endl;

  return (0);
}
```

For this example, if a lowercase "f" is in the string, the memchr() function will report "character found at location: 11."

Comparing Characters in Strings

This example highlights the memicmp() function. This function compares two strings contained in *buf1* and *buf2*. This function is insensitive to the case of the string characters.

```
//
// memcmp.cpp : Defines the entry point for the console application.
// Demonstrating the use of the memicmp() function
// to compare two string buffers.
// Copyright (c) Chris H. Pappas and William H. Murray, 2000
//

#include "stdafx.h"
#include <iostream>
#include <cstring>

using namespace std;

char buf1[40],
     buf2[40];
```

```
int main(int argc, char* argv[])
{
  strcpy(buf1,"Well, are they identical or not?");
  strcpy(buf2,"Well, are they identicle or not?");
  /* 0 - identical strings except for case */
  /* x - any integer, means not identical */

  cout << endl << memicmp(buf1,buf2,40);
  /* returns a non-zero value */

  return (0);
}
```

If it weren't for the fact that "identical" (or is it "identicle"?) was spelled incorrectly in the second string, both strings would have been the same. A nonzero value, -1, is returned by memicmp() for this example.

Loading the Buffer with memset()

Often it is necessary to load or clear a buffer with a predefined character. In those cases you might consider using the memset() function, shown here:

```
//
// memset.cpp : Defines the entry point for the console application.
// Demonstrating the use of the memset() function
// to set the contents of a string buffer.
// Copyright (c) Chris H. Pappas and William H. Murray, 2000
//

#include "stdafx.h"
#include <iostream>
#include <cstring>

using namespace std;

char buf[20];

int main(int argc, char* argv[] )
{
  cout << "The contents of buf: " << memset(buf,'+',15);
  buf[15] = '\0';

  return (0);
}
```

In this example, the buffer is loaded with 15 + characters and a null character. The program will print 15 + characters to the screen.

Working with String Functions

The prototypes for using several string-manipulating functions contained in cstring are shown in Table 14-9.

Function	Description
int strcmp(const char * s1, const char *s2)	Compares two strings
size_t strcspn(const char * s1, const char * s2)	Finds a substring in a string
char * strcpy(char * s1, const char * s2)	Copies a string
char * strerror(int errnum)	ANSI-supplied number
char * _strerror(char * s)	User-supplied message
size_t strlen(const char * s)	Null-terminated string
char * strlwr(char * s)	Converts string to lowercase
char * strncat(char * s1, const char *s2, size_t n)	Appends *n* **char** s2 to s1
int strncmp(const char * s1, char * s2, size_t n)	Compares first *n* characters of two strings
int strnicmp(const char * s1, const char * s2, size_t n)	Compares first *n* characters of two strings (case insensitive)
char * strncpy(char * s1, const char * s2, size_t n)	Copies *n* characters of s2 to s1
char * strnset(char * s, int ch, size_t n)	Sets first *n* characters of string to **char** setting
char * strpbrk(const char * s1, const char * s2)	Locates character from **const** s2 in s1
char * strrchr(const char * s, int ch)	Locates last occurrence of *ch* in string

Table 14-9.   *String Manipulating Functions*

Function	Description
char * strrev(char * s)	Converts string to reverse
char * strset(char * s, int ch)	Sets string with *ch*
size_t strspn(const char * s1, const char * s2)	Searches s1 with **char** set in s2
char * strstr(const char * s1, const char * s2)	Searches s1 with s2
char * strtok(char * s1, char * s2)	Finds token in s1. s1 contains token(s), s2 contains the delimiters
char * strupr(char * s)	Converts string to uppercase

Table 14-9. *String Manipulating Functions (continued)*

PROGRAMMING FOUNDATIONS

Here, *s* is a pointer to a string, while *s1* and *s2* are pointers to two strings. Usually *s1* points to the string to be manipulated and *s2* points to the string doing the manipulation. *ch* is a character value.

Comparing the Contents of Two Strings

The following program uses the strcmp() function and reports how one string compares to another.

```
//
// strcmp.cpp : Defines the entry point for the console application.
// Demonstrating the use of the strcmp() function
// to compare two strings.
// Copyright (c) Chris H. Pappas and William H. Murray, 2000
//

#include "stdafx.h"
#include <iostream>
#include <cstring>

using namespace std;
```

```
char s1[45] = "A group of characters makes a good string.";
char s2[45] = "A group of characters makes a good string?";
int answer;

int main(int argc, char* argv[] )
{
  answer = strcmp(s1,s2);

  if( answer > 0 ) cout << "s1 is greater than s2";
    else if( answer == 0 ) cout << "s1 is equal to s2";
      else cout << "s1 is less than s2";

  return (0);
}
```

Can you predict which of the preceding strings would be greater? Can you do it without running the program? The answer is that *s1* is less than *s2*.

Searching for Several Characters in a String

The next program searches a string for the first occurrence of one or more characters:

```
//
// strspn.cpp : Defines the entry point for the console application.
// Demonstrating the use of the strcspn() function to find
// the occurrence of one of a group of characters.
// Copyright (c) Chris H. Pappas and William H. Murray, 2000
//

#include "stdafx.h"
#include <iostream>
#include <cstring>

using namespace std;

char s1[35];
int answer;

int main(int argc, char* argv[] )
{
  strcpy(s1,"We are looking for great strings." );
  answer = strcspn(s1,"abc");
```

```
    cout << "The first a,b,c appeared at position "
         << answer+1;

    return (0);
}
```

This program will report the position of the first occurrence of an "a", a "b", or a "c". A 1 is added to the answer since the first character is at index position zero. This program reports an "a" at position 4.

Finding the First Occurrence of a Single Character in a String

Have you ever wanted to check a sentence for the occurrence of a particular character? You might consider using the strchr() function. The following application looks for the first blank or space character in the string.

```
//
// strchr.cpp : Defines the entry point for the console application.
// Demonstrating the use of the strchr() function to
// locate the first occurrence of a character in a string.
// Copyright (c) Chris H. Pappas and William H. Murray, 2000
//

#include "stdafx.h"
#include <iostream>
#include <cstring>

using namespace std;

char s1[20] = "What is a friend?";
char *answer;

int main(int argc, char* argv[] )
{
  answer = strchr(s1,' ');

  cout << "After the first blank: " << answer << endl;

  return (0);
}
```

What is your prediction on the outcome after execution? Run the program and see.

Finding the Length of a String

The strlen() function reports the length of any given string. Here is a simple example:

```
//
// strlen.cpp : Defines the entry point for the console application.
// Demonstrating the use of the strlen() function to
// determine the length of a string.
// Copyright (c) Chris H. Pappas and William H. Murray, 2000
//

#include "stdafx.h"
#include <iostream>
#include <cstring>

using namespace std;

char *s1="String length is measured in characters!";

int main(int argc, char* argv[] )
{
  cout << "The string length is "<< strlen(s1);

  return (0);
}
```

In this example, the strlen() function reports on the total number of characters contained in the string. In this example, there are 40 characters.

Locating One String in Another String

The strstr() function searches a given string within a group (a string) of characters, as shown here:

```
//
// strstr.cpp : Defines the entry point for the console application.
// Demonstrating the use of the strstr() function to
// locate a string within a string.
// Copyright (c) Chris H. Pappas and William H. Murray, 2000
//

#include "stdafx.h"
#include <iostream>
#include <cstring>
```

```
using namespace std;

int main(int argc, char* argv[] )
{
  char *s1="There is always something you miss.";
  char *s2="way";

  cout << "\n" << strstr(s1,s2);

  return (0);
}
```

This program sends the remainder of the string to the printf() function after the first occurrence of "way." The string printed to the screen is "ways something you miss."

Converting Characters to Uppercase

A handy function to have in a case-sensitive language is one that can convert the characters in a string to another case. The strupr() function converts lowercase characters to uppercase, as shown here:

```
//
// strupr.cpp : Defines the entry point for the console application.
// Demonstrating the use of the strupr() function to
// convert lowercase letters to uppercase.
// Copyright (c) Chris H. Pappas and William H. Murray, 2000
//

#include "stdafx.h"
#include <iostream>
#include <cstring>

using namespace std;

char s1[] = "Uppercase characters are easier to read.";
char *s2;

int main(int argc, char* argv[] )
{
  s2 = strupr(s1);
  cout << "The results: " << s2;

  return (0);
}
```

This program converts each lowercase character to uppercase. Note that only lowercase letters will be changed.

The Math Functions (cmath)

The functions prototyped in the cmath header file permit a great variety of mathematical, algebraic, and trigonometric operations.

The math functions are relatively easy to use and understand for those familiar with algebraic and trigonometric concepts. The most popular math functions are shown in Table 14-10.

Function	Description
abs()	Returns absolute value of **integer** argument
acos(), acosl()	Arc cosine
asin(), asinl()	Arc sine
atan(), atanl()	Arc tangent
atan2(), atan2l()	Arc tangent of two numbers
ceil(), ceill()	Greatest **integer**
cos(), cosl()	Cosine
cosh(), coshl()	Hyberbolic cosine
exp(), expl()	Exponential value
fabs(), fabsl()	Absolute value
floor(), floorl()	Smallest value
fmod(), fmodl()	Modulus operator
frexp(), frexpl()	Split mantissa and exponent
hypot(), hypotl()	Hypotenuse
labs()	Returns absolute value of **long** argument
ldexp(), ldexpl()	x times 2 to the exp power

Table 14-10.   *Popular Math Functions*

Function	Description
log(), logl()	Natural log
log10(), log10l()	Common log
modf(), modfl()	Mantissa and exponent
pow(), powl()	x to y power
pow10(), pow10l()	x raised by power of 10
sin(), sinl()	Sine
sinh(), sinhl()	Hyperbolic sine
sqrt(), sqrtl()	Square root
tan(), tanl()	Tangent
tanh(), tanhl()	Hyperbolic tangent

Table 14-10.   *Popular Math Functions (continued)*

PROGRAMMING FOUNDATIONS

Note

*Functions accept and return **double** values except where noted. Functions ending in "l" accept and return **long double** values.*

Many of these functions were demonstrated in earlier chapters. When using trigonometric functions, remember that angle arguments are always specified in radians.

Programmers desiring complex number arithmetic must resort to using **struct complex** and the _cabs() function described in cmath. Following is the only structure available for complex arithmetic in Visual C++:

```
struct complex {double x,double y}
```

This structure is used by the _cabs() function. The _cabs() function returns the absolute value of a complex number.

Building a Table of Trigonometric Values

Since math functions have already been used extensively in this book, the only example for this section involves an application that will generate a table of sine, cosine, and tangent values for the angles from zero to 45 degrees.

This application also takes advantage of the special C++ formatting abilities. Study the following listing to determine how the output will be sent to the screen:

```cpp
//
// math.cpp : Defines the entry point for the console application.
// A program that demonstrates the use of several
// math functions.
// Copyright (c) Chris H. Pappas and William H. Murray, 2000
//

#include "stdafx.h"
#include <iostream>
#include <iomanip>
#include <cmath>

using namespace std;

#define PI 3.14159265359

int main(int argc, char* argv[] )
{
  int i;
  double x,y,z,ang;

  for( i = 0; i <= 45; i++ ) {
    ang=PI*i/180;  // convert degrees to radians
    x = sin(ang);
    y = cos(ang);
    z = tan(ang);
    // formatting output columns
    cout << setiosflags(ios::left) << setw(8)
         << setiosflags(ios::fixed) << setprecision(6);
    // data to print
    cout << i << "\t" << x << "\t" <<
            y << "\t" << z << "\n";
  }

  return (0);
}
```

This application uses the sin(), cos(), and tan() functions to produce a formatted trigonometric table. The angles are stepped from zero to 45 degrees and are converted to radians before being sent to each function. This particular C++ formatting is discussed in more detail in Chapter 18.

Following is a partial output from this application:

```
0 0.000000 1.000000 0.000000
1 0.017452 0.999848 0.017455
2 0.034899 0.999391 0.034921
 .    .        .        .
 .    .        .        .
 .    .        .        .
28 0.469472 0.882948 0.531709
29 0.484810 0.874620 0.554309
30 0.500000 0.866025 0.577350
31 0.515038 0.857167 0.600861
32 0.529919 0.848048 0.624869
 .    .        .        .
 .    .        .        .
 .    .        .        .
43 0.681998 0.731354 0.932515
44 0.694658 0.719340 0.965689
45 0.707107 0.707107 1.000000
```

The Time Functions (ctime)

Table 14-11 shows some of the time and date functions found in ctime.

Names	Description
asctime()	Converts date and time to an ASCII string and uses tm structure
ctime()	Converts date and time to a string
difftime()	Calculates the difference between two times
gmtime()	Converts date and time to GMT using tm structure
localtime()	Converts date and time to tm structure
strftime()	Allows formatting of date and time data for output
time()	Obtains current time (system)
tzset()	Sets time variables for environment variable TZ

Table 14-11.   *Time and Date Functions*

These functions offer a variety of ways to obtain time and/or date formats for programs. A discussion of the syntax for each function is included in the next section.

Time and Date Structures and Syntax

Many of the date and time functions described in the previous section use the *tm* structure defined in ctime. This structure is shown here:

```
struct tm   {
    int   tm_sec;
    int   tm_min;
    int   tm_hour;
    int   tm_mday;
    int   tm_mon;
    int   tm_year;
    int   tm_wday;
    int   tm_yday;
    int   tm_isdst;
};
```

The syntax for calling each date and time function differs according to the function's ability. The syntax and parameters for each function are shown in Table 14-12.

Function	Description
char * ASCTIME(CONST STRUCT tm * tblock)	Converts the structure into a 26-character string.
	For example: Sun June 1, 10:18:20 2000\n\0.
char * CTIME(CONST TIME_T *time)	Converts a time value, pointed to by * time into a 26-char string (see asctime()).
Double difftime(time_t time2, time_t time1)	Calculates the difference between *time2* and *time1* and returns a **double**.

Table 14-12. *Time and Date Function Parameters*

Function	Description
struct tm * GMTIME(CONST TIME_T * TIMER)	Accepts address of a value returned by the function time() and returns a pointer to the structure with GMT information.
struct tm * LOCALTIME(CONST TIME_T * TIMER)	Accepts address of a value returned by the function time() and returns a pointer to the structure with local time information.
size_t strftime (char * s, SIZE_T maxsize, const char * fmt, const struct tm * t)	Formats date and time information for output. *S* points to the string information, *maxsize* is maximum string length, *fmt* represents the format, and *t* points to a structure of type tm. The formatting options include: ■ %a Abbreviate weekday name ■ %A Full weekday name ■ %b Abbreviate month name ■ %B Full month name ■ %c Date and time information ■ %d Day of month (01 to 31) ■ %H Hour (00 to 23) ■ %I Hour (00 to 12) ■ %j Day of year (001 to 366) ■ %m Month (01 to 12) ■ %M Minutes (00 to 59) ■ %p AM or PM ■ %S Seconds (0 to 59) ■ %U Week number (00 to 51), Sunday is first day

Table 14-12. *Time and Date Function Parameters (continued)*

PROGRAMMING
FOUNDATIONS

Function	Description
	■ %w Weekday (0 to 6)
	■ %W Week number (00 to 51), Monday is first day
	■ %x Date
	■ %X Time
	■ %y Year, without century (00 to 99)
	■ %Y Year, with century
	■ %Z Time zone name
	■ %% Character %
time_t time(time_t *timer)	Returns the time in seconds since 00:00:00 GMT, January 1, 2000.
void _tzset (void)	Sets the global variables *daylight*, *timezone0*, and *tzname0* based on the environment string.

Table 14-12. *Time and Date Function Parameters (continued)*

The TZ environment string uses the following syntax:

```
TZ = zzz[+/-]d[d]{lll}
```

Here, zzz represents a three-character string with the local time zone, for example, "EST" for Eastern Standard Time. The *[+/]d[d]* argument contains an adjustment for the local time zone's difference from GMT. Positive numbers are a westward adjustment, while negative numbers are an eastward adjustment. For example, a five (5) would be used for EST. The last argument, *{lll}*, represents the local time zone's daylight savings time, for example, EDT for Eastern Daylight Savings Time.

Several of these functions are used in example programs in the next section.

Working with the localtime() and asctime() Functions

Many times it is necessary to obtain the time and date in a programming application. The next program returns these values by using the localtime() and asctime() functions:

```
//
// asctim.cpp : Defines the entry point for the console application.
// Demonstrating the use of the localtime() and asctime()
// functions.
// Copyright (c) Chris H. Pappas and William H. Murray, 2000
//

#include "stdafx.h"
#include <ctime>
#include <iostream>

using namespace std;

struct tm *date_time;
time_t timer;

int main(int argc, char* argv[] )
{
  time(&timer);
  date_time=localtime(&timer);

  printf("The present date and time is: %s\n",
  asctime(date_time));

  return (0);
}
```

This program formats the time and date information in the manner shown here:

```
The present date and time is: Sat May 31 13:16:20 2000
```

Working with the gmtime() and asctime() Functions

There are other functions that you can also use to return time and date information. The next program is similar to the last example, except that the gmtime() function is used:

```
//
// cmtime.cpp : Defines the entry point for the console application.
// Demonstrating the use of the gmtime() and asctime()
// functions.
// Copyright (c) Chris H. Pappas and William H. Murray, 2000
```

```
//

#include "stdafx.h"
#include <ctime>
#include <iostream>

using namespace std;

int main(int argc, char* argv[] )
{
  struct tm *date_time;
  time_t timer;

  time(&timer);
  date_time=gmtime(&timer);

  cout << asctime(date_time);

  return (0);
}
```

The following date and time information was returned by this program:

```
Sat May 31 14:13:25
```

Working with the strftime() Function

The strftime() function provides the greatest formatting flexibility of all the date and time functions. The following program illustrates several formatting options:

```
//
// strstm.cpp : Defines the entry point for the console application.
// Demonstrating the use of the strftime() function.
// Copyright (c) Chris H. Pappas and William H. Murray, 2000
//

#include "stdafx.h"
#include <ctime>
#include <iostream>

using namespace std;
```

```
int main(int argc, char* argv[] )
{
  struct tm *date_time;
  time_t timer;
  char str[80];

  time(&timer);
  date_time = localtime(&timer);
  strftime(str,80,"It is %X on %A, %x",
           date_time);
  cout << "\n" << str;

  return (0);
}
```

Here is a sample of the output for this program:

```
It is 17:18:45 on Saturday, 05/31/00
```

You may find that the strftime() function is not portable from one system to another. Use it with caution if portability is a consideration.

Working with the ctime() Function

The following C++ program illustrates how to make a call to the ctime() function. This program shows how easy it is to obtain date and time information from the system:

```
//
// ctime.cpp : Defines the entry point for the console application.
// Demonstrating the use of the ctime() function.
// Copyright (c) Chris H. Pappas and William H. Murray, 2000
//

#include "stdafx.h"
#include <ctime>
#include <iostream>

using namespace std;

time_t longtime;

int main(int argc, char* argv[] )
{
```

```
    time(&longtime);

    cout << "The time and date are " <<
            ctime(&longtime) << "\n";

    return (0);
}
```

The output, sent to the screen, would appear in the following format:

```
The time and date are Sat May 31 14:23:27 2000
```

Creating a Time Delay Routine

Usually it is desirable for programs to execute as quickly as possible. However, there are times when slowing down information makes it easier for the user to view and understand. The time_delay() function in the following application delays program execution. The delay variable is in seconds. For this example, there is a two-second delay between each line of output to the screen:

```
//
// tdelay.cpp : Defines the entry point for the console application.
// A C program that demonstrates how to create a delay
// function for slowing program output.
// Copyright (c) Chris H. Pappas and William H. Murray, 2000
//

#include "stdafx.h"
#include <iostream>
#include <ctime>

using namespace std;

void time_delay(int);

int main(int argc, char* argv[] )
{
  int i;

  for( i = 0; i < 25; i++ ) {
    time_delay(2);
```

```
      cout << "The count is " << i << endl;
   }

   return (0);
}

void time_delay(int t)
{
   long initial,final;
   long ltime;

   initial = time(&ltime);
   final = initial+t;

   while (time(&ltime) < final);

   return;
}
```

What other uses might the time_delay() function have? One case might be where the computer is connected to an external data sensing device, such as a thermocouple or strain gauge. The function could be used to take readings every minute, hour, or day.

What's Coming?

In this chapter you have examined many of the functions programmers use that are built-in to C and C++ compiler libraries. These built-in functions save you from "reinventing the wheel" when you need a special routine. These routines offer extensive support for character, string, math, and time and date functions. Most importantly, you learned that the library functions are portable from one computer to another and from one operating system to another. There are some functions, however, that are system- or compiler-dependent. Using these functions efficiently requires you to know where to locate the library functions and how to call them properly.

The next chapter begins a new section of this book dealing with object-oriented programming. You'll find that many of the library functions discussed in this chapter can be extended to object-oriented programming techniques.

The Complete Reference

Visual C++.NET

Part III

Foundations for Object-Oriented Programming

The
Complete
Reference

Visual C++.NET

Chapter 15

Object-Oriented Programming Foundations

T he previous chapters have concentrated on Visual C++ syntax presented in a procedure-oriented environment. There is another Visual C++ environment that will provide great power to your solutions and projects: the object-oriented environment. This chapter will discuss the terms and definitions most frequently encountered by the object-oriented programmer. As you prepare to enter the world of object-oriented programming, you should know that except for your current version of the Microsoft Visual C++ compiler, no special hardware is required.

When a program is written and compiled into an executable format, an .exe file is created. Take a moment to think about just what that means. In file type terms, it means that a *.exe is a *. exe is a *.exe. In other words, no matter whether the source file is interpreted (as in the case of the native BASIC language), compiled (as in Pascal, FORTRAN, C, and C++), compiled *and* interpreted (as in Java), or assembled (as in the case of assembly language), once the translator generates the final executable form, each one will run on the same microprocessor!

This means that regardless of the source syntax, all of the program's instructions are translated down to machine language (adds, subtracts, compares, jumps, loops, and so on), and are native to the microprocessor. If you know assembly language, you already know just how close a language can be to the actual microprocessor's native tongue. As a language becomes more "high-level," you simply force the interpreter or compiler to do more work in getting your English-like statements translated into something the computer understands. And, in the case of *all* object-oriented languages, even more translation work is required.

However, the burden of work is on the translator. Since you do not buy a new computer to run object-oriented programs, object-oriented languages are inherently incapable of providing any additional microprocessor horsepower than, say, assembly language! Stop for a moment to ponder this last statement.

The real question to ask is "What is the real difference in object-oriented languages such as C++?" In a word, packaging! Consider this simple analogy. For the purpose of argument, imagine a program that declares and uses 100 integer variables. Messy, yes, but a program such as this is structurally possible. Now, imagine you are in a Programming 101 computer course and your instructor begins teaching the topic of Arrays. "Ah," you say, "what a logical and syntactical way to clean up this mess of 100 separate, standalone integer variables!" However, you also know that the rewritten array version did not give your program any more horsepower; it just streamlined logical and syntactical efficiency. In a similar sense, that is all that object-oriented programming does.

Object-oriented programming languages streamline and repackage concepts that you, as a programmer, already know! What *are* new are those language constructs unique to C and C++, not found in other programming languages, that form the foundational building blocks to C++'s object-oriented capabilities. For example, C's keyword **static** is a non-object-oriented language feature. However, **static** can be used in object-oriented programs. If you are new to object-oriented design and syntax, your problem will not be learning how to repackage what you already know—such as how to write a function (called *member functions* or *methods* in OOP terminology)—but instead, how to incorporate C and C++'s new constructs in conjunction with the repackaging.

Here is one more fundamental concept you need to understand. You do not need to use object-oriented syntax to write a Windows 98 or 2000 application. Likewise, you can use object-oriented syntax to write DOS applications! Object-oriented syntax is a separate issue from what a program needs structurally to run under a multitasking operating system like Windows, or under the now-fading command-line MS-DOS mode. Beginning OOPs and Windows programmers often incorrectly view the two requirements as one entity.

More confusion is added to the mix when companies use product-specific re-combinations of this packaging of "standard Windows syntax." Using all of the objects available in the Visual C++ compiler package, for example, can initially be an overwhelming experience. To avoid this, Microsoft has pre-selected "standard" Windows objects and repackaged the already repackaged horsepower. Microsoft calls this double repackaging MFC (Microsoft Foundation Class Library).

Using the information discussed in the previous paragraphs, sit back and relax. In this chapter you will see what you already know as a programmer become the underpinnings to object-oriented horsepower. They only thing standing in your way is terminology. Many of the procedural language fundamentals you already use have new names in an object-oriented world. For example, in this chapter you will learn how the C++ class type (an actual object-definition syntax/concept) is an outgrowth of the C and C++ **struct** type (a regular procedural language record-definition syntax/concept)!

There Is Nothing New Under the Sun

Advertisers know that a product will sell better if the word *new* appears somewhere on the product's label. If, however, the saying "There is nothing new under the sun" is applied to programming, the conclusion would have to be that object-oriented programming is not a new programming concept at all. Scott Guthery stated in 1989 that "Object-oriented programming has been around since subroutines were invented in the 1940s." ("Are the Emperor's New Clothes Object-Oriented?", *Dr. Dobb's Journal*, December 1989.) The article continued by suggesting that objects, the foundation of object-oriented programming, have appeared in earlier languages, such as FORTRAN II.

Considering these statements, why are we only hearing about object-oriented programming at the start of the new millennium? Why is it being touted as the newest programming technique of the century? It seems that the bottom line is packaging. OOP concepts may have been available in 1940, but we certainly didn't have them packaged in a usable container.

Early programmers growing up with the BASIC language often wrote large programs without the use of structured programming concepts. Pages and pages of programming code were tied together with one- or two-letter variables that had a global scope. The use of GOTO statements abounded. The code was a nightmare to read, understand, and debug. Adding new features to such a BASIC program was like unlocking Pandora's box. To say the least, the code was very difficult to maintain.

In the 1960s, structured programming concepts were introduced suggesting the use of meaningful variable names, global and local variable scope, and a procedure-oriented top-down programming approach. Applying these concepts made code easier to read, understand, and debug. Program maintenance was improved because the program could now be studied and altered one procedure at a time. Programming languages such as Ada, C, and Pascal encouraged a structured approach to programming problems.

Bjarne Stroustrup, considered the father of C, developed the language at Bell Labs in the early 1980s. He may well be the father of object-oriented programming, as we know it in the C++ language. Jeff Duntemann stated that "Object-oriented programming is structured Structured Programming. It's the second derivative of software development, the Grand Unifying Theory of program structure" ("Dodging Steamships," *Dr. Dobb's Journal*, July 1989). Indeed, what you'll see as we go along is that object-oriented programming, using C++, builds on foundations established earlier in the C language. Even though C++ is the foundational language for object-oriented programming, it is still possible to write unstructured code or procedure-oriented code. The choice is yours.

There might not be anything new under the sun if Scott Guthery's statements are taken to mean "programming concepts," but this chapter introduces you to the most elegant packaging method for a programming concept you have ever seen. At last we truly have the tools, with languages such as C++, to enter the golden age of object-oriented programming.

Traditional Structured Programming

The earlier chapters in this book were devoted to teaching traditional procedure-oriented structured programming techniques for solving C++ problems. These chapters introduced you to fundamental C++ syntax in a familiar programming environment. Procedure-oriented programming is common among all structured languages, including C, C++, Pascal, and PL/I. A procedure-oriented C++ program is structured in such a way that there is typically a main function and possibly one or more functions (subroutines) that are called from the main function. This is a top-down approach. The main function is typically short, shifting the work to the remaining functions in the program. Program execution flows from the top of the main function and terminates at the bottom of the same function.

In this approach, code and data are separate. Procedures define what is to happen to data, but the two never become one. You'll see that this changes in object-oriented programming. The procedural approach suffers from several disadvantages, chiefly program maintenance. When additions or deletions must be made to the program code, such as in a database program, the entire program must often be reworked to include the new routines. This approach takes enormous amounts of time in both development and debugging. A better approach toward program maintenance is needed.

Object-Oriented Programming

Object-oriented programs (OOPs) function differently from the traditional procedural approach. They require a new programming strategy that is often difficult for traditional procedure-oriented programmers to grasp. In this and the following four chapters you will be introduced to the concepts that make up object-oriented programming in C++. If you have already written or examined program code for Windows 98 or 2000, you have had a taste of one of the concepts used in object-oriented programming—that a program consists of a group of objects that are often related. With C++, objects are formed by using the new class data type. A class provides a set of values (data) and the operations (methods or member functions) that act on those values. The resulting objects can be manipulated by using messages.

It is the message component of object-oriented languages that is also common to Windows programs. In object-oriented programming, objects hold not only the data (member data) but also the methods (member functions) for working on that data. The two items have been combined into one working concept. Simply put, objects contain data and the methods for working on that data.

There are three distinct advantages offered to the programmer by object-oriented programming. The first is program maintenance. Programs are easier to read and understand, and object-oriented programming controls program complexity by allowing only the necessary details to be viewed by the programmer. The second advantage is program alteration (adding or deleting features). It is possible to make additions and deletions to programs, such as in a database program, by simply adding or deleting objects. New objects can inherit everything from a parent object, and the new objects need only to add or delete items that differ. The third advantage is that you can use objects numerous times. Well-designed objects can be saved in a toolkit of useful routines that can easily be inserted into new code, with few or no changes to that code.

It is often possible to convert procedure-oriented C programs to C++, and vice versa, by making simple program alterations. For example, a C **printf** statement can be switched in a C++ **cout** for I/O streams. This is an easy switch because the conversion is from and to a procedural programming structure. However, object-oriented programming is exclusively in the C++ realm because C does not provide the vital link—the abstract data-type class. It is therefore more difficult to convert a procedure-oriented program to an object-oriented form. Programs have to be reworked, with traditional functions being replaced with objects. In some cases, it turns out to be easier to discard the old program and create an object-oriented program from the ground up. This can be considered a distinct disadvantage.

C++ and Object-Oriented Programming

Object-oriented programming concepts cross language boundaries. Microsoft Pascal, for example, was one of the first languages to allow the use of objects. What does C++ have that makes it a suitable language for developing object-oriented programs? The answer is simply the class data type. It is C++'s class type, built on C's **struct** type, that gives the language the ability to build objects. Also, C++ brings several additional features to object-oriented programming, not included in other languages, that simply make use of objects. C++'s advantages include strong typing, operator overloading, and less emphasis on the preprocessor. It is true that you can do object-oriented programming with other products and in other languages, but with C++ the benefits are outstanding. This is a language that was designed, not retrofitted, for object-oriented programming.

In the next section of this chapter, you will learn some object-oriented terminology. These terms and definitions will help you form a solid understanding of this programming technique. Be prepared: The new terminology will be your biggest hurdle as you enter the world of object-oriented programming.

Object-Oriented Terminology

Much of the terminology of object-oriented programming is language independent; that is, it is not associated with a specific language such as Pascal or C++. Therefore, many of the following definitions apply to the various implementations of object-oriented languages. Chapter 16 discusses terms that are more specific to C++.

Object-oriented programming is a programming technique that allows you to view concepts as a variety of objects. By using objects, you can represent the tasks that are to be performed, their interaction, and any given conditions that must be observed. A data structure often forms the basis of an object; thus, in C or C++, the **struct** type can form an elementary object. Communicating with objects can be done through the use of messages, as mentioned earlier. Using messages is similar to calling a function in a procedure-oriented program. When an object receives a message, methods contained within the object respond. Methods, also called member functions, are similar to the functions of procedure-oriented programming. However, methods are part of an object.

The C++ class is an extension of the C and C++ **struct** type and forms the required abstract data type for object-oriented programming. The class can contain closely related items that share attributes. Stated more formally, an object is simply an instance of a class. In Figure 15-1, the Lincoln automobile class is illustrated.

Assume that the Lincoln automobile class is described in the program's code. This class might include a description of items that are common to all Lincolns, and data concerning maintenance intervals. At run time, three additional subclasses of the Lincoln class can be created. They could include the Lincoln LS, Town Car, Continental, and Navigator. The additional derived subclasses might include details of features and data common to each individual model. For example, a Navigator is an object that describes a particular type of Lincoln automobile. It is a derived subclass, or child class of the Lincoln class.

If a message is sent to the instance of the Lincoln class (similar to a call to a function) with instructions to check the rear hatch or the four-wheel-drive mechanism, that message could be utilized only by the Navigator object of the class. Only the Lincoln Navigator has a rear hatch and four-wheel drive.

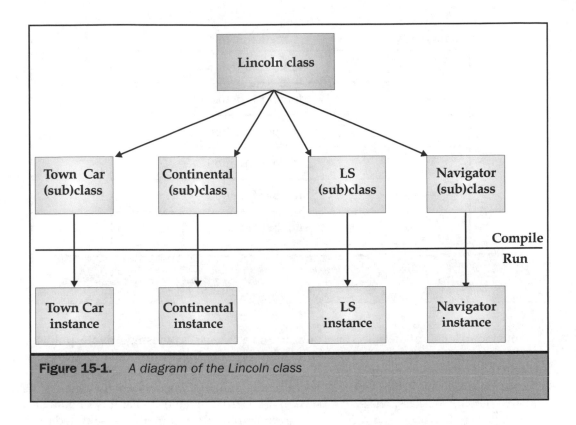

Figure 15-1. *A diagram of the Lincoln class*

Ultimately, there should emerge class libraries containing many object types. Then instances of those object types could be used to piece together program code. You will see interesting examples of this when Windows class libraries are described in Chapters 21 and 22.

Before you examine these terms in closer detail, it is a good idea to become familiar with several additional concepts that relate to C++ and object-oriented programming, as described in the next few sections.

Encapsulation

Encapsulation refers to the way each object combines its member data and member functions (methods) into a single structure. Figure 15-2 illustrates how you can combine data fields and methods to build an object.

Typically, an object's description is part of a C++ class and includes a description of the object's internal structure, how the object relates with other objects, and some form of protection that isolates the functional details of the object from outside the class. The C++ class structure does all of this.

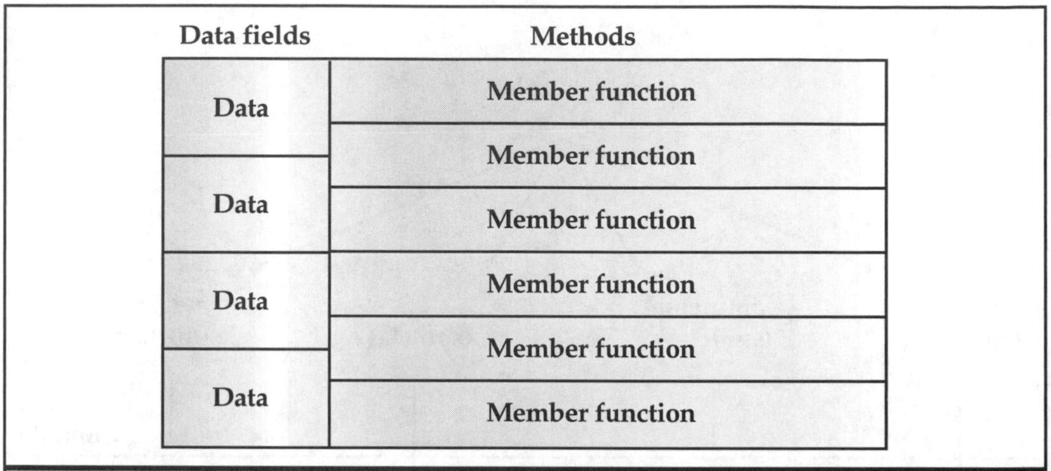

Figure 15-2.   *Data fields and methods combined to build an object*

Functional details of the object are controlled in a C++ class by using private, public, and/or protected descriptors. In object-oriented programming, the public section is typically used for the interface information (methods) that makes the class reusable across applications. If data or methods are contained in the public section, they are available outside the class. The private section of a class limits the availability of data or methods to the class itself. A protected section containing data or methods is limited to the class and any derived subclasses.

Class Hierarchy

The C++ class actually serves as a template or pattern for creating objects. The objects formed from the class description are *instances* of the class. It is possible to develop a class hierarchy where there is a parent class and several child classes. In C++, the basis for doing this revolves around *derived* classes. Parent classes represent more generalized tasks, while derived child classes are given specific tasks to perform. For example, the Lincoln class discussed earlier might contain data and methods common to the entire Lincoln line, such as engines, instrumentation, batteries, braking ability, and handling. Child classes derived from the parent, such as LS, Town Car, Continental, and Navigator, could contain items specific to the class. Recall that the Navigator is the only vehicle in the Lincoln line with a rear hatch and four-wheel drive.

Inheritance

Inheritance in object-oriented programming allows a class to inherit properties from a class of objects. The parent class serves as a pattern for the derived class and can be altered in several ways. (In the next chapter you will learn that member functions can be overloaded, new member functions can be added, and member access privileges can be changed.) If an object inherits its attributes from a single parent, it is called *single inheritance*. If an object inherits its attributes from multiple parents, it is called *multiple inheritance*. Inheritance is an important concept since it allows reuse of a class definition without requiring major code changes. Inheritance encourages the reuse of code since child classes are extensions of parent classes.

Polymorphism

Another important object-oriented concept that relates to the class hierarchy is that common messages can be sent to the parent class objects and all derived subclass objects. In formal terms, this is called *polymorphism*.

Polymorphism allows each subclass object to respond to the message format in a manner appropriate to its definition. Imagine a class hierarchy for gathering data. The parent class might be responsible for gathering the name, social security number, occupation, and number of years of employment for an individual. Child classes could then be used to decide what additional information would be added based on occupation. In one case a supervisory position might include yearly salary, while in another case a sales position might include an hourly rate and commission information. Thus, the parent class gathers general information common to all child classes while the child classes gather additional information relating to specific job descriptions. Polymorphism allows a common data-gathering message to be sent to each class. Both the parent and child classes respond in an appropriate manner to the message. Polymorphism encourages extendibility of existing code.

Virtual Functions

Polymorphism gives objects the ability to respond to messages from routines when the object's exact type is not known. In C++, this ability is a result of late binding. With late binding, the addresses are determined dynamically at run time, rather than statically at compile time, as in traditional compiled languages. This static (fixed) method is often called *early binding*. Function names are replaced with memory addresses. Late binding accomplishes this by using virtual functions, which are defined in the parent class when subsequent derived classes will overload the function by redefining the function's implementation. When virtual functions are used, messages are passed as a pointer. The pointer points to the location instead of directly to the object.

Virtual functions utilize a table for address information. The table is initialized at run time by using a constructor. A constructor is invoked whenever an object of its class is created. The job of the constructor here is to link the virtual function with the table of address information. During the compile operation, the address of the virtual function is not known; rather, it is given the position in the table (determined at run time) of addresses that will contain the address for the function.

A First Look at the C++ Class

It has already been stated that the C++ class type is an extension of the **struct** type. In this section, you learn how you can use the **struct** type in C++ to form a primitive class, complete with data and members. Next, you examine the formal syntax for defining a class and see several simple examples of its implementation. The section discusses the differences between a primitive **struct** class type and an actual C++ class, and presents several simple examples to illustrate class concepts. (Chapter 16 is devoted to a detailed analysis of the C++ class as it applies to object-oriented programming.)

A Structure as a Primitive Class

Chapter 12 discussed structures for C++. In many respects, the structure in C++ is an elementary form of a class. The keyword **struct** is used to define a structure. Examine the following code:

```cpp
//
//  sqroot.cpp
//  C++ program using the keyword "struct" to illustrate a
//  primitive form of class. Here several member functions
//  are defined within the structure.
//  Copyright (c) Chris H. Pappas and William H. Murray, 2001
//

#include "stdafx.h"
#include <iostream>
#include <cmath>

using namespace std;

struct math_operations {
    double data_value;

    void set_value(double ang) {data_value = ang;}
    double get_square(void) {double answer;
                            answer = data_value * data_value;
                            return (answer);}
    double get_square_root(void) {double answer;
                                answer = sqrt(data_value);
                                return (answer);}
} math;

int main(int argc, char* argv[])
```

```
{
    // set numeric value to 35.63
    math.set_value(35.63);

    cout << "The square of the number is: "
         << math.get_square() << endl << endl;
    cout << "The square root of the number is: "
         << math.get_square_root() << endl << endl;

    return 0;
}
```

The first thing to notice in this code is that the structure definition contains member data and functions. While it is common to see data declarations as part of a structure, this is probably the first time you have seen member functions defined within the structure definition. There was no mention of member functions in the discussion of the **struct** type in Chapter 12 because there was no need for their use at that time. These member functions can act on the data contained in the structure (or class) itself.

Recall that a class can contain member data and functions. By default, in a **struct** declaration in C++, member data and functions are public. (A public section is one in which the data and functions are available outside the structure.) Here is the output sent to the screen when the program is executed:

```
The square of the number is: 1269.5
The square root of the number is: 5.96909
```

In this example, the structure definition contains a single data value:

```
double data_value;
```

Next, three member functions are defined. Actually, the code for each function is contained within the structure:

```
void set_value(double ang) {data_value = ang;}
double get_square(void) {double answer;
                         answer = data_value * data_value;
                         return (answer);}
double get_square_root(void) {double answer;
                              answer = sqrt(data_value);
                              return (answer);}
```

The first member function is responsible for initializing the variable, *data_value*. The remaining two member functions return the square and square root of *data_value*. Notice that the member functions are not passed a value; *data_value* is available to them as members of the structure. Both member functions return a double.

The program's main() function sets the value of *data_value* to 35.63 with a call to the member function, set_value():

```
math.set_value(35.63);
```

Notice that the name *math* has been associated with the structure math_operations.

The remaining two member functions return values to the **cout** stream:

```
cout << "The square of the number is: "
     << math.get_square() << endl << endl;
cout << "The square root of the number is: "
     << math.get_square_root() << endl << endl;
```

This example contains a structure with member data and functions. The functions are contained within the structure definition. You won't find an example simpler than this one.

In the next program, the **struct** keyword is still used to develop a primitive class, but this time the member functions are written outside the structure. This is the way you will most commonly see structures and classes defined.

This example contains a structure definition with one data member, *data_value*, and seven member functions. The member functions return information for various trigonometric values:

```
//
//   TStruct.cpp
//   C++ program using the keyword "struct" to illustrate a
//   primitive form of class. This program uses a structure
//   to obtain trigonometric values for an angle.
//   Copyright (c) Chris H. Pappas and William H. Murray, 2001
//

#include "stdafx.h"
#include <iostream>
#include <cmath>

using namespace std;
```

```
const double DEG_TO_RAD=0.0174532925;

struct degree {
    double data_value;

    void set_value(double);
    double get_sine(void);
    double get_cosine(void);
    double get_tangent(void);
    double get_secant(void);
    double get_cosecant(void);
    double get_cotangent(void);
} deg;

void degree::set_value(double ang)
{
    data_value = ang;
}

double degree::get_sine(void)
{
    double answer;

    answer = sin(DEG_TO_RAD * data_value);
    return (answer);
}

double degree::get_cosine(void)
{
    double answer;

    answer = cos(DEG_TO_RAD * data_value);
    return (answer);
}

double degree::get_tangent(void)
{
    double answer;

    answer = tan(DEG_TO_RAD * data_value);
    return (answer);
}
```

```cpp
double degree::get_secant(void)
{
    double answer;

    answer = 1.0 / sin(DEG_TO_RAD * data_value);
    return (answer);
}

double degree::get_cosecant(void)
{
    double answer;

    answer = 1.0 / cos(DEG_TO_RAD * data_value);
    return (answer);
}

double degree::get_cotangent(void)
{
    double answer;

    answer=1.0 / tan(DEG_TO_RAD * data_value);
    return (answer);
}

int main(int argc, char* argv[])
{
    // set angle to 25.0 degrees
    deg.set_value(25.0);

    cout << "The sine of the angle is: "
        << deg.get_sine() << endl;
    cout << "The cosine of the angle is: "
        << deg.get_cosine() << endl;
    cout << "The tangent of the angle is: "
        << deg.get_tangent() << endl;
    cout << "The secant of the angle is: "
        << deg.get_secant() << endl;
    cout << "The cosecant of the angle is: "
        << deg.get_cosecant() << endl;
    cout << "The cotangent of the angle is: "
        << deg.get_cotangent() << endl << endl;

    return 0;
}
```

Notice that the structure definition contains the prototypes for the member functions. The variable *deg* is associated with the degree structure type:

```
struct degree {
  double data_value;

  void set_value(double);
  double get_sine(void);
  double get_cosine(void);
  double get_tangent(void);
  double get_secant(void);
  double get_cosecant(void);
  double get_cotangent(void);
} deg;
```

Immediately after the structure is defined, the various member functions are developed and listed. The member functions are associated with the structure or class by means of the scope operator (::). Other than the use of the scope operator, the member functions take on the appearance of normal functions.

Examine the first part of the main() function:

```
// set angle to 25.0 degrees
deg.set_data(25.0);
```

Here the value 25.0 is being passed as an argument to the set_value() function. Observe the syntax for this operation. The set_value() function itself is very simple:

```
void degree::set_value(double ang)
{
  data_value = ang;
}
```

The function accepts the argument and assigns the value to the class variable, *data_value*. This is one way of initializing class variables. From this point forward in the class, *data_value* is accessible by each of the six member functions. The job of the member functions is to calculate the sine, cosine, tangent, secant, cosecant, and cotangent of the given angle. The respective values are printed to the screen from the main() function with statements similar to the following:

```
cout << "The sine of the angle is: "
     << deg.get_sine() << endl;
```

Use the dot notation, commonly used for structures, to access the member functions. Pointer variables can also be assigned to a structure or class, in which case the arrow operator is used. You will see examples of this in Chapter 16.

The Syntax and Rules for C++ Classes

The definition of a C++ class begins with the keyword *class*. The class name (tag type) immediately follows the keyword. The framework of the class is very similar to the **struct** type definition you have already seen:

```
class type {
  type var1
  type var2
  type var3

      .
      .
      .

public:
  member function 1
  member function 2
  member function 3
  member function 4

      .
      .
      .

} name associated with class type;
```

Member variables immediately follow the class declaration. These variables are, by default, private to the class and can be accessed only by the member functions that follow. Member functions typically follow a public declaration. This allows access to the member functions from calling routines external to the class. All class member functions have access to public, private, and protected parts of a class.

The following is an example of a class that is used in the next programming example:

```
class degree {
  double data_value;

public:
  void set_value(double);
  double get_sine(void);
  double get_cosine(void);
  double get_tangent(void);
```

```
  double get_secant(void);
  double get_cosecant(void);
  double get_cotangent(void);
} deg;
```

This class has a type (tag name) degree. A private variable, *data_value*, will share degree values among the various member functions. Seven functions make up the function members of the class. They are set_value(), get_sine(), get_cosine(), get_tangent(), get_secant(), get_cosecant(), and get_cotangent(). The name that is associated with this class type is *deg*. Unlike this example, the association of a variable name with the class name is most frequently made in the main() function.

Does this class definition look familiar? It is basically the structure definition from the previous example converted to a true class.

A Simple C++ Class

In a C++ class, the visibility of class members is private by default. That is, member variables are accessible only to member functions of the class. If the member functions are to have visibility beyond the class, you must explicitly specify that visibility.

The conversion of the last program's structure to a true C++ class is simple and straightforward. First, the **struct** keyword is replaced by the class keyword. Second, the member functions that are to have public visibility are separated from the private variable of the class with the use of a public declaration. Examine the complete program:

```
//
//  TClass.cpp
//  C++ program illustrates a simple but true class and
//  introduces the concept of private and public.
//  This program uses a class to obtain the trigonometric
//  value for a given angle.
//  Copyright (c) Chris H. Pappas and William H. Murray, 2001
//

#include "stdafx.h"
#include <iostream>
#include <cmath>

using namespace std;

const double DEG_TO_RAD = 0.0174532925;
```

```cpp
class degree {
    double data_value;

public:
    void set_value(double);
    double get_sine(void);
    double get_cosine(void);
    double get_tangent(void);
    double get_secant(void);
    double get_cosecant(void);
    double get_cotangent(void);
} deg;

void degree::set_value(double ang)
{
    data_value = ang;
}

double degree::get_sine(void)
{
    double answer;

    answer = sin(DEG_TO_RAD * data_value);
    return (answer);
}

double degree::get_cosine(void)
{
    double answer;

    answer = cos(DEG_TO_RAD * data_value);
    return (answer);
}

double degree::get_tangent(void)
{
    double answer;

    answer = tan(DEG_TO_RAD * data_value);
    return (answer);
}

double degree::get_secant(void)
```

```
{
    double answer;

    answer = 1.0 / sin(DEG_TO_RAD * data_value);
    return (answer);
}

double degree::get_cosecant(void)
{
    double answer;

    answer = 1.0 / cos(DEG_TO_RAD * data_value);
    return (answer);
}

double degree::get_cotangent(void)
{
    double answer;

    answer = 1.0 / tan(DEG_TO_RAD * data_value);
    return (answer);
}

int main(int argc, char* argv[])
{
    // set angle to 25.0 degrees
    deg.set_value(25.0);

    cout << "The sine of the angle is: "
         << deg.get_sine() << endl;
    cout << "The cosine of the angle is: "
         << deg.get_cosine() << endl;
    cout << "The tangent of the angle is: "
         << deg.get_tangent() << endl;
    cout << "The secant of the angle is: "
         << deg.get_secant() << endl;
    cout << "The cosecant of the angle is: "
         << deg.get_cosecant() << endl;
    cout << "The cotangent of the angle is: "
         << deg.get_cotangent() << endl << endl;
    return 0;
}
```

In this example, the body of the program remains the same. The structure definition has been converted to a true, but elementary, class definition with private and public parts.

Note that the variable, *data_value*, is private to the class (by default) and as a result is accessible only by the member functions of the class. The member functions themselves have been declared public in visibility and are accessible from outside the class. Each class member, however, whether public or private, has access to all other class members, public or private.

Here is the output from the program:

```
The sine of the angle is: 0.422618
The cosine of the angle is: 0.906308
The tangent of the angle is: 0.466308
The secant of the angle is: 2.3662
The cosecant of the angle is: 1.10338
The cotangent of the angle is: 2.14451
```

Again, class member functions are usually defined immediately after the class has been defined and before the main() function of the program. Nonmember class functions are still defined after the main() function and are prototyped in the normal fashion.

What's Coming?

In this chapter you learned terms and definitions common to most object-oriented languages. You also learned concepts that separate procedure-oriented languages from object-oriented languages.

In the next chapter, details of C++ classes will be examined more closely.

The
Complete
Reference

Visual C++.NET

Chapter 16

Working with
C++ Classes

A primitive C++ class can be created by using the struct keyword, as you learned in the previous chapter. You also learned how to create several elementary C++ classes by using the class keyword. Both types of examples illustrated the simple fact that classes can contain member data and member functions (methods) that act on that data. In this chapter, you will learn more details about C++ classes—nesting of classes and structures, the use of constructors and destructors, overloading member functions, friend functions, operator overloading, derived classes, virtual functions, and other miscellaneous topics. These class structures create objects that form the foundation of object-oriented programs.

The programming flexibility offered to the C++ programmer is, to a large degree, a result of the various data types discussed in earlier chapters. The C++ class gives you another advantage: the benefits of a structure and the ability to limit access to specific data to functions that are also members of the class. As a result, classes are one of the greatest contributions to programming made by C++. The added features of the class over earlier structures include the ability to initialize and protect sensitive functions and data.

Consider, for example, the increase in programming power you have gained with each new data type. Vectors, or one-dimensional arrays, allow a group of like-data types to be held together. Next, structures allow related items of different data types to be combined in a group. Finally, the C++ class concept takes you one step further with abstract data types. A class allows you to implement a member data type and associate member functions with the data. Using classes gives you the storage concept associated with a structure along with the member functions to operate on the member variables.

Features Specific to Classes

The syntax for correctly creating an elementary C++ class was illustrated in the previous chapter. However, classes have extended capabilities that go far beyond this simple syntax. This section is devoted to exploring these capabilities with an eye toward object-oriented programming. In the next chapter, class objects will be woven into more complicated object-oriented programs.

Working with a Simple Class

In this section we'll present a short review of a simple class based on the definitions from Chapter 15. Remember that a class starts with the keyword **class** followed by a class name (tag). In the following example, the class tag name is **car**. If the class contains member variables, they are defined at the start of the class. Their declaration type is private, by default. This example defines three member variables: mileage, tire_pressure, and speed. Class member functions follow the member variable list. Typically, the member functions are declared public. A private declaration limits the member variables to member functions within the class. This is often referred to as *data hiding*. A public declaration makes the member functions available outside of the class:

```
class car {
    int    mileage;
    int    tire_pressure;
    float speed;

public:
    int maintenance(int);
    int wear_record(int);
    int air_resistance(float);
} mycar;
```

Notice that three member functions are prototyped within the class definition. They are maintenance(), wear_record(), and air_resistance(). All three return an **int** type. Typically, however, the contents of the member functions are defined outside the class definition—usually, immediately after the class itself.

Let's continue the study of classes with a look at additional class features.

Nesting Classes

In Chapter 12 you learned that structures can be nested. This also turns out to be true for C++ classes. When using nested classes, you must take care not to make the resulting declaration more complicated than necessary. The following examples illustrate the nesting concept.

Nesting Structures Within a Class

The next listing is a simple example of how two structures can be nested within a class definition. Using nesting in this fashion is both common and practical.

```
//
//  wages.cpp
//  C++ program illustrates the use of nesting concepts
//  in classes. This program calculates the wages for
//  the named employee.
//  Copyright (c) Chris H. Pappas and William H. Murray, 2001
//

#include "stdafx.h"
#include <iostream>
```

```cpp
using namespace std;

char newline;

class employee {
    struct emp_name {
        char firstname[20];
        char middlename[20];
        char lastname[20];
    } name;
    struct emp_hours {
        double hours;
        double base_sal;
        double overtime_sal;
    } hours;

public:
    void emp_input(void);
    void emp_output(void);
};

void employee::emp_input()
{
    cout << "Enter first name of employee: ";
    cin >> name.firstname;
    cin.get(newline);    // flush carriage return
    cout << "Enter middle name of employee: ";
    cin >> name.middlename;
    cin.get(newline);
    cout << "Enter last name of employee:  ";
    cin >> name.lastname;
    cin.get(newline);

    cout << "Enter total hours worked:  ";
    cin >> hours.hours;
    cout << "Enter hourly wage (base rate):   ";
    cin >> hours.base_sal;
    cout << "Enter overtime wage (overtime rate): ";
    cin >> hours.overtime_sal;
    cout << "\n\n";
}

void employee::emp_output()
```

```
{
    cout << name.firstname << " " << name.middlename
        << " " << name.lastname << endl;
    if (hours.hours <=  40)
        cout << "Base Pay:  $"
            << hours.hours * hours.base_sal << endl;
        else {
            cout << "Base Pay:  $"
                << 40 * hours.base_sal << endl;
            cout << "Overtime Pay: $"
                << (hours.hours - 40) * hours.overtime_sal
                << endl;
        }
}

int main(int argc, char* argv[])
{
    employee acme_corp;     // associate acme_corp with class

    acme_corp.emp_input();
    acme_corp.emp_output();
    return 0;
}
```

In the next example, two classes are nested within the employee class definition. The use of nesting, as you can see, can be quite straightforward.

```
class employee {
    class emp_name {
        char firstname[20];
        char middlename[20];
        char lastname[20];
    } name;
    class emp_hours {
        double hours;
        double base_salary;
        double overtime_sal;
    } hours;

public:
    void emp_input(void);
    void emp_output(void);
};
```

The employee class includes two nested classes, **emp_name** and **emp_hours**. The nested classes are part of the private section of the employee class and are not visible outside the class. In other words, the visibility of the nested classes is not the same as the owning employee class definition. The individual member variables, for this example, are accessed through the member functions (public, by default), emp_input() and emp_output().

The member functions, emp_input() and emp_output(), are of type void and do not accept arguments. The emp_input() function prompts the user for employee data that will be passed to the nested structures (classes). The data collected includes the employee's full name, the total hours worked, the regular pay rate, and the overtime pay rate. Output is generated when the emp_output() function is called. The employee's name, base pay, and overtime pay will be printed to the screen:

```
Enter first name of employee: Peter
Enter middle name of employee: Harry
Enter last name of employee: Jones
Enter total hours worked: 52
Enter hourly wage (base rate): 7.50
Enter overtime wage (overtime rate): 10.00

Peter Harry Jones
Base Pay:  $300.00
Overtime Pay: $120.00
```

The int main(int argc, char* argv[]) function in this program is fairly short. This is because most of the work is being done by the member functions of the class:

```
employee acme_corp;     // associate acme_corp with class

acme_corp.emp_input();
acme_corp.emp_output();
```

The variable *acme_corp*, representing the Acme Computer Corporation, is associated with the employee class. To request a member function, the dot operator is used. Next, acme_corp.emp_input() is called to collect the employee information, and then acme_corp.emp_output() is used to calculate and print the payroll results.

An Alternate Nesting Form

There is an alternate way to perform nesting. The following form of nesting is also considered acceptable syntax:

```
class cars {
    int mileage;
public:
    void trip(int t);
    int speed(float s);
};

class contents {
    int count;
public:
    cars mileage;
    void rating(void);
{
```

In this portion of code, *cars* becomes nested within the contents class. Nested classes, whether inside or outside, have the same scope.

Working with Constructors and Destructors

A constructor is a class member function. Constructors are useful for initializing class variables or allocating memory storage. The constructor always has the same name as the class it is defined within. Constructors have additional versatility: They can accept arguments and be overloaded. A constructor is executed automatically when an object of the class type is created. Free store objects are objects created with the new operator and serve to allocate memory for the objects created. Constructors are generated by the Visual C++ compiler if they are not explicitly defined.

A destructor is a class member function typically used to return memory allocated from free store memory. The destructor, like the constructor, has the same name as the class it is defined in, preceded by the tilde character (~). Destructors are the complement to their constructor counterparts. A destructor is automatically called when the delete operator is applied to a class pointer or when a program passes beyond the scope of a class object. Destructors, unlike their constructor counterparts, cannot accept an argument and may not be overloaded. Destructors are also generated by the Visual C++ compiler if they are not explicitly defined.

A Simple Constructor and Destructor

The following listing represents the first example involving the use of constructors and destructors. Here a constructor and destructor are used to signal the start and end of a coin conversion example. This program illustrates that constructors and destructors are called automatically:

```cpp
//
//  coins.cpp
//  C++ program illustrates the use of constructors and
//  destructors in a simple program.
//  This program converts cents into appropriate coins:
//  (quarters, dimes, nickels, and pennies).
//  Copyright (c) Chris H. Pappas and William H. Murray, 2001
//

#include "stdafx.h"
#include <iostream>

using namespace std;

const int QUARTER = 25;
const int DIME = 10;
const int NICKEL = 5;

class coins {
    int number;

public:
    coins() {cout << "Begin Conversion!\n\n";}      // constructor
    ~coins() {cout << "\nFinished Conversion!\n";} // destructor
    void get_cents(int);
    int quarter_conversion(void);
    int dime_conversion(int);
    int nickel_conversion(int);
};

void coins::get_cents(int cents)
{
    number = cents;
    cout << number << " cents, converts to:"
        << endl;
}

int coins::quarter_conversion()
{
```

```
        cout << number / QUARTER << " quarter(s), ";
        return(number % QUARTER);
}

int coins::dime_conversion(int d)
{
        cout << d / DIME << " dime(s), ";
        return(d % DIME);
}

int coins::nickel_conversion(int n)
{
        cout << n / NICKEL << " nickel(s), and ";
        return(n % NICKEL);
}

int main(int argc, char* argv[])
{
        int c, d, n, p;

        cout << "Enter the cash, in cents, to convert: ";
        cin >> c;

        // associate cash_in_cents with coins class.
        coins cash_in_cents;

        cash_in_cents.get_cents(c);
        d = cash_in_cents.quarter_conversion();
        n = cash_in_cents.dime_conversion(d);
        p = cash_in_cents.nickel_conversion(n);
        cout << p << " penny(ies)." << endl;
        return 0;
}
```

This program uses four member functions. The first function passes the number of pennies to the private class variable *number*. The remaining three functions convert cash, given in cents, to the equivalent cash in quarters, dimes, nickels, and pennies. Notice in particular the placement of the constructor and destructor in the class definition. The constructor and destructor function descriptions contain nothing more than a message that will be printed to the screen. Constructors are not specifically called by a program. Their appearance on the screen is your key that the constructor and destructor were automatically called when the object was created and destroyed.

```
class coins {
    int number;

public:
    coins() {cout << "Begin Conversion!\n\n";}      // constructor
    ~coins() {cout << "\nFinished Conversion!\n";}  // destructor
    void get_cents(int);
    int quarter_conversion(void);
    int dime_conversion(int);
    int nickel_conversion(int);
};
```

Here is an example of the output from this program:

```
Enter the cash, in cents, to convert: 159
Begin Conversion!

159 cents, converts to:
6 quarter(s), 0 dime(s), 1 nickel(s), and 4 penny(ies).
Finished Conversion!
```

In this example, the function definition is actually included within the constructor and destructor. When the function definition is included with member functions, it is said to be implicitly defined. Member functions can be defined in the typical manner or declared explicitly as inline functions.

Why not expand this example to include dollars and half-dollars!

Initializing Member Variables with Constructors

Another practical use for constructors is for initialization of private class variables. In the previous examples, class variables were set using separate member functions. In the next example, the original class of the previous program is modified slightly to eliminate the need for user input. In this case, the variable *number* will be initialized to 431 pennies:

```
class coins {
    int number;

public:
```

```
    coins() {number = 431;}                         // constructor
    ~coins() {cout << "\nFinished Conversion!";}   // destructor
    int quarter_conversion(void);
    int dime_conversion(int);
    int nickel_conversion(int);
};
```

The route to class variables is always through class member functions. Remember that the constructor is considered a member function.

Creating and Deleting Free Store Memory

Perhaps the most significant reason for using a constructor is in utilizing free store memory. In the next example, a constructor is used to allocate memory for the string1 pointer with the new operator. A destructor is also used to release the allocated memory back to the system when the object is destroyed. This is accomplished with the use of the delete operator:

```
class string_operation {
    char *string1;
    int  string_len;

public:
    string_operation(char *) {string1 = new char[string_len];}
    ~string_operation() {delete string1;}
    void input_data(char *);
    void output_data(char *);
};
```

The memory allocated by new to the pointer string can only be deallocated with a subsequent call to delete. For this reason, you will usually see memory allocated to pointers in constructors and deallocated in destructors. This also ensures that if the variable assigned to the class passes out of its scope, the allocated memory will be returned to the system. These operations make memory allocation dynamic and are most useful in programs that utilize linked lists.

The memory used by data types, such as **int** and **float**, is automatically restored to the system.

Overloading Class Member Functions

Class member functions can be overloaded just like ordinary C++ functions. Overloading functions means that more than one function can have the same function name in the current scope. It becomes the compiler's responsibility to select the correct function based on the number and type of arguments used during the function call. The first example in this section illustrates the overloading of a class function named number(). This overloaded function will return the absolute value of an integer or double the integer with the use of the math functions abs(), which accepts and returns integer values, and fabs(), which accepts and returns double values. With an overloaded function, the argument types determine which member function will actually be used:

```cpp
//
//   absol.cpp
//   C++ program illustrates member function overloading.
//   Program determines the absolute value of an integer
//   and a double.
//   Copyright (c) Chris H. Pappas and William H. Murray, 2001
//

#include "stdafx.h"
#include <iostream>
#include <cmath>

using namespace std;

class absolute_value {
public:
    int number(int);
    double number(double);
};

int absolute_value::number(int test_data)
{
    int answer;

    answer = abs(test_data);
    return (answer);
}

double absolute_value::number(double test_data)
{
    double answer;

    answer = fabs(test_data);
    return (answer);
}
```

```
int main(int argc, char* argv[])
{
    absolute_value neg_number;

    cout << "The absolute value is "
         << neg_number.number(-583) << endl;
    cout << "The absolute value is "
         << neg_number.number(-583.1749)
         << endl << endl;
    return 0;
}
```

Notice that the dot operator is used in conjunction with the member function name to pass a negative integer and negative double values. The program selects the proper member function based on the type of argument (integer or double) passed along with the function name. The positive value returned by each function is printed to the screen:

```
the absolute value is 583
the absolute value is 583.1749
```

In another example, angle information is passed to member functions in one of two formats—a double or a string. With member function overloading, it is possible to process both types:

```
//
// overld.cpp
// C++ program illustrates overloading two class member
// functions. The program allows an angle to be entered
// in decimal or deg/min/sec format. One member function
// accepts data as a double, the other as a string. The
// program returns the sine, cosine, and tangent.
// Copyright (c) Chris H. Pappas and William H. Murray, 2001
//

#include "stdafx.h"
#include <iostream>
#include <cmath>
#include <string>
```

```
using namespace std;

const double DEG_TO_RAD = 0.0174532925;

class trigonometric {
    double angle;
    double answer_sine;
    double answer_cosine;
    double answer_tangent;

public:
    void trig_calc(double);
    void trig_calc(char *);
};

void trigonometric::trig_calc(double degrees)
{
    angle = degrees;
    answer_sine = sin(angle * DEG_TO_RAD);
    answer_cosine = cos(angle * DEG_TO_RAD);
    answer_tangent = tan(angle * DEG_TO_RAD);
    cout << "\nFor an angle of " << angle
            << " degrees." << endl;
    cout << "The sine is " << answer_sine << endl;
    cout << "The cosine is " << answer_cosine << endl;
    cout << "The tangent is " << answer_tangent << endl;
}

void trigonometric::trig_calc(char *dat)
{
    char *deg, *min, *sec;

    deg = strtok(dat, "d ");
    min = strtok(0, "m ");
    sec = strtok(0, "s ");
    angle = atof(deg) + ((atof(min)) / 60.0) + ((atof(sec)) / 360.0);
    answer_sine = sin(angle * DEG_TO_RAD);
    answer_cosine = cos(angle * DEG_TO_RAD);
    answer_tangent = tan(angle * DEG_TO_RAD);
    cout << "\nFor an angle of " << angle
            << " degrees." << endl;
```

```
        cout << "The sine is " << answer_sine << endl;
        cout << "The cosine is " << answer_cosine << endl;
        cout << "The tangent is " << answer_tangent << endl;
}

int main(int argc, char* argv[])
{
    trigonometric data;

    data.trig_calc(75.0);

    char str1[] = "35d 75m 20s";
    data.trig_calc(str1);

    data.trig_calc(145.72);

    char str2[] = "65d 45m 30s";
    data.trig_calc(str2);

    cout << endl;

    return 0;
}
```

This program makes use of a very powerful built-in function, strtok(), prototyped in the string library. The syntax for using strtok() is straightforward:

```
char *strtok(string1, string2);   //locates token in string1
  char *string1;                   //string that has token(s)
  const char *string2;             //string with delimiter chars
```

The strtok() function will scan the first string, string1, looking for a series of character tokens. For this example, the tokens representing degrees, minutes, and seconds are used. The actual length of the tokens can vary. The second string, string2, contains a set of delimiters. Spaces, commas, or other special characters can be used for delimiters. The tokens in string1 are separated by the delimiters in string2. Because of this, all of the tokens in string1 can be retrieved with a series of calls to the strtok() function; strtok() alters string1 by inserting a null character after each token is retrieved. The function returns a pointer to the first token the first time it is called. Subsequent calls return a pointer to the next token, and so on. When there are no more tokens in the string, a null pointer is returned.

This example permits angle readings formatted as decimal values, or in degrees, minutes, and seconds of arc. For the latter case, strtok() uses the symbol (d) to find the first token. For minutes, a minute symbol (m) will pull out the token containing the number of minutes. Finally, the (s) symbol is used to retrieve seconds.

This program produces the following formatted output:

```
For an angle of 75 degrees.
The sine is 0.965926
The cosine is 0.258819
The tangent is 3.732051

For an angle of 36.305556 degrees.
The sine is 0.592091
The cosine is 0.805871
The tangent is 0.734722

For an angle of 145.72 degrees.
The sine is 0.563238
The cosine is -0.826295
The tangent is -0.681642

For an angle of 65.833333 degrees.
The sine is 0.912358
The cosine is 0.409392
The tangent is 2.228568
```

Class member function overloading gives programs and programmers flexibility when dealing with different data formats. If you are not into math or engineering programs, can you think of any application that interests you where this feature might be helpful? Consider this possibility: If you are the cook in your household, you could develop an application that modifies recipes. You could write a program that would accept data as a decimal value or in mixed units. For example, the program might allow you to enter "1 pint 1.75 cups" or "1 pint 1 cup 2 tbs."

Friend Functions

Classes have another important feature—the ability to hide data. Recall that member data is private by default in classes—that is, sharable only with member functions of the class. It is almost ironic, then, that there exists a category of functions specifically designed to override this feature. Functions of this type, called *friend functions*, allow the sharing of private class information with nonmember functions. Friend functions, not defined in the class itself, can share the same class resources as member functions.

Friend functions offer the advantage that they are external to the class definition, as shown here:

```
//
// secs.cpp
// C++ program illustrates the use of friend functions.
// Program will collect a string of date and time
// information from system. Time information will
// be processed and converted into seconds.
// Copyright (c) Chris H. Pappas and William H. Murray, 2001
//

#include "stdafx.h"
#include <iostream>
#include <ctime>          // for tm & time_t structure
#include <string>         // for strtok function prototype

using namespace std;

class time_class {
    long secs;
    friend char * present_time(time_class);    //friend
public:
    time_class(char *);
};

time_class::time_class(char *tm)
{
    char *hours, *minutes, *seconds;

    // data returned in the following string format:
    // (day month date hours:minutes:seconds year)
    // Thus, need to skip over three tokens, i.e.,
    // skip day, month, and date
    hours = strtok(tm," ");
    hours = strtok(0," ");
    hours = strtok(0," ");

    // collect time information from string
    hours = strtok(0,":");
    minutes = strtok(0,":");
    seconds = strtok(0," ");
```

```
        // convert data to long type and accumulate seconds.
        secs = atol(hours) * 3600;
        secs+= atol(minutes) * 60;
        secs+= atol(seconds);
    }

    char * present_time(time_class);          // prototype

    int main(int argc, char* argv[])
    {
        // get the string of time & date information
        struct tm *ptr;
        time_t ltime;
        ltime = time(NULL);
        ptr = localtime(&ltime);

        time_class tz(asctime(ptr));

        cout << "The date/time string information: "
             << asctime(ptr) << endl;
        cout << "The time converted to seconds: "
             << present_time(tz) << endl << endl;
        return 0;
    }

    char * present_time(time_class tz)
    {
        char *ctbuf;
        ctbuf = new char[40];
        long int seconds_total;

        seconds_total = tz.secs;
        ltoa(seconds_total, ctbuf, 10);
        return (ctbuf);
    }
```

Notice in the class definition the use of the keyword **friend** along with the description of the present_time() function. When you examine the program listing, you will notice that this function, external to the class, appears after the int main(int argc, char* argv[]) function description. In other words, it is written as a traditional C++ function, external to member functions of the defined class.

This program has a number of additional interesting features. In the function int main(int argc, char* argv[]), the system's time is obtained with the use of *time_t* and its associated structure *tm*. In this program, *ltime* is the name of the variable associated with *time_t*. Local time is initialized and retrieved into the pointer, ptr, with the next two lines of code. By using asctime(ptr), the pointer will point to an ASCII string of date and time information:

```
struct tm *ptr;
time_t ltime;
ltime = time(NULL);
ptr = localtime(&ltime);

time_class tz(asctime(ptr));
```

The date and time string is formatted in this manner:

```
day month date hours:minutes:seconds year \n \0
```

For example:

```
Mon Aug 28 13:12:21 2000
```

There is a more detailed discussion of built-in functions, including those prototyped in time.h, in Chapter 14.

The string information that is retrieved is sent to the class by associating tz with the class **time_class**:

```
time_class tz(asctime(ptr));
```

A constructor, time_class(char *), is used to define the code required to convert the string information into integer data. This is accomplished by using the strtok() function. The date/time information is returned in a rather strange format. To process this information, strtok() must use a space as the delimiter in order to skip over the day, month, and date information in the string. In this program the variable, hours, initially serves as a junk collector for unwanted tokens. The next delimiter is a colon (:), which is used in collecting both hour and minute tokens from the string. Finally, the number of seconds can be retrieved by reading the string until another space is encountered. The string information is then converted to a long type and the appropriate number of seconds. The variable, *secs*, is private to the class but accessible to the friend function.

The friend function takes the number of accumulated seconds, tz.seconds, and converts it back to a character string. The memory for storing the string is allocated with the new operator. This newly created string is a result of using the friend function.

The program prints two pieces of information:

```
The date/time string information: Mon Aug 28 09:31:14 2000

The time converted to seconds: 34274
```

First, **cout** sends the string produced by asctime() to the screen. This information is obtainable from time_t() and is available to the int main(int argc, char* argv[]) function. Second, the system time is printed by passing present_time to the **cout** stream.

While friend functions offer some interesting programming possibilities when programming with C++ classes, they should be used with caution.

The this Pointer

The keyword **this** is used to identify a self-referential pointer that is implicitly declared in C++, as follows:

```
class_name *this;    //class_name is class type.
```

The **this** pointer is used to point to the object for which the member function is invoked and is only accessible in member functions of the class (**struct** or **union**) type. It can also be used to include a link on a doubly linked list or when writing constructors involving memory allocations as you see in the following example:

```
class class_name {
  int x,y,z;
  char chr;

public:
  class_name(size) {this = new(size);}
  ~class_name(void);
};
```

Operator Overloading

You have learned that it is possible to overload member functions in a class. In this section, you will learn that it is also possible to overload C++ operators. In C++, new definitions can be applied to such familiar operators as +, -, *, and / in a given class.

The concept of operator overloading is common in numerous programming languages, even if it is not specifically implemented. For example, all compiled languages make it possible to add two integers, two floats, or two doubles (or their equivalent types) with the + operator. This is the essence of operator overloading—using the same operator on different data types. In C++ it is possible to extend this simple concept even further. In most compiled languages it is not possible, for example, to take a complex number, matrix, or character string and add it together with the + operator.

These operations are valid in all programming languages:

```
3 + 8
3.3 + 7.2
```

These operations are typically not valid operations:

```
(4 - j4) + (5 + j10)
(15d 20m 45s) + (53d 57m 40s)
"combine " + "strings"
```

If the last three operations were possible with the + operator, the workload of the programmer would be greatly reduced when designing new applications. The good news is that in C++, the + operator can be overloaded and the previous three operations can be made valid. Many additional operators can also be overloaded. Operator overloading is used extensively in C++. You will find examples throughout the various Microsoft C++ libraries.

Overloading Operators and Function Calls

In C++, the operators shown in Table 16-1 can be overloaded.

+	-	*0	/	=	<	>	+=	-=
*0=	/=	<<	>>	>>=	<<=	==	!=	<=
>=	++	—	%	&	^^	!	|	~
&=	^=	|=	&&	||	%=	[]	()	new
Delete								

Table 16-1. *Operators that Can Be Overloaded in C++*

The main restrictions are that the syntax and precedence of the operator must remain unchanged from its originally defined meaning. Another important point is that operator overloading is valid only within the scope of the class in which overloading occurs.

Overloading Syntax

In order to overload an operator, the operator keyword is followed by the operator itself:

```
type operator opr(param list)
```

For example:

```
angle_value operator +(angle_argument);
```

Here, **angle_value** is the name of the class type, followed by the **operator** keyword, then the operator itself (+), and a parameter to be passed to the overloaded operator.

Within the scope of a properly defined class, several angles specified in degrees/minutes/seconds could be directly added together:

```
char str1[] = "37d 15m 56s";
angle_value angle1(str1);

char str2[] = "10d 44m 44s";
angle_value angle2(str2);

char str3[] = "75d 17m 59s";
angle_value angle3(str3);

char str4[] = "130d 32m 54s";
angle_value angle4(str4);

angle_value sum_of_angles;

sum_of_angles = angle1 + angle2 + angle3 + angle4;
```

In this example, the symbol for degrees is (d), for minutes (m), and for seconds (s).

The carry information from seconds-to-minutes and from minutes-to-hours must be handled properly. A carry occurs in both cases when the total number of seconds or minutes exceeds 59. This doesn't have anything to do with operator overloading directly, but the program must take this fact into account if a correct total is to be produced, as shown here:

```cpp
//
//   opover.cpp
//   C++ program illustrates operator overloading.
//   Program will overload the "+" operator so that
//   several angles, in the format degrees, minutes, seconds,
//   can be added directly.
//   Copyright (c) Chris H. Pappas and William H. Murray, 2001
//

#include "stdafx.h"
#include <iostream>
#include <string>

using namespace std;

int totaldegrees, totalminutes, totalseconds;

class angle_value {
    int degrees, minutes, seconds;

    public:
    angle_value() {degrees = 0,
                   minutes = 0,
                   seconds = 0;}  // constructor
    angle_value(char *);
    angle_value operator +(angle_value);
 };

angle_value::angle_value(char *angle_sum)
{
    degrees = atoi(strtok(angle_sum, "d"));
    minutes = atoi(strtok(0, "m"));
    seconds = atoi(strtok(0, "s"));
}

angle_value angle_value::operator+(angle_value angle_sum)
{
    angle_value ang;
    ang.seconds = (seconds + angle_sum.seconds) % 60;
    ang.minutes = ((seconds + angle_sum.seconds) / 60 +
```

```
                        minutes+angle_sum.minutes)%60;
        ang.degrees = ((seconds + angle_sum.seconds) / 60 +
                        minutes + angle_sum.minutes) / 60;
        ang.degrees += degrees + angle_sum.degrees;
        totaldegrees = ang.degrees;
        totalminutes = ang.minutes;
        totalseconds = ang.seconds;
        return ang;
}
int main(int argc, char* argv[])
{
        char str1[] = "37d 15m 56s";
        angle_value angle1(str1);

        char str2[] = "10d 44m 44s";
        angle_value angle2(str2);

        char str3[] = "75d 17m 59s";
        angle_value angle3(str3);

        char str4[] = "130d 32m 54s";
        angle_value angle4(str4);

        angle_value sum_of_angles;

        sum_of_angles = angle1 + angle2 + angle3 + angle4;
        cout << "The sum of the angles is "
             << totaldegrees << "d "
             << totalminutes << "m "
             << totalseconds << "s "   << endl << endl;

    return 0;
}
```

The following portion of code shows how the mixed units are added together. Here the + operator is to be overloaded:

```
    .
    .
    .
  ang.seconds = (seconds + angle_sum.seconds) % 60;
  ang.minutes = ((seconds + angle_sum.seconds) / 60 +
                 minutes + angle_sum.minutes) % 60;
```

```
ang.degrees = ((seconds + angle_sum.seconds) / 60 +
               minutes + angle_sum.minutes) / 60;
ang.degrees+ = degrees + angle_sum.degrees;
  .
  .
  .
```

The divide and modulus operations are performed on the sums to ensure correct carry information.

Further details of the program's operation are omitted since you have seen most of the functions and modules in earlier examples. However, it is important to remember that when you overload operators, proper operator syntax and precedence must be maintained.

The output from this program shows the sum of the four angles to be as follows:

```
The sum of the angles is 253d 51m 33s
```

Is this answer correct?

Derived Classes

A derived class can be considered an extension or inheritance of an existing class. The original class is known as a base or parent class and the derived class as a subclass or child class. As such, a derived class provides a simple means for expanding or customizing the capabilities of a parent class, without the need for recreating the parent class itself. With a parent class in place, a common interface is possible with one or more of the derived classes.

Any C++ class can serve as a parent class, and any derived class will reflect its description. The derived class can add additional features to those of the parent class. For example, the derived class can modify access privileges, add new members, or overload existing ones. When a derived class overloads a function declared in the parent class, it is said to be a virtual member function. You will see that virtual member functions are very important to the concept of object-oriented programming.

Derived Class Syntax

You describe a derived class by using the following syntax:

```
class derived-class-type :(public/private/protected) . . .
      parent-class-type { . . . .};
```

For example, in creating a derived class, you might write this:

```
class retirement:public consumer { . . . .};
```

In this case, the derived class tag is **retirement**. The parent class has public visibility, and its tag is **consumer**.

A third visibility specifier is often used with derived classes—a protected specifier. A protected specifier is the same as a private specifier, with the added feature that class member functions and friends of derived classes are given access to the class.

Using Derived Classes

The following example is used to illustrate the concept of a derived class. The parent class collects and reports information on a consumer's name, address, city, state, and ZIP code. Two similar child classes are derived. One derived child class maintains information on a consumer's accumulated airline mileage, while the second reports information on a consumer's accumulated rental car mileage. Both derived child classes inherit information from the parent class. Study the listing and see what you can discern about these derived classes:

```
//
//  dercls.cpp
//  C++ program illustrates derived classes.
//  The parent class contains name, street, city,
//  state, and zip information. Derived classes add
//  either airline or rental car mileage information
//  to parent class information.
//  Copyright (c) Chris H. Pappas and William H. Murray, 2001
//

#include "stdafx.h"
#include <iostream>
#include <string>

using namespace std;

char newline;

class consumer {
    char name[60],
         street[60],
         city[20],
         state[15],
```

```
            zip[10];
public:
    void data_output(void);
    void data_input(void);
};

void consumer::data_output()
{
    cout << "Name: " << name << endl;
    cout << "Street: " << street << endl;
    cout << "City: " << city << endl;
    cout << "State: " << state << endl;
    cout << "Zip: " << zip << endl;
}

void consumer::data_input()
{
    cout << "Enter The Consumer's Full Name: ";
    cin.get(name, 59, '\n');
    cin.get(newline);         //flush carriage return
    cout << "Enter the Street Address: ";
    cin.get(street, 59, '\n');
    cin.get(newline);
    cout << "Enter the City: ";
    cin.get(city, 19, '\n');
    cin.get(newline);
    cout << "Enter the State: ";
    cin.get(state, 14, '\n');
    cin.get(newline);
    cout << "Enter the Five-Digit Zip Code: ";
    cin.get(zip, 9, '\n');
    cin.get(newline);
}

class airline:public consumer {
    char airline_type[20];
    float acc_air_miles;
public:
    void airline_consumer();
    void disp_air_mileage();
};

void airline::airline_consumer()
```

```
{
    data_input();
    cout << "Enter Airline Type: ";
    cin.get(airline_type, 19, '\n');
    cin.get(newline);
    cout << "Enter Accumulated Air Mileage: ";
    cin >> acc_air_miles;
    cin.get(newline);          //flush carriage return
}

void airline::disp_air_mileage()
{
    data_output();

    cout << "Airline Type: " << airline_type
         << endl;
    cout << "Accumulated Air Mileage: "
         << acc_air_miles << endl;
}

class rental_car:public consumer {
    char rental_car_type[20];
    float acc_road_miles;
public:
    void rental_car_consumer();
    void disp_road_mileage();
};

void rental_car::rental_car_consumer()
{
    data_input();
    cout << "Enter Rental_car Type: ";
    cin.get(rental_car_type, 19, '\n');
    cin.get(newline);          //flush carriage return
    cout << "Enter Accumulated Road Mileage: ";
    cin >> acc_road_miles;
    cin.get(newline);
}

void rental_car::disp_road_mileage()
{
    data_output();
```

```
    cout << "Rental Car Type: "
         << rental_car_type << endl;
    cout << "Accumulated Mileage: "
         << acc_road_miles << endl;
}

int main(int argc, char* argv[])
{
    //associate variable names with classes
    airline jetaway;
    rental_car varooom;

    //get airline information
    cout << "\n--Airline Consumer--\n";
    jetaway.airline_consumer();


    //get rental_car information
    cout << "\n--Rental Car Consumer--\n";
    varooom.rental_car_consumer();

    //now display all consumer information
    cout << "\n--Airline Consumer--\n";
    jetaway.disp_air_mileage();
    cout << "\n--Rental Car Consumer--\n";
    varooom.disp_road_mileage();

    cout << endl;

    return 0;
}
```

In this example, the parent class is of type **consumer**. The private part of this class accepts consumer information for name, address, city, state, and ZIP code. The public part describes two functions, data_output() and data_input(). You have seen functions similar to these to gather class information in earlier programs. The first derived child class is **airline**:

```
class airline:public consumer {
  char airline_type[20];
  float acc_air_miles;
```

```
public:
  void airline_consumer(void);
  void disp_air_mileage(void);
};
```

This derived child class contains two functions, airline_consumer() and disp_air_mileage(). The first function, airline_consumer(), uses the parent class to obtain name, address, city, state, and ZIP code, and attaches the airline type and accumulated mileage:

```
void airline::airline_consumer()
{
  data_input();
  cout << "Enter Airline Type: ";
  cin.get(airline_type, 19, '\n');
  cin.get(newline);
  cout << "Enter Accumulated Air Mileage: ";
  cin >> acc_air_miles;
  cin.get(newline);        //flush carriage return
}
```

Do you understand how the derived class is being used? A call to the function data_input() is a call to a member function that is part of the parent class. The remainder of the derived class is involved with obtaining the additional airline type and accumulated mileage.

The information on accumulated air mileage can be displayed for a consumer in a similar manner. The parent class function, data_output(), prints the information gathered by the parent class (name, address, and so on), while disp_air_mileage() attaches the derived child class's information (airline type and mileage) to the output. The process is repeated for the rental car consumer.

Thus, one parent class serves as the data-gathering base for two derived child classes, each obtaining its own specific information.

The following is a sample output from the program:

```
--Airline Consumer--
Name: Peter J. Smith
Street: 401 West Summit Avenue
City: Middletown
State: Delaware
Zip: 19804
```

```
Airline Type: US AIR
Accumulated Air Mileage: 55321.0

--Rental Car Consumer--
Name: Harry Z. Beener
Street: 511 West Pacific Road
City: Longtown
State: New York
Zip: 25888
Rental Car Type: Audi
Accumulated Road Mileage: 33446.5
```

Experiment with this program by entering your own database of information. You might also consider adding additional member functions to the consumer class.

What's Coming?

In this chapter you learned extensive information about C++ classes. This information included nesting, constructors and destructors, overloading friend functions, and derived classes.

Now that you have learned about the class structure, you are ready for a complete look at I/O in C++ in the following chapter.

The Complete Reference

Visual C++.NET

Chapter 17

Complete I/O in C++

C hapter 11 introduced the concept of iostream objects, **cin** and **cout**, along with the put to (insertion) operator, <<; and the get from (extraction) operator, >>. In this chapter you will learn about the classes behind C++ I/O streams.

This chapter also introduces several additional topics relating to the development of C++ code, such as how to use C library functions in a C++ program.

Using enum Types in C++

User-defined enumerated types behave differently in C++ from their C counterparts. For example, C *enum* types are compatible with the type *int*. This means they can be cross-assigned with no complaints from the compiler. However, in C++ the two types are incompatible.

Another difference between C and C++ enumerated types involves the syntax shorthand when you define C++ *enum* variables. The following example program highlights the enumerated type differences between the two languages:

```
//
//   enum.cpp
//   C++ program demonstrates how to use enumerated types and
//   how C++ enumerated types differ from C enumerated types.
//   Copyright (c) Chris H. Pappas and William H. Murray, 2001
//

#include "stdafx.h"
#include <iostream>

using namespace std;

typedef enum boolean { FALSE, TRUE };

int main(int argc, char* argv[])
{
    // enum boolean bflag = 0; legal C,
    // but illegal C++ statement
    boolean bcontinue, bflag = FALSE;

    bcontinue = (boolean)1;

    bflag = bcontinue;

    return 0;
}
```

This code starts by defining the enumerated type *boolean*, which is a standard type in several other high-level languages. Because of the ordering of the definition—FALSE, then TRUE—the compiler assigns a zero to FALSE and a 1 to TRUE. This is perfect for their logical use in a program.

The statement, commented-out in the main() program, represents a legal C statement. Remember, when you define enumerated variables in C, such as *bflag,* you must use the **enum** keyword with the enumerated type's tag field—in this case, *boolean.* Since C **enum** types are compatible with **int** types, it is also legal to initialize a variable with an integer value. This statement would not get past the C++ compiler. The second statement in main() shows the legal C++ counterpart.

The final two statements in the program show how to use enumerated types. Notice that in C++, an explicit cast (*boolean*), is needed to convert the 1 to a *boolean* compatible type.

User-defined types cannot be directly input from or output to a file, as you may recall. Either they must go through a conversion routine or you can custom overload the >> and << operators, as discussed in Chapter 12.

Reference Variables

The reference variable is a C++ feature that can really be appreciated because it simplifies the syntax and readability of the more confusing pointer notation. Remember that by using pointer parameters, a program could pass something to a function either call-by-reference or call-by-variable, which enables the function to change the item passed. In contrast, call-by-value sends a copy of the variable's contents to the function. Any change to the variable in this case is a local change not reflected in the calling routine.

In the next example, the program passes an *stStudent* structure to a function, using the three possible calling methods: call-by-value, call-by-reference with pointer notation, and call-by-reference using the simpler C++ reference type. If the program were sending the entire array to the subroutine, by default, the array parameter would be passed call-by-reference. However, single structures within the array, by default, are passed call-by-value:

```
//
//  refvar.cpp
//  C++ program demonstrating how the C++ reference type
//  eliminates the more confusing pointer notation.
//  The program also demonstrates how to pass a single
//  array element, call by value, variable, and reference.
//  Copyright (c) Chris H. Pappas and William H. Murray, 2001
//

#include "stdafx.h"
#include <iostream>
using namespace std;
```

```
struct stStudent {
    char    pszName[66],
            pszAddress[66],
            pszCity[26],
            pszState[3],
            pszPhone[13];
    int     icourses;
    float   GPA;
};

void vByValueCall     (stStudent  stAStudent);
void vByVariableCall  (stStudent *pstAStudent);
void vByReferenceCall (stStudent &rstAStudent);

int main(int argc, char* argv[])
{
    stStudent astLargeClass[100];

    astLargeClass[0].icourses = 10;

    vByValueCall     ( astLargeClass[0]);
    cout << astLargeClass[0].icourses << "\n";
    // icourses still 10

    vByVariableCall  (&astLargeClass[0]);
    cout << astLargeClass[0].icourses << "\n";
    // icourses = 20

    vByReferenceCall ( astLargeClass[0]);
    cout << astLargeClass[0].icourses << "\n";
    // icourses = 30

    return 0;
}

void vByValueCall(stStudent  stAStudent)
{
    stAStudent.icourses += 10;
    // normal structure syntax
}

void vByVariableCall(stStudent *pstAStudent)
{
```

```
        pstAStudent->icourses += 10;
        // pointer syntax
}

void vByReferenceCall(stStudent &rstAStudent)
{
        rstAStudent.icourses += 10;
        // simplified reference syntax
}
```

Notice that the following portion of code has spliced together each function's prototype, along with its matching invoking statement:

```
void vByValueCall      (stStudent   stAStudent);
     vByValueCall      ( astLargeClass[0]    );

void vByVariableCall   (stStudent *pstAStudent);
     vByVariableCall   (&astLargeClass[0]       );

void vByReferenceCall (stStudent &rstAStudent);
     vByReferenceCall ( astLargeClass[0]     );
```

FOUNDATIONS FOR OBJECT-ORIENTED PROGRAMMING

One immediate advantage of this style is the simpler syntax needed to send a reference variable, *astLargeClass[0]* (the last statement), over the equivalent pointer syntax, *&astLargeClass[0]*. At this point the difference may appear small. However, as your algorithms become more complicated, this simpler syntax can avoid unnecessary precedence-level conflicts with other operators such as the pointer *dereference operator* (*) and the dot *member operator* (.), which qualifies structure fields.

The next three statements were pulled out of the program's respective functions to show the syntax for using the structure within each function:

```
stAStudent.icourses   += 10;  // normal structure syntax
pstAStudent->icourses += 10;  // pointer syntax
rstAStudent.icourses  += 10;  // simplified reference syntax
```

The last two statements make a permanent change to the passed *stStudent* structure because the structure was passed call-by-reference (variable). Notice that the last statement did not require the pointer operator.

The difference between the first and third statements is dramatic. Although they look identical, the first statement references only a copy of the *stStudent* structure. In this case, when *stAstudent.icourses* is incremented, it is done only to the function's local copy. Exiting the function returns the structure to bit-oblivion, along with the incremented value. This explains why the program outputs 10, 20, 30 instead of 20, 30, 40.

Default Arguments

A function can be prototyped in C++ by using default arguments. This means that if the invoking statement omits certain fields, predefined default values will be supplied by the function. Default argument definitions cannot be spread throughout a function's prototype; they must be the last formal parameters defined. The following example program demonstrates how to define and use such a function:

```cpp
//
//  defrag.cpp
//  C++ program demonstrates how to prototype functions
//  with default arguments. Default arguments must always
//  be the last formal parameters defined.
//  Copyright (c) Chris H. Pappas and William H. Murray, 2001
//

#include "stdafx.h"
#include <iostream>

using namespace std;

void fdefault_argument(char ccode = 'Q', int ivalue = 0,
                       double fvalue = 0);

int main(int argc, char* argv[])
{
    fdefault_argument('A', 2, 12.34);
    fdefault_argument();

    return 0;
}

void fdefault_argument(char ccode, int ivalue, double fvalue)
{
    if(ccode == 'Q')
        cout << "\n\nUsing default values only.";
        cout << "\nivalue = " << ivalue;
        cout << "\nfvalue = " << fvalue << endl << endl;
}
```

Notice that in this program, all three formal parameter types have been given
default values. The function fdefault() checks the CCODE value to switch on or off an
appropriate message. The output from the program is straightforward:

```
ivalue = 2
fvalue = 12.34

Using default values only.
ivalue = 0
fvalue = 0
```

Careful function prototyping, using default argument assignment, can be an
important approach to avoiding unwanted side effects. This is one means of guaranteeing
that dynamically allocated variables will not have garbage values if the user did not
supply any. Another way to initialize dynamically allocated memory is with the
function memset().

The memset() Function

The memset() function can be used to initialize a dynamically allocated byte, or bytes,
to a specific character. The prototype for memset() looks like this:

```
void *memset(void *dest, int cchar, size_t count);
```

Once the memset() function is called, *dest* points to *count* bytes of memory initialized
to the character *cchar*. The following example program demonstrates a dynamic
structure declaration:

```
//
//  memset.cpp
//  C++ program demonstrating the function memset(),
//  which can initialize dynamically allocated memory.
//  Copyright (c) Chris H. Pappas and William H. Murray, 2001
//

#include "stdafx.h"
#include <iostream>
#include <memory>

using namespace std;
```

```
struct keybits {
    unsigned char rshift, lshift,  ctrl,   alt,
                      scroll, numlock, caplock, insert;
};

int main(int argc, char* argv[])
{
    keybits *pstkinitialized;

    pstkinitialized = new keybits;
    memset(pstkinitialized, 0, sizeof(keybits));

    return 0;
}
```

Because of the memset() function, the dynamically allocated structure pointed to by *pstkinitialized* contains all zeros. The call to the function memset() also used the sizeof() operator instead of hardwiring the statement to a "magic number." The use of sizeof() allows the algorithm to automatically adjust to the size of any object passed to it. Remember, too, that C++ does not require the **struct** keyword to precede a structure tag field (keybits) when defining structure variables, as is the case with *pstkinitialized*.

Formatting Output

The next example continues the development of C++ formatted output initially introduced in Chapter 11. The first program demonstrates how to print a table of factorials using long doubles with the default right justification:

```
//
//  fact1.cpp
//  A C++ program that prints a table of
//  factorials for the numbers from 1 to 25.
//  Program uses the long double type.
//  Formatting includes precision, width, and fixed,
//  with default of right justification when printing.
//  Copyright (c) Chris H. Pappas and William H. Murray, 2001
//

#include "stdafx.h"
#include <iostream>
#include <iomanip>
```

```
using namespace std;

int main(int argc, char* argv[])
{
    long double number, factorial;

    number = 1.0;
    factorial = 1.0;

    cout.precision(0);              // no decimal place
    cout.setf(ios::fixed);          // use fixed format

    for(int i = 0; i < 25; i++) {
        factorial *= number;
        number = number + 1.0;
        cout.width(30);             // width of 30 characters
        cout << factorial << endl << endl;
    }
    return 0;
}
```

The precision(), width(), and setf() class members functions were repeated in the loop. The output from the program takes on the following form:

```
                             1

                             2

                             6

                            24

                           120

                           720

                          5040

                         40320

                        362880

                       3628800

                      39916800

                     479001600

                    6227020800

                   87178291200

                 1307674368000

                20922789888000

               355687428096000

              6402373705728000
```

```
      121645100408832000
     2432902008176640000
    51090942171709440000
   1124000727777607680000
  25852016738884976640000
 620448401733239439360000
15511210043330985984000000
```

The next program/output pair demonstrates how to vary output column width and override the default right justification:

```cpp
//
//   fact2.cpp
//   A C++ program that prints a table of
//   factorials for the numbers from 1 to 15.
//   Program uses the long double type.
//   Formatting includes precision, width, alignment,
//   and format of large numbers.
//   Copyright (c) Chris H. Pappas and William H. Murray, 2001
//

#include "stdafx.h"
#include <iostream>
#include <iomanip>

using namespace std;

int main(int argc, char* argv[])
{
    long double number, factorial;

    number = 1.0;
    factorial = 1.0;

    cout.precision(0);              // no decimal point
    cout.setf(ios::left);           // left justify numbers
    cout.setf(ios::fixed);          // use fixed format

    for(int i = 0; i < 25; i++) {
        factorial *= number;
        number = number + 1.0;
        cout.width(30);             // width of 30 characters
        cout << factorial << endl << endl;
```

```
    }

    return 0;
}
```

The left-justified output takes on the following form:

```
1
2
6
24
120
720
5040
40320
362880
3628800
39916800
479001600
6227020800
87178291200
1307674368000
20922789888000
355687428096000
6402373705728000
121645100408832000
2432902008176640000
51090942171709440000
1124000727777607680000
25852016738884976640000
620448401733239439360000
15511210043330985984000000
```

The next example prints out a table of numbers, their squares, and their square roots. The program demonstrates how easy it is to align columns, pad with blanks, fill spaces with zeros, and control numeric precision in C++:

```
//
//   sqrt.cpp
//   A C++ program that prints a table of
//   numbers, squares, and square roots for the
//   numbers from 1 to 15. Program uses the type
//   double. Formatting aligns columns, pads blank
```

FOUNDATIONS FOR OBJECT-ORIENTED PROGRAMMING

```cpp
//   spaces with '0' character, and controls
//   precision of answer.
//   Copyright (c) Chris H. Pappas and William H. Murray, 2001
//

#include "stdafx.h"
#include <iostream>
#include <iomanip>
#include <cmath>

using namespace std;

int main(int argc, char* argv[])
{
    double number, square, sqroot;

    cout << "num\t" << "square\t\t" << "square root\n";
    cout << "_____\n";

    number = 1.0;
    cout.setf(ios::fixed);        // use fixed format

    for(int i = 1; i < 16; i++) {
        square = number * number; // find square
        sqroot = sqrt(number);    // find square root

        cout.fill('0');           // fill blanks with zeros
        cout.width(2);            // column 2 characters wide
        cout.precision(0);        // no decimal place
        cout << number << "\t";

        cout.width(6);            // column 6 characters wide
        cout.precision(1);        // print 1 decimal place
        cout << square << "\t\t";

        cout.width(8);            // column 8 characters wide
        cout.precision(6);        // print 6 decimal places
        cout << sqroot << endl;

        number += 1.0;
    }
```

```
      cout << endl;

      return 0;
}
```

The formatted output takes on the following form:

num	square	square root
01	0001.0	1.000000
02	0004.0	1.414214
03	0009.0	1.732051
04	0016.0	2.000000
05	0025.0	2.236068
06	0036.0	2.449490
07	0049.0	2.645751
08	0064.0	2.828427
09	0081.0	3.000000
10	0100.0	3.162278
11	0121.0	3.316625
12	0144.0	3.464102
13	0169.0	3.605551
14	0196.0	3.741657
15	0225.0	3.872983

I/O Options

Chapter 15 introduced the concepts and syntax for object-oriented classes, constructors, destructors, member functions, and operators. This understanding is required for a deeper understanding of C++ I/O.

C++, like C, does not have any built-in I/O routines. Instead, all C++ compilers come bundled with object-oriented iostream classes. These standard I/O class objects have a cross-compiler syntax consistency because they were developed by the authors of the C++ language. If you are trying to write a C++ application that is portable to other C++ compilers, you will want to use these iostream classes. The Visual C++ compiler provides the following five ways to perform C++ I/O:

ANSI C buffered I/O   C also supports buffered functions such as fread() and fwrite(). These STDIO.H library functions perform their own buffering before calling the direct I/O base routines.

C console and port I/O C provides additional I/O routines that have no C++ equivalent, such as _getch(), _ungetch(), and _kbhit(). All non-Windows applications can use these functions, which give direct access to the hardware.

Microsoft Foundation Class library The Microsoft CFile class found in the Foundation Class library provides C++ and Windows applications with objects for disk I/O. Using this library of routines guarantees that your application will be portable and easy to maintain.

Microsoft iostream class library The iostream class library provides C++ programs with object-oriented I/O. This I/O can be used in place of functions such as scanf(), printf(), fscanf(), and fprintf(). However, while these iostream classes are not required by C++ programs, many of the character-mode objects, such as **cin**, **cout**, **cerr**, and **clog**, are incompatible with the Windows graphical user interface.

Unbuffered C library I/O The C compiler provides unbuffered I/O through functions such as _read() and _write(). These functions are very popular with C programmers because of their efficiency and the ease with which they can be customized.

The iostream Class List

All of the I/O objects defined in the iostream class library share the same abstract stream base class, called **ios**, with the exception of the stream buffer classes. These derived classes fall into the four broad categories shown in Table 17-1.

Input Stream Classes	Description
Istream	Used for general-purpose input or as a parent class for other derived input classes
Ifstream	Used for file input

Table 17-1. *The Four ios Class Categories*

Input Stream Classes	Description
Istream_withassign	Used for **cin** input
Istrstream	Used for string input

Output Stream Classes	Description
Ostream	Used for general-purpose output or as a parent class for other derived output streams
Ofstream	Used for file output
Ofstream_withassign	Used for **cout**, **cerr**, and **clog**
ostrstream	Used for string output

Input/Output Stream Classes	Description
iostream	Used for general-purpose input and output, or as a parent class for other derived I/O streams
fstream	File I/O stream class
strstream	String I/O stream class
stdiostream	Standard I/O stream class

Stream Buffer Classes	Description
streambuf	Used as a parent class for derived objects
filebuf	Disk file stream buffer class
strstreambuf	Stream buffer class for strings
stdiobuf	Stream buffer class for standard file I/O

Table 17-1.   *The Four ios Class Categories (continued)*

Figure 17-1 illustrates the interrelationship between these **ios** stream classes.

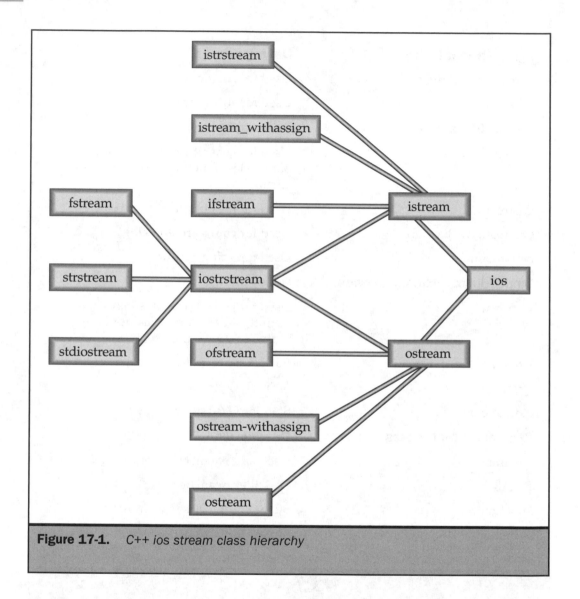

Figure 17-1. C++ ios stream class hierarchy

All ios-derived **iostream** classes use a streambuf class object for the actual I/O processing. The iostream class library uses the three derived buffer classes with streams as shown in Table 17-2.

Derived classes usually expand upon their inherited parent class definitions. This is why it is possible to use an operator or member function for a derived class that doesn't directly appear to be in the derived class's definition.

Buffered Class	Description
filebuf	Provides buffered disk file I/O
strstreambuf	Provides an in-memory array of bytes to hold the stream data
stdiobuf	Provides buffered disk I/O with all buffering done by the standard I/O system

Table 17-2.   *Buffered Classes*

Often, because of this fact, it will be necessary to research back to the root or parent class definition. Since C++ derives so many of its classes from the **ios** class, a portion of ios.h follows. You will be able to use this as an easy reference for understanding any class derived from **ios**:

```
#ifndef EOF
#define EOF (-1)
#endif

class streambuf;
class ostream;

class ios {

public:
    enum io_state { goodbit    = 0x00,
                    eofbit     = 0x01,
                    failbit    = 0x02,
                    badbit     = 0x04 };

    enum open_mode { in        = 0x01,
                     out       = 0x02,
                     ate       = 0x04,
                     app       = 0x08,
                     trunc     = 0x10,
                     nocreate  = 0x20,
                     noreplace = 0x40,
                     binary    = 0x80 }; // not in latest spec.
```

```
enum seek_dir { beg=0, cur=1, end=2 };

enum {  skipws      = 0x0001,
        left        = 0x0002,
        right       = 0x0004,
        internal    = 0x0008,
        dec         = 0x0010,
        oct         = 0x0020,
        hex         = 0x0040,
        showbase    = 0x0080,
        showpoint   = 0x0100,
        uppercase   = 0x0200,
        showpos     = 0x0400,
        scientific  = 0x0800,
        fixed       = 0x1000,
        unitbuf     = 0x2000,
        stdio       = 0x4000
                            };

static const long basefield;    // dec | oct | hex
static const long adjustfield;  // left | right | internal
static const long floatfield;   // scientific | fixed

ios(streambuf*);               // differs from ANSI
virtual ~ios();

inline long flags() const;
inline long flags(long _l);

inline long setf(long _f,long _m);
inline long setf(long _l);
inline long unsetf(long _l);

inline int width() const;
inline int width(int _i);
inline ostream* tie(ostream* _os);
inline ostream* tie() const;

inline char fill() const;
inline char fill(char _c);

inline int precision(int _i);
inline int precision() const;
```

```
    inline int rdstate() const;
    inline void clear(int _i = 0);

//  NOTE: inline operator void*() const;
    operator void *() const { if(state&(badbit|failbit) ) \
                              return 0; return (void *)this; }
    inline int operator!() const;

    inline int  good() const;
    inline int  eof() const;
    inline int  fail() const;
    inline int  bad() const;
```

The programs in the following sections use a derived class based on some parent class. Some of the example program code uses derived class member functions, while other statements use inherited characteristics. These examples will help you understand the many advantages of derived classes and of inherited characteristics. While these concepts may appear difficult or frustrating at first, you'll quickly appreciate how you can inherit functionality from a predefined class simply by defining a derived class based on the predefined one.

Input Stream Classes

The **ifstream** class used in the next example program is derived from fstreambase and istream. It provides input operations on a filebuf. The program concentrates on text stream input:

```
//
//  ifstrm.cpp
//  C++ program demonstrating how to use ifstream class,
//  derived from the istream class.
//  Copyright (c) Chris H. Pappas and William H. Murray, 2001
//
//  Valid member functions for ifstream include:
//          ifstream::open        ifstream::rdbuf
//
//  Valid member functions for istream include:
//          istream::gcount       istream::get
//          istream::getline      istream::ignore
//          istream::istream      istream::peek
//          istream::putback      istream::read
//          istream::seekg        istream::tellg

#include "stdafx.h"
```

```
#include <fstream>
#include <iostream>

using namespace std;

#define iCOLUMNS 80

int main(int argc, char* argv[])
{
    char cOneLine[iCOLUMNS];

    ifstream ifMyInputStream("ifstrm.cpp", ios::in);
    while(ifMyInputStream) {
        ifMyInputStream.getline(cOneLine, iCOLUMNS);
        cout << '\n' << cOneLine;
    }
    ifMyInputStream.close();

    return 0;
}
```

The ifstream constructor is used first to create an ifstream object and connect it to an open file descriptor, *ifMyInputStream*. The syntax uses the name of a file, including a path if necessary ("ifstrm.cpp"), along with one or more open modes (for example, ios::in | ios::nocreate | ios::binary). The default is text input. The optional ios::nocreate parameter tests for the file's existence. The *ifMyInputStream* file descriptor's integer value can be used in logical tests, such as if and while statements, and the value is automatically set to zero on EOF.

The getline() member function inherited from the **iostream** class allows a program to read whole lines of text up to a terminating null character. Function getline() has three formal parameters: a *char *: the number of characters to input, including the null character; and an optional delimiter (default = '\n').

cOneLine meets the first parameter requirement since char array names are technically pointers to characters. The number of characters to be input matches the array's definition, or *iCOLUMNS*. No optional delimiter was defined. However, if you knew your input lines were delimited by a special character—for example, '*'—you could have written the getline() statement like this:

```
ifMyInputStream.getline(cOneLine,iCOLUMNS,'*');
```

The example program continues by printing the string and then manually closes the file ifMyInputStream.close().

Output Stream Classes

All **ofstream** classes are derived from fstreambase and ostream and allow a program to perform formatted and unformatted output to a streambuf. The output from this program is used later in this chapter in the section titled "Binary Files" to contrast text output with binary output.

The following example uses the ofstream constructor, which is very similar to its ifstream counterpart, described earlier. It expects the name of the output file, "myostrm.out", and the open mode, ios::out.

```
//
// ostrm.cpp
// C++ program demonstrating how to use the ofstream class
// derived from the ostream class.
// Copyright (c) Chris H. Pappas and William H. Murray, 2001

// Valid ofstream member functions include:
//          ofstream::open      ofstream::rdbuf

// Valid ostream member functions include:
//          ostream::flush      ostream::ostream
//          ostream::put        ostream::seekp
//          ostream::tellp      ostream::write

#include "stdafx.h"
#include <fstream>
#include <iostream>

using namespace std;

#define iSTRING_MAX 40

int main(int argc, char* argv[])
{
    int i = 0;
    long ltellp;
    char pszString[iSTRING_MAX] = "Sample test string\n";

    // file opened in the default text mode
    ofstream ofMyOutputStream("myostrm.out",ios::out);
```

```
// write string out character by character
// notice that '\n' IS translated into 2 characters

while(pszString[i] != '\0') {
    ofMyOutputStream.put(pszString[i]);
    ltellp = ofMyOutputStream.tellp();
    cout << "\ntellp value: " << ltellp;
    i++;
}



// write entire string out with write member function

ltellp = ofMyOutputStream.tellp();
cout << "\ntellp's value before writing 2nd string: "
    << ltellp;
ofMyOutputStream.write(pszString,strlen(pszString));
ltellp = ofMyOutputStream.tellp();
cout << "\ntellp's updated value: " << ltellp;

ofMyOutputStream.close();

cout << endl << endl;

return 0;
}
```

The initial **while** loop prints out the *pszString*, character by character, with the put() member function. After each character is output, the variable *ltellp* is assigned the current put pointer's position as returned by the call to the tellp() member function. It is important that you stop at this point to take a look at the output generated by the program, shown at the end of this section.

The string variable *pszString* is initialized with 19 characters plus a '\0' null terminator, bringing the count to a total of 20. However, although the program output generates a *tellp* count of 1...20, the 20th character is not the '\0' null terminator. This is because in text mode, the *pszString*'s '\n' is translated into a 2-byte output—one for the carriage return (19th character) and the second for the linefeed (20th character). The null terminator is not output.

The last portion of the program calculates the output pointer's position before and after using the write() member function to print *pszString* as a whole string. Notice that the printed *tellp* values show that the function write() also translates the single null terminator into a two-character output. If the character translation had not occurred, *tellp*'s last value would be 39 (assuming put() left the first count at 20, not 19). The abbreviated output from the program looks like this:

```
tellp value: 1
tellp value: 2
tellp value: 3
      .
      .
      .
tellp value: 17
tellp value: 18
tellp value: 20
tellp's value before writing 2nd string: 20
tellp's updated value: 40
```

Fortunately, istream-derived class member functions such as get() and read() automatically convert the 2-byte output back to a single '\n'. The program highlights the need for caution when dealing with file I/O. If the file, created by this program, were used later as an input file and opened in binary mode, a disaster would occur. This is because binary files do not use such translation; the file positions and contents would be incorrect.

Buffered Stream Classes

The **streambuf** class is the foundation for C++ stream I/O. This general class defines all of the basic operations that can be performed with character-oriented buffers. The **streambuf** class is also used to derive file buffers (**filebuf** class) and the **istream** and **ostream** classes that contain pointers to **streambuf** objects.

Any derived classes based on the **ios** class inherit a pointer to a **streambuf**. The **filebuf** class, as seen in Figure 17-2, is derived from **streambuf** and specializes the parent class to handle files.

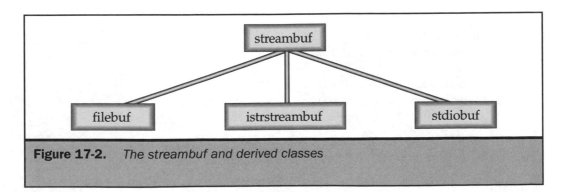

Figure 17-2.   *The streambuf and derived classes*

The following example begins by defining two **filebuf** handles, *fbMyInputBuf* and *fbMyOutputBuf*, using the open() member function to create each text file:

```
//
//   filbuf.cpp
//   C++ program demonstrating how to use filebuf class.
//   Copyright (c) Chris H. Pappas and William H. Murray, 2001
//
//   Valid member functions include:
//           filebuf::attach        filebuf::close
//           filebuf::fd            filebuf::~filebuf
//           filebuf::filebuf       filebuf::is_open
//           filebuf::open          filebuf::overflow
//           filebuf::seekoff       filebuf::setbuf
//           filebuf::sync          filebuf::underflow
//

#include "stdafx.h"
#include <cstdlib>             // exit() prototype
#include <fstream>             // ios::in and ios::out
#include <iostream>

//   NOTE:  use of older style header files
//       no longer used:
//       #include <fcntl.h>    // _O_TEXT and _O_WRONLY
//           use ios::in and ios::out
//       #include <process.h> // exit() prototype

using namespace std;

int main(int argc, char* argv[])
{
    char ch;
    int iLineCount = 0;
    filebuf fbMyInputBuf, fbMyOutputBuf;

    fbMyInputBuf.open("filbuf.cpp", ios::in);
    if(fbMyInputBuf.is_open() == 0) {
        cerr << "Can't open input file";
        cout << endl << endl;
        exit (1);
    }
```

```
        istream is(&fbMyInputBuf);

        fbMyOutputBuf.open("output.dat", ios::out);
        if(fbMyOutputBuf.is_open() == 0) {
            cerr << "Can't open output file";
            cout << endl << endl;
            exit (2);
        }

        ostream os(&fbMyOutputBuf);

        while(is) {
            is.get(ch);
            os.put(ch);
            iLineCount += (ch == '\n');
        }

        fbMyInputBuf.close();
        fbMyOutputBuf.close();

        cout << "You had " << iLineCount << " lines in your file";
        cout << endl << endl;

        return 0;
}
```

Assuming there were no file-creation errors, each handle is then associated with an appropriate **istream** (input) and **ostream** (output) object. With both files opened, the **while** loop performs a simple echo print from the input stream is.get() to the output stream os.put(), counting the number of linefeeds, '\n'. The overloaded close() member function manually closes each file.

String Stream Class

The **streambuf** class can be used to extend the capabilities of the **iostream** class. Figure 17-1, shown earlier, illustrated the relationship between the **ios** and derived classes. It is the **ios** class that provides the derived classes with the programming interface and formatting features. However, it is the **streambuf** public members and virtual functions that do all the work. All derived **ios** classes make calls to these routines.

All buffered **streambuf** objects manage a fixed memory buffer called a *reserve area*. This reserve area can be divided into a get area for input and a put area for output. If an application requires, the get and put areas may overlap. Your program can use protected member functions to access and manipulate the two separate get and put pointers for character I/O. Each application determines the behavior of the buffers and pointers based on the program's implementation of the derived class.

There are two constructors for **streambuf** objects. They take on the following form:

```
streambuf::streambuf();
streambuf::streambuf(char* pr, int nLength);
```

The first constructor is used indirectly by all **streambuf** derived classes. It sets all the internal pointers of the streambuf object to null. The second constructor creates a streambuf object that is attached to an existing character array. The following program demonstrates how to declare a string strstreambuf object derived from the **streambuf** base class. Once the *stbMyStreamBuf* object is created, the program outputs a single character using the sputc() member function and then reads the character back in with the sgetc() member function:

```cpp
//
//   strbuf.cpp
//   C++ program demonstrating how to use the streambuf class.
//   Copyright (c) Chris H. Pappas and William H. Murray, 2001
//

#include "stdafx.h"
#include <strstream>
#include <iostream>

using namespace std;

#define iMYBUFFSIZE 1024

 int main(int argc, char* argv[])
{
    char c;

    strstreambuf stbMyStreamBuf(iMYBUFFSIZE);
    // output single character to buffer
    stbMyStreamBuf.sputc('A');
    c = stbMyStreamBuf.sgetc();
    cout << c << endl << endl;

    return 0;
}
```

There are two separate pointers for streambuf-based objects—a put to and a get from. Each is manipulated independently of the other. The reason the sgetc() member function retrieves the 'A' is to return the contents of the buffer at the location to which the get pointer points. The sputc() moves the put pointer but does not move the get pointer and does not return a character from the buffer.

Table 17-3 gives the names and explanations for all **streambuf** public members and highlights which functions manipulate the put and get pointers.

Table 17-4 gives the names and explanations for all **streambuf** virtual functions.

Table 17-5 gives the names and explanations for all streambuf-protected members.

Public Member	Meaning
Sgetc	Returns the character pointed to by the get pointer. However, sgetc does not move the pointer.
Sgetn	Gets a series of characters from the **streambuf** buffer.
Sputc	Puts a character in the put area and moves the put pointer.
Sputn	Puts a sequence of characters into the **streambuf** buffer and then moves the put pointer.
Snextc	Moves the get pointer and returns the next character.
Sbumpc	Returns the current character and then moves the get pointer.
Stossc	Advances the get pointer one position. However, stossc does not return a character.
sputbackc	Attempts to move the get pointer back one position. Character put back must match one from previous get.
out_waiting	Reports the number of characters in the put area.
in_avail	Reports the number of characters in the get area.
Dbp	Outputs **streambuf** buffer statistics and pointer values.

Table 17-3.   *Members of streambuf*

Virtual Function	Meaning
Seekoff	Seeks to the specified offset
Seekpos	Seeks to the specified position
overflow	Clears out the put area
underflow	Fills the get area, if necessary
pbackfail	Extends the sputbackc() function
Setbuf	Tries to attach a reserve area to the **streambuf**
Sync	Clears out the put and get area

Table 17-4.   *Virtual Functions of streambuf*

Protected Member	Meaning
Allocate	Allocates a buffer by calling doalloc
doallocate	Allocates a reserve area (virtual function)
Base	Returns a pointer to the beginning of the reserve area
Ebuf	Returns a pointer to the end of the reserve area
Blen	Returns the size of the reserve area
Pbase	Returns a pointer to the beginning of the put area
Pptr	Returns the put pointer
Gptr	Returns the get pointer
Eback	Returns the lower bound of the get area
Epptr	Returns a pointer to the end of the put area
Egptr	Returns a pointer to the end of the get area
Setp	Sets all the put area pointers

Table 17-5.   *Protected Members of streambuf*

Protected Member	Meaning
Setg	Sets all the get area pointers
Pbump	Increments/decrements the put pointer
Gbump	Increments/decrements the get pointer
Setb	Sets up the reserve area
unbuffered	Sets or tests the streambuf buffer state variable

Table 17-5. *Protected Members of streambuf (continued)*

The **streambuf** class comes equipped with almost every function a programmer could possibly need for manipulating a stream buffer. Since the **streambuf** class is used to derive file buffers (**filebuf** class) and **istream** and **ostream** classes, they all inherit **streambuf** characteristics.

Binary Files

Most of the example programs presented so far have used standard text files, or streams, as they are more appropriately called. This is not surprising since streams were originally designed for text, and text, therefore, is their default I/O mode.

Standard text files, or streams, contain a sequence of characters including carriage returns and linefeeds. In text mode, there is no requirement that individual characters remain unaltered as they are written to or read from a file. This can cause problems for certain types of applications. For example, the ASCII value for the newline character is a decimal 10. However, it could also be written as an 8-bit, hexadecimal 0A. In both C and C++ programs, it is considered to be the single character constant '\n'.

Under MS-DOS-compatible operations, the newline character is physically represented as a character pair—carriage return (decimal 13)/linefeed (decimal 10). Normally, this isn't a problem since the program automatically maps the two-character sequence into the single newline character on input, reversing the sequence on output. The problem is that a newline character occupies 1 byte, while the CR/LF pair occupies 2 bytes of storage.

Binary files, or streams, contain a sequence of bytes with a one-to-one correspondence to the sequence found in the external device (disk, tape, or terminal). In a binary file, no character translations will occur. For this reason, the number of bytes read or written will be the same as that found in the external device.

When an application is developed that needs to read an executable file, the file should be read as a binary file. Likewise, binary files should be used when reading or writing pure data files, like databases. Performing this action guarantees that no alteration of the data occurs except those changes performed explicitly by the application.

The following program is identical to ostrm.cpp, described earlier in this chapter, except that the output file mode has been changed from text to ios::binary:

```cpp
//
// binary.cpp
// This program is a modification of ostrm.cpp and
// demonstrates binary file output.
// Copyright (c) Chris H. Pappas and William H. Murray, 2001
// Valid ofstream member functions include:
//          ofstream::open     ofstream::rdbuf
// Valid ostream member functions include:
//          ostream::flush     ostream::ostream
//          ostream::put       ostream::seekp
//          ostream::tellp     ostream::write

#include "stdafx.h"
#include <fstream>
#include <iostream>

using namespace std;

#define iSTRING_MAX 40

int main(int argc, char* argv[])
{
    int i = 0;
    long ltellp;
    char pszString[iSTRING_MAX] = "Sample test string\n";
    // file opened in binary mode!
    ofstream ofMyOutputStream("myostrm.out",
                        ios::out | ios::binary);

    // write string out character by character
    // notice that '\n' is NOT translated into 2 characters!
    while(pszString[i] != '\0') {
        ofMyOutputStream.put(pszString[i]);
        ltellp = ofMyOutputStream.tellp();
        cout << "\ntellp value: " << ltellp;
        i++;
    }
```

```
// write entire string out with write member function
ltellp = ofMyOutputStream.tellp();
cout << "\ntellp's value before writing 2nd string: "
     << ltellp;
ofMyOutputStream.write(pszString, strlen(pszString));
ltellp = ofMyOutputStream.tellp();
cout << "\ntellp's updated value: " << ltellp
     << endl << endl;

ofMyOutputStream.close();

return 0;
}
```

The abbreviated output, seen in the following listing, illustrates the one-to-one relationship between a file and the data's internal representation:

```
tellp value: 1
tellp value: 2
tellp value: 3
     .
     .
     .
tellp value: 17
tellp value: 18
tellp value: 19
tellp's value before writing 2nd string: 19
tellp's updated value: 38
```

The string *pszString*, which has 19 characters plus a '\0' null string terminator, is output exactly as stored, without the appended '\0' null terminator. This explains why tellp() reports a multiple of 19 at the completion of each string's output.

Combining C and C++ Code

In earlier discussions, such as those in Chapter 6, you saw how the **extern** keyword specifies that a variable or function has external linkage. This means that the variable or function referenced is defined in some other source file or later on in the same file.

In C and C++, the **extern** keyword can be used with a string. The string indicates that another language's linkage conventions are being used for the identifier(s) being defined. For C++ programs, the default string is "C++".

In C++, functions are overloaded by default. This causes the C++ compiler to assign a new name to each function. You can prevent the compiler from assigning a new name to each function by preceding the function definition with extern "C". This is necessary so that C functions and data can be accessed by C++ code. Naturally, this is only done for one of a set of functions with the same name. Without this override, the linker would find more than one global function with the same name. The syntax for using extern "C" takes this form:

```
extern "C" freturn_type fname(param_type(s) param(s))
```

The following listing demonstrates how extern "C" is used with a single-function prototype:

```
extern "C" int fprintf(FILE *stream, char *format, ...);
```

To modify a group of function prototypes, a set of braces, {}, is needed:

```
extern "C"
  {
       .
       .
       .
  }
```

The next code segment modifies the getc() and putc() function prototypes:

```
extern "C"
  {
       int getc(FILE *stream);
       int putc(int c, FILE *stream);
  }
```

The following example program demonstrates how to use extern "C":

```
//
//   clink.cpp
//   C++ program demonstrating how to link C++ code
//   to C library functions.
//   Copyright (c) Chris H. Pappas and William H. Murray, 2001
```

```
//

#include "stdafx.h"
#include <iostream>

using namespace std;

#define iMAX 9

extern "C" int imycompare(const void *pi1, const void *pi2);

int main(int argc, char* argv[])
{
    int iarray[iMAX] = { 1, 9, 2, 8, 3, 7, 4, 6, 5};

    for(int i = 0; i < iMAX; i++)
        cout << iarray[i] << " ";

    cout << endl;

    qsort(iarray,iMAX,sizeof(int),imycompare);

    for(i = 0; i < iMAX; i++)
        cout << iarray[i] << " ";

    cout << endl << endl;

  return 0;
}

extern "C" int imycompare(const void *pi1, const void *pi2)
{
    return( *(int *)pi1 - *(int *)pi2);
}
```

All Visual C++ include files use extern "C". This makes it possible for a C++ program to use the C run-time library functions. Rather than repeat extern "C" for every definition in these header files, the following conditional statement pair surrounds all C header file definitions:

```
// 3-statements found at the beginning of header file.
```

```
#ifdef __cplusplus
extern "C" {
#endif


// 3-statements found at the end of the header file.

#ifdef __cplusplus
}
#endif
```

When compiling a C++ program, the compiler automatically defines the __cplusplus name. This in turn makes the extern "C" { statement and the closing brace, }, visible only when needed.

Designing Unique Manipulators

The concept of stream manipulators was first introduced in Chapter 11. Manipulators are used with the insertion, <<, and extraction, >>, operators, exactly as if they represented data for output or variables to receive input. As the name implies, however, manipulators can carry out arbitrary operations on the input and output streams.

Several of the example programs used the built-in manipulators dec, hex, oct, setw, and setprecision. Now you will learn how to write your own custom manipulators. To gradually build your understanding of the syntax necessary to create your own manipulators, the example programs begin with the simplest type of manipulator, one with no parameters, and then move on to ones with parameters.

Manipulators Without Parameters

A custom manipulator can be created any time to repeatedly insert the same character sequence into the output stream. For example, maybe your particular application needs to flag the user to an important piece of data. You even want to beep the speaker to get the user's attention just in case he or she isn't looking directly at the monitor. Without custom manipulators, your output statements would look like this:

```
cout << '\a' << "\n\n\t\tImportant data: "
     << fcritical_mass << endl;
```

Every time you wanted to grab the user's attention, you would repeat the bell prompt, '\a', and the "...Important data: " string. An easier approach is to define a manipulator, called *beep*, that automatically substitutes the desired sequence. The beep manipulator also makes the statement easier to read:

```
cout << beep << fcritical_mass << endl;
```

The following program demonstrates how to define and use the beep() function:

```
//
//   beep.cpp
//   C++ program demonstrates how to create your own
//   non-parameterized manipulator.
//   Note: This program does not generate a sound!
//   Copyright (c) Chris H. Pappas and William H. Murray, 2001
//

#include "stdafx.h"
#include <iostream>

using namespace std;

ostream& beep(ostream& os) {
    return os << '\a' << "\n\n\t\t\tImportant data: ";
}

int main(int argc, char* argv[])
{
    double fcritical_mass = 12459876.12;

    cout << beep << fcritical_mass
        << endl << endl;

    return 0;
}
```

The globally defined beep() function uses an ostream& formal parameter and returns the same ostream&. Beep works because it is automatically connected to the stream's insertion operator, <<. The stream's << operator is overloaded to accept this kind of function with the following inline function:

```
Inline ostream& ostream::operator<<(ostream& (*f)(ostream&)) {
  (*f)(*this);
```

FOUNDATIONS FOR
OBJECT-ORIENTED
PROGRAMMING

```
    return *this;
}
```

The inline function associates the << operator with the custom manipulator by accepting a pointer to a function sent to an ostream& type and that returns the same. This is exactly how beep() is prototyped. Now when << is used with beep(), the compiler dereferences the overloaded operator, finding where function beep() sits, and then executes it. The overloaded operator returns a reference to the original ostream. Because of this, you can combine manipulators, strings, and other data with the << operators.

Manipulators with One Parameter

The **iostream** class library, prototyped in the Standard C++ library, iomanip, defines a special set of macros for creating parameterized macros. One of the simplest parameterized macros you can write accepts an **int** parameter.

The following example program demonstrates the syntax necessary to create a single-parameter custom manipulator:

```cpp
//
//   manip1.cpp
//   C++ program demonstrating how to create and use
//   one-parameter custom manipulators.
//   Copyright (c) Chris H. Pappas and William H. Murray, 2001
//

#include "stdafx.h"
#include <iomanip>
#include <string>
#include <iostream>

using namespace std;

_Smanip<int> number_base(int base)
{
    return setbase(base);
}

int main(int argc, char* argv[])
{
    cout << number_base(16);

    for(int j=0; j<=20; j++) {
        cout << j << endl;
    }
```

```
        cout << endl << endl;

        return 0;
}
```

The number_base custom-parameterized manipulator accepts a single value, base, representing the numeric radix to be used when representing numbers. The iomanip header file defines a template Smanip<int>. The definition for this template includes all of the constructs necessary to manipulate the radix information we desire. When number_base is inserted into the stream, it calls the setbase() to change the current base to the new base.

The output from this application follows:

```
0
1
2
3
4
5
6
7
8
9
a
b
c
d
e
f
10
11
12
13
14
```

Acceptable bases or radix values include 8 (octal), 10 (decimal), and 16 (hexadecimal).

Manipulators with Multiple Parameters

Quoting from Microsoft's documentation "If your current application is very iostream intensive, you may choose *not* to link with the new Standard C++ library." The following application shows a prototype for a manipulator, fc, using the older style header files.

This example should be familiar. Actually, it is the same code (sqrt.cpp) seen earlier in this chapter to demonstrate how to format numeric output. However, the program has been rewritten using a two-parameter custom manipulator to format the data.

The first modification to the program involves a simple structure definition to hold the format manipulator's actual parameter values:

```
struct stwidth_precision {
    int iwidth;
    int iprecision;
};
```

When you create manipulators that take arguments other than *int* or *long*, you must use the IOMANIPdeclare macro. This macro declares the classes for your new data type. The definition for the format manipulator begins with the OMANIP macro:

```
OMANIP(stwidth_precision) format(int iwidth, int iprecision)
{
    stwidth_precision stWidth_Precision;
    stWidth_Precision.iwidth = iwidth;
    stWidth_Precision.iprecision = iprecision;
    return OMANIP (stwidth_precision)(ff, stWidth_Precision);
}
```

In this example, the custom manipulator is passed two integer arguments, *iwidth* and *iprecision*. The first value defines the number of spaces to be used by format, and the second value specifies the number of decimal places. Once format has initialized the stWidth_Precision structure, it calls the constructor, which creates and returns an __OMANIP object. The object's constructor then calls the ff() function, which sets the specified parameters:

```
static ostream& ff(ostream& os, stwidth_precision
                stWidth_Precision)
{
    os.width(stWidth_Precision.iwidth);
    os.precision(stWidth_Precision.iprecision);
    os.setf(ios::fixed);
    return os;
}
```

The complete program follows:

```
//
//   manip2.cpp
//   This C++ program is the same as sqrt.cpp, except
//   that it uses custom parameterized
//   manipulators to format the output.
//   A C++ program that prints a table of
//   numbers, squares, and square roots for the
//   numbers from 1 to 15. Program uses the type
//   double. Formatting aligns columns, pads blank
//   spaces with '0' character, and controls
//   precision of answer.
//   Copyright (c) Chris H. Pappas and William H. Murray, 2001
//

#include "stdafx.h"
#include <iomanip.h>
#include <math.h>
#include <iostream.h>

struct stwidth_precision {
    int iwidth;
    int iprecision;
};

IOMANIPdeclare(stwidth_precision);

static ostream& ff(ostream& os, stwidth_precision
                    stWidth_Precision)
{
    os.width(stWidth_Precision.iwidth);
    os.precision(stWidth_Precision.iprecision);
    os.setf(ios::fixed);
    return os;
}

OMANIP(stwidth_precision) format(int iwidth, int iprecision)
{
    stwidth_precision stWidth_Precision;
    stWidth_Precision.iwidth = iwidth;
    stWidth_Precision.iprecision = iprecision;
    return OMANIP (stwidth_precision)(ff, stWidth_Precision);
}
```

```
int main(int argc, char* argv[])
{
    double number, square, sqroot;

    cout << "num\t" << "square\t\t" << "square root\n";
    cout << "_____\n";

    number = 1.0;

    //cout.setf(ios::fixed);        // use fixed format
    for(int i = 1; i < 16; i++) {
        square = number * number; // find square
        sqroot = sqrt(number);    // find square root

        cout.fill('0');               // fill blanks with zeros
        //   cout.width(2);           // column 2 characters wide
        //   cout.precision(0);       // no decimal place
        cout << format(2, 0) << number << "\t";

        //   cout.width(6);           // column 6 characters wide
        //   cout.precision(1);       // print 1 decimal place
        cout << format(6, 1) << square << "\t\t";

        //   cout.width(8);           // column 8 characters wide
        //   cout.precision(6);       // print 6 decimal places
        cout << format(8, 6) << sqroot << endl;

        number += 1.0;
    }

    cout << endl << endl;

    return 0;
}
```

All of the code replaced by the call to format has been left in the listing for comparison. Notice how the format custom manipulator streamlines each output statement.

At this point, you may wish to change this code from the older style C++ library to the new Standard C++ library. To perform this feat, we recommend you first print a copy of both iomanip.h and iomanip.

What's Coming?

In this chapter you examined the details of I/O in C++ that allow custom formatting and parameterized macros. You also learned how to work with binary files in addition to the more common text files.

With the discussion of advanced C++ object-oriented I/O completed, you are ready to tackle object-oriented design philosophies. Chapter 18 explains how important good class design is to a successful object-oriented program solution.

Chapter 18

Working in an Object-Oriented Environment

C++ appears to be the language of choice among object-oriented programmers. However, other languages are available. Every object-oriented language shares several common features. Bertrand Meyer, in his book *Object-Oriented Software Construction* (Prentice Hall) suggests that there are seven features standard to true object-oriented programs as a whole:

- Abstract data types
- Classes
- Inheritance
- Inheritance (multiple)
- Memory management (automatic)
- Object-based modularization
- Polymorphism

In Chapter 17 you learned that Visual C++ classes provide these features to the object-oriented programmer. You might also conclude that to do true object-oriented programming, you must work in a language, such as C++, that is itself object oriented. There are valid arguments against this notion, as you will see later in this book. For example, programs written for Microsoft Windows contain many of the seven previously mentioned features, even though they can be written in C.

An Object-Oriented Stack

Chapter 15 introduced many object-oriented concepts. For example, the C++ class was introduced as an abstract data type that provides the encapsulation of data structures and the operations on those structures (member functions). In this capacity the C++ class serves as the mechanism for forming objects. The following simple example of object creation with a C++ class demonstrates the implementation of an object-oriented stack.

The traditional FILO (first-in, last-out) manner is used for the stack operations in this example. The stack class provides six member functions or methods: clear(), top(), empty(), full(), push(), and pop(). Examine the following listing and observe how these member functions are implemented:

```
//
//  stack.cpp
//  C++ program illustrates object-oriented programming
//  with a classical stack operation using a string of
//  characters.
//  Copyright (c) Chris H. Pappas and William H. Murray, 2001
//
```

```
#include "stdafx.h"
#include <iostream>

using namespace std;

#define maxlen 80

class stack {
    char str1[maxlen];
    int  first;

public:
    void clear(void);
    char top(void);
    int  empty(void);
    int  full(void);
    void push(char chr);
    char pop(void);
};

void stack::clear(void)
{
    first = 0;
}

char stack::top(void)
{
    return (str1[first]);
}

int stack::empty(void)
{
    return (first == 0);
}

int stack::full(void)
{
    return (first == maxlen - 1);
}

void stack::push(char chr)
{
    str1[++first] = chr;
```

```
}

char stack::pop(void)
{
    return (str1[first--]);
}

int main(int argc, char* argv[])
{
    stack mystack;
    char str[11] = "0123456789";
    int length;

    // clear the stack
    mystack.clear();

    // load the string, char by char, on the stack
    cout << "\nLoad character data on stack" << endl;
    length = strlen(str);
    for(int i = 0; i < length; i++) {
        if (!mystack.full())
            mystack.push(str[i]);
        cout << str[i] << endl;
    }

    // unload the stack, char by char
    cout << "\nUnload character data from stack" << endl;
    while (!mystack.empty())
        cout << mystack.pop() << endl;
    cout << endl << endl;

    return 0;
}
```

In this application, characters from a string are pushed, one character at a time, onto the stack. Then the stack is unloaded one character at a time. Loading and unloading are done from the stack top, so the first character information loaded on the stack is pushed down most deeply in the stack.

Notice in the following listing that the character for the number zero was pushed onto the stack first. It should be no surprise that it is the last character popped off the stack:

```
Load character data on stack
0
```

```
1
2
3
4
5
6
7
8
9

Unload character data from stack
9
8
7
6
5
4
3
2
1
0
```

This example lacks many of the more advanced object-oriented concepts such as memory management, inheritance, and polymorphism. However, the example is a complete object-oriented program. The power of object-oriented thinking becomes more apparent as more and more of Meyer's seven points are actually implemented.

An Object-Oriented Linked List in C++

A linked-list program was developed in Chapter 13 using a traditional procedural programming approach in C++. When using the procedure-oriented approach, you learned that the linked-list program is difficult to alter and maintain. In this chapter, a linked-list program using objects is developed that will allow you to create a list of employee information. It will also be possible to add and delete employees from the list. To limit the size of the linked-list program, no user interface will be used for gathering employee data. Data for the linked list has been hardwired in the main() function. Examples of how to make this program interactive and able to accept information from the keyboard have been shown in earlier chapters.

This program is slightly more involved than the application presented in Chapter 13. It includes, in addition to linked-list concepts, all seven of the object-oriented concepts listed earlier.

Creating a Parent Class

Several child classes derived from a common parent class are used in this example. The parent class for this linked-list example is named NNR. Here, the letters NNR represent the Nineveh National Research Company that develops computer-related books and software. The linked-list program is a database that will keep pertinent information and payroll data on company employees. The purpose of the parent class NNR is to gather information common to all subsequent derived child classes. For this example, that common information includes an employee's last name, first name, occupation title, social security number, and year hired at the company. The parent class NNR has three levels of isolation: public, protected, and private. The protected section of this class shows the structure for gathering data common to each derived child class. The public section (member functions) shows how that information will be intercepted from the function main():

```
// PARENT CLASS
class NNR {

friend class payroll_list;

protected:
    char lstname[20];
    char fstname[15];
    char job_title[30];
    char social_sec[12];
    double year_hired;
    NNR *pointer;
    NNR *next_link;

public:
    NNR(char *lname, char *fname, char *ss,
        char *job, double y_hired)
    {
        strcpy(lstname, lname);
        strcpy(fstname, fname);
        strcpy(social_sec, ss);
        strcpy(job_title, job);
        year_hired = y_hired;
        next_link = 0;
    }
        .
        .
        .
        .
```

A **friend** class, named payroll_list, is used by the parent class and all derived child classes. When you study the full program listing later in this chapter, notice that all derived child classes share this common variable, too. (Remember how the terms "private" and "public" relate to encapsulation concepts used by object-oriented programmers.)

A Derived Child Class

Four derived child classes are used in this program. Each of these is derived from the parent class NNR shown in the last section. This segment illustrates one child class, **salespersons**, that represents the points common to all four derived classes. A portion of this derived class is shown next. The derived child class satisfies the object-oriented concept of inheritance.

```
//SUB OR DERIVED CHILD CLASS
class salespersons:public NNR {

friend class payroll_list;

private:
    double disk_sales;
    double comm_rate;

public:
    salespersons(char *lname, char *fname, char *ss,
                 char *job, double y_hired,
                 double d_sales, double c_rate):
                 NNR(lname, fname, ss,
                 job, y_hired)
    {
        disk_sales = d_sales;
        comm_rate = c_rate;
    }
        .
        .
        .
        .
```

The **salespersons** child class gathers information and adds it to the information already gathered by the parent class. This in turn forms a data structure composed of last name, first name, social security number, year hired, the total sales, and the appropriate commission rate.

Here is the remainder of the child class description:

```
        .
        .
        .
        .


    void fill_sales(double d_sales)
    {
        disk_sales = d_sales;
    }


    void fill_comm_rate(double c_rate)
    {
        comm_rate = c_rate;
    }


    void add_info()
    {
        pointer = this;
    }


    void send_info()
    {
        NNR::send_info();
        cout << "\n Sales (disks): " << disk_sales;
        cout << "\n Commission Rate: " << comm_rate;
    }

};
```

Instead of add_info() setting aside memory for each additional linked-list node by using the new free store operator, the program uses each object's this pointer. The pointer is being assigned the address of an NNR node.

Output information on a particular employee is constructed in a unique manner. In the case of the **salespersons** class, notice that send_info() makes a request to NNR's send_info() function. NNR's function prints the information common to each derived class; then the salespersons' send_info() function prints the information unique to the particular child class. For this example, this information includes the sales and the commission rate.

It would also have been possible to print the information about the salesperson completely from within the child class, but the method used allows another advantage of object-oriented programming to be illustrated, and that is the use of virtual functions.

Using a Friend Class

The **friend** class, payroll_list, contains the means for printing the linked list and for the insertion and deletion of employees from the list. Here is a small portion of this class:

```
//FRIEND CLASS
class payroll_list {

private:
    NNR *location;

public:
    payroll_list()
    {
        location = 0;
    }

    void print_payroll_list();

    void insert_employee(NNR *node);

    void remove_employee_id(char *social_sec);

};
        .
        .
        .
        .
```

FOUNDATIONS FOR
OBJECT-ORIENTED
PROGRAMMING

Notice that messages sent to the member functions print_payroll_list(), insert_employee(), and remove_employee_id() form the functional part of the linked-list program.

Consider the function print_payroll_list(), which begins by assigning the pointer to the list to the pointer variable *present*. While the pointer *present* is not zero, it will continue to point to employees in the linked list, direct them to send_info, and update the pointer until all employees have been printed. The next section of code shows how this is achieved:

```
        .
        .
        .
        .

void payroll_list::print_payroll_list()
```

```
{
    NNR *present = location;

    while(present != 0) {
        present -> send_info();
        present = present -> next_link;
    }
}
        .
        .
        .
```

We discussed earlier that the variable *pointer* contains the memory address of nodes inserted via add_info(). This value is used by insert_employee() to form the link with the linked list. The insertion technique inserts data alphabetically by an employee's last name. Thus, the linked list is always ordered alphabetically by last name.

A correct insertion is made by the application by comparing the last name of a new employee with those already in the list. When a name (*node->lstname*) already in the list is found that is greater than the *current_node->lstname,* the first **while** loop ends. This is a standard linked-list insert procedure that leaves the pointer variable, *previous_node,* pointing to the node behind where the new node is to be inserted and leaves *current_node* pointing to the node that will follow the insertion point for the new node.

Once the insertion point is determined, the program creates a new link or node by calling node->add_info(). The *current_node* is linked to the new node's *next_link.* The last decision that must be made is whether or not the new node is to be placed as the front node in the list or between existing nodes. The program establishes this by examining the contents of the pointer variable *previous_node.* If the pointer variable is zero, it cannot be pointing to a valid previous node, so *location* is updated to the address of the new node. If *previous_node* contains a nonzero value, it is assumed to be pointing to a valid previous node. In this case, *previous_node->next_link* is assigned the address of the new node's address, or *node->pointer.*

```
        .
        .
        .
        .
void payroll_list::insert_employee(NNR *node)
{
    NNR *current_node = location;
    NNR *previous_node = 0;

    while (current_node != 0 &&
           strcmp(current_node -> lstname,
```

```
                           node -> lstname) < 0) {
         previous_node = current_node;
         current_node = current_node -> next_link;
     }
     node -> add_info();
     node -> pointer -> next_link = current_node;
     if (previous_node == 0)
         location = node -> pointer;
     else
         previous_node -> next_link = node -> pointer;
 }
          .
          .
          .
          .
```

Items can be removed from the linked list only by knowing the employee's social security number. This technique adds a level of protection against accidentally deleting an employee.

As you examine remove_employee_id(), shown in the next listing, note that the structure used for examining the nodes in the linked list is almost identical to that of insert_employee(). However, the first **while** loop leaves the *current_node* pointing to the node to be deleted, not the node after the one to be deleted:

```
          .
          .
          .
          .
void payroll_list::remove_employee_id(char *social_sec)
{
    NNR *current_node = location;
    NNR *previous_node = 0;

    while(current_node != 0 &&
          strcmp(current_node -> social_sec,
          social_sec) != 0) {
        previous_node = current_node;
        current_node = current_node -> next_link;
    }

    if(current_node != 0 && previous_node == 0) {
        location = current_node -> next_link;
        delete current_node;
```

```
    }
    else if(current_node != 0 && previous_node != 0) {
        previous_node -> next_link = current_node -> next_link;
        delete current_node;
    }
}
```

The first compound **if** statement takes care of deleting a node in the front of the list. The program accomplishes this by examining the contents of *previous_node* to see if it contains a zero. If it does, then the front of the list, location, needs to be updated to the node following the one to be deleted. This is achieved with the following line:

```
current_node->next_link
```

The second **if** statement takes care of deleting a node between two existing nodes. This requires the node behind to be assigned the address of the node after the one being deleted:

```
previous_node->next_link=current_node->next_link.
```

Now that the important pieces of the program have been examined, the next section puts them together to form a complete program.

Examining the Complete Program

The following listing is the complete operational object-oriented linked-list program. The only thing it lacks is an interactive user interface. When the program is executed, it will add nine employees, with their different job titles, to the linked list and then print the list. Next, the program will delete two employees from the list. This is accomplished by supplying their social security numbers. The altered list is then printed. The main() function contains information on which employees are added and deleted:

```
//
//  nnr.cpp
//  C++ program illustrates object-oriented programming
//  with a linked list. This program keeps track of
//  employee data at Nineveh National Research (NNR).
//  Copyright (c) Chris H. Pappas and William H. Murray, 2001
//

#include "stdafx.h"
#include <iostream>
```

```cpp
using namespace std;

// PARENT CLASS
class NNR {

friend class payroll_list;

protected:
    char lstname[20];
    char fstname[15];
    char job_title[30];
    char social_sec[12];
    double year_hired;
    NNR *pointer;
    NNR *next_link;

public:
    NNR(char *lname, char *fname, char *ss,
        char *job, double y_hired)
    {
        strcpy(lstname, lname);
        strcpy(fstname, fname);
        strcpy(social_sec, ss);
        strcpy(job_title, job);
        year_hired = y_hired;
        next_link = 0;
    }

    NNR()
    {
        lstname[0] = NULL;
        fstname[0] = NULL;
        social_sec[0] = NULL;
        job_title[0] = NULL;
        year_hired = 0;
        next_link = 0;
    }

    void fill_lstname(char *l_name)
    {
        strcpy(lstname, l_name);
    }
```

```cpp
    void fill_fstname(char *f_name)
    {
        strcpy(fstname, f_name);
    }

    void fill_social_sec(char *soc_sec)
    {
        strcpy(social_sec, soc_sec);
    }

    void fill_job_title(char *o_name)
    {
        strcpy(job_title, o_name);
    }

    void fill_year_hired(double y_hired)
    {
        year_hired = y_hired;
    }

    virtual void add_info() {
    }

    virtual void send_info()
    {
        cout << "\n\n" << lstname << ", " << fstname
             << "\n Social Security: #" << social_sec;
        cout << "\n Job Title: " << job_title;
        cout << "\n Year Hired: " << year_hired;
    }

};

//SUB OR DERIVED CHILD CLASS
class administration:public NNR {

friend class payroll_list;

private:
    double yearly_salary;

public:
    administration(char *lname,char *fname, char *ss,
                char *job,double y_hired,
```

```
                      double y_salary):
                 NNR(lname, fname, ss,
                 job, y_hired)
    {
        yearly_salary = y_salary;
    }

    administration():NNR()
    {
        yearly_salary = 0.0;
    }

    void fill_yearly_salary(double salary)
    {
        yearly_salary = salary;
    }

    void add_info()
    {
        pointer = this;
    }

    void send_info()
    {
        NNR::send_info();
        cout << "\n Yearly Salary: $" << yearly_salary;
    }

};


//SUB OR DERIVED CHILD CLASS
class salespersons:public NNR {

friend class payroll_list;

private:
    double disk_sales;
    double comm_rate;

public:
    salespersons(char *lname,char *fname,char *ss,
                 char *job, double y_hired,
                 double d_sales, double c_rate):
```

```
                NNR(lname, fname, ss,
                job, y_hired)
{
    disk_sales = d_sales;
    comm_rate = c_rate;
}

salespersons():NNR()
{
    disk_sales = 0.0;
    comm_rate = 0;
}

void fill_sales(double d_sales)
{
    disk_sales = d_sales;
}

void fill_comm_rate(int c_rate)
{
    comm_rate = c_rate;
}

void add_info()
{
    pointer = this;
}

void send_info()
{
    NNR::send_info();
    cout << "\n Sales (disks): " << disk_sales;
    cout << "\n Commission Rate: " << comm_rate;
}

};


//SUB OR DERIVED CHILD CLASS
class technicians:public NNR {

friend class payroll_list;

private:
```

```cpp
        double hourly_salary;

public:
    technicians(char *lname, char *fname, char *ss, char *job,
                double y_hired, double h_salary):
                NNR(lname, fname, ss, job, y_hired)
    {
        hourly_salary = h_salary;
    }

    technicians():NNR()
    {
        hourly_salary = 0.0;
    }

    void fill_hourly_salary(double h_salary)
    {
        hourly_salary = h_salary;
    }

    void add_info()
    {
        pointer = this;
    }

    void send_info()
    {
        NNR::send_info();
        cout << "\n Hourly Salary: $" << hourly_salary;
    }

};


//SUB OR DERIVED CHILD CLASS
class supplies:public NNR {

friend class payroll_list;

private:
    double hourly_salary;

public:
    supplies(char *lname, char *fname, char *ss, char *job,
```

```
                  double y_hired, double h_salary):
                  NNR(lname, fname, ss,
                  job, y_hired)
     {
         hourly_salary = h_salary;
     }

     supplies():NNR()
     {
         hourly_salary = 0.0;
     }

     void fill_hourly_salary(double h_salary)
     {
         hourly_salary = h_salary;
     }

     void add_info()
     {
         pointer = this;
     }

     void send_info()
     {
         NNR::send_info();
         cout << "\n Hourly Salary: $" << hourly_salary;
     }

};


//FRIEND CLASS
class payroll_list {

private:
     NNR *location;

public:
     payroll_list()
     {
         location = 0;
     }

  void print_payroll_list();
```

```
  void insert_employee(NNR *node);

  void remove_employee_id(char *social_sec);

};

void payroll_list::print_payroll_list()
{
    NNR *present = location;

    while(present != 0) {
        present -> send_info();
        present = present -> next_link;
    }
}

void payroll_list::insert_employee(NNR *node)
{
    NNR *current_node = location;
    NNR *previous_node = 0;
    while (current_node !=  0 &&
            strcmp(current_node -> lstname,
            node -> lstname) < 0) {
        previous_node = current_node;
        current_node = current_node -> next_link;
    }
    node -> add_info();
    node -> pointer -> next_link = current_node;
    if (previous_node == 0)
        location = node -> pointer;
    else
        previous_node -> next_link = node -> pointer;
}

void payroll_list::remove_employee_id(char *social_sec)
{
    NNR *current_node = location;
    NNR *previous_node = 0;

    while(current_node !=  0 &&
            strcmp(current_node -> social_sec,
            social_sec) !=  0) {
        previous_node = current_node;
```

```
            current_node = current_node -> next_link;
    }

    if(current_node !=  0 && previous_node  ==  0) {
        location = current_node -> next_link;
        // delete current_node;
        // needed if new() used in add_info()
    }
    else if(current_node !=  0 && previous_node !=  0) {
        previous_node -> next_link = current_node -> next_link;
        // delete current_node;
        // needed if new() used in add_info()
    }
}

int main(int argc, char* argv[])
{
    payroll_list workers;

    // static data to add to linked list
    salespersons salesperson1("Harddrive",  "Harriet",  "313-56-7884",
                              "Salesperson",  1985,  6.5,  7.5);
    salespersons salesperson2("Flex",  "Frank",  "663-65-2312",
                              "Salesperson",  1985,  3.0,  3.2);
    salespersons salesperson3("Ripoff",  "Randle",  "512-34-7612",
                              "Salesperson",  1987,  9.6,  6.8);
    technicians techperson1("Align",  "Alice",  "174-43-6781",
                              "Technician",  1989,  12.55);
    technicians techperson2("Tightscrew",  "Tom",  "682-67-5312",
                              "Technician",  1992,  10.34);
    administration vice_president1("Stuckup",  "Stewart",
                              "238-18-1119",  "Vice President",
                              1980,  40000.00);
    administration vice_president2("Learnedmore",  "Lawrence",
                              "987-99-9653",  "Vice President",
                              1984,  45000.00);
    supplies supplyperson1("Allpart",  "Albert",  "443-89-3772",
                              "Supplies",  1983,  8.55);
    supplies supplyperson2("Ordermore",  "Ozel",  "111-44-5399",
                              "Supplies",  1988,  7.58);

    // add the nine workers to the linked list
    workers.insert_employee(&techperson1);
    workers.insert_employee(&vice_president1);
```

```
        workers.insert_employee(&salesperson1);
        workers.insert_employee(&supplyperson1);
        workers.insert_employee(&supplyperson2);
        workers.insert_employee(&salesperson2);
        workers.insert_employee(&techperson2);
        workers.insert_employee(&vice_president2);
        workers.insert_employee(&salesperson3);

        // print the linked list
        workers.print_payroll_list();

        // remove two workers from the linked list
        workers.remove_employee_id("238-18-1119");
        workers.remove_employee_id("512-34-7612");

        cout << "\n\n**********************************";

        // print the revised linked list
        workers.print_payroll_list();

        cout << endl << endl;

        return (0);
}
```

As you study the complete listing, see if you understand how employees are inserted and deleted from the list. If it is still a little confusing, go back and study each major section of code discussed in earlier sections.

Output from the Linked-List

The linked-list program sends output to the monitor. Here is a sample output sent to the screen:

```
Align, Alice
 Social Security: #174-43-6781
 Job Title: Technician
 Year Hired: 1989
 Hourly Salary: $12.55

Allpart, Albert
 Social Security: #443-89-3772
 Job Title: Supplies
 Year Hired: 1983
```

```
Hourly Salary: $8.55

Flex, Frank
 Social Security: #663-65-2312
 Job Title: Salesperson
 Year Hired: 1985
 Sales (disks): 3
 Commission Rate: 3

Harddrive, Harriet
 Social Security: #313-56-7884
 Job Title: Salesperson
 Year Hired: 1985
 Sales (disks): 6.5
 Commission Rate: 7

Learnedmore, Lawrence
 Social Security: #987-99-9653
 Job Title: Vice President
 Year Hired: 1984
 Yearly Salary: $45000

Ordermore, Ozel
 Social Security: #111-44-5399
 Job Title: Supplies
 Year Hired: 1988
 Hourly Salary: $7.58

Ripoff, Randle
 Social Security: #512-34-7612
 Job Title: Salesperson
 Year Hired: 1987
 Sales (disks): 9.6
 Commission Rate: 6

Stuckup, Stewart
 Social Security: #238-18-1119
 Job Title: Vice President
 Year Hired: 1980
 Yearly Salary: $40000

Tightscrew, Tom
 Social Security: #682-67-5312
 Job Title: Technician
```

```
Year Hired: 1992
Hourly Salary: $10.34


*************************************

Align, Alice
 Social Security: #174-43-6781
 Job Title: Technician
 Year Hired: 1989
 Hourly Salary: $12.55

Allpart, Albert
 Social Security: #443-89-3772
 Job Title: Supplies
 Year Hired: 1983
 Hourly Salary: $8.55

Flex, Frank
 Social Security: #663-65-2312
 Job Title: Salesperson
 Year Hired: 1985
 Sales (disks): 3
 Commission Rate: 3

Harddrive, Harriet
 Social Security: #313-56-7884
 Job Title: Salesperson
 Year Hired: 1985
 Sales (disks): 6.5
 Commission Rate: 7

Learnedmore, Lawrence
 Social Security: #987-99-9653
 Job Title: Vice President
 Year Hired: 1984
 Yearly Salary: $45000

Ordermore, Ozel
 Social Security: #111-44-5399
 Job Title: Supplies
 Year Hired: 1988
 Hourly Salary: $7.58
```

```
Tightscrew, Tom
 Social Security: #682-67-5312
 Job Title: Technician
 Year Hired: 1992
 Hourly Salary: $10.34
```

The first section of the list contains the nine employee names that were used to create the original list. The last part of the list shows the list after two employees are deleted.

What's Coming?

We're sure your interest in object-oriented programming has increased after working through this chapter. You will really be interested in the Windows applications developed in Chapters 20 through 27. These particular Windows applications make use of Microsoft's Foundation Class (MFC) library. This library contains the reusable classes that make programming under Windows ME, 2000, and XP much easier. As you study these chapters, you will see the concepts you have mastered in this chapter applied to the Windows environment.

Chapter 19

Templates and the Standard Template Library

The Standard Template Library, or STL, encapsulates the pure raw horsepower of the C++ language and includes efficient algorithms typically developed within a good Data Structures course. It is similar, in a way, to having struggled for years learning how to graph mathematical equations on graph paper, only to be given a graphing calculator that does all the work for you.

The Standard Template Library can be viewed as an extensible framework that contains components for language support, diagnostics, general utilities, strings, locales, standard template library (containers, iterators, algorithms, numerics) and input/output.

STL's Recent Past

With the ever increasing popularity of C++ and Microsoft Windows controlled environments of Windows ME and 2000, many third-party vendors evolved into extremely profitable commodities by providing libraries of routines designed to handle the storage and processing of data. In an attempt to maintain C++'s viability as a programming language of choice, and to keep the ball rolling by maintaining strict control of the languages' formal definition, the ANSI/ISO C++ added a new approach to defining these libraries—Standard Template Library, or STL.

STL was developed by Alexander Stepanov and Meng Lee of Hewlett Packard. STL is expected to become the standard approach to storing and processing data. Major compiler vendors have incorporated the STL into their products. The Standard Template Library is more than just a minor addition to the world's most popular programming language; it represents a revolutionary new capability. The STL brings a surprisingly mature set of generic containers and algorithms to the C++ programming language, adding a dimension to the language that simply did not exist before.

Taking Advantage of the STL

Many of the features of the STL can be picked up easily with the information you have already learned about C++. However, the capabilities of the STL are enormous and cannot be approached in one introductory chapter. We recommend our book *Visual C++ Templates* (Prentice Hall, 2000). This 500-page text covers all of the details of the STL.

Although the STL is large and its syntax can be initially intimidating, it is actually quite easy to use once you understand how it is constructed and what elements it employs. At the core of the STL are three foundational items: containers, algorithms, and iterators. These libraries work together allowing you to generate, in a portable format, frequently employed algorithmic solutions, such as array creation, element insertion/deletion, sorting, and element output. But the STL goes even further by providing internally clean, seamless, and efficient integration of iostreams and exception handling.

The ANSI C/C++ Committees

The ANSI C/C++ committees are responsible for giving us portable C and C++ code by filing in the missing details for the formal language descriptions of both C and C++ as developed by their authors, Dennis Ritchie and Bjarne Stroustrup, respectively. It is the ANSI/ISO C++ Committee that continues to guarantee C++'s portability far into this millennium, with exacting standards for the STL.

The ANSI/ISO C++ committee's current standards exceed their past recommendations, which historically decided only to codify existing practices and resolve ambiguities and contradictions among existing translator implementations. The C++ committee's changes are innovative. In most cases, the changes implement features that committee members admired in other languages, features that they view as deficiencies in traditional C++, or features that they've always wanted in a programming language. A great deal of thought and discussion have been invested in each change, and consequently, the committee feels that the new C++ definition, along with the evolutionary definition of STL, is the best definition of C++ possible today.

Most of these recommended changes consist of language additions that should not affect existing code. Old programs should still compile with newer compilers as long as the old codes do not coincidentally use any of the new keywords as identifiers. However, even experienced C++ programmers may be surprised by how much of C++ has evolved even without discussing the STL (e.g., the use of namespaces, new-style type casting, and runtime type information discussed in Chapters 2 and 3).

STL's Makeup

Conceptually, STL encompasses three separate algorithmic problem solvers. The three most important are containers, algorithms, and iterators. A container is a way that stored data is organized in memory (e.g., an array, stack, queue, linked list, or binary-tree). However, there are many other kinds of containers, and the STL includes the most useful. The STL containers are implemented by template classes so they can be easily customized to hold different data types.

All the containers have common management member functions defined in their template definitions: insert(), erase(), begin(), end(), size(), capacity(), and so on. Individual containers have member functions that support their unique requirements.

Algorithms are behaviors or functionality applied to containers to process their contents in various ways. For example, there are algorithms to sort, copy, search, and merge container contents. In the STL, algorithms are represented by template functions. These functions are not member functions of the container classes. Instead, they are standalone functions. Indeed, one of the surprising characteristics of the STL is that its algorithms are so general. You can use them not only on STL containers, but also on ordinary C++ arrays or any other application-specific container.

A standard suite of algorithms provides for searching for, copying, reordering, transforming, and performing numeric operations on the objects in the containers. The same algorithm is used to perform a particular operation for all containers of all object types!

Once you have decided on a container type and data behaviors, the only thing left is to interact the two with iterators. Iterators can be thought of as generalized pointers that point to elements within a container. Iterators can be incremented, as you can a pointer, so they point to each successive element in the container. Iterators are a key part of the STL because they connect algorithms with containers.

Containers

All STL library syntax incorporates the full use of C++ templates (data type independent syntax). As we discuss the container types, remember they are implemented as templates; the types of objects they contain are determined by the template arguments given when the program instantiates the containers. There are several major types of containers: vectors (or dynamic arrays), deques (or double-ended queues), linear lists, bitset, map, and multimap.

Sequence containers store finite sets of objects of the same type in a linear organization. An array of names is a sequence. You use one of the sequence types—vector, list, or deque—for a particular application, depending on its retrieval requirements.

bitset Class

The **bitset** class supports operations on a set of bits, such as, flip(), reset(), set(), size(), to_string, and so on.

deque Class

A deque sequence is similar to a vector sequence except that a deque sequence allows fast inserts and deletes at the beginning as well as at the end of the container. Random inserts and deletes are less efficient.

list Class

A list sequence provides bi-directional access; it allows you to perform inserts and deletes anywhere without undue performance penalties. Random access is simulated by forward or backward iteration to the target object. A list consists of noncontiguous objects linked with forward and backward pointers.

map Class

The **map** class provides associative containers with unique keys mapped to specific values.

multimap Class

The **multimap** class is very similar to the **map** class in raw horsepower except for one minor difference: the availability of a non-unique key mapped to specific values.

vector Class

Vector sequences allow random data access. A vector is an array of contiguous homogeneous objects with an instance counter or pointer to indicate the end of the vector sequence. Random access is facilitated through the use of a subscript operation. Vector sequences allow you to append entries to and remove entries from the end of the dynamic structure without undue overhead. Inserts and deletes from the middle, however naturally, take longer due to the time involved in shifting the remaining entries to make room for the new or deleted item.

Container Adapters

STL supports three adapter containers, which can be combined with one of the sequence containers just discussed. First, select the appropriate application-specific container. Next, instantiate a container adapter class by naming the existing container in the declaration:

```
queue< list< bank_customer_struct > >TellerOneQueue;
```

The example instantiates a queue container, one of the three adapter containers supported by the STL, by using the list container as the underlying data structure built around a hypothetical bank customer waiting for an available teller.

Container adapters hide the public interface of the underlying container and implement their own. A queue data structure, for example, resembles a list but has its own requirements for its user interface. STL incorporates three standard adapter containers: stack, queue, and priority_queue.

FOUNDATIONS FOR OBJECT-ORIENTED PROGRAMMING

priority_queue Class

A priority_queue is similar to a queue adapter in that all items added to the queue are at the end of the list. However, unlike a queue adapter that removes items only from the front of the list, a priority_queue adapter removes the highest priority item within the list first!

queue Class

Regardless of whether or not the storage sequence container is a vector or linked list, the queue adapter uses this underlying scheme to add items to the end of the list, using the push() method, and to delete or remove items from the front of the list, using pop(). The acronym for a queue algorithm is First In First Out, or FIFO.

stack Class

The stack adapter provides the logical operations of push() and pop(), enabling the standard Last In First Out, or LIFO, solution. Stacks are great for certain types of problem solutions like evaluating an Infix arithmetic expression that has been translated into Postfix for the purposes of unambiguous evaluation.

Algorithms

Algorithms act on containers and are similar to container adapters. Algorithms provide for container initializations, sorting, searching, and data transformations. Interestingly, algorithms are not implemented as class methods, but instead are standalone template functions. For this reason they not only work on STL containers, but standard C++ arrays or with container classes you create yourself.

Typical algorithmic behaviors include find()—to locate a specific item; count()—letting you know how many items are in the list; equal()—for comparisons; and search(), copy(), swap(), fill(), sort(), and so on.

Iterators

Whenever an application needs to move through the elements of a container, it uses an iterator. Iterators are similar to pointers used to access individual data items. In the STL, an iterator is represented by an object of an iterator class. You can increment an iterator with the C++ increment operator ++, moving it to the address of the next element. The dereference operator, *, can be used to access individual members within the selected item. Special iterators are capable of remembering the location of specific container elements.

There are different classes of iterators that must be used with specific container types. The three major classes of iterators are: forward, bi-directional, and random access:

- Backward iterators work like the forward iterator counterparts, except backward.

- Bidirectional iterators can move forward as well as backward, and cannot be assigned or updated to point to any element in the middle of the container.

- Forward iterators can only advance forward through the container, one item at a time. They cannot move backward, nor can they be updated to point to any location in the middle of the container.

- Random-access iterators go one step further than bidirectional iterators in that they do allow the application to perform arbitrary location jumps within the container.

Additionally, the STL defines two specialized categories known as input and output iterators. Input and output iterators can point to specific devices. For example, an input iterator may point to a user-defined input file, or cin, and can be used to perform sequential reads into the container. Likewise, an output iterator may point to a user-defined output file, or cout, performing the logical inverse operation of sequentially outputting container elements.

Unlike forward, backward, bi-directional, and random-access iterators, input and output iterators cannot store their current values. The first four iterators must hold their values in order for them to know where they are within the container. The last two, input and output, do not structurally represent the same type of information because they are pointers to devices, and therefore have no memory capabilities.

Additional STL Elements

The STL also defines additional components beyond containers, algorithms, and iterators:

Allocators   For managing memory allocation for an individual container.

Comparison function   A unique binary predicate comparing two elements and returning true only if the first argument is less than the second.

Function objects   Including plus, minus, multiply, divide, modulus, negate, equal_to, not_equal_to, greater, greater_equal, less, less_equal, logical_and, logical_or, logical_not, and so on.

Predicates   Which are unary or binary in nature, meaning they work on either one operand or two, and always return either true or false.

Templates Out of Structures

The STL makes excellent use of pointers, overloaded subroutines, and overloaded operators, but it also relies heavily on templates. But before looking at an STL example, take a look at this straightforward C code section that uses the **#define** and concatenation **(##)** preprocessor statements to define a binary tree node:

```
C Example
#define BINARY_TREE( t )
typedef struct _tree_##t {
  t data;
  struct _tree_##t *left;
  struct _tree_##t *right;
} BINARY_TREE_##;
```

Notice how the preprocessor substitutes the argument *t* with whichever data type the user chose:

```
BINARY_TREE( int );
BINARY_TREE( float );
BINARY_TREE( my_structure );
```

Then it totally redefines the node. For example, for **int** data types, the binary tree node's definition would take on this form:

```
typedef struct _tree_int {
  int data;
```

```
    struct _tree_int *left;
    struct _tree_int *right;
} BINARY_TREE_int;
```

This is just a minor example of the inherit sophistication and modularity provided by the C++ language. Remember, the previous examples are all-legal in C and require no additional C++ syntax and sophistication!

However, for as slick as this example is, there is one inherent problem. Unlike inline functions, which can also be used to generate macros, **#define** defined macros have no error-checking capabilities. The **#define** statements are strictly string search and replace operations performed by pass one of Visual C++'s two pass compile. Obviously, in order to generate reliable and portable code, some other means was necessary for generating robust definitions—the C++ template.

The template Keyword

Templates were one of the last features added to C++ before the ANSI/ISO C++ standardization process began. As Bjarne Stroustrup (author of C++) states, "Templates were considered essential for the design of proper container classes.... For many people, the largest single problem with C++ is the lack of an extensive standard library. A major problem in producing such a library is that C++ does not provide a sufficiently general facility for defining 'container classes' such as lists, vectors, and associative arrays." It is the incorporation of templates into the C++ language that led directly to the development of the STL, a standardized library of container classes and algorithms using template classes and functions.

template Syntax

At this point you have a good understanding of functions and function calls. The function contains a modularly designed, reusable, single problem-solving algorithm. The function call passes the actual values needed by the function at a particular instance in the execution of the calling routine's algorithm.

C++ templates use parameters in an entirely new way: to create new functions and classes. In addition, unlike parameters passing to functions, templates create these new functions and classes at compile-time, rather than run-time.

The straightforward syntax for templates takes on this form:

```
template <argument_list> declaration
```

After the **template** keyword and argument_list, the programmer supplies the template declaration, where you define the parameterized version of a class or function. It's up to the Visual C++ compiler to generate different versions of the class or function based on the arguments passed to the template when it is used.

Template Functions!

To understand how templates function in the STL, you need to understand that there are two types of templates: class templates and function templates. Function templates generate functions, while class templates generate classes.

The following example defines a function template that squares any data type:

```
template <class Type>
Type squareIt( Type x ) { return x * x; } //function template
```

The function template squareIt(), can be passed any appropriate data type. For example:

```
void main( void )
{

  cout << "The square of the integer 9 is: " << squareIt( 9 ) << endl;
  cout << "The square of the unsigned int 255 is: " << squareIt( 255U )
       << endl;
  cout << "The square of the float 10.0: " << squareIt( 10.0 ) << endl;
  //...
}
```

These three statements cause the compiler to generate, at compile-time, three unique function bodies:

```
int square(int x) { return x * x; }
unsigned int square(unsigned int x) { return x * x; }
double square(double x) { return x * x; }
```

Notice that one instance is for integer data, another for unsigned integer data, and a third for floating-point values.

Template Classes

The second category of templates is a class template. The following example defines a simple array container class template:

```
template < class Type, int MAX_ELEMENTS >
class Array {
  protected:
    Type *pTypeArray;
  public:
```

```
    //constructor
    Array()  { pTypeArray  = new Type[ MAX_ELEMENTS ]; }

    //destructor
    ~Array() { delete[] pTypeArray; }
  // ...
};
```

The template class definition creates an array container class of any Type! The first argument to the template defines what type of elements the array will hold, while the second argument defines how many rows, or number of elements, the array will hold. The array's Type can be anything from a simple standard C++ data type such as **int**, or as complex as an application-specific structure or complex object.

A program instantiates an actual tangible instance of the template class definition with almost a function-like syntax:

```
void main( void )
{
  Array < float, 10 >  fArray;
  Array < int, 25 > iArray;
  Array < MY_STRUCTURE_DEFINITION, MAX_RECORDS > strucArray;
  Array < MY_CLASS_DEFINITION, iRunTimeUsersChoice > classArray;
  //...
}
```

For each instantiation, the compiler generates a brand new version of the **Array** class for every different combination of types passed to it. This is done at compile-time by performing a substitution of the arguments wherever they appear in the formal template definition.

STL: Even Better than Templates

In theory, C++ templates fill the need for easy-to-use container classes. But in real life, it wasn't always that simple because several obstacles got in the way. First, depending on the implementation of template container classes either from compiler or third-party vendors, template-based containers could be noticeably slower than their C counterparts. For instance, many template-based container classes relied on inheritance to do their jobs, and certain kinds of inheritance can measurably slow down a program.

Another problem with templates was compatibility. If you happened to use templates from two different vendors, there could be compatibility conflicts between them since there was no standard. But this was a lesser problem than customization. To some extent, customizing code is a normal part of working with templates. Take a class called

VehicleSalesRecord, for instance. For this class to work with a linked-list template you would have to define operations like less-than (<), the equivalence operator (==), and possibly a greater-than operator (>)—providing these operations or requirements for every class was part of the overhead of working with any template.

Traditionally, to work with container templates, a programmer needed to customize the objects in the container, not the container template itself. The problem occurs when you need to modify the way a template works. For example, imagine you want to customize the way the items are sorted. With most template-based classes, you need to decipher someone else's code, modify the template source code, and re-compile your program. That assumes you have access to the original template definition. And template code modification doesn't lend itself to preserving the original intent behind templates. With the inherent slowness in template-based container classes, and their being historically nonstandard (and not easy to customize), there needed to be a better way—welcome to the STL!

In the following section, we'll demonstrate many STL advantages by illustrating the use of the <vector> template class. The concepts you will learn about this template class also apply to many other STL template classes. The study of the <vector> template class will be reinforced with example code.

The <vector> Template

In STL, <vector> containers are logically and syntactically very similar to simple C++ arrays. The advantage of <vector> containers is that they are not statically allocated arrays, as in traditional array syntax, but are dynamic in the sense of linked-list technology. This means that the <vector> container can grow and shrink its size to maximize the use of RAM.

The term *vector* is commonly used to mean an indexed collection of similarly typed values. In C++ we can represent this abstract concept as a one-dimensional array. Recall that an array is a fixed-size collection of values of homogeneous data types, indexed by integer keys. The number of elements held by the array is provided as part of the declaration. The following, for example, creates a traditional array of ten float values:

```
float fArray[10];
```

Legal index values range from zero to one less than the size of the collection. Values are accessed using the subscript operator. A programmer can think of the elements of an array as being placed end to end in memory. The underlying C++ language provides only a primitive mechanism for the support of one-dimensional arrays, and this mechanism provides few safeguards. Most importantly, index values are *not* checked against declared bounds at run time.

The problem is compounded by the fact that there is no way to determine from the value of a simple C++ array the extent, or number of elements, it should contain. Furthermore, there are even fewer high-level operations defined for the array type than there are for character strings. By adding a new abstraction layer on top of the basic language framework many of these deficiencies can be corrected.

Templatized Vectors

A vector viewed as a data abstraction is different in one very important respect from the data types we have previously investigated. As an abstract concept, the idea of a vector describes an incomplete data type. The solution of any particular problem might require a vector of integers, a vector of floating-point values, or even a vector of strings. In order to abstract the concept of a vector, out of these more concrete realizations, we need a facility to parameterize a type description with another type. That is, we need some way to describe the idea of a vector of type T, where T represents an unknown type.

Within a vector class description the unknown parameter type T can be used in any situation requiring the use of a type name. This allows you to declare an instance variable as a pointer to T, and we can declare an operator as returning a T reference. In the copy constructor we need to refer to an object of the same type as the receiver. Although only the keyword **vector** is used, it is implicitly assumed to mean vector of T.

Instantiating Vectors

In order to use a template class as a type, you have to provide bindings for the unknown argument types. This is accomplished by providing the element type in a list, again surrounded by angle brackets:

```
// overloaded <vector> constructors
vector<int> iVector(5,0);
vector<float> fVector(20);
vector<string> szVector(10,"xyz");
```

For example, the first line of code in the previous listing declares a vector of five integer values, each entry initialized to 0. The second line declares a vector consisting of 20 un-initialized, float-precision values. The final line of code declares a vector of ten strings, all initialized to the string "xyz".

Understanding Vector Template Functions

The following template function max(), which appears in the STL, is used to compute the maximum of two arguments. This functionality is parameterized using the template syntax:

```
template <class T> max(T a, T b)
{
  if( a < b )
      return b;
  return a;
}
```

The template function will work as long as the arguments are of a type that can be compared. Thus, the function will work with integers, floating-point precision, and strings. Many of the template functions used by the <vector> template library use this data-independent syntax.

Accessing <vector> Elements

Accessing an individual <vector> element is no more difficult than accessing a simple array element. The syntax looks identical:

```
standardArrayElementReference[ 1 ];
myVectorInstanceElementReference[ 1 ];
```

The syntax changes slightly when traversing an entire <vector> versus an array. Look at the two equivalent statements that follow:

```
// traversing a simple array
for( int offset = 0; offset < MAX_ELEMENTS; offset++)...
// traversing a <vector> instance
vector<int>::iterator iteratorOffset;
for( iteratorOffset = myVector.front();
     iteratorOffset != myVector.end();
     iteratorOffset++)...
```

Similar to the <string> template, the <vector> template contains a type definition for the name iterator. This permits an iterator to be easily declared for any particular type of vector value. The template functions begin() and end() yield random access iterators for the vector. Again, note that the iterators yielded by these operations can become invalidated after insertions or removal of elements.

Insertion and Removal of <vector> Elements

The <vector> template functions push_back(), insert(), pop_back(), and erase() are used to insert and remove <vector> elements. The template function push_back() takes a new value as argument, and inserts the element at the end of the vector, increasing the size of the vector by one. The more general template function insert() takes as arguments an iterator and a value, and inserts the new element preceding the position specified by the iterator. Again, the size of the vector is increased by one.

The <vector> template function pop_back() removes the last element of the vector, reducing the size of the vector by one. The more general template function erase() is overloaded. In the easier form a single location is specified using an iterator, and the value denoted by the iterator is removed from the vector. Again, the size of the vector is reduced by one. The more general form of erase() takes two iterator arguments, which specify a range of values within the vector. All elements within this range are removed, regardless of the number of elements being removed.

The template function swap() takes as argument another vector that holds the same type of elements. The values of the two vectors are then exchanged; after the operation all values from the argument will be held by the receiving vector, and all elements in the current vector will be held by the argument.

Two Different Vector Size Descriptors

Recall that unlike a standard C++ array (which has a fixed size determined by the declaring statement), <vector> vectors are dynamic in size (growing and shrinking as needed). However, vectors have two different sizes associated with them. The first is the number of elements currently in the vector; the second is the maximum size to which the vector can grow, without actually allocating that new storage. The <vector> template function size() fulfills the first category—returning the actual number of vector elements, while capacity() returns your "wish list" for the total number of elements to be stored.

Inserting and deleting vector elements always changes the vector's size but may or may not change its capacity. An insertion that causes the size to exceed the capacity generally results in a new block of memory being allocated to hold the vector elements. Values are then copied into this new memory using the assignment operator appropriate to the element type, and the old memory is deleted. This can generate a significant performance hit on your algorithm should the vector be large in size.

The <vector> template function reserve() is a directive to the vector, indicating that the vector is expected to grow to at least the given size. If the argument used with reserve() is larger than the current capacity, then a reallocation occurs and the argument value becomes the new capacity. If subsequent inserts cause the vector to grow even larger than this new value, the vector can grow even larger. The reserved value is not a fixed delimiter, but an application's best-guess at the maximum vector size. When the capacity is already in excess of the reserved size request, no reallocation takes place. Remember, calling reserve() does *not* change the actual size of the vector, nor the element values themselves.

Caution is the word when dealing with pointers to vectors, as a reallocation invalidates *all* references, pointers, and iterators denoting elements being held by a vector:

```
vector<double>::iterator FrontOfVectorConstant;
FrontOfVectorConstant = myVector.begin();
// code using FrontOfVectorConstant instead
// of myVector.begin()...
```

This means that it is dangerous to lock onto an iterator's address, thinking that the address associated with the pointer will *never* change.

Other <vector> Operations

While the <vector> template does not directly provide any template function that can be used to determine if a specific value is contained in the collection, the generic <algorithm> template functions find() or count() can be used for these purposes. The <algorithm> template with its more <vector> related components is shown in Table 19-1.

Related <algorithm> Template Functions	Description
copy()	Copies one sequence into another.
count()	Counts the elements that match a target value, incrementing a counter.
count_if()	Counts elements that satisfy the unary template function passed to it, incrementing a counter.
fill()	Fills a vector with a given initial value.
find()	Finds a value for which the template function passed to it returns true, returning an iterator for the matching element's location.
find_if()	Finds a value in the container, returning an iterator to the matching element.
for_each()	Executes a template function passed to it, on each container element.
iter_swap()	Swaps the values specified by two iterators.
max_element()	Finds the largest value in a collection.
min_element()	Finds the smallest value in a collection.
replace()	Replaces the target element with a new value.
replace_if()	Replaces elements for which unary template function passed to it returns true, with replacement value.
reverse()	Reverses the container's elements.
sort()	Places elements in ascending order.
transform()	Transforms elements using the unary template function passed to it, from source container to destination container.

Table 19-1.   *<algorithm> Related <vector> Template Functions*

Table 19-2 gives the <algorithm> template functions that can be used with sort().

Related <algorithm> Template Functions	Description
binary_search()	Searches for elements within a container, returning true or false.
inplace_merge()	Merges two adjacent sorted sequences into one.
lower_bound()	Finds the first element larger than or equal to the specified value, returns an iterator pointing to the match.
merge()	Merges two sorted collections into a third container.
upper_bound()	Finds the first element greater than the value specified, returns an iterator pointing to the match.

Table 19-2.   *<algorithm> Template Functions Used with sort()*

We'll make use of numerous template functions in the examples at the end of this chapter.

<vector> Template Syntax

The following listing gives the syntax for the <vector> template:

```
namespace std {
template<class T, class A>
    class vector;
template<class A>
    class "vector<bool, A>;
//    TEMPLATE FUNCTIONS
template<class T, class A>
    bool operator==(
        const vector<T, A>& lhs,
        const vector<T, A>& rhs);
template<class T, class A>
    bool operator!=(
        const vector<T, A>& lhs,
```

```
                const vector<T, A>& rhs);
template<class T, class A>
    bool operator<(
        const vector<T, A>& lhs,
        const vector<T, A>& rhs);
template<class T, class A>
    bool "operator>(
        const vector<T, A>& lhs,
        const vector<T, A>& rhs);
template<class T, class A>
    bool operator<=(
        const vector<T, A>& lhs,
        const vector<T, A>& rhs);
template<class T, class A>
    bool ="operator>=(
        const vector<T, A>& lhs,
        const vector<T, A>& rhs);
template<class T, class A>
    void swap(
        const vector<T, A>& lhs,
        const vector<T, A>& rhs);
    };
```

You must include the STL standard header <vector> to define the container template class vector and three supporting templates:

```
template<class T, class A = allocator<T> >
    class vector {
public:
    typedef A allocator_type;
    typedef A::size_type size_type;
    typedef A::difference_type difference_type;
    typedef A::reference reference;
    typedef A::const_reference const_reference;
    typedef A::value_type value_type;
    typedef T0 iterator;
    typedef T1 const_iterator;
    typedef reverse_iterator<iterator, value_type,
        reference, A::pointer, difference_type>
            reverse_iterator;
    typedef reverse_iterator<const_iterator, value_type,
```

```
        const_reference, A::const_pointer, difference_type>
            const_reverse_iterator;
    explicit vector(const A& al = A());
    explicit vector(size_type n, const T& v = T(), const A& al = A());
    vector(const vector& x);
    vector(const_iterator first, const_iterator last,
        const A& al = A());
    void reserve(size_type n);
    size_type capacity() const;
    iterator begin();
    const_iterator begin() const;
    iterator end();
    iterator end() const;
    reverse_iterator rbegin();
    const_reverse_iterator rbegin() const;
    reverse_iterator rend();
    const_reverse_iterator rend() const;
    void resize(size_type n, T x = T());
    size_type size() const;
    size_type max_size() const;
    bool empty() const;
    A get_allocator() const;
    reference at(size_type pos);
    const_reference at(size_type pos) const;
    reference operator[](size_type pos);
    const_reference operator[](size_type pos);
    reference front();
    const_reference front() const;
    reference back();
    const_reference back() const;
    void push_back(const T& x);
    void pop_back();
    void assign(const_iterator first, const_iterator last);
    void assign(size_type n, const T& x = T());
    iterator insert(iterator it, const T& x = T());
    void insert(iterator it, size_type n, const T& x);
    void insert(iterator it,
        const_iterator first, const_iterator last);
    iterator erase(iterator it);
    iterator erase(iterator first, iterator last);
    void clear();
```

```
    void swap(vector x);
protected:
    A allocator;
    };
```

   While the implementation of the <vector> template can be intimidating, you will see that using this template is straightforward. Two examples at the end of this chapter will illustrate these concepts.

<vector> Template typedefs

Table 19-3 defines the typedefs used by the <vector> template.

Overloaded Operator	Description
`typedef A allocator_type;`	The type is a synonym for the template parameter A.
`typedef A::const_reference const_reference;`	The type describes an object that can serve as a constant reference to an element of the controlled sequence.
`typedef A::difference_type difference_type;`	The signed integer type describes an object that can represent the difference between the addresses of any two elements in the controlled sequence.
`typedef A::reference reference;`	The type describes an object that can serve as a reference to an element of the controlled sequence.

Table 19-3.   *typedefs Used by the <vector> Template*

Overloaded Operator	Description
`typedef A::size_type size_type;`	The unsigned integer type describes an object that can represent the length of any controlled sequence.
`typedef A::value_type value_type;`	The type is a synonym for the template parameter T.
`typedef reverse_iterator<const_iterator, value_type, const_reference, A::const_ pointer, difference_type>` `      const_reverse_iterator;`	The type describes an object that can serve as a constant reverse iterator for the controlled sequence.
`typedef reverse_iterator<iterator, value_type, reference, A::pointer, difference_type>` `      reverse_iterator;`	The type describes an object that can serve as a reverse iterator for the controlled sequence.
`typedef T0 iterator;`	The type describes an object that can serve as a random-access iterator for the controlled sequence.
`typedef T1 const_iterator;`	The type describes an object that can serve as a constant random-access iterator for the controlled sequence.

Table 19-3.   *typedefs Used by the <vector> Template (continued)*

<vector> Overloaded Operators

Table 19-4 lists the overloaded operators used in the <vector> template.

Overloaded Operator Template Function	Description
```bool operator!=(const vector <T, A>& lhs, const vector <T, A>& rhs);```	The template function returns !(lhs == rhs).
```bool operator<(const vector <T, A>& lhs, const vector <T, A>& rhs);```	The template function overloads operator< to compare two objects of template class vector. The function returns lexicographical_compare(lhs. begin(), lhs. end(), rhs.begin(), rhs.end()).
```bool operator<=(const vector <T, A>& lhs, const vector <T, A>& rhs);```	The template function returns !(rhs < lhs).
```bool operator==(const vector <T, A>& lhs, const vector <T, A>& rhs);```	The template function overloads operator== to compare two objects of template class vector. The function returns lhs.size() == rhs.size() && equal(lhs. begin(), lhs. end(), rhs.begin()).
```bool operator>(const vector <T, A>& lhs, const vector <T, A>& rhs);```	The template function returns rhs < lhs.
```bool operator>=(const vector <T, A>& lhs, const vector <T, A>& rhs);```	The template function returns !(lhs < rhs).
```void swap(const vector <T, A>& lhs,```	The template function executes lhs.swap(rhs).

Table 19-4. *Overloaded <vector> Template Operators*

<vector> Template Methods

The <vector> template provides the methods shown in Table 19-5. This table lists the template methods along with a short description of each method and returned values.

Template Method	Description
`A get_allocator() const;`	Returns `allocator`.
`bool empty() const;`	Returns true for an empty controlled sequence.
`const_iterator begin() const;` `iterator begin();`	Returns a random-access iterator that points at the first element of the sequence (or just beyond the end of an empty sequence).
`const_iterator end() const;` `iterator end();`	Returns a random-access iterator that points just beyond the end of the sequence.
`const_reference at(size_type pos) const;` `reference at(size_type pos);`	Returns a reference to the element of the controlled sequence at position `pos`. If that position is invalid, the function throws an object of class `out_of_range`.
`const_reference operator[](size_type pos) const;` `reference operator[](size_type pos);`	Returns a reference to the element of the controlled sequence at position `pos`. If that position is invalid, the behavior is undefined.
`const_reverse_iterator rbegin() const;` `reverse_iterator rbegin();`	Returns a reverse iterator that points just beyond the end of the controlled sequence. Pointer to the beginning of the reverse sequence.
`const_reverse_iterator rend() const;` `reverse_iterator rend();`	Returns a reverse iterator that points at the first element of the sequence (or just beyond the end of an empty sequence). Pointer to the end of the reverse sequence.

Table 19-5. *<vector> Template Methods*

Template Method	Description
``explicit vector(const A& al = A());
explicit vector(size_type n, const
T& v = T(), const A& al = A());
vector(const vector& x);
vector(const_iterator first,
const_iterator last,
const A& al = A());```	Vector constructors store the allocator object al (or, for the copy constructor, x.get_allocator()) in allocator and initialize the controlled sequence. The first constructor implies an empty initial controlled sequence. The second constructor supplies a repetition of n elements of value x. The third constructor requests a copy of the sequence controlled by x. The last constructor specifies the sequence [first, last).
``Iterator erase(iterator it);
iterator erase(iterator first,
iterator last);```	The first member function removes the element of the controlled sequence pointed to by it. The second member function removes the elements of the controlled sequence in the range [first, last). Both return an iterator that designates the first element remaining beyond any elements removed, or end() if no such element exists. Erasing N elements causes N destructor calls and an assignment for each of the elements between the insertion point and the end of the sequence. No reallocation occurs, so iterators and references become invalid only from the first element erased through the end of the sequence.
``Iterator insert(iterator it,
const T& x = T());
void insert(iterator it, size_type n,
const T& x);
void insert(iterator it,
const_iterator first,
const_iterator last);```	Each member function inserts, before the element pointed to by it in the controlled sequence, a sequence specified by the remaining operands. The first member function inserts a single element with value x and returns an iterator that points to the newly inserted element. The second member function inserts a repetition of n elements of value x. The last member function inserts the sequence [first, last).

Table 19-5.   *<vector> Template Methods (continued)*

Template Method	Description
`reference back();` `const_reference back() const;`	Returns a reference to the last element of the controlled sequence, which must be non-empty.
`reference front();` `const_reference front() const;`	Returns a reference to the first element of the controlled sequence, which must be non-empty.
`size_type capacity() const;`	Returns the storage currently allocated to hold the controlled sequence, a value at least as large as `size()`.
`size_type max_size() const;`	Returns the length of the longest sequence that the object can control.
`size_type size() const;`	Returns the length of the controlled sequence.

`void assign(const_iterator first,`
`const_iterator last);`
`void assign(size_type n, const T& x = T());`
	The first member function replaces the sequence controlled by `*this` with the sequence [`first`, `last`). The second member function replaces the sequence controlled by `*this` with a repetition of n elements of value x.

`void clear() const;`	Calls `erase( begin(), end())`.
`void pop_back();`	The member function removes the last element of the controlled sequence, which must be non-empty.
`void reserve(size_type n);`	Guarantees that `capacity()` returns at least n.
`void resize(size_type n, T x = T());`	Guarantees `size()` returns n. If it must lengthen the controlled sequence, it appends elements with value x.
`void swap(vector& str);`	Swaps the controlled sequences between `*this` and `str`. If `allocator == str.allocator`, it does so in constant time. Otherwise, it performs a number of element assignments and constructor calls proportional to the number of elements in the two controlled sequences.

Table 19-5. *<vector> Template Methods (continued)*

The template class describes an object that controls a varying-length sequence of elements of type T. The sequence is stored as an array of T. The object allocates and frees storage for the sequence it controls through a protected object named allocator, of class A. Such an allocator object must have the same external interface as an object of template class allocator. Note that allocator is not copied when the object is assigned.

Vector reallocation occurs when a member function must grow the controlled sequence beyond its current storage capacity. Other insertions and erasures may alter various storage addresses within the sequence. In all such cases, iterators or references that point at altered portions of the controlled sequence become invalid.

Sample Code

The following sample applications demonstrate many of the more frequently used <vector> template functions, overloaded operators, and areas of caution when using this template library.

The vector1.cpp Application

This first application demonstrates the dimensioning of vector containers, from the initial instantiation of the vector, to dynamically allocated "guess" length, to actually increasing the size of the container:

```
//
// vector1.cpp
// Testing <vector>
// push_back(), size(), capacity(), max_size(), reserve(), resize()
// Copyright (c) Chris H. Pappas and William H. Murray, 2001
//

#include "stdafx.h"
#include <vector>
#include <iomanip>
#include <iostream>

using namespace std ;

typedef vector<int> iVector;

int main(int argc, char* argv[])
{
    // Instantiation of 0 element integer vector.
    iVector iVectorInstance;

    // Inserting a 5, at the end of the vector
```

```
    iVectorInstance.push_back(5);

    // Current vector statistics.
    cout << "Current statistics:" << endl;
    cout << "iVectorInstance's current size: "
         << setw(10) << iVectorInstance.size() << endl;
    cout << "iVectorInstance's maximum size: "
         << iVectorInstance.max_size() << endl;
    cout << "iVectorInstance's capacity    : "
         << setw(10) << iVectorInstance.capacity() << endl;

    // See if there is room for a total of 15 elements
    iVectorInstance.reserve(15);
    cout << "\nReserving storage for 15 elements:" << endl;
    cout << "iVectorInstance's size is      : "
         << setw(10) << iVectorInstance.size() << endl;
    cout << "iVectorInstance's maximum size: "
         << setw(10) << iVectorInstance.max_size() << endl;
    cout << "iVectorInstance's capacity is : "
         << setw(10) << iVectorInstance.capacity() << endl;

    // Demanding room for at least 25 elements.
    iVectorInstance.resize(25);
    cout << "\nAfter resizing storage for 25 elements:"
         << endl;
    cout << "iVectorInstance's size is      : "
         << setw(10) << iVectorInstance.size() << endl;
    cout << "iVectorInstance's maximum size: "
         << iVectorInstance.max_size() << endl;
    cout << "iVectorInstance's capacity is : "
         << setw(10) << iVectorInstance.capacity() << endl;

    cout << endl << endl;

    return 0;
}
```

The program begins with the following type definition:

```
typedef vector<int> iVector;
```

This type definition defines iVector as an integer vector type. Next the iVectorInstance is instantiated:

```
iVector iVectorInstance;\
```

Notice that the container does *not* specify any fixed length. The first action on the vector is to insert the integer value 5, into the container using the push_back() template function:

```
iVectorInstance.push_back(5);
```

The next series of statements output the containers size(), max_size(), and capacity(), all with template functions:

```
cout << "Current statistics:" << endl;
cout << "iVectorInstance's current size: "
    <<  setw(10) << iVectorInstance.size() << endl;
cout << "iVectorInstance's maximum size: "
    <<  iVectorInstance.max_size() << endl;
cout << "iVectorInstance's capacity    : "
    <<  setw(10) << iVectorInstance.capacity() << endl;
```

This series of statements repeats the same statistics based on two container size-changing statements. The first takes on this form:

```
iVectorInstance.reserve(15);
```

Remember that reserve() only checks to see if the requested size could indeed fit in available RAM, but does *not* actually increase the actual size of the container. The second dimension change comes from the following statement:

```
iVectorInstance.resize(25);
```

Unlike reserve(), resize() physically increases the maximum number of elements. Look at the output from the program and notice the effect on the various container statistics:

```
Current statistics:
iVectorInstance's current size:          1
```

FOUNDATIONS FOR OBJECT-ORIENTED PROGRAMMING

```
iVectorInstance's maximum size: 1073741823
iVectorInstance's capacity     :            1

Reserving storage for 15 elements:
iVectorInstance's size is      :            1
iVectorInstance's maximum size: 1073741823
iVectorInstance's capacity is :            15

After resizing storage for 25 elements:
iVectorInstance's size is      :            25
iVectorInstance's maximum size: 1073741823
iVectorInstance's capacity is :            25
```

Notice that the reserve() request did *not* change the number of elements from 1 to 15, but *did* change the capacity to 15. However, resize() changed both the *size* and *capacity*. Also observe the maximum_size(), which returns the length of the longest sequence that the object can control and remains constant.

The vector2.cpp Application

This next example demonstrates how to access vector elements using iterators and various insert() and erase() operations. Pay particular attention to how you syntactically and logically access vector elements:

```cpp
//
// vector2.cpp
// Testing <vector>
// push_back(), insert(), delete(), begin(), end()
// Copyright (c) Chris H. Pappas and William H. Murray, 2001
//

#include "stdafx.h"
#include <vector>
#include <iostream>

using namespace std ;

typedef vector<char> cVector;

int main(int argc, char* argv[])
{
    // Instantiation of 0 element integer vector.
```

```
cVector cVectorInstance;

// Inserting five vowels
cVectorInstance.push_back('A');
cVectorInstance.push_back('E');
cVectorInstance.push_back('I');
cVectorInstance.push_back('O');
cVectorInstance.push_back('Y');

// Accessing vector elements using array syntax - DANGEROUS
for(int i = 0; i < 5; i++)
  cout << cVectorInstance[i];
cout << endl;

// Accessing vector elements using iterators - BEST APPROACH
vector<char>::iterator p = cVectorInstance.begin();
while(p != cVectorInstance.end()) {
  cout << *p;
  p++;
}
cout << endl;

// Inserting a NEW fifth element extending the vector's size
p = cVectorInstance.begin();
p += 4; // moves pointer to fifth element's address
cVectorInstance.insert(p, 'U');

// Accessing the NEW list
p = cVectorInstance.begin();
while(p != cVectorInstance.end()) {
  cout << *p;
  p++;
}
cout << endl;

// Deleting the sixth element 'Y'
p = cVectorInstance.end();
cVectorInstance.erase(--p);

// Printing the modified container
p = cVectorInstance.begin();
while(p != cVectorInstance.end()) {
  cout << *p;
```

```
        p++;
    }

    cout << endl << endl;

    return 0;
}
```

Most of the initial program statements should now look familiar to you so the discussion begins with the two methods for accessing container elements:

```
// Accessing vector elements using array syntax - DANGEROUS
for(int i = 0; i < 5; i++)
    cout << cVectorInstance[i];
cout << endl;
```

While this **for** loop works, it is not the most generalized approach and breaks many of the STL rules. In particular, it is hardwired to the element count. The better, standard STL approach below uses the begin() and end() template functions, along with the iterator p to perform the task:

```
// Accessing vector elements using iterators - BEST APPROACH
vector<char>::iterator p = cVectorInstance.begin();
while(p != cVectorInstance.end()) {
    cout << *p;
    p++;
}
```

The next three statements insert a new fifth vowel into the container, preceding the current fifth element of Y:

```
p = cVectorInstance.begin();
    p += 4; // moves pointer to fifth element's address
    cVectorInstance.insert(p,'U');
```

The re-initialization of p is necessary since the previous loop moved the pointer beyond the end of the vector container. Pointer arithmetic is next employed to move p to the address of the fifth element, followed by a call to the insert() template function. This function accepts an iterator, p, and valid element type, U.

In order to output the updated container, iterator p needs resetting:

```
p = cVectorInstance.begin();
    while(p != cVectorInstance.end()) {
        cout << *p;
        p++;
    }
```

The final two statements:

```
p = cVectorInstance.end();
cVectorInstance.erase(-p);
```

Here, p is reset one more time, only this time to the end of the container. Caution: The template function end() returns an interator *one beyond the end* of the container. This explains the prefix decrement of p in the template function call statement (–p). Finally, the template function erase() removes the element at the specified location. The template function could have removed a range of values with just a slightly different syntax:

```
cVectorInstance.erase(initializedIterator, initializedIterator + n);
```

The output from the program takes on this form:

```
AEIOY
AEIOY
AEIOUY
AEIOU
```

Study the program listing, once again, and be certain you understand how the characters were actually inserted and deleted.

What's Coming?

This chapter presented the essence of the ANSI/ISO Standard Template Library available with your Microsoft Visual C++ compiler. You learned the history of the STL, examined a logical overview of the library, and learned various STL terms and definitions.

This chapter highlighted the fact that even "experienced" C++ programmers might be surprised to see just how much C++ has changed within this past year, even without the topic of STL.

Finally, the STL <vector> container was used to illustrate concepts common to most STL containers. Then with coded examples, you learned about various dimension descriptors, template functions, and how to traverse a vector container with iterators.

Additional work with the STL will be presented in Chapter 26 as we look at various Windows applications.

The
Complete
Reference

Visual C++.NET

Part IV

Windows and Wizards

Visual C++.NET

Chapter 20

Concepts and Tools for Windows Applications

663

S tarting in this section, you are about to make a quantum jump with your programming skills. While the core programming techniques of the previous 19 chapters have been complicated enough, we're about to add another layer to that complexity—Windows programming!

Microsoft's main development language for 32-bit Windows applications is C++. In the past, assembly language has played a major role in speed-sensitive situations but you will find that the majority of code for Windows itself is written in C++. Microsoft has provided all of the necessary tools, with this version of the compiler, for developing 32-bit Windows programs from within the language environment. This chapter will deal with the features that relate to a 32-bit approach to Windows application development.

All of the Windows applications in this book are designed with the development tools provided with the Microsoft Visual C++ compiler. When installing your Microsoft Visual C++ compiler, make sure that the setup program includes all of the available tools for Windows ME and 2000 application development.

This chapter is divided into three major sections. The first section deals with the language, definitions, and terms used with Windows. This section also includes a discussion of the graphics-based environment. The second section is devoted to a discussion of those Windows items most frequently used by application developers. Here, Windows components such as borders, icons, bitmaps, and so on are examined. The third section includes a description of Windows resources and many of the Visual C++ tools provided for building them. Windows resources include icons, cursors, bitmaps, menus, hot keys, dialog boxes, and fonts.

| Note | *Throughout the remainder of this book the term Windows will refer to both the Windows ME and Windows 2000 programming environments.* |

Windows Fundamentals

Windows applications can be developed using either a procedure-oriented or object-oriented approach in C++. Either approach brings together point-and-shoot control, pop-up menus, and the ability to run applications written specially for the Windows environment. The purpose of this portion of the chapter is to introduce you to Windows concepts and vocabulary fundamentals. The graphics user interface is the interface of the millennium, and Windows gives you the ability to develop that code now!

The Windows Environment

Windows is a graphics-based multitasking operating system. Programs developed for this environment (those written specifically for Windows) all have a consistent look and command structure. To the user, this makes learning each successive Windows application easier.

To help in the development of Windows applications, Windows provides numerous built-in functions that allow for the easy implementation of pop-up menus, scroll bars, dialog boxes, icons, and many other features that represent a user-friendly interface. It is easy to take advantage of the extensive graphics programming language provided with Windows and easily format and output text in a variety of fonts and pitches.

Windows permits the application's treatment of the video display, keyboard, mouse, printer, serial port, and system timers in a hardware-independent manner. Device or hardware independence allows the same application to run identically on a variety of computers with differing hardware configurations.

 For those interested in the Java programming language, pay particular attention to this chapter. Many of the terms and concepts once relegated to C++ Windows application development have found their way into many Java applications and applets.

Windows Advantages

There are numerous advantages, for Windows users and programmers alike, over the older DOS text-based environment. Windows provides several major programming capabilities that include a standardized graphics interface, a multitasking capability, an OOP approach in programming, memory control, hardware independence, and the use of dynamic link libraries (DLLs).

The Graphics User Interface (GUI)

The most noticeable Windows feature is the standardized graphics user interface, which is also the most important one for the user. All versions of Windows are based on the same standardized interface. The consistent interface uses pictures, or *icons,* to represent disk drives, files, subdirectories, and many of the operating system commands and actions. Figure 20-1 shows a typical Windows application.

In Windows, program names appear in caption bars. Many of the basic file manipulation functions are accessed through the program's menus by pointing and clicking with the mouse. Most Windows programs provide both a keyboard and a mouse interface. Although you can access most Windows functions with just the keyboard, the mouse is the preferred tool of most users.

A similar look and feel is common to all Windows applications. Once a user learns how to manipulate common Windows commands, each new application becomes easier to master. For example, compare the Microsoft Excel screen shown in Figure 20-2 with the Microsoft Word screen shown in Figure 20-3.

These screens illustrate the similarity between applications, including common File and Edit options. Compare the options in both of these applications with the Paint application illustrated earlier in Figure 20-1.

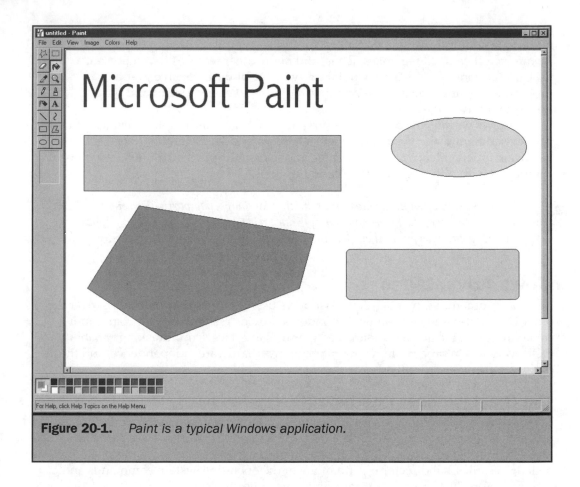

Figure 20-1.   *Paint is a typical Windows application.*

The consistent user interface provides advantages for the programmer also. For example, it is possible to tap into built-in Windows functions for constructing menus and dialog boxes. All menus have the same style keyboard and mouse interface because Windows, rather than the programmer, handles its implementation.

The Multitasking Environment

The Windows multitasking environment allows the user to have several applications, or several instances of the same application, running at the same time. The screen in Figure 20-4 shows three Windows applications running at the same time. Each application occupies a rectangular window on the screen. At any given time, the user can move the windows on the screen, switch between different applications, change the windows' sizes, and exchange information from window to window.

	A	B	C	D	E	F	G	H	I	J
9	CST-105-1A	Computer Applications	3	20	W	8:00AM-9:50AM	AT004	Poliquin, M.		
10	CST-105L2A	Laboratory	0	20	M	8:00AM-9:50AM	AT002	Poliquin, M.		
11										
12	CST-105-1B	Computer Applications	3	20	R	8:00AM-9:50AM	AT004	Poliquin, M.		
13	CST-105L2B	Laboratory	0	20	T	8:00AM-9:50AM	AT002	Poliquin, M.		
14										
15	CST-105-1C	Computer Applications	3	20	W	8:00AM-9:50AM	D211	Wasson, B.	Multimedia Classroom	
16	CST-105L2C	Laboratory	0	20	F	8:00AM-9:50AM	AT002	Bryden, P.		
17										
18	CST-105-1D	Computer Applications	3	20	W	10:00AM-11:50AM	D211	Wasson, B.	Multimedia Classroom	
19	CST-105L2D	Laboratory	0	20	M	10:00AM-11:50AM	AT002	Wasson, B.		
20										
21	CST-105-1E	Computer Applications	3	20	W	11:00AM-12:50PM	D116	Hinton, R.	Multimedia Classroom	
22	CST-105L2E	Laboratory	0	20	F	11:00AM-12:50PM	AT002	Hinton, R.		
23										
24	CST-105-1F	Computer Applications	3	20	T	11:00AM-12:50PM	AT004	Hinton, R.		
25	CST-105L2F	Laboratory	0	20	R	11:00AM-12:50PM	AT002	Hinton, R.		
26										
27	CST-105-1G	Computer Applications	3	20	R	10:00AM-11:50AM	D211	Wasson, B.	Multimedia Classroom	
28	CST-105L2G	Laboratory	0	20	T	10:00AM-11:50AM	AT002	Wasson, B.		
29										
30	CST-105-1H	Computer Applications	3	20	T	1:00PM-2:50PM	AT004	Hinton, R.		
31	CST-105L2H	Laboratory	0	20	R	1:00PM-2:50PM	AT002	Hinton, R.		
32										
33	CST-105-1J	Computer Applications	3	20	M	12:00PM-1:50PM	D116	Poliquin, M.	Multimedia Classroom	
34	CST-105L2J	Laboratory	0	20	W	12:00PM-1:50PM	AT002	Poliquin, M.		
35										
36	CST-105-1K	Computer Applications	3	20	M	3:00PM-4:50PM	AT004	Bryden, P.		
37	CST-105L2K	Laboratory	0	20	W	3:00PM-4:50PM	AT002	Bryden, P.		
38										
39	CST-105-1S	Computer Applications	3	20	T	12:00PM-1:50PM	D116	Lander, M.	Multimedia Classroom	
40	CST-105L2S	Laboratory	0	20	M	12:00PM-1:50PM	AT002	Lander, M.	SPANISH SPANISH	
41										
42	CST-105-70	Computer Applications	3	20	T	6:00PM-7:50PM	D211	Wasson, B.	Multimedia Classroom	
43	CST-105L71	Laboratory	0	20	T	8:00PM-9:50PM	AT002	Wasson, B.		
44										

Figure 20-2. *Microsoft's Excel program*

The example shown in Figure 20-4 is a group of three concurrently running processes—well, not really. In reality, only one application can be using the processor at any one time. The distinction between a task that is processing and one that is merely running is important. There is also a third state to consider. An application may be in the active state. An *active application* is one that is receiving the user's attention. Just as there can be only one application that is processing at any given instant, so too there can be only one active application at a time. However, there can be any number of concurrently running tasks. Partitioning of the microprocessor's processing time, called *time slicing*, is the responsibility of Windows. It is Windows that controls the sharing of the microprocessor by using a variety of techniques including queued input or messages.

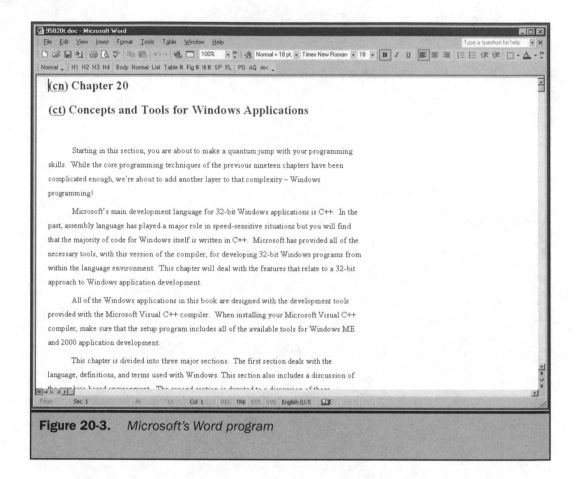

Figure 20-3. *Microsoft's Word program*

Before multitasking was achieved under Windows, applications assumed they had exclusive control of all the computer's resources, including the input and output devices, memory, the video display, and even the CPU itself. Under Windows, all of these resources must be shared. Thus, for example, memory management is controlled by Windows instead of the application.

Advantages of Using a Queued Input

Memory, as you have learned, is a shared resource under Windows. However, so are most input devices such as the keyboard and mouse. Thus, when you develop a Windows program in C++, it is no longer possible to read directly from the keyboard using the C++ I/O stream. With Windows, an application does not make explicit calls to read from the keyboard or mouse. Rather, Windows receives all input from the keyboard, mouse, and timer in the system queue. It is the queue's responsibility to redirect the input to the appropriate program since more than one application can be running. This redirection is achieved by copying the message from the system queue into the application's queue. At this point, when the application is ready to process the input, it reads from its queue and dispatches a message to the correct window.

Input is accessed with the use of a uniform format called an *input message*. All input messages specify the system time, state of the keyboard, scan code of any depressed key, position of the mouse, and which mouse button has been pressed (if any), as well as information specifying which device generated the message.

Keyboard, mouse, and timer messages all have identical formats and are processed in a similar manner. Further, with each message, Windows provides a device-independent virtual keycode that identifies the key, regardless of which keyboard it is on, and the device-dependent scan code generated by the keyboard, as well as the status of other keys on the keyboard, including NUM LOCK, ALT, SHIFT, and CTRL.

The keyboard and mouse are a shared resource. One keyboard and one mouse must supply all the input information for each program running under Windows. Windows sends all keyboard input messages directly to the currently active window. Mouse messages, on the other hand, are handled differently. Mouse messages are sent to the window that is physically underneath the mouse cursor, the window with the current focus.

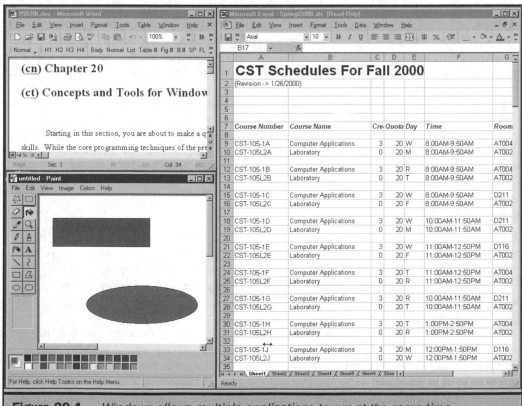

Figure 20-4.   *Windows allows multiple applications to run at the same time.*

Another shared resource is timer messages. *Timer messages* are similar to keyboard and mouse messages. Windows allows a program to set a system timer so that one of its windows receives a message at periodic intervals. This timer message goes directly into the application's message queue. It is also possible for other messages to be passed into an application's message queue as a result of the program's calling certain Windows functions.

OOPs and Windows Messages

Object-oriented programming has become very popular, but Windows has always employed a pseudo-OOP environment. The message system under Windows is the underlying structure used to disseminate information in the multitasking environment. From the application's perspective, a message is a notification that some event of interest has occurred that may or may not need a specific action. The user may initiate these events by clicking or moving the mouse, changing the size of a window, or making a menu selection. The events can also be initiated by the application itself. For example, a graphics-based spreadsheet could finish a recalculation that results in the need to update a graphics bar chart. In this situation, the application would send an "update window" message to itself.

Windows itself can also generate messages, as in the case of the "close session" message, in which Windows informs each application of the intent to shut down.

When considering the role of messages in Windows, use the following points. It is the message system that allows Windows to achieve its multitasking capabilities. The message system makes it possible for Windows to share the processor among different applications. Each time Windows sends a message to the application program, it also grants processor time to the application. In reality, the only way an application can get access to the microprocessor is when it receives a message. Also, messages enable an application to respond to events in the environment. These events can be generated by the application itself, by other concurrently running applications, by the user, or by Windows. Each time an event occurs, Windows makes a note and distributes an appropriate message to the interested applications.

Managing Memory

One of the most important shared resources under Windows is system memory. When more than one application is running at the same time, each application must cooperate to share memory in order not to exhaust the total resources of the system. Likewise, as new programs are started and old ones are terminated, memory can become fragmented. Windows is capable of consolidating free memory space by moving blocks of code and data in memory.

It is also possible to over commit memory in Windows. For example, an application can contain more code than can actually fit into memory at one time. Windows can discard currently unused code from memory and later reload the code from the program's executable file.

Windows applications can share routines located in other executable files. The files that contain shareable routines are called *dynamic link libraries (DLLs)*.

Windows includes the mechanism to link the program with the DLL routines at run time. Windows itself is comprised of a large set of dynamic link libraries. To facilitate all of this, Windows programs use a new format of executable file called the *New Executable format*. These files include the information Windows needs to manage the code and data segments and to perform the dynamic linking.

Independence from User Hardware

Windows also provides hardware or device independence. Windows frees the application developer from having to build programs that take into consideration every possible monitor, printer, and input device available for computers. For example, DOS applications had to be written to include drivers for every possible device the application would encounter. In order to make a DOS application capable of printing on any printer, the application designer had to furnish a different driver for every printer. This required many software companies to write essentially the same device driver over and over again—a LaserJet driver for Microsoft Word for DOS, one for Microsoft Works, and so on.

Under Windows, a device driver for each hardware device is written once. This device driver can be supplied by Microsoft, the application vendor, or the user. As you know, Microsoft includes a large variety of hardware drivers with Windows.

It is hardware independence that makes programming a snap for the application developer. The application interacts with Windows rather than with any specific device. It doesn't need to know what printer is hooked up. The application instructs Windows to draw a filled rectangle, and Windows worries about how to accomplish it on the installed hardware. Likewise, each device driver works with every Windows application. Developers save time, and users do not have to worry about whether each new Windows application will support their hardware configuration.

Hardware independence is achieved by specifying the minimum capabilities the hardware must have. These capabilities are the minimum specifications required ensuring that the appropriate routines will function correctly. Every routine, regardless of its complexity, is capable of breaking itself down into the minimal set of operations required for a given device. This is a very impressive feature. For example, not every plotter is capable of drawing a circle by itself. As an application developer, however, you can still use the routines for drawing a circle, even if the plotter has no specific circle capabilities. Since every plotter connected to Windows must be capable of drawing a line, Windows is capable of breaking down the circle routine into a series of small lines.

Windows can specify a set of minimum capabilities to ensure that your application will receive only valid, predefined input. Windows has predefined the set of legal keystrokes allowed by applications. The valid keystrokes are very similar to those produced by the PC compatible keyboard. Should a manufacturer produce a keyboard that contains additional keys that do not exist in the Windows list of acceptable keys, the manufacturer would also have to supply additional software that would translate these illegal keystrokes into Windows' legal keystrokes. This predefined Windows legal input covers all the input devices, including the mouse. Therefore, even if someone should develop a four-button mouse, you don't have to worry. The manufacturer would supply the software necessary to convert all mouse input to the Windows predefined possibilities of mouse-button clicks.

Dynamic Link Libraries (DLLs)

Dynamic link libraries, or DLLs, provide much of Windows' functionality. They are used to enhance the base operating system by providing a powerful and flexible graphics user interface. Dynamic link libraries contain predefined functions that are linked with an application program when it is loaded (dynamically), instead of when the executable file is generated (statically). Dynamic link libraries use the .DLL file extension.

Storing frequently used routines in separate libraries was not an invention of the Windows product. For example, the C++ language depends heavily on libraries to implement standard functions and streams for different systems. The linker makes copies of run-time library functions, such as strlen() into a program's executable file. Libraries of functions save each programmer from having to re-create a new procedure for a common operation such as reading in a character or formatting output. Programmers can easily build their own libraries to include additional capabilities, such as changing a character font or justifying text. Making the function available as a general tool eliminates redundant design—a key feature in OOP.

Windows libraries are dynamically linked. In other words, the linker does not copy the library functions into the program's executable file. Instead, while the program is executing, it makes calls to the function in the library. Naturally, this conserves memory. No matter how many applications are running, there is only one copy of the library in RAM at a given time, and this library can be shared.

When a call is made to a Windows function, the C++ compiler must generate machine code for a far inter-segment call to the function located in a code segment in one of the Windows libraries. This presents a problem since, until the program is actually running inside Windows, the address of the Windows function is unknown. Doesn't this sound suspiciously similar to the concept of late binding, discussed in the OOP section of this book? The solution to this problem in Windows is called *delayed binding* or *dynamic linking*. Starting with Windows 3.0 and Microsoft C 6.0, the linker allows a program to have calls to functions that cannot be fully resolved at link time. Only when the program is loaded into memory, to be run, are the far function calls resolved.

Special Windows *import libraries* are included with the C++ compiler; they are used to properly prepare a Windows program for dynamic linking. For example, the import library user32.dll is the import library that contains a record for each Windows function that your program can call. This record defines the Windows module that contains this function and, in many cases, an ordinal value that corresponds to the function in the module.

Windows applications typically make a call to the Windows PostMessage() function. When your application is linked at compile time, the linker finds the PostMessage() function listed in user32.lib. The linker obtains the ordinal number for the function and embeds this information in the application's executable file. When the application is run, Windows connects the call your application makes with the actual PostMessage() function.

The Executable Format for Windows

An executable file format was developed for Windows and is called the New Executable format. This new format includes a *new-style header* capable of holding information about dynamic link library functions.

For example, DLL functions are included for the KERNEL, USER, and GDI modules. These libraries contain routines that help programs carry out various chores, such as sending and receiving messages. The library modules provide functions that can be called from the application program or from other library modules. To the module that contains the functions, the functions are known as *exports*. The New Executable format identifies these exported functions with a name and an ordinal number. Included in the New Executable format is an *Entry Table* section that indicates the address of each of these exported functions within the module.

From the perspective of the application program, the library functions that an application uses are known as *imports*. These imports use the various relocation tables and can identify the far calls that the application makes to an imported function. Almost all Windows programs contain at least one exported function. This window function is usually located in one of the library modules and is the one that receives window messages.

This new format also provides the additional information on each of the code and data segments in a program or library. Typically, code segments are flagged as moveable and discardable, while data segments are flagged as moveable. This allows Windows to move code and data segments in memory and even discard code segments if additional memory is needed. If Windows later decides it needs a discarded code segment, it can reload the code segment from the original executable file. Windows has another category called *load on call*. This defines a program or library code segment that will not be loaded into memory at all unless a function in the code segment is called from another code segment. Through this sophisticated memory-management scheme, Windows can simultaneously run several programs in a memory space that would normally be sufficient for only one program.

Originally, Windows depended on a module-definition file to specify the linker options just discussed. However, the linker provided with Visual C++ now provides equivalent command-line options for most module-definition statements. Thus, a program now designed for Windows does not usually require a module definition file to access these capabilities.

Programming Concepts and Vocabulary for Windows

The Windows programming environment is uniquely different for most programmers. The uniqueness occurs because Windows includes new programming concepts and its own special vocabulary. These new concepts and vocabulary can be broken down into two major categories: the features of Windows that are visible to the user (menus, dialog boxes, icons, and so on) and the invisible features (messages, function access, and so on). There is a standard vocabulary associated with Windows programming development designed to give application developers the ability to communicate effectively with one another. Thus, all Windows features have been given a name and an associated usage. In this section you will learn a variety of Windows terms that will give you the ability to confidently discuss and develop Windows applications.

What Is a Windows Window?

A Windows window appears to the user as a rectangular portion of the display device; its appearance is independent of the particular application at hand. To an application, however, the window is a rectangular area of the screen that is under the direct control of the application. The application has the ability to create and control everything about the main window, including its size and shape. When the user starts a program, a window is created. Each time the user clicks a window option, the application responds. Closing a window causes the application to terminate. The use of windows conveys to the user the multitasking capabilities of Windows. By partitioning the screen into different windows, the user can direct input to a specific application within the multitasking environment by using the keyboard or a mouse to select one of the concurrently running applications. Windows then intercepts the user's input and allocates any necessary resources (such as the microprocessor) as needed.

The Layout of a Window

Features such as borders, control boxes, About boxes, and so on, are common to all Windows applications. It is this common interface that gives Windows a comforting predictability from one application to another. Notice in Figure 20-5 the fundamental components of a typical Windows window.

Border

A window has a *border* surrounding it. The border is made up of lines that frame the rectangular outline of the window. To the novice, the border may appear only to delineate one application's screen viewport from another. Upon closer examination of the border, however, a different conclusion will be drawn. For example, by positioning the mouse pointer over a border and holding down the left mouse button, the user can change the size of the active window.

Title Bar

The name of the application program is displayed at the top of the window in the *title bar*. Title bars are located at the top of each associated window. Title bars indicate which applications are currently running. By default, the active application uses a different color in the title bar area than a non-active application.

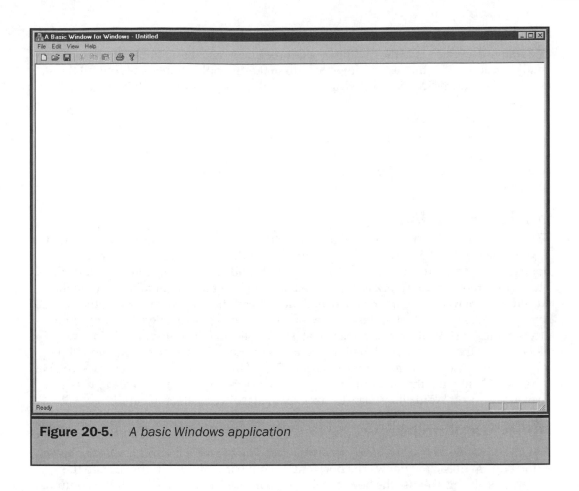

Figure 20-5.   *A basic Windows application*

Control Icon

A *control icon* is used by each Windows application. The control icon is a small image in each window's upper-left corner. Clicking the mouse pointer on the control icon (referred to as clicking the control icon) causes Windows to display the system menu.

System Menu

The *system menu* is opened by clicking the control icon. The system menu provides standard application options such as Restore, Move, Size, Minimize, Maximize, and Close.

Minimize Icon

Each Windows application typically displays three iconic images in the upper-right hand corner of the window. The first icon on the left, a dash or underline symbol, allows the application to be minimized.

Restore Down Icon

The *restore down icon* is in the middle of the three iconic images and appears as two very small windows. Use the restore down icon to make an application's window fill the entire screen. If this icon is selected, all other application windows will be covered.

Close Window Icon

The *close window* icon is on the right of the three iconic images and appears as an "X" symbol. Use the close window icon to quickly exit an application. When this icon is selected for an application, the application ends and other applications move to the foreground.

Vertical Scroll Bar

An application can show a *vertical scroll bar* if desired. The vertical scroll bar is located against the right-hand edge of the application's window. The vertical scroll bar has opposite-pointing arrows at its extremes, a colored band, and a transparent window block. The transparent window block is used to visually represent the orientation between the currently displayed contents and the overall document (the colored band). Use the vertical scroll bar to select which of multiple pages of output are to be displayed. Clicking either arrow typically shifts the display one line at a time. Clicking the transparent window block, below the up arrow, and dragging it causes screen output to be quickly updated to any portion of the application's screen output. One of the best uses of the vertical scroll bar is for quickly moving through a multi-page word processing document. Word processors such as Microsoft Word allow users to take advantage of vertical scroll bars.

Horizontal Scroll Bar

It is also possible to display a *horizontal scroll bar*. The horizontal scroll bar is displayed at the bottom of each window. The horizontal scroll bar is similar in function to the vertical scroll bar. You use the horizontal scroll bar to select which of multiple columns of information you would like displayed. Clicking either arrow causes the screen image to typically be shifted one column at a time. Clicking the transparent window block, to the right of the left-pointing arrow, and dragging it causes the screen output to be quickly updated to any horizontally shifted portion of the application's screen output. One of the best uses for the horizontal scroll bar is for quickly moving through the multiple columns of a spreadsheet application, where the number of columns of information cannot fit into one screen width. Horizontal scroll bars are especially helpful in programs like Microsoft Excel.

Menu Bar

An optional *menu bar* can also be displayed just below the title bar in a window. Use the menu bar for making menu and submenu selections. Pointing and clicking a menu command or, alternately, using a hot-key combination makes menu selections. Hot-key combinations often use the ALT key in conjunction with the underlined letter in a command. For example, you would press the F key for the command File.

Client Area

The *client area* usually occupies the largest portion of each window. The client area is the primary output area for the application. Managing the client area is the responsibility of the application program. Additionally, only the application can output to the client area.

A Procedure-Oriented Windows Class

The basic components of a window help define the standard appearance of an application. There are also occasions when an application will create two windows with a similar appearance and behavior. Windows Paint is one such example. The fashion in which Paint allows the user to clip or copy a portion of a graphics image is achieved by running two instances (or copies) of Paint. Information is then copied from one instance to the other. Each instance of Paint looks and behaves like its counterpart. This requires each instance to create its own window with an identical appearance and functionality.

Windows that are created in this manner look alike and behave in a similar fashion. These windows are said to be of the same *window class*. However, windows that you create can take on different characteristics. They may be different sizes, placed in different areas of the display, have different text in the caption bars, have different display colors, use different mouse cursors, and so on.

Every created window must be based on a window class. With applications developed in C++ using traditional function calls, several window classes are registered by the Windows application during its initialization phase. Your application may register additional classes of its own. In order to allow several windows to be created and based on the same window class, Windows specifies some of a window's characteristics as parameters to the CreateWindow() function, while others are specified in a window class structure. Also, when you register a window class, the class becomes available to all programs running under Windows. For object-oriented applications using Microsoft's Foundation Classes, much of this registration work is already done through the use of predefined objects. Chapter 21 teaches you how to write applications in the Windows procedure-oriented environment, while Chapters 22 and 23 concentrate on the object-oriented environment using the Microsoft Foundation Class (MFC) library.

Windows of similar appearance and behavior can be grouped together into classes, thereby reducing the amount of information that needs to be maintained. Since each window class has its own shareable window class structure, there is no needless replication of the window class' parameters. Also, two windows of the same class use the same function and any of its associated subroutines. This feature saves time and storage because there is no code duplication.

OOPs and Windows

Traditional procedure-oriented C++ programs take on the characteristics of object-oriented programs under Windows. Recall that in object-oriented programming, an *object* is an abstract data type that consists of a data structure and various functions that act on the data structure. Likewise, objects receive messages that can cause them to function differently.

A Windows *graphics object*, for example, is a collection of data that can be manipulated as a whole entity and that is presented to the user as part of the visual interface. In particular, a graphics object implies both the data and the presentation of data. Menus, title bars, control boxes, and scroll bars are examples of graphics objects. The next sections describe several new graphics objects that affect the user's view of an application.

Icons

An icon is a small graphics object used to remind the user of a particular operation, idea, or product. For example, a spreadsheet application when minimized could display a very small histogram icon to remind the user that the application is running. Double-clicking the histogram would then cause Windows to bring the application to active status. Icons can be very powerful tools. They are good for gaining the user's attention, as in the case of an error warning, and also when presenting choices to the user. Windows provides several stock icons including a question mark, an exclamation point, an asterisk, an upturned palm icon, and so on. It is also possible to design your own device-independent color icons with the Microsoft C++ compiler's resource editor.

Cursors

Cursors are also Windows graphics symbols that are used to follow the movement of the pointing device. The graphics symbol is capable of changing shapes to indicate particular Windows actions. For example, the standard Windows arrow cursor changes to the small hourglass cursor to indicate a pause while a selected command is being executed. Windows provides several stock cursors: a diagonal arrow, a vertical arrow, an hourglass, a cross hair, an I-beam, and several others. You can also use the Microsoft C++ compiler's resource editor to create your own cursors.

Carets

Carets are symbols an application places in a window to show the user where input will be received. Carets are distinguished from other screen markers because they blink. Most of the time, mouse input is associated with cursor and keyboard input with a caret. However, the mouse can move or change the input emphasis of a caret. To help clarify the difference between a cursor and a caret, Windows carets behave most similarly to the old DOS style cursor. One of the carets provided for you automatically, when entering a dialog box, is the I-beam caret. Unlike icons and cursors, an application must create its own carets using special functions. There are no stock carets.

Message Boxes

The *message box* is another common Windows graphics object. Message boxes are pop-up windows that contain a title, an icon, and a message. Figure 20-6 is the standard message box presented when terminating a Windows notepad session.

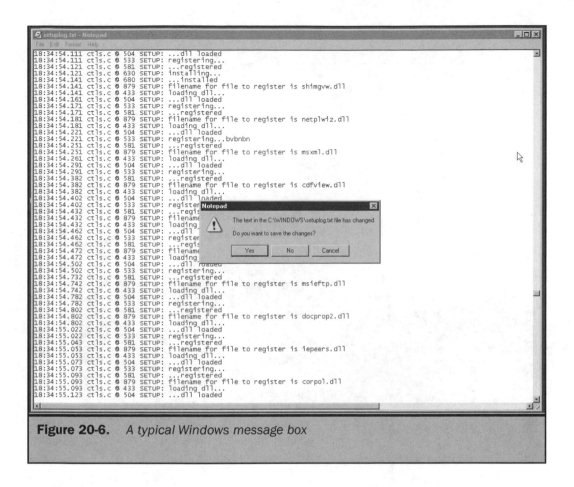

Figure 20-6.   *A typical Windows message box*

The application needs to supply the message title, the message itself, and instructions on which stock icon to use (if any) and indicate if a stock response is allowed (such as OK). Additional stock user responses include Yes/No, Yes/No/Cancel, OK/Cancel, and Retry/Cancel. Stock icons include IconHand, IconQuestion, IconExclamation, IconAsterisk, and so on.

Windows Dialog Boxes

A *dialog box* is similar to a message box in that it too is a pop-up window. Dialog boxes, however, are primarily used to receive input from the user rather than to just present output. A dialog box allows an application to receive information, one field at a time or one box's worth of information at a time, rather than a character at a time. Figure 20-7 shows a typical Windows dialog box. Windows does the graphic design of a dialog box automatically for you.

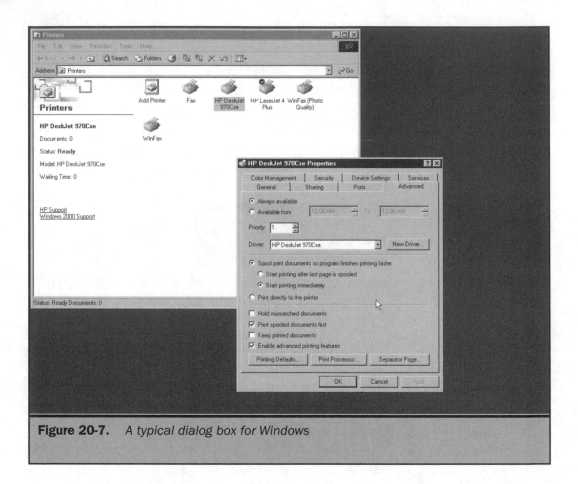

Figure 20-7.   *A typical dialog box for Windows*

The layout of a dialog box is normally done with the compiler's resource editor.

Fonts

A *font* is a graphics object or resource that defines a complete set of characters from one typeface. These characters are all of a certain size and style that can be manipulated to give text a variety of appearances. A *typeface* is a basic character design, defined by certain serifs and stroke widths. For instance, your application can use any of the different fonts provided with Windows including System, Courier, and Times Roman, or custom fonts that you define and include in the application program's executable file. By using built-in routines, Windows allows for the dynamic modification of a font, including boldface, italics, underline, and changing the size of the font. Windows provides all of the necessary functions for displaying text anywhere within the client area. Additionally, because of Windows device independence, an application's output will have a consistent appearance from one output device to the next. TrueType font technology, first introduced with Windows 3.1, provides improved fonts for the screen and printer under all current versions of Windows.

Bitmaps

Bitmaps serve as a photographic image of the display (in pixels) and are stored in memory. Bitmaps are used whenever an application must display a graphics image quickly. Since bitmapped images are transferred directly from memory, they can be displayed more quickly than by executing the code necessary to re-create the image. There are two basic uses for bitmaps. First, bitmaps are used to draw pictures on the display. For example, Windows uses many small bitmaps for drawing arrows in scroll bars; displaying the check marks when selecting pop-up menu options; and drawing the system menu box, the size box, and many others. Bitmaps are also used for creating brushes. Brushes allow you to paint and fill objects on the screen.

There are two disadvantages to using bitmaps. First, depending on their size, bitmaps can occupy an unpredictably large portion of memory. For each pixel that is being displayed, there needs to be an equivalent representation in memory. Displaying the same bitmap on a color monitor versus a monochrome monitor would also require more memory. On a monochrome monitor, one bit can be used to define a pixel as being on or off. However, on a color monitor that can display 16 colors, each pixel would require 4 bits, or a nibble, to represent its characteristics. Also, as the resolution of the display device increases, so too does the memory requirement for the bitmap. Another disadvantage of bitmaps is that they contain only a static picture. For example, if an automobile is represented by a bitmap, there is no way to access the picture's various components, such as tires, hood, window, and so on. However, if the automobile had been constructed from a series of primitive drawing routines, an application would be able to change the data sent to these routines and modify individual items in the picture. For example, an application could modify the roof line and convert a sedan to a convertible. You can create or modify bitmaps with the compiler's resource editor.

Pens

Windows uses information on the current pen when it draws a shape on the screen. *P*ens are used to draw lines and outline shapes. Pens have three basic characteristics: line width, style (dotted, dashed, solid), and color. Windows always has a pen for drawing black lines and one for drawing white lines available to each application. It is also possible to create your own unique pens. For example, you might want to create a thick, light-gray line to outline a portion of the screen or a dot-dash-dot line for spreadsheet data analysis.

Brushes

Windows uses *brushes* to paint colors and fill areas with predefined patterns. Brushes have a minimum size of 8x8 pixels and, like pens, have three basic characteristics: size, pattern, and color. With their 8x8-pixel minimum size, brushes are said to have a pattern, not a style as pens do. The pattern may be a solid color, hatched, diagonal, or any other user-definable combination.

Windows Messages

As you have learned, an application does not write directly to the screen under Windows. Neither does an application directly process hardware interrupts or output directly to the printer. Instead, an application uses the appropriate Windows functions or waits for an appropriate message to be delivered. Application development under Windows must now incorporate the processing of the application and the user's view of the application through Windows.

The Windows message system is the underlying structure used to disseminate information in a multitasking environment. From the application's viewpoint, a message is seen as a notification that some event of interest has occurred that may or may not need a specific response. These events may have been initiated on the part of the user, such as clicking or moving the mouse, changing the size of a window, or making a menu selection. However, the signaled event could also have been generated by the application itself.

The overall effect of this process is that your application must now be totally oriented toward the processing of messages. It must be capable of awakening, determining the appropriate action based on the type of message received, taking that action to completion, and returning to sleep.

Windows applications are significantly different from their older DOS counterparts. Windows provides an application program with access to hundreds of function calls directly or indirectly through foundation classes. These function calls are handled by several main modules including the KERNEL, GDI (graphics device interface), and USER modules. The KERNEL is responsible for memory management, loading and running an application, and scheduling. The GDI contains all of the routines to create and display graphics. The USER module takes care of all other application requirements.

The next section takes a closer look at the message system by examining the format and sources of messages and looking at several common message types and the ways in which both Windows and your application process messages.

The Windows Message Format

Messages are used to notify a program that an event of interest has occurred. Technically, a message is not just of interest to the application, but also to a specific window within that application. Therefore, every message is addressed to a window.

Actually only one message system exists under Windows—the system message queue. However, each program currently running under Windows also has its own program message queue. The USER module must eventually transfer each message in the system message queue to a program's message queue. The program's message queue stores all messages for all windows in that program.

Four parameters are associated with all messages, regardless of their type: a window handle, a message type, and two additional 32-bit parameters. The first parameter specified in a window message is the handle of the window to which the message is addressed.

These are the parameters for 32-bit Windows applications. The parameters used for earlier 16-bit Windows 3.x applications differed.

Table 20-1 shows a list of data types frequently used with Win32 functions.

Data Type	Description
HANDLE	Defines a 32-bit unsigned integer that is used as a handle.
HWND	Defines a 32-bit unsigned integer that is used as the handle to a window.
HDC	Defines a handle to a device context.
LONG	Specifies a 32-bit signed integer.
LPSTR	Defines a 32-bit pointer.
NULL	Specifies an integral zero value often used to trigger function default parameters or actions.
UINT	Specifies a 32-bit unsigned integer.
WCHAR	Specifies a 16-bit UNICODE character used to represent all of the symbols known for all of the world's written languages.

Table 20-1.   *Frequently Used Win32 Data Types*

Handles are always used when writing procedure-oriented Windows applications. Remember that a handle is a unique number that identifies many different types of objects, such as windows, controls, menus, icons, pens and brushes, memory allocation, output devices, and even window instances. Under Windows, each loaded copy of a program is called an instance. When programming in the MFC object-oriented environment, handles are not part of the parameter list but are processed internally by MFC.

Since Windows allows more than one copy of the same application to be run at the same time, the operating system needs to keep track of each of these instances. It does this by attaching a unique instance handle to each running copy of the application.

The instance handle is usually used as an index into an internally maintained table. By referencing a table element, rather than an actual memory address, Windows can dynamically rearrange all resources simply by inserting a new address into the resource's table position. For example, if Windows associates a particular application's resource with table lookup position 16, then no matter where Windows moves the resource in memory, table position 16 will contain the resource's current location.

WINDOWS AND WIZARDS

Windows conserves memory resources because of the way multiple instances of the same application are handled.

The instance of an application has a very important role. It is the instance of an application that defines all of the objects necessary for the functioning of the application. This can include controls, menus, dialog boxes, and much more, along with new window classes.

The second parameter in a message is the *message type*. This is one of the identifiers specified in several header files unique to Windows. These header files can be pointed to with the use of windows.h. With Windows, each message type begins with a two-character mnemonic, followed by the underscore character, and finally a descriptor. The most frequently encountered type of message in traditional procedure-oriented C++ Windows applications is the window message. Windows messages include WM_CREATE, WM_PAINT, WM_CLOSE, WM_COPY, WM_PASTE, etc. Other message types include control window messages (BM_), edit control messages (EM_), and list box messages (LB_). An application can also create and register its own message type. This permits the use of private message types.

The last two parameters provide additional information necessary to interpret the message. The contents of these last two parameters will therefore vary depending on the message type. Examples of the types of information that would be passed include which key was just struck, the position of the mouse, the position of the vertical or horizontal scroll bar elevators, and the selected pop-up menu item.

Generating Messages

It is the message-passing concept that allows Windows to be multitasking. Thus, Windows must process all messages. There are four basic sources for a message. An application can receive a message from the user, from Windows itself, from the application program itself, or from other applications.

User messages include keystroke information, mouse movements, point-and-click coordinates, any menu selections, the location of scroll bar elevators, and so on. The application program will devote a great deal of time to processing user messages. User-originated messages indicate that the person running the program wants to change the way the application is viewed.

A message is sent to an application whenever a state change is to take effect. An example of this would be when the user clicks an application's icon indicating that they want to make that application the active application. In this case, Windows tells the application that its main window is being opened, that its size and location are being modified, and so on. Depending on the current state of an application, Windows-originated messages can be processed or ignored.

Currently, most applications written for Windows do not take full advantage of the fourth type of message source, inter-task communication. However, this category will become increasingly important as more and more applications take advantage of this Windows integration capability. Microsoft's dynamic data exchange protocol (DDE) was the first to take advantage of this feature.

Responding to Messages

Traditional procedure-oriented C++ Windows applications have a procedure for processing each type of message they may encounter. Different windows can respond differently to messages of the same type. For example, one application may have created two windows that respond to a mouse-button click in two different ways. The first window could respond to a mouse-button click by changing the background color, while the second window may respond to the mouse-button click by placing a crosshatch on a spreadsheet. It is because the same message can be interpreted differently by different windows that Windows addresses each message to a specific window within an application. Not only will the application have a different procedure to handle each message type, it will also need a procedure to handle each message type for each window. The window procedure groups together all the message type procedures for an application.

The Message Loop

A basic component of all Windows applications is the message-processing loop. The location of the message loop in procedure-oriented applications is easy to identify. In object-oriented code, the message loop is processed in the CWinAPP foundation class.

Each C++ application performs the operation internally. These applications contain procedures to create and initialize windows, followed by the message-processing loop and finally some code required to close the application. The message loop is responsible for processing a message delivered by Windows to the main body of the program. Here, the program acknowledges the message and then requests Windows to send it to the appropriate window procedure for processing. When the message is received, the window procedure executes the desired action.

Two factors that can influence the sequence in which a message is processed are the message queue and the dispatching priority. Messages can be sent from one of two queues—either the system queue or the application's message queue. Messages, regardless of the source, are first placed in the system queue. When a given message reaches the front of the queue, it is sent to the appropriate application's message queue. This dual-mode action allows Windows to keep track of all messages and permits each application to concern itself with only those messages that pertain to it.

Messages are placed in the queues as you would expect: FIFO (first in first out) order. These are called *synchronous messages*. Most Windows applications use this type of dispatching method. However, there are occasions when Windows will push a message to the end of the queue, thereby preventing it from being dispatched. Messages of this type are called *asynchronous messages*. Care must be taken when sending an asynchronous message that overrides the application's normal sequence of processing.

Several types of asynchronous messages exist, including paint, timer, and quit messages. A timer message, for example, causes a certain action to take effect at a specified time, regardless of the messages to be processed at that moment. A timer message has priority and will cause all other messages in the queue to be pushed farther from the queue front.

A few asynchronous messages can be sent to other applications. This is unique because the receiving application doesn't put the message into its queue. Rather, the received message directly calls the application's appropriate window procedure, where it is immediately executed.

How does Windows dispatch messages that are pending for several applications at the same time? Windows handles this problem in one of two ways. One method of message processing is called *dispatching priority*. Whenever Windows loads an application, it sets the application's priority to zero. Once the application is running, however, the application can change its priority. With everything else being equal, Windows will settle any message-dispatching contention by sending messages to the highest priority application.

One example of a high-priority program would be a data communications application. Tampering with an application's priority level is not recommended and is very uncommon. Windows has another method for dispatching messages to concurrent applications of the same priority level. Whenever Windows sees that a particular application has a backlog of unprocessed messages, it hangs on to the new message while continuing to dispatch other new messages to the other applications.

Accessing Windows Functions

As you have learned, Windows provides the application developer with hundreds of functions. Examples of these functions include DispatchMessage(), PostMessage(), RegisterWindowMessage(), and SetActiveWindow(). For C++ programmers using the Microsoft Foundation Classes (MFCs), many of these functions are dispatched automatically. However, many can be called directly and inter-mixed with the use of MFC objects.

Calling Convention for Functions

Function declarations under 16-bit Windows 3.x included the **pascal** modifier, which was more efficient under DOS. Windows does not use this modifier for 32-bit applications. As you have learned, the parameters to all Windows functions are passed via the system stack. The parameters for the function are pushed from the rightmost parameter to the leftmost parameter, in a normal C++ fashion. Upon return from the function, the calling procedure must adjust the stack pointer to a value equal to the number of bytes originally pushed onto the stack.

The Windows Header File: windows.h

The windows.h header file provides a path to over a thousand constant declarations, **typedef** declarations, and hundreds of function prototypes. One of the main reasons a Windows application takes longer to compile than a non-Windows C++ program is the size of this and associated header files. The windows.h header file (and associated header files) is an integral part of all programs. Traditionally, windows.h is a required include file in all C++ Windows applications. When using the Microsoft Foundation Class library in C++ the windows.h header file is included via the afxwin.h header file.

Usually, the **#define** statements found in windows.h or its associated files map a numeric constant with a text identifier. For example:

```
#define WM_CREATE 0x0001
```

In this case, the Visual C++ compiler will use the hexadecimal constant 0x0001 as a replacement for WM_CREATE during preprocessing.

Other **#define** statements may appear a bit unusual. For example:

```
#define NEAR near
#define VOID void
```

In Visual C++, both **near** and **void** are reserved words. Your applications should use the uppercase **NEAR** and **VOID** for one very good reason: if you port your application to another compiler, it will be much easier to change the **#define** statements within the header file than to change all of the occurrences of a particular identifier in your application.

Components that Make Up a Windows Application

There are several important steps that are common in developing all Windows applications:

- Create the WinMain() and associated Windows functions in C++. You can also utilize foundation classes, such as CWinAPP, in C++.

- Create the menu, dialog box, and any additional resource descriptions and put them into a resource script file.

- (Optional) Use the appropriate resource editor in the Visual C++ compiler to create unique cursors, icons, and bitmaps.

- (Optional) Use the appropriate resource editor in the Visual C++ compiler to create dialog boxes.

- Compile and link all C/C++ language sources and resource files using a project file.

The actual creation of a Windows application requires the use of several new development tools. Before developing applications in C++, an understanding of these tools is needed. The next section briefly discusses the tools supplied with the Visual C++ compiler as they relate to creating a Windows application.

WINDOWS AND WIZARDS

Visual C++ Windows Development Tools

The Visual C++ compiler contains several resource editors. The individual editors are available by selecting View | Resource View. Right-click the project's .rc file and you will be given the option of adding any type of Windows resource you desire for the project. These editors allow for the quick definition of icons, cursors, and bitmaps. They also provide a convenient method for creating your own unique fonts and make it easy to create dialog-box descriptions for data entry.

Resources have the capability of turning ordinary Windows applications into truly exciting graphical presentations. When you develop icons, cursors, menus, bitmaps, and more for your application, the graphical flare gives your program presentation a quality appearance. Resource files also let you add user-interactive components to your program such as menus, keyboard accelerators, and dialog boxes.

Graphics objects such as icons, cursors, carets, message boxes, dialog boxes, fonts, bitmaps, pens, and brushes are all examples of resources. A *resource* represents data that is included in an application's executable file. Technically speaking, however, it does not reside in a program's normal data segment. When Windows loads a program into memory for execution, it usually leaves all of the resources on the disk. Consider, as an example, when the user first requests to see an application's About box. Before Windows can display the About box it must first access the disk to copy this information from the program's executable file into memory.

The resource compiler, rc.exe, is a compiler for Windows resources. Many times a Windows application will use its own resources, such as dialog boxes, menus, and icons. Each one of these resources must be predefined in a file called a *resource file* or *resource script file*. These files are created with the resource editors previously mentioned. Resource script files can be compiled into resource files by the resource compiler. This information is then added to the application's final executable file. This method allows Windows to load and use the resources from the executable file.

The use of resources and additional compilers adds an extra layer of complexity to application development, but one that is easily incorporated with the project utility.

Project Files

Project files provide an efficient means of overseeing the compilation of resources and program code as well as keeping the executable version of an application up to date. They accomplish their incremental operation by keeping track of the dates and times of their source files.

Project files include information about the compile and link process for the particular program. Programmers often have the choice of changing libraries, hardware platforms, software platforms, etc. Project files, as you already know, are created within the integrated C++ editing environment. In many cases, the default project file setup can be used with just minor adjustments for program titles and a file list to include in the build operation.

Project files also support incremental compiles and links. For example, consider a Windows application that simulates the flight of an arrow. During the development process you decide to create your own unique cursor instead of pointing with the standard arrow provided by Windows. You create a cursor that looks like an apple with an arrow through it. When the application is recompiled incrementally, the program only really needs to accommodate the changes in the cursor resource file, apple.cur. The project utility will ensure that only the information about the new cursor is updated during recompilation, speeding up the overall operation.

Resource Details

Customizing a Windows application with your own icons, pointers, and bitmaps is easy when you use the resource editors provided with the C++ compiler. These editors give you a complete environment in which to develop graphical resources. The editors will also help you create menus and dialog boxes—the basic means of data entry in Windows. In this section you learn how to use these editors to create icons, cursors, menus, and dialog boxes. The editors can also help you manipulate individual bitmaps, keyboard accelerators, and strings.

Icons, Cursors, and Bitmaps

This section describes the general operation of three editors. A specific editor is capable of producing an icon, cursor, or bitmap. Although each is a separate editor, they share many common features. As an example of the use of these image editors, a custom icon and cursor will be created for an application in the next chapter. Icons and cursors are both really small bitmaps. The resource editors for designing icons and cursors allow you to create device-independent bitmap images. The icons and cursors created with these editors are functionally device independent with respect to resolution.

This image-file format allows for the tailoring of a bitmap that has a consistent look on each particular display resolution. For example, one icon might consist of four definitions (called DIBs): one designed for monochrome displays, one for CGAs, one for EGAs, and one for VGAs. Whenever the application displays the icon, it simply refers to it by name; Windows then automatically selects the icon image best suited to the current display. Figure 20-8 shows the icon editor window during the construction of a custom icon.

Initially, a color palette appears at the left of the editor for selecting the drawing color. Associated with this palette is a color box that shows the currently selected value. You can also create custom colors.

A large editing area is provided for drawing the icons, cursors, or bitmaps. The area is initially divided into smaller cells with a 32x32 grid. The editor also provides a small View window to allow you to observe the graphics in true size.

Designing a Custom Icon and Cursor

To create an icon or cursor we recommend simply editing the default icon and cursor provided by the project Wizard. Simply select View | Resource View and expand the list of resources as you see on the right of Figure 20-8.

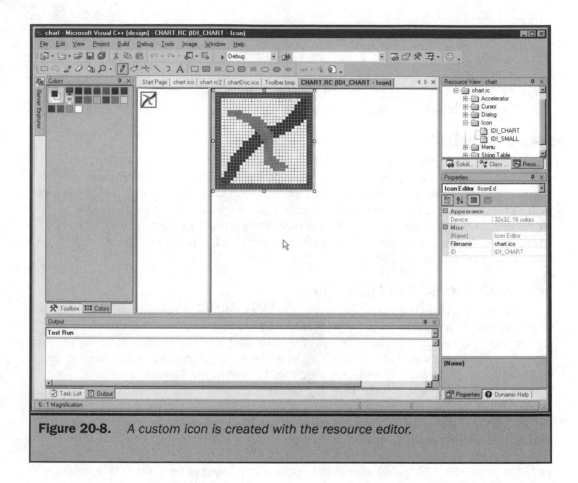

Figure 20-8.   *A custom icon is created with the resource editor.*

In Figure 20-8, we cleared the default icon and went about drawing our own custom icon for the project.

These editors can provide a broad spectrum of painting colors for icons and a selection of dithered colors for cursors. Click the color choice from the palette of colors shown. Now it is possible to draw the icon, cursor, or bitmap to your program's specification. You can also create custom colors. Be sure to save your final results by selecting File | Save or File | Save As.

Figure 20-9 shows the editor window with a new and completed cursor design. When looking at the completed icon or cursor designs, you will note that there are actually two renditions of the design. The larger one, within the editing area, allows your eyes to easily create an image. The smaller version, to the left, represents the actual size of the design, as it will appear in the application's window.

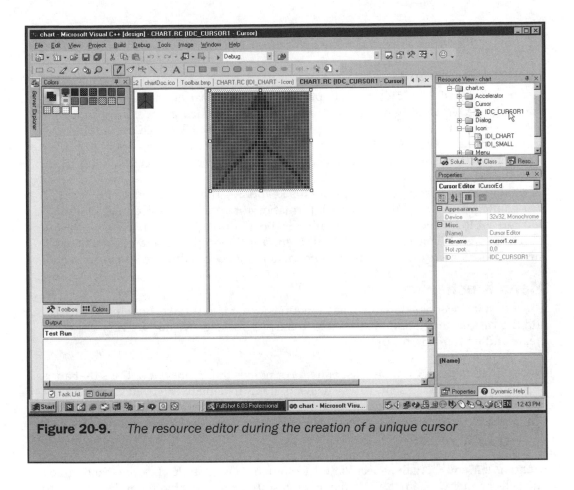

Figure 20-9.   *The resource editor during the creation of a unique cursor*

It takes a great deal of patience and practice to create a meaningful icon, cursor, or bitmap. This process often requires several trial-and-error attempts. Whenever you come up with a design that looks good, stop and save a copy of it. It is too easy to get your design to a point where you really like it only to make one additional change and ruin hours of work.

The first time you select File | Save, the editor prompts you for a filename. If you are creating an icon, the file system will automatically append an .ico file extension. The .cur file extension is used for cursors. (Note that the file extension *must* be .ico or .cur, respectively.) If you are simply modifying an existing icon or cursor, the file will already have a default name. If you are creating several possible designs, make certain you choose the Save As option, *not* Save. Save overwrites your original file, but Save As allows you to create multiple copies.

When you are creating cursors, you can select an optional hotspot. The hotspot button is located just above the drawing palette. The cursor *hotspot* is a point that will be used to return the current screen coordinates during the application's use. The hotspot on this cursor is located at the tip of the arrow.

Designing Menus

Menus are one of Windows' most important tools for creating interactive programs. Menus form the gateway for easy, consistent interfacing across applications. In their simplest form, menus allow the user to point and click selections that have been predefined. These selections include screen color choices, sizing options, and file operations. More advanced menu options allow the user to select dialog boxes from the menu list.

Dialog boxes permit data entry from the keyboard. They allow the user to enter string, integer, and even real number information for applications. However, before you can get to a dialog box, you typically must pass through a menu.

The project Wizard creates a default menu for the project with a File and Help menu. This menu resource can be expanded, eliminated, or edited to suit your needs.

Menu Mechanics

The following sections describe what a menu is, what it looks like, how it is created, and the various menu options available to the programmer. Menus are very easy to create and implement in a program.

What Is a Menu?   A *menu* is a list of items or names that represent options that an application can take. In some cases, the list of items in a menu can even be bitmap images. The user can select an option by using the mouse, the keyboard, or a hot key. Windows, in turn, responds by sending a message to the application stating which command was selected.

Creating a Menu   Again, select View | Resource View. Double-click the existing .rc file and select a menu resource. Click the menu resource provided by the project's Wizard. The menu will appear and can then be edited within the menu editor. An alternative technique is to use the compiler's text editor to specify a menu resource, but we strongly advise using the editors provided.

The menu resource editor is capable of creating or reading menu descriptions contained in resource script files (.rc) or compiled resource files (.res). Resource script files are simply uncompiled text files. If a header file is available describing constants used in a menu's description, these can be added at the start of the menu's description. For example, the constant IDM_ABOUT might be identified with 40 in a header file.

Figure 20-10 shows the default project menu being edited in the editor.

Different styles and attributes for application menus can be included in this file. These styles and attributes include check marks to indicate the status of an item or define styles for an item's text (normal or grayed) and separator lines to divide menus (menu bar breaks), align menu items in column format, and assign a help attribute to a menu item.

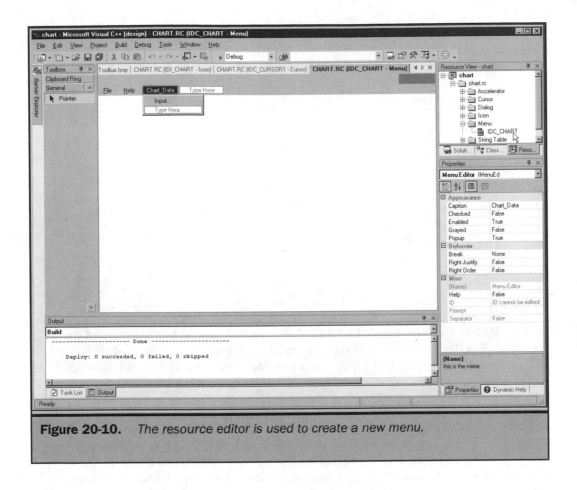

Figure 20-10. *The resource editor is used to create a new menu.*

Menus and the Resource Compiler   By following a set of simple rules, Windows will draw and manage menus for you. In so doing, Windows will produce consistent menus from one application to another. The resource compiler will compile menu resource information. The compiled file, a file with an .res file extension, will be combined with your application at link time. At this time, the compiler and linker will create the final executable file (.exe).

The structure of a simple menu is quite easy to understand. Here is a resource script file:

```
///////////////////////////////////////////////////////
//
// Menu
//
```

```
IDC_CHART MENU DISCARDABLE
BEGIN
    POPUP "&File"
    BEGIN
        MENUITEM "E&xit",              IDM_EXIT
    END
    POPUP "&Help"
    BEGIN
        MENUITEM "&About ...",         IDM_ABOUT
    END
    POPUP "Chart_Data"
    BEGIN
        MENUITEM "Input...",           IDD_CHARTDATA_INPUT
    END
END
```

By studying this listing, you can identify a number of additional menu keywords such as **MENU**, **POPUP**, and **MENUITEM**. You can use brackets ({}) instead of the keywords **BEGIN** and **END**. It is also easy to identify the menu items that will appear in this menu: Exit, About, and Input. The three dots following a menu selection indicate a dialog box to the user.

Menu Keywords and Options   The name of this program's menu definition is IDC_CHART. The menu definition name is followed by the keyword **MENU**. This particular example describes three pop-up menus, File, Exit and Chart_Data, which will appear on the menu bar. Pop-up menus are arranged from left to right on the menu bar. If several pop-up items are used, an additional bar is provided automatically. Only one pop-up menu can be displayed at a time.

You can use an ampersand to produce an underscore under the character that follows the ampersand in the selection list. The ampersand allows the menu item to be selected from the keyboard. Notice, for example, that the "A" in the About Box choice has been preceded with an ampersand. This means that this menu item can be selected with the ALT-A key combination. Menu items can also be selected by positioning the mouse pointer on the menu item and clicking the left button. When a pop-up menu is selected, Windows pops the menu to the screen immediately under the selected item on the menu bar. Each **MENUITEM** describes one menu item in this example. For example, "Chart_Data" provides the Input menu item.

Identification numbers or constants from a header file appear to the right of the menu items. If numbers are present, they can be replaced with values identified in header files, for example, IDM_ABOUT, IDM_EXIT, and IDD_CHARTDATA_INPUT. IDM stands for the identification number of a menu item. IDD stands for the identification number of a dialog box resource. This form of ID has become very popular but is not required. What is important, however, is that each menu item has a unique identification associated with it.

The project Wizard will keep a list of these identification numbers in a separate file, as shown in the following listing:

```
//{{NO_DEPENDENCIES}}
// Microsoft Developer Studio generated include file.
// Used by chart.rc
//
#define IDC_MYICON                      2
#define IDD_CHART_DIALOG                102
#define IDS_APP_TITLE                   103
#define IDD_ABOUTBOX                    103
#define IDM_ABOUT                       104
#define IDM_EXIT                        105
#define IDI_CHART                       107
#define IDI_SMALL                       108
#define IDC_CHART                       109
#define IDR_MAINFRAME                   128
#define IDC_CURSOR1                     129
#define IDD_CHARTDATA_INPUT             130
#define IDD_DIALOG1                     131
#define IDC_EDIT1                       1000
#define IDC_EDIT2                       1001
#define IDC_STATIC                      -1

// Next default values for new objects
//
#ifdef APSTUDIO_INVOKED
#ifndef APSTUDIO_READONLY_SYMBOLS
#define _APS_NEXT_RESOURCE_VALUE        132
#define _APS_NEXT_COMMAND_VALUE         32771
#define _APS_NEXT_CONTROL_VALUE         1002
#define _APS_NEXT_SYMED_VALUE           110
#endif
#endif
```

Can you find the numeric values associated with the menu ID values?

Keyboard Accelerators   Keyboard accelerators are most often used by menu designers as a sort of "fast-key" combination for selecting menu items. For example, a menu may have 12 color items for selecting a background color. The user can point and click the menu for each color in the normal fashion or, with a keyboard accelerator, simply hit a special key combination. If a keyboard accelerator is used, the function keys (F1 to F12) for example, could be used for color selection without the menu popping up at all.

WINDOWS AND WIZARDS

Dialog Box Data Entry

You have already learned that menus are considered a means of simple data entry. This section investigates a more significant means of data entry—the dialog box. While data can be entered directly into the application's client area, dialog boxes are the preferred entry form for maintaining consistency across Windows programs.

Dialog boxes allow the user to check items in a window list, set buttons for various choices, directly enter strings and integers from the keyboard, and indirectly enter real numbers (floats). A special form of control can also be used in a dialog box. *Combo boxes* allow a combination of a single-line edit field and list boxes. The dialog box is the programmer's key to serious data entry in Windows programs. The dialog box is also the programmer's secret for ease of programming since Windows handles all necessary program overhead.

Dialog boxes can be called when selected as a choice from a menu and appear as a pop-up window to the user. To distinguish a dialog box choice from ordinary selections in a menu, three dots (an ellipsis) follow the dialog option name. In a previous section, the About Box and Input... menu items referred to dialog box selections.

The graphical design of a dialog box is eventually converted to a resource script file. The specifications that make up a dialog box are typically produced with the dialog box resource editor. The resource editor is designed to read and save dialog resource files in the text (.rc) and compiled format (.res). Text files make it easy to combine several menu and dialog box specifications in one file.

Dialog Box Concepts   Dialog boxes are actually "child" windows that pop up when selected from the user's menu. When various dialog box buttons, check boxes, and so on are selected, Windows provides the means necessary for processing the message information.

Dialog boxes can be produced in two basic styles—modal and modeless. Modal dialog boxes are the most popular and are used for the example developed in the next chapter. When a modal dialog box is created, no other options within the current program will be available until the user ends the dialog box by clicking an OK or Cancel button. The OK button will process any new information selected by the user, while the Cancel button will return the user to the original window without processing new information. Windows expects the ID values for these push buttons to be 1 and 2, respectively.

Modeless dialog boxes are more closely related to ordinary windows. A pop-up window can be created from a parent window, and the user can switch back and forth between the two. The same thing is permitted with a modeless dialog box. Modeless dialog boxes are preferred when a certain option must remain on the screen, such as a color select dialog box.

Dialog Box Design

If you are creating a new dialog box from scratch for your project you should use the dialog box resource editor. The next few sections discuss the fundamentals of using the resource editor to create and modify a dialog box. Microsoft's on-line help utility will provide additional information for more advanced features and editing.

Reconsider the dialog box resource script file, shown earlier in this chapter, to convince yourself of the need of a resource editor for dialog boxes. The resource editor allows you to design the dialog box in a graphical environment.

Examine the dialog box resource script file, shown earlier. Ask yourself the following questions. Where do all those terms come from? What do all those numbers mean? How could I figure all of this out without the resource editor? I would have to create, size, and place dialog boxes and their associated controls on the screen experimentally. The resource editor, on the other hand, will do all this for you automatically. Except for being able to make the claim that you created a dialog box without the resource editor at least once in your life, there is no reason for designing dialog boxes without the graphical environment of the editor.

Dialog Box Mechanics

Select View | Resource View. Double-click the existing .rc file and select the dialog box option from the list of possible resources. Right-click the DIALOG item and choose the Insert Dialog option. A screen similar to the one in Figure 20-11 should appear.

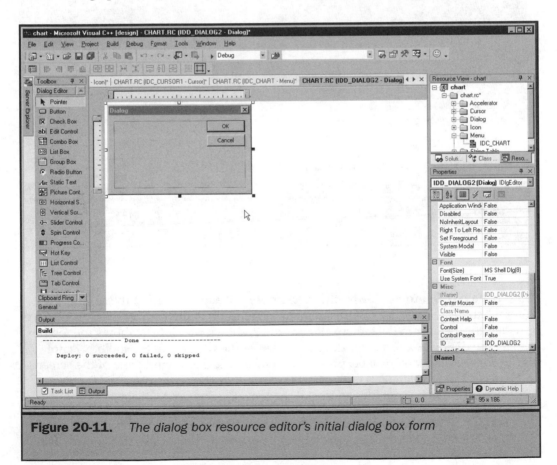

Figure 20-11. *The dialog box resource editor's initial dialog box form*

The screen now contains the initial outline for the new dialog box. This initial dialog box can be moved about the screen and sized to fit your needs. The screen in Figure 20-12 shows the initial dialog box with the OK button moved to a new position.

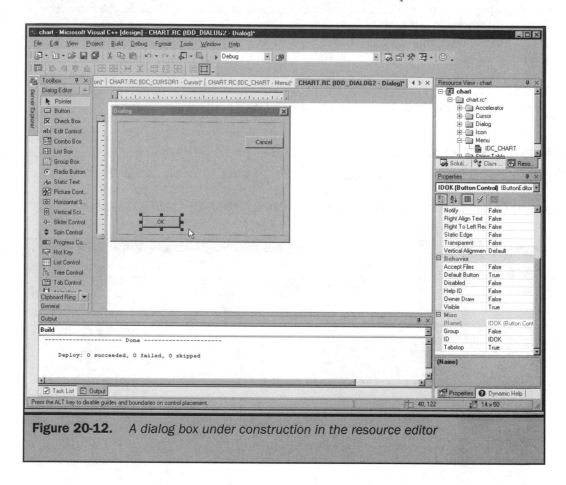

Figure 20-12.   *A dialog box under construction in the resource editor*

Placing Toolbox Controls   By far the most important aspect of using the resource editor when designing dialog boxes is an understanding of the various controls that are provided for the user in the toolbox. Figure 20-12, shown previously, shows the toolbox used by the dialog box resource editor to the left of the window. If the toolbox is not displayed, click the toolbox label presented in the vertical left-hand pane of the screen.

Here is a brief explanation of the most important toolbox controls. The Visual C++ 7.0 compiler's toolbox provides an icon of the tool along with a text label.

Static Text control   Allows the insertion of labels and strings within the dialog box. These can be used, for example, to label an Edit Box. Select this control using the toolbox icon with the upper- and lowercase characters.

The Group Box control   Creates a rectangular outline within a dialog box to enclose a group of controls that are to be used together. A group box contains a label on its upper-left edge. Select this control using the toolbox icon with the rectangular outline with text on the upper edge.

The Check Box control   Creates a small square box, called a check box, with a label to its right. Check boxes are usually marked or checked by clicking with the mouse, but they can also be selected with the keyboard. Several check boxes usually appear together in a dialog box; they allow the user to check one or more features at the same time. Select this control using the toolbox icon with the "x" or check mark located in a small rectangular region.

The Combo Box control   Is made up of two elements. It is a combination of a single-line edit field (also called a Static Text control) and a List Box control. With a combo box, the user has the ability to enter something into the edit box or scroll through the list box looking for an appropriate selection. Windows provides several styles of combo boxes. Select this control using the toolbox icon with three rectangular areas. This control is located under the Check Box control.

The Horizontal Scroll Bar control   Allows horizontal scroll bars to be created for the dialog box. These are usually used in conjunction with another window or control that contains text or graphics information. Select this control using the toolbox icon with the left and right directional arrows.

The Spin control   Creates two small rectangular areas, one on top of the other. The top area has an upward pointing arrow and the bottom a downward pointing arrow. This control functions like the thumb-wheel control on the new Microsoft mouse, allowing you to click selections up or down. Select this control using the toolbox icon with the two pyramid shapes (one upright and one upside down).

The Slider control   Initially creates a horizontal slider button and track. The control can be changed to a vertical Slider control by changing the property of the control once it is placed in the dialog box. Slider controls are used frequently in place of scroll bars when simpler actions are required. Select this control using the toolbox icon with the slider button and horizontal track.

The List control   Contains a rectangular area for a list of items (these may be small iconic images) and a vertical scroll bar. This control is similar to the List Box control, but contains the vertical scroll bar. Select this control using the toolbox icon with the nine small images within the rectangular area.

The Tab control   Is used when a dialog box is to contain a large amount of information. Instead of creating a complicated dialog box with one screen, the tab control allows the user to flip to different pages within the dialog box. Each page then contains just a portion of the overall information. Select this control using the toolbox icon with the small tab folder.

The Rich Edit control   Allows the user to enter and edit multiple lines of text. Formatting can be applied as well as embedded OLE objects. Select this control using the toolbox icon with underlined "ab" characters.

WINDOWS AND WIZARDS

The Picture control   Allows a rectangular area to be placed in the dialog box where a bitmapped image can be placed. Select this control using the toolbox icon with the small picture.

The Edit Box control   Creates a small interactive rectangle on the screen in which the user can enter string information. The edit box can be sized to accept short or long strings. This string information can be processed directly as character or numeric integer data and indirectly as real-number data in the program. The edit box is the most important control for data entry. Select this control using the toolbox icon with the lower case "ab" characters.

The Button control   Is a small, slightly rounded, rectangular button that can be sized. The button contains a label within it. The user uses buttons for an immediate choice such as accepting or canceling the dialog box selections made. Select this control using the toolbox icon with the rounded rectangular shape.

The Radio Button control   Creates a small circle, called a radio button, with a label to its right. Radio buttons, like check boxes, typically appear in groups. However, unlike check boxes, only one radio button can be selected at a time in any particular group. Select this control using the toolbox icon with the small bull's eye.

The List Box control   Creates a rectangular outline with a vertical scroll bar. List boxes are useful when scrolling is needed to allow the user to select a file from a long directory listing. Select this control using the toolbox icon with the rectangular area and an upward and downward facing arrow.

The Vertical Scroll Bar control   Allows vertical scroll bars to be created for the dialog box. These are usually used in conjunction with another window or control that contains text or graphics information. Select this control using the toolbox icon with the upward and downward facing arrows.

The Progress control   Produces a small bar that an application can use to indicate the progress of an operation. The progress bar is filled from left to right. Select this control using the toolbox icon with the small progress bar image.

The Hot Key control   Enables the creation of a hot key. A hot key is a key or key combination that allows the quick selection of items such as menu selections and so on. Select this control using the toolbox icon with the button and finger combination.

The Tree control   Displays a list of data in a tree structure. This control is helpful when you wish to convey to the user a hierarchical structure. Select this control using the toolbox icon with the small tree structure image.

The Animate control   Supports the displays of an AVI clip (Audio Video Interleaved). The clip is created as a short series of bitmap frames. This is the technique used for making animated cursors. Select this control using the toolbox icon with the two file frames.

The Custom Control control   Allows the use of existing custom or user controls. This technique has been replaced by the use of ActiveX controls and is included to be backward compliant. Developers should elect to use ActiveX controls. Select this control using the toolbox icon with the image of a person.

You can place controls from this toolbox in the current dialog box outline by selecting the appropriate control from the toolbox, positioning the mouse pointer in the dialog box, and clicking the mouse button. If the placement is not where you desired, you can use the mouse for repositioning. It is also possible to size the controls once they are placed.

Editing a Dialog Box

In this section, we'll complete our dialog box design. Figure 20-13 shows the default dialog box for this project, with a static text and edit box added to the design.

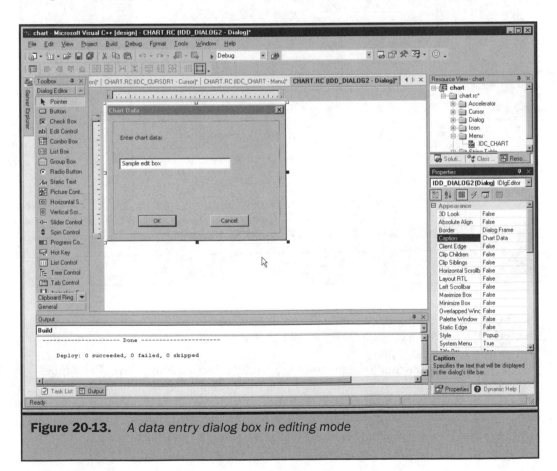

Figure 20-13.   *A data entry dialog box in editing mode*

The mouse can be used to place, size, and position the static text box and edit controls. Clicking the mouse within the dialog box, after positioning it, will allow editing of the actual text string. Figure 20-14 shows a completed data entry dialog box.

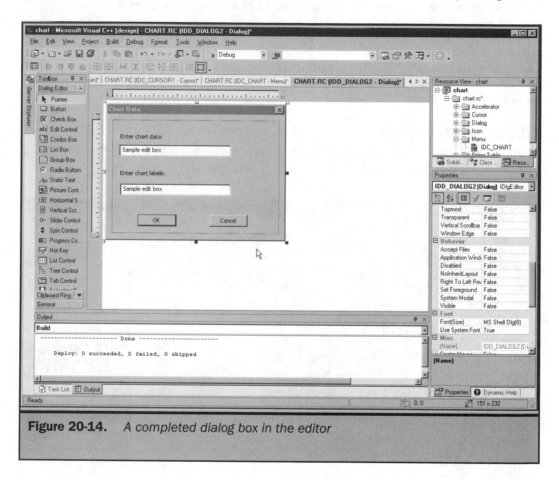

Figure 20-14.   *A completed dialog box in the editor*

The strings currently displayed in the static text control, in this figure, are entered by changing the control's caption. Simply right-click a particular control and examine and edit any desired control property.

The dialog box information can then be saved by selecting File | Save. Remember that the resource editor will save this file in the text (.rc) or compiled resource form (.res). Using the resource editor to create dialog boxes is a skill learned with practice. Large dialog boxes, utilizing many controls, will initially take hours to design. Again, use the detailed information contained in the Help menu or your Microsoft user's manuals. Start with simple dialog boxes and work toward more complicated designs.

Examining the Resource Script   You can examine the script file information once the resource is saved as an .rc file. Use any ASCII text editor to see how the data entry dialog box description appears.

The following listing shows a portion of the resource script file that describes this dialog box:

```
IDD_DIALOG1 DIALOGEX 0, 0, 228, 146
STYLE DS_MODALFRAME | WS_POPUP | WS_CAPTION | WS_SYSMENU
CAPTION "Chart Data"
FONT 8, "MS Sans Serif"
BEGIN
    DEFPUSHBUTTON      "OK",IDOK,34,115,50,14
    PUSHBUTTON         "Cancel",IDCANCEL,151,114,50,14
    LTEXT              "Enter chart data:",IDC_STATIC,17,15,89,16
    EDITTEXT           IDC_EDIT1,17,36,177,16,ES_AUTOHSCROLL
    LTEXT              "Enter chart labels:",IDC_STATIC,18,65,88,18
    EDITTEXT           IDC_EDIT2,19,80,176,17,ES_AUTOHSCROLL
END
```

The name of this dialog box is IDD_DIALOG1. The editor has affixed various segment values along with size specifications for the box. The various style options further identify the dialog box as one that has a modal frame, is a pop-up type, and so on. Several controls are listed.

The first and second controls are for the OK and CANCEL push buttons. The text within the first set of double quotes specifies what will appear within the push button. The labels for the ID values for the push button are a system default.

The two LTEXT controls represent two static text controls where the text will be left justified. The dialog box is completed with two EDITTEXT controls that allow a user to type in values from the keyboard.

Remember that it is not necessary to view this information at all. The resource editor will convert the graphics dialog box you see on the screen directly into a compiled resource file (.res). The only time you will need this information is when you are entering dialog box specifications from a book or magazine.

Resource Statements

A project's resource information is usually contained in a file with an .rc file extension. Suppose a project uses a resource script file called myres.rc:

```
myicon ICON myicon.ico
mycursor CURSOR mycursor.cur
mybitmap BITMAP mybitmap.bmp
```

Remember that myres.rc is a resource script or text file that defines three new resources. The names of the three resources are myicon, mycursor, and mybitmap. **ICON**, **CURSOR**, and **BITMAP** are reserved keywords defining the type of the resource. These are followed by the actual filenames containing the resource information, for example, myicon.ico, mycursor.cur, and mybitmap.bmp.

There are five additional options that can be included with each single-line statement. These options follow the resource-type keyword and include PRELOAD, LOADONCALL, FIXED, MOVEABLE, and DISCARDABLE. The first two options define load options; the latter define memory options. For example:

```
resourceID resource-type [[load-option]] [[memory-option]]
         filename
```

The PRELOAD option automatically loads the resource whenever the application is run. LOADONCALL loads the resource only when it is called.

If a FIXED memory option is selected, the resource remains at a fixed memory address. Selecting MOVEABLE allows Windows to move the resource to compact and conserve memory. The last choice, DISCARDABLE, allows Windows to discard the resource if it is no longer needed. However, it can be reloaded should a call be made requesting the particular resource. For example, making mybitmap LOADONCALL and DISCARDABLE is as simple as entering the following modified single-line statement into the resource script:

```
myicon ICON myicon.ico
mycursor CURSOR mycursor.cur
mybitmap BITMAP LOADONCALL DISCARDABLE mybitmap.bmp
```

Compiling Resources

Resource script files must be compiled into resource files. The resource compiler is responsible for this operation. The resource compiler can be run from the command line or, more typically, with the use of the project utility.

The command to run the resource compiler includes the name of the resource script file, the name of the executable file that will receive the compiler's binary format output, and any optional instructions.

The syntax for using the resource compiler from the command line is simple. From the command line, type:

```
rc [[compiler options]] filename.rc [[executable filename]]
```

For example, invoking the resource compiler with the example resource script described earlier would look like one of the following three lines:

```
rc myres
rc myres.rc
rc -r myres.rc
```

The first two examples read the myres.rc resource script file, create the compiled resource file myres.res, and copy the resources into the executable file myres.exe. The third command performs the same actions except that it does *not* put the resource into myres.exe. If the third command were executed, the myres.res binary file could be added to the myres.exe file at a later date by using the following command structure:

```
rc myres.res
```

This causes the resource compiler to search for the compiled resource file (.res) and places it into the executable file (.exe) of the same filename.

What's Coming?

This chapter has examined many terms and definitions common to the Windows ME, 2000, and XP programming environments. You have also learned specific information regarding applications that can be developed with both procedure-oriented and object-oriented approaches.

In addition to the information contained in this chapter, the Microsoft user's guides provide a wealth of information on each of these topics. While using the various resource editors, avail yourself of the extensive built-in help engine that is available. Details on the creation of actual Windows resources can be found in the books mentioned in earlier chapters and in various magazine articles. Developing serious Windows code is a major undertaking, but don't forget to have fun while learning.

In Chapter 21 you'll expand your Windows application talents by learning how to use various Wizards included with your C++ compiler.

WINDOWS AND WIZARDS

Visual C++.NET

Chapter 21

Wizards and Procedure-Oriented Windows Applications

The previous chapter concentrated on Windows terms, definitions, and tools in order to prepare you for the procedure-oriented applications developed in this chapter. The most attractive features of Windows applications are the common visual interface, device independence, and concurrent execution. It is now time to put theory to practice and develop applications with these exciting features.

This chapter teaches you how to write procedure-oriented Windows applications in C++ using various Wizards provided with your Visual C++ compiler. Later, in Chapters 22 and 23 you will learn how to create object-oriented Windows applications. These applications incorporate the Microsoft's Foundation Class (MFC) library into your code. Even if you plan to do all of your development work in object-oriented C++, this is still an important chapter for you to study. By studying the applications developed in this chapter, you'll have a much better understanding of how the Microsoft Foundation Class library aids in C++ code development.

An Application Framework

This section describes the various components that make up a project named swp (simple windows program). The swp project incorporates all of the Windows components minimally necessary to create and display a window (a main window with a border, a title bar, a system menu, and maximize/minimize boxes), draw a diagonal line, print a text message, and allow you to gracefully exit the application. You'll also learn that the swp project (and its related files) is a template for almost all Windows procedure-oriented applications. Understanding code, such as that used in this project, will save you time and help foster an understanding of how Windows applications are put together and why they work.

Table 21-1 summarizes frequently encountered data types that were discussed in Chapter 20.

Type	Description
CALLBACK	Replaces FAR PASCAL in application's callback routine.
HANDLE	A 32-bit unsigned integer that is used as a handle.
HDC	A handle to a device context.
HWND	A 32-bit unsigned integer that is used as the handle to a window.
LONG	A 32-bit signed integer.

Table 21-1. *Frequently Encountered Win32 Types*

Type	Description
LPARAM	Type used for declaration of lParam.
LPCSTR	LPCSTR is the same as LPSTR, but is used for read-only string pointers.
LPSTR	A 32-bit pointer.
LPVOID	A generic pointer type. It is equivalent to (void *).
LRESULT	Used for the return value of a window procedure.
NULL	An integral zero value. It is frequently used to trigger default parameters or actions for a function.
UINT	An unsigned integer type. The host environment determines the size of UINT. For Windows 95 and NT it is 32 bits.
WCHAR	A 16-bit UNICODE character. WCHAR is used to represent all of the symbols for all of the world's languages.
WINAPI	Replaces FAR PASCAL in API declarations.
WPARAM	Used for the declaration of wParam.

Table 21-1.   *Frequently Encountered Win32 Types (continued)*

There are a number of structures that are frequently encountered by Windows programmers. Table 21-2 will serve as a quick reference for these structures.

Structure	Description
MSG	Defines the fields of an input message.
PAINTSTRUCT	Defines the paint structure used when drawing inside a window.
RECT	Defines a rectangle.
WNDCLASS	Defines a window class.

Table 21-2.   *Frequently Encountered Win32 Structures*

WINDOWS AND WIZARDS

We're now ready to examine the components of a Windows application using these tools.

Windows Application Components

Windows applications contain two common and essential elements, the WinMain() function and a window function. The main body of your application is named WinMain(). WinMain() serves as the entry point for the Windows application and acts similarly to the main function in standard C++ programs.

The window function, not to be confused with WinMain(), has a unique role. Recall that a Windows application never directly accesses any window functions. When a Windows application attempts to execute a standard window function, it makes a request to Windows to carry out the specified task. For this reason, all Windows applications must have a call back window function. The call back function is registered with Windows and is called back whenever Windows executes an operation on a window.

The WinMain() Function

A WinMain() function is required by all Windows applications. This is the point at which program execution begins and usually ends. The WinMain() function is responsible for

- Creating and initiating the application's message processing loop (which accesses the program's message queue)
- Performing any required initializations
- Registering the application's window class type
- Terminating the program, usually upon receiving a WM_QUIT message

Four parameters are passed to the WinMain() function from Windows. The following code segment illustrates these required parameters as they are used in the swp.cpp file of the swp project:

```
int APIENTRY WinMain(HINSTANCE hInstance,
                     HINSTANCE hPreInstance,
                     LPSTR     lpCmdLine,
                     int       nCmdShow)
```

The first formal parameter to WinMain() is *hInstance,* which contains the instance handle of the application. This number uniquely identifies the program when it is running under Windows.

The second formal parameter, *hPreInstance,* will always contain a NULL indicating that there is no previous instance of this application.

MS-DOS versions of Windows (Windows 3.3 and earlier) used hPreInstance to indicate whether there were any previous copies of the program loaded. Under operating systems, such as Windows ME and 2000, each application runs in its own separate address space. For this reason, under Windows ME and 2000, hPreInstance will never return a valid previous instance, just NULL.

The third parameter, *lpCmdLine*, is a long pointer to a null-terminated string that represents the application's command-line arguments. Normally, *lpszCmdLine* contains a NULL if the application was started using the Windows Run command.

The fourth and last formal parameter to WinMain() is *nCmdShow*. The **int** value stored in *nCmdShow* represents one of the many Windows predefined constants defining the possible ways a window can be displayed, such as SW_SHOWNORMAL, SW_SHOWMAXIMIZED, or SW_SHOWMINIMIZED.

WNDCLASSEX

The WinMain() function registers the application's main window class. Every window class is based on a combination of user-selected styles, fonts, caption bars, icons, size, placement, and so on. The window class serves as a template that defines these attributes.

Under earlier versions of Windows running over DOS, registered window classes became available to all programs running under Windows. For this reason, the programmer had to use caution when naming and registering classes to make certain that those names used did not conflict with any other application window classes. Windows ME and 2000 require that every instance (each copy of an application) must register its own window class.

Basically, the same standard C++ structure type is used for all Windows class definitions. The following example is taken directly from winuser.h, which is an **#include** file referenced in windows.h. The header file contains a **typedef** statement defining the structure type WNDCLASSEX:

```
typedef struct _WNDCLASSEX {
    UINT     style;
    WNDPROC  lpfnWndProc;
    int      cbClsExtra;
    int      cbWndExtra;
    HANDLE   hInstance;
    HICON    hIcon;
    HCURSOR  hCursor;
    HBRUSH   hbrBackground;
    LPCTSTR  lpszMenuName;
    LPCTSTR  lpszClassName;
    HICON    hIconSm;
} WNDCLASSEX;
```

Windows provides several predefined window classes, but most applications define their own window classes. To define a window class, your application must define a structure variable of the following type:

```
WNDCLASSEX wcex;
```

The *wcex* structure is then filled with information about the window class. The following sections describe the various fields within the WNDCLASSEX structure. Some of the fields may be assigned a NULL, directing Windows to use predefined values, while others must be given specific values.

style   The style field names the class style. The styles can be combined with the bitwise OR operator. The style field is made up of a combination of the values shown in Table 21-3.

Value	Meaning
CS_BYTEALIGNCLIENT	Aligns a client area on a byte boundary
CS_BYTEALIGNWINDOW	Aligns a window on the byte boundary
CS_CLASSDC	Provides the window class a display context
CS_DBLCLKS	Sends a double-click message to the window
CS_GLOBALCLASS	States that the window class is an application Global class
CS_HREDRAW	Redraws the window when horizontal size changes
CS_NOCLOSE	Inhibits the close option from the system menu
CS_OWNDC	Each window receives an instance for its own Display context (DC)
CS_PARENTDC	Sends the parent window's display context (DC) To the window class
CS_SAVEBITS	Saves that part of a screen that is covered by another window
CS_VREDRAW	Redraws the window when the vertical size changes

Table 21-3.   *Frequently Used Windows Styles*

lpfnWndProc   *lpfnWndProc* receives a pointer to the window function that will carry out all of the tasks for the window.

cbClsExtra   *cbClsExtra* gives the number of bytes that must be allocated after the window class structure. It can be set to NULL.

cbWndExtra   *cbWndExtra* gives the number of bytes that must be allocated after the window instance. It can be set to NULL.

hInstance   *hInstance* defines the instance of the application registering the window class. This must be an instance handle and cannot be set to NULL.

hIcon   *hIcon* defines the icon to be used when the window is minimized. This can be set to NULL.

hCursor   *hCursor* defines the cursor to be used with the application. This handle can be set to NULL. The cursor is valid only within the application's client area.

hbrBackground   *hbrBackground* provides the identification for the background brush. This can be a handle to the physical brush or it can be a color value. Color values must be selected from one of the standard colors in the following list. A value of 1 must be added to the selected color.

```
COLOR_ACTIVEBORDER

COLOR_ACTIVECAPTION

COLOR_APPWORKSPACE

COLOR_BACKGROUND

COLOR_BTNFACE

COLOR_BTNSHADOW

COLOR_BTNTEXT

COLOR_CAPTIONTEXT

COLOR_GRAYTEXT

COLOR_HIGHLIGHT

COLOR_HIGHLIGHTTEXT

COLOR_INACTIVEBORDER

COLOR_INACTIVECAPTION

COLOR_MENU

COLOR_MENUTEXT

COLOR_SCROLLBAR
```

```
COLOR_WINDOW

COLOR_WINDOWFRAME

COLOR_WINDOWTEXT
```

If *hbrBackground* is set to NULL, the application paints its own background.

lpszMenuName   *lpszMenuName* is a pointer to a null-terminated character string. The string is the resource name of the menu. This item can be set to NULL.

lpszClassName   *lpszClassName* is a pointer to a null-terminated character string. The string is the name of the window class.

hIconSm   This member is used as the handle to the small icon associated with a window class. Predefined window classes are available but most programmers define their own window class.

Defining a Window Class

An application can define its own window class by defining a structure of the appropriate type and then filling the structure's fields with the information about the window class.

The following listing is from the swp project, created later in this chapter, and demonstrates how the WNDCLASSEX structure has been defined and initialized:

```
WNDCLASSEX wcex;

    wcex.cbSize = sizeof(WNDCLASSEX);
    wcex.style          = CS_HREDRAW | CS_VREDRAW;
    wcex.lpfnWndProc    = (WNDPROC)WndProc;
    wcex.cbClsExtra     = 0;
    wcex.cbWndExtra     = 0;
    wcex.hInstance      = hInstance;
    wcex.hIcon          = LoadIcon(hInstance, (LPCTSTR)IDI_SWP);
    wcex.hCursor        = LoadCursor(NULL, IDC_ARROW);
    wcex.hbrBackground  = (HBRUSH)(COLOR_WINDOW+1);
    wcex.lpszMenuName   = (LPCSTR)IDC_SWP;
    wcex.lpszClassName  = szWindowClass;
    wcex.hIconSm        = LoadIcon(wcex.hInstance, (LPCTSTR)IDI_SMALL);

    return RegisterClassEx(&wcex);
```

The *wcex.style* window class style has been set to CS_HREDRAW bitwise ORed with CS_VREDRAW. All window class styles have identifiers in winuser.h that begin with "CS_". Each identifier represents a bit value. The bitwise OR operation, |, is used to combine these bit flags. The two parameters used (CS_HREDRAW and CS_VREDRAW) instruct Windows to redraw the entire client area whenever the horizontal or vertical size of the window is changed.

The second parameter, *wcex*.lpfnWndProc, indicates the current instance of the application and is assigned the pointer address to the window function that will carry out all of the window's tasks. For the swp project, the function is called WndProc().

The next two fields, *wcApp.cppbClsExtra* and *wcApp.cppbWndExtra*, are frequently assigned 0. These fields are used to optionally indicate the count of extra bytes that may have been reserved at the end of the window class structure and the window data structure used for each window class.

The next field in WNDCLASSEX, *wcex.hInstance*, is assigned the instance handle returned in *hInstance* after WinMain() is invoked.

The swp project uses the IDI_SWP icon. This value is used for the *wcex.hIcon* parameter. Note that the icon is loaded with a call to the LoadIcon() function.

The *wcex.hCursor* field is assigned a handle to the instance's cursor, which in this example is IDC_ARROW (representing the default tilted arrow cursor). This assignment is accomplished through a call to the LoadCursor() function.

The *wcex.hbrBackground* parameter is used to set the background color of the client area within the application's window. The brush color is selected from a group of predefined brush colors. In this case COLOR_WINDOW+1 will select a white brush.

The *wcex.lpszMenuName* parameter is used to identify the name of the application's menu. By default, you will learn that the application Wizard creates a default menu and assigns the following IDC_SWP value to it.

The *wcex.lpszClassName* parameter is assigned the generic name *szWindowClass* for the swp project.

 WndProc() can be a user-defined function name and does not have to be the predefined function name assigned by the Wizard. The function must be prototyped before the assignment statement.

The final parameter, *wcex.hIconSm* is assigned the IDI_SMALL default icon ID. This icon is generated by the application Wizard. The icon can be edited, by the programmer, at a later date. The LoadIcon() function is used to load this resource into the application.

When all of these parameters are specified and accepted, the return value calls the RegisterClassEx() to register the window class.

Creating a Window

A window is displayed when a message is received and processed by InitInstance(). Since all windows are patterned after some predefined and registered class type, simply defining and then registering a window class has nothing to do with actually displaying a window in a Windows application. Examine the following code:

```
BOOL InitInstance(HINSTANCE hInstance, int nCmdShow)
{
```

```
    HWND hWnd;

    hInst = hInstance;

    hWnd = CreateWindow(szWindowClass, szTitle,
                        WS_OVERLAPPEDWINDOW,
                        CW_USEDEFAULT, 0,
                        CW_USEDEFAULT, 0,
                        NULL, NULL, hInstance, NULL);

    if (!hWnd)
    {
        return FALSE;
    }

    ShowWindow(hWnd, nCmdShow);
    UpdateWindow(hWnd);

    return TRUE;
}
```

Notice that a window is created with a call to the CreateWindow() function. This process is common for all versions of Windows. While the window class defines the general characteristics of a window, allowing the same window class to be used for many different windows, the parameters for CreateWindow() specify more detailed information about the window. If the function call is successful, CreateWindow() returns the handle of the newly created window. Otherwise, the function returns a NULL value.

The parameter information for the CreateWindow() function falls under the following categories: class, title, style, screen position, window's parent handle, menu handle, instance handle, and 32 bits of additional information.

The first field, *szWindowClass* (assigned earlier), defines the window's class, followed by the title to be used for the window's title bar. The style of the window is the third parameter (WS_OVERLAPPEDWINDOW). This standard Windows style represents a normal overlapped window with a caption bar, a system menu icon, minimize, maximize, and terminate icons, and a window frame.

The next six parameters (either CS_USEDEFAULT or NULL) represent the initial x and y positions and x and y size of the window, along with the parent window handle and window menu handle. Each of these fields has been assigned a default value. The *hInstance* field contains the instance of the program, followed by no additional parameters (NULL).

Showing and Updating a Window

Under Windows, the ShowWindow() function is needed to actually display a window. The following portion of code, from the swp.cpp file of the swp project, demonstrates this:

```
ShowWindow(hWnd,nCmdShow);
```

The handle of the window created by the call to CreateWindow() is held in the *hWnd* parameter. The second parameter to ShowWindow(), *nCmdShow*, determines how the window is initially displayed. This display mode is also referred to as the window's visibility state.

The *nCmdShow* parameter can specify that the window be displayed as a normal window (SW_SHOWNNORMAL) or in several other possible forms. For example, substituting *nCmdShow* with the winuser.h constant SW_SHOWMINNOACTIVE, as shown in the following line of code, causes the window to be drawn as an icon:

```
ShowWindow(hWnd,SW_SHOWMINNOACTIVE);
```

Other display possibilities include SW_SHOWMAXIMIZED, which causes the window to be active and fill the entire display, along with its counterpart, SW_SHOWMINIMIZED.

The final step in displaying a window requires a call to the Windows UpdateWindow() function:

```
UpdateWindow(hWnd);
```

A call to ShowWindow() with a SW_SHOWNORMAL parameter causes the function to erase the window's client area with the background brush specified in the window's class. It is the call to UpdateWindow() that generates the familiar WM_PAINT message, causing the client area to be painted.

The Message Loop

With everything in place, the application is ready to perform its main task: processing messages. Recall that Windows does not send input from the mouse or keyboard directly to an application. Windows places all input into the application's message queue. The message queue can contain messages generated by Windows or messages posted by other applications. Examine the following code:

```
// Main message loop:
    while (GetMessage(&msg, NULL, 0, 0))
    {
```

```
      if (!TranslateAccelerator(msg.hwnd, hAccelTable, &msg))
      {
          TranslateMessage(&msg);
          DispatchMessage(&msg);
      }
  }
```

The application needs a message-processing loop once the call to WinMain() has created and displayed the window. The most common approach is to use a standard **while** loop as shown in the previous listing.

The GetMessage() Function The next message to be processed from the application's message queue can be obtained with a call to the Windows GetMessage() function:

```
  while (GetMessage(&msg, NULL, 0, 0))
```

The GetMessage() function copies the message into the message structure pointed to by the long pointer, &msg, and sends the message structure to the main body of the program.

The NULL parameter instructs the function to retrieve any of the messages for any window that belongs to the application. The last two parameters, 0 and 0, tell GetMessage() not to apply any message filters. Message filters can restrict retrieved messages to specific categories such as keystrokes or mouse moves. These filters are referred to as *wMsgFilterMin* and *wMsgFilterMax* and specify the numeric filter extremes to apply.

Control can be returned to Windows at any time before the message loop is begun. For example, an application will normally make certain that all steps leading up to the message loop have executed properly. This can include making sure that each window class is registered and has been created. However, once the message loop has been entered, only one message can terminate the loop. Whenever the message to be processed is WM_QUIT, the value returned is FALSE. This causes the processing to proceed to the main loop's closing routine. The WM_QUIT message is the only way for an application to get out of the message loop.

The TranslateMessage() Function Virtual-key messages can be converted into character messages with the TranslateMessage() function. The function call is required only by applications that need to process character input from the keyboard. This ability can be very useful because it allows the user to make menu selections without having to use the mouse.

The TranslateMessage() function creates an ASCII character message (WM_CHAR) from a WM_KEYDOWN and WM_KEYUP message. As long as this function is included in the message loop, the keyboard interface will also be in effect.

The DispatchMessage() Function   Windows sends current messages to the correct window procedures with the DispatchMessage() function. This function makes it easy to add additional windows and dialog boxes to your application. DispatchMessage() automatically routes each message to the appropriate window procedure.

The Window Function

Recall that all applications must include a WinMain() function and a Windows call back function. Since a Windows application never directly accesses any Windows function, each application must make a request to Windows to carry out any specified operation.

A call back function is registered with Windows and is called back whenever Windows executes an operation on a window. The length of the actual code for the call back function will vary with each application. The window function itself may be very small, processing only one or two messages, or it may be large and complex.

The following code segment (minus application-specific statements) shows the call back window function, WndProc(), as it is used in the swp project:

```
LRESULT CALLBACK WndProc(HWND hWnd, UINT message,
                         WPARAM wParam, LPARAM lParam)
{
    int wmId, wmEvent;
    PAINTSTRUCT ps;
    HDC hdc;

    switch (message)
    {
    case WM_COMMAND:
        wmId    = LOWORD(wParam);
        wmEvent = HIWORD(wParam);
        // Parse the menu selections:
        switch (wmId)
        {
        case IDM_ABOUT:
            DialogBox(hInst, (LPCTSTR)IDD_ABOUTBOX, hWnd,
                      (DLGPROC)About);
            break;
        case IDM_EXIT:
            DestroyWindow(hWnd);
            break;
        default:
            return DefWindowProc(hWnd, message,
                                 wParam, lParam);
        }
        break;
    case WM_PAINT:
```

```
            hdc = BeginPaint(hWnd, &ps);
            // TODO: Add any drawing code here...
            EndPaint(hWnd, &ps);
            break;
        case WM_DESTROY:
            PostQuitMessage(0);
            break;
        default:
            return DefWindowProc(hWnd, message,
                                 wParam, lParam);
    }
    return 0;
}
```

Windows expects the name referenced by the *wcex.lpfnWndProc* field of the window class structure definition to match the name used for the call back function. WndProc() will be the name used for the call back function for all subsequent windows created from this window class.

Windows has several hundred different Windows messages that it can send to the window function. These messages are labeled with identifiers that begin with "WM_". For example, WM_COMMAND, WM_DESTROY, WM_INITDIALOG, and WM_PAINT are used quite frequently. These identifiers are also known as symbolic constants.

The first parameter to WndProc() is *hWnd*. The handle *hWnd* is a handle to the window to which Windows will send the message. Since it is possible for one window function to process messages for several windows created from the same window class, this handle is used by the window function to determine which window is receiving the message.

The second parameter to the function, *message*, specifies the actual message being processed as defined in winuser.h. The last two parameters, *wParam* and *lParam*, specify any additional information needed to process each specific message. Frequently, the value returned to each of these parameters is NULL. This means that they can be ignored. At other times, the parameters contain a 2-byte value and a pointer, or two word values.

The WndProc() function continues by defining two important variables: *hdc* specifies the display context handle, and *ps* specifies a PAINTSTRUCT structure needed to store client area information. The other variables, *wmId* and *wmEvent* are needed to process menu and dialog box selections.

The call back function is used to examine the type of message it is about to process and then select the appropriate action to be taken. This selection process usually takes place within a standard C++ **switch-case** statement.

Processing WM_PAINT Messages

This application will process WM_COMMAND, WM_PAINT, and WM_DESTROY messages. As an example, we'll investigate how WM_PAINT messages are handled in this application. Many Windows messages can be generated at any given time. WM_PAINT handles all windows paint messages. Here the Windows function BeginPaint() can be called. This function prepares the specified window for painting and fills a PAINTSTRUCT (&ps) with information about the area to be painted. The BeginPaint() function also returns a handle to the device context for the given window.

Because Windows is a multitasking operating system, it is possible for one application to display its window or dialog box over another application's client area. This creates a problem whenever the window or dialog box is closed: a hole appears on the screen where the dialog box was displayed. Windows handles this problem by sending the active application a WM_PAINT message. In this case, Windows requests that the active application update its client area.

Except for the first WM_PAINT message, which is sent by the call to UpdateWindow() in WinMain(), additional WM_PAINT messages are sent under the following conditions:

- When forcing a WM_PAINT message with a call to the InvalidateRect() or InvalidateRgn() function

- When resizing a window

- When using the ScrollWindow() function

- Whenever a portion of a client area has been hidden by a menu or dialog box that has just been closed

Here is how the process works. Any portion of an application's client area that has been corrupted by the overlay of a dialog box, for example, has that area of the client area marked as invalid. Windows makes the redrawing of a client area efficient by keeping track of the diagonal coordinates of this invalid rectangle. It is the presence of an invalid rectangle that prompts Windows to send the WM_PAINT message.

If several portions of the client area are invalidated, Windows will adjust the invalid rectangle coordinates to encapsulate all invalid regions. In other words, Windows does not send a WM_PAINT message for each invalid rectangle.

The call to InvalidateRect() allows Windows to mark the client area as invalid, thereby forcing a WM_PAINT message. An application can obtain the coordinates of the invalid rectangle by calling the GetUpdateRect() function. A call to the ValidateRect() function validates any rectangular region in the client area and deletes any pending WM_PAINT messages.

The EndPaint() function is called when the WndProc() function ends its processing of the WM_PAINT messages. This function is called whenever the application is finished outputting information to the client area. It tells Windows that the application has finished processing all paint messages and that it is now OK to remove the display context.

Processing the WM_DESTROY Message

When the Close option is selected by the user from an application's system menu, Windows posts a WM_DESTROY message to the application's message queue. The application terminates after it retrieves this message.

The DefWindowProc() Function

The DefWindowProc() function call, in the default section of WndProc()'s switch statement, is needed to empty the application's message queue of any unrecognized and/or unprocessed messages. This function ensures that all of the messages posted to the application are processed.

Creating a Procedure-Oriented Project with the Application Wizard

To create a procedure-oriented Windows application using the Visual C++ Application Wizard, simply start by opening the New Project dialog box as shown in Figure 21-1.

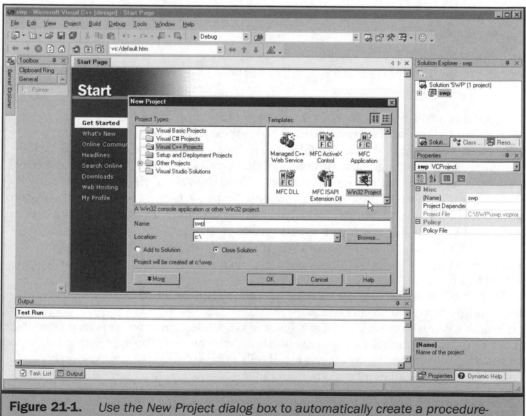

Figure 21-1. Use the New Project dialog box to automatically create a procedure-oriented Windows project.

This dialog box can be opened by selecting File | New Menu Item. You will be given a choice of creating a project or file. Choose the project option.

While in the New Project dialog box, select the Win32 Project option, name the new project (swp in this example) and set the location for the project's files (c:\ in this case). When you have completed these steps, click the OK button to open the next dialog box.

The Win32 Application Wizard dialog box will be opened next, as shown in Figure 21-2.

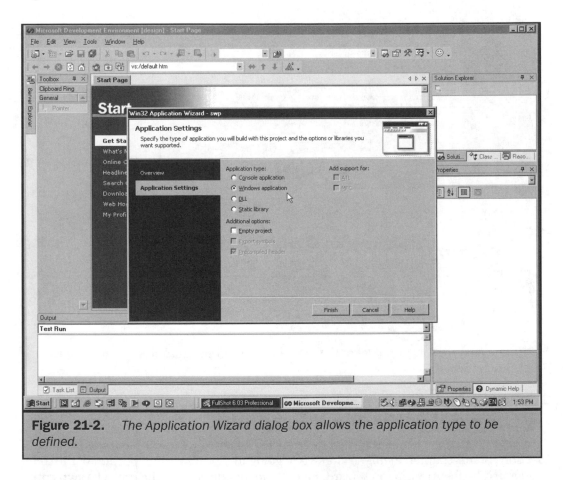

Figure 21-2. *The Application Wizard dialog box allows the application type to be defined.*

For procedure-oriented Windows applications, make sure the Windows Application button, on the Application Settings page, is selected. When the Finish button is selected, the Application Wizard will automatically create a number of files, including a basic source code file or template.

Figure 21-3 shows the Visual C++ design window with the source code file for the swp project opened.

At this point the project could be compiled, linked, and executed. However, all you would see would be the simple window shown in Figure 21-4.

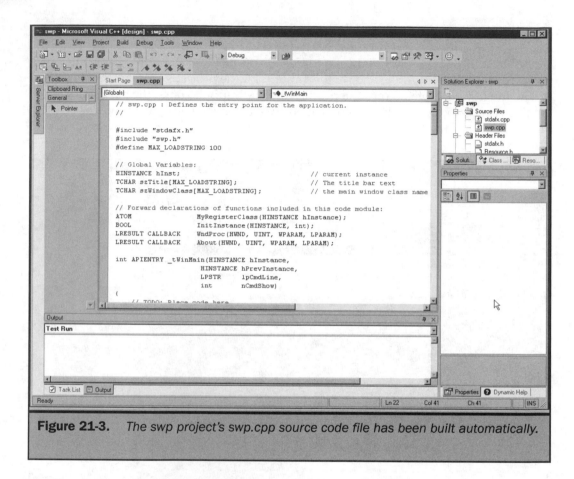

Figure 21-3.   *The swp project's swp.cpp source code file has been built automatically.*

In the next section, you'll learn how to add some simple graphics to the client area of this window.

A Complete Windows Program

We have been discussing portions of a completed swp project throughout the previous sections of this chapter. In this section we're going to modify a small portion of the code generated by the Application Wizard. Find the following code in the project's swp.cpp source code file:

```
case WM_PAINT:
    hdc = BeginPaint(hWnd, &ps);
    // TODO:  Add any drawing code here...
    EndPaint(hWnd, &ps);
    break;
```

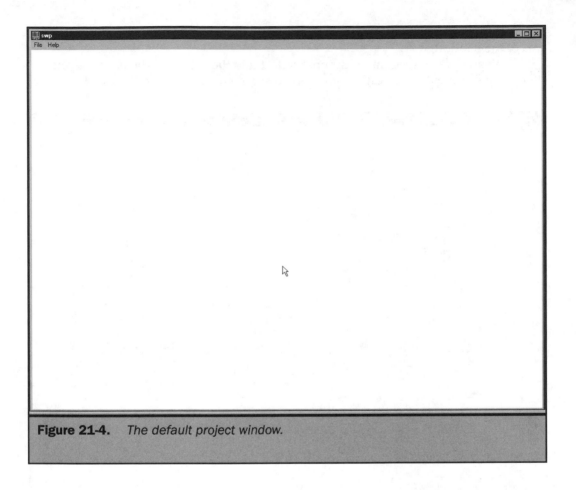

Figure 21-4. *The default project window.*

Now, modify the previous portion of code to match the code in the following listing:

```
case WM_PAINT:
    hdc = BeginPaint(hWnd, &ps);

    MoveToEx(hdc,0,0,NULL);
    LineTo(hdc,639,429);
    MoveToEx(hdc,300,0,NULL);
    LineTo(hdc,50,300);

    TextOut(hdc,120,30,"<- a few lines ->",17);

    EndPaint(hWnd, &ps);
    break;
```

This is all of the code necessary to draw two lines and draw some text in the client area of the window.

Once you have entered this additional code, build the project in the usual manner. When you execute the application, you should see a screen similar to Figure 21-5.

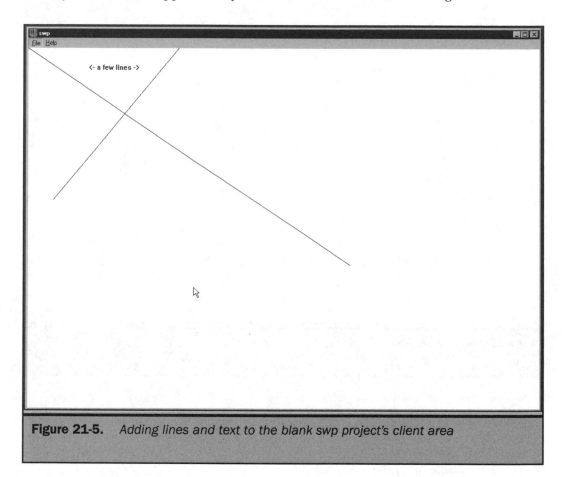

Figure 21-5. *Adding lines and text to the blank swp project's client area*

It is within the WM_PAINT portion of the swp.cpp source code file that you can experiment with a wide variety of Windows GDI graphics drawing functions. These drawing functions are often called drawing primitives.

Now, you can experiment with other GDI graphics primitives such as ellipses, chords, pie wedges, and rectangles. In the next section, you will see how these GDI primitives work.

Drawing an Ellipse

The Ellipse() function is used for drawing an ellipse or a circle. The center of the ellipse is also the center of an imaginary rectangle described by the points *x1,y1* and *x2,y2*, as shown in Figure 21-6.

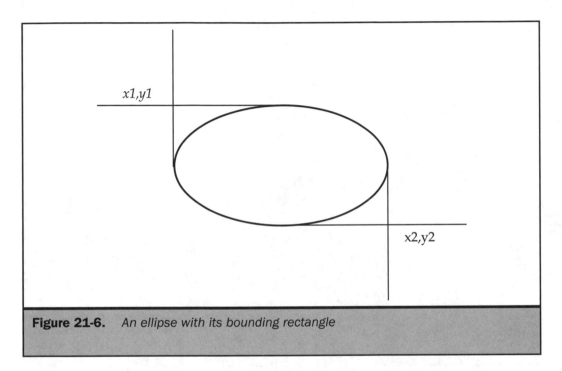

Figure 21-6. *An ellipse with its bounding rectangle*

An ellipse is a closed figure and filled with the current brush. The handle for the device context is given by *hdc*. All other parameters are of type **int**. This function returns a type **BOOL**.

The syntax for the command is:

```
Ellipse(hdc,x1,y1,x2,y2)
```

For example, the following code draws a small ellipse in the user's window:

```
Ellipse(hdc,200,200,275,250);
TextOut(hdc,210,215,"<- an ellipse",13);
```

Figure 21-7 shows how the ellipse will appear on the screen.

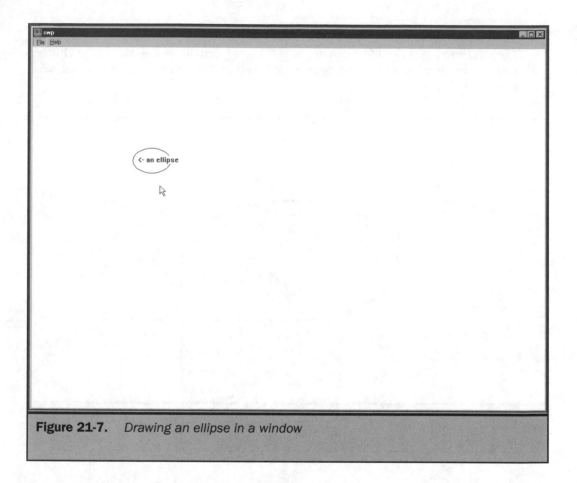

Figure 21-7. *Drawing an ellipse in a window*

Drawing other shapes in the client area is just as easy as drawing lines or text.

Drawing a Chord

The Chord() function is a closed figure with a line between two arc points, *x3,y3* and *x4,y4*. Figure 21-8 shows these points.

A chord is filled with the current brush. The handle for the device context is given by *hdc*. All other parameters are of type **int**. This function returns a type **BOOL**.

The syntax for the command is:

```
Chord(hdc,x1,y1,x2,y2,x3,y3,x4,y4)
```

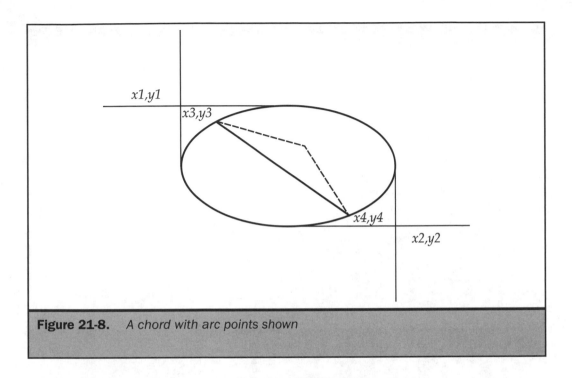

Figure 21-8. *A chord with arc points shown*

For example, the following code draws a small chord in the user's window:

```
Chord(hdc,550,20,630,80,555,25,625,70);
TextOut(hdc,470,30," A Chord ->",11);
```

Figure 21-9 shows the chord section and its location on the user's screen.

Drawing a Pie Wedge

Use the Pie() function for drawing pie-shaped wedges. The center of the elliptical arc is also the center of an imaginary rectangle described by the points *x1,y1* and *x2,y2*, as shown in Figure 21-10.

The starting and ending points of the arc are points *x3,y3* and *x4,y4*. Two lines are drawn from each end point to the center of the rectangle. Drawing is done in a counterclockwise direction. The pie wedge is filled because it is a closed figure. The handle for the device context is given by *hdc*. All other parameters are of type **int**. This function returns a type **BOOL**.

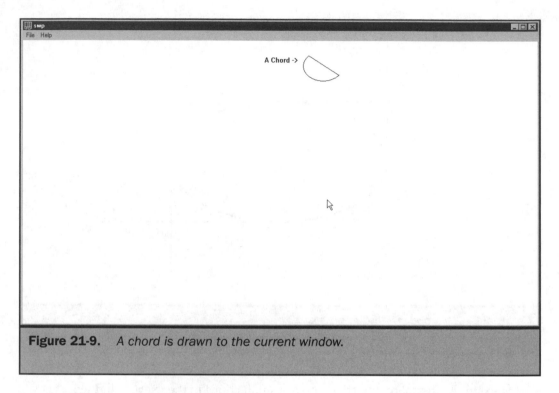

Figure 21-9. *A chord is drawn to the current window.*

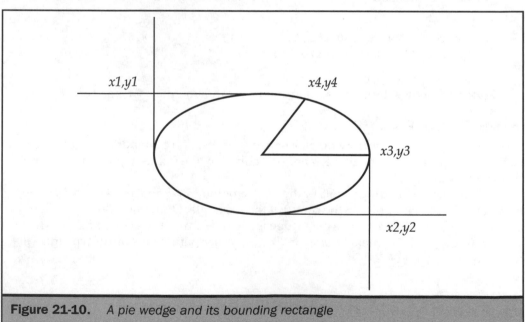

Figure 21-10. *A pie wedge and its bounding rectangle*

The syntax for the command is:

```
Pie(hdc,x1,y1,x2,y2,x3,y3,x4,y4)
```

For example, the following code draws a small pie-shaped wedge in the window:

```
Pie(hdc,300,50,400,150,300,50,300,100);
TextOut(hdc,350,80,"<- A Pie Wedge",14);
```

Figure 21-11 shows the pie wedge on the screen.
Pie wedge sizes can vary from a thin sliver to a full pie shape.

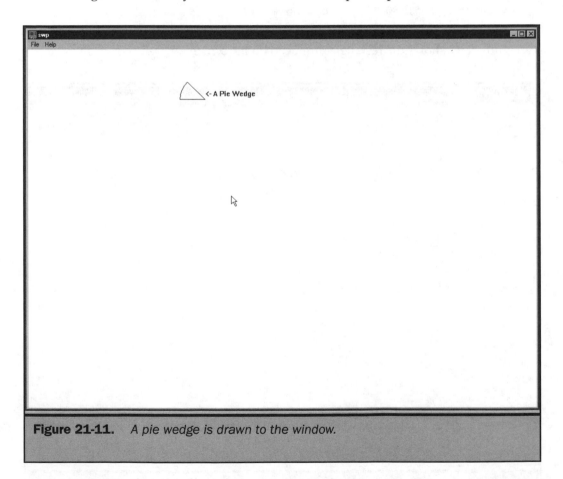

Figure 21-11.   *A pie wedge is drawn to the window.*

Drawing a Rectangle

The Rectangle() function draws a rectangle or box described by *x1,y1* and *x2,y2*. Again, the rectangle is filled because it is a closed figure. The handle for the device context is given by *hdc*. All other parameters are of type **int**. This function returns a type **BOOL**.

The syntax for the command is:

```
Rectangle(hdc,x1,y1,x2,y2)
```

As an example, the following code draws a rectangular figure in the user's window:

```
Rectangle(hdc,50,300,150,400);
TextOut(hdc,160,350,"<- A Rectangle",14);
```

Figure 21-12 shows the rectangle produced on the screen.

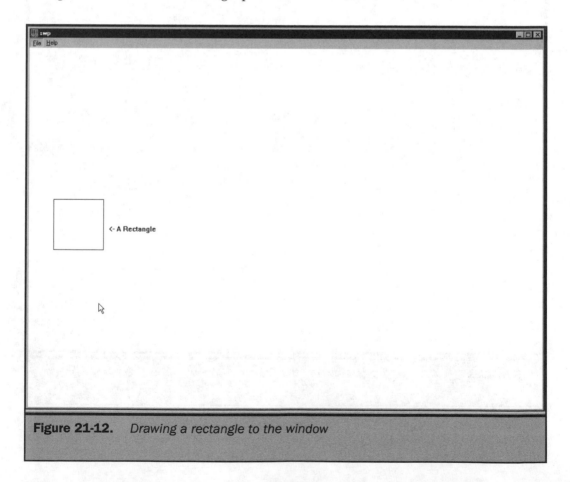

Figure 21-12.   *Drawing a rectangle to the window*

You'll find that rectangles can be sized from tiny dots to shapes that fill the whole screen. However, without additional work their lines are always drawn horizontally and vertically—never at an angle!

Another Practical Project

The previous section described the development of a simple project named swp. The next project illustrates how the same basic code can be modified to draw a sine wave in the client area of a window.

Create a new project named Sine, as you did in the previous section. Alter the Sine.cpp source code file to match the bolded portion of code in the following complete listing:

```
//
// Sine.cpp
// An application that draws a sine wave.
// Developed using swp.cpp as a template.
// Copyright (c) William H. Murray and Chris H. Pappas, 2001
//

#include "stdafx.h"
#include "Sine.h"
#include <windows.h>
#include <math.h>
#define MAX_LOADSTRING 100
#define pi 3.14159265359

// Global Variables:
HINSTANCE hInst;                         // current instance
TCHAR szTitle[MAX_LOADSTRING];           // The title bar text
TCHAR szWindowClass[MAX_LOADSTRING];     // The title bar text

// Foward declarations of functions included in this code module:
ATOM            MyRegisterClass(HINSTANCE hInstance);
BOOL            InitInstance(HINSTANCE, int);
LRESULT CALLBACK    WndProc(HWND, UINT, WPARAM, LPARAM);
LRESULT CALLBACK    About(HWND, UINT, WPARAM, LPARAM);

int APIENTRY WinMain(HINSTANCE hInstance,
                     HINSTANCE hPrevInstance,
                     LPSTR     lpCmdLine,
                     int       nCmdShow)
{
```

```
      // TODO: Place code here.
    MSG msg;
    HACCEL hAccelTable;

    // Initialize global strings
    LoadString(hInstance, IDS_APP_TITLE, szTitle, MAX_LOADSTRING);
    LoadString(hInstance, IDC_SINE, szWindowClass, MAX_LOADSTRING);
    MyRegisterClass(hInstance);

    // Perform application initialization:
    if (!InitInstance (hInstance, nCmdShow))
    {
        return FALSE;
    }

    hAccelTable = LoadAccelerators(hInstance, (LPCTSTR)IDC_SINE);

    // Main message loop:
    while (GetMessage(&msg, NULL, 0, 0))
    {
        if (!TranslateAccelerator(msg.hwnd, hAccelTable, &msg))
        {
            TranslateMessage(&msg);
            DispatchMessage(&msg);
        }
    }

    return msg.wParam;
}


//
//   FUNCTION: MyRegisterClass()
//
//   PURPOSE: Registers the window class.
//
//   COMMENTS:
//
//     This function and its usage are only necessary if
//     you want this code to be compatible with Win32
//     systems prior to the 'RegisterClassEx' function that
//     was added to Windows 95. It is important to call this
//     function so that the application will get 'well formed'
//     small icons associated with it.
//
```

```
ATOM MyRegisterClass(HINSTANCE hInstance)
{
    WNDCLASSEX wcex;

    wcex.cbSize = sizeof(WNDCLASSEX);

    wcex.style          = CS_HREDRAW | CS_VREDRAW;
    wcex.lpfnWndProc    = (WNDPROC)WndProc;
    wcex.cbClsExtra     = 0;
    wcex.cbWndExtra     = 0;
    wcex.hInstance      = hInstance;
    wcex.hIcon          = LoadIcon(hInstance,
                                    (LPCTSTR)IDI_SINE);
    wcex.hCursor        = LoadCursor(NULL, IDC_ARROW);
    wcex.hbrBackground  = (HBRUSH)(COLOR_WINDOW+1);
    wcex.lpszMenuName   = (LPCSTR)IDC_SINE;
    wcex.lpszClassName  = szWindowClass;
    wcex.hIconSm        = LoadIcon(wcex.hInstance,
                                    (LPCTSTR)IDI_SMALL);


    return RegisterClassEx(&wcex);
}


//
//   FUNCTION: InitInstance(HANDLE, int)
//
//   PURPOSE: Saves instance handle and creates main window
//
//   COMMENTS:
//
//        In this function, we save the instance handle in a
//        global variable and create and display the main
//        program window.
//
BOOL InitInstance(HINSTANCE hInstance, int nCmdShow)
{
   HWND hWnd;

   hInst = hInstance; // Store instance handle

   hWnd = CreateWindow(szWindowClass, szTitle,
                    WS_OVERLAPPEDWINDOW,
                    CW_USEDEFAULT, 0, CW_USEDEFAULT,
                    0, NULL, NULL, hInstance, NULL);
```

```cpp
    if (!hWnd)
    {
        return FALSE;
    }

    ShowWindow(hWnd, nCmdShow);
    UpdateWindow(hWnd);

    return TRUE;
}


//
//   FUNCTION: WndProc(HWND, unsigned, WORD, LONG)
//
//   PURPOSE:  Processes messages for the main window.
//
//   WM_COMMAND    - process the application menu
//   WM_PAINT      - Paint the main window
//   WM_DESTROY    - post a quit message and return
//
//
LRESULT CALLBACK WndProc(HWND hWnd, UINT message,
                         WPARAM wParam, LPARAM lParam)
{
    int wmId, wmEvent;
    PAINTSTRUCT ps;
    HDC hdc;

    double y;
    int i;

    switch (message)
    {
    case WM_COMMAND:
        wmId    = LOWORD(wParam);
        wmEvent = HIWORD(wParam);
        // Parse the menu selections:
        switch (wmId)
        {
        case IDM_ABOUT:
            DialogBox(hInst, (LPCTSTR)IDD_ABOUTBOX,
                      hWnd, (DLGPROC)About);
            break;
```

```
        case IDM_EXIT:
            DestroyWindow(hWnd);
            break;
        default:
            return DefWindowProc(hWnd, message,
                                 wParam, lParam);
        }
        break;
    case WM_PAINT:
        hdc = BeginPaint(hWnd, &ps);

        // draw the x & y coordinate axes
        MoveToEx(hdc, 100, 50, NULL);
        LineTo(hdc, 100, 350);
        MoveToEx(hdc, 100, 200, NULL);
        LineTo(hdc, 500, 200);
        MoveToEx(hdc, 100, 200, NULL);

        // draw the sine wave
        for (i = 0; i < 400; i++) {
            y = 120.0 * sin(pi * i * (360.0 / 400.0) / 180.0);
            LineTo(hdc, i + 100, (int) (200.0 - y));
        }

        EndPaint(hWnd, &ps);
        break;
    case WM_DESTROY:
        PostQuitMessage(0);
        break;
    default:
        return DefWindowProc(hWnd, message, wParam, lParam);
    }
    return 0;
}


// Message handler for about box.
LRESULT CALLBACK About(HWND hDlg, UINT message,
                       WPARAM wParam, LPARAM lParam)
{
    switch (message)
    {
    case WM_INITDIALOG:
        return TRUE;
```

```
    case WM_COMMAND:
        if (LOWORD(wParam) == IDOK ||
            LOWORD(wParam) == IDCANCEL)
        {
            EndDialog(hDlg, LOWORD(wParam));
            return TRUE;
        }
        break;
    }
    return FALSE;
}
```

Examine the source code just listed and compare it with the previous swp.cpp source code. As you can see, this application only needs minor changes to the swp.cpp source code to create an entirely new application.

Notice that new variables are declared in WndProc():

```
double y;
int i;
```

The actual sine wave plotting takes place under WM_PAINT. The coordinate axes are drawn with several calls to the MoveToEx() and LineTo() functions:

```
// draw the x & y coordinate axes
MoveToEx(hdc, 100, 50, NULL);
LineTo(hdc, 100, 350);
MoveToEx(hdc, 100, 200, NULL);
LineTo(hdc, 500, 200);
MoveToEx(hdc, 100, 200, NULL);
```

The sine wave is drawn and scaled in one operation. In this application, the waveform will extend 120 pixels above and below the horizontal axis. The sin() function from math.h is used to generate the sine values. The use of the constant pi is needed to convert angles from degrees to radians.

```
// draw the sine wave
for (i = 0; i < 400; i++) {
    y = 120.0 * sin(pi * i * (360.0 / 400.0) / 180.0);
    LineTo(hdc, i + 100, (int)(200.0 - y));
}
```

Since this application was designed to work in the default drawing mode, the program draws directly in screen pixels. On a VGA monitor, the figure will fill the entire screen. Figure 21-13 shows the output of the program on a 1024x768 graphics screen. As you can see the graphic does not fill the entire window.

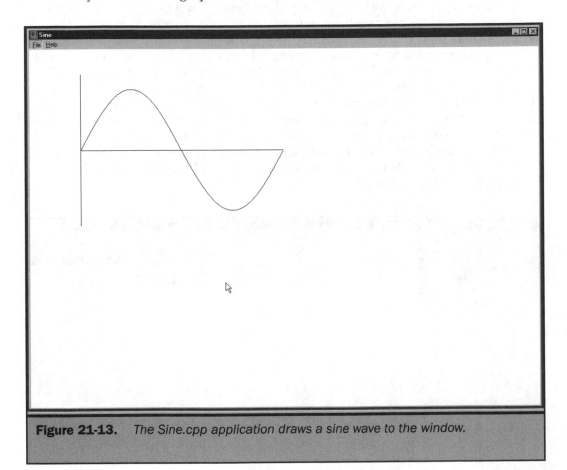

Figure 21-13. *The Sine.cpp application draws a sine wave to the window.*

Changes in figure size, such as this, are usually considered undesirable, and you'll see a technique for avoiding these variations in the pie chart project that follows.

Creating a Pie Chart Application

A pie chart is a useful business application that also allows you to incorporate many of the resources studied in the last chapter into a presentation-quality program. This particular pie chart will use a menu, the default About dialog box, and a data entry dialog box for user input. Recall that you learned how to design these items in the previous chapter. The data entry dialog box will prompt the user to enter up to ten numbers that define the size of each pie wedge. These integer numbers are then scaled in order to make each pie slice proportional in the 360-degree pie chart. Slices are colored in a sequential manner. The sequence is defined by the programmer and contained in the global array *lColor[]*. The program also allows the user to enter a title for the pie chart that is centered below the pie figure. You may wish to continue the development of this example by adding a legend, label, or value for each pie slice.

Create the project in the normal manner by selecting File | New and then choosing the Project option. From the New Project dialog box, select the Win32 Project option. Name the new project pie and set the directory for C:\. The Win32 Application Wizard dialog box will then allow you to select the Application Settings. From the Application Settings, select the Windows Application option. When you click the Finish button, the Win32 Application Wizard will create the template code for this project.

Use the Visual Studio's View menu to set the view to Resource View. If you expand the pie.rc file, as shown in the right pane of Figure 21-14, a list of possible resources for the project will be displayed.

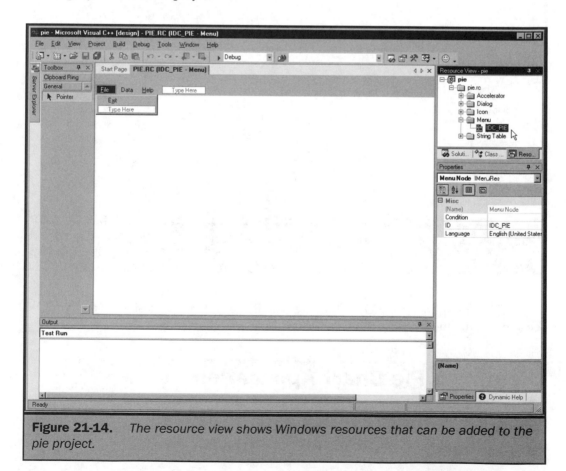

Figure 21-14. *The resource view shows Windows resources that can be added to the pie project.*

The first thing we'll alter in this project is the default menu bar. Left-click the menu item in the Resource View pane. The expanded menu resource list will then display IDC_PIE, which is the ID value for the default menu in this project. Left-double-click this item to bring up and display the project's menu in the design pane. This is the pane just to the left of the Resource View pane, shown earlier in Figure 21-14.

A new menu can be added to the menu bar by simply typing the new menu title on the menu bar. In Figure 21-14, we added a new menu named Data to the menu bar. In a similar manner, individual menu items, for any menu on the menu bar, can be added by typing the menu item in the space provided. In Figure 21-14, we have already added a menu item named Chart Values to the new Data menu.

The menu alteration is now complete for this project. Recall that a menu item followed by (…) ellipses means that the menu item, during operation, will bring up a dialog box.

Now, we need to add a new dialog box resource. Return to the Resource View pane and select the Dialog resource by left-clicking that item. Since we need to add a new dialog box, right-click the Dialog resource item to bring up a list of options. From the list, select Insert DIALOG. The Resource View pane in Figure 21-15 shows that we have already added another dialog box to the list. This dialog box is given the ID value of IDD_DIALOG1 by default.

A default dialog box is created immediately, as you learned in the previous chapter. Alter the default dialog box so that it takes on the appearance of the dialog box shown in the design pane of Figure 21-15.

This dialog box uses eleven Static Text and Edit Control controls. The Static Text controls are placed along the left vertical edge of the dialog box and the Edit Control controls just to the right of each of them. To view the control toolbox, select the tab named Toolbox, shown on the left-hand edge of Figure 21-15. When this tab is selected, a palette of optional controls will be displayed. Simply drag-and-drop any desired control from the toolbox onto the design pane. Patience and careful control placement will determine how useful your dialog box will be to the user. Optional grid lines can be selected to make control placement easier. This can be done by selecting Format | Guide Settings.

In order to be able to communicate with menus, dialog boxes, and the various controls placed in the dialog boxes, some type of ID value is needed. The Resource Editor assigns a number of default ID values to these items. Along with the ID values, each menu, dialog box, and control also has a group of properties that describe their capabilities.

Figure 21-16 shows a property pane for the Edit Control for the first pie wedge.

While it is not necessary to describe each of these default properties until needed, you should note that we changed the ID value of this control to IDC_DATA1. This better reflects the use of the control rather than the default IDC_EDIT1 assigned by the Resource Editor. Subsequently, we then changed all of the other Edit Box controls to reflect this change. Note that the test, "Sample edit box," will not appear in a working dialog box.

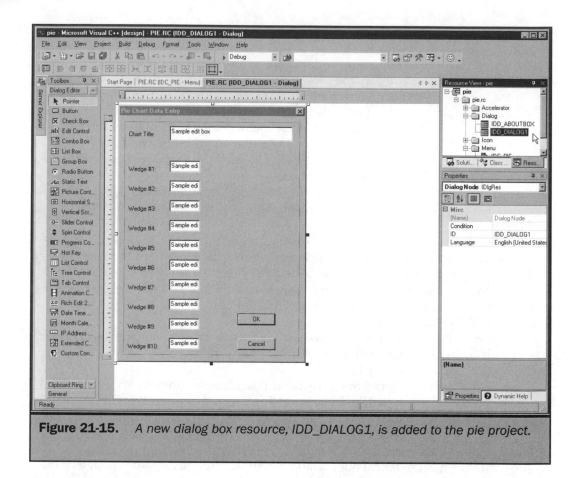

Figure 21-15. *A new dialog box resource, IDD_DIALOG1, is added to the pie project.*

The description of menu and dialog box information will eventually appear in its script form in the pie.rc resource script file. You can view this file from within the Visual C++ Studio, or by using a simple editor like Notepad. Here is a portion of the pie.rc file, edited for clarity:

```
//Microsoft Developer Studio generated resource script.
//
#include "resource.h"
    .
    .
    .
/////////////////////////////////////////////////////////////////
//
// Menu
//
```

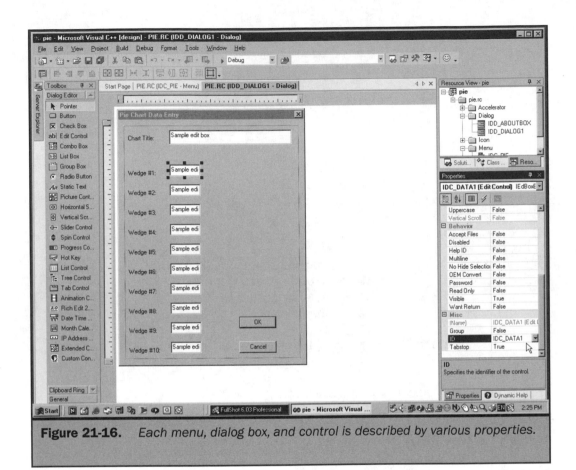

Figure 21-16.   *Each menu, dialog box, and control is described by various properties.*

```
IDC_PIE MENU DISCARDABLE
BEGIN
    POPUP "&File"
    BEGIN
        MENUITEM "E&xit",                       IDM_EXIT
    END
    POPUP "Data"
    BEGIN
        MENUITEM "Chart Values...",             IDM_INPUT
    END
    POPUP "&Help"
    BEGIN
        MENUITEM "&About ...",                  IDM_ABOUT
    END
```

```
END
    .
    .
    .
//////////////////////////////////////////////////////////
//
// Dialog
//

IDD_ABOUTBOX DIALOG DISCARDABLE  22, 17, 230, 75
STYLE DS_MODALFRAME | WS_CAPTION | WS_SYSMENU
CAPTION "About"
FONT 8, "System"
BEGIN
    ICON            IDI_PIE,IDC_MYICON,14,9,16,16
    LTEXT           "pie Version 1.0",IDC_STATIC,
                    49,10,119,8,SS_NOPREFIX
    LTEXT           "Copyright (C) 2000",IDC_STATIC,
                    49,20,119,8
    DEFPUSHBUTTON   "OK",IDOK,195,6,30,11,WS_GROUP
END

IDD_DIALOG1 DIALOGEX 0, 0, 244, 298
STYLE DS_MODALFRAME | DS_CENTER | WS_POPUP | WS_CAPTION
                    | WS_SYSMENU
CAPTION "Pie Chart Data Entry"
FONT 8, "MS Sans Serif"
BEGIN
    DEFPUSHBUTTON   "OK",IDOK,156,240,50,14
    PUSHBUTTON      "Cancel",IDCANCEL,156,270,50,14
    LTEXT           "Wedge #1:",IDC_STATIC,12,60,37,8
    LTEXT           "Wedge #2:",IDC_STATIC,12,84,37,8
    LTEXT           "Wedge #3:",IDC_STATIC,12,108,37,8
    LTEXT           "Wedge #4:",IDC_STATIC,12,132,37,8
    LTEXT           "Wedge #5:",IDC_STATIC,12,156,37,8
    LTEXT           "Wedge #6:",IDC_STATIC,12,180,37,8
    LTEXT           "Wedge #7:",IDC_STATIC,12,204,37,8
    LTEXT           "Wedge #8:",IDC_STATIC,12,228,37,8
    LTEXT           "Wedge #9:",IDC_STATIC,12,252,37,8
    LTEXT           "Wedge #10:",IDC_STATIC,12,276,41,8
    EDITTEXT        IDC_DATA1,66,54,40,14,ES_AUTOHSCROLL
    EDITTEXT        IDC_DATA2,66,78,40,14,ES_AUTOHSCROLL
    EDITTEXT        IDC_DATA3,66,102,40,14,ES_AUTOHSCROLL
    EDITTEXT        IDC_DATA4,66,126,40,14,ES_AUTOHSCROLL
```

```
        EDITTEXT          IDC_DATA5,66,150,40,14,ES_AUTOHSCROLL
        EDITTEXT          IDC_DATA6,66,174,40,14,ES_AUTOHSCROLL
        EDITTEXT          IDC_DATA7,66,198,40,14,ES_AUTOHSCROLL
        EDITTEXT          IDC_DATA8,66,222,40,14,ES_AUTOHSCROLL
        EDITTEXT          IDC_DATA9,66,246,40,14,ES_AUTOHSCROLL
        EDITTEXT          IDC_DATA10,66,270,40,14,ES_AUTOHSCROLL
        LTEXT             "Chart Title:",IDC_STATIC,12,18,42,12
        EDITTEXT          IDC_TEXT1,66,12,162,18,ES_AUTOHSCROLL
END
        .
        .
        .
```

Remember that the pie.rc file is simply the text file equivalent to the menu and dialog boxes that were developed by the resource editors and discussed in the previous chapter. Can you find the IDC_DATA1 to IDC_DATA10 ID values for each edit box control in this listing?

In order to be able to access the menu, menu items, and dialog box information, alterations to the pie.cpp source code file will be needed. These changes are in addition to the code that will be required to draw the pie chart. You will notice that this source code file is much longer than previous source code files in this chapter because of the new menu and dialog box procedures. However, as you study the listing you should still see familiar components that have been common to all previous Windows source code files in this chapter. The bolded lines of code, shown in the next listing, were added to the template code generated by the Application Wizard.

```
//
// pie.cpp
// A Pie Chart Application with Resources
// Copyright (c) William H. Murray and Chris H. Pappas, 2001
//

#include "stdafx.h"
#include "pie.h"
#include <math.h>

#define MAX_LOADSTRING 100
#define radius            180
#define maxnumwedge       10
#define pi                3.14159265359


// Global Variables:
HINSTANCE hInst;                              // current instance
```

WINDOWS AND WIZARDS

```
TCHAR szTitle[MAX_LOADSTRING];          // The title bar text
TCHAR szWindowClass[MAX_LOADSTRING];    // The title bar text

ATOM                MyRegisterClass(HINSTANCE hInstance);
BOOL                InitInstance(HINSTANCE, int);
LRESULT CALLBACK    WndProc(HWND, UINT, WPARAM, LPARAM);
LRESULT CALLBACK    About(HWND, UINT, WPARAM, LPARAM);
LRESULT CALLBACK    PieDlgProc(HWND, UINT, WPARAM, LPARAM);

char szTString[80] = "(pie chart title area)";
unsigned int iWedgesize[maxnumwedge] = {5, 20, 10, 15};
long lColor[maxnumwedge] = {0x0L, 0xFFL, 0xFF00L, 0xFFFFL,
                            0xFF0000L, 0xFF00FFL,
                            0xFFFF00L, 0xFFFFFFL,
                            0x8080L, 0x808080L};

int APIENTRY WinMain(HINSTANCE hInstance,
                     HINSTANCE hPrevInstance,
                     LPSTR     lpCmdLine,
                     int       nCmdShow)
{
    // TODO: Place code here.
    MSG msg;
    HACCEL hAccelTable;

    // Initialize global strings
    LoadString(hInstance, IDS_APP_TITLE, szTitle,
            MAX_LOADSTRING);
    LoadString(hInstance, IDC_PIE,
            szWindowClass, MAX_LOADSTRING);
    MyRegisterClass(hInstance);

    // Perform application initialization:
    if (!InitInstance (hInstance, nCmdShow))
    {
        return FALSE;
    }

    hAccelTable = LoadAccelerators(hInstance,
                                   (LPCTSTR)IDC_PIE);

    // Main message loop:
    while (GetMessage(&msg, NULL, 0, 0))
    {
```

```
        if (!TranslateAccelerator(msg.hwnd,
                                  hAccelTable,
                                  &msg))
        {
            TranslateMessage(&msg);
            DispatchMessage(&msg);
        }
    }

    return msg.wParam;
}

ATOM MyRegisterClass(HINSTANCE hInstance)
{
    WNDCLASSEX wcex;

    wcex.cbSize = sizeof(WNDCLASSEX);

    wcex.style          = CS_HREDRAW | CS_VREDRAW;
    wcex.lpfnWndProc    = (WNDPROC)WndProc;
    wcex.cbClsExtra     = 0;
    wcex.cbWndExtra     = 0;
    wcex.hInstance      = hInstance;
    wcex.hIcon          = LoadIcon(hInstance,
                                (LPCTSTR)IDI_PIE);
    wcex.hCursor        = LoadCursor(NULL, IDC_ARROW);
    wcex.hbrBackground  = (HBRUSH)(COLOR_WINDOW+1);
    wcex.lpszMenuName   = (LPCSTR)IDC_PIE;
    wcex.lpszClassName  = szWindowClass;
    wcex.hIconSm        = LoadIcon(wcex.hInstance,
                                (LPCTSTR)IDI_SMALL);

    return RegisterClassEx(&wcex);
}

BOOL InitInstance(HINSTANCE hInstance, int nCmdShow)
{
    HWND hWnd;

    hInst = hInstance; // Store instance handle

    hWnd = CreateWindow(szWindowClass, szTitle,
                    WS_OVERLAPPEDWINDOW,
                    CW_USEDEFAULT, 0,
```

```
                        CW_USEDEFAULT, 0,
                        NULL, NULL, hInstance, NULL);

    if (!hWnd)
    {
        return FALSE;
    }

    ShowWindow(hWnd, nCmdShow);
    UpdateWindow(hWnd);

    return TRUE;
}

LRESULT CALLBACK WndProc(HWND hWnd, UINT message,
                         WPARAM wParam, LPARAM lParam)
{
    int wmId, wmEvent;
    PAINTSTRUCT ps;
    HDC hdc;

    HBRUSH hBrush;
    static int xClientView, yClientView;

    unsigned int iTotalWedge[maxnumwedge+1];
    int i, iNWedges;

    iNWedges = 0;
    for (i = 0; i < maxnumwedge; i++) {
        if(iWedgesize[i] != 0) iNWedges++;
    }

    iTotalWedge[0] = 0;

    for (i=0 ; i < iNWedges; i++)
        iTotalWedge[i+1] = iTotalWedge[i] + iWedgesize[i];

    switch (message)
    {
    case WM_SIZE:
        xClientView = LOWORD(lParam);
        yClientView = HIWORD(lParam);
        break;
     case WM_COMMAND:
```

```
        wmId     = LOWORD(wParam);
        wmEvent = HIWORD(wParam);
        // Parse the menu selections:
        switch (wmId)
        {
        case IDM_ABOUT:
            DialogBox(hInst, (LPCTSTR)IDD_ABOUTBOX,
                        hWnd, (DLGPROC)About);
            break;
        case IDM_INPUT:
            DialogBox(hInst, (LPCTSTR) IDD_DIALOG1,
                        hWnd, (DLGPROC)PieDlgProc);
            InvalidateRect(hWnd, NULL, TRUE);
            UpdateWindow(hWnd);
            break;
        case IDM_EXIT:
            DestroyWindow(hWnd);
            break;
        default:
            return DefWindowProc(hWnd, message,
                                    wParam, lParam);
        }
        break;
    case WM_PAINT:
        hdc = BeginPaint(hWnd, &ps);

        SetMapMode(hdc, MM_ISOTROPIC);
        SetWindowExtEx(hdc, 500, 500, NULL);
        SetViewportExtEx(hdc, xClientView,
                        -yClientView, NULL);
        SetViewportOrgEx(hdc, xClientView / 2,
                        yClientView / 2, NULL);

        if (xClientView > 200)
            TextOut(hdc, (int) strlen(szTString) * (-8 / 2),
                    240, szTString,(int) strlen(szTString));

        for(i = 0; i < iNWedges; i++) {
            hBrush = CreateSolidBrush(lColor[i]);
            SelectObject(hdc, hBrush);
            Pie(hdc, -200, 200, 200, -200,
                (int)(radius * cos(2 * pi * iTotalWedge[i] /
                iTotalWedge[iNWedges])),
                (int)(radius * sin(2 * pi * iTotalWedge[i] /
```

```
                                    iTotalWedge[iNWedges])),
                               (int)(radius * cos(2 * pi * iTotalWedge[i+1] /
                               iTotalWedge[iNWedges])),
                               (int)(radius * sin(2 * pi * iTotalWedge[i+1] /
                               iTotalWedge[iNWedges])));
            }

        ValidateRect(hWnd,NULL);
        EndPaint(hWnd, &ps);
        break;
    case WM_DESTROY:
        PostQuitMessage(0);
        break;
    default:
        return DefWindowProc(hWnd, message, wParam, lParam);
    }
    return 0;
}


// Message handler for about box.
LRESULT CALLBACK About(HWND hDlg, UINT message,
                    WPARAM wParam, LPARAM lParam)
{
    switch (message)
    {
    case WM_INITDIALOG:
        return TRUE;

    case WM_COMMAND:
        if (LOWORD(wParam) == IDOK ||
            LOWORD(wParam) == IDCANCEL)
        {
            EndDialog(hDlg, LOWORD(wParam));
            return TRUE;
        }
        break;
    }
    return FALSE;
}


// Message handler for data entry dialog box.
LRESULT CALLBACK PieDlgProc(HWND hDlg, UINT message,
                            WPARAM wParam, LPARAM lParam)
{
```

```
    switch (message)
    {
    case WM_INITDIALOG:
        return FALSE;

    case WM_COMMAND:
        switch (wParam)
        {
            case IDOK:
                GetDlgItemText(hDlg, IDC_TEXT1,
                                    szTString, 80);
                iWedgesize[0] = GetDlgItemInt(hDlg, IDC_DATA1,
                                              NULL, 0);
                iWedgesize[1] = GetDlgItemInt(hDlg, IDC_DATA2,
                                              NULL, 0);
                iWedgesize[2] = GetDlgItemInt(hDlg, IDC_DATA3,
                                              NULL, 0);
                iWedgesize[3] = GetDlgItemInt(hDlg, IDC_DATA4,
                                              NULL, 0);
                iWedgesize[4] = GetDlgItemInt(hDlg, IDC_DATA5,
                                              NULL, 0);
                iWedgesize[5] = GetDlgItemInt(hDlg, IDC_DATA6,
                                              NULL, 0);
                iWedgesize[6] = GetDlgItemInt(hDlg, IDC_DATA7,
                                              NULL, 0);
                iWedgesize[7] = GetDlgItemInt(hDlg, IDC_DATA8,
                                              NULL, 0);
                iWedgesize[8] = GetDlgItemInt(hDlg, IDC_DATA9,
                                              NULL, 0);
                iWedgesize[9] = GetDlgItemInt(hDlg, IDC_DATA10,
                                              NULL, 0);
                EndDialog(hDlg, TRUE);
                break;
            case IDCANCEL:
                EndDialog(hDlg, FALSE);
                break;
            default:
                return FALSE;
        }
        break;
    default:
        return FALSE;
    }
    return TRUE;
}
```

In the next section we'll look at the important components that make up the complete pie source code file.

The pie.cpp Source Code

The C++ source code for pie.cpp allows the user to develop a pie chart with as many as ten pie slices. The application will allow the user to input the data on pie-slice sizes directly to a dialog box. In addition to data on pie sizes, the user may enter the title of the pie chart. Don't let the size of this code listing scare you; much of the code you see is an extension of the source code used in other projects in this chapter. You might want to compare the source code listing for this project to the source code listing of the sine project. The discussion in this section will concentrate on the new features in this project, namely menu and dialog box resources.

The following piece of code initiates a request to display the data entry dialog box when the user selects the appropriate menu item:

```
case IDM_INPUT:
    DialogBox(hInst, (LPCTSTR) IDD_DIALOG1,
              hWnd, (DLGPROC)PieDlgProc);
    InvalidateRect(hWnd, NULL, TRUE);
    UpdateWindow(hWnd);
    break;
```

Dialog box information is then processed with the case **IDOK** statement under the *PieDlgProc* procedure:

```
case WM_COMMAND:
    switch (wParam)
    {
        case IDOK:
            GetDlgItemText(hDlg, IDC_TEXT1,
                           szTString, 80);
            iWedgesize[0] = GetDlgItemInt(hDlg, IDC_DATA1,
                                          NULL, 0);
            iWedgesize[1] = GetDlgItemInt(hDlg, IDC_DATA2,
                                          NULL, 0);
            iWedgesize[2] = GetDlgItemInt(hDlg, IDC_DATA3,
                                          NULL, 0);
            .
            .
            .
```

The chart title is returned as a text string with the GetDlgItemText() function. Numeric information, on wedge sizes, is returned using the GetDlgItemInt() function. This function translates the "numeric" string information entered by the user into an integer that can be a signed or unsigned number. The GetDlgItemInt() function requires four parameters. The handle and ID number are self-explanatory. The third parameter, which is NULL in this case, is used to flag a successful conversion. The fourth parameter is used to indicate signed and unsigned numbers. In this case, a zero states that the dialog box is returning unsigned numbers. These numbers are saved in the global array *iWedgesize[ ]* for future use.

The major work in this application is done in the WndProc() function. Various pieces of information and data are sent as messages and examined by the five case statements. Study the code and make sure you can find these "message" case statements: WM_SIZE, WM_COMMAND, WM_PAINT, and WM_DESTROY.

Determining the size of the client or application window is achieved with the help of WM_SIZE. Windows sends a message to WM_SIZE any time the window is resized. In this case, the size will be returned in two variables, *xClientView* and *yClientView*. This information will be used by WM_PAINT to scale the pie chart to the window.

Dialog boxes can be opened with messages sent to WM_COMMAND. Notice that WM_COMMAND contains three case statements. IDM_ABOUT is the ID for the About box procedure, while IDM_INPUT is the ID for the data entry dialog box. IDM_EXIT allows a graceful exit from the application.

The routines for actually drawing the pie wedges are processed under WM_PAINT.

The mapping mode is changed to MM_ISOTROPIC from the default text mode, MM_TEXT. When in the MM_TEXT mapping mode, drawings are made in "pixel" coordinates with point 0,0 in the upper-left corner of the window. This is why the sine project, discussed earlier, did not change size as the window size was changed.

```
SetMapMode(hdc, MM_ISOTROPIC);
SetWindowExtEx(hdc, 500, 500, NULL);
SetViewportExtEx(hdc, xClientView, -yClientView,NULL);
SetViewportOrgEx(hdc, xClientView / 2, yClientView / 2,NULL);
```

Table 21-4 shows additional mapping modes available under Windows ME and 2000.

MM_ISOTROPIC allows you to select the extent of both the X and Y axes. The mapping mode is changed by calling the function SetMapMode(). When the function SetWindowExt() is called, with both parameters set to 500, the height and width of the client or application area are equal. These are logical sizes, which Windows adjusts (scales) to fit the physical display device. The display size values are used by the SetViewportExt() function. The negative sign for the *y* coordinate specifies increasing *y* values from the bottom of the screen. It should be no surprise that these are the values previously obtained under WM_SIZE.

Value	Meaning
MM_ANISOTROPIC	Maps one logical unit to an arbitrary physical unit. The X and Y axes are scaled.
MM_HIENGLISH	Maps one logical unit to 0.001 inch. Positive y is up.
MM_HIMETRIC	Maps one logical unit to 0.01 millimeter. Positive y is up.
MM_ISOTROPIC	Maps one logical unit to an arbitrary physical unit. X and Y unit lengths are equal.
MM_LOENGLISH	Maps one logical unit to 0.01 inch. Positive y points up.
MM_LOMETRIC	Maps one logical unit to 0.1 millimeter. Positive y points up.
MM_TEXT	Maps one logical unit to one pixel. Positive y points down. This is the default mode.
MM_TWIPS	Maps one logical unit to ½₀ of a printer's point. Positive y points up.

Table 21-4. *Mapping Modes for Windows Applications*

For this example, the pie chart will be placed on a traditional *x,y* coordinate system, with the center of the chart at 0,0. The SetViewportOrgEx() function is used for this purpose.

The pie chart title is printed to the screen using the coordinates for the current mapping mode. The program centers the title on the screen by estimating the size of the character font and knowing the string length. For really small windows, the title is not printed.

```
if (xClientView > 200)
    TextOut(hdc, (int) strlen(szTString) * (-8 / 2),
            240, szTString, (int) strlen(szTString));
```

Before actually discussing how the pie wedges are plotted, let's return to the beginning of the *WndProc* procedure in order to gain an understanding of how the wedges are scaled to fit a complete circle. There are several pieces of code that are very important.

This code determines how many wedges the user has requested:

```
iNWedges = 0;
for (i = 0; i < maxnumwedge; i++) {
    if(iWedgesize[i] != 0) iNWedges++;
}
```

It is assumed that there is at least one wedge of some physical size, so the array *iWedgesize[ ]* can be scanned for the first zero value. For each nonzero value returned, *iNWedges* will be incremented. Thus, when leaving this routine, *iNWedges* will contain the total number of wedges for this plot.

A progressive total on wedge size values will be returned to the *iTotalWedge[ ]* array. These values will help determine where one pie slice ends and the next begins. For example, if the user entered 5, 10, 7, and 20 for wedge sizes, *iTotalWedge[ ]* would contain the values 0, 5, 15, 22, and 42. Study the following code to make sure you understand how these results are achieved:

```
iTotalWedge[0] = 0;
for (i = 0; i < iNWedges; i++)
    iTotalWedge[i+1] = iTotalWedge[i] + iWedgesize[i];
```

The values contained in *iTotalWedge[ ]* are needed in order to calculate the beginning and ending angles for each pie wedge. You might recall that the Pie() function accepts nine parameters. The first parameter is the handle, and the next four specify the coordinates of the bounding rectangle. In this case, for the mapping mode chosen, they are -200, 200, 200, and -200. The remaining four parameters are used to designate the starting x,y pair and the ending x,y pair for the pie arc. To calculate x values, the cosine function is used, and to calculate y values, the sine function is used. For example, the first x position is determined by multiplying the radius of the pie by the cosine of 2*pi*iTotalWedge[0]. The 2*pi value is needed in the conversion of degrees to radians. The y value is found with the sine function in an identical way. Those two values serve as the x,y starting coordinates for the first slice. The ending coordinates are found with the same equations, but using the next value in *iTotalWedge[ ]*. In order to scale each of these points to make all slices proportional and fit a 360-degree pie, each coordinate point is divided by the grand total of all individual slices. This total is the last number contained in *iTotalWedge[ ]*. Observe how this calculation is achieved in the next piece of code:

```
for(i = 0; i < iNWedges; i++) {
    hBrush = CreateSolidBrush(lColor[i]);
    SelectObject(hdc, hBrush);
```

```
Pie(hdc, -200, 200, 200, -200,
    (int)(radius * cos(2 * pi * iTotalWedge[i] /
        iTotalWedge[iNWedges])),
    (int)(radius * sin(2 * pi * iTotalWedge[i] /
        iTotalWedge[iNWedges])),
    (int)(radius * cos(2 * pi * iTotalWedge[I + 1] /
        iTotalWedge[iNWedges])),
    (int)(radius * sin(2 * pi * iTotalWedge[I + 1] /
        iTotalWedge[iNWedges])));
}
```

In order to draw and fill all slices, a loop is used. This loop will index through all *iNWedge* values.

Figure 21-17 shows the default pie chart plot, and Figure 21-18 shows a unique pie chart application.

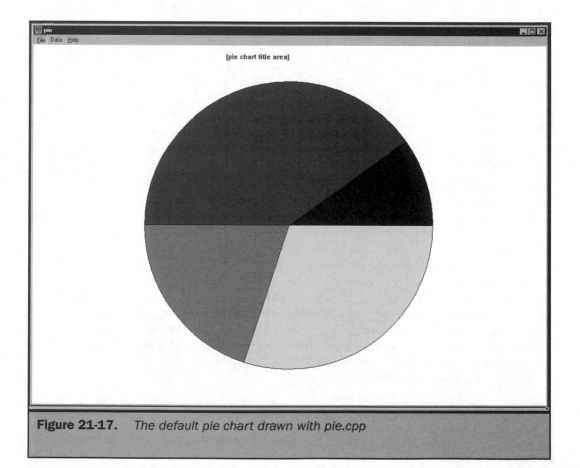

Figure 21-17. *The default pie chart drawn with pie.cpp*

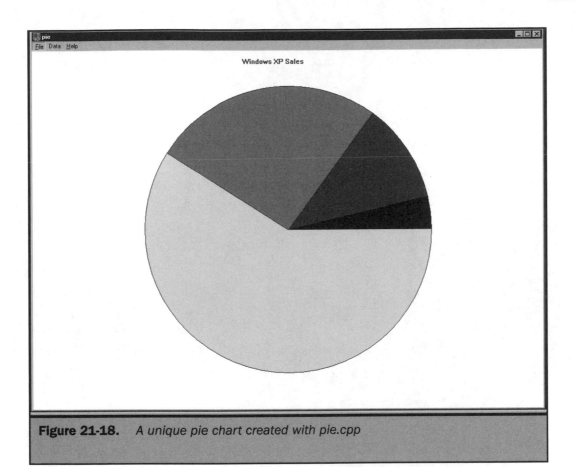

Figure 21-18.   *A unique pie chart created with pie.cpp*

Isn't it interesting how easy it was to create this robust application using the Visual Studio Application Wizard and several lines of your own code!

What's Coming?

Most C++ programmers are familiar with the procedure-oriented programming techniques presented in this chapter. However, there has been another method of Windows application development co-existing with the procedure-oriented approach presented in this chapter. That approach is the object-oriented method favored by Microsoft and many programmers.

C++ Windows applications can take advantage of object-oriented concepts and include the advantages of Microsoft's Foundation Class library. The Microsoft Foundation Class library provides the programmer with access to reusable code—a chief advantage of C++. Many authors and programmers are suggesting that all Windows applications be developed with object-oriented programming techniques. These techniques will be the primary focus in the remainder of this book.

The
Complete
Reference

Visual C++.NET

Chapter 22

Microsoft Foundation
Class Library
Fundamentals

759

I n the previous chapter you learned that even the simplest Windows applications, when combined with resources such as menus and dialog boxes, can be difficult and time-consuming to develop.

Microsoft's Visual C++ compiler provides an up-to-date 32-bit Foundation Class library containing a new set of object-oriented programming tools for the exclusive development of 32-bit Windows applications. The Microsoft Foundation Class (MFC) library encapsulates all normal procedure-oriented windows functions and provides support for control bars, property sheets, OLEO, ActiveX controls, and much, much more. In addition, database support is provided for a wide range of database sources including DAO and ODBC. You'll also find that the MFC supports the development of Internet applications in C++. Ah, the NET in the Visual Studio 7.0 NET!

This chapter discusses the advantages of using the Microsoft Foundation Class library for object-oriented Windows code development. The MFC library will make Windows application development easier. Also examined in this chapter are MFC terms, definitions, and techniques that are common across all MFC versions. The material you learn in this chapter can be applied to all of the MFC application code developed in the remaining chapters of this book. It is easy to determine the role of the MFC library when you realize that basically one chapter of this book is devoted to conventional procedure-oriented programming while all of the remaining chapters are devoted to object-oriented programming with the MFC!

We recommend that you take the time to review object-oriented terminology and programming techniques discussed earlier in Chapters 15 through 19 before tackling the MFC terminology presented in this chapter.

The MFC is a powerful toolkit for the object-oriented programmer. Consider the following analogy. If procedure-oriented Windows developers could be considered as having a hammer and crosscut saw in their toolkit, the object-oriented C++ Windows developer, using the MFC, is equipped with a pneumatic hammer and circular power saw.

The Need for a Foundation Class Library

The MFC library provides programmers with easy-to-use objects. Windows, from its very inception, has followed many principles of object-oriented programming design, within the framework of a non-object-oriented language like C. Many of these features were discussed in the previous two chapters. The marriage of C++ and Windows is a natural relationship that can take full advantage of object-oriented features. The MFC development team designed a comprehensive implementation of the Windows Application Program Interface (API). This C++ library encapsulates the most important data structures and API function calls within a group of reusable classes.

Class libraries such as the MFC offer many advantages over the traditional function libraries used by C programmers and discussed in the previous two chapters.

This list includes many of the usual advantages of C++ classes, such as:

■ Elimination of function and variable name collisions

- Encapsulation of code and data within the class
- Inheritance
- Reduced code size resulting from well-designed class libraries
- Resulting classes appearing to be natural extensions of the language

With the use of the MFC library, the code required to establish a window has been reduced to approximately one-third of the length of a conventional procedure-oriented application. This allows you, the developer, to spend less time communicating with Windows and more time developing your application's code.

MFC Design Considerations

The Foundation Class library design team set rigorous design principles that had to be followed in the implementation of the MFC library. These principles and guidelines include the following:

- Allow the mixing of traditional function calls with the use of new class libraries.
- Balance power and efficiency in the design of class libraries.
- Make the transition from standard API function calls to the use of class libraries as simple as possible.
- Produce a class library that can migrate easily to evolving platforms, such as from Windows 3.1 to 95 to 98 to ME to XP or from Windows NT to 2000 to XP.
- Utilize the power of C++ without overwhelming the programmer.

The design team felt that good code design had to start with the MFC library itself. The C++ foundation classes are designed to be small in size and fast in execution time. Their simplicity makes them very easy to use, and their execution speed is close to the bulkier function libraries of C.

These classes were designed in a fashion that requires minimal relearning of function names for seasoned Windows programmers. Carefully naming and designing classes achieved this feature. In fact, Microsoft identifies this feature as the "single characteristic that sets the MFC apart from other class libraries."

The MFC team also designed the Foundation Class library to allow a "mixed-mode" operation. That is, classes and traditional function calls can be intermixed in the same source code. Functions, such as SetCursor() and GetSystemMetrics() require direct calls, even when using the MFC.

Microsoft was also aware that class libraries should be usable. Some class libraries, provided earlier by other manufacturers, were designed with too high a level of abstraction. These "heavy classes," as Microsoft called them, tended to produce applications that were large in size and slow in execution. The MFC library provides a reasonable level of abstraction while keeping code sizes small.

WINDOWS AND WIZARDS

The development team designed the original MFC library to be dynamic rather than static. The dynamic architecture has allowed the classes to be scaled to the growing Windows 95, 98, and NT environments we now have.

Key Features of the MFC Library

Class libraries for Windows are available from other compiler manufacturers, but Microsoft claims several real advantages for its MFC library.

- An extensive exception-handling design that makes application code less subject to failure. Support for "out of memory," and so on, is provided.

- Better diagnostics support through the ability to send information about objects to a file. Also included is the ability to validate member variables.

- Complete support for all Windows functions, controls, messages, GDI (Graphics Device Interface) graphics primitives, menus, and dialog boxes.

- Determination of the type of a data object at run time. This allows for a dynamic manipulation of a field when classes are instantized.

- Elimination of many **switch/case** statements that are a source of error. All messages are mapped to member functions within a class. This direct message-to-method mapping is available for all messages.

- Small code with a fast implementation. As mentioned earlier, the MFC library adds only a small amount of object code overhead and executes almost as quickly as conventional C Windows applications.

- Support for the Component Object Model (COM).

- Use of the same naming convention as the conventional Windows API. Thus, the action of a class is immediately recognized by its name.

The experienced Windows programmer will immediately appreciate two of these features: the familiar naming convention and the message-to-method mapping. If you reexamine the source code for the applications developed in Chapter 21, you will see extensive use of the error-prone **switch/case** statements. Also notice that these applications make extensive use of API function calls. Both groups of problems are eliminated or reduced when you use the MFC.

Professional developers will certainly appreciate Microsoft's dedication to better diagnostics and the small code overhead imposed by the MFC library. Now programmers can take advantage of the MFC library without gaining a size penalty on their application's code.

The bottom line is that the MFC library is the only real ball game in town! The MFC has become the de facto standard used by the majority of C++ compiler manufacturers.

It All Begins with CObject

Libraries such as the MFC library often start with a few parent classes. Additional classes are then derived from the parent classes. CObject is one parent class used extensively in developing Windows applications. The MFC library header files located in the mfc/include subdirectory provide a wealth of information on defined classes.

Let's take a brief look at an edited version of CObject that is defined in the afx.h header file:

```
//////////////////////////////////////////////////////////////
// class CObject is the root of all compliant objects

class AFX_NOVTABLE CObject
{
public:

// Object model (types, destruction, allocation)
    virtual CRuntimeClass* GetRuntimeClass() const;
    virtual ~CObject() = 0;  //virtual destructors necessary

    // Diagnostic allocations
    void* PASCAL operator new(size_t nSize);
    void* PASCAL operator new(size_t, void* p);
    void PASCAL operator delete(void* p);
#if _MSC_VER >= 1200
    void PASCAL operator delete(void* p, void* pPlace);
#endif

#if defined(_DEBUG) && !defined(_AFX_NO_DEBUG_CRT)
    // for file name/line number tracking using DEBUG_NEW
    void* PASCAL operator new(size_t nSize,
                             LPCSTR lpszFileName,
                             int nLine);
#if _MSC_VER >= 1200
    void PASCAL operator delete(void *p,
                               LPCSTR lpszFileName,
                               int nLine);
#endif
#endif

protected:
    CObject();
private:
    CObject(const CObject& objectSrc);
```

```
    void operator=(const CObject& objectSrc);

// Attributes
public:
    BOOL IsSerializable() const;
    BOOL IsKindOf(const CRuntimeClass* pClass) const;

// Overridables
    virtual void Serialize(CArchive& ar);

#if defined(_DEBUG) || defined(_AFXDLL)
    // Diagnostic Support
    virtual void AssertValid() const;
    virtual void Dump(CDumpContext& dc) const;
#endif

// Implementation
public:
    static const CRuntimeClass classCObject;
#ifdef _AFXDLL
    static CRuntimeClass* PASCAL GetThisClass();
#endif
};
```

This code has been edited slightly for clarity, but is essentially the same code that you will find in the header file.

Upon inspection of the CObject listing, notice the components that make up this class definition. First, CObject is divided into public, protected, and private parts. CObject also provides normal and dynamic type checking and serialization. Recall that dynamic type checking allows the type of object to be determined at run time. The state of the object can be saved to a storage medium, such as a disk, through a concept called *persistence*. Object persistence allows object member functions to also be persistent, permitting retrieval of object data.

Child classes are derived from parent classes. CGdiObject is an example of a class derived from CObject. Here is the CGdiObject definition as found in afxwin.h. Again, this listing has been edited for clarity:

```
//////////////////////////////////////////////////////////////////
// CGdiObject abstract class for CDC SelectObject

class CGdiObject : public CObject
{
    DECLARE_DYNCREATE(CGdiObject)
```

```
public:

// Attributes
    HGDIOBJ m_hObject;          // must be first data member
    operator HGDIOBJ() const;
    HGDIOBJ GetSafeHandle() const;

    static CGdiObject* PASCAL FromHandle(HGDIOBJ hObject);
    static void PASCAL DeleteTempMap();
    BOOL Attach(HGDIOBJ hObject);
    HGDIOBJ Detach();

// Constructors
    CGdiObject(); // must Create a derived class object
    BOOL DeleteObject();

// Operations
    int GetObject(int nCount, LPVOID lpObject) const;
    UINT GetObjectType() const;
    BOOL CreateStockObject(int nIndex);
    BOOL UnrealizeObject();
    BOOL operator==(const CGdiObject& obj) const;
    BOOL operator!=(const CGdiObject& obj) const;

// Implementation
public:
    virtual ~CGdiObject();
#ifdef _DEBUG
    virtual void Dump(CDumpContext& dc) const;
    virtual void AssertValid() const;
#endif
};

/////////////////////////////////////////////////////////////////
// CGdiObject subclasses (drawing tools)

class CPen : public CGdiObject
{
    DECLARE_DYNAMIC(CPen)

public:
    static CPen* PASCAL FromHandle(HPEN hPen);

// Constructors
```

766   Visual C++.NET: The Complete Reference

```
    CPen();
    CPen(int nPenStyle, int nWidth, COLORREF crColor);
    CPen(int nPenStyle, int nWidth, const LOGBRUSH* pLogBrush,
        int nStyleCount = 0, const DWORD* lpStyle = NULL);
    BOOL CreatePen(int nPenStyle, int nWidth, COLORREF crColor);
    BOOL CreatePen(int nPenStyle, int nWidth,
                    const LOGBRUSH* pLogBrush,
                    int nStyleCount = 0,
                    const DWORD* lpStyle = NULL);
    BOOL CreatePenIndirect(LPLOGPEN lpLogPen);

// Attributes
    operator HPEN() const;
    int GetLogPen(LOGPEN* pLogPen);
    int GetExtLogPen(EXTLOGPEN* pLogPen);

// Implementation
public:
    virtual ~CPen();
#ifdef _DEBUG
    virtual void Dump(CDumpContext& dc) const;
#endif
};
        .
        .
        .
// Additional drawing tools follow in this file (authors)
```

CGdiObject and its member functions (methods) allow drawing items such as stock and custom pens, brushes, and fonts to be created and used in a Windows application. Classes, such as CPen (see previous listing), are further derived from the CGdiObject class.

Microsoft has provided complete source code for the MFC library in order to allow the utmost in programming flexibility and customization. However, for the beginner, it is not even necessary to know how the various classes are defined in order to use them efficiently.

For example, in traditional procedure-oriented Windows applications, the DeleteObject() function is called with the following syntax:

```
DeleteObject(hBRUSH);    //hBRUSH is the brush handle
```

In object-oriented applications, using the MFC library, the same results can be achieved by accessing the member function with the following syntax:

```
newbrush.DeleteObject(); //newbrush is current brush
```

As you can see, switching between procedure-oriented Windows function calls and class library objects can be intuitive. Microsoft has used this approach in developing all Windows classes, making the transition from traditional function calls to MFC library objects very easy.

Key MFC Classes

The following is an abbreviated list of important 32-bit MFC classes derived from CObject.

```
CObject
    CException
        CMemoryException
        CFileException
        CArchiveException
        CDaoException
        CNotSupportedException
        CUserException
        COleException
        COleDispatchException
        CDBException
        CResourceException
    CFile
        CStdioFile
        CMemFile
        COleStreamFile
        CSocketFile
    CDC
        CClientDC
        CWindowDC
        CPaintDC
        CMetaFileDC
    CGdiObject
        CPen
        CBrush
        CFont
```

```
        CBitmap
        CPalette
        CRgn
    CMenu
    CArray
    CByteArray
    CWordArray
    CDWordArray
    CPtrArray
    CObArray
    CStringArray
    CUIntArray
    CList
    CPtrList
    CObList
    CStringList
    CMap
    CMapWordToPtr
    CMapPtrToWord
    CMapPtrToPtr
    CMapWordToOb
    CMapStringToPtr
    CMapStringToOb
    CMapStringToString
    CDatabase
    CRecordSet
    CLongBinary
    CCmdTarget
        CWinThread
            CWinApp
                COleControlModule
        CDocTemplate
            CSingleDocTemplate
            CMultiDocTemplate
        COleObjectFactory
            COleTemplateServer
        COleDataSource
        COleDropSource
        COleDropTarget
        COleMessageFilter
        CConnectionPoint
    CDocument
```

```
        COleDocument
            COleLinkingDoc
                COleServerDoc
                    CRichEditDoc
CDocItem
    COleClientItem
        CRichEditCntrItem
    COleServerItem
CWnd
    CFrameWnd
        CMDIChildWnd
        CMDIFrameWnd
        CMiniFrameWnd
        COleIPFrameWnd
    CControlBar
        CToolBar
        CStatusBar
        CDialogBar
        COleResizeBar
    CSplitterWnd
    CPropertySheet
    CDialog
        CCommonDialog
            CColorDialog
            CFileDialog
            CFindReplaceDialog
            CFontDialog
            COleDialog
                COleInsertDialog
                COleChangeIconDialog
                COlePasteSpecialDialog
                COleConvertDialog
                COleBusyDialog
                COleLinksDialog
                    COleUpdateDialog
                COleChangeSourceDialog
                COlePageSetupDialog
                CPrintDialog
        COlePropertyPage
        CPropertyPage
    CView
        CCtrlView
            CEditView
```

```
                        CListView
                        CRichEditView
                        CTreeView
                CScrollView
                    CFormView
                        CDaoRecordView
                        CRecordView
            CAnimateCtrl
            CButton
                CBitmapButton
            CComboBox
            CEdit
            CHeaderCtrl
            CHotKeyCtrl
            CListBox
                CCheckListBox
                CDragListBox
            CListCtrl
            COleControl
            CProgresCtrl
            CRichEditCtrl
            CScrollBar
            CSliderCtrl
            CSpinButtonCtrl
            CStatic
            CStatusBarCtrl
            CTabCtrl
            CToolbarCtrl
            CToolTipCtrl
            CTreeCtrl
```

From this list you can see and understand the general strategy in deriving one class or a group of classes from a parent class. The next list is an abbreviated list of the 34-bit run-time object model support provided by the MFC.

CArchive	CFieldExchange
CCmdUI	CFileStatus
CCommandLineInfo	CFontHolder
CCreateContext	CMemoryState
CDataExchange	CMultiLock
CDataFieldExchange	COleCurrency
CDumpContext	COleDataObject

COleDateTime	CRuntimeClass
COleDateTimeSpan	CSingleLock
COleDispatchDriver	CSize
COleVariant	CString
CPictureHolder	CTime
CPoint	CTimeSpan
CPrintInfo	CTypedPtrArray
CPropExcahnge	CTypedPtrList
CRect	CTypedPtrMap
CRectTracker	CWaitCursor

You'll want to put a bookmark at this spot. These two lists will help you as you continue to study the MFC library in the remaining chapters of this book.

A MFC Word Processor Application

In this section we'll develop a simple MFC word processor application using the Application Wizard. This application will allow you to do simple text editing.

From the Microsoft Visual C++ main menu bar, select File | New. Now select the Project option from the displayed list. This will open the New Project dialog box as shown in Figure 22-1.

Examine Figure 22-1 and make sure you select the options highlighted in this figure for your project. Name the project Editor and set the default build location to C:\.

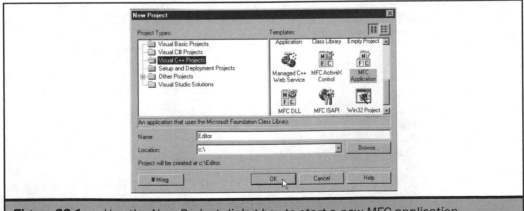

Figure 22-1.   *Use the New Project dialog box to start a new MFC application.*

When everything is correct, click the OK button with the mouse to start the MFC Application Wizard, as shown in Figure 22-2.

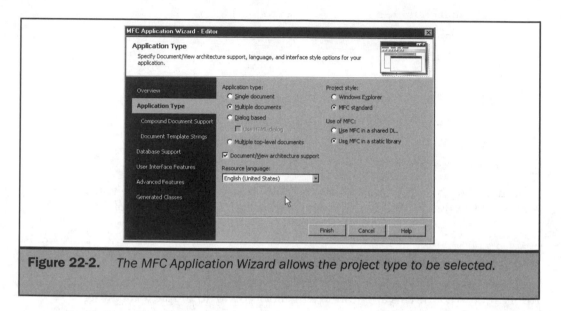

Figure 22-2. *The MFC Application Wizard allows the project type to be selected.*

Make sure your options are set to those shown in Figure 22-2. Once in the Wizard, the Application type can be set by clicking Application Type, as shown in this figure. Now, check the Compound Document Support for the project by clicking that dialog box option, as shown in Figure 22-3.

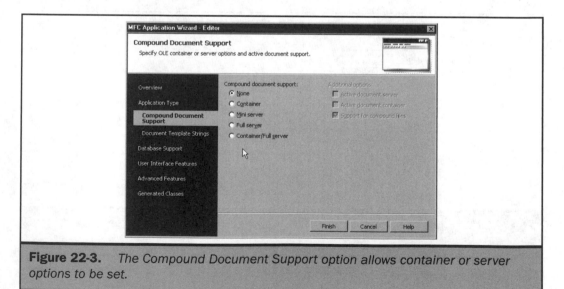

Figure 22-3. *The Compound Document Support option allows container or server options to be set.*

For this project, no compound document support is needed. Now select Document Template Strings from the options list, as shown in Figure 22-4.

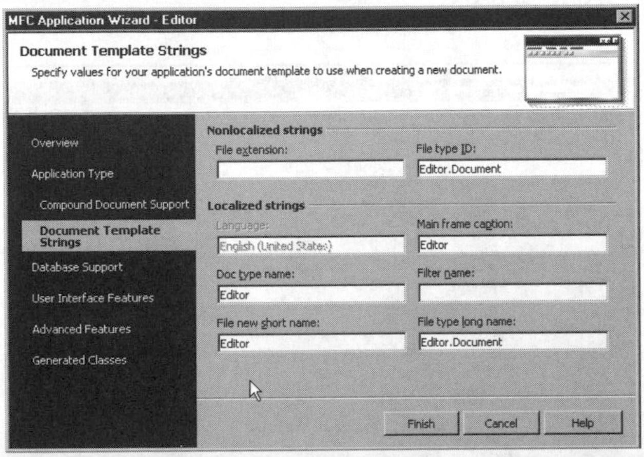

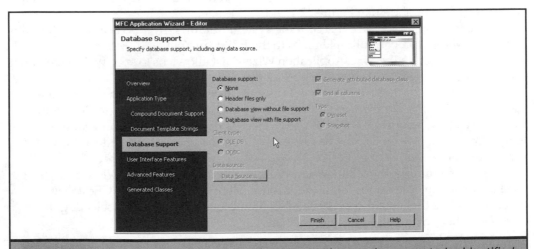

Figure 22-4.   *The Document Template Strings option allows document options to be set.*

This feature allows you to specify the document template strings, shown in Figure 22-4, when the project is created. For this application, we'll just use the suggested default values. If your project demands database support, select the Database Support option as shown in Figure 22-5.

Figure 22-5.   *Database support allows database options and sources to be identified in a new project.*

This project will not use database support. Make sure the default items, shown in Figure 22-5, match those in your project.

The User Interface Features option, shown in Figure 22-6, allows frame styles and toolbars to be specified for a project.

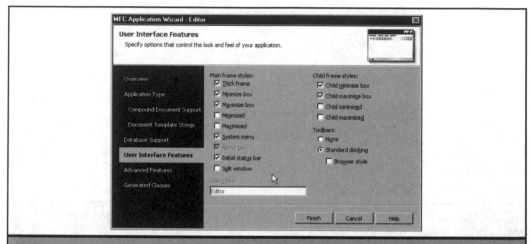

Figure 22-6.   *The User Interface Features option allows frame and toolbar options to be set for the project.*

This project will use the default user interface features specified in this project. Make sure these are the same features selected for your project.

The next MFC Application Wizard project option can be set from the Advanced Features option, as shown in Figure 22-7.

Again, for this project, we'll accept the system defaults. In this case, we will add printing and ActiveX control capabilities to the Editor project.

The final option in the MFC Application Wizard list allows us to specify the Generated Classes for the project, as shown in Figure 22-8.

For this project, all of the system defaults are acceptable except the Base Class specification. For this simple word processor application, we'll want to use CEditView as the base class. You'll see we've already selected this class when you examine Figure 22-8. When you click the Base Class option, the list will expand to show several options.

So for this example, the CEditorView class, derived from the CEditView class, is used to create the base for this application's user-defined view classes. CEditView describes a class that can be used to develop a simple text editor. After selecting the class, click the Finish button to build the template files for the project.

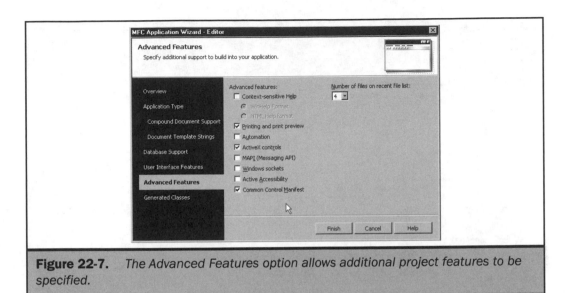

Figure 22-7. *The Advanced Features option allows additional project features to be specified.*

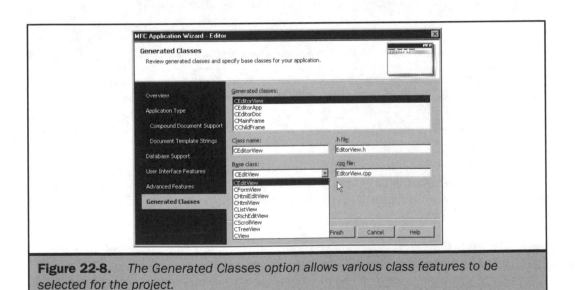

Figure 22-8. *The Generated Classes option allows various class features to be selected for the project.*

Figure 22-9 shows an expanded Solution Explorer pane to the right of the figure.

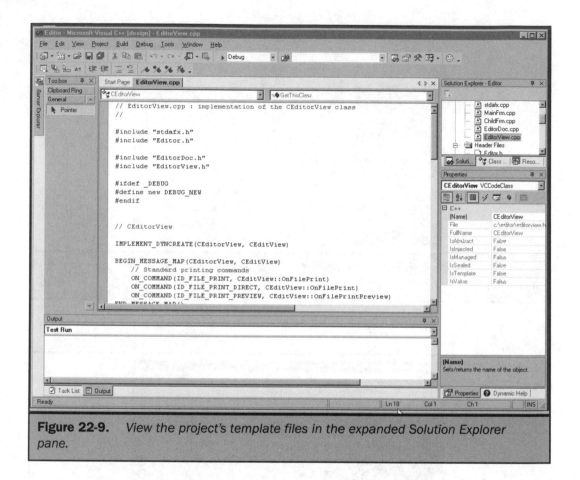

Figure 22-9. *View the project's template files in the expanded Solution Explorer pane.*

To examine the contents of any of the project's various files, simply highlight the desired file in the Solution Explorer pane to bring the contents of that file into Visual Studio's editor pane. In Figure 22-9, the EditorView.cpp file has been selected and is shown in the editor pane.

> **Note**
>
> *The* CEditView *class supplies the necessary functionality of an edit control. Now your template can print, find and replace, cut, copy, paste, clear, and undo. Since the* CEditView *class is derived from the* CView *class, its objects can be used with documents and document templates. By default, this class handles ID_FILE_PRINT, ID_EDIT_ CUT, ID_EDIT_COPY, ID_EDIT_PASTE, ID_EDIT_CLEAR, ID_EDIT_UNDO, ID_EDIT_SELECT_ALL, ID_EDIT_FIND, ID_EDIT_REPLACE, and ID_EDIT_ REPEAT.*

The Editor application, currently being built, will eventually use one message handler, but we're saving the details on that message handler for later!

Building the Application

This application can now be compiled and linked in the normal manner. When the compile and link process has been completed, an executable file will be present in the appropriate subdirectory. To test the application, run the application from the Debug menu. You should be able to open existing text files or create new files. Figure 22-10 shows the Editor project with two separate text files opened.

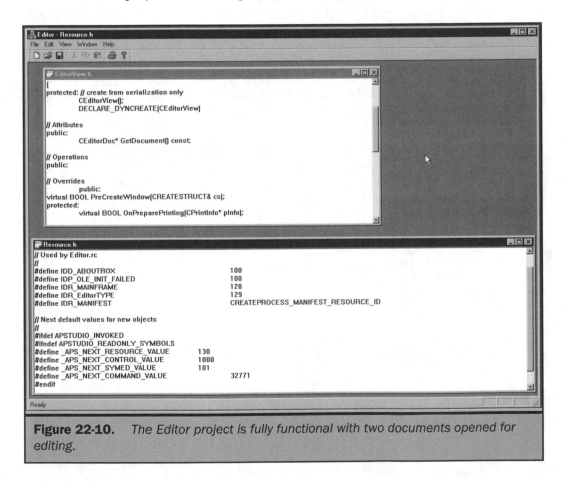

Figure 22-10. *The Editor project is fully functional with two documents opened for editing.*

Isn't this amazing? You haven't written any code, but just used various Wizard options to create a completely functional word processor application. In the next section we'll examine the code produced by the MFC Application Wizard and discuss any additions we plan to add to the project.

Examining MFC Application Wizard Code

The MFC Application Wizard generates five important source code files for the initial Editor application. These files are named Editor.cpp, MainFrm.cpp, EditorDoc.cpp, ChildFrm.cpp, and EditorView.cpp. Each of these source code files has an associated header file: Editor.h, MainFrm.h, EditorDoc.h, ChildFrm.h, and EditorView.h. The header files contain the declarations of the specific classes in each C++ source code file.

The code contained in the five separate source code files, for any given project, could be contained in a single source code file. Microsoft decided that the code should be separated so that for larger projects it would be more manageable.

You may want to review the object-oriented topics discussed in Chapters 15 through 19 before tackling the following sections. While the MFC Application Wizard is easy to use, the code it generates requires a complete understanding of object-oriented coding practices.

The Editor.cpp Source Code File   The Editor.cpp file serves as the main file for the application. It contains the CEditorApp class. The following listing contains a slightly edited version of this file:

```
// Editor.cpp : Defines class behaviors for the application.
//

#include "stdafx.h"
#include "Editor.h"
#include "MainFrm.h"

#include "ChildFrm.h"
#include "EditorDoc.h"
#include "EditorView.h"


#ifdef _DEBUG
#define new DEBUG_NEW
#endif


/////////////////////////////////////////////////////////////////
// CEditorApp

BEGIN_MESSAGE_MAP(CEditorApp, CWinApp)
    ON_COMMAND(ID_APP_ABOUT, OnAppAbout)
    // Standard file based document commands
    ON_COMMAND(ID_FILE_NEW, CWinApp::OnFileNew)
    ON_COMMAND(ID_FILE_OPEN, CWinApp::OnFileOpen)
    // Standard print setup command
    ON_COMMAND(ID_FILE_PRINT_SETUP, CWinApp::OnFilePrintSetup)
END_MESSAGE_MAP()
```

```
////////////////////////////////////////////////////////
// CEditorApp construction

CEditorApp::CEditorApp()
{
    // TODO: add construction code here,
    // Place all significant initialization in InitInstance
}


////////////////////////////////////////////////////////
// The one and only CEditorApp object

CEditorApp theApp;
////////////////////////////////////////////////////////
// CEditorApp initialization

BOOL CEditorApp::InitInstance()
{
    // Initialize OLE libraries
    if (!AfxOleInit())
    {
        AfxMessageBox(IDP_OLE_INIT_FAILED);
        return FALSE;
    }
    AfxEnableControlContainer();
    SetRegistryKey(_T("Local MFC Application Wizard-Generated
    Applications"));
    LoadStdProfileSettings(4); // Load standard INI file options
    CMultiDocTemplate* pDocTemplate;
    pDocTemplate = new CMultiDocTemplate(IDR_EditorTYPE,
        RUNTIME_CLASS(CEditorDoc),
        RUNTIME_CLASS(CChildFrame), // custom MDI child frame
        RUNTIME_CLASS(CEditorView));
    AddDocTemplate(pDocTemplate);
    // create main MDI Frame window
    CMainFrame* pMainFrame = new CMainFrame;
    if (!pMainFrame->LoadFrame(IDR_MAINFRAME))
        return FALSE;
    m_pMainWnd = pMainFrame;
    CCommandLineInfo cmdInfo;
    ParseCommandLine(cmdInfo);
    if (!ProcessShellCommand(cmdInfo))
        return FALSE;
    // The main window initialized - show and update
    pMainFrame->ShowWindow(m_nCmdShow);
```

```cpp
    pMainFrame->UpdateWindow();
    return TRUE;
}


/////////////////////////////////////////////////////////////////
// CAboutDlg dialog used for App About

class CAboutDlg : public CDialog
{
public:
    CAboutDlg();

// Dialog Data
    enum { IDD = IDD_ABOUTBOX };

protected:
    virtual void DoDataExchange(CDataExchange* pDX);

// Implementation
protected:
    DECLARE_MESSAGE_MAP()
};

CAboutDlg::CAboutDlg() : CDialog(CAboutDlg::IDD)
{
}

void CAboutDlg::DoDataExchange(CDataExchange* pDX)
{
    CDialog::DoDataExchange(pDX);
}

BEGIN_MESSAGE_MAP(CAboutDlg, CDialog)
END_MESSAGE_MAP()

// App command to run the dialog
void CEditorApp::OnAppAbout()
{
    CAboutDlg aboutDlg;
    aboutDlg.DoModal();
}


/////////////////////////////////////////////////////////////////
// CEditorApp message handlers
```

The message map, near the top of the listing, belongs to the CEditorApp class. This message map specifically links the ID_APP_ABOUT, ID_FILE_NEW, ID_FILE_OPEN, and ID_FILE_PRINT_SETUP messages with their member functions OnAppAbout(), CWinApp::OnFileNew(), CWinApp::OnFileOpen(), and CWinAppOnFilePrintSetup(). Also notice in the listing that a constructor, an initial instance InitInstance(), and a member function OnAppAbout() are implemented.

This application will use a multiple-document interface instead of the single-document interface used in the previous example:

```
CMultiDocTemplate* pDocTemplate;
pDocTemplate = new CMultiDocTemplate(IDR_EditorTYPE,
    RUNTIME_CLASS(CEditorDoc),
    RUNTIME_CLASS(CChildFrame),
    RUNTIME_CLASS(CEditorView));
AddDocTemplate(pDocTemplate);
```

The About dialog box is derived from the CDialog class. There are no initial CEditorApp commands, as you can see from the end of the listing.

The MainFrm.cpp Source Code File The MainFrm.cpp file, shown here, contains the frame class CMainFrame. This class is derived from *CFrameWnd* and is used to control all multiple-document-interface (MDI) frame features. Pay particular attention to the portion of the listing set in a bold font.

```
// MainFrm.cpp : implementation of the CMainFrame class
//

#include "stdafx.h"
#include "Editor.h"

#include "MainFrm.h"

#ifdef _DEBUG
#define new DEBUG_NEW
#endif


/////////////////////////////////////////////////////////////
// CMainFrame

IMPLEMENT_DYNAMIC(CMainFrame, CMDIFrameWnd)

BEGIN_MESSAGE_MAP(CMainFrame, CMDIFrameWnd)
    ON_WM_CREATE()
```

```cpp
END_MESSAGE_MAP()

static UINT indicators[] =
{
    ID_SEPARATOR,              // status line indicator
    ID_INDICATOR_CAPS,
    ID_INDICATOR_NUM,
    ID_INDICATOR_SCRL,
};

/////////////////////////////////////////////////////////////
// CMainFrame construction/destruction

CMainFrame::CMainFrame()
{
    // TODO: add member initialization code here
}

CMainFrame::~CMainFrame()
{
}


int CMainFrame::OnCreate(LPCREATESTRUCT lpCreateStruct)
{
    if (CMDIFrameWnd::OnCreate(lpCreateStruct) == -1)
        return -1;

    if (!m_wndToolBar.CreateEx(this, TBSTYLE_FLAT,
                            WS_CHILD | WS_VISIBLE |
                            CBRS_TOP | CBRS_GRIPPER |
                            CBRS_TOOLTIPS | CBRS_FLYBY |
                            CBRS_SIZE_DYNAMIC) ||
        !m_wndToolBar.LoadToolBar(IDR_MAINFRAME))
    {
        TRACE0("Failed to create toolbar\n");
        return -1;        // fail to create
    }

    if (!m_wndStatusBar.Create(this) ||
        !m_wndStatusBar.SetIndicators(indicators,
          sizeof(indicators)/sizeof(UINT)))
```

```
        {
            TRACE0("Failed to create status bar\n");
            return -1;        // fail to create
        }
        // TODO: Delete these three lines if you don't want
        // the toolbar to be dockable
        m_wndToolBar.EnableDocking(CBRS_ALIGN_ANY);
        EnableDocking(CBRS_ALIGN_ANY);
        DockControlBar(&m_wndToolBar);

        return 0;
}

BOOL CMainFrame::PreCreateWindow(CREATESTRUCT& cs)
{
        if( !CMDIFrameWnd::PreCreateWindow(cs) )
            return FALSE;
        // TODO: Modify the Window class or styles here by
        // modifying the CREATESTRUCT cs

        return TRUE;
}

/////////////////////////////////////////////////////////////////
// CMainFrame diagnostics

#ifdef _DEBUG
void CMainFrame::AssertValid() const
{
        CMDIFrameWnd::AssertValid();
}

void CMainFrame::Dump(CDumpContext& dc) const
{
        CMDIFrameWnd::Dump(dc);
}

#endif //_DEBUG

/////////////////////////////////////////////////////////////////
// CMainFrame message handlers
```

When you examine this listing, you will notice that the message map does handle ON_WM_CREATE messages. The constructor and destructor, however, still contain no code.

However, notice the inclusion of this small portion of code:

```
static UINT indicators[] =
{
    ID_SEPARATOR,               // status line indicator
    ID_INDICATOR_CAPS,
    ID_INDICATOR_NUM,
    ID_INDICATOR_SCRL,
};
```

Recall that the MFC Application Wizard was asked to generate a template with an initial toolbar and status bar. This group of custom controls will require ID values for the various status-line indicators.

The inclusion of the toolbar and status bar is handled by the second portion of bolded code, shown in the MainFrm.cpp listing.

The member functions AssertValid() and Dump() use definitions contained in the parent class. CMainFrame initially contains no message handlers.

The EditorDoc.cpp Source Code File   The EditorDoc.cpp file, shown here, contains the CEditorDoc class, which is unique to this application. This file is used to hold document data and to load and save files.

```
// EditorDoc.cpp : implementation of the CEditorDoc class
//

#include "stdafx.h"
#include "Editor.h"

#include "EditorDoc.h"

#ifdef _DEBUG
#define new DEBUG_NEW
#endif


/////////////////////////////////////////////////////////////////
// CEditorDoc

IMPLEMENT_DYNCREATE(CEditorDoc, CDocument)

BEGIN_MESSAGE_MAP(CEditorDoc, CDocument)
```

```
END_MESSAGE_MAP()

///////////////////////////////////////////////////////////
// CEditorDoc construction/destruction

CEditorDoc::CEditorDoc()
{
    // TODO: add one-time construction code here

}

CEditorDoc::~CEditorDoc()
{
}

BOOL CEditorDoc::OnNewDocument()
{
    if (!CDocument::OnNewDocument())
        return FALSE;

    // TODO: add reinitialization code here
    // (SDI documents will reuse this document)

    return TRUE;
}

///////////////////////////////////////////////////////////
// CEditorDoc serialization

void CEditorDoc::Serialize(CArchive& ar)
{
    // CEditView's edit control handles all serialization
    ((CEditView*)m_viewList.GetHead())->SerializeRaw(ar);
}

///////////////////////////////////////////////////////////
// CEditorDoc diagnostics

#ifdef _DEBUG
void CEditorDoc::AssertValid() const
{
    CDocument::AssertValid();
}
```

```
void CEditorDoc::Dump(CDumpContext& dc) const
{
    CDocument::Dump(dc);
}
#endif //_DEBUG


/////////////////////////////////////////////////////////////////
// CEditorDoc commands
```

When you examine this listing, you will again notice that the message map, constructor, and destructor contain no code. Several member functions can be used to provide vital document support. OnNewDocument() uses the definition provided by the parent class. Serialize() supports persistent objects.

```
    ((CEditView*)m_viewList.GetHead())->SerializeRaw(ar);
```

This line of code provides the functionality to the file I/O menu commands, allowing text files to be created, opened, and saved.

The member functions AssertValid() and Dump() use definitions contained in the parent class. There are no initial CEditorDoc commands.

The EditorView.cpp Source Code File   The EditorView.cpp file, shown next, provides the view of the document. In this implementation, CEditorView is derived from the CEditView class:

```
// EditorView.cpp : implementation of the CEditorView class
//

#include "stdafx.h"
#include "Editor.h"

#include "EditorDoc.h"
#include "EditorView.h"
#include "EditorView.h"

#ifdef _DEBUG
#define new DEBUG_NEW
#endif


/////////////////////////////////////////////////////////////////
// CEditorView
```

```
IMPLEMENT_DYNCREATE(CEditorView, CEditView)

BEGIN_MESSAGE_MAP(CEditorView, CEditView)
    ON_WM_RBUTTONDOWN()

    // Standard printing commands
    ON_COMMAND(ID_FILE_PRINT, CEditView::OnFilePrint)
    ON_COMMAND(ID_FILE_PRINT_DIRECT, CEditView::OnFilePrint)
    ON_COMMAND(ID_FILE_PRINT_PREVIEW,
               CEditView::OnFilePrintPreview)
END_MESSAGE_MAP()

/////////////////////////////////////////////////////////////
// CEditorView construction/destruction

CEditorView::CEditorView()
{
    // TODO: add construction code here

}

CEditorView::~CEditorView()
{
}

BOOL CEditorView::PreCreateWindow(CREATESTRUCT& cs)
{
    // TODO: Modify the Window class or styles here by
    //   modifying the CREATESTRUCT cs

    BOOL bPreCreated = CEditView::PreCreateWindow(cs);
    cs.style &= ~(ES_AUTOHSCROLL|WS_HSCROLL); // word-wrapping

    return bPreCreated;
}

/////////////////////////////////////////////////////////////
// CEditorView printing

BOOL CEditorView::OnPreparePrinting(CPrintInfo* pInfo)
{
    // default CEditView preparation
    return CEditView::OnPreparePrinting(pInfo);
}
```

```
void CEditorView::OnBeginPrinting(CDC* pDC, CPrintInfo* pInfo)
{
    // Default CEditView begin printing
    CEditView::OnBeginPrinting(pDC, pInfo);
}

void CEditorView::OnEndPrinting(CDC* pDC, CPrintInfo* pInfo)
{
    // Default CEditView end printing
    CEditView::OnEndPrinting(pDC, pInfo);
}

/////////////////////////////////////////////////////////////////////
// CEditorView diagnostics

#ifdef _DEBUG
void CEditorView::AssertValid() const
{
    CEditView::AssertValid();
}

void CEditorView::Dump(CDumpContext& dc) const
{
    CEditView::Dump(dc);
}

CEditorDoc* CEditorView::GetDocument() const
{
    ASSERT(m_pDocument->IsKindOf(RUNTIME_CLASS(CEditorDoc)));
    return (CEditorDoc*)m_pDocument;
}
#endif //_DEBUG

/////////////////////////////////////////////////////////////////////
// CEditorView message handlers

void CEditorView::OnRButtonDown(UINT nFlags, CPoint point)
{
  char szTimeStr[20];
  CTime tm=CTime::GetCurrentTime();

  sprintf(szTimeStr, "It's now  %02d:%02d:%02d",
          tm.GetHour(),tm.GetMinute(),
          tm.GetSecond());
```

```
    MessageBox(szTimeStr, "Is it time to quit yet?",
            MB_OK);

    CEditView::OnRButtonDown(nFlags, point);
}
```

When you examine the message map, you will see that it contains ON_WM_RBUTTONDOWN. This is needed to support the portion of code we added at the end of the listing. The listing also contains ID_FILE_PRINT and ID_FILE_PREVIEW, which are provided when the CEditorView class is used. The constructor and destructor are empty.

You will also have to edit the associated header file, EditorView.h, slightly. The addition to the standard file is shown in bold in the following listing:

```
// EditorView.h : interface of the CEditorView class
//
/////////////////////////////////////////////////////////////////

#pragma once


class CEditorView : public CEditView
{
protected: // create from serialization only
    CEditorView();
    DECLARE_DYNCREATE(CEditorView)

// Attributes
public:
    CEditorDoc* GetDocument() const;

// Operations
public:

// Overrides
    public:
virtual BOOL PreCreateWindow(CREATESTRUCT& cs);
protected:
    virtual BOOL OnPreparePrinting(CPrintInfo* pInfo);
    virtual void OnBeginPrinting(CDC* pDC, CPrintInfo* pInfo);
    virtual void OnEndPrinting(CDC* pDC, CPrintInfo* pInfo);

// Implementation
```

```
public:
    virtual ~CEditorView();
#ifdef _DEBUG
    virtual void AssertValid() const;
    virtual void Dump(CDumpContext& dc) const;
#endif

protected:

// Generated message map functions
protected:

    afx_msg void OnRButtonDown(UINT nFlags, CPoint point);

    DECLARE_MESSAGE_MAP()
};

#ifndef _DEBUG  // debug version in EditorView.cpp
inline CEditorDoc* CEditorView::GetDocument() const
   { return (CEditorDoc*)m_pDocument; }
#endif
```

CEditorView handles document printing with OnPreparePrinting(), OnBeginPrinting(), and OnEndPrinting(). The member functions AssertValid() and Dump() use definitions contained in the parent class.

The message handler code for OnRButtonDown() is an easy enhancement to the application:

```
void CEditorView::OnRButtonDown(UINT nFlags, CPoint point)
{
  char szTimeStr[20];
  CTime tm = CTime::GetCurrentTime();

  sprintf(szTimeStr, "It's now  %02d:%02d:%02d",
          tm.GetHour(), tm.GetMinute(),
          tm.GetSecond());

  MessageBox(szTimeStr, "Is it time to quit yet?",
             MB_OK);

  CEditView::OnRButtonDown(nFlags, point);
}
```

Now, when the user clicks the right mouse button while using the text editor, a small dialog box will pop up on the screen and display the current time.

Figure 22-11 shows the application running with one text file open and the current time displayed in a dialog box.

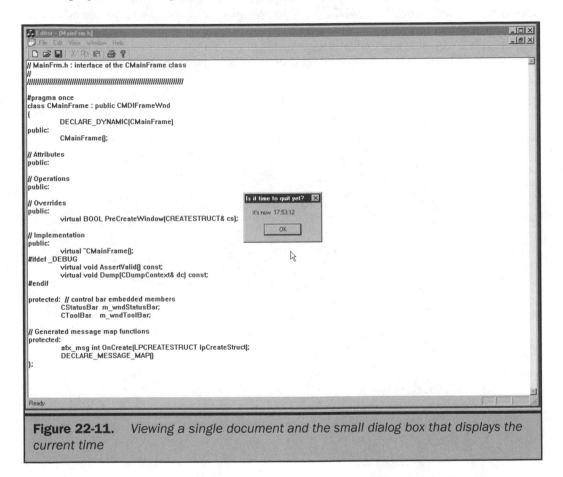

Figure 22-11.   *Viewing a single document and the small dialog box that displays the current time*

Want to know what time it is while you are working? Maybe it's time to quit? Simply right-click while over a document to pop-up a message box with the current time.

In the next chapter you will learn a more automated method for adding features such as the ability to intercept mouse button clicks to your applications.

What's Coming?

Reusable classes are one of the main drawing cards in C++ for simplified design and application maintenance. The MFC library for Windows allows C++ to be extended in a natural way, making these classes appear to be part of the language itself. In the next chapter you'll explore many additional features of the MFC library as you develop applications that include robust charting programs that use user-defined menus and dialog boxes.

Chapter 23

Wizards and MFC
Windows Applications

C hapter 20 contained information on various Windows building blocks such as menus, dialog boxes, keyboard accelerators, and so on that apply to all development platforms. In Chapter 22 you learned the theory and specifications of the Microsoft Foundation Class library and looked at an application built entirely by Visual C++ Wizards. This chapter continues the work in these earlier chapters and builds more robust applications using the MFC.

In this chapter you will find three complete MFC library Windows applications that will help you understand the MFC library even better and give you practice using various Visual C++ Wizards. The examples in this chapter are graded, that is, each example builds upon the knowledge you gain from the previous example. It is imperative, therefore, that you study each application in the order in which they appear. By the time you get to the third application, you will be working with a complex Windows application that uses several Windows resources, depends heavily on the MFC library, and produces a useful professional grade application.

The modifications to the code generated by the Visual C++ Wizards can be quite long. If you are entering them from the keyboard, do so carefully. Remember as you type that these modifications are still far simpler than writing all of the code from scratch.

Drawing in the Client Area

The first application in this chapter is named gdi. The gdi project will draw several graphics shapes in the window's client area. These are the same GDI drawing primitives discussed (and used separately) in Chapter 21. You will also learn how to modify the default menu, the About dialog box, the title in the title bar, and the icon used in the dialog box.

Using the Application Wizard

The first step in creating the gdi project is to use the Application Wizard to generate the template code for the project.

Open the New Project dialog box, as shown in Figure 23-1, from the Visual C++ File menu.

Make sure the project name and path match those shown in the figure. Click OK to open the next dialog box. Figure 23-2 shows the options we have selected for this project's Application Type.

Again, check to make sure that your project settings match those in the figure. Select Compound Document Support to set OLE container information, as shown in Figure 23-3.

The Document Template Strings option allows various project titles and documents to be set. Figure 23-4 shows that we will accept the default strings for this project.

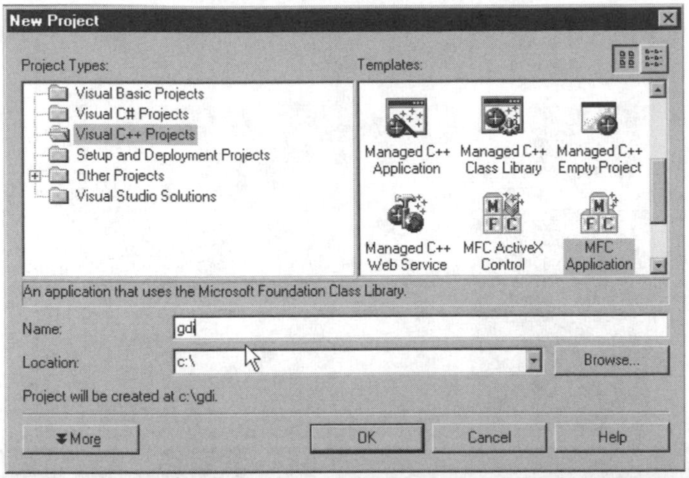

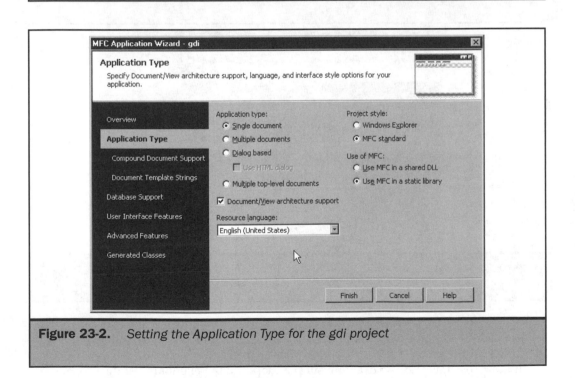

Figure 23-1.   *Create a new MFC project named gdi with the Application Wizard.*

Figure 23-2.   *Setting the Application Type for the gdi project*

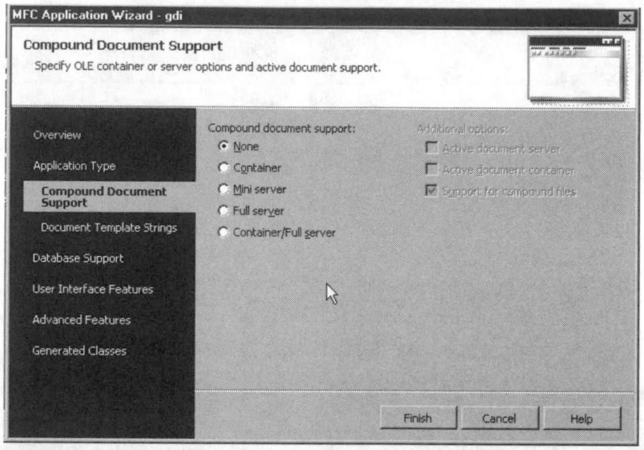

Figure 23-3.   *Compound Document Support is not needed for this project.*

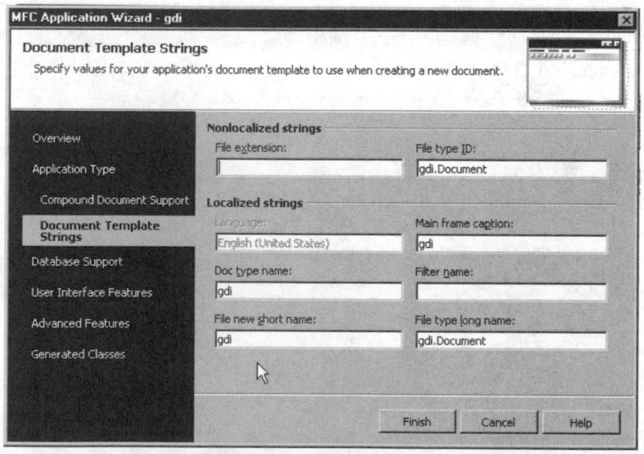

Figure 23-4.   *The Document Template Strings option is not modified for the project.*

The Database Support option, shown in Figure 23-5, allows a data source to be identified for the project.

In this project, we will be drawing simple shapes to the client area of the screen. Thus, no database support is needed.

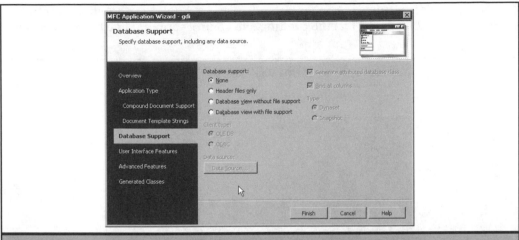

Figure 23-5. *The Database Support option is not used in this project.*

The User Interface Features option, shown in Figure 23-6, allows various toolbars, windows styles, and frame styles to be set.

We have modified the default User Interface Features slightly since this project will just draw some graphics to the client area. We have no need for a toolbar or status bar. Make sure those options are unchecked when you create your project.

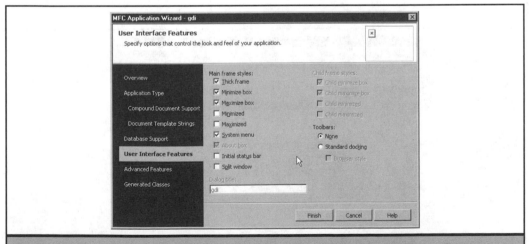

Figure 23-6. *The User Interface Features for this project have been modified.*

The Advanced Features option, by default, includes printing and ActiveX control support. Figure 23-7 shows that the printing and control support have been unchecked.

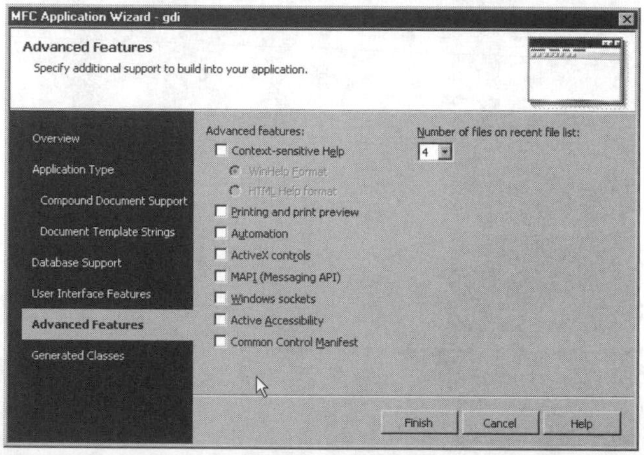

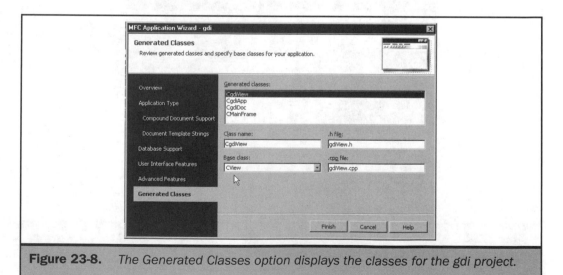

Figure 23-7. *The Advanced Features options are not used in this project.*

Finally, it is possible to view the various classes that will be automatically generated for this project by selecting the Generated Classes option. Figure 23-8 shows a list of classes for the gdi project.

Figure 23-8. *The Generated Classes option displays the classes for the gdi project.*

When you have examined the various classes, select the Finish button. This will set the Application Wizard in motion, generating all of the files necessary to create a template for your project.

Modifying Template Code

In order to draw graphics shapes in the client area, we'll have to modify a portion of the gdiView.cpp source code file. From the Solution Explorer pane, select the gdiView.cpp source code file. Scroll the code in this file until you find the portion titled CgdiView drawing. In the following listing, the code we've added to this section is shown in a bold font:

```cpp
/////////////////////////////////////////////////////////////
// CgdiView drawing

void CgdiView::OnDraw(CDC* pDC)
{
    CgdiDoc* pDoc = GetDocument();
    ASSERT_VALID(pDoc);

    static DWORD dwColor[9]={RGB(0,0,0),          //black
                             RGB(255,0,0),        //red
                             RGB(0,255,0),        //green
                             RGB(0,0,255),        //blue
                             RGB(255,255,0),      //yellow
                             RGB(255,0,255),      //magenta
                             RGB(0,255,255),      //cyan
                             RGB(127,127,127),    //gray
                             RGB(255,255,255)};   //white
    int xcoord;
    POINT polylpts[4],polygpts[5];

    CBrush newbrush;
    CBrush* oldbrush;
    CPen   newpen;
    CPen* oldpen;

    // draws a wide black diagonal line
    newpen.CreatePen(PS_SOLID,6,dwColor[0]);
    oldpen=pDC->SelectObject(&newpen);
    pDC->MoveTo(0,0);
    pDC->LineTo(640,430);
    pDC->TextOut(70,20,"<-diagonal line",15);
    // delete pen objects
    pDC->SelectObject(oldpen);
```

```
        newpen.DeleteObject();

        // draws a blue arc
        newpen.CreatePen(PS_DASH,1,dwColor[3]);
        oldpen=pDC->SelectObject(&newpen);
        pDC->Arc(100,100,200,200,150,175,175,150);
        pDC->TextOut(80,180,"small arc->",11);
        // delete pen objects
        pDC->SelectObject(oldpen);
        newpen.DeleteObject();

    // draws a wide green chord
    newpen.CreatePen(PS_SOLID,8,dwColor[2]);
    oldpen=pDC->SelectObject(&newpen);
    pDC->Chord(550,20,630,80,555,25,625,70);
    pDC->TextOut(485,30,"chord->",7);
    // delete pen objects
    pDC->SelectObject(oldpen);
    newpen.DeleteObject();

    // draws and fills a red ellipse
    newpen.CreatePen(PS_SOLID,1,dwColor[1]);
    oldpen=pDC->SelectObject(&newpen);
    newbrush.CreateSolidBrush(dwColor[1]);
    oldbrush=pDC->SelectObject(&newbrush);
    pDC->Ellipse(180,180,285,260);
    pDC->TextOut(210,215,"ellipse",7);
    // delete brush objects
    pDC->SelectObject(oldbrush);
    newbrush.DeleteObject();
    // delete pen objects
    pDC->SelectObject(oldpen);
    newpen.DeleteObject();

    // draws and fills a blue circle with ellipse function
    newpen.CreatePen(PS_SOLID,1,dwColor[3]);
    oldpen=pDC->SelectObject(&newpen);
    newbrush.CreateSolidBrush(dwColor[3]);
    oldbrush=pDC->SelectObject(&newbrush);
    pDC->Ellipse(380,180,570,370);
    pDC->TextOut(450,265,"circle",6);
    // delete brush objects
    pDC->SelectObject(oldbrush);
    newbrush.DeleteObject();
```

```
// delete pen objects
pDC->SelectObject(oldpen);
newpen.DeleteObject();

// draws a black pie wedge and fills with green
newpen.CreatePen(PS_SOLID,1,dwColor[0]);
oldpen=pDC->SelectObject(&newpen);
newbrush.CreateSolidBrush(dwColor[2]);
oldbrush=pDC->SelectObject(&newbrush);
pDC->Pie(300,50,400,150,300,50,300,100);
pDC->TextOut(350,80,"<-pie wedge",11);
// delete brush objects
pDC->SelectObject(oldbrush);
newbrush.DeleteObject();
// delete pen objects
pDC->SelectObject(oldpen);
newpen.DeleteObject();

// draws a black rectangle and fills with gray
newbrush.CreateSolidBrush(dwColor[7]);
oldbrush=pDC->SelectObject(&newbrush);
pDC->Rectangle(50,300,150,400);
pDC->TextOut(160,350,"<-rectangle",11);
// delete brush objects
pDC->SelectObject(oldbrush);
newbrush.DeleteObject();

// draws a black rounded rectangle and fills with blue
newbrush.CreateHatchBrush(HS_CROSS,dwColor[3]);
oldbrush=pDC->SelectObject(&newbrush);
pDC->RoundRect(60,310,110,350,20,20);
pDC->TextOut (120,310,"<------rounded rectangle",24);
// delete brush objects
pDC->SelectObject(oldbrush);
newbrush.DeleteObject();

// draws several green pixels
for(xcoord=400;xcoord<450;xcoord+=3)
  pDC->SetPixel(xcoord,150,0L);
pDC->TextOut(455,145,"<-pixels",8);

// draws several wide magenta lines with polyline
newpen.CreatePen(PS_SOLID,3,dwColor[5]);
oldpen=pDC->SelectObject(&newpen);
```

```
        polylpts[0].x=10;
        polylpts[0].y=30;
        polylpts[1].x=10;
        polylpts[1].y=100;
        polylpts[2].x=50;
        polylpts[2].y=100;
        polylpts[3].x=10;
        polylpts[3].y=30;
        pDC->Polyline(polylpts,4);
        pDC->TextOut(10,110,"polyline",8);
        // delete pen objects
        pDC->SelectObject(oldpen);
        newpen.DeleteObject();

        // draws a wide cyan polygon and
        // fills with diagonal yellow
        newpen.CreatePen(PS_SOLID,4,dwColor[6]);
        oldpen=pDC->SelectObject(&newpen);
        newbrush.CreateHatchBrush(HS_FDIAGONAL,dwColor[4]);
        oldbrush=pDC->SelectObject(&newbrush);
        polygpts[0].x=40;
        polygpts[0].y=200;
        polygpts[1].x=100;
        polygpts[1].y=270;
        polygpts[2].x=80;
        polygpts[2].y=290;
        polygpts[3].x=20;
        polygpts[3].y=220;
        polygpts[4].x=40;
        polygpts[4].y=200;
        pDC->Polygon(polygpts,5);
        pDC->TextOut(70,210,"<-polygon",9);
        // delete brush objects
        pDC->SelectObject(oldbrush);
        newbrush.DeleteObject();
        // delete pen objects
        pDC->SelectObject(oldpen);
        newpen.DeleteObject();

}
```

After adding this code, you can build and execute the project. You should see a figure similar to Figure 23-9 on your screen.

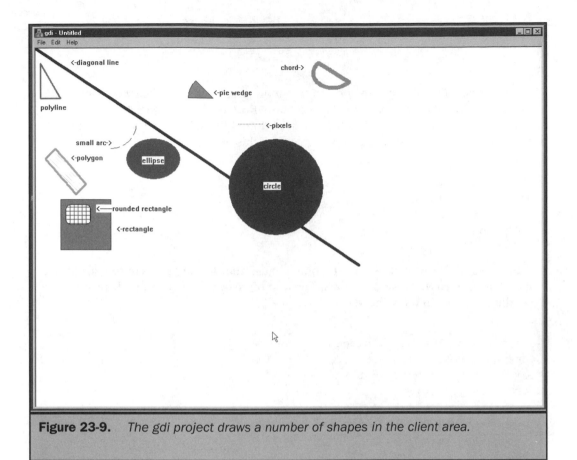

Figure 23-9.   *The gdi project draws a number of shapes in the client area.*

Basically, the screen has turned out exactly as we have planned. However, there are still a few details that we have to discuss.

Examining the Modified Code

Here is a portion of code the source code listing contained in the OnDraw() message handler function. An array is created to hold the RGB values for nine unique brush and pen colors. You'll see how colors are picked from this array:

```
static DWORD dwColor[9]={RGB(0,0,0),          //black
                         RGB(255,0,0),        //red
                         RGB(0,255,0),        //green
                         RGB(0,0,255),        //blue
                         RGB(255,255,0),      //yellow
                         RGB(255,0,255),      //magenta
                         RGB(0,255,255),      //cyan
```

```
                    RGB(127,127,127),  //gray
                    RGB(255,255,255)}; //white
```

The CBrush and CPen classes permit brush or pen objects to be passed to any CDC (base class for display context) member function. Brushes can be solid, hatched, or patterned, and pens can draw solid, dashed, or dotted lines. Here is the syntax that is required to create a new brush and pen object for this example:

```
CBrush newbrush;
CBrush* oldbrush;
CPen  newpen;
CPen* oldpen;
```

Since each GDI primitive's code is somewhat similar to the others in the group, we will only examine two typical sections. The first piece of code is used to draw a wide black diagonal line in the window:

```
// draws a wide black diagonal line
newpen.CreatePen(PS_SOLID,6,dwColor[0]);
oldpen=pDC->SelectObject(&newpen);
pDC->MoveTo(0,0);
pDC->LineTo(640,430);
pDC->TextOut(70,20,"<-diagonal line",15);
// delete pen objects
pDC->SelectObject(oldpen);
newpen.DeleteObject();
```

The pen object is initialized by the CreatePen() function to draw black solid lines six logical units wide. Once the pen is initialized, the SelectObject() member function is overloaded for the pen object class and attaches the pen object to the device context. The previously attached object is returned. The MoveTo() and LineTo() functions set the range for the diagonal line that is drawn by the selected pen. Finally, a label is attached to the figure with the use of the TextOut() function.

Brushes can be handled in a similar way. In the following code, the brush is initialized to be a hatched brush filled with blue crosses (HS_CROSS). The brush object is selected in the same way the pen object was selected:

```
// draws a black rounded rectangle and fills with blue
newbrush.CreateHatchBrush(HS_CROSS,dwColor[3]);
```

```
oldbrush=pDC->SelectObject(&newbrush);
pDC->RoundRect(60,310,110,350,20,20);
pDC->TextOut (120,310,"<------rounded rectangle",24);
// delete brush objects
pDC->SelectObject(oldbrush);
newbrush.DeleteObject();
```

The RoundRect() function draws a rounded rectangle in black at the given screen coordinates. A label is also printed for this figure.

The remaining shapes are drawn to the screen using a similar technique.

Additional Project Details

When you examined Figure 23-9 earlier, you might have noticed a few rough edges for this project. First, the title in the project's title bar reads "gdi – Untitled." Second, the project's menu provides the template for File, Edit, and Help menus. However, we have no intention of implementing some of these features. You may want to correct these jagged edges before completing the project.

Modifying the Title Bar String

If you want to modify the title bar string for this project you will need to switch the view to the Resource View. This can be done by selecting View | Resource View. Figure 23-10 shows the Resource View with the String Table resource opened.

At the top of this list is the ID value for the string we wish to modify. Locate IDR_MAINFRAME in the ID list and modify the caption to match the caption shown in Figure 23-10. It is just that simple, but be careful because you must type it exactly as shown.

The reason the word "Untitled" was showing up was that this template-designed code would allow us to open a document (see the Editor project in Chapter 22). The opened document's name would replace the word Untitled in all such applications. For this project, and the remaining projects in this chapter, no external documents are used. Thus, a more professional appearance suggests a short description of the project instead of the word "Untitled."

Modifying the Default Menu

Projects are created with a default menu providing File, Edit, and Help options. These menus, in turn, provide numerous menu options. In many cases, project developers do not need the menus or have no intention of implementing the code for the menu items. To polish the project for a more professional appearance, the menu and menu items often need to be modified.

Again, using the Resource View, select the menu resource as shown in Figure 23-11.

WINDOWS AND WIZARDS

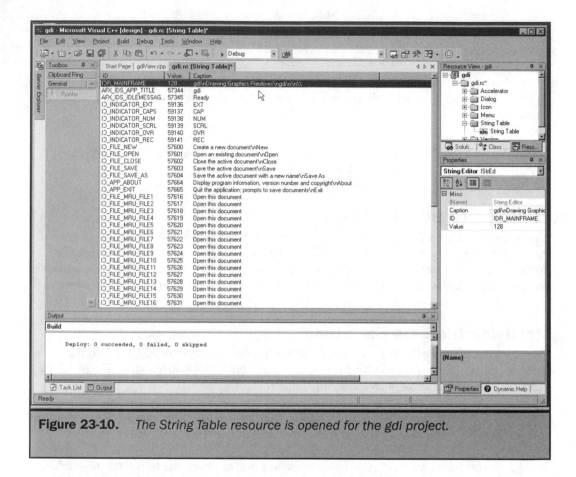

Figure 23-10.   *The String Table resource is opened for the gdi project.*

Menus or menu items can be deleted in this editor. Place the mouse over the menu or menu item, highlight the item, then press the DELETE key to remove the selected item. If you examine Figure 23-11, you'll see that we've already removed the Edit menu and several menu items in the File menu.

The File menu, after editing, provides the Exit option. The Help menu provides a view of the project's About dialog box.

Changing the About Box Icon

The Application Wizard creates a default About dialog box that includes a default icon with the letters MFC. Now, there is nothing wrong with this icon. In fact, it was very nicely designed. The problem, however, is that every project will begin to take on the same appearance if modifications are not made. The About box icon is very easy to change by simply modifying the default icon.

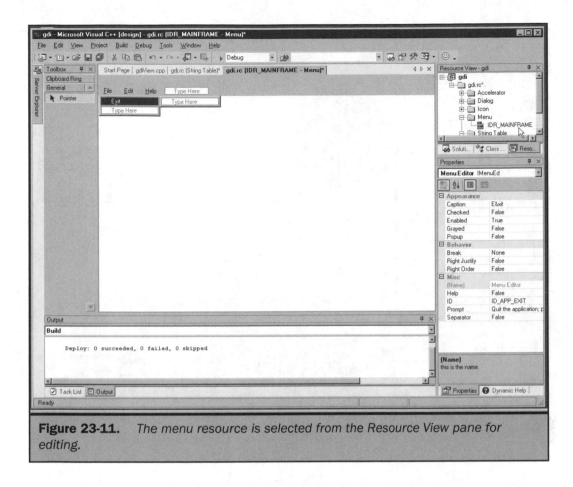

Figure 23-11. *The menu resource is selected from the Resource View pane for editing.*

From the Resource View, select IDR_MAINFRAME in the Resource View pane, as shown in Figure 23-12.

When you select this ID value with the mouse, the default icon will appear in the design window. The icon can now be modified by selecting a color from the palette of colors shown to the left of this figure and an appropriate drawing tool selected from the toolbar. Figure 23-12 shows the modification we made to the original default icon.

Changing the About Box Appearance

About boxes, by tradition, usually include the project name, developer's name, and any necessary copyright information. The default About dialog box contains all of this information except the name(s) of the developers.

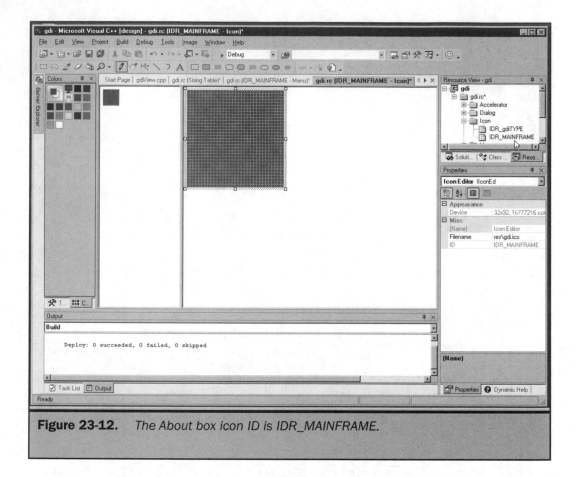

Figure 23-12.   *The About box icon ID is IDR_MAINFRAME.*

The default About box can be modified by selecting the About dialog box resource. This resource is found under the Dialog resources in the resource view pane. Select the About dialog box with the mouse and bring the dialog box into the editor.

Figure 23-13 shows a modification we've made to the About dialog box.

The size of the dialog box is increased first by dragging the lower-right corner of the dialog box down and to the right while in the editor. A new Static Text control is added in the center of the About dialog box by first dragging the copyright notice lower in the figure. The caption is changed in the new Static Text control by altering the control's properties. Can you see all of this in Figure 23-13?

When you examine Figure 23-13, notice that the icon, designed in the previous section, has already made its appearance in the dialog box.

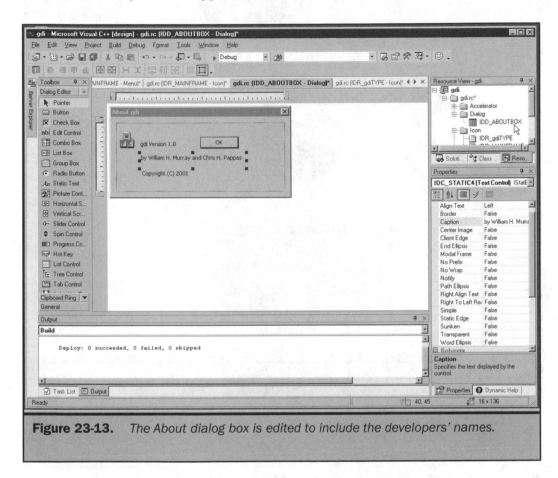

Figure 23-13.   *The About dialog box is edited to include the developers' names.*

Testing the Modifications

Build the application once again. When you execute the project, you should see a screen that looks similar to Figure 23-14.

As you examine the screen, notice a new title in the title bar area, a modified menu bar, and finally an About box with modified icon and text.

These modifications are simple to make and really add a professional look to any MFC project.

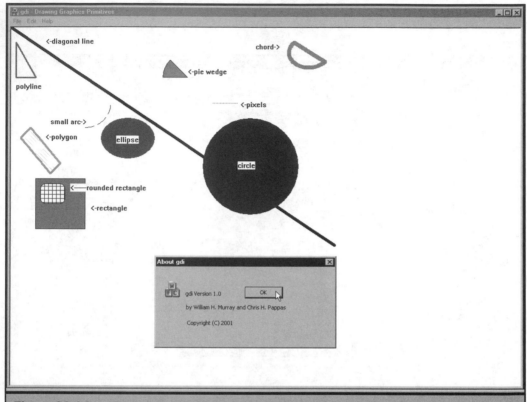

Figure 23-14.   *The edited modifications now show up in the project.*

A Fourier Series Application with Resources

The next application for this chapter is a project named Fourier. The Fourier project will draw a Fourier series waveform in the window's client area. This application uses, in addition to the default project resources, a data entry dialog box.

Building the Fourier Template Code

The Fourier template code can be built exactly the same way you built the template code for the GDI project described earlier in this chapter. Return to this example and follow the steps necessary to create a project named Fourier with the Application Wizard. Here is a brief summary of the features you'll need for the Application Wizard:

■ Create a new project named Fourier

- Application Type: set for Single document support
- Compound Document Support: none needed
- Document Template Strings: none modified for this project
- Database Support: none for this project
- User Interface Features: toolbars—none, status bar—none
- Advanced Features: uncheck Printing And Print Preview as well as ActiveX Controls

Once the settings have been entered, click Finish to generate the template for the Fourier project.

The project is now ready for any modifications we wish to make.

Adding a Dialog Box Resource

This project will require an additional dialog box. A dialog box resource can be added to the project by first displaying the Resource View pane. Figure 23-15 shows the Add Resource dialog box to the right of the figure.

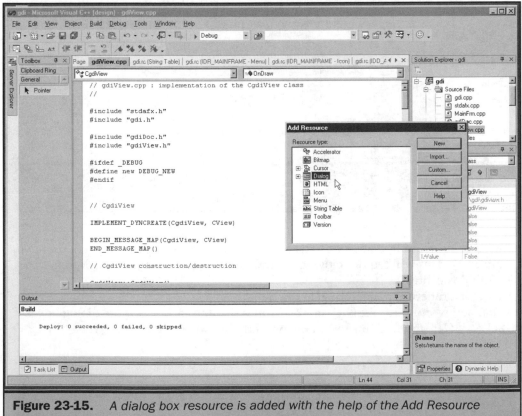

Figure 23-15. *A dialog box resource is added with the help of the Add Resource dialog box.*

Right-click the Dialog option shown in the Resource View pane and select the Insert Dialog option. This should bring you into the dialog box editor, as shown in Figure 23-16.

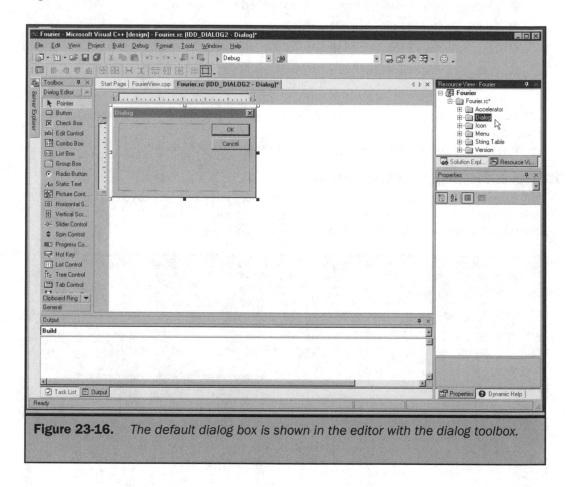

Figure 23-16. *The default dialog box is shown in the editor with the dialog toolbox.*

Modify the default dialog box to take on the appearance of the dialog box shown in Figure 23-17. This will require moving controls, adding three Static Text controls and two Edit Box controls.

Use the Properties pane, shown to the right in Figure 23-17, to alter the properties of the dialog box and controls. For example, notice that the caption for the dialog box is Data Entry. Can you find this text in the property box for this dialog box?

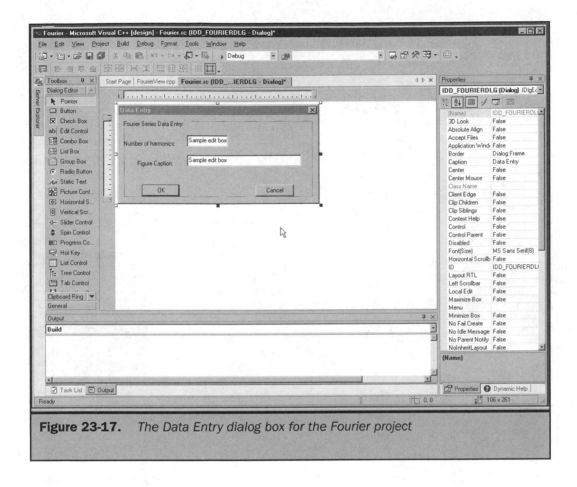

Figure 23-17.   *The Data Entry dialog box for the Fourier project*

While viewing the properties for the various controls, it is possible to view the ID values assigned to the various controls within the dialog box. Figure 23-18 shows all of the ID values in the Properties pane.

You might find it helpful to write these ID values down for future reference. Of course, you can always return to the Properties pane to view them again.

Altering the Menu Resource

We'll need to modify the default menu, as we did for the GDI project discussed earlier. From the Resource View pane, open the menu resource as shown in Figure 23-19.

You will need to delete the Edit menu and also all of the unsupported menu items in the File menu. Next, add the Data Entry menu item to the File menu, as shown in Figure 23-19.

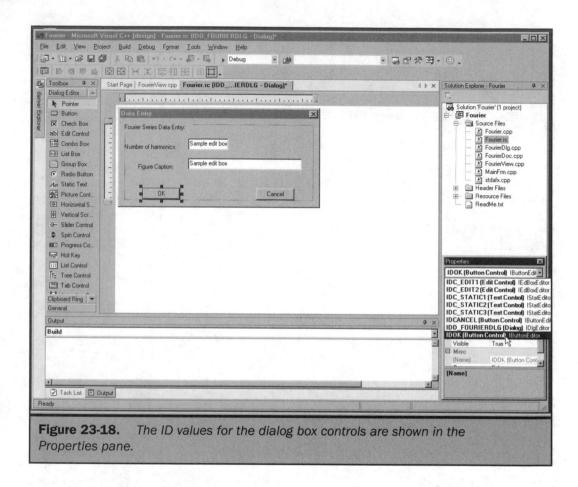

Figure 23-18. *The ID values for the dialog box controls are shown in the Properties pane.*

This menu item will allow the user to open the Data Entry dialog box we created in the previous section.

Fourier Title Bar and About Box

The title bar for the Fourier project can be altered by opening the String Table from the Resource View pane, as shown in Figure 23-20.

Change the string, identified by IDR_MAINFRAME, to match the text shown in Figure 23-20. This will change the text displayed in the project's title bar.

The About box and About box icon can be changed at this point, too. If you have forgotten how to do this, return to the description provided in the GDI project section for complete steps. At this point, create a unique icon and About box for the Fourier project.

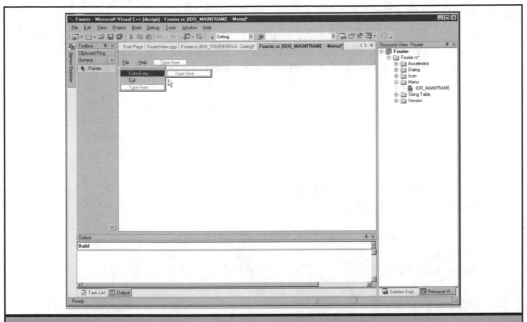

Figure 23-19.   *Modifying the Fourier project's menu resource*

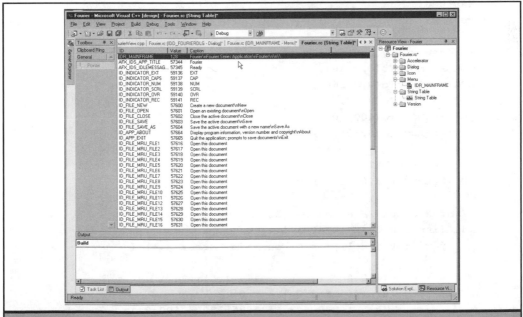

Figure 23-20.   *Various project strings are visible in the String Table resource.*

WINDOWS AND WIZARDS

Fourier Drawing Code

Let's briefly examine the code that will be used to draw the Fourier series waveform. This code resides in the FourierView.cpp file under the OnDraw() method. The modifications we have made to the template code are shown in a bold font:

```
/////////////////////////////////////////////////////////////
// CFourierView drawing

void CFourierView::OnDraw(CDC* pDC)
{
    CFourierDoc* pDoc = GetDocument();
    ASSERT_VALID(pDoc);

    // all remaining code for Fourier Series
    int ang;
    double y, yp;

    pDC->SetMapMode(MM_ISOTROPIC);
    pDC->SetWindowExt(500, 500);
    pDC->SetViewportExt(m_cxClient, -m_cyClient);
    pDC->SetViewportOrg(m_cxClient / 20, m_cyClient / 2);

    ang = 0;
    yp = 0;

    // draw x & y coordinate axes
    pDC -> MoveTo(0, 240);
    pDC -> LineTo(0, -240);
    pDC -> MoveTo(0, 0);
    pDC -> LineTo(400, 0);
    pDC -> MoveTo(0, 0);

    // draw a label
    pDC->TextOut(420, 10, pDoc -> mytext);

    // draw actual Fourier waveform
    for (int i = 0; i <= 400; i++) {
        for (int j = 1; j <= pDoc -> myterms; j++) {

            y = (250.0 / ((2.0 * j) - 1.0)) * \
                sin(((j * 2.0 ) - 1.0) * \
                (ang * 2.0 * 3.14159265359 / 400.0));
```

```
        yp += y;
    }
    pDC -> LineTo(i, (int)yp);
    yp -= yp;
    ang++;
    }
}
```

In order to prevent the scaling problems described in the previous example, a scalable drawing surface is created. You may wish to review the purpose of these functions in Chapter 20.

As shown in the following code, the mapping mode is changed to MM_ISOTROPIC with the SetMapMode() function. The MM_ISOTROPIC mapping mode uses arbitrary drawing units:

```
pDC -> SetMapMode(MM_ISOTROPIC);
```

The next line of code shows the window's extent set to 500 units in both the X and Y directions:

```
pDC -> SetWindowExt(500, 500);
```

This simply means that the X and Y axes will always have 500 units, regardless of the size of the window. The viewport extent is set to the currently reported window size, as shown here:

```
pDC -> SetViewportExt(m_cxClient, -m_cyClient);
```

In this case, you will see all 500 units in the window.

Note *Using a negative value when specifying the Y viewport extent forces Y to increase in the upward direction.*

As the following code shows, the viewport origin is set midway on the Y axis a short distance (a fifth of the length) from the left edge of the X axis:

```
pDC -> SetViewportOrg(m_cxClient/20, m_cyClient/2);
```

Next, X and Y coordinate axes are drawn in the window. Compare the values shown here to the axes shown in screen shots later in this section:

```
// draw x & y coordinate axes
pDC -> MoveTo(0, 240);
pDC -> LineTo(0, -240);
pDC -> MoveTo(0, 0);
pDC -> LineTo(400, 0);
pDC -> MoveTo(0, 0);
```

The technique for drawing the Fourier wave, shown below, uses two **for** loops. The *i* variable controls the angle used by the sine function, and the *j* variable holds the value for the current Fourier harmonic. Each point plotted on the screen is a summation of all the Fourier harmonics for a given angle. Thus, if you request that the application draw 1000 harmonics, approximately 400,000 separate calculations will be made.

```
// draw actual Fourier waveform
for (int i = 0; i <= 400; i++) {
    for (int j = 1; j <= pDoc -> myterms; j++) {
        y = (250.0 / ((2.0 * j) - 1.0)) * \
            sin(((j * 2.0 ) - 1.0) * \
            (ang * 2.0 * 3.14159265359 / 400.0));
        yp += y;
    }
    pDC -> LineTo(i, (int)yp);
    yp -= yp;
    ang++;
}
```

The LineTo() function is used to connect each calculated point, forming a waveform drawn with a solid line.

Before the figure is completed, a label is printed in the window just to the right of the X axis:

```
// draw a label
pDC->TextOut(420, 10, pDoc -> mytext);
```

Remember that all objects drawn within the client area will be scaled to the viewport. This program eliminates the sizing problem of earlier examples and requires only a little additional coding. Add all of this code to your project at this time.

Code for Sizing Graphics

We want this project to size the graphics in the client area so that regardless of the
size of the window, the graphics will be drawn proportionately. We wrote the code
necessary for this operation in the previous section using SetMapMode() through
SetViewportOrg(). However, two of the functions in this section use the *m_cxClient* and
m_cyClient member variables. What values are being returned in these variables? The
values returned give information on the size of the client area. In order to obtain this
information, we'll have to add a member function, OnSize(), to the project.

Open the Class View pane, as shown on the right of Figure 23-21.

Right-click the CFourierView class to display the option list also shown in
Figure 23-21.

Select the Add option from the option list and select Add Function from the two
options provided.

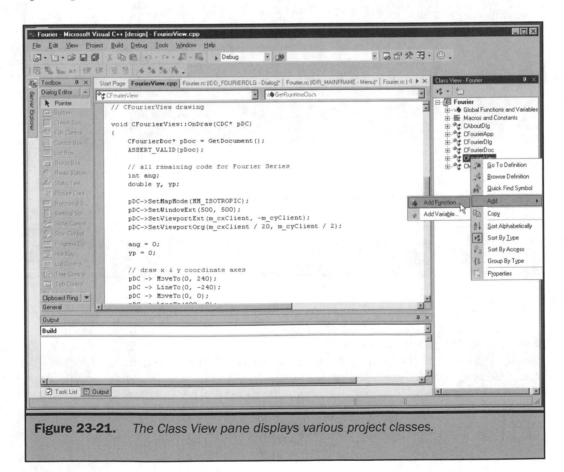

Figure 23-21.   *The Class View pane displays various project classes.*

Selecting the Add Function option opens the Add Member Function Wizard, as shown in Figure 23-22.

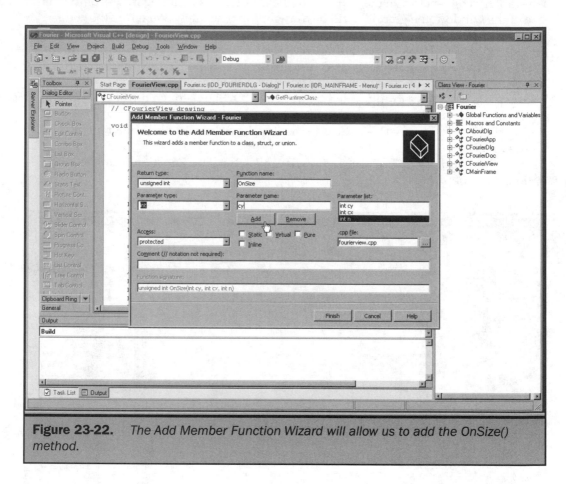

Figure 23-22. *The Add Member Function Wizard will allow us to add the OnSize() method.*

Examine Figure 23-22 and notice the various entries to the dialog box fields. Parameters for a given method are added one at a time. Observe that three parameters have been added: *nType*, *cx*, and *cy*.

Clicking Finish will add this method to the FourierView.cpp source code file. We'll now need two member variables for this method. To add member variables, right-click the CFourierView class to display the option list shown earlier in Figure 23-21.

Select the Add option from the option list and select Add Variable from the two options provided.

Selecting the Add Variable option opens the Add Member Variable Wizard, as shown in Figure 23-23.

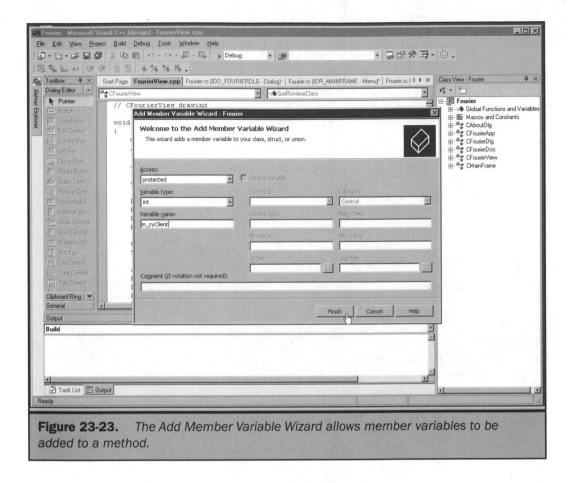

Figure 23-23. *The Add Member Variable Wizard allows member variables to be added to a method.*

Figure 23-23 shows the *m_cyClient* member variable as it is being added to the method. You'll also have to add the *m_cxClient* member variable.

At this point, the following code has been added to the FourierView.cpp file to support the OnSize() method and member variables. The bolded lines of code were added by us to the recently added OnSize() method:

```
void CFourierView::OnSize(unsigned int nType, int cx, int cy)
{
    CView::OnSize(nType, cx, cy);

    m_cxClient = cx;
    m_cyClient = cy;
}
```

A quick look of the FourierView.h header file shows that support for both the method and member variables have been added. Here is a portion of the header file:

```
// FourierView.h : interface of the CFourierView class
//
///////////////////////////////////////////////////////////

#pragma once


class CFourierView : public CView
{
protected: // create from serialization only
    CFourierView();
    DECLARE_DYNCREATE(CFourierView)

    .

    .

    .
// Generated message map functions
protected:
    DECLARE_MESSAGE_MAP()
void OnSize(unsigned int nType, int cx, int cy);

int m_cyClient;

int m_cxClient;

};
```

The next item that requires our attention is the new dialog box resource. In the next section you'll learn how to set up a path of communications between the dialog box resource and the project.

Dialog Box Interfacing

Earlier in this section, we designed a new dialog box resource that will allow the user to enter data for the application. Specifically, the dialog box we created allows the user to enter the number of Fourier harmonics and a label for the project. It is now our job to interface the dialog box information with the project. This is typically accomplished with an additional class.

Open the Class View pane and right-click Fourier. This will open a list of options. From this list, select Add and then Add Class. When this selection is made, the Add Class dialog will open. From the right pane of this dialog, select the template for an MFC Class. When the Open button is selected, the MFC Class Wizard dialog box will open, as shown in Figure 23-24.

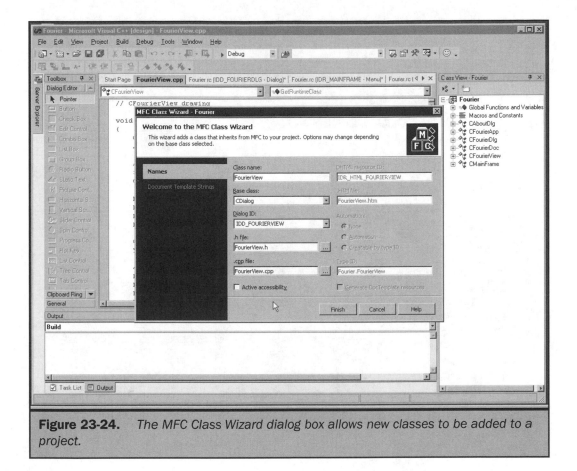

Figure 23-24. *The MFC Class Wizard dialog box allows new classes to be added to a project.*

As you can see by viewing this figure, the class we add, CFourierDlg, will be based on the CDialog base class. The dialog ID value is one we have assigned to the previously created dialog box, IDD_FOURIERVIEW. Support for this dialog box is provided in the FourierDlg.cpp and FourierDlg.h files.

Set the various data fields to those shown in Figure 23-24 and click Finish. You'll have to add support for two member variables, *m_text* and *m_terms* using the techniques described earlier in this section relating to member variables. The variable *m_terms* will be used to return an integer value. The *m_text* variable will return a type CString that will hold an optional label for the graph. You may have to type *CString* into the type field if it is not available from the pull-down selection.

We are now ready to add a member function to the CFourierView class in the FourierView.cpp source code file. Open the Add Member Function Wizard, as you did when adding the OnSize() method in the previous section. The method or member function we wish to add is OnFourier(), as shown in Figure 23-25.

When you are done, make sure the following changes have been made to the files described in the following sections.

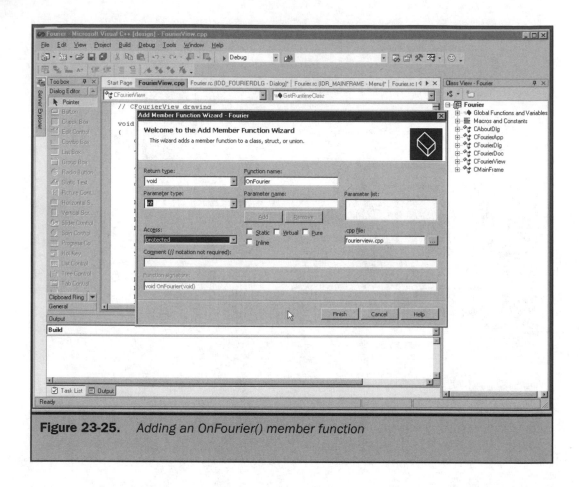

Figure 23-25.   *Adding an OnFourier() member function*

FourierDlg.cpp and FourierDlg.h

The following portion of code is taken from the FourierDlg.cpp source code file. The code shown in a bold font should exist or be added to this listing:

```
// FourierDlg.cpp : implementation file
//

#include "stdafx.h"
#include "Fourier.h"
#include "FourierDlg.h"
        .
        .
        .


IMPLEMENT_DYNAMIC(CFourierDlg, CDialog)
```

```
CFourierDlg::CFourierDlg(CWnd* pParent /*=NULL*/)
    : CDialog(CFourierDlg::IDD, pParent)
{
    m_terms = 4;            //set default value in edit control
    m_text = _T("Title"); //set default value in edit control
}
        .
        .
        .

void CFourierDlg::DoDataExchange(CDataExchange* pDX)
{
    CDialog::DoDataExchange(pDX);

    DDX_Text(pDX, IDC_EDIT1, m_terms);  // make data exchange
    DDX_Text(pDX, IDC_EDIT2, m_text); // make data exchange
    DDV_MinMaxUInt(pDX, m_terms, 1, 100000);
}
```

Note that the "4" and the word "Title" shown in this listing provided the default values for the edit box controls.

Next, the following edited portion of code is taken from the FourierDlg.h header file. The code shown in a bold font should also exist or be added to this listing:

```
/////////////////////////////////////////////////////////////
// CFourierDlg dialog

class CFourierDlg : public CDialog
{
    DECLARE_DYNAMIC(CFourierDlg)
        .
        .
        .
// Dialog Data
    enum { IDD = IDD_FOURIERVIEW };
        .
        .
        .
DECLARE_MESSAGE_MAP()
public:
    int m_terms;
    CString m_text;
};
```

WINDOWS AND WIZARDS

The variables and values shown in this code should be obvious in terms of their use in the interface of the dialog box with the project.

The MFC library supports regular and modal dialog boxes with the CDialog class. For very simple dialog boxes such as About boxes, the MFC can be used directly. For data entry dialog boxes, however, the class will have to be derived from an existing class. The dialog box for this example is derived from CDialog. Modal dialog boxes must be dismissed before other actions can be taken in an application.

In a derived modal dialog class, member variables and functions can be added to specify the behavior of the dialog box. Member variables can also be used to save data entered by the user or to save data for display. Classes derived from CDialog require their own message maps, with the exception of the OnInitDialog(), OnOK(), and OnCancel() functions.

In this simple example, the CFourierDlg() is derived from the CDialog class. The parent window is the owner for this modal dialog box.

The dialog box will actually return data to the application when the user clicks the OK dialog box button. If either the OK or the Cancel button is clicked, the dialog box closes and is removed from the screen. When the dialog box closes, the member functions access its member variables to retrieve information entered by the user.

FourierDoc.cpp and FourierDoc.h

Document files, such as FourierDoc.cpp, provide document support for MFC projects. Typically, string information provided by various resources will be held in these files. We'll use the document files to pass information from the dialog box to the project.

The following edited portion of code is taken from the FourierDoc.cpp source code file. The code shown in a bold font should exist or be added to this listing:

```
// FourierDoc.cpp : implementation of the CFourierDoc class
//

#include "stdafx.h"
#include "Fourier.h"
#include "FourierDoc.h"

     .

     .

     .

/////////////////////////////////////////////////////////////////
// CFourierDoc construction/destruction

CFourierDoc::CFourierDoc()
{
    myterms = 4;
    mytext = "Title";
```

```
}
    .
    .
    .
```

The "4" and the word "Title" provide information for the window when it is initially drawn.

The next portion of edited code is taken from the FourierDoc.h header file. The code shown in a bold font should exist or be added to this listing:

```
// FourierDoc.h : interface of the CFourierDoc class
/////////////////////////////////////////////////////////////

#pragma once

class CFourierDoc : public CDocument
{
protected: // create from serialization only
    CFourierDoc();
    DECLARE_DYNCREATE(CFourierDoc)

    int myterms;
    CString mytext;

    .
    .
    .
/////////////////////////////////////////////////////////////
```

Next, we'll examine the changes to the FourierView.cpp source code file and the FourierView.h header file.

FourierView.cpp and FourierView.h

The next portion of edited code is taken from the FourierView.cpp source code file. The code shown in a bold font should exist or be added to this listing. Note that a large portion of code is not shown in this listing for clarity:

```
// FourierView.cpp : implementation of the CFourierView class
//

#include "stdafx.h"
#include "Fourier.h"
```

```
#include "FourierDoc.h"
#include "FourierView.h"

#include "FourierDlg.h"
#include "math.h"
      .
      .
      .

IMPLEMENT_DYNCREATE(CFourierView, CView)

BEGIN_MESSAGE_MAP(CFourierView, CView)
    ON_WM_SIZE()
    ON_COMMAND(ID_FILE_DATAENTRY, OnFourier)
END_MESSAGE_MAP()
      .
      .
      .
//////////////////////////////////////////////////////////////
// CFourierView message handlers

void CFourierView::OnSize(UINT nType, int cx, int cy)
{
    CView::OnSize(nType, cx, cy);

    m_cxClient = cx;
    m_cyClient = cy;
}

void CFourierView::OnFourier(void)
{
    CFourierDlg dlg (this);
    int result = dlg.DoModal();

    if(result == IDOK) {
        CFourierDoc* pDoc = GetDocument();
        ASSERT_VALID(pDoc);
        pDoc -> myterms = dlg.m_terms;
        pDoc -> mytext  = dlg.m_text;
        Invalidate();
    }
}
```

The user is permitted to enter a chart label and an integer representing the number of Fourier harmonics to draw. If the user clicks the OK button, the data entry dialog box is removed from the window and the client area is updated, as shown in the following portion of code.

CFourierDlg was derived from CDialog and discussed earlier. Notice, however, that it is at this point in the application that data is actually retrieved. The user entered this data in the dialog box. The information is returned when the user clicks the dialog box OK button.

The information is passed from the dialog box to the project's document code. The member variables are accessed to provide the transfer to the local variables *myterms* and *mytext*.

```
pDoc -> myterms = dlg.m_terms;
pDoc -> mytext  = dlg.m_text;
```

The next portion of edited code is taken from the FourierView.h header file. The code shown in a bold font should exist or be added to this listing:

```
// FourierView.h : interface of the CFourierView class
//
/////////////////////////////////////////////////////////////
    .
    .
    .
// Generated message map functions
protected:
    DECLARE_MESSAGE_MAP()
private:

protected:
    void OnSize(unsigned int nType, int cx, int cy);
    void OnFourier(void);

    int m_cxClient;
    int m_cyClient;
};
    .
    .
    .
```

DECLARE_MESSAGE_MAP is used frequently to state that the class overrides the handling of certain messages. This technique is more space efficient than the use of virtual functions.

There is an ON_COMMAND() function in FourierView.cpp that corresponds to the OnFourier() method in this listing:

```
ON_COMMAND(ID_FILE_DATAENTRY, OnFourier)
```

This line of code associates the menu item in the project's File menu with the data entry dialog box.

Testing the Fourier Project

Compile the Fourier project in the normal manner. When the Fourier project is executed, a default waveform is drawn in the client area. The default waveform is created with four harmonics and is shown in Figure 23-26.

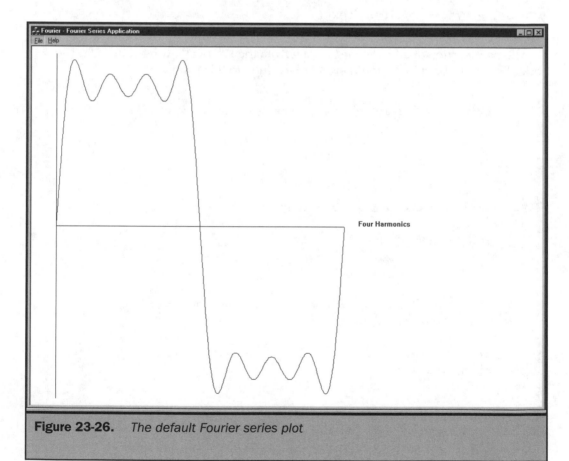

Figure 23-26.   *The default Fourier series plot*

Figure 23-27 shows the plot when 40 harmonics are drawn.

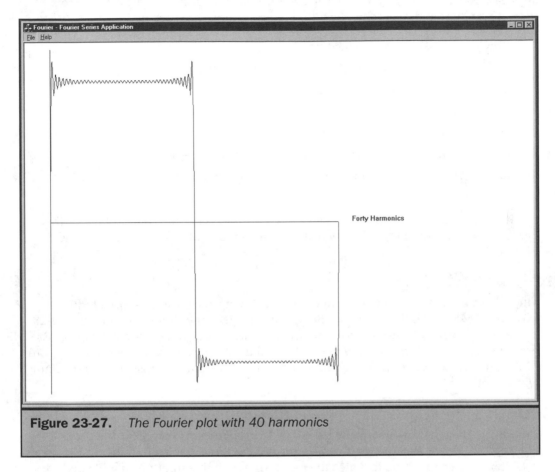

Forty Harmonics

Figure 23-27.   *The Fourier plot with 40 harmonics*

As the number of harmonics increases, the figure drawn in the client area will approach a perfect square wave. You can experiment with various values and note how the drawing time increases for very large numbers of harmonics.

A Bar Chart with Resources

The final project in this chapter, BarChart, will draw a presentation-quality bar chart in the window's client area. This application also makes use of several Windows resources, including a menu, an About dialog box, and a data entry dialog box.

The template code for this project is created in exactly the same manner as the other applications in this chapter. When using the Application Wizard, simply name this project BarChart and make sure the following conditions are specified:

- Create a new project named BarChart
- Application Type: set for Single document support
- Compound Document Support: none needed
- Document Template Strings: none modified for this project
- Database Support: none for this project
- User Interface Features: toolbars—none, status bar—none
- Advanced Features: uncheck Printing And Print Preview as well as ActiveX Controls

Once the settings have been entered, click Finish to generate the template for the BarChart project. The project is now ready for the modifications we'll make to the project.

Title Bar String

The title in the title bar can be changed by modifying the string resource IDR_MAINFRAME. To do this, bring up the Resource View pane, as shown in Figure 23-28.

Select the String Table resource from the Resource View pane to view the list of this project's string resources. Modify the IDR_MAINFRAME resource, as shown in Figure 23-28. The project will now display this string in the title bar area instead of the default word "untitled."

Menu

Once again, use the Resource View pane to select the menu resource for the project. Figure 23-29 shows the Resource View pane and the menu bar itself in the design area.

Alter the default menu to match the menu shown in this figure. You will need to delete the Edit menu and insert the Data Entry menu, assigning it an ID of IDM_INPUT. In addition, don't forget to delete any menu items in the File menu that you do not plan to implement. For this project, we just left the Exit menu item in this menu.

About Box Icon

We'll create a custom About box icon for the project. Use the Resource View pane to select the icon identified by IDR_MAINFRAME. When this item is selected, you'll be able to view the default icon for the project. Use the various editing tools provided in the toolbar and the palette of colors provided to the left of the design area, as shown in Figure 23-30.

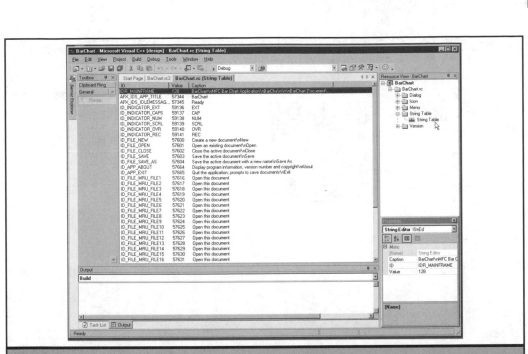

Figure 23-28.   *The Resource View pane shows all of this project's resources.*

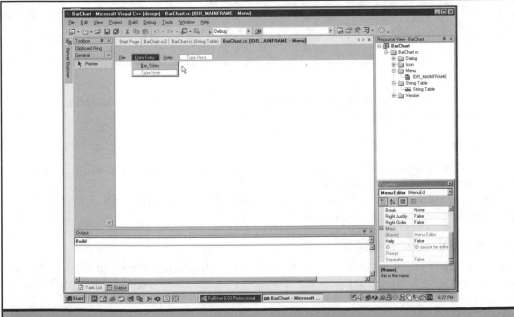

Figure 23-29.   *The menu is altered for the BarChart project.*

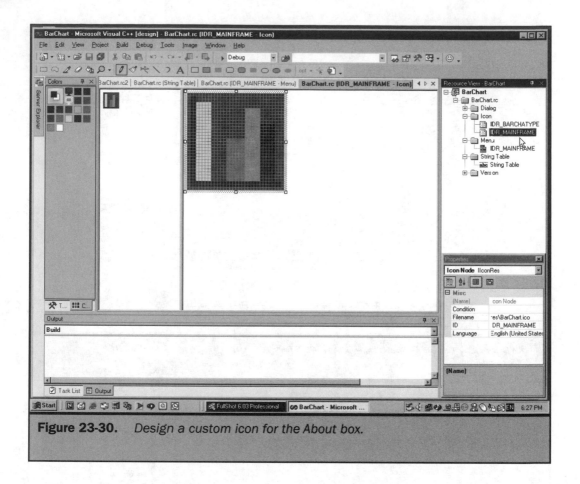

Figure 23-30.   *Design a custom icon for the About box.*

Here is a good place to let your artistic talents help you design a functional and practical icon for the project.

About Box

The About box, shown in Figure 23-31, is a modified version of the default dialog box created by the Application Wizard.

Notice, in this figure, that the new icon is present. This will only occur if you compile the project after creating the new iconic image.

Data Entry Dialog Box

The next step in this project is to design a data entry dialog box that will allow the user to enter a title, axis labels, bar heights, and labels for the chart's legend. Figure 23-32 shows the data entry dialog box we designed for the project.

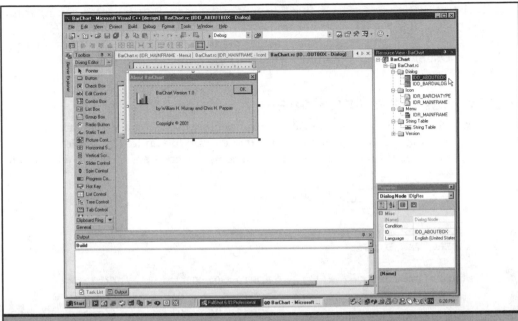

Figure 23-31.   *Modify the About dialog box to include your name.*

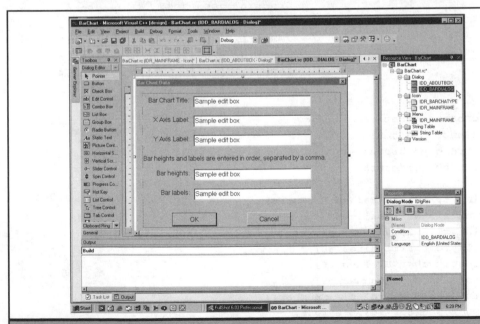

Figure 23-32.   *A good dialog box design is well laid out, easy to read, and functional.*

Notice five Static Text controls, five Edit Box controls, two Push Button controls and a group box. Change the ID of the box to IDD_BARDATADIALOG.

At this point, you'll also get a little practice aligning and sizing controls within a dialog box. Dialog boxes, in our opinion, are the most difficult part of the project for most programmers.

Core BarChart Drawing Code

In this section we'll briefly examine the code that will be used to draw the bar chart in the client area. This code resides in the BarChartView.cpp file under the OnDraw() method. The modifications we have made to the template code are shown in a bold font:

```
void CBarChartView::OnDraw(CDC* pDC)
{
    CBarChartDoc* pDoc = GetDocument();
    ASSERT_VALID(pDoc);

    static DWORD dwColor[12] = {RGB(0, 0, 0),          //black
                                RGB(255, 0, 0),        //red
                                RGB(0, 255, 0),        //green
                                RGB(0, 0, 255),        //blue
                                RGB(255, 255, 0),      //yellow
                                RGB(255, 0, 255),      //magenta
                                RGB(0, 255, 255),      //cyan
                                RGB(125, 125, 0),      //blend 1
                                RGB(125, 0, 125),      //blend 2
                                RGB(0, 125, 125),      //blend 3
                                RGB(125, 125, 125),    //blend 4
                                RGB(255, 255, 255)};   //white

    CFont newfont;
    CFont* oldfont;
    CBrush newbrush;
    CBrush* oldbrush;

    int i,iNBars,iBarWidth,iBarMax;
    int ilenMaxLabel;
    int x1, x2, y1, y2, z1, z2;
    static char LValues[80];
    static char HValues[80];
    int iBarSize[maxnumber];
    int iBarSizeScaled[maxnumber];
    char sbuffer[10], *strptr;
    char szBarLabel[12][20];
    static char *n, *p;
```

```
// make copies of data for re-drawing
strcpy(HValues, pDoc -> GHValues);
strcpy(LValues, pDoc -> GLValues);

// parse string to get bar heights
iNBars = 0;
i = 0;
n = HValues;
p = strtok(n, ",");
while ((n != NULL)) {
    iBarSize[i] = atoi(n);
    p = strtok(NULL, ",");
    n = p;
    iNBars++;
    i++;
}


// parse string to get bar labels
i = 0;
n = LValues;
p = strtok(n, ",");
while ((n != NULL)) {
    strcpy(szBarLabel[i], n);
    p = strtok(NULL, ",");
    n = p;
    i++;
}


iBarWidth = 400 / iNBars;

// Find bar with maximum height and scale
iBarMax = iBarSize[0];
for(i = 0; i < iNBars; i++)
    if (iBarMax < iBarSize[i]) iBarMax = iBarSize[i];

// Convert maximum y value to a string
strptr = _itoa(iBarMax, sbuffer, 10);
ilenMaxLabel = strlen(sbuffer);

// Scale bars in array. Highest bar = 270
for (i = 0; i < iNBars; i++)
    iBarSizeScaled[i] = iBarSize[i] * (270 / iBarMax);
```

```cpp
// Create custom viewport and map mode
pDC -> SetMapMode(MM_ISOTROPIC);
pDC -> SetWindowExt(640, 480);
pDC -> SetViewportExt(m_cxClient, m_cyClient);
pDC -> SetViewportOrg(0, 0);

// Draw text if window is large enough
if ((m_cxClient > 300) && (m_cyClient > 200)) {
    newfont.CreateFont(20, 12, 900, 900, FW_NORMAL,
                       FALSE, FALSE, FALSE,
                       OEM_CHARSET, OUT_DEFAULT_PRECIS,
                       CLIP_DEFAULT_PRECIS,
                       DEFAULT_QUALITY,
                       34,
                       "Arial");
  oldfont = pDC -> SelectObject(&newfont);
  pDC -> TextOut(50,
                 200 + (strlen(pDoc -> YString) * 10 / 2),
                 pDoc -> YString, strlen(pDoc -> YString));
  pDC -> SelectObject(oldfont);
  newfont.DeleteObject();

    newfont.CreateFont(20, 12, 0, 0, FW_NORMAL,
                       FALSE, FALSE, FALSE, OEM_CHARSET,
                       OUT_DEFAULT_PRECIS,
                       CLIP_DEFAULT_PRECIS,
                       DEFAULT_QUALITY,
                       34,
                       "Arial");
  oldfont = pDC -> SelectObject(&newfont);
  pDC -> TextOut((300 - (strlen(pDoc -> TString) * 10 / 2)),
                 15, pDoc -> TString,
                 strlen(pDoc -> TString));
  pDC -> TextOut((300 - (strlen(pDoc -> XString) * 10 / 2)),
                 365, pDoc -> XString,
                 strlen(pDoc -> XString));
  pDC -> TextOut((90 - ilenMaxLabel * 12), 70,
                 strptr, ilenMaxLabel);
  pDC -> SelectObject(oldfont);
  newfont.DeleteObject();
}

// Draw coordinate axis
pDC -> MoveTo(99, 49);
```

```
    pDC -> LineTo(99, 350);
    pDC -> LineTo(500, 350);
    pDC -> MoveTo(99, 350);

    // Initial values
    x1 = 100;
    y1 = 350;
    z1 = 50;
    z2 = z1 + 15;
    x2 = x1 + iBarWidth;

    // Draw each bar
    for(i = 0; i < iNBars; i++) {
        newbrush.CreateSolidBrush(dwColor[i]);
        oldbrush = pDC -> SelectObject(&newbrush);
        y2 = 350 - iBarSizeScaled[i];
        pDC -> Rectangle(x1, y1, x2, y2);
        x1 = x2;
        x2 += iBarWidth;

        // Draw labels
        if ((strlen(szBarLabel[0]) != 0) && (m_cxClient > 300) &&
            (m_cyClient > 200)) {
            pDC -> Rectangle(545, z1, 560, z2);
            pDC -> TextOut(565, z1, szBarLabel[i],
                              strlen(szBarLabel[i]));
            z1 = z2 + 15;
            z2 += 30;
        }
    pDC -> SelectObject(&newbrush);
    newbrush.DeleteObject();
    }
```

Just as we did for the Fourier project, we'll add code that will allow the bar chart to be sized with the window. The details for creating a scalable drawing surface using special functions were explained in Chapter 20.

The first step is to change the mapping mode to MM_ISOTROPIC with the SetMapMode() function. The MM_ISOTROPIC mapping mode uses arbitrary drawing units:

```
pDC -> SetMapMode(MM_ISOTROPIC);
```

The next line of code shows the window's extent set to 640 units in X and 480 units in the Y direction:

```
pDC -> SetWindowExt(640, 480);
```

This simply means that the X and Y axes will always have the same number of drawing units regardless of the size of the window. The viewport extent is set to the currently reported window size, as shown here:

```
pDC -> SetViewportExt(m_cxClient, m_cyClient);
```

In this case, you will see all of the drawing units in the window. The following code shows the viewport origin is set to 0,0. This position is at the top-left portion of the window:

```
pDC -> SetViewportOrg(0, 0);
```

Next, X and Y coordinate axes are drawn in the window. Compare the values shown here to the axes shown in screen shots later in this section:

```
// Draw coordinate axis
pDC -> MoveTo(99, 49);
pDC -> LineTo(99, 350);
pDC -> LineTo(500, 350);
pDC -> MoveTo(99, 350);
```

Notice that since the origin was set to 0,0, the starting points of the axes had to be offset on the chart. This is a distinctly different approach than that used in the Fourier project.

The technique for drawing the individual bar chart bars and legend labels is straightforward, as you can see in the following portion of code:

```
// Draw each bar
for(i = 0; i < iNBars; i++) {
    newbrush.CreateSolidBrush(dwColor[i]);
    oldbrush = pDC -> SelectObject(&newbrush);
    y2 = 350 - iBarSizeScaled[i];
    pDC -> Rectangle(x1, y1, x2, y2);
    x1 = x2;
    x2 += iBarWidth;
```

```
            // Draw labels
            if ((strlen(szBarLabel[0]) != 0) && (m_cxClient > 300) &&
                (m_cyClient > 200)) {
                pDC -> Rectangle(545, z1, 560, z2);
                pDC -> TextOut(565, z1, szBarLabel[i],
                                strlen(szBarLabel[i]));
                z1 = z2 + 15;
                z2 += 30;
            }
            pDC -> SelectObject(&newbrush);
            newbrush.DeleteObject();
        }
```

We'll get back to this code in a later section. The maximum number of bars, *maxnumbar*, is set to 12 at the start of the application:

```
#define maxnumbar 12
```

This value can be changed slightly, but remember that a good bar chart doesn't crowd too many bars onto a single chart.

Because the application keeps track of the client area size (using the OnSize() method), this bar chart can be scaled to fit the current window size.

Bar colors are selected from the *dwColor[]* array in a sequential manner. If the bar chart has three bars, they will be black, red, and green. Colors can be exchanged if you so desire.

The **CFont** and **CBrush** classes permit a font or brush object to be passed to any CDC (base class for display context) member function. New fonts will be needed to draw the chart title and axes labels. Brushes were discussed earlier in this chapter. Here is the syntax used to create a new font and brush object:

```
CFont newfont;
CFont* oldfont;
CBrush newbrush;
CBrush* oldbrush;
```

Manipulating Bar Data

Before plotting a bar chart, it is first necessary to determine how many bar values are going to be plotted. The user has entered a number of bar values in a dialog box. These values, entered as a string, are separated by a comma. We'll use the following parser to separate the string values, convert them to numeric values, and place them in an array. For each value placed in the array, the count in *iNBars* is incremented:

```
// parse string to get bar heights
iNBars = 0;
i = 0;
n = HValues;
p = strtok(n, ",");
while ((n != NULL)) {
    iBarSize[i] = atoi(n);
    p = strtok(NULL, ",");
    n = p;
    iNBars++;
    i++;
}
```

The strtok() function is used in this example as the heart of the parser routine. The atoi() function converts the string value to an integer and places it in the *iBarSize[]* array. The legend labels are parsed in a similar manner.

The actual data values are returned whenever the data entry dialog box is closed. The width of each bar drawn in the chart is dependent upon the total number of bars. The chart will always be drawn to the same width. Individual bar width is determined with this calculation:

```
iBarWidth = 400 / iNBars;
```

The height of each bar is determined relative to the largest bar value entered by the user. The largest bar value is always drawn to the same chart height. The size of the largest bar value is easy to determine:

```
// Find bar with maximum height and scale
iBarMax = iBarSize[0];
for(i = 0; i < iNBars; i++)
    if (iBarMax < iBarSize[i]) iBarMax = iBarSize[i];
```

This chart will also print the height of the largest bar value next to the vertical axis. The _itoa() function is used to convert this value to a string:

```
// Convert maximum y value to a string
strptr = _itoa(iBarMax, sbuffer, 10);
ilenMaxLabel = strlen(sbuffer);
```

The remaining bars in the array are then scaled to the largest bar's value:

```
// Scale bars in array. Highest bar = 270
for (i = 0; i < iNBars; i++)
  iBarSizeScaled[i] = iBarSize[i] * (270 / iBarMax);
```

The height of the largest bar in the data set is set to 270. All bars are scaled to the largest bar.

Drawing Text to the Window

When a project requires several fonts or orientations, various font functions must be used. Let's look at how these fonts can be created. There are actually two ways to create and manipulate fonts in Windows: use the CreateFont() or CreateFontIndirect() functions. This example uses the CreateFont() function.

What Is a Font?   A *font* can be defined as a complete set of characters of the same typeface and size. Fonts include letters, punctuation marks, and additional symbols. The size of a font is measured in points. For example, 12-point Arial, 12-point Times New Roman, 14-point Times New Roman, and 12-point Lucida Bright are all different fonts. A *point* is the smallest unit of measure used in typography. There are 12 points in a *pica* and 72 points (6 picas) in an inch.

A *typeface* is a basic character design that is defined by a stroke width and a serif (a smaller line used to finish off a main stroke of a letter, as you can see at the top and bottom of the uppercase letter "M"). As mentioned above, a font represents a complete set of characters from one specific typeface, all with a certain size and style, such as italics or bold. Usually the system owns all of the font resources and shares them with application programs. Fonts are not usually compiled into the final executable version of a program.

Projects such as BarChart treat fonts like other drawing objects. Windows supplies several fonts: System, Terminal, Courier, Helvetica, Modern, Roman, Script, and Times Roman, as well as several TrueType fonts. These are called *GDI_supplied fonts*.

The CreateFont() Function Syntax   The CreateFont() function selects a logical font from the GDI's pool of physical fonts that most closely matches the characteristics specified by the developer when the function is called. Once the logical font is created it can be selected by any device. The syntax for the CreateFont() function is:

```
CreateFont (Height,Width,Escapement,Orientation,Weight,
            Italic,Underline,StrikeOut,CharSet,
            OutputPrecision,ClipPrecision,Quality,
            PitchAndFamily,Facename)
```

Using the CreateFont() function, with its 14 parameters, requires quite a bit of skill. Table 23-1 gives a brief description of the CreateFont() parameters.

CreateFont() Parameters	Description
(LONG) Height	Desired font height in logical units
(LONG) Width	Average font width in logical units
(LONG) Escapement	Angle (in tenths of a degree) for each line written in the font
(LONG) Orientation	Angle (in tenths of a degree) for each character's baseline
(LONG) Weight	Weight of font (from 0 to 1000); 400 is normal, 700 is bold
(BYTE) Italic	Italic font
(BYTE) Underline	Underline font
(BYTE) StrikeOut	Struck out fonts (redline)
(BYTE) CharSet	Character set (ANSI-CHARSET, OEM-CHARSET)
(BYTE) OutputPrecision	How closely output must match the requested specifications (OUT-CHARACTER PRECIS, OUT-DEFAULT-PRECIS, OUT-STRING-PRECIS, OUT-STROKE-PRECIS)
(BYTE) ClipPrecision	How to clip characters outside of clipping range (CLIP-CHARACTER PRECIS, CLIP-DEFAULT-PRECIS, CLIP-STROKE-PRECIS)
(BYTE) Quality	How carefully the logical attributes are mapped to the physical font (DEFAULT-QUALITY, DRAFT-QUALITY, PROOF-QUALITY)
(BYTE) PitchAndFamily	Pitch and family of font (DEFAULT-PITCH, FIXED-PITCH, PROOF-QUALITY, FF-ROMAN, FF-SCRIPT, FF-DECORATIVE, FF-DONTCARE, FF-MODERN, FF-SWISS)
(CHAR) Facename	A string pointing to the typeface name of the desired font

Table 23-1.   *CreateFont() Parameters*

The first time the CreateFont() function is called by the application, the parameters are set to the following values:

```
Height = 20

Width  = 12

Escapement = 900

Orientation = 900

Weight = FW_NORMAL

Italic = FALSE

Underline = FALSE

StrikeOut = FALSE

CharSet = OEM_CHARSET

OutputPrecision = OUT_DEFAULT_PRECIS

ClipPrecision = CLIP_DEFAULT_PRECIS

Quality = DEFAULT_QUALITY

PitchAndFamily = 34

Facename = "Arial"
```

An attempt will then be made by Windows to find a font to match the preceding specifications. This font will be used to print a vertical string of text in the window. The next time CreateFont() is called, the parameters are set to the following values:

```
Height = 20

Width  = 12

Escapement = 0

Orientation = 0

Weight = FW_NORMAL

Italic = FALSE

Underline = FALSE

StrikeOut = FALSE

CharSet = OEM_CHARSET

OutputPrecision = OUT_DEFAULT_PRECIS

ClipPrecision = CLIP_DEFAULT_PRECIS

Quality = DEFAULT_QUALITY

PitchAndFamily = 34

Facename = "Arial"
```

WINDOWS AND WIZARDS

Again, an attempt will be made by Windows to find a match to the preceding specifications. Examine the listing and notice that only *Escapement* and *Orientation* were changed. Both of these parameters use angle values specified in tenths of a degree. In the first case, 900 represents an angle of 90.0 degrees. In the second case, 0 represents 0.0 degrees. The *Escapement* parameter rotates the line of text from horizontal to vertical. *Orientation* rotates each character, in the first case, by 90.0 degrees.

Here is how the vertical axis label was printed in this application:

```
newfont.CreateFont(20, 12, 900, 900, FW_NORMAL,
                   FALSE, FALSE, FALSE,
                   OEM_CHARSET,
                   OUT_DEFAULT_PRECIS,
                   CLIP_DEFAULT_PRECIS,
                   DEFAULT_QUALITY,
                   34,
                   "Arial");
oldfont = pDC -> SelectObject(&newfont);
pDC -> TextOut(50, 200 + (strlen(pDoc -> YString) * 10 / 2),
               pDoc -> YString, strlen(pDoc -> YString));
```

Note that the string, *YString*, is declared in BarChartDoc.h and initialized in BarChartDoc.cpp.

When you develop your own applications, be sure to examine the online documentation on the CreateFont() function and the additional typefaces that may be available for your use.

Drawing the Bars

The program now prepares for drawing each bar. As the following code shows, the first bar always starts at position 100,350 on the chart, as defined by *x1* and *y1*. The width of the first bar and all subsequent bars is calculated from the last drawing position and the width of each bar. The second x value is defined by *x2*.

```
// Initial values
x1 = 100;
y1 = 350;
z1 = 50;
z2 = z1 + 15;
x2=x1 + iBarWidth;
```

Note *The z variables are used for the legend values.*

Bars are drawn (by the program) by retrieving the scaled bar height value from *iBarSizeScaled[]* array. This scaled value, saved in *y2*, is used in the Rectangle() function. Since the Rectangle() function draws a closed figure, the figure will be filled with the current brush color. The color value selected from the array is incremented during each pass through the loop. Here is a portion of code to show how this is achieved:

```
for(i = 0; i < iNBars; i++) {
    newbrush.CreateSolidBrush(dwColor[i]);
    oldbrush = pDC -> SelectObject(&newbrush);
    y2 = 350 - iBarSizeScaled[i];
    pDC -> Rectangle(x1, y1, x2, y2);
    x1 = x2;
    x2 += iBarWidth;
```

After each bar is drawn, the values in *x1* and *x2* are updated to point to the next bar's position. This process is repeated in the **for** loop until all the bars are drawn.

If you examine the portion of code that follows this **for** loop in the original listing, you'll see that the chart's legend is drawn in a similar manner.

Code for Sizing Graphics

We want this project, like the Fourier project, to size the graphics in the client area so that regardless of the size of the window, the graphics will be drawn proportionately. The code needed for this support is contained in the OnDraw() method and uses the SetMapMode() through SetViewportOrg() functions already described. Two of the functions in this section use the *m_cxClient* and *m_cyClient* member variables. The values returned by these functions give information on the size of the client area. In order to obtain this information, we'll have to add a member function, OnSize(), to the project.

Open the Class View pane as you have done for other projects. Right-click the CBarChartView class to display the option list. Then select the Add option from the option list. Next, select Add Function from the two additional options that are provided.

Selecting the Add Function option opens the Add Member Function Wizard, as shown in Figure 23-33.

Examine Figure 23-33 and notice the various entries to the dialog box fields. Parameters for a given method are added one at a time. Observe that three parameters have been added: *nType*, *cx*, and *cy*.

Clicking Finish will add this method to the BarChartView.cpp source code file. We'll also need two member variables for this method. To add member variables, right-click the CBarChartView class to display the option list. Select the Add option from the option list and select Add Variable from the two additional options that are provided.

Selecting the Add Variable option opens the Add Member Variable Wizard, as shown in Figure 23-34.

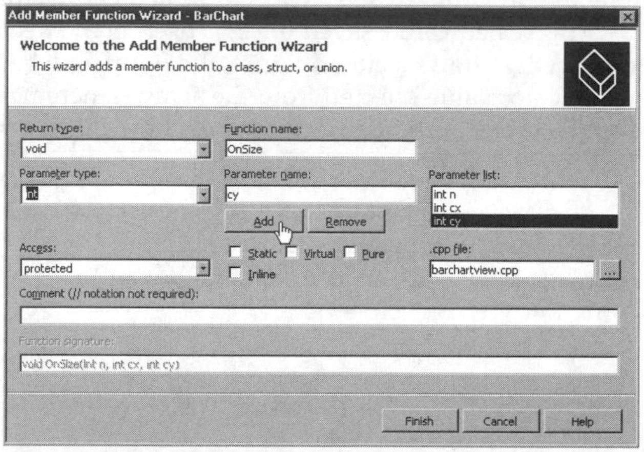

Figure 23-33.   *The Add Member Function Wizard will allow us to add the OnSize() method.*

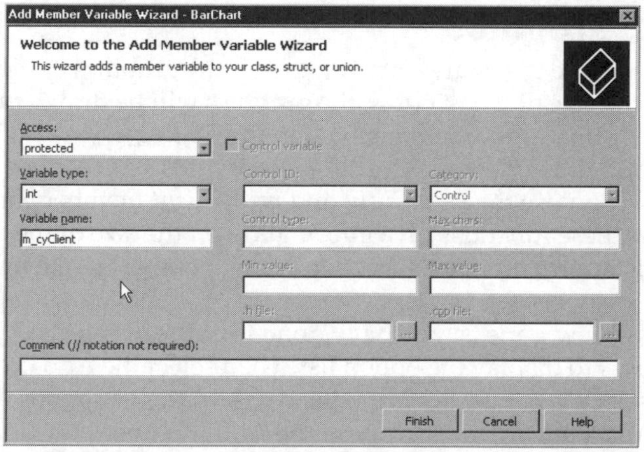

Figure 23-34.   *The Add Member Variable Wizard allows member variables to be added to a method.*

Figure 23-34 shows the *m_cyClient* member variable as it is being added to the method. You'll also have to add the *m_cxClient* member variable.

At this point, the following code has been added to the BarChartView.cpp file to support the OnSize() method and member variables. The bolded lines of code were added by us to the recently added OnSize() method:

```
void CBarChartView::OnSize(UINT nType, int cx, int cy)
{
    CView::OnSize(nType, cx, cy);

    m_cxClient = cx;
    m_cyClient = cy;
}
```

You might want to examine the BarChartView.h header file to see that both the method and member variables have been added.

The next item that requires our attention is the new dialog box resource. In the next section you'll learn how to set up a path of communications between the dialog box resource and the project.

Dialog Box Interfacing

Earlier in this section, we designed a dialog box resource that will allow the user to enter data for the application. We must now provide a bridge for data exchange between the dialog box information and the project code. This bridge is typically accomplished with an additional class.

Open the Class View pane and right-click the BarChart. This will open a list of options. From this list, select Add and then Add Class. When this selection is made, the Add Class dialog will open. From the right pane of this dialog, select the template for an MFC Class. When the Open button is selected, the MFC Class Wizard dialog box will open, as shown in Figure 23-35.

As you can see by viewing this figure, the class we add will be based on the CDialog base class. The dialog ID value is one previously assigned to the dialog box, IDD_BARDATADIALOG. Support for this dialog box is provided in the BarChartDlg.cpp and BarChartDlg.h files.

Set the various data fields to those shown in Figure 23-35 and click Finish. Now you'll have to add support for five CString member variables, *m_TString*, *m_XString*, *m_YString*, *m_GHValues*, and *m_GLValues*. The *m_TString* variable is used to hold the title for the chart. The *m_XString* and *m_YString* variables hold the axis labels. The *m_GHValues* variable stores the bar heights entered by the user while the *m_GLValues* variable holds the legend labels. When you are done, click Finish.

We are now ready to add a member function to the BarChartView.cpp source code file. Open the Add Member Function Wizard, as you did when adding the OnSize() method in the previous section. The method or member function we wish to add is OnInput(), as shown in Figure 23-36.

The next task is to make sure the following changes have been made to the files described in the following sections.

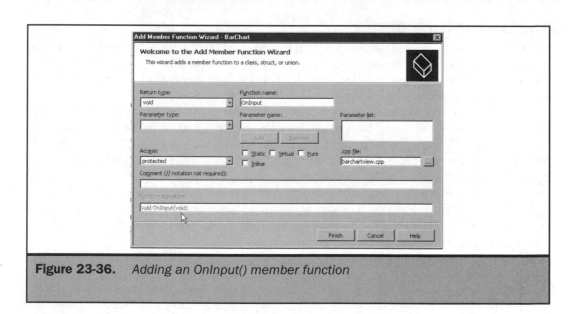

Figure 23-35. *The MFC Class Wizard dialog box allows new classes to be added to a project.*

Figure 23-36. *Adding an OnInput() member function*

BarDataDialog.cpp and BarDataDialog.h

The following portion of code is taken from the BarDataDialog.cpp source code file. The code shown in a bold font should exist or be added to this listing:

```
// BarDataDialog.cpp : implementation file
```

```
//

#include "stdafx.h"
#include "BarChart.h"
#include "BarDataDialog.h"

#ifdef _DEBUG
#define new DEBUG_NEW
#endif

/////////////////////////////////////////////////////////////////
// CBarDataDialog dialog


CBarDataDialog::CBarDataDialog(CWnd* pParent /*=NULL*/)
    : CDialog(CBarDataDialog::IDD, pParent)
{
    //{{AFX_DATA_INIT(CBarDataDialog)
    m_TString = _T("Bar Chart Title");
    m_XString = _T("x-axis label");
    m_YString = _T("y-axis label");
    m_GHValues = _T("30, 20, 25, 35");
    m_GLValues = _T("#1, #2, #3, #4");
    //}}AFX_DATA_INIT
}

void CBarDataDialog::DoDataExchange(CDataExchange* pDX)
{
    CDialog::DoDataExchange(pDX);
    //{{AFX_DATA_MAP(CBarDataDialog)
    DDX_Text(pDX, IDD_TITLE, m_TString);
    DDX_Text(pDX, IDD_XLABEL, m_XString);
    DDX_Text(pDX, IDD_YLABEL, m_YString);
    DDX_Text(pDX, IDD_P, m_GHValues);
    DDX_Text(pDX, IDD_L, m_GLValues);
    //}}AFX_DATA_MAP
}

BEGIN_MESSAGE_MAP(CBarDataDialog, CDialog)
    //{{AFX_MSG_MAP(CBarDataDialog)
    //}}AFX_MSG_MAP
END_MESSAGE_MAP()

/////////////////////////////////////////////////////////////////
// CBarDataDialog message handlers
```

```
void CBarDataDialog::OnOK()
{
        CDialog::OnOK();
}
```

Note that the values in quotes for the five member variables provided the default values shown in the edit box controls.

Next, the following edited portion of code is taken from the BarDataDialog.h header file. The code shown in a bold font should also exist or be added to this listing:

```
// BarDataDialog.h : header file
//


/////////////////////////////////////////////////////////////
// CBarDataDialog dialog

class CBarDataDialog : public CDialog
{
// Construction
public:
    CBarDataDialog(CWnd* pParent = NULL);

// Dialog Data
    enum { IDD = IDD_BARDIALOG };
      .
      .
      .
public:
    CString m_TString;
    CString m_XString;
    CString m_YString;
    CString m_GHValues;
    CString m_GLValues;
};
```

BarChartDoc.cpp and BarChartDoc.h

The following edited portion of code is taken from the BarChartDoc.cpp source code file. The code shown in a bold font should exist or be added to this listing:

```
// BarChartDoc.cpp : implementation of the CBarChartDoc class
```

```
//
     .
     .
     .
/////////////////////////////////////////////////////////////
// CBarChartDoc construction/destruction

CBarChartDoc::CBarChartDoc()
{
    TString = "Bar Chart Title";
    XString = "x-axis label";
    YString = "y-axis label";
    GHValues = "30, 20, 25, 35";
    GLValues = "#1, #2, #3, #4";
}
     .
     .
     .
```

The values between the quote marks provide initial information for the bar chart when it is initially drawn.

The next portion of edited code is taken from the BarChartDoc.h header file. The code shown in a bold font should exist or be added to this listing:

```
// BarChartDoc.h : interface of the CBarChartDoc class
//
/////////////////////////////////////////////////////////////

class CBarChartDoc : public CDocument
{
protected: // create from serialization only
    CBarChartDoc();
    DECLARE_DYNCREATE(CBarChartDoc)

    CString TString;
    CString XString;
    CString YString;
    CString GHValues;
    CString GLValues;
     .
     .
     .
```

Next, we'll examine the changes to the BarChartView.cpp source code file and the BarChartView.h header file.

BarChartView.cpp and BarChartView.h

The next portion of edited code is taken from the BarChartView.cpp source code file. The code shown in a bold font should exist or be added to this listing. Note that a large portion of code is not shown in this listing for clarity:

```cpp
// BarChartView.cpp : implementation of the CBarChartView class
//

#include "stdafx.h"
#include "BarChart.h"
#include "BarChartDoc.h"
#include "BarChartView.h"
#include "BarDataDialog.h"        // add for resource information

CBarDataDialog dlg;

#define maxnumber 12

#ifdef _DEBUG
#define new DEBUG_NEW
#endif


/////////////////////////////////////////////////////////////
// CBarChartView

IMPLEMENT_DYNCREATE(CBarChartView, CView)

BEGIN_MESSAGE_MAP(CBarChartView, CView)
    //{{AFX_MSG_MAP(CBarChartView)
    ON_WM_SIZE()
    ON_COMMAND(IDM_INPUT, OnInput)
    //}}AFX_MSG_MAP
END_MESSAGE_MAP()


/////////////////////////////////////////////////////////////
// CBarChartView construction/destruction

CBarChartView::CBarChartView()
{
}
```

```
CBarChartView::~CBarChartView()
{
}
    .
    .
    .

void CBarChartView::OnDraw(CDC* pDC)
{
    CBarChartDoc* pDoc = GetDocument();
    ASSERT_VALID(pDoc);
    .
    .
    .

}

/////////////////////////////////////////////////////////////////
// CBarChartView message handlers

void CBarChartView::OnSize(UINT nType, int cx, int cy)
{
    CView::OnSize(nType, cx, cy);

    m_cxClient = cx;
    m_cyClient = cy;
}

void CBarChartView::OnInput()
{
    CBarDataDialog dlg (this);
    int result = dlg.DoModal();

    if(result == IDOK) {
        CBarChartDoc* pDoc = GetDocument();
        ASSERT_VALID(pDoc);

        pDoc -> TString = dlg.m_TString;
        pDoc -> XString = dlg.m_XString;
        pDoc -> YString = dlg.m_YString;
        pDoc -> GHValues = dlg.m_GHValues;
        pDoc -> GLValues = dlg.m_GLValues;

        InvalidateRect(NULL, TRUE);
    }
}
```

Notice how the member variable information is transferred to the variables declared in the BarChartDoc.h file. This occurs when the user selects the OK button in the dialog box.

The next portion of edited code is taken from the BarChartView.h header file. The code shown in a bold font should exist or be added to this listing:

```
// BarChartView.h : interface of the CBarChartView class
//
/////////////////////////////////////////////////////////////////

class CBarChartView : public CView
{
    .
    .
    .
// Generated message map functions
protected:
    //{{AFX_MSG(CBarChartView)
    //}}AFX_MSG
    DECLARE_MESSAGE_MAP()

    void OnSize(UINT nType, int cx, int cy);
    void OnInput(void);

    int m_cxClient;
    int m_cyClient;
};
    .
    .
    .
```

DECLARE_MESSAGE_MAP is used frequently to state that the class overrides the handling of certain messages. This technique is more space efficient than the use of virtual functions.

There is an ON_COMMAND() function in BarChartView.cpp that corresponds to the OnInput() method in this listing:

```
    ON_COMMAND(IDM_INPUT, OnInput)
```

This line of code associates the menu item in the project's Data Entry menu with the data entry dialog box.

Testing the BarChart Project

Compile the BarChart project in the normal manner. When the BarChart project is executed, a default bar chart is drawn in the client area. The default chart is shown in Figure 23-37.

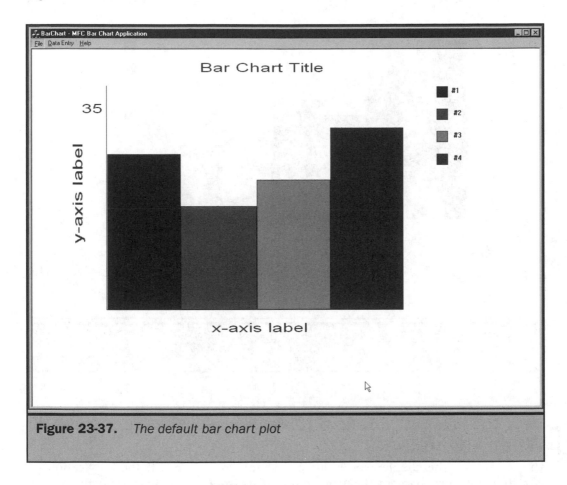

Figure 23-37.   *The default bar chart plot*

Figure 23-38 shows what a little imagination can generate.

Experiment with various bar sizes and legend labels. Try sizing and resizing the window. What do you observe?

You can continue the development of this application by adding axis tick marks or making the bars 3-D. Customization is limited only by your imagination.

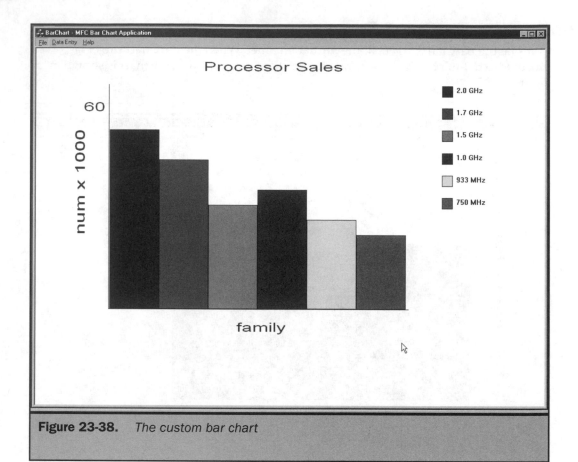

Figure 23-38.   *The custom bar chart*

What's Coming?

The examples in this chapter were built upon templates created with the Application Wizard. In the next chapter you will learn some C# essentials and then apply that knowledge in developing several command-line programs and a Windows project. As you continue to build applications using Wizards, you will find that the code building process becomes easier and more intuitive.

The
Complete
Reference

Visual C++.NET

Part V

Advanced Programming Concepts

Visual C++.NET

Chapter 24

C# Windows
Applications

In Chapters 20 through 23 you have learned how to develop Windows applications using both the procedure-oriented and object-oriented C++ programming techniques. The techniques presented in these chapters have changed little in the past ten years save for the introduction of various Wizards for object-oriented code development.

In this chapter we will look at an entirely new approach to developing object-oriented Windows applications. This approach uses the C# language, objects, and a variety of Wizards from Visual Studio. When you observe the techniques for developing these C# Windows applications, you will find that they contain the best elements of C#'s drag-and-drop design, the power of a C language platform, and access to the full Windows API (Application Program Interface).

If you thought the C++ code design of Chapters 20 through 23 was pure drudgery, wait until you start developing object-oriented Windows applications with C#. Applications almost fall together! What's more, you'll be designing applications in minutes, what would take C++ programmers, using the traditional programming techniques, hours or days to design.

Visual Basic programmers have had access to this powerful design environment for years. Now you have access to the same rich design environment with the power of the C# language. In preparation for this chapter, you may want to review the material on C# presented earlier in Chapter 4.

Creating a C# Windows Application: CircleArea

In this section you will learn the fundamentals for creating a complete C# Windows application.

C# projects are started the same way all of our C++ applications have been started in previous chapters. From within the design environment of Visual Studio, start a new project named CircleArea. Choose the C# language and a Windows design template as shown in Figure 24-1.

You will see that the C# Wizards are very similar to the C++ Wizards you have already used in earlier chapters.

Forms and Modules

Every C# Windows project is comprised of forms and code modules. Forms are used to store the visual elements of an application. Code modules contain the programming code necessary to implement the application, describe the form and controls, and provide any necessary links between the controls and C# code added to the project. The form and code information can be shared with other modules making up the complete project. With Visual Studio.NET these modules can be written in other languages such as Visual C++, Visual Basic, and so on.

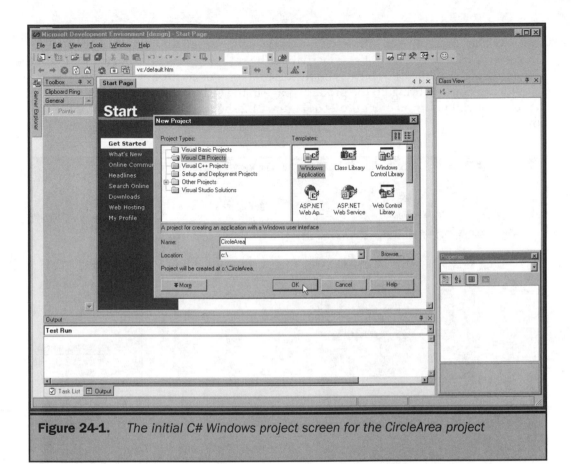

Figure 24-1. *The initial C# Windows project screen for the CircleArea project*

The Solution Explorer

C# Windows projects use the Solution Explorer to keep track of all of the components that make up a complete application. To the upper-right of your screen (refer to Figure 24-1) you will see the Solution Explorer pane. Notice that it already has at least one entry: Form1.cs. Every C# Windows project needs at least one form. This initial form, Form1.cs, is automatically entered into the project design area and is displayed in the center of the screen.

Controls and Properties

Every form has associated with it a property page. The property page contains the initial code that acts upon any controls placed in the form. Recall that Windows controls can be selected from the toolbox. For example, the TextBox control allows a program to output text or the user to enter data. A Button control can be used to cause a particular action to take place, or many other frequently needed program or user interactions. You can get to any form's or control's property page by selecting View | Properties Window or by pressing F4 while the mouse is on the desired form or control.

Either action will bring up the property page in the Properties pane, shown earlier in the lower-right portion of Figure 24-1. Figure 24-2 shows the initial code page for Form1.

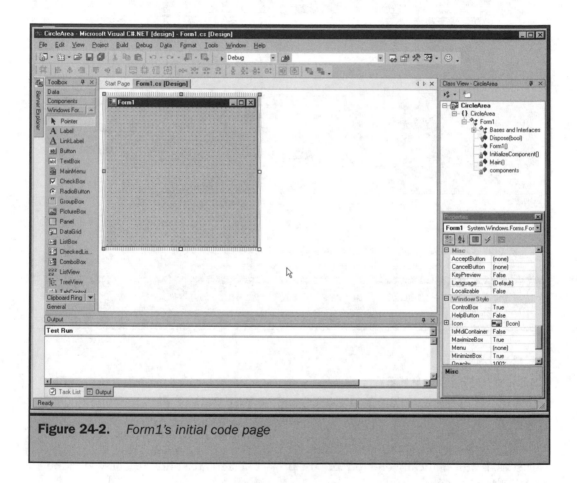

Figure 24-2. *Form1's initial code page*

Open the toolbox to view the list of controls that can be added to the form. Modify the size and shape of form1 by adding three Label controls, three TextBox controls, and one Button control to the form, as shown in Figure 24-3.

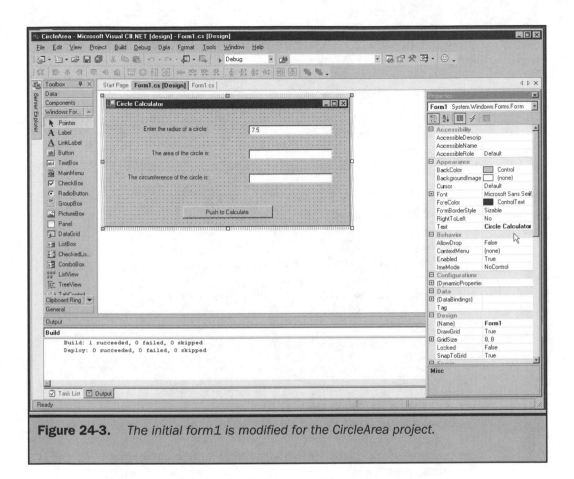

Figure 24-3. *The initial form1 is modified for the CircleArea project.*

When all of the controls have been sized, placed, and modified to match those shown in Figure 24-3, double-click the Button control. By doing this, a button click event handler (method) will be added to the code for this project. This method can then be modified to do what the programmer desires when the user clicks the button. The initial code for this method takes on this form:

```
private void button1_Click(object sender, System.EventArgs e)
{

}
```

To view the code for the whole project, use the code view by pressing the F7 button, or selecting View | Code View. You should see project code that looks similar to the following listing:

```
using System;
using System.Drawing;
using System.Collections;
using System.ComponentModel;
using System.Windows.Forms;
using System.Data;

namespace CircleArea
{
    /// <summary>
    /// Summary description for Form1.
    /// </summary>
    public class Form1 : System.Windows.Forms.Form
    {
        /// <summary>
        /// Required designer variable.
        /// </summary>
        ///

        // variable declaration
        public double radius = 7.5;

        private System.ComponentModel.Container components =
            null;
        private System.Windows.Forms.Label label3;
        private System.Windows.Forms.Label label2;
        private System.Windows.Forms.Label label1;
        private System.Windows.Forms.Button button1;
        private System.Windows.Forms.TextBox textBox3;
        private System.Windows.Forms.TextBox textBox2;
        private System.Windows.Forms.TextBox textBox1;

        public Form1()
        {
            //
            // Required for Windows Form Designer support
            //
            InitializeComponent();

            //
```

```
    // TODO: Add any constructor code after
    // InitializeComponent call
    //
}


/// <summary>
/// Clean up any resources being used.
/// </summary>
protected override void Dispose( bool disposing )
{
    if( disposing )
    {
        if (components != null)
        {
            components.Dispose();
        }
    }
    base.Dispose( disposing );
}


#region Windows Form Designer generated code
/// <summary>
/// Required method for Designer support - do
/// not modify the contents of this method
/// with the code editor.
/// </summary>
private void InitializeComponent()
{
    this.textBox2 = new System.Windows.Forms.TextBox();
    this.textBox3 = new System.Windows.Forms.TextBox();
    this.textBox1 = new System.Windows.Forms.TextBox();
    this.button1 = new System.Windows.Forms.Button();
    this.label1 = new System.Windows.Forms.Label();
    this.label2 = new System.Windows.Forms.Label();
    this.label3 = new System.Windows.Forms.Label();
    this.SuspendLayout();
    //
    // textBox2
    //
    this.textBox2.Location = new System.Drawing.
                                    Point(280, 80);
    this.textBox2.Name = "textBox2";
    this.textBox2.Size = new System.Drawing.
                                    Size(168, 20);
```

```
this.textBox2.TabIndex = 4;
this.textBox2.Text = "";
//
// textBox3
//
this.textBox3.Location = new System.Drawing.
                              Point(280, 128);
this.textBox3.Name = "textBox3";
this.textBox3.Size = new System.Drawing.
                              Size(168, 20);
this.textBox3.TabIndex = 5;
this.textBox3.Text = "";
//
// textBox1
//
this.textBox1.Location = new System.Drawing.
                              Point(280, 32);
this.textBox1.Name = "textBox1";
this.textBox1.Size = new System.Drawing.
                              Size(168, 20);
this.textBox1.TabIndex = 1;
this.textBox1.Text = " 7.5";
//
// button1
//
this.button1.Location = new System.Drawing.
                              Point(152, 192);
this.button1.Name = "button1";
this.button1.Size = new System.Drawing.
                              Size(176, 24);
this.button1.TabIndex = 6;
this.button1.Text = "Push to Calculate";
this.button1.Click += new System.EventHandler
                              (this.button1_Click);
//
// label1
//
this.label1.Location = new System.Drawing.
                              Point(72, 32);
this.label1.Name = "label1";
this.label1.Size = new System.Drawing.
                              Size(144, 24);
this.label1.TabIndex = 0;
this.label1.Text = "Enter the radius of a circle:";
//
```

```
// label2
//
this.label2.Location = new System.Drawing.
                         Point(88, 80);
this.label2.Name = "label2";
this.label2.Size = new System.Drawing.
                         Size(128, 24);
this.label2.TabIndex = 2;
this.label2.Text = "The area of the circle is:";
//
// label3
//
this.label3.Location = new System.Drawing.
                         Point(40, 128);
this.label3.Name = "label3";
this.label3.Size = new System.Drawing.
                         Size(176, 24);
this.label3.TabIndex = 7;
this.label3.Text = "The circumference of
                     the circle is:";
//
// Form1
//
this.AutoScaleBaseSize = new System.Drawing.
                             Size(5, 13);
this.ClientSize = new System.Drawing.
                     Size(480, 229);
this.Controls.AddRange
    (new System.Windows.Forms.
    Control[] {
             this.label3,
             this.label2,
             this.label1,
             this.textBox3,
             this.textBox2,
             this.textBox1,
             this.button1});
this.Name = "Form1";
this.Text = "Circle Calculator";
this.ResumeLayout(false);

}
#endregion
```

```
/// <summary>
/// The main entry point for the application.
/// </summary>
[STAThread]
static void Main()
{
    Application.Run(new Form1());
}

private void button1_Click(object sender,
    System.EventArgs e)
{   double radius = Convert.ToDouble(textBox1.Text);
    textBox2.Text = (radius * radius * 22 / 7).
                    ToString();
    textBox3.Text = (radius * 2.0 * 22 / 7).
                    ToString();
}
    }
}
```

The code shown in bold is code we added to the project to make it functional. Add this code to your project at this time, then compile and run the application. You should see a screen similar to that shown in Figure 24-4.

When the Push to Calculate button is clicked, the application will calculate the area and the circumference of a circle, with the radius given by the user.

In the following sections, we'll examine various C# Windows application design options in more detail.

Default Project Code

In this section we'll examine various key aspects of the default project code as generated by the C# Windows Application Wizard.

Namespaces

Various namespaces are added to the initial project by the Wizard to provide a wide range of project options:

```
using System;
using System.Drawing;
using System.Collections;
using System.ComponentModel;
using System.WinForms;
using System.Data;
```

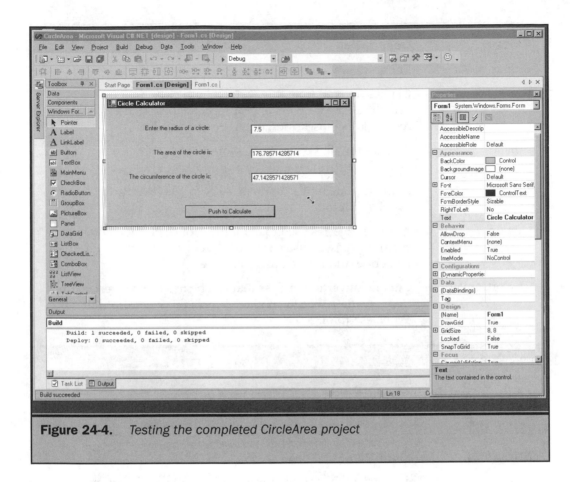

Figure 24-4.   *Testing the completed CircleArea project*

Let's examine the System.Drawing namespace as a representative example. Use the Help menu to select System.Drawing.

The Help screen will show the various classes available in this namespace. Table 24-1 shows a description of several classes taken from this reference.

The reference to the System.Drawing namespace also lists various structures used by the various classes. For example, Table 24-2 shows several structures and their descriptions.

In addition, you'll also find a list of any special Delegates and Enumerations for the namespace. For this chapter, we'll concentrate on the various classes available in any given namespace.

Class	Description
Bitmap	Encapsulates a GDI+ bitmap.
Brush	Classes derived from this abstract base class define objects used to fill the interiors of graphical shapes such as rectangles, ellipses, pies, polygons, and paths.
Brushes	Brushes for all the standard colors.
ColorConverter	ColorConverter is a class that can be used to convert colors from one data type to another. Access this class through the TypeDescriptor.
Cursor	A cursor object is used to paint the mouse pointer. Different cursor shapes are used as visual queues to inform the user what operation the mouse will have.
CursorConverter	CursorConverter is a class that can be used to convert colors from one data type to another. Access this class through the TypeDescriptor.

Table 24-1. *Classes Available in System.Drawing Namespace*

Structure	Description
Point	This is a class that represents a single (X,Y) coordinate and various interesting operations on such a coordinate.
Rectangle	Rectangle stores the location and size of a rectangular region. For more advanced region functions use a Region object.
RectangleF	RectangleF stores the location and size of a rectangular region. For more advanced region functions use a Region object.

Table 24-2. *Structures Used in System.Drawing Namespace*

Designer Variables

The next portion of project code lists the designer variables for all of the controls that you added to the form. For this example, they include:

```
/// <summary>
///     Required designer variable
/// </summary>
private System.ComponentModel.Container components =

private System.Windows.Forms.Label label3;
private System.Windows.Forms.Label label2;
private System.Windows.Forms.Label label1;
private System.Windows.Forms.Button button1;
private System.Windows.Forms.TextBox textBox3;
private System.Windows.Forms.TextBox textBox2;
private System.Windows.Forms.TextBox textBox1;
```

We don't think you would be surprised to learn that each of these controls is described in the System.WinForms namespace. Use the Help option if you want to discover more information about each of these controls.

Project Initialization

The project is initialized for Form1 by using the following portion of code:

```
public Form1()
{
    //
    // Required for Windows Form Designer support
    //
    InitializeComponent();

    //
    // TODO: Add any constructor code after
    // InitializeComponent call
    //
}
```

This portion of code makes a call to *InitializeComponent()* that appears later in the code listing.

Clean up for the project is accomplished with another small portion of code:

```
/// <summary>
/// Clean up any resources being used.
/// </summary>
protected override void Dispose( bool disposing )
{
    if( disposing )
    {
        if (components != null)
        {
            components.Dispose();
        }
    }
    base.Dispose( disposing );
}
```

In the next section, we'll see how the designer converted our graphical layout into code that initializes each form and control in the project.

Control and Form Initialization

The following partial listing shows how the Wizard converts the form design into actual code for each control placed in the form:

```
#region Windows Form Designer generated code
/// <summary>
/// Required method for Designer support - do
/// not modify the contents of this method
/// with the code editor.
/// </summary>
private void InitializeComponent()
{
    this.textBox2 = new System.Windows.Forms.TextBox();
    this.textBox3 = new System.Windows.Forms.TextBox();
    this.textBox1 = new System.Windows.Forms.TextBox();
    this.button1 = new System.Windows.Forms.Button();
    this.label1 = new System.Windows.Forms.Label();
    this.label2 = new System.Windows.Forms.Label();
    this.label3 = new System.Windows.Forms.Label();
    this.SuspendLayout();
    //
    // textBox2
    //
```

```
this.textBox2.Location = new System.Drawing.
                                Point(280, 80);
this.textBox2.Name = "textBox2";
this.textBox2.Size = new System.Drawing.
                                Size(168, 20);
this.textBox2.TabIndex = 4;
this.textBox2.Text = "";
//
// textBox3
//
this.textBox3.Location = new System.Drawing.
                                Point(280, 128);
this.textBox3.Name = "textBox3";
this.textBox3.Size = new System.Drawing.
                                Size(168, 20);
this.textBox3.TabIndex = 5;
this.textBox3.Text = "";
        .
        .
        .
```

For example, the second label control, *label2*, is specified with four properties. These properties include *Location*, *Text*, *Size*, and *TabIndex*. Each of the values assigned to these properties was determined by where the control was placed in the form and its order with respect to the other controls.

It is possible to alter control properties in the code or in the designer window.

Application's Entry Point

Every C, C++, and C# application has a main entry point. The main entry point for this application is described at the end of the code listing:

```
/// <summary>
/// The main entry point for the application.
/// </summary>
[STAThread]
    static void Main()
    {
        Application.Run(new Form1());
    }
```

For most simple cases, the portion of code will not vary much from one application to another.

Responding to Events

In the previous section, you learned that we could add a method to our project that would respond to a mouse button click. These methods are frequently referred to as *event handlers*. Each control has its own group of events that it will respond to. You can view a list of these events by using the Help menu and entering the control name followed by the word "event". For example, a search for button events yields the following list:

```
Click (inherited from Control)

ControlAdded (inherited from Control)

ControlRemoved (inherited from Control)

CreateHandle (inherited from Control)

DestroyHandle (inherited from Control)

DoubleClick Occurs when the user double clicks the Button.

DragDrop (inherited from RichControl)

DragEnter (inherited from RichControl)

DragLeave (inherited from RichControl)

DragOver (inherited from RichControl)

Enter (inherited from Control)

GiveFeedback (inherited from RichControl)

GotFocus (inherited from Control)

Help (inherited from RichControl)

Invalidate (inherited from RichControl)

KeyDown (inherited from Control)

KeyPress (inherited from Control)

KeyUp (inherited from Control)

Layout (inherited from Control)

Leave (inherited from Control)

LostFocus (inherited from Control)

MouseDown (inherited from Control)

MouseEnter (inherited from Control)

MouseHover (inherited from Control)

MouseLeave (inherited from Control)

MouseMove (inherited from Control)

MouseUp (inherited from Control)
```

```
MouseWheel (inherited from Control)

Move (inherited from Control)

Paint (inherited from RichControl)

PropertyChanged (inherited from Control)

QueryContinueDrag (inherited from RichControl)

Resize (inherited from Control)

Validated (inherited from Control)

Validating (inherited from Control)
```

For a description of any particular event, position the mouse over the event name and left-click. For example, left-clicking the mouse over the click method yields the following description:

```
private void ControlName_Click(
   object sender,
   EventArgs e
);
```

The parameters are *sender* and the source of the event *e*. *EventArgs* contains the event data. For example, *ExtendedInfo* holds a reference to an object that manages the event's state.

Events can be generated by the user, such as a mouse click, but they can also be generated by the system itself. Whenever you want a control to respond to an event, simply put the instructions in a method.

Changing Properties with Code

Many of the properties for a control can be changed while the application is executing. For example, you may want to change the text shown in the Button control after the user has made the first selection.

You can change the text displayed in the Button control by adding the following line of code to the *button1_Click* method (event handler).

```
private void button1_Click(object sender, System.EventArgs e)
{
    radius = Convert.ToDouble(textBox1.Text);
    textBox2.Text = (radius * radius * 22 / 7).ToString();
    textBox3.Text = (radius * 2.0 * 22 / 7).ToString();
    button1.Text = "Do you want to try another?";
}
```

The syntax for changing an object's properties using code is to use the object's name, followed by a period, then the property's name. On the right side of the assignment operator you put a legal substitute. Figure 24-5 shows the results of this modification.

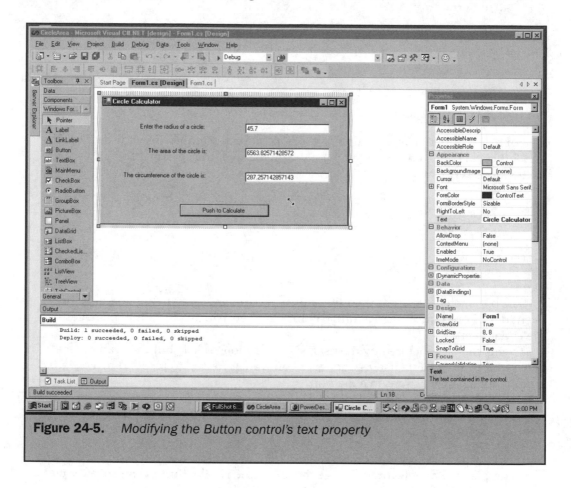

Figure 24-5.   *Modifying the Button control's text property*

Other properties are just as easy to modify. Pick a couple, such as color or font size, and experiment.

Creating a C# Windows Application: Tester

No doubt, you are already thinking of several projects you would like to create for Windows using C#. Before you do, however, we need to investigate some drawing capabilities for this environment. This project will be as simple as the last.

Create a new Windows C# project, just as you did the last one, but name this project Tester. In the Tester project, we're going to test several drawing functions.

When the designer shows you form1 in the drawing area, go to the code view and modify this project's code to match that of the following listing. This project will not use any controls.

```
using System;
using System.Drawing;
using System.Collections;
using System.ComponentModel;
using System.Windows.Forms;
using System.Data;

using System.Drawing.Drawing2D;

namespace Tester
{
    /// <summary>
    /// Summary description for Form1.
    /// </summary>
    public class Form1 : System.Windows.Forms.Form
    {
        /// <summary>
        /// Required designer variable.
        /// </summary>
        private System.ComponentModel.Container components =
            null;

        public Form1()
        {
            //
            // Required for Windows Form Designer support
            //
            InitializeComponent();

            //
            // TODO: Add any constructor code after
            // InitializeComponent call
            //
        }

        /// <summary>
        /// Clean up any resources being used.
        /// </summary>
        protected override void Dispose( bool disposing )
        {
```

```
        if( disposing )
        {
            if (components != null)
            {
                components.Dispose();
            }
        }
        base.Dispose( disposing );
    }

    #region Windows Form Designer generated code
    /// <summary>
    /// Required method for Designer support - do
    /// not modify the contents of this method
    /// with the code editor.
    /// </summary>
    private void InitializeComponent()
    {
        this.components = new System.ComponentModel.
                          Container();
        this.Size = new System.Drawing.
                    Size(1024, 768);
        this.Text = "C# Windows Drawing Primitives";
        this.AutoScaleBaseSize = new System.Drawing.
                                 Size(5, 13);
    }
    #endregion

    /// <summary>
    /// The main entry point for the application.
    /// </summary>
    [STAThread]
    static void Main()
    {
        Application.Run(new Form1());
    }

    protected override void OnPaint(PaintEventArgs e)
    {
        Graphics g = e.Graphics;

        // draw wide red line
        Pen mypen1 = new Pen(Color.Red);
```

```
        mypen1.Width = 15;
        g.DrawLine(mypen1, 1000, 45, 200, 700);

        // change end caps and draw line
        mypen1.StartCap = LineCap.Round;
        mypen1.EndCap = LineCap.Round;
        g.DrawLine(mypen1, 700, 100, 800, 300);

        // draw a blue arc
        Pen mypen2 = new Pen(Color.Blue);
        mypen2.Width = 5;
        Rectangle rect1 = new Rectangle(10,20,200,300);
        g.DrawArc(mypen2, rect1, 20, 100);

        // draw a yellow ellipse
        Pen mypen3 = new Pen(Color.Yellow);
        mypen3.Width = 3;
        g.DrawEllipse(mypen3, 500, 50, 80, 300);

        // draw an aquamarine ellipse (circle)
        Pen mypen4 = new Pen(Color.Aquamarine);
        mypen4.Width = 6;
        g.DrawEllipse(mypen4, 50, 500, 100, 100);

        // draw a purple pie slice with
        // a dashed line style
        Pen mypen5 = new Pen(Color.Purple);
        mypen5.Width = 4;
        mypen5.DashStyle = DashStyle.Dash;
        Rectangle rect2 = new Rectangle(400,200,600,400);
        g.DrawPie(mypen5, rect2, 20, 60);

        // draw a filled rectangle
        Brush mybrush1 = new SolidBrush(Color.LimeGreen);
        g.FillRectangle(mybrush1, 900, 200, 80, 100);

        // draw a filled circle
        Brush mybrush2 = new SolidBrush(Color.Orange);
        g.FillEllipse(mybrush2, 100, 25, 150, 150);
    }
  }
}
```

We're going to do our drawing on form1. Actually, another form could be created just for this purpose. We've added the *OnPaint()* method and the System.Drawing.Drawing2D namespace in order to provide the drawing options we desire for the project.

Applications for C# Windows can make use of a wide variety of drawing methods that start with Draw or Fill. If you examine the previous listing, you'll find *DrawLine()*, *DrawRectangle()*, *FillRectangle()*, and so on.

If you enter this code and execute the project, your screen should appear like Figure 24-6 if you are operating with a 1024x768 resolution.

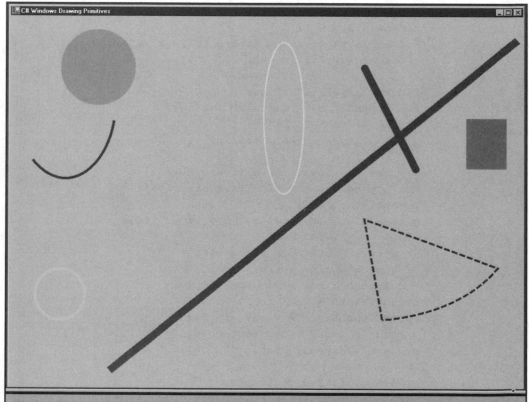

Figure 24-6.   *Several graphics shapes are drawn with C# Windows drawing primitives.*

The following list contains the most frequently used classes provided by the System.Drawing namespace:

AddMetafileComment()	DrawString()	GetNearestColor()
BeginContainer()	EndContainer()	GetType()
Clear()	EnumerateMetafile()	InitializeLifetime Service()
Dispose()	Equals()	IntersectClip()
DrawArc()	ExcludeClip()	IsVisible()
DrawBezier()	FillClosedCurve()	MeasureString()
DrawBeziers()	FillEllipse()	MeasureStringRegion()
DrawClosedCurve()	FillPath()	MultiplyTransform()
DrawCurve()	FillPie()	ReleaseHDC()
DrawEllipse()	FillPolygon()	ResetClip()
DrawIcon()	FillRectangle()	ResetTransform()
DrawIconUnstretched()	FillRectangles()	Restore()
DrawImage()	FillRegion()	RotateTransform()
DrawImageUnscaled()	Flush()	Save()
DrawLine()	FromHDC()	ScaleTransform()
DrawLines()	FromHWND()	SetClip()
DrawPath()	FromImage()	ToString()
DrawPie()	GetHalftonePalette()	TransformPoints()
DrawPolygon()	GetHashCode()	TranslateClip()
DrawRectangle()	GetHDC()	TranslateTransform()
DrawRectangles()	GetLifetimeService()	

In addition to the classes provided by the System.Drawing namespace, the System.Drawing.Drawing2D namespace provides additional functionality to this project. The following listing shows the most frequently used classes in this namespace:

AdjustableArrowCap()	GraphicsState()
Blend()	HatchBrush()
ColorBlend()	LinearGradientBrush()
CustomLineCap()	Matrix()
GraphicsContainer()	PathData()
GraphicsPath()	PathGradientBrush()
GraphicsPathIterator()	RegionData()

Along with the various classes included in this namespace are the enumerations included in the following listing:

CombineMode	LineJoin
CompositingMode	MatrixOrder
CompositingQuality	PathPointType
CoordinateSpace	PenAlignment
DashStyle	PenType
FillMode	PixelOffsetMode
FlushIntention	QualityMode
HatchStyle	RenderingHint
InterpolationMode	SmoothingMode
LinearGradientMode	WarpMode
LineCap	WrapMode

The classes and enumerations provided in the previous lists will let you experiment further with this project. Why not try adding text or varying the colors of the various objects?

If you master these drawing primitives you are well on your way to developing the same type of robust applications that were developed in Chapters 20 through 23.

What's Coming?

The examples in this chapter were built upon templates created with the C# Windows Application Wizard. We are confident that this type of code development will revolutionize Windows application development. Look for whole books on C# and Windows that will explain all of the nuances of the language.

In the next chapter we'll return to the MFC and learn how the STL can be incorporated into Windows code.

The
Complete
Reference

Visual C++.NET

Chapter 25

The STL and Windows

I n this chapter we'll investigate the use of the Standard Template Library (STL) in MFC Windows applications. In particular, we'll see how the <complex> template class can be used to perform complex arithmetic.

There are two examples at the end of this chapter. One example is a non-Windows application to illustrate the simple use of the <complex> template class. The second example is a MFC Windows application that draws several vectors to the screen, then calculates the sum.

Complex Numbers

In order for you to fully understand the <complex> template, a brief review of what complex numbers are might be in order. If you work in the area of mathematics, engineering, or physics you have probably used complex numbers in calculations at one time or another. Complex numbers, in the real world, result from vectors (no relationship to STL vectors) or, better yet, phasors that have a magnitude and direction and can be described on an x-y coordinate system. The positive and negative X-axis represents the real component of a vector or phasor, while the Y-axis represents the imaginary component of a vector or phasor. In engineering statics, vectors and phasors are often used to represent a force moving in a certain direction. In electrical engineering, vectors and phasors are often used to represent voltages and currents and their associated phase angles.

There are three ways to represent complex numbers, vectors, or phasors: polar form, rectangular form, or exponential form. For example, imagine a vector or phasor with a magnitude of 40 at an angle of 30 degrees measured counterclockwise from the positive X-axis.

Polar Form   In polar form, this vector could be represented as:

40 /_ 30 deg

Rectangular Form   In rectangular form, the real component is found using:

40 * cos 30 = 40 * 0.86603 = 34.641

The imaginary component is:

40 * sin 30 = 40 * 0.5 = 20

This vector could now be presented as:

34.641 + j20

Exponential Form   In exponential form, the vector is represented as:

$40 * e^{j30}$

Because vectors and phasors contain both real and imaginary components, they are called complex numbers.

It has always been difficult to perform mathematical operations on complex numbers using a computer since most mathematical operators are not overloaded. For example, it is not possible to add, subtract, multiply, or divide complex numbers without operators overloaded for such purposes or by having a template to handle all of that work for you.

Vectors or phasors represented in rectangular form are easy to add and subtract. For example:

$$(20 + j50) - (30 + j20) = -10 + j30$$

$$(20 + j20) + (30 + j20) = 50 + j50$$

Multiplication and division of vectors and phasors, in rectangular form, is not as easy, but not impossible. However, the easiest way to multiply and divide vectors and phasors is by working with them in polar form. For example:

$$(44.72 \text{ / } 63.44 \text{ deg}) * (36.05 \text{ / } 33.7 \text{ deg}) = (44.72 * 36.05) \text{ / } (63.44 + 33.7) \text{ deg}$$

$$= 1612.156 \text{ / } 97.14 \text{ deg}$$

$$(20 \text{ / } 50 \text{ deg}) \text{ / } (15 \text{ / } 30 \text{ deg}) = (20 \text{ / } 15) \text{ / } (50 \text{ deg} - 30 \text{ deg})$$

$$= 1.333 \text{ / } 20 \text{ deg}$$

As a result of these various forms, conversion from one form to another is typical in most arithmetic operations involving vectors and phasors. The calculations can be tedious when using a calculator or computer program that cannot handle complex numbers.

If you would like more information on the use of complex numbers we recommend any good technical mathematics book, electrical engineering book dealing with ac circuits, or any college physics book.

In the following section, we'll investigate the capabilities of the <complex> template. Then in the sample application section of this chapter you'll see how the <complex> template can be used in three separate applications.

The <complex> Template Syntax

The standard C++ header <complex> is used to define the template class complex and a large number of supporting template functions. The following listing gives the syntax for the <complex> template:

```
namespace std {
#define __STD_COMPLEX
//    TEMPLATE CLASSES
template<class T>
    class complex;
class "complex<float>;
class "complex<double>;
class "complex<long double>;
//    TEMPLATE FUNCTIONS
template<class T>
```

```
        complex<T> operator+(const complex<T>& lhs,
                             const complex<T>& rhs);
template<class T>
        complex<T> operator+(const complex<T>& lhs,
                             const T& rhs);
template<class T>
        complex<T> operator+(const T& lhs,
                             const complex<T>& rhs);
template<class T>
        complex<T> operator-(const complex<T>& lhs,
                             const complex<T>& rhs);
template<class T>
        complex<T> operator-(const complex<T>& lhs,
                             const T& rhs);
template<class T>
        complex<T> operator-(const T& lhs,
                             const complex<T>& rhs);
template<class T>
        complex<T> operator*(const complex<T>& lhs,
                             const complex<T>& rhs);
template<class T>
        complex<T> operator*(const complex<T>& lhs,
                             const T& rhs);
template<class T>
        complex<T> operator*(const T& lhs,
                             const complex<T>& rhs);
template<class T>
        complex<T> operator/(const complex<T>& lhs,
                             const complex<T>& rhs);
template<class T>
        complex<T> operator/(const complex<T>& lhs,
                             const T& rhs);
template<class T>
        complex<T> operator/(const T& lhs,
                             const complex<T>& rhs);
template<class T>
        complex<T> operator+(const complex<T>& lhs);
template<class T>
        complex<T> operator-(const complex<T>& lhs);
template<class T>
        bool operator==(const complex<T>& lhs,
                        const complex<T>& rhs);
template<class T>
        bool operator==(const complex<T>& lhs, const T& rhs);
```

```
template<class T>
    bool operator==(const T& lhs, const complex<T>& rhs);
template<class T>
    bool operator!=(const complex<T>& lhs,
                    const complex<T>& rhs);
template<class T>
    bool operator!=(const complex<T>& lhs,
                    const T& rhs);
template<class T>
    bool operator!=(const T& lhs, const complex<T>& rhs);
template<class E, class Ti, class T>
    basic_istream<E, Ti>& "operator>>(basic_istream<E, Ti>& is,
        complex<T>& x);
template<class E, class T, class U>
    basic_ostream<E, T>& operator<<(basic_ostream<E, T>& os,
        const complex<U>& x);
template<class T>
    T real(const complex<T>& x);
template<class T>
    T imag(const complex<T>& x);
template<class T>
    T abs(const complex<T>& x);
template<class T>
    T arg(const complex<T>& x);
template<class T>
    T norm(const complex<T>& x);
template<class T>
    complex<T> conjg(const complex<T>& x);
template<class T>
    complex<T> polar(const T& rho, const T& theta = 0);
template<class T>
    complex<T> cos(const complex<T>& x);
template<class T>
    complex<T> cosh(const complex<T>& x);
template<class T>
    complex<T> exp(const complex<T>& x);
template<class T>
    complex<T> log(const complex<T>& x);
template<class T>
    complex<T> log10(const complex<T>& x);
template<class T>
    complex<T> pow(const complex<T>& x, int y);
template<class T>
    complex<T> pow(const complex<T>& x, const T& y);
```

```
template<class T>
    complex<T> pow(const complex<T>& x, const complex<T>& y);
template<class T>
    complex<T> pow(const T& x, const complex<T>& y);
template<class T>
    complex<T> sin(const complex<T>& x);
template<class T>
    complex<T> sinh(const complex<T>& x);
template<class T>
    complex<T> sqrt(const complex<T>& x);
    };
```

At the time of this writing, the complex conjugate of a complex number is found by using conj(), not conjg(), as it appears in Microsoft's references.

For this template class, functions that return multiple values will return an imaginary part in the half-open interval given by (-pi, pi].

Table 25-1 lists and describes the template functions for <complex>.

Template Functions

```
complex<T> operator+(const complex<T>& lhs, const complex<T>& rhs);
complex<T> operator+(const complex<T>& lhs, const T& rhs);
complex<T> operator+(const T& lhs, const complex<T>& rhs);
complex<T> operator-(const complex<T>& lhs, const complex<T>& rhs);
complex<T> operator-(const complex<T>& lhs, const T& rhs);
complex<T> operator-(const T& lhs, const complex<T>& rhs);
complex<T> operator*(const complex<T>& lhs, const complex<T>& rhs);
complex<T> operator*(const complex<T>& lhs, const T& rhs);
complex<T> operator*(const T& lhs, const complex<T>& rhs);
complex<T> operator/(const complex<T>& lhs, const complex<T>& rhs);
complex<T> operator/(const complex<T>& lhs, const T& rhs);
complex<T> operator/(const T& lhs, const complex<T>& rhs);
complex<T> operator+(const complex<T>& lhs);
```

Table 25-1. *Frequently Used Template Functions for <complex>*

```
complex<T> operator-(const complex<T>& lhs);

bool operator==(const complex<T>& lhs, const complex<T>& rhs);

bool operator==(const complex<T>& lhs, const T& rhs);

bool operator==(const T& lhs, const complex<T>& rhs);

bool operator!=(const complex<T>& lhs, const complex<T>& rhs);

bool operator!=(const complex<T>& lhs, const T& rhs);

bool operator!=(const T& lhs, const complex<T>& rhs);

basic_istream<E, Ti>& "operator>>(basic_istream<E, Ti>& is,
complex<T>& x);

basic_ostream<E, T>& operator<<(basic_ostream<E, T>& os,
const complex<U>& x);
```

Table 25-1.   *Frequently Used Template Functions for <complex> (continued)*

The methods in this template class are listed and described in Table 25-2. All of the normal operations needed for manipulating complex numbers are provided with this template.

Template Method	Description
template<class T> T abs(const complex<T>& x);	Returns the magnitude of x.
template<class T> T arg(const complex<T>& x);	Returns the phase angle of x.
template<class T> complex<T> conjg (const complex<T>& x);	Returns the conjugate of x. Note: use conj(), at this time, to find the complex conjugate.

Table 25-2.   *Template Methods for <complex>*

Template Method	Description
template<class T> complex<T> cos (const complex<T>& x);	Returns the cosine of x.
template<class T> complex<T> cosh (const complex<T>& x);	Returns the hyperbolic cosine of x.
template<class T> complex<T> exp (const complex<T>& x);	Returns the exponential of x.
template<class T> T imag(const complex<T>& x);	Returns the imaginary part of x.
template<class T> complex<T> log (const complex<T>& x);	Returns the logarithm of x. The branch cuts occur along the negative real axis.
template<class T> complex<T> log10 (const complex<T>& x);	Returns the base 10 logarithm of x. The branch cuts occur along the negative real axis.
template<class T> T norm(const complex<T>& x);	Returns the squared magnitude of x.

template<class T>
 	
  complex<T> polar(const T& rho,
 	
  const T& theta = 0);
	Returns a complex value. The magnitude is rho and the phase angle is theta.

template<class T>
 	
  complex<T> pow(const complex<T>& x,
 	
  int y);
	Each function converts both operands to the given return type, then returns the converted x to the power y. The branch cut for x occurs along the negative real axis.

Table 25-2. *Template Methods for <complex> (continued)*

Template Method	Description
template<class T> complex<T> pow (const complex<T>& x, const T& y);	
template<class T> complex<T> pow (const complex<T>& x, const complex<T>& y);	
template<class T> complex<T> pow (const T& x, const complex<T>& y);	
template<class T> T real(const complex<T>& x);	Returns the real part of x.
template<class T> complex<T> sin (const complex<T>& x);	Returns the imaginary sine of x.
template<class T> complex<T> sinh; (const complex<T>& x)	Returns the hyperbolic sine of x.
template<class T> complex<T> sqrt (const complex<T>& x);	Returns the square root of x. The phase angle occurs in the half-open interval (-pi/2, pi/2]. The branch cuts occur along the negative real axis.

Table 25-2.   *Template Methods for <complex> (continued)*

The <complex> template class describes an object. This object stores two objects of type T. One object represents the real part of a complex number and the other object the imaginary part of the complex number. Objects of class T have a public constructor, destructor, copy constructor, and assignment operator. Class T objects can be assigned integer or floating-point values or **cast** to the desired values. Arithmetic operators are defined for the appropriate floating-point types.

The example programs that follow at the end of this chapter illustrate many of these methods and operators.

In the following three sections, you'll see how the template class handles three floating-point types: float, double, and long double. For this version of Visual C++, a value of any other type T is **cast** to a double for actual calculations. The return type, a double, is assigned back to the object of type T.

The class complex <float>

The class complex <float> describes an object that stores two objects of type float. One object represents the real part of a complex number and the second object the imaginary part of the complex number.

```
class complex<float> {
public:
  complex(float re = 0, float im = 0);
  explicit complex(const complex<double>& x);
  explicit complex(const complex<long double>& x);
  // remainder identical to template class complex
};
```

Note that the only difference is in the defined constructors. The first constructor initializes the real part to *re* and the imaginary part *im*. Two final constructors initialize the real part to x.real() and the imaginary part to x.imag().

The class complex <double>

The class complex <double> describes an object that stores two objects of type double. One object represents the real part of a complex number and the second object the imaginary part of the complex number.

```
class complex<double> {
public:
  complex(double re = 0, double im = 0);
  complex(const complex<float>& x);
  explicit complex(const complex<long double>& x);
  // remainder identical to template class complex
};
```

Again, the only difference is in the defined constructors. The first constructor initializes the real part to *re* and the imaginary part *im*. Two final constructors initialize the real part to x.real() and the imaginary part to x.imag().

The class complex <long double>

The class complex <long double> describes an object that stores two objects of type long double. One object represents the real part of a complex number and the second object the imaginary part of the complex number.

```
class complex<long double> {
public:
  complex(long double re = 0, long double im = 0);
  complex(const complex<float>& x);
  complex(const complex<double>& x);
  // remainder identical to the template class complex
};
```

Again, the only difference is in the defined constructors. The first constructor initializes the real part to *re* and the imaginary part *im*. Two final constructors initialize the real part to x.real() and the imaginary part to x.imag().

A Simple <complex> Application

The first complex arithmetic application, complex1.cpp, shows how to use complex numbers to solve a simple series ac circuit problem involving a resistor, capacitor, and inductor. Reactance values for capacitors and inductors are complex quantities determined by the component values and the frequency used in the circuit.

```
// Complex1.cpp : Defines entry point for console application.
// An electrical circuit has a resistance of 80 ohms
// an inductive reactance of 70 ohms and a capacitive
// reactance of 130 ohms connected in series.
// Determine the impedance of the circuit and the phase
// angle between the voltage and current.
// Results printed in both rectangular and polar formats.
// Chris H. Pappas and William H. Murray, 2001

#include "stdafx.h"
#include <iostream>
#include <complex>
```

```
using namespace std;

int main(int argc, char* argv[])
{
    double pi = 3.14159265359;

    complex<double> x1, x2, x3, z1;

    // phasor one
    x1.real(80.0);          //resistor = 30.0 +j0.0
    // phasor two
    x2.imag(70.0);          //ind react = 0.0 +j70.0
    // phasor three
    x3.imag(-130);          //cap react = 0.0 -j130

    // complex arithmetic calculation
    z1 = x1 + x2 + x3;

    // results in rectangular form
    cout << "The answer in rectangular format is: "
        << z1 << endl << endl;
    // results in polar form
    cout << "The answer in polar format is: "
        << sqrt(norm(z1)) << " at /_ " << arg(z1)
        << " radians (or " << arg(z1) * 180.0 / pi
        << " degrees)" << endl << endl;

    return 0;
}
```

This application merely adds the three vectors together, so it is quite simple. The results are reported to the screen in both rectangular and polar forms. The output for this application is

```
The answer in rectangular format is: (80, -60)

The answer in polar format is: 100 at /_ -0.643501 radians
                               (or -36.8699 degrees)
```

This application was certainly easy enough, yet it used the real power of the <complex> template. In the next example, we'll weave complex arithmetic into a MFC windows application.

A Windows Application Using the STL and MFC

The second <complex> application, complex2.cpp, is a graphical application that you'll build in the normal manner using Visual Studio Wizards and the MFC.

For a quick review of Wizards and the MFC, refer to Chapter 23. You can build this application using the steps outlined in this chapter. When you start the Application Wizard, name this project complex2 and make sure you select MFC Windows application for the application type.

The next step, once the template code has been generated, is to examine the complex2View.cpp source code file and find the OnDraw() method. Once you find this method, add the code shown in a bold font in the following listing:

```cpp
// Complex2View.cpp : implementation of the CComplex2View class
//

#include "stdafx.h"
#include "Complex2.h"

#include "Complex2Doc.h"
#include "Complex2View.h"

#include <complex>
#include "Complex2View.h"

using namespace std;

#ifdef _DEBUG
#define new DEBUG_NEW
#endif


/////////////////////////////////////////////////////////////////
// CComplex2View

IMPLEMENT_DYNCREATE(CComplex2View, CView)

BEGIN_MESSAGE_MAP(CComplex2View, CView)
    ON_WM_SIZE()
END_MESSAGE_MAP()


/////////////////////////////////////////////////////////////////
// CComplex2View construction/destruction

CComplex2View::CComplex2View()
```

```cpp
{
    // TODO: add construction code here

}

CComplex2View::~CComplex2View()
{
}

BOOL CComplex2View::PreCreateWindow(CREATESTRUCT& cs)
{
    // TODO: Modify the Window class or styles here modifying
    //   the CREATESTRUCT cs

    return CView::PreCreateWindow(cs);
}

/////////////////////////////////////////////////////////////////
// CComplex2View drawing

void CComplex2View::OnDraw(CDC* pDC)
{
    CComplex2Doc* pDoc = GetDocument();
    ASSERT_VALID(pDoc);

    CPen bluepen, greenpen, magentapen, redpen;
    CPen* oldpen;

    complex<double> x1, x2, x3, temp;

    // phasor one
    x1 = polar(-50.0, -0.523598);   //-50.0 /_ -30 deg

    // phasor two
    x2.real(70.0);                   //70.0 + j40.0
    x2.imag(40.0);

    // phasor three
    x3.real(-40.0);                  //-40.0 + j50.0
    x3.imag(50.0);

    // set mapping modes and viewport
    pDC->SetMapMode(MM_ISOTROPIC);
    pDC->SetWindowExt(250, 250);
```

```
    pDC->SetViewportExt(m_cxClient, -m_cyClient);
    pDC->SetViewportOrg(m_cxClient / 2, m_cyClient / 2);

    // draw coordinate axes
    pDC->MoveTo(-120, 0);
    pDC->LineTo(120, 0);
    pDC->MoveTo(0, -100);
    pDC->LineTo(0, 100);

    // draw first phasor with blue pen
    bluepen.CreatePen(PS_DASHDOT, 0, RGB(0, 0, 255));
    oldpen = pDC -> SelectObject(&bluepen);
    pDC -> MoveTo(0, 0);
    pDC -> LineTo((int) real(x1), (int) imag(x1));
    DeleteObject(oldpen);

    temp = x1 + x2;   // add first two phasors

    // draw second phasor with green pen
    greenpen.CreatePen(PS_DASHDOT, 0, RGB(0, 255, 0));
    oldpen = pDC -> SelectObject(&greenpen);
    pDC -> LineTo((int) real(temp), (int) imag(temp));
    DeleteObject(oldpen);

    temp += x3;      // add in last phasor

    // draw third phasor with magenta pen
    magentapen.CreatePen(PS_DASHDOT, 0, RGB(255, 0, 255));
    oldpen = pDC -> SelectObject(&magentapen);
    pDC -> LineTo((int) real(temp), (int) imag(temp));
    DeleteObject(oldpen);

    // draw sum of phasors with wide red pen
    redpen.CreatePen(PS_SOLID, 3, RGB(255, 0, 0));
    oldpen = pDC -> SelectObject(&redpen);
    pDC -> LineTo(0, 0);
    DeleteObject(oldpen);
}

/////////////////////////////////////////////////////////////////
// CComplex2View diagnostics

#ifdef _DEBUG
void CComplex2View::AssertValid() const
```

```
{
    CView::AssertValid();
}

void CComplex2View::Dump(CDumpContext& dc) const
{
    CView::Dump(dc);
}

CComplex2Doc* CComplex2View::GetDocument() const // non-debug version
is inline
{
    ASSERT(m_pDocument->IsKindOf(RUNTIME_CLASS(CComplex2Doc)));
    return (CComplex2Doc*)m_pDocument;
}
#endif //_DEBUG


/////////////////////////////////////////////////////////////////////
/////////
// CComplex2View message handlers
```

To complete this application a few more steps are necessary. First, add the following code to the start of the Complex2View.cpp file, just under the other **#include** statements:

```
#include <complex>

using namespace std;
```

Next, in order to be able to size the graphics with the window size, we'll add a WM_SIZE message handler as we have done with other MFC projects.

Code for Sizing Graphics

The graphics will be sized in the client area so that regardless of the size of the window, the graphics will be drawn proportionately to the client area size. The code necessary for this operation is already present in the OnDraw() method. However, what is still missing are the two member variables: *m_cxClient* and *m_cyClient*. Recall from Chapter 23 that these member variables return information on the size of the client area. In order to obtain this information, we'll have to add a member function, OnSize(), to the project.

Open the Class View pane, as shown on the right of Figure 25-1.

Right-click the CComplex2View class to display the option list also shown in Figure 25-1.

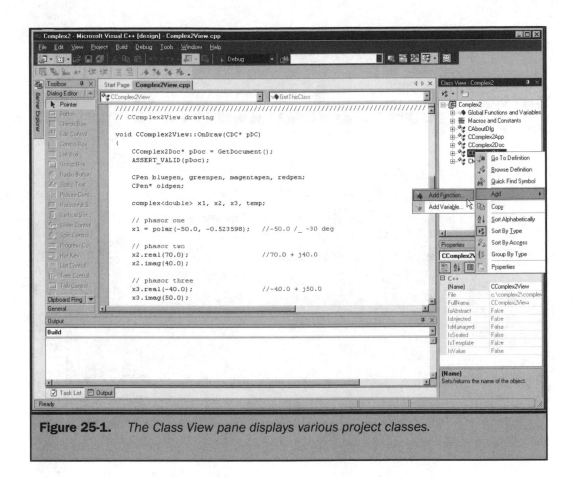

Figure 25-1. *The Class View pane displays various project classes.*

Select the Add option from the option list and select Add Function from the two options provided.

Selecting the Add Function option opens the Add Member Function Wizard, as shown in Figure 25-2.

Examine Figure 25-2 and notice the various entries to the dialog box fields. Parameters for a given method are added one at a time. Observe that three parameters have been added: *nType*, *cx*, and *cy*.

Clicking Finish will add this method to the Complex2View.cpp source code file. We'll now need the two previously mentioned member variables for this method. To add member variables, right-click the mouse on the CComplex2View class to display the option list shown earlier in Figure 25-1.

Select the Add option from the option list and select Add Variable from the two options provided.

Selecting the Add Variable option opens the Add Member Variable Wizard, as shown in Figure 25-3.

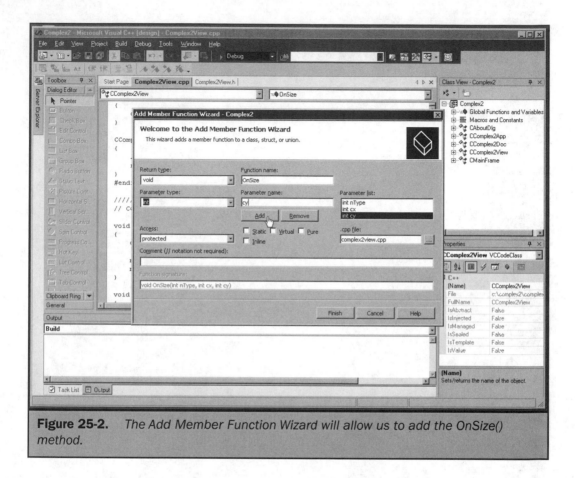

Figure 25-2.   *The Add Member Function Wizard will allow us to add the OnSize()*
method.

Figure 25-3 shows the *m_cyClient* member variable as it is being added to the
method. You'll also have to add the *m_cxClient* member variable.

At this point, the following code has been added to the Complex2View.cpp file to
support the OnSize() method and member variables. The bolded lines of code were
added by us to the recently added OnSize() method.

```cpp
void CComplex2View::OnSize(UINT nType, int cx, int cy)
{
    CView::OnSize(nType, cx, cy);

    m_cxClient = cx;
    m_cyClient = cy;
}
```

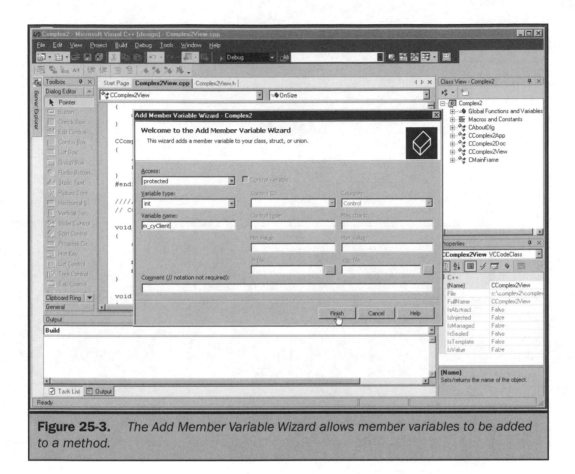

Figure 25-3.   *The Add Member Variable Wizard allows member variables to be added to a method.*

If you open the Complex2View.h header file you will observe that both the method and member variables have been added to this file.

The only thing left is to compile and execute this application.

Testing the Complex2 Application

Figure 25-4 shows the output sent to the window by the Complex2 application.

The three phasors are shown with dash-dot line segments and the result of adding the phasors together is shown with a solid wide red line.

We're sure you'll agree that adding graphing capabilities to complex number arithmetic opens new possibilities to engineering and mathematical calculations.

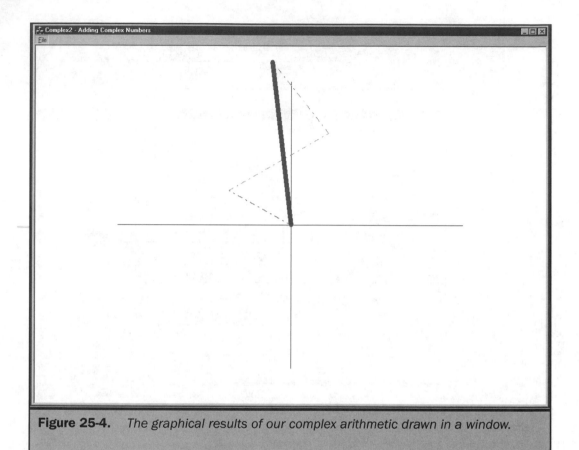

Figure 25-4.   *The graphical results of our complex arithmetic drawn in a window.*

Summary

Combining the capabilities of the STL and MFC has opened new doors and provides a powerful tool when dealing with complex numbers. For a complete treatment of the MFC and STL, you may wish to purchase *MFC Programming in C++ with the Standard Template Libraries* by Murray and Pappas (Prentice-Hall, 2000).

Chapter 26

Getting Started with OLE

The concepts and definitions used with the tools in Microsoft OLE will be introduced in this chapter. OLE, at its inception, simply stood for Object Linking and Embedding. However, as Microsoft expanded its power and features, its abilities exceeded this definition. Microsoft no longer refers to this product as anything but OLE. By definition, OLE is an object-based technology for sharing information and services across process and machine boundaries.

OLE tools allow programmers to develop interconnected applications—*compound documents*—which are dynamically linked together. These compound documents include linked or embedded objects in addition to data.

Developing OLE-compliant containers and servers without the use of Microsoft's Wizards and the MFC is foolish, because you will have to write literally thousands of lines of code, much of it redundant from one OLE application to another.

This chapter shows you how to build OLE-compliant applications with the Visual Studio AppWizard. The program developer can transcend the mundane tasks of repetitive programming code by using the AppWizard's dynamic templates. The AppWizard also allows you, the programmer, to introduce features into your applications without having to worry about the details of the implementation. With the AppWizard, implementing OLE in an application has become very, very simple!

A container application is developed in this chapter with the use of the AppWizard. The information you learn from this application can be applied to a server application that you can develop on your own.

OLE Features and Specifications

OLE offers additional features that are not directly related to compound documents. These features specify methods for handling drag-and-drop, data transfer, file management, and so on. This section contains an overview of these concepts.

Objects

Procedure-oriented Windows programming makes extensive use of API function calls. Sometimes it is difficult to see the implementation language (C or C++) because these applications seem to contain nothing but function calls!

In Chapters 22 and 23 you observed a movement away from a procedure-oriented programming approach and toward an object-oriented approach. The MFC library provides the tools for this transition. With OLE, additional tools for object-oriented programming have become available.

The object-oriented *component object model* is a binary specification or standard that allows two unrelated applications to communicate with each other. The communication takes place through interfaces implemented on the object. When an object conforms to this standard, it is called a *Component Object Model* or *COM object*.

A component object can be instantiated through a component object library—which contains functions that support this instantiation. A *component object* is a Windows object with a unique class ID. The object's functions, contained in the library and referred to as an *interface*, can be called via a returned pointer. This process allows the creation of objects that are not dependent upon the programming language. The library also *marshals* how function calls and function parameters are handled between processes.

Files

OLE allows the use of stream and storage objects—*compound files*—that streamline file manipulation. The stream object most closely resembles a single file, and the storage object resembles a file directory. This structured storage concept shields you from the actual location of data on a disk.

Microsoft's long-range plans include the development of a common file structure so that all files can be easily browsed.

Data

Uniform data transfers are made through a *data object*. OLE uses pointers to a data object. This helps connect the data source to the data receiver. The data object, in turn, handles how data is actually exchanged. Thus, to the programmer, data transfers that use the Clipboard will be handled in the same manner as those that use drag-and-drop.

Embedding

Compound documents can hold information from a variety of unrelated sources. For example, a Microsoft Word document can contain an Excel chart and a Paint bitmap.

Before OLE, items such as charts and bitmaps could be copied to other documents via the Clipboard. Once the objects were "pasted" into the receiving document, they retained no knowledge of their former life. They were static, dead images. If changes eventually had to be made to these objects, the user had to return to the application that originally generated the object, make the changes on the original, and go through the cut-and-paste transfer process once again.

In this case, the Word document would be called the *container*, and Excel and Paint would be called the *servers*. A container holds an object or objects created by other applications, whereas a server is the source of an object or objects used by other applications.

An Embedded Object

As a simple example of embedding objects, this section will teach you how to embed a Paint object into a Microsoft Word document. Here Word will serve as the container, and Paint will function as the server. Use the following steps to embed an object:

1. Open Microsoft Word. Figure 26-1 shows a typical Word screen with a small amount of text written in the window.

2. From the Insert menu, select the Object menu item, as shown in Figure 26-2.

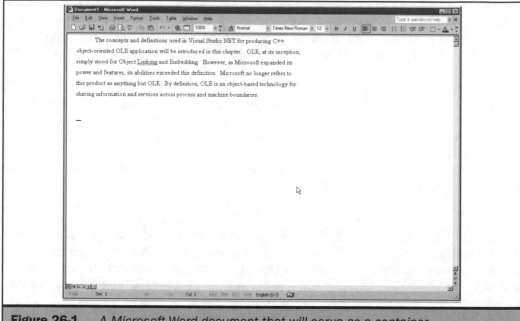

Figure 26-1.   *A Microsoft Word document that will serve as a container*

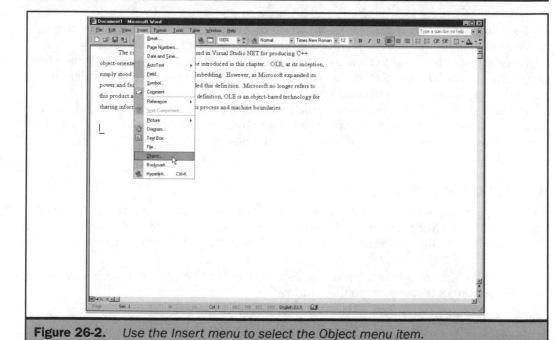

Figure 26-2.   *Use the Insert menu to select the Object menu item.*

Once the menu item is selected, the Object dialog box will appear, as shown in Figure 26-3.

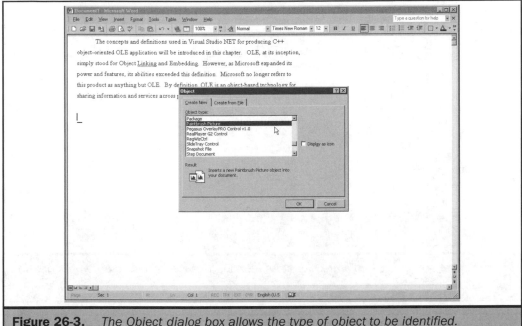

Figure 26-3.   *The Object dialog box allows the type of object to be identified.*

3. From the Object dialog box, choose Paintbrush Picture as the object to embed. Paint will be opened automatically, as shown in Figure 26-4, and the drawing surface will appear on the Word document.

4. Use Paint to draw the object that you wish to embed in the Word document. In this example, several simple graphic shapes were drawn in the Paint drawing area, as shown in Figure 26-5.

5. When you are done creating the embedded object, select File | Save to save your work—just in case!

6. Now, open the document once again. You should see the new object embedded within the Word document, as shown in Figure 26-6.

Now the embedded object can also be edited. A single left-click, while it is over the embedded graphics, will bring the editing rectangle to the foreground, as shown in Figure 26-7.

Now here is the magic. Use the mouse to stretch the height and width of the object, as shown in Figure 26-8.

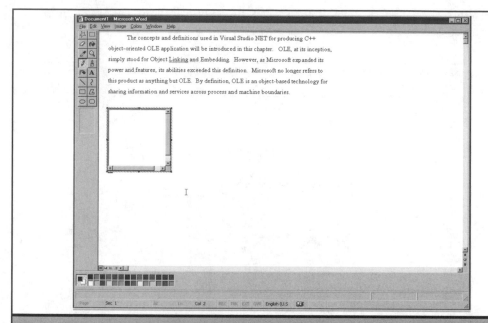

Figure 26-4. *Paintbrush picture has been identified as the object to be embedded in the Word document.*

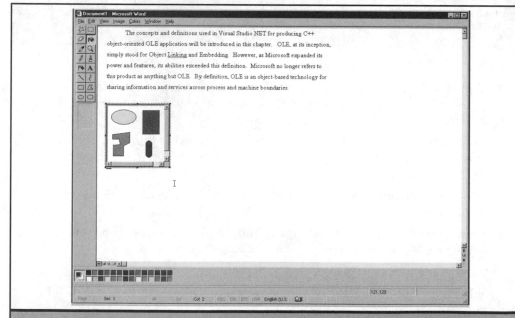

Figure 26-5. *The graphics to be embedded are completed in Paint.*

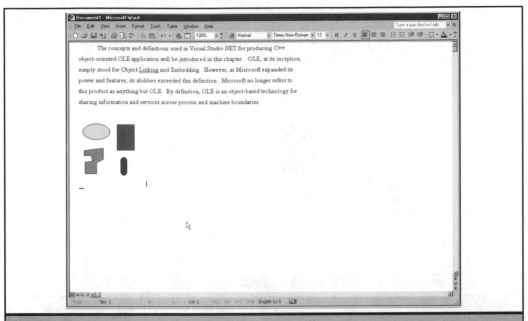

Figure 26-6.   *The embedded object is now part of the Word document.*

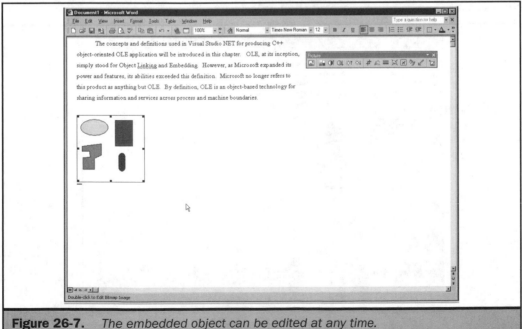

Figure 26-7.   *The embedded object can be edited at any time.*

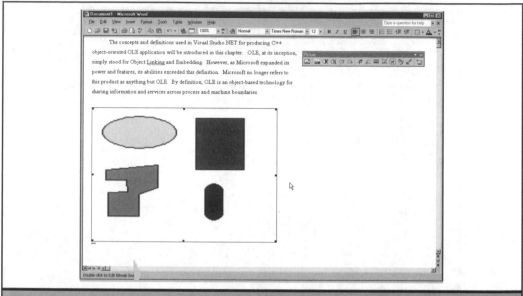

Figure 26-8.   *Embedded objects can be moved or changed by blocking the object.*

If you double-click the embedded object, surprise—you are back in Paint. Figure 26-9 shows that the embedding process is dynamic!

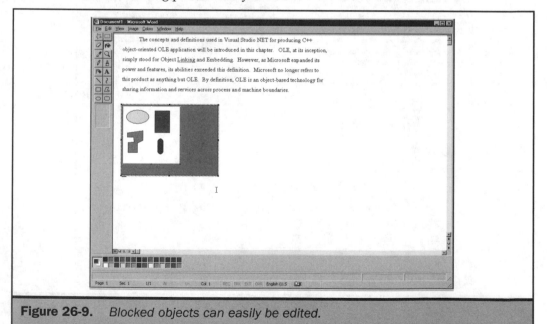

Figure 26-9.   *Blocked objects can easily be edited.*

Embedded objects can be moved, changed, and edited at any time.

Linking

OLE supports a dynamic linking process between applications. When applications are linked, data can be shared instantaneously between the applications. In the past, linking was difficult because it was too easy for users to break the links. With OLE, *file monikers* prevent most of the link breakage problems. File monikers, based on a path in the file system, are used to identify COM objects that are saved in their own files.

Developing a Container Application

In Chapter 23, a simple single-document interface (SDI) project was created and named "gdi". The container application in this chapter will be patterned closely after that example. We'll call this application "Cnt," which is shorthand for container.

This application uses two important OLE classes, **COleClientItem** and **COleDocument**. **COleDocument** manages a list of **COleClientItem** items. **COleClientItem** itself manages the embedded or linked objects and the required communications.

The important thing to remember as you view the container code in the next sections is that the code is completely generated by the AppWizard. This container template code can be enhanced with your specific application features to turn it into a full-blown product. In this chapter, however, no additional features were added to the basic template.

Using the AppWizard

The AppWizard is used here in the same way it was used in Chapters 22 and 23, however a few options will be changed. You might want to review those chapters for a more detailed explanation of each step in the creation process. This section will outline the most important steps for building the Cnt container project.

1. Start a MFC Application project in the normal manner from the Visual Studio. Name the project Cnt.

2. Once the AppWizard is started, create a single-document interface, as shown in Figure 26-10.

3. Select Container under Compound Document Support and also choose Support For Compound Files under Additional Options, as shown in Figure 26-11.

4. Do not make changes to the Document Template Strings for this project (see Figure 26-12).

5. Select None under Database Support, as shown in Figure 26-13, for this project.

6. Use Figure 26-14 to help you select the User Interface Features for the project.

7. Select the Advanced Features for this project as shown in Figure 26-15. Note in particular that printing and ActiveX control options have been requested.

8. View the classes that will be generated for the project, shown in Figure 26-16, then click Finish to complete the specification process. The panels, or panes, to the right of your display can now be used to view the various classes and files created for the Cnt project.

9. As a final step, compile the project in the normal manner. When the process is complete, the subdirectory specified at the start of the project will contain an executable file named Cnt.exe. We will test this container project a little later in this chapter.

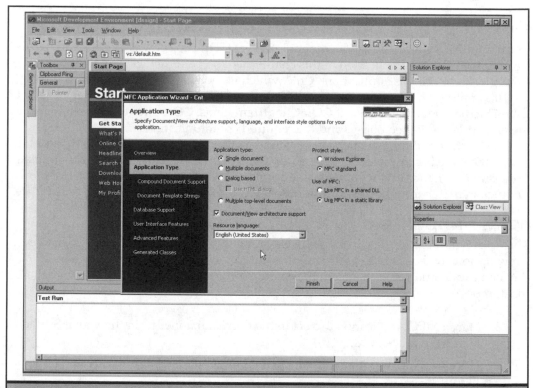

Figure 26-10.   *Application Type: Single Document option is selected*

A Look at Project Files

The files generated by the AppWizard produce a fully operable container application named Cnt. The AppWizard creates a variety of project files. Most of these files you are already familiar with from Chapters 22 and 23. In the following sections, we'll examine several source code files that have a significant bearing on the Cnt project. As you examine these files, remember to examine the associated header file, too.

Figure 26-11. *Compound Document Support: Project will be a container application*

Figure 26-12. *Document Template Strings: No changes are made to the project's strings*

Figure 26-13. *Database Support: No database support will be needed for this container*

Figure 26-14. *User Interface Features: Select the features shown in this figure for your project*

Figure 26-15.   *Advanced Features: Chose Printing and ActiveX control support*

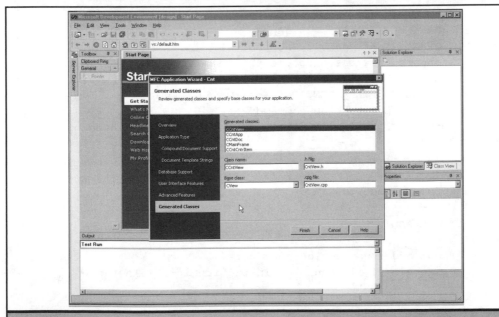

Figure 26-16.   *Generated Classes: Examine the classes for the project then click Finish*

The Container File: Cnt.cpp

The code used in the container Cnt.cpp source code file is almost identical to that used in other projects contained in Chapters 22 and 23. However, there are some features that you might want to examine.

The following listing is a slightly modified version of the Cnt.cpp source code file:

```cpp
// Cnt.cpp : Defines the class behaviors for the application.
//

#include "stdafx.h"
#include "Cnt.h"
#include "MainFrm.h"

#include "CntDoc.h"
#include "CntView.h"

#ifdef _DEBUG
#define new DEBUG_NEW
#endif


/////////////////////////////////////////////////////////////////
// CCntApp

BEGIN_MESSAGE_MAP(CCntApp, CWinApp)
    ON_COMMAND(ID_APP_ABOUT, OnAppAbout)
    // Standard file based document commands
    ON_COMMAND(ID_FILE_NEW, CWinApp::OnFileNew)
    ON_COMMAND(ID_FILE_OPEN, CWinApp::OnFileOpen)
    // Standard print setup command
    ON_COMMAND(ID_FILE_PRINT_SETUP, CWinApp::OnFilePrintSetup)
END_MESSAGE_MAP()


/////////////////////////////////////////////////////////////////
// CCntApp construction

CCntApp::CCntApp()
{
    // TODO: add construction code here,
    // Place all significant initialization in InitInstance
}


/////////////////////////////////////////////////////////////////
// The one and only CCntApp object
```

```
CCntApp theApp;
/////////////////////////////////////////////////////////////
// CCntApp initialization

BOOL CCntApp::InitInstance()
{
    CWinApp::InitInstance();      // Initialize OLE libraries
    if (!AfxOleInit())
    {
        AfxMessageBox(IDP_OLE_INIT_FAILED);
        return FALSE;
    }
    AfxEnableControlContainer();
    // Standard initialization
    SetRegistryKey(_T("Local AppWizard-Generated Applications"));
    LoadStdProfileSettings(4);
    // Register the application's document templates.
    CSingleDocTemplate* pDocTemplate;
    pDocTemplate = new CSingleDocTemplate(
        IDR_MAINFRAME,
        RUNTIME_CLASS(CCntDoc),
        RUNTIME_CLASS(CMainFrame),   // main SDI frame window
        RUNTIME_CLASS(CCntView));
    pDocTemplate->SetContainerInfo(IDR_CNTR_INPLACE);
    AddDocTemplate(pDocTemplate);
    // Parse command line for standard shell commands
    CCommandLineInfo cmdInfo;
    ParseCommandLine(cmdInfo);
    if (!ProcessShellCommand(cmdInfo))
        return FALSE;
    m_pMainWnd->ShowWindow(SW_SHOW);
    m_pMainWnd->UpdateWindow();

    return TRUE;
}


/////////////////////////////////////////////////////////////
// CAboutDlg dialog used for App About

class CAboutDlg : public CDialog
{
public:
    CAboutDlg();
```

```
// Dialog Data
    enum { IDD = IDD_ABOUTBOX };

protected:
    virtual void DoDataExchange(CDataExchange* pDX);

// Implementation
protected:
    DECLARE_MESSAGE_MAP()
};

CAboutDlg::CAboutDlg() : CDialog(CAboutDlg::IDD)
{
}


void CAboutDlg::DoDataExchange(CDataExchange* pDX)
{
    CDialog::DoDataExchange(pDX);
}


BEGIN_MESSAGE_MAP(CAboutDlg, CDialog)
END_MESSAGE_MAP()

// App command to run the dialog
void CCntApp::OnAppAbout()
{
    CAboutDlg aboutDlg;
    aboutDlg.DoModal();
}


/////////////////////////////////////////////////////////////
// CCntApp message handlers
```

There is an interesting section of code in this file that deserves a mention. Under OLE, in-place editing is supported. *In-place editing* means that when an object is embedded in a container, such as our Cnt application, its menu replaces the container's menu. For example, if an Excel spreadsheet object is embedded in Cnt, Cnt's menu will change to that of Excel's!

This menu change is handled by MFC, via OLE, almost automatically. The MFC makes this possible by having three menu sources available: IDR_MAINFRAME, IDR_DOCTYPE, and IDR_CNTR_INPLACE (the name of the last IDR is specific to your application). When no object is embedded in the container application, IDR_MAINFRAME is used. When a document is opened, IDR_DOCTYPE is used. Finally, when an object has been embedded in the container, IDR_CNTR_INPLACE is used.

The Container File: CntDoc.cpp

The code used in the container CntDoc.cpp source code, shown here, contains some additional code that does not appear in the applications of Chapter 22 and 23. You may want to compare these files and examine the differences.

```cpp
// CntDoc.cpp : implementation of the CCntDoc class
//

#include "stdafx.h"
#include "Cnt.h"

#include "CntDoc.h"
#include "CntrItem.h"

#ifdef _DEBUG
#define new DEBUG_NEW
#endif


/////////////////////////////////////////////////////////////
// CCntDoc

IMPLEMENT_DYNCREATE(CCntDoc, COleDocument)

BEGIN_MESSAGE_MAP(CCntDoc, COleDocument)
    // Enable default OLE container implementation
    ON_UPDATE_COMMAND_UI(ID_EDIT_PASTE,
                         COleDocument::OnUpdatePasteMenu)
    ON_UPDATE_COMMAND_UI(ID_EDIT_PASTE_LINK,
                         COleDocument::OnUpdatePasteLinkMenu)
    ON_UPDATE_COMMAND_UI(ID_OLE_EDIT_CONVERT,
                         COleDocument::OnUpdateObjectVerbMenu)
    ON_COMMAND(ID_OLE_EDIT_CONVERT,
               COleDocument::OnEditConvert)
    ON_UPDATE_COMMAND_UI(ID_OLE_EDIT_LINKS,
                         COleDocument::OnUpdateEditLinksMenu)
    ON_COMMAND(ID_OLE_EDIT_LINKS,
               COleDocument::OnEditLinks)
    ON_UPDATE_COMMAND_UI_RANGE(ID_OLE_VERB_FIRST,
                         ID_OLE_VERB_LAST,
                         COleDocument::OnUpdateObjectVerbMenu)
END_MESSAGE_MAP()


/////////////////////////////////////////////////////////////
// CCntDoc construction/destruction
```

```
CCntDoc::CCntDoc()
{
    // Use OLE compound files
    EnableCompoundFile();

    // TODO: add one-time construction code here

}

CCntDoc::~CCntDoc()
{
}

BOOL CCntDoc::OnNewDocument()
{
    if (!COleDocument::OnNewDocument())
        return FALSE;

    // TODO: add reinitialization code here
    // (SDI documents will reuse this document)

    return TRUE;
}


/////////////////////////////////////////////////////////////
// CCntDoc serialization

void CCntDoc::Serialize(CArchive& ar)
{
    if (ar.IsStoring())
    {
        // TODO: add storing code here
    }
    else
    {
        // TODO: add loading code here
    }

    // the base class COleDocument enables serialization
    // of the container document's COleClientItem objects.
    COleDocument::Serialize(ar);
}
```

```
//////////////////////////////////////////////////////////
// CCntDoc diagnostics

#ifdef _DEBUG
void CCntDoc::AssertValid() const
{
    COleDocument::AssertValid();
}

void CCntDoc::Dump(CDumpContext& dc) const
{
    COleDocument::Dump(dc);
}
#endif //_DEBUG


//////////////////////////////////////////////////////////
// CCntDoc commands
```

The most significant change in this file comes with the expansion of the message map, as shown in bold type.

The message map will now allow the implementation of the default OLE container. You can also see that the constructor calls the EnableCompoundFile() function. This is required for a container application.

The Container File: CntView.cpp

The container CntView.cpp source code file also has some major changes in comparison to the applications of Chapters 22 and 23. Examine the following partial listing for this source code file and note, in particular, the additions to the message map.

```
// CntView.cpp : implementation of the CCntView class
//

#include "stdafx.h"
#include "Cnt.h"

#include "CntDoc.h"
#include "CntrItem.h"
#include "CntView.h"

#ifdef _DEBUG
#define new DEBUG_NEW
```

```cpp
#endif

/////////////////////////////////////////////////////////////
// CCntView

IMPLEMENT_DYNCREATE(CCntView, CView)

BEGIN_MESSAGE_MAP(CCntView, CView)
    ON_WM_DESTROY()
    ON_WM_SETFOCUS()
    ON_WM_SIZE()
    ON_COMMAND(ID_OLE_INSERT_NEW, OnInsertObject)
    ON_COMMAND(ID_CANCEL_EDIT_CNTR, OnCancelEditCntr)
    ON_COMMAND(ID_FILE_PRINT, OnFilePrint)
    ON_COMMAND(ID_FILE_PRINT_DIRECT, CView::OnFilePrint)
    ON_COMMAND(ID_FILE_PRINT_PREVIEW,
                CView::OnFilePrintPreview)
END_MESSAGE_MAP()
        .
        .
        .
/////////////////////////////////////////////////////////////
// CCntView drawing

void CCntView::OnDraw(CDC* pDC)
{
    CCntDoc* pDoc = GetDocument();
    ASSERT_VALID(pDoc);

    // TODO: add draw code for native data here
    // TODO: also draw all OLE items in the document

    // Draw the selection at an arbitrary position. This
    // code should be removed once your real drawing code
    // is implemented. This position corresponds exactly
    // to the rectangle returned by CCntCntrItem,
    //  to give the effect of in-place editing.

    // TODO: remove this code when final draw code is complete.

    if (m_pSelection == NULL)
    {
        POSITION pos=pDoc->GetStartPosition();
```

```
            m_pSelection=(CCntCntrItem*)pDoc->GetNextClientItem(pos);
    }
    if (m_pSelection != NULL)
{
    CSize size;
    CRect rct;
    GetClientRect(&rct);


    if (SUCCEEDED(m_pSelection->GetExtent(&size, m_pSelection-
>m_nDrawAspect)))
    {
        pDC->HIMETRICtoLP(&size);
        rct.right = size.cx;
        rct.bottom = size.cy;
    }
    m_pSelection->Draw(pDC, rct);
    }
}
    .
    .
    .
void CCntView::OnSize(UINT nType, int cx, int cy)
{
    CView::OnSize(nType, cx, cy);
    COleClientItem* pActiveItem = GetDocument()-> \
                                    GetInPlaceActiveItem(this);
    if (pActiveItem != NULL)
        pActiveItem->SetItemRects();
}
    .
    .
    .
```

So that the application can handle drawing (i.e., inserted objects) for the CCntView container, the OnDraw() member function has to be altered by the AppWizard. This portion of code was shown in bold type in the file. Here is just a small portion of that code:

```
if (m_pSelection != NULL)
{   CSize size;     CRect rct;     GetClientRect(&rct);
    if (SUCCEEDED(m_pSelection->GetExtent(&size, m_pSelection-
>m_nDrawAspect)))    {         pDC->HIMETRICtoLP(&size);
rct.right = size.cx;         rct.bottom = size.cy;     }
m_pSelection->Draw(pDC, rct);      }
```

This code determines the OLE object's size and converts it to the container's mapping mode. Thus it appears in the same location and with the same size, relative to the container's window, each time it is displayed. Other additions include OnInitialUpdate(), IsSelected(), OnInsertObject(), OnCancelEdit(), OnSetFocus(), and OnSize(). These signal when an OLE object is selected or otherwise being manipulated. OnInsertObject() runs COleInsertDialog. Any additional code for these functions must be supplied by you, the programmer.

The Container File: CntrItem.cpp

The container CntrItem.cpp source code file, shown here as an edited listing, is responsible for the implementation of the **CCntCntrItem** class:

```
// CntrItem.cpp : implementation of the CCntCntrItem class
//

#include "stdafx.h"
#include "Cnt.h"

#include "CntDoc.h"
#include "CntView.h"
#include "CntrItem.h"
     .
     .
     .
void CCntCntrItem::OnChange(OLE_NOTIFICATION nCode, DWORD dwParam)
{
    ASSERT_VALID(this);

    COleClientItem::OnChange(nCode, dwParam);

    // When an item is being edited (either in-place or fully open)
    //  it sends OnChange notifications for changes in the state of the
    //  item or visual appearance of its content.

    // TODO: invalidate the item by calling UpdateAllViews
    //  (with hints appropriate to your application)

    GetDocument()->UpdateAllViews(NULL);
        // for now just update ALL views/no hints
}


BOOL CCntCntrItem::OnChangeItemPosition(const CRect& rectPos)
```

```
{
    ASSERT_VALID(this);

    // During in-place activation CCntCntrItem::OnChangeItemPosition
    //  is called by the server to change the position of the in-place
    //  window. Usually, this is a result of the data in the server
    //  document changing such that the extent has changed or as a
result
    //  of in-place resizing.
    //
    // The default here is to call the base class, which will call
    //  COleClientItem::SetItemRects to move the item
    //  to the new position.

    if (!COleClientItem::OnChangeItemPosition(rectPos))
        return FALSE;

    // TODO: update any cache you may have of the item's
rectangle/extent

    return TRUE;
}

void CCntCntrItem::OnGetItemPosition(CRect& rPosition)
{
    ASSERT_VALID(this);

    // During in-place activation, CCntCntrItem::OnGetItemPosition
    //  will be called to determine the location of this item. The
default
    //  implementation created from AppWizard simply returns a hard-
coded
    //  rectangle. Usually, this rectangle would reflect the current
    //  position of the item relative to the view used for activation.
    //  You can obtain the view by calling
CCntCntrItem::GetActiveView.

    // TODO: return correct rectangle (in pixels) in rPosition

    rPosition.SetRect(10, 10, 210, 210);
}
```

```
void CCntCntrItem::OnActivate()
{
    // Allow only one inplace activate item per frame
    CCntView* pView = GetActiveView();
    ASSERT_VALID(pView);
    COleClientItem* pItem = GetDocument()-
>GetInPlaceActiveItem(pView);
    if (pItem != NULL && pItem != this)
        pItem->Close();

    COleClientItem::OnActivate();
}
            .
            .
            .
```

The primary purpose of this file is to help monitor the position and size of the item in the drawing. Examine the portions of code set in bold type. This code, by default, returns the location of the object at a prearranged location designated by a CRect() at 10, 10 and 210, 210. These values can be changed manually or automatically. In the next section you'll see how to use the container application to accept an object from a server.

Testing the Container Application

The container application can now be tested. Remember that the container application was produced as a template, without additional functionality added. However, what you will see in the next few pages is a very complete and functioning application.

The container application can be run directly from the integrated environment of the Visual Studio. Figure 26-17 shows the initial container window.

This container can use objects from any server. For this example we'll insert an Excel spreadsheet into the container. To select Excel as the server, choose Edit | Insert New Object. This will open the Insert Object dialog box as shown in Figure 26-18.

From the Insert Object dialog box, choose Microsoft Excel Worksheet as the object to embed in the container.

Figure 26-19 shows the initial insertion of the object into the container document with data entered in various cells.

Don't forget, you gained all of this functionality without writing one line of code. The AppWizard has made it very easy to develop OLE container and server applications. As a little project, why not create your own server application? Then to test your skills further, insert a server object from this application into the Cnt container.

Figure 26-17.   *The initial window for the Cnt container application*

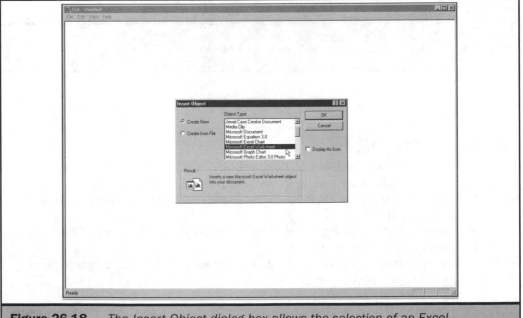

Figure 26-18.   *The Insert Object dialog box allows the selection of an Excel Worksheet.*

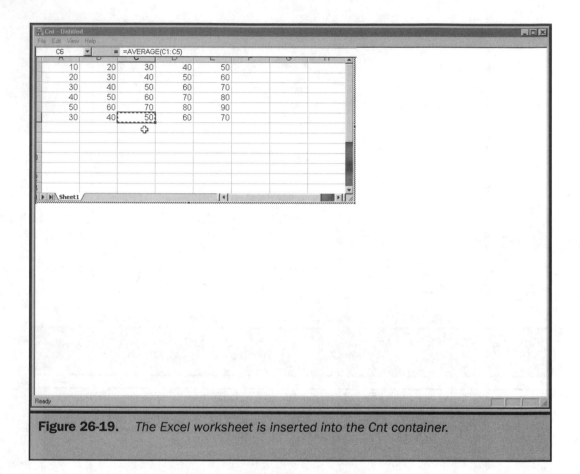

Figure 26-19. *The Excel worksheet is inserted into the Cnt container.*

What's Coming?

OLE is truly a complicated subject, but one worthy of your attention. The smart money is on building OLE applications with the help of the AppWizard and the MFC library. Once you master OLE concepts, using the AppWizard makes actual project creation a snap.

For additional study we recommend examining articles on OLE and COM that can be found in the *Microsoft Systems Journal*.

In the next chapter we will take a look at another subject: ActiveX controls. Now we're really getting into power programming.

Chapter 27

Getting Started with ActiveX Controls

You are already familiar with a wide variety of Windows controls such as radio buttons, check boxes, list boxes, and so on. Many developers also design their own controls. This special group of controls is known as ActiveX or custom controls. As Windows evolved from 3.*x* to 95, 98, ME, NT, 2000, and XP, so have custom controls. Custom controls really had their beginning with Microsoft's Visual Basic programming language. Visual Basic made it easy to implement new controls that were not part of the standard group of Windows controls. These custom controls, originally known as VBXs (after their original file extension .vbx), were specialty items. They were actually small Dynamic-Link Libraries (DLLs) with .vbx file extensions. Custom controls have now evolved into 32-bit controls with new abilities. These new controls use an .ocx file extension. A good example of a custom control is a custom slide bar that might be used to control the volume in a CD-ROM player application.

There is a commercial market for well-designed custom controls. However, custom controls developed commercially can also be much more complicated. Some include complete spreadsheet, image, and database capabilities within the control!

Many programmers have developed custom controls using Visual Basic and then incorporated them into their C++ applications. Obviously, the C++ language has needed its own mechanism for creating custom controls. At the same time Microsoft was developing a solution, they began the migration from 16-bit Windows 3.1 to 32-bit Windows 95 and NT. As it turns out, the hardware-specific 16-bit VBX controls will not serve the new 32-bit multiple platform environments as well as programmers desired. Microsoft decided that rather than expand the VBX specifications, it would redesign the custom control architecture to include the 32-bit platforms, thus the new control specifications with .ocx file extensions. Under Windows 95, 98, ME, NT, and 2000, OCX controls are the natural replacement for the older VBX custom controls of Visual Basic. These new custom controls will also serve container applications such as Microsoft Access, Excel, Word, PowerPoint, and so on. The term "custom control" has largely been replaced with "ActiveX control."

The good news concerning controls for the C++ developer is that Visual Studio.NET has a built-in Microsoft C++ Wizard that helps build the control. This Wizard is officially called the *MFC ActiveX ControlWizard.* The Wizard builds the ActiveX control using object-oriented C++ code and takes full advantage of the MFC.

During development, your controls can be tested with the ActiveX Test Container tool or in any application capable of accepting these controls. For example, Microsoft Word and Excel are applications that can make full use of ActiveX controls.

ActiveX Controls

ActiveX controls can be placed alongside standard controls such as radio buttons, push buttons, check boxes, and so on. Therefore, you might find a dialog box containing a few radio buttons, check boxes, and an ActiveX control. ActiveX controls, however, are inherently more difficult to implement than the standard controls we have worked with up to this point.

Unless a commercial vendor has supplied an ActiveX control to you, the programmer will be responsible for the design and complete implementation of the control and its properties. The problem is now twofold. First, during the design phase the programmer must create, write, and compile the code that draws the control and implements all of the controls, methods, and so on. This code eventually becomes a tiny dynamic link library with an .ocx file extension. Second, the application that is to use the ActiveX control must now interface with the control's methods, data, and so on. The programmer, again, must properly design this interface.

A properly designed ActiveX control must be independent from the application in which it is used. In other words, it must be completely re-entrant. Remember that an ActiveX control is really a separate dynamic link library that is not linked to any particular application. A separate instance for data for each use of the control is required for re-entrance in a DLL. The only communications allowed between an application and an ActiveX control are via messages. Hence, an ActiveX control must be defined in a dynamic link library.

Control Design Criterion

When entering the design phase for an ActiveX control, several decisions must be made to create an ActiveX control as appealing and functional as possible.

First, you must decide how the ActiveX control will be drawn and displayed. Here, some talent will be required to produce ActiveX controls that are both functional and attractive.

Next, the ActiveX control should be designed to take advantage of changes in control properties resulting from the automation interface of the control. Note that for ActiveX controls designed in this way property pages will allow the user to change properties at run time. Arguments should be assigned ActiveX controls in order to control events, set their names, and determine when they should be fired. A control's methods should be defined in terms of arguments and return types.

Finally, the persistence of a control's various property states must be determined and implemented.

The COleControl Class

ActiveX controls are derived from MFC's COleControl class. Examine the code in the next listing. This listing contains a highly edited and shortened portion of the AFXCTL.H header file. If you are interested in examining the full header file, you should be able to locate it in the mfc\include subdirectory. Be warned, however, that this file is approximately 30 pages in length.

```
// This is a part of the Microsoft Foundation Classes
// C++ library.
// Copyright (C) 1992-2001 Microsoft Corporation
// All rights reserved.
//
        .
```

```
        .
        .
        .
//////////////////////////////////////////////////////////////
// Stock events

#define EVENT_STOCK_CLICK() \
    { afxEventStock, DISPID_CLICK, _T("Click"), VTS_NONE },

#define EVENT_STOCK_DBLCLICK() \
    { afxEventStock, DISPID_DBLCLICK, _T("DblClick"),
      VTS_NONE },

#define EVENT_STOCK_KEYDOWN() \
    { afxEventStock, DISPID_KEYDOWN, _T("KeyDown"),
      VTS_PI2 VTS_I2 },

#define EVENT_STOCK_KEYPRESS() \
    { afxEventStock, DISPID_KEYPRESS, _T("KeyPress"),
      VTS_PI2 },

#define EVENT_STOCK_KEYUP() \
    { afxEventStock, DISPID_KEYUP, _T("KeyUp"),
      VTS_PI2 VTS_I2 },

#define EVENT_STOCK_MOUSEDOWN() \
    { afxEventStock, DISPID_MOUSEDOWN, _T("MouseDown"), \
      VTS_I2 VTS_I2 VTS_XPOS_PIXELS VTS_YPOS_PIXELS },

#define EVENT_STOCK_MOUSEMOVE() \
    { afxEventStock, DISPID_MOUSEMOVE, _T("MouseMove"), \
      VTS_I2 VTS_I2 VTS_XPOS_PIXELS VTS_YPOS_PIXELS },

#define EVENT_STOCK_MOUSEUP() \
    { afxEventStock, DISPID_MOUSEUP, _T("MouseUp"), \
      VTS_I2 VTS_I2 VTS_XPOS_PIXELS VTS_YPOS_PIXELS },

#define EVENT_STOCK_ERROREVENT() \
    { afxEventStock, DISPID_ERROREVENT, _T("Error"), \
      VTS_I2 VTS_PBSTR VTS_SCODE VTS_BSTR VTS_BSTR \
      VTS_I4 VTS_PBOOL },

#define EVENT_STOCK_READYSTATECHANGE() \
    { afxEventStock, DISPID_READYSTATECHANGE, \
      _T("ReadyStateChange"), \
```

```
        VTS_I4 },

// Shift state values for mouse and keyboard events
#define SHIFT_MASK        0x01
#define CTRL_MASK         0x02
#define ALT_MASK          0x04

// Button values for mouse events
#define LEFT_BUTTON       0x01
#define RIGHT_BUTTON      0x02
#define MIDDLE_BUTTON     0x04


/////////////////////////////////////////////////////////////////
// Stock properties

#define DISP_PROPERTY_STOCK(theClass, szExternalName, \
        dispid, pfnGet, pfnSet, vtPropType) \
        { _T(szExternalName), dispid, NULL, vtPropType, \
        (AFX_PMSG)(void (theClass::*)(void))&pfnGet, \
        (AFX_PMSG)(void (theClass::*)(void))&pfnSet, 0, \
        afxDispStock }, \

#define DISP_STOCKPROP_APPEARANCE() \
        DISP_PROPERTY_STOCK(COleControl, "Appearance", \
        DISPID_APPEARANCE, \
        COleControl::GetAppearance, \
        COleControl::SetAppearance, VT_I2)

#define DISP_STOCKPROP_BACKCOLOR() \
        DISP_PROPERTY_STOCK(COleControl, "BackColor", \
        DISPID_BACKCOLOR, \
        COleControl::GetBackColor, COleControl::SetBackColor, \
        VT_COLOR)

#define DISP_STOCKPROP_BORDERSTYLE() \
        DISP_PROPERTY_STOCK(COleControl, "BorderStyle", \
        DISPID_BORDERSTYLE, \
        COleControl::GetBorderStyle, \
        COleControl::SetBorderStyle, VT_I2)

#define DISP_STOCKPROP_CAPTION() \
        DISP_PROPERTY_STOCK(COleControl, "Caption", \
        DISPID_CAPTION, \
        COleControl::GetText, COleControl::SetText, VT_BSTR)
```

```
#define DISP_STOCKPROP_ENABLED() \
        DISP_PROPERTY_STOCK(COleControl, "Enabled",
        DISPID_ENABLED, \
        COleControl::GetEnabled,
        COleControl::SetEnabled, VT_BOOL)

#define DISP_STOCKPROP_FONT() \
        DISP_PROPERTY_STOCK(COleControl, "Font",
        DISPID_FONT, \
        COleControl::GetFont, COleControl::SetFont,
        VT_FONT)

#define DISP_STOCKPROP_FORECOLOR() \
        DISP_PROPERTY_STOCK(COleControl, "ForeColor",
        DISPID_FORECOLOR, \
        COleControl::GetForeColor, COleControl::SetForeColor,
        VT_COLOR)

#define DISP_STOCKPROP_HWND() \
        DISP_PROPERTY_STOCK(COleControl, "hWnd",
        DISPID_HWND, \
        COleControl::GetHwnd, SetNotSupported, VT_HANDLE)

#define DISP_STOCKPROP_TEXT() \
        DISP_PROPERTY_STOCK(COleControl, "Text", DISPID_TEXT, \
        COleControl::GetText, COleControl::SetText, VT_BSTR)

#define DISP_STOCKPROP_READYSTATE() \
        DISP_PROPERTY_STOCK(COleControl, "ReadyState",
        DISPID_READYSTATE, \
        COleControl::GetReadyState, SetNotSupported, VT_I4)

///////////////////////////////////////////////////////////
// Stock methods

#define DISP_FUNCTION_STOCK(theClass, szExternalName, dispid,
        pfnMember, vtRetVal, vtsParams) \
        { _T(szExternalName), dispid, vtsParams, vtRetVal, \
        (AFX_PMSG)(void (theClass::*)(void))&pfnMember, \
        (AFX_PMSG)0, 0, afxDispStock }, \

#define DISP_STOCKFUNC_REFRESH() \
        DISP_FUNCTION_STOCK(COleControl, "Refresh",
```

```
        DISPID_REFRESH, \
        COleControl::Refresh, VT_EMPTY, VTS_NONE)

#define DISP_STOCKFUNC_DOCLICK() \
        DISP_FUNCTION_STOCK(COleControl, "DoClick", \
        DISPID_DOCLICK, \
        COleControl::DoClick, VT_EMPTY, VTS_NONE)

        .
        .
        .
/////////////////////////////////////////////////////////////////
// CFontHolder - helper class for dealing with font objects

class CFontHolder
{
// Constructors
public:
    explicit CFontHolder(LPPROPERTYNOTIFYSINK pNotify);

// Attributes
    LPFONT m_pFont;

// Operations
    void InitializeFont(
            const FONTDESC* pFontDesc = NULL,
            LPDISPATCH pFontDispAmbient = NULL);
    void SetFont(LPFONT pNewFont);
    void ReleaseFont();
    HFONT GetFontHandle();
    HFONT GetFontHandle(long cyLogical, long cyHimetric);
    CFont* Select(CDC* pDC, long cyLogical, long cyHimetric);
    BOOL GetDisplayString(CString& strValue);
    LPFONTDISP GetFontDispatch();
    void QueryTextMetrics(LPTEXTMETRIC lptm);

// Implementation
public:
    ~CFontHolder();
    void SetFontNotifySink(LPPROPERTYNOTIFYSINK pNotify);

protected:
    DWORD m_dwConnectCookie;
    LPPROPERTYNOTIFYSINK m_pNotify;
};
```

```
        .
        .
        .

// Firing functions for stock events
void FireKeyDown(USHORT* pnChar, short nShiftState);
void FireKeyUp(USHORT* pnChar, short nShiftState);
void FireKeyPress(USHORT* pnChar);
void FireMouseDown(short nButton, short nShiftState,
    OLE_XPOS_PIXELS x, OLE_YPOS_PIXELS y);
void FireMouseUp(short nButton, short nShiftState,
    OLE_XPOS_PIXELS x, OLE_YPOS_PIXELS y);
void FireMouseMove(short nButton, short nShiftState,
    OLE_XPOS_PIXELS x, OLE_YPOS_PIXELS y);
void FireClick();
void FireDblClick();
void FireError(SCODE scode, LPCTSTR lpszDescription,
            UINT nHelpID = 0);
void FireReadyStateChange();

// Changing size and/or rectangle
BOOL GetRectInContainer(LPRECT lpRect);
BOOL SetRectInContainer(LPCRECT lpRect);
void GetControlSize(int* pcx, int* pcy);
BOOL SetControlSize(int cx, int cy);
    .
    .
    .

// Stock events
void KeyDown(USHORT* pnChar);
void KeyUp(USHORT* pnChar);
void ButtonDown(USHORT iButton, UINT nFlags, CPoint point);
void ButtonUp(USHORT iButton, UINT nFlags, CPoint point);
void ButtonDblClk(USHORT iButton, UINT nFlags,
                CPoint point);

// Masks to identify used stock events and properties
void InitStockEventMask();
void InitStockPropMask();
DWORD GetStockEventMask() const;
DWORD GetStockPropMask() const;
    .
    .
    .
```

```
// Message Maps
protected:
    //{{AFX_MSG(COleControl)
    afx_msg void OnKeyDown(UINT nChar, UINT nRepCnt,
                           UINT nFlags);
    afx_msg void OnKeyUp(UINT nChar, UINT nRepCnt,
                         UINT nFlags);
    afx_msg void OnChar(UINT nChar, UINT nRepCnt, UINT nFlags);
    afx_msg void OnMouseMove(UINT nFlags, CPoint point);
    afx_msg void OnLButtonDown(UINT nFlags, CPoint point);
    afx_msg void OnLButtonUp(UINT nFlags, CPoint point);
    afx_msg void OnLButtonDblClk(UINT nFlags, CPoint point);
    afx_msg void OnMButtonDown(UINT nFlags, CPoint point);
    afx_msg void OnMButtonUp(UINT nFlags, CPoint point);
    afx_msg void OnMButtonDblClk(UINT nFlags, CPoint point);
    afx_msg void OnRButtonDown(UINT nFlags, CPoint point);
    afx_msg void OnRButtonUp(UINT nFlags, CPoint point);
    afx_msg void OnRButtonDblClk(UINT nFlags, CPoint point);
    afx_msg void OnInitMenuPopup(CMenu*, UINT, BOOL);
    afx_msg void OnMenuSelect(UINT nItemID, UINT nFlags,
                              HMENU hSysMenu);
    afx_msg LRESULT OnSetMessageString(WPARAM wParam,
                                       LPARAM lParam);
    afx_msg void OnEnterIdle(UINT nWhy, CWnd* pWho);
    afx_msg void OnCancelMode();
    afx_msg void OnPaint(CDC* pDC);
    afx_msg BOOL OnEraseBkgnd(CDC* pDC);
    afx_msg void OnSysKeyDown(UINT nChar, UINT nRepCnt,
                              UINT nFlags);
    afx_msg void OnSysKeyUp(UINT nChar, UINT nRepCnt,
                            UINT nFlags);
    afx_msg int  OnMouseActivate(CWnd *pDesktopWnd,
                                 UINT nHitTest, UINT message);
    afx_msg LRESULT OnSetText(WPARAM wParam, LPARAM lParam);
    afx_msg BOOL OnNcCreate(LPCREATESTRUCT lpCreateStruct);
    afx_msg void OnDestroy();
    afx_msg  void OnKillFocus(CWnd* pNewWnd);
    afx_msg void OnSetFocus(CWnd* pOldWnd);
    afx_msg void OnNcPaint();
    afx_msg void OnNcCalcSize(BOOL bCalcValidRects,
                              NCCALCSIZE_PARAMS* lpncsp);
    afx_msg UINT OnNcHitTest(CPoint point);
    afx_msg void OnNcLButtonDown(UINT nHitTest, CPoint point);
    afx_msg BOOL OnSetCursor(CWnd* pWnd, UINT nHitTest,
```

```
                                UINT message);
    afx_msg UINT OnGetDlgCode();
    afx_msg int OnCreate(LPCREATESTRUCT lpCreateStruct);
    afx_msg void OnSize(UINT nType, int cx, int cy);
    afx_msg void OnMove(int x, int y);
    afx_msg void OnShowWindow(BOOL bShow, UINT nStatus);
    //}}AFX_MSG

    afx_msg LRESULT OnOcmCtlColorBtn(WPARAM wParam,
                                    LPARAM lParam);
    afx_msg LRESULT OnOcmCtlColorDlg(WPARAM wParam,
                                    LPARAM lParam);
    afx_msg LRESULT OnOcmCtlColorEdit(WPARAM wParam,
                                    LPARAM lParam);
    afx_msg LRESULT OnOcmCtlColorListBox(WPARAM wParam,
                                        LPARAM lParam);
    afx_msg LRESULT OnOcmCtlColorMsgBox(WPARAM wParam,
                                        LPARAM lParam);
    afx_msg LRESULT OnOcmCtlColorScrollBar(WPARAM wParam,
                                        LPARAM lParam);
    afx_msg LRESULT OnOcmCtlColorStatic(WPARAM wParam,
                                        LPARAM lParam);

    DECLARE_MESSAGE_MAP()

    // button handler helpers
    void OnButtonUp(USHORT nButton, UINT nFlags, CPoint point);
    void OnButtonDown(USHORT nButton, UINT nFlags,
                    CPoint point);
    void OnButtonDblClk(USHORT nButton, UINT nFlags,
                        CPoint point);
    .
    .
    .
// Interface Maps
public:
    // IPersistStorage
    BEGIN_INTERFACE_PART(PersistStorage, IPersistStorage)
        INIT_INTERFACE_PART(COleControl, PersistStorage)
        STDMETHOD(GetClassID)(LPCLSID);
        STDMETHOD(IsDirty)();
        STDMETHOD(InitNew)(LPSTORAGE);
        STDMETHOD(Load)(LPSTORAGE);
        STDMETHOD(Save)(LPSTORAGE, BOOL);
```

```
        STDMETHOD(SaveCompleted)(LPSTORAGE);
        STDMETHOD(HandsOffStorage)();
    END_INTERFACE_PART_STATIC(PersistStorage)

    // IPersistStreamInit
    BEGIN_INTERFACE_PART(PersistStreamInit, IPersistStreamInit)
        INIT_INTERFACE_PART(COleControl, PersistStreamInit)
        STDMETHOD(GetClassID)(LPCLSID);
        STDMETHOD(IsDirty)();
        STDMETHOD(Load)(LPSTREAM);
        STDMETHOD(Save)(LPSTREAM, BOOL);
        STDMETHOD(GetSizeMax)(ULARGE_INTEGER *);
        STDMETHOD(InitNew)();
    END_INTERFACE_PART_STATIC(PersistStreamInit)

    // IPersistMemory
    BEGIN_INTERFACE_PART(PersistMemory, IPersistMemory)
        INIT_INTERFACE_PART(COleControl, PersistMemory)
        STDMETHOD(GetClassID)(LPCLSID);
        STDMETHOD(IsDirty)();
        STDMETHOD(Load)(LPVOID, ULONG);
        STDMETHOD(Save)(LPVOID, BOOL, ULONG);
        STDMETHOD(GetSizeMax)(ULONG*);
        STDMETHOD(InitNew)();
    END_INTERFACE_PART_STATIC(PersistMemory)
        .
        .
        .
```

Our intention in showing this partial listing was not to explain each section of the listing in detail, but to provide you with a reference as we introduce some new terms used with ActiveX controls. You'll find several of the captions for those sections set in a bold font.

Events

Events are actions or responses that are triggered by the control's reaction to an action on the control—for example, a keypress or mouse button click. KeyUp and KeyDown are examples of stock events.

A new OLE class is derived from Microsoft's COleControl parent class. The new class will be able to use a new map that enables messages. These messages or events are sent to the application using the control. This application is called the *control container*. The application or container will receive information about an event when something happens to the control. This event could be as simple as clicking the mouse within the control.

Using event parameters can provide additional information. Examine the message map area of the previous listing.

A control communicates with its application (container) by firing events. ActiveX provides stock and custom events to be used by your control. See the sections marked "Stock events" in the previous listing. Stock events are handled by the COleControl as a default. Custom events might be used to signal the application (container) when a control event occurs, such as receiving a message.

Methods and Properties

The control must expose a set of methods (functions) and properties (interface) to the application using the control in order to make an ActiveX control interactive. Methods are control functions that permit external code to alter characteristics of the control. Typical characteristics include appearance, properties, or behavior. Control properties, on the other hand, include the color, text, font, and other elements used in the control. Methods and properties form the basic mechanism whereby the application (container) communicates with the control. This communication allows the appearance and values of the control to be changed. The developer, while using the Visual Studio NET ClassWizard, defines methods and properties. Find the section defining stock methods in the previous listing. Stock methods are implemented automatically by the COleControl class. The programmer can add custom methods if additional custom features are needed by the control.

A primary interface to the control allows early bound access to the control's methods and properties. Here, object methods are exposed as methods, and properties as get/set method pairs. IDispatch is used for late bound access. The application using the control (container) decides which type of binding is provided to the user. IProvideClassInfo returns a CoClass TypeInfo, which describes the control.

ActiveX controls also provide extended properties, methods, and events. Usually this is control-specific information needed only by the application (container).

Persistence

Controls support persistence to streams through IPersistStream and persistence to storage through IPersistStorage. Both implementations can be found in the "Interface Maps" section of the previous listing. IPersistStorage is necessary for continued support of compound document applications (containers). IPersistStream allows embedded controls to be saved to streams, where feasible.

Persistence permits the ActiveX control to read or write property values to and from a file or stream. An application (container) can use persistence to store property values for the control. These values can then be retrieved if a new instance of the control is created.

An example, not shown in the previous listing, is the parameter PX_Blob that is used to exchange a control property that stores Binary Large Object (BLOB) data. In a similar manner, PX_Bool is used to exchange a control property of type BOOL.

Containers that Hold ActiveX Controls

The standard compound document interface required for an in-place embedding container has the attributes necessary for a control container. In addition to the container attributes inherent in this type of container, the container must also provide two additional items: events and ambient properties.

An ActiveX control actually serves as a converter when dealing with events. As such, a control must convert events from the user into events that are meaningful to the container. For each event so converted, the container must supply an entry point in order to respond to the event.

Ambient properties refer to container properties that typically apply to all controls in the container. These include default colors and fonts.

Designing a Simple ActiveX Control

In this section, you will learn the step-by-step approach to creating a simple ActiveX control template. Then we will modify the template to create a unique control for our use.

The code generated for the ActiveX control is MFC library code. If you need to review object-oriented coding techniques using the MFC, study the material in Chapters 22 through 26.

From this point on, the MFC ActiveX ControlWizard will be referred to simply as the ControlWizard.

A Basic Control

From the Visual Studio.NET menu bar, select the File | New menu item. From the New Project dialog box, select the MFC ActiveX Control option, as shown in Figure 27-1. Name this project TDCtrl.

There are three categories of project options that can be changed: Application Settings, Control Names, and Control Settings. Figure 27-2 shows the Application Settings options.

For this simple ActiveX control, no Application Settings will be selected. Next, let's view the Control Names option. Figure 27-3 shows a large number of Control Name options that can be altered.

Again, for this project, no changes will be made to the default names supplied with this option. Various Control Settings options are shown in Figure 27-4.

Un addition to the default Control Settings options, we have also checked the Available in Insert Object dialog option. This will allow the new control to be listed with other insertable objects in such applications as Microsoft Word, Excel, and so on.

When the Finish button is clicked, the ControlWizard will generate the files necessary to create the basic control.

At this point it is possible to use the Visual Studio's Test Container to examine the new control or to simply use an application, such as Microsoft Word or Excel.

Figure 27-5 shows the technique for inserting an object in a Microsoft Word document.

ADVANCED PROGRAMMING CONCEPTS

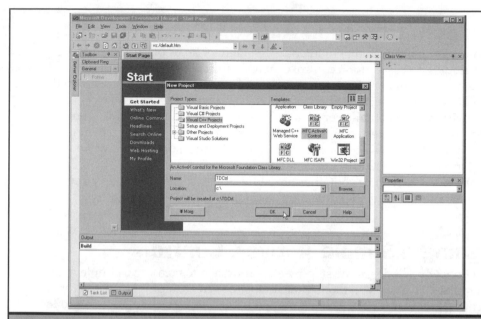

Figure 27-1. Use the New Project dialog box to select the MFC ActiveX Control option.

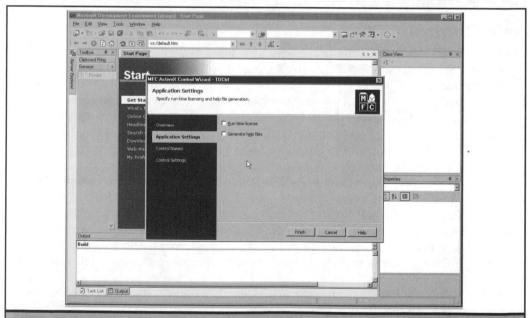

Figure 27-2. Application Settings options

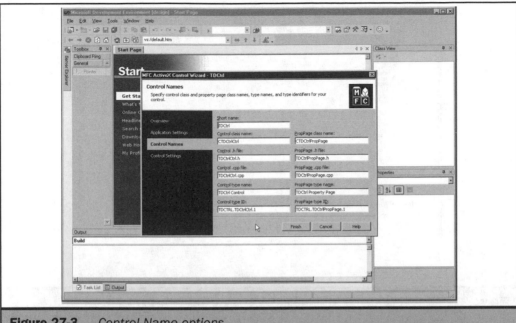

Figure 27-3.   *Control Name options*

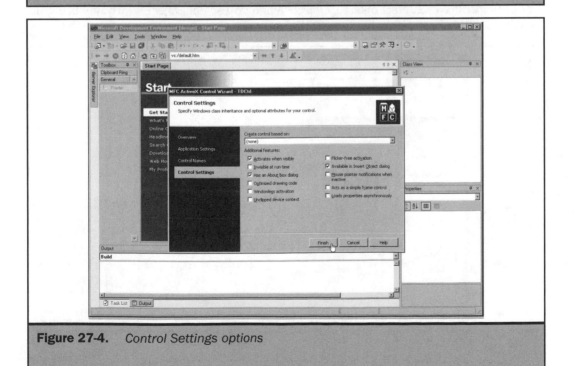

Figure 27-4.   *Control Settings options*

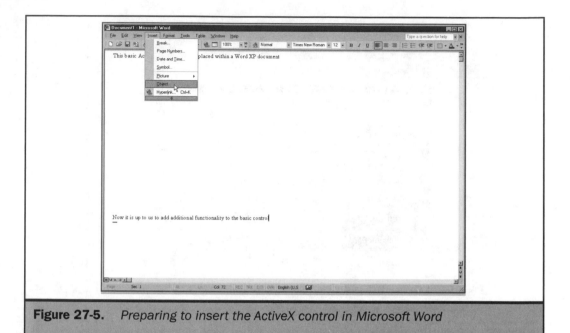

Figure 27-5. *Preparing to insert the ActiveX control in Microsoft Word*

In Microsoft Word select Insert | Object. When you select Object, Word will bring up the Object dialog box shown in Figure 27-6.

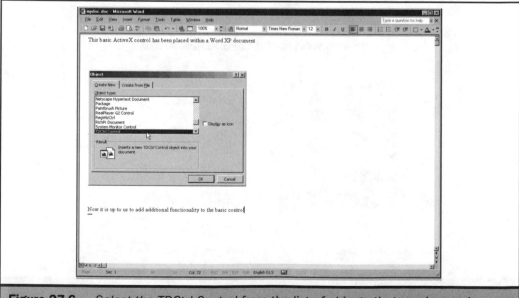

Figure 27-6. *Select the TDCtrl Control from the list of objects that can be used.*

Scroll down the list of available objects until you find TDCtrl Control. Select this ActiveX control and click OK. The ActiveX control will be inserted immediately into the Word document at the current cursor location, as shown in Figure 27-7. The build process created a new control with the filename TDCTRL.OCX. This file is located in the debug subdirectory of your project. As you can see, the actual control is graphically just the ellipse shape that you see surrounded by a design frame. At this point the control is not really functional. We will have to add some code to this template to create a unique control for our purposes.

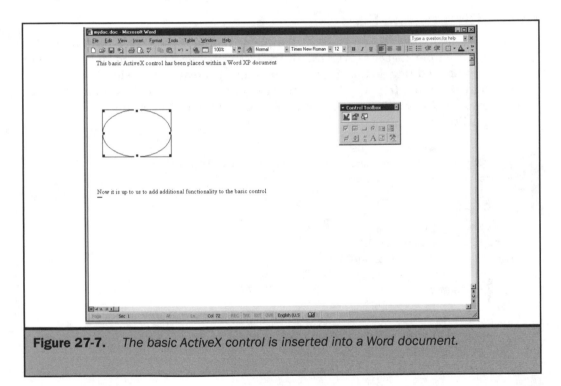

Figure 27-7.   *The basic ActiveX control is inserted into a Word document.*

Before we modify the template code, let's look at some of the code generated by the ControlWizard. We'll examine the code specifically related to the changes we're about to make to the template.

Looking at Important Code

A detailed analysis of the code for the whole TDCtrl project is beyond the scope of this book. Actually, it would probably require a whole book itself. However, you don't have to be an automobile mechanic to drive a car, and you certainly don't have to understand every nuance of program code to build effective ActiveX controls. You have learned the basics of how the MFC combines object-oriented objects into complete applications.

The ControlWizard generates four C++ source code files for most ActiveX controls. In this example they are named stdafx.cpp, TDCtrl.cpp, TDCtrlCtrl.cpp, and TDCtrlPropPage.cpp. These files are supported with their appropriate support header files.

The stdafx.cpp file is used to include all the standard header files that your ActiveX control will need. The TDCtrl.cpp file is responsible for the implementation of the CTDCtrlApp class and the registration of the subsequent DLL file.

In the following sections we examine the role of the TDCtrlCtrl.cpp and TDCtrlPropPage.cpp files in more detail.

The TDCtrlCtrl.cpp File

The TDCtrlCtrl.cpp file provides the actual implementation of the ActiveX control's OLE class. In this example, that class is CTDCtrlCtrl. This is the file you will most likely spend most of your time editing. In this file, you will be able to create unique implementations of your ActiveX control from the default ActiveX control created by the ControlWizard.

Let's examine the specific code allotted to the default ActiveX control. Study the following listing:

```
// TDCtrlCtrl.cpp : Implementation of the CTDCtrlCtrl
// ActiveX Control class.

#include "stdafx.h"
#include "TDCtrl.h"
#include "TDCtrlCtrl.h"
#include "TDCtrlPropPage.h"

#ifdef _DEBUG
#define new DEBUG_NEW

#endif

IMPLEMENT_DYNCREATE(CTDCtrlCtrl, COleControl)

/////////////////////////////////////////////////////////////
// Message map

BEGIN_MESSAGE_MAP(CTDCtrlCtrl, COleControl)
    ON_OLEVERB(AFX_IDS_VERB_EDIT, OnEdit)
    ON_OLEVERB(AFX_IDS_VERB_PROPERTIES, OnProperties)
END_MESSAGE_MAP()

/////////////////////////////////////////////////////////////
// Dispatch map
```

```
BEGIN_DISPATCH_MAP(CTDCtrlCtrl, COleControl)
    DISP_FUNCTION_ID(CTDCtrlCtrl, "AboutBox", DISPID_ABOUTBOX,
                    AboutBox, VT_EMPTY, VTS_NONE)
END_DISPATCH_MAP()


/////////////////////////////////////////////////////////////
// Event map

BEGIN_EVENT_MAP(CTDCtrlCtrl, COleControl)
END_EVENT_MAP()


/////////////////////////////////////////////////////////////
// Property pages

// TODO: Add more property pages as needed.
//        Remember to increase the count!
BEGIN_PROPPAGEIDS(CTDCtrlCtrl, 1)
    PROPPAGEID(CTDCtrlPropPage::guid)
END_PROPPAGEIDS(CTDCtrlCtrl)


/////////////////////////////////////////////////////////////
// Initialize class factory and guid

IMPLEMENT_OLECREATE_EX(CTDCtrlCtrl, "MyTDCTRL.TDCtrlCtrl.1",
                    0xfc6dd0a, 0xe4d5, 0x479e, 0x94, 0xe7,
                    0x40, 0x4d, 0xa9, 0xe9, 0xd0, 0xa4)


/////////////////////////////////////////////////////////////
// Type library ID and version

IMPLEMENT_OLETYPELIB(CTDCtrlCtrl, _tlid,
                    _wVerMajor, _wVerMinor)


/////////////////////////////////////////////////////////////
// Interface IDs

const IID BASED_CODE IID_DTDCtrl =
        { 0x27FF99B3, 0x7145, 0x48F5, { 0xBD, 0x3C, 0x39,
                                        0xA6, 0xE6, 0xD3,
                                        0x1A, 0x12 } };
const IID BASED_CODE IID_DTDCtrlEvents =
        { 0x8EFB8C08, 0xD5C3, 0x4C2E, { 0xAE, 0xA2, 0xCA,
                                        0x63, 0x44, 0x44,
```

```
                                          0x82, 0x68 } };

/////////////////////////////////////////////////////////////
// Control type information

static const DWORD BASED_CODE _dwTDCtrlOleMisc =
    OLEMISC_ACTIVATEWHENVISIBLE |
    OLEMISC_SETCLIENTSITEFIRST |
    OLEMISC_INSIDEOUT |
    OLEMISC_CANTLINKINSIDE |
    OLEMISC_RECOMPOSEONRESIZE;

IMPLEMENT_OLECTLTYPE(CTDCtrlCtrl, IDS_TDCTRL, _dwTDCtrlOleMisc)

/////////////////////////////////////////////////////////////
// CTDCtrlCtrl::CTDCtrlCtrlFactory::UpdateRegistry -
// Adds or removes system registry entries for CTDCtrlCtrl

BOOL CTDCtrlCtrl::CTDCtrlCtrlFactory::UpdateRegistry \
                                    (BOOL bRegister)
{
    // TODO: Verify that your control follows apartment-model
    // threading rules.
    // Refer to MFC TechNote 64 for more information.
    // If your control does not conform to the apartment-model
    // rules, then you must modify the code below, changing
    // the 6th parameter from
    // afxRegInsertable | afxRegApartmentThreading to
    // afxRegInsertable.

    if (bRegister)
        return AfxOleRegisterControlClass(
            AfxGetInstanceHandle(),
            m_clsid,
            m_lpszProgID,
            IDS_TDCTRL,
            IDB_TDCTRL,
            afxRegInsertable | afxRegApartmentThreading,
            _dwTDCtrlOleMisc,
            _tlid,
            _wVerMajor,
            _wVerMinor);
```

```
        else
            return AfxOleUnregisterClass(m_clsid, m_lpszProgID);
}


/////////////////////////////////////////////////////////////////
// CTDCtrlCtrl::CTDCtrlCtrl - Constructor

CTDCtrlCtrl::CTDCtrlCtrl()
{
    InitializeIIDs(&IID_DTDCtrl, &IID_DTDCtrlEvents);
    // TODO: Initialize your control's instance data here.
}


/////////////////////////////////////////////////////////////////
// CTDCtrlCtrl::~CTDCtrlCtrl - Destructor

CTDCtrlCtrl::~CTDCtrlCtrl()
{
    // TODO: Cleanup your control's instance data here.
}


/////////////////////////////////////////////////////////////////
// CTDCtrlCtrl::OnDraw - Drawing function

void CTDCtrlCtrl::OnDraw(
            CDC* pdc, const CRect& rcBounds,
            const CRect& rcInvalid)
{
    // TODO: Replace following code with your drawing code.
    pdc->FillRect(rcBounds, \
    CBrush::FromHandle((HBRUSH)GetStockObject(WHITE_BRUSH)));
    pdc->Ellipse(rcBounds);
}


/////////////////////////////////////////////////////////////////
// CTDCtrlCtrl::DoPropExchange - Persistence support

void CTDCtrlCtrl::DoPropExchange(CPropExchange* pPX)
{
    ExchangeVersion(pPX, MAKELONG(_wVerMinor, _wVerMajor));
    COleControl::DoPropExchange(pPX);
```

```
            // TODO: Call PX_ functions for persistent property.
        }


        /////////////////////////////////////////////////////////////
        // CTDCtrlCtrl::OnResetState - Reset control to default state

        void CTDCtrlCtrl::OnResetState()
        {
            COleControl::OnResetState();   // Resets defaults
                                           // found in DoPropExchange

            // TODO: Reset any other control state here.
        }


        /////////////////////////////////////////////////////////////
        // CTDCtrlCtrl::AboutBox - Display an "About" box to the user

        void CTDCtrlCtrl::AboutBox()
        {
            CDialog dlgAbout(IDD_ABOUTBOX_TDCTRL);
            dlgAbout.DoModal();
        }


        /////////////////////////////////////////////////////////////
        // CTDCtrlCtrl message handlers
```

The message map, dispatch map, and event map are automatically created and edited by various Visual Studio NET Wizards. Under most circumstances, you will not edit these maps directly.

Recall that message maps are important because they provide an alternative to the **switch** statement used in procedure-oriented programs to handle messages. Automation includes techniques to call methods and access properties across several applications. These requests are dispatched via the dispatch map. The event map helps process ActiveX control events.

Examine the listing and notice the section of code used to implement the type library. In general, ActiveX controls need to exchange information concerning various properties and methods. The best way to provide this information is through a type library.

As you continue reading down the listing, you will see code for updating the system registry as well as constructor code for initializing instances of the control.

The OnDraw() method is going to be of immediate interest to us because it is this section of code that draws the graphics for the control. In the default control provided by the ControlWizard, the default shape is an Ellipse().

```
void CTDCtrlCtrl::OnDraw(
          CDC* pdc, const CRect& rcBounds,
          const CRect& rcInvalid)
{
    // TODO: Replace following code with your drawing code.
    pdc->FillRect(rcBounds, \
    CBrush::FromHandle((HBRUSH)GetStockObject(WHITE_BRUSH)));
    pdc->Ellipse(rcBounds);
}
```

The ControlWizard also designed a default About box for this project. The contents of this simple dialog box can be edited to suit your project's needs or used as is. You'll find the resource information in the TDCtrl.rc resource file. The About dialog box is brought to the screen with the following portion of code:

```
void CTDCtrlCtrl::AboutBox()
{
    CDialog dlgAbout(IDD_ABOUTBOX_TDCTRL);
    dlgAbout.DoModal();
}
```

Notice that the default About box is a standard modal dialog box of the type we have been using since Chapter 22.

The TDCtrlPropPage.cpp File

The TDCtrlPropPage.cpp source code file is used to derive the CTDCtrlPropPage class from Microsoft's COlePropertyPage class. Examine the following listing:

```
// TDCtrlPropPage.cpp : Implementation of the CTDCtrlPropPage
// property page class.

#include "stdafx.h"
#include "TDCtrl.h"
#include "TDCtrlPropPage.h"

#ifdef _DEBUG
#define new DEBUG_NEW
#endif

IMPLEMENT_DYNCREATE(CTDCtrlPropPage, COlePropertyPage)
```

```
/////////////////////////////////////////////////////////
// Message map

BEGIN_MESSAGE_MAP(CTDCtrlPropPage, COlePropertyPage)
END_MESSAGE_MAP()


/////////////////////////////////////////////////////////
// Initialize class factory and guid

IMPLEMENT_OLECREATE_EX(CTDCtrlPropPage,
                       "MyTDCTRL.TDCtrlPropPage.1",
                       0xfe1919bf, 0x301d, 0x4500, 0xa3, 0x9e,
                       0xe3, 0xfb, 0xb8, 0x21, 0x3e, 0x82)


/////////////////////////////////////////////////////////
// CTDCtrlPropPage::CTDCtrlPropPageFactory::UpdateRegistry -
// Adds or removes system registry entries for CTDCtrlPropPage

BOOL CTDCtrlPropPage::CTDCtrlPropPageFactory::UpdateRegistry \
                    (BOOL bRegister)
{
    if (bRegister)
        return AfxOleRegisterPropertyPageClass \
                (AfxGetInstanceHandle(),
                 m_clsid, IDS_TDCTRL_PPG);
    else
        return AfxOleUnregisterClass(m_clsid, NULL);
}


/////////////////////////////////////////////////////////
// CTDCtrlPropPage::CTDCtrlPropPage - Constructor

CTDCtrlPropPage::CTDCtrlPropPage() :
    COlePropertyPage(IDD, IDS_TDCTRL_PPG_CAPTION)
{
}


/////////////////////////////////////////////////////////
// CTDCtrlPropPage::DoDataExchange - Moves data between
                                    // page and properties
```

```
void CTDCtrlPropPage::DoDataExchange(CDataExchange* pDX)
{
    DDP_PostProcessing(pDX);
}


/////////////////////////////////////////////////////////////////
// CTDCtrlPropPage message handlers
```

The AfxOleRegisterPropertyPageClass() function is used to register the property page class with the registration database. This permits the property page to be used by other containers that are made aware of ActiveX controls. The registry, with the property page name and its location on the system, will be updated after this function is called.

Notice in this file that COlePropertyPage, from which our CTDCtrlPropPage class is derived, can use the constructor to identify the dialog-template resource on which the property page is based and also the string resource containing the caption.

The DoDataExchange() function is generally used by the framework to exchange and validate dialog data. Here the specific job is to move data between the page and properties of the control.

Customizing the Basic Control

The ClassWizard can be used to modify the default custom control produced by the ControlWizard. To modify the default custom control described in the previous section, the following features will be added to the project.

- The TDCtrl control will always draw a rectangle instead of the default ellipse.

- The TDCtrl surface will be a unique color.

- The TDCtrl control will respond to a mouse event within the control and print the current system time and date within the control.

All of these new features can be added to the control by just working with the TDCtrlCtrl.cpp and TDCtrlCtrl.h files. In the next section, we'll add several of the new features.

Altering the Shape, Size, and Colors of the TDCtrl

From within Visual Studio, use the View menu to select the Class View menu item. Click this item to display the Class View pane for the project. This pane is shown on the right of Figure 27-8.

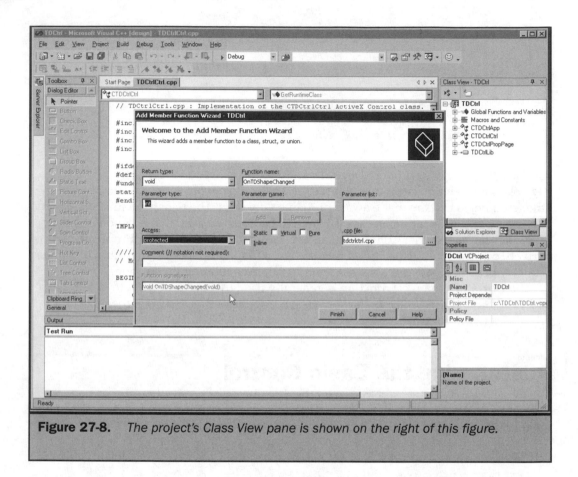

Figure 27-8. *The project's Class View pane is shown on the right of this figure.*

Now, let's make the following modifications to the project in order to allow the shape and color properties of the control to be modified:

1. Select CTDCtrlCtrl from the Class name list box.

2. Right-click this function and select Add from the list of items. When this option is selected, you will be presented with three additional choices; select Add Function. This will display the Add Member Function Wizard dialog box, shown earlier in Figure 27-8.

3. Add the function OnTDShapeChanged(), with the return type and parameters shown in the figure.

4. Right-click the CTDCtrlCtrl class and select Add from the list of items. When this option is selected, you will be presented with three additional choices;

select Add Variable. This will display the Add Member Variable Wizard dialog box shown in Figure 27-9.

5. Add the member variable m_tDShape, using a BOOL return type, shown in Figure 27-9.

6. Accept these values by clicking Finish.

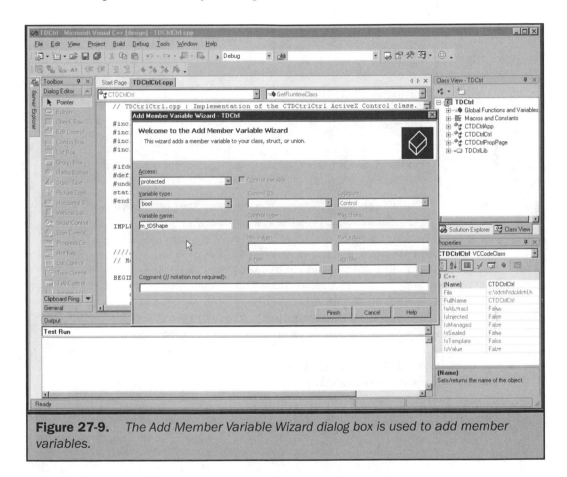

Figure 27-9.   *The Add Member Variable Wizard dialog box is used to add member variables.*

The ClassWizard will create the code to add the OnTDShapeChanged() method to the project. We'll alter the CTDCtrlCtrl class's dispatch map to accommodate this new method. Note that a declaration for the OnTDShapeChanged() function is added to the TDCtrlCtrl.h header file.

Now it becomes our job to write the code that reacts to the changes we desire to intercept.

Return to the TDCtrlCtrl.cpp File

The following listing shows the code we've modified in the TDCtrlCtrl.cpp file. This file is identical to the default file returned by the ControlWizard, except for the lines of code set in a bold font. Make these changes to your file, too:

```cpp
/////////////////////////////////////////////////////////////////
// CTDCtrlCtrl::OnDraw - Drawing function

void CTDCtrlCtrl::OnDraw(
            CDC* pdc, const CRect& rcBounds,
            const CRect& rcInvalid)
{
    CBrush* pOldBrush;
    CBrush NewBrush;
    CPen* pOldPen;
    CPen NewPen;

    pdc -> FillRect(rcBounds, CBrush::FromHandle((HBRUSH) \
                GetStockObject(WHITE_BRUSH)));

    NewPen.CreatePen(PS_SOLID, 3 , RGB(0, 0, 0));
    pOldPen = (CPen*)pdc -> SelectObject(&NewPen);

    // Create a yellow brush
    NewBrush.CreateSolidBrush(RGB(255, 255, 0));
    pOldBrush = (CBrush*)pdc -> SelectObject(&NewBrush);

    // Draw and fill the rectangle
    pdc -> Rectangle(rcBounds);

    pdc -> SelectObject(pOldPen);
    pdc -> SelectObject(pOldBrush);
}
```

Notice that the modified control is drawn with the Rectangle() function and filled with a yellow brush.

Mouse Events

In this section, the TDCtrl control will be altered to respond to mouse events. If the cursor is on the TDCtrl control when the left mouse button is depressed, the TDCtrl will change to a light gray color and report the system date and time to the control. The color change, date, and time information are indicators that a control "hit" has occurred.

Here is a list of steps needed to implement the "hit" features:

1. Select CTDCtrlCtrl from the Class name list box.

2. Right-click this function and select Add from the list of items. When this option is selected, you will be presented with three additional choices; select Add Function. This will display the Add Member Function Wizard dialog box.

3. Add the function, HitTDCtrl(), with the return type and parameter list:

   ```
   void CTDCtrlCtrl::HitTDCtrl(CDC* pdc);
   ```

4. Repeat the process and add an OnLButtonDown() message handler function, using the following return type and parameter list:

   ```
   void CTDCtrlCtrl::OnLButtonDown(UINT nFlags, CPoint point);
   ```

5. Repeat the process again and add an OnLButtonUp() message handler function, using the following return type and parameter list:

   ```
   void CTDCtrlCtrl::OnLButtonUp(UINT nFlags, CPoint point);
   ```

6. Right-click the CTDCtrlCtrl() function once again and select Add from the list of items. When this option is selected, you will be presented with three additional choices; select Add Variable. This will display the Add Variable dialog box.

7. Add the variable OLE_COLOR m_hitTDCtrl.

Now, we'll have to add code to make each of the added methods functional. We'll examine this code in the next section.

The TDCtrlCtrl.h Header File

In the following listing, the TDCtrlCtrl.h header file is listed in its entirety. All additions that were added to the original project's template code are shown in a bold font:

```
#pragma once

// TDCtrlCtrl.h : Declaration of ActiveX Control class.

//////////////////////////////////////////////////////////////////
// CTDCtrlCtrl : See TDCtrlCtrl.cpp for implementation.

class CTDCtrlCtrl : public COleControl
{
    DECLARE_DYNCREATE(CTDCtrlCtrl)
```

```cpp
// Constructor
public:
    CTDCtrlCtrl();

// Overrides
public:
    virtual void OnDraw(CDC* pdc, const CRect& rcBounds,
                        const CRect& rcInvalid);
    virtual void DoPropExchange(CPropExchange* pPX);
    virtual void OnResetState();

// Implementation
protected:
    ~CTDCtrlCtrl();


    DECLARE_OLECREATE_EX(CTDCtrlCtrl)  //Class factory and guid
    DECLARE_OLETYPELIB(CTDCtrlCtrl)    //GetTypeInfo
    DECLARE_PROPPAGEIDS(CTDCtrlCtrl)   //Property page IDs
    DECLARE_OLECTLTYPE(CTDCtrlCtrl)    //Type and misc status

// Message maps
    afx_msg void OnLButtonDown(UINT nFlags, CPoint point);
    afx_msg void OnLButtonUp(UINT nFlags, CPoint point);
    afx_msg void OnTDShapeChanged();
    DECLARE_MESSAGE_MAP()

// Dispatch maps
    DECLARE_DISPATCH_MAP()

    afx_msg void AboutBox();

// Event maps
    DECLARE_EVENT_MAP()

// Dispatch and event IDs
public:
    enum {
    };
protected:
    void OnTDShapeChanged(void);
```

```
    bool m_tDShape;
    BOOL InTDCtrl(CPoint& point);        //Hit the control?
    void HitTDCtrl(CDC* pdc);
    void OnLButtonDown(UINT nFlags, CPoint point);
    void OnLButtonUp(UINT nFlags, CPoint point);
    OLE_COLOR m_hitTDCtrl;
};
```

Make sure the bolded lines in this listing are also in your project. The code will now be added to the source code listing to make the control respond to mouse events within the control.

Return to the TDCtrlCtrl.cpp File

In order to ensure completeness, let's list the entire TDCtrlCtrl.cpp source code file before looking at individual ports. Again, any changes to the original template code are now shown in a bold font:

```
// TDCtrlCtrl.cpp : Implementation of the ActiveX Control class

#include "stdafx.h"
#include "TDCtrl.h"
#include "TDCtrlCtrl.h"
#include "TDCtrlPropPage.h"

#ifdef _DEBUG
#define new DEBUG_NEW
#endif

IMPLEMENT_DYNCREATE(CTDCtrlCtrl, COleControl)


////////////////////////////////////////////////////////////
// Message map

BEGIN_MESSAGE_MAP(CTDCtrlCtrl, COleControl)
    ON_WM_LBUTTONDOWN()
    ON_WM_LBUTTONUP()
    ON_OLEVERB(AFX_IDS_VERB_EDIT, OnEdit)
    ON_OLEVERB(AFX_IDS_VERB_PROPERTIES, OnProperties)
END_MESSAGE_MAP()


////////////////////////////////////////////////////////////
```

```
// Dispatch map

BEGIN_DISPATCH_MAP(CTDCtrlCtrl, COleControl)
    DISP_PROPERTY(CTDCtrlCtrl, "HitTDCtrl",
                    m_hitTDCtrl, VT_COLOR)
    DISP_PROPERTY_NOTIFY(CTDCtrlCtrl, "TDShape",
                            m_tDShape, OnTDShapeChanged, VT_BOOL)
    DISP_STOCKPROP_BACKCOLOR()
    DISP_FUNCTION_ID(CTDCtrlCtrl, "AboutBox", DISPID_ABOUTBOX,
                    AboutBox, VT_EMPTY, VTS_NONE)
END_DISPATCH_MAP()

/////////////////////////////////////////////////////////////
// Event map

BEGIN_EVENT_MAP(CTDCtrlCtrl, COleControl)
END_EVENT_MAP()

/////////////////////////////////////////////////////////////
// Property pages

// TODO: Add more property pages as needed.
//    Remember to increase the count!
BEGIN_PROPPAGEIDS(CTDCtrlCtrl, 1)
    PROPPAGEID(CTDCtrlPropPage::guid)
END_PROPPAGEIDS(CTDCtrlCtrl)


/////////////////////////////////////////////////////////////
// Initialize class factory and guid

IMPLEMENT_OLECREATE_EX(CTDCtrlCtrl, "MyTDCTRL.TDCtrlCtrl.1",
                    0xfc6dd0a, 0xe4d5, 0x479e, 0x94,
                    0xe7, 0x40, 0x4d, 0xa9, 0xe9,
                    0xd0, 0xa4)

/////////////////////////////////////////////////////////////
// Type library ID and version

IMPLEMENT_OLETYPELIB(CTDCtrlCtrl, _tlid,
                    _wVerMajor, _wVerMinor)
```

```
//////////////////////////////////////////////////////////
// Interface IDs

const IID BASED_CODE IID_DTDCtrl =
        { 0x27FF99B3, 0x7145, 0x48F5, { 0xBD, 0x3C, 0x39,
          0xA6, 0xE6, 0xD3, 0x1A, 0x12 } };
const IID BASED_CODE IID_DTDCtrlEvents =
        { 0x8EFB8C08, 0xD5C3, 0x4C2E, { 0xAE, 0xA2, 0xCA,
          0x63, 0x44, 0x44, 0x82, 0x68 } };


//////////////////////////////////////////////////////////
// Control type information

static const DWORD BASED_CODE _dwTDCtrlOleMisc =
    OLEMISC_ACTIVATEWHENVISIBLE |
    OLEMISC_SETCLIENTSITEFIRST |
    OLEMISC_INSIDEOUT |
    OLEMISC_CANTLINKINSIDE |
    OLEMISC_RECOMPOSEONRESIZE;

IMPLEMENT_OLECTLTYPE(CTDCtrlCtrl, IDS_TDCTRL,
                     _dwTDCtrlOleMisc)


//////////////////////////////////////////////////////////
// CTDCtrlCtrl::CTDCtrlCtrlFactory::UpdateRegistry -
// Adds or removes system registry entries for CTDCtrlCtrl

BOOL CTDCtrlCtrl::CTDCtrlCtrlFactory::UpdateRegistry \
                                    (BOOL bRegister)
{
    // TODO: Verify that your control follows apartment-model
    // threading rules. Refer to MFC TechNote 64 for more
    // information. If your control does not conform to the
    // apartment-model rules, then you must modify the code
    // below, changing the 6th parameter from
    // afxRegInsertable | afxRegApartmentThreading to
    // afxRegInsertable.

    if (bRegister)
        return AfxOleRegisterControlClass(
            AfxGetInstanceHandle(),
            m_clsid,
```

```
                    m_lpszProgID,
                    IDS_TDCTRL,
                    IDB_TDCTRL,
                    afxRegInsertable | afxRegApartmentThreading,
                    _dwTDCtrlOleMisc,
                    _tlid,
                    _wVerMajor,
                    _wVerMinor);
        else
            return AfxOleUnregisterClass(m_clsid, m_lpszProgID);
}


/////////////////////////////////////////////////////////////
// CTDCtrlCtrl::CTDCtrlCtrl - Constructor

CTDCtrlCtrl::CTDCtrlCtrl()
{
    InitializeIIDs(&IID_DTDCtrl, &IID_DTDCtrlEvents);
    // TODO: Initialize your control's instance data here.
}


/////////////////////////////////////////////////////////////
// CTDCtrlCtrl::~CTDCtrlCtrl - Destructor

CTDCtrlCtrl::~CTDCtrlCtrl()
{
    // TODO: Cleanup your control's instance data here.
}


/////////////////////////////////////////////////////////////
// CTDCtrlCtrl::OnDraw - Drawing function

void CTDCtrlCtrl::OnDraw(CDC* pdc, const CRect& rcBounds,
                        const CRect& rcInvalid)
{
    CBrush* pOldBrush;
    CBrush NewBrush;
    CPen* pOldPen;
    CPen NewPen;

    pdc -> FillRect(rcBounds, CBrush::FromHandle((HBRUSH) \
                GetStockObject(WHITE_BRUSH)));
```

```
    NewPen.CreatePen(PS_SOLID, 3, RGB(0, 0, 0));
    pOldPen = (CPen*)pdc -> SelectObject(&NewPen);

    // Create a yellow brush
    NewBrush.CreateSolidBrush(RGB(255, 255, 0));
    pOldBrush = (CBrush*)pdc -> SelectObject(&NewBrush);

    // Draw and fill the rectangle
    pdc -> Rectangle(rcBounds);

    pdc -> SelectObject(pOldPen);
    pdc -> SelectObject(pOldBrush);
}


/////////////////////////////////////////////////////////////
// CTDCtrlCtrl::DoPropExchange - Persistence support

void CTDCtrlCtrl::DoPropExchange(CPropExchange* pPX)
{
    ExchangeVersion(pPX, MAKELONG(_wVerMinor, _wVerMajor));
    COleControl::DoPropExchange(pPX);

    // TODO: Call PX_ functions for each persistent
    // custom property.
    // Use a light-gray color to show a hit
    PX_Long(pPX,_T("HitTDCtrl"), (long &)m_hitTDCtrl,
            RGB(200, 200, 200));
}


/////////////////////////////////////////////////////////////
// CTDCtrlCtrl::OnResetState - Reset control to default state

void CTDCtrlCtrl::OnResetState()
{
    COleControl::OnResetState();   // Resets defaults

    // TODO: Reset any other control state here.
}


/////////////////////////////////////////////////////////////
// CTDCtrlCtrl::AboutBox - Display an "About" box to the user
```

```cpp
void CTDCtrlCtrl::AboutBox()
{
    CDialog dlgAbout(IDD_ABOUTBOX_TDCTRL);
    dlgAbout.DoModal();
}


/////////////////////////////////////////////////////////////
// CTDCtrlCtrl message handlers

void CTDCtrlCtrl::OnTDShapeChanged(void)
{
    SetModifiedFlag();
}

void CTDCtrlCtrl::OnLButtonDown(UINT nFlags, CPoint point)
{
    // TODO: Add message handler code here and/or call default
    CDC* pdc;

    //Blink a color change for control
    pdc = GetDC();
    HitTDCtrl(pdc);
    ReleaseDC(pdc);

    COleControl::OnLButtonDown(nFlags, point);
}

void CTDCtrlCtrl::OnLButtonUp(UINT nFlags, CPoint point)
{
    // TODO: Add message handler code here and/or call default
    InvalidateControl();

    COleControl::OnLButtonUp(nFlags, point);
}

void CTDCtrlCtrl::HitTDCtrl(CDC* pdc)
{
    CBrush* pOldBrush;
    CBrush hitBrush(TranslateColor(m_hitTDCtrl));
    CRect rc;
    TEXTMETRIC tm;
```

```
    struct tm *date_time;
    time_t timer;

    // Background mode to transparent
    pdc -> SetBkMode(TRANSPARENT);

    GetClientRect(rc);

    pOldBrush = pdc -> SelectObject(&hitBrush);

    // Draw and fill the rectangle
    pdc -> Rectangle(rc);

    // Get time and date
    time(&timer);
    date_time = localtime(&timer);
    const CString& strtime = asctime(date_time);

    // Get Font information then print
    pdc -> GetTextMetrics(&tm);
    pdc -> SetTextAlign(TA_CENTER | TA_TOP);
    pdc -> ExtTextOut((rc.left + rc.right) / 2,
                    (rc.top + rc.bottom - tm.tmHeight) / 2,
                     ETO_CLIPPED, rc, strtime,
                     strtime.GetLength() - 1, NULL);
    pdc -> SelectObject(pOldBrush);
}
```

Some of this code has already been explained, so we'll concentrate on the new features. The control's face will change color when the user clicks the left mouse button within the rectangular area. The event notification, in part, is handled by the DoPropExchange() function. Here is the DoPropExchange() function and modification showing the new line in a bold font:

```
void CTDCtrlCtrl::DoPropExchange(CPropExchange* pPX)
{
    ExchangeVersion(pPX, MAKELONG(_wVerMinor, _wVerMajor));
    COleControl::DoPropExchange(pPX);

    // TODO: Call PX_ functions for each persistent
    // custom property.
```

```
    // Use a light-gray color to show a hit
    PX_Long(pPX, _T("HitTDCtrl"), (long &)m_hitTDCtrl,
        RGB(200, 200, 200));
}
```

This function is responsible for initializing the *m_hitTDCtrl* member variable to a light gray color. The variable *m_hitTDCtrl* must be cast to a long since it is an unsigned long value.

The following portion of code is added to the OnLButtonDown() function in order to check to make sure the left mouse button was clicked within the face of the clock. If it was, the HitTDCtrl() function will be called to change the color of the clock face from yellow to light gray:

```
void CTDCtrlCtrl::OnLButtonDown(UINT nFlags, CPoint point)
{
    // TODO: Add message handler code here and/or call default
    CDC* pdc;

    //Blink a color change for control
    pdc = GetDC();
    HitTDCtrl(pdc);
    ReleaseDC(pdc);

    COleControl::OnLButtonDown(nFlags, point);
}
```

When the left mouse button is released, the OnLButtonUp() function merely invalidates the control, forcing a repaint in the face to yellow.

When the mouse is left-clicked within the control, the HitTDCtrl() function will be called. This is the code used by this function:

```
void CTDCtrlCtrl::HitTDCtrl(CDC* pdc)
{
    CBrush* pOldBrush;
    CBrush hitBrush(TranslateColor(m_hitTDCtrl));
    CRect rc;
    TEXTMETRIC tm;
    struct tm *date_time;
    time_t timer;
```

```
    // Background mode to transparent
    pdc -> SetBkMode(TRANSPARENT);

    GetClientRect(rc);

    pOldBrush = pdc -> SelectObject(&hitBrush);

    // Draw and fill the rectangle
    pdc -> Rectangle(rc);

    // Get time and date
    time(&timer);
    date_time = localtime(&timer);
    const CString& strtime = asctime(date_time);

    // Get Font information then print
    pdc -> GetTextMetrics(&tm);
    pdc -> SetTextAlign(TA_CENTER | TA_TOP);
    pdc -> ExtTextOut((rc.left + rc.right) / 2,
                      (rc.top + rc.bottom - tm.tmHeight) / 2,
                      ETO_CLIPPED, rc, strtime,
                      strtime.GetLength() - 1, NULL);
    pdc -> SelectObject(pOldBrush);
}
```

The code in this function selects the light gray brush, defined earlier, and repaints the entire TDCtrl control area. The time and date information is accessed with normal C++ date and time functions.

Testing the Finished Control

Microsoft Word can be used once again to test the final version of the TDCtrl control. For this example, open Microsoft Word and insert the control by selecting it from the list of registered controls. When the control is inserted it can be resized as shown in Figure 27-10. You may have to exit design mode of the control first.

Now position the cursor over the control and click the left mouse button to see the current time and date information on a light gray background, as shown in Figure 27-11.

You may want to continue experimenting with this ActiveX control. Why not try altering another control property?

ADVANCED
PROGRAMMING CONCEPTS

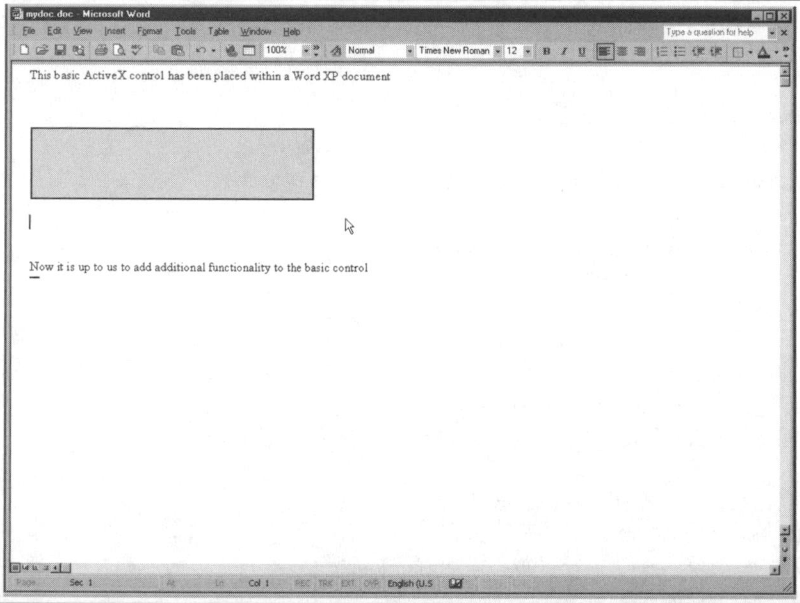

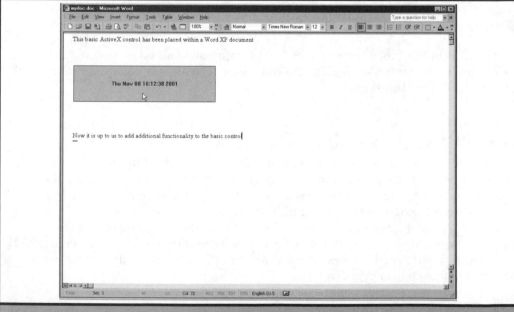

Figure 27-10. *The final TDCtrl control, with a yellow background, is inserted and resized.*

Figure 27-11. *The time and date arc displayed when a mouse hit occurs.*

Summary

If the topic of ActiveX controls is of real interest to you, you'll want to read additional sources of information. The *Microsoft Systems Journal* contains a wealth of material on ActiveX controls.

ActiveX controls can also be designed in Microsoft's Visual Basic. Some programmers prefer the use of Visual Basic when designing ActiveX controls because of its drag-and-drop design capabilities.

The Complete Reference

Visual C++.NET

Chapter 28

Dynamic Link Libraries

D ynamic Link Libraries (DLLs) are in many ways similar to other Visual C++.NET libraries in that they give the programmer an easy way to distribute new functions and other resources. DLLs differ from other Visual C++.NET libraries in that they are linked to the application at run time rather than during the compile/link cycle. This process is described as *dynamic linking* rather than *static linking*. Static linking occurs when linking C++ run-time libraries to an application at compile/link time. DLLs also offer the advantage, in a multitasking environment, of sharing both functions and resources.

DLLs can be divided into two distinct categories: conventional API-based DLLs written in C or C++ (without objects) and MFC object-based DLLs. API DLLs have the advantage of being portable from one compiler to another. DLLs based on the MFC are, of course, restricted to compilers using a licensed version of the MFC.

Since our focus in this book has been on the MFC, we'll demonstrate the development of a simple DLL with the use of the MFC library.

A MFC-Based Dynamic Link Library

A MFC-based DLL can be created and compiled in a manner similar to the MFC Windows applications of Chapters 22 through 27 in this book, but with some subtle changes. The Framer project will use the Application Wizard to create a dynamic link library. By using the Wizard, all necessary header, resource, and source code files will be created automatically. Follow these steps to complete the Framer project.

1. Use the Visual C++ NET File | New menu option to bring up the New Project dialog box, as shown in Figure 28-1.

2. Select the MFC DLL option, shown in this figure and name the new project Framer.

3. Click OK to start the MFC Application Wizard.

4. The MFC DLL Wizard will now appear on the screen, as shown in Figure 28-2.

5. Use the Applications Settings option to set the DLL type to a Regular DLL using shared MFC DLL, as shown in Figure 28-3.

6. Click Finish to generate the base code for the project.

Like other Application Wizard templates, the code that was generated for the Framer project is functional—it just doesn't do anything. We'll have to add our own unique code to this DLL.

The two files that are of greatest interest to us are the Framer.h and Framer.cpp files.

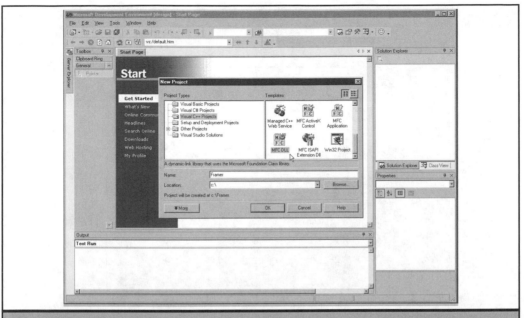

Figure 28-1. *The New Project dialog box allows you to create a MFC DLL project.*

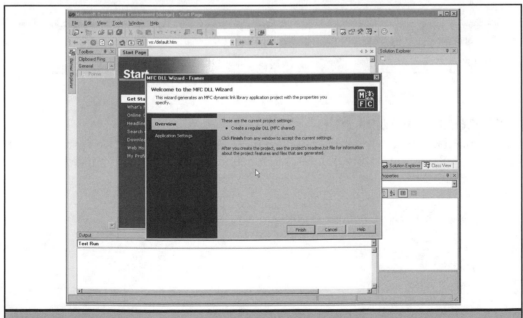

Figure 28-2. *Use the MFC DLL Wizard to set project options.*

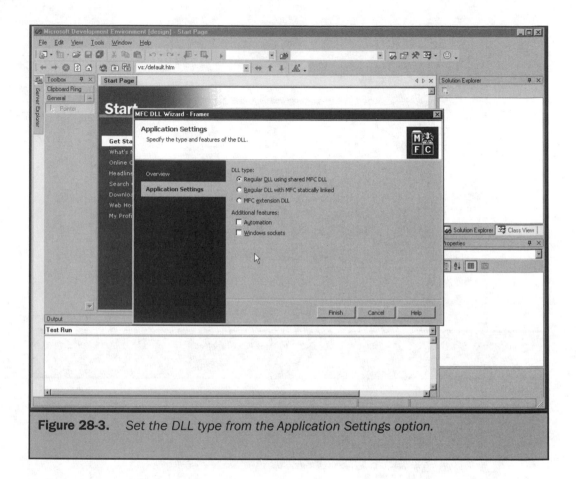

Figure 28-3. *Set the DLL type from the Application Settings option.*

The Framer.h Header File

The Framer.h header file is used to hold any function prototypes that we wish to export. In this example, DateAndTime() is the only function we've included in this code. Here is a listing of this file:

```
// Framer.h : main header file for the Framer DLL
//

#pragma once

#ifndef __AFXWIN_H__
    #error include 'stdafx.h' before this file for PCH
#endif
```

```
#include "resource.h"          // main symbols

__declspec( dllexport ) void WINAPI DateAndTime();

/////////////////////////////////////////////////////////////
// CFramerApp
// See Framer.cpp for the implementation of this class
//

class CFramerApp : public CWinApp
{
public:
    CFramerApp();

// Overrides
    DECLARE_MESSAGE_MAP()
};
```

Microsoft uses the extended attribute syntax—for example, __declspec—for simplifying and standardizing Microsoft-specific extensions to the C++ language. Here the **__declspec** keyword indicates that an instance of the type will be stored with a Microsoft-specific storage-class attribute.

The explicit use of the **dllexport** keyword eliminates the need for EXPORT statements in a module definition file (Framer.def). Developers of C-based DLLs are familiar with the practice of identifying all exported functions in the module definition file. That practice is now outdated.

The Framer.cpp Source Code File

The specific DLL code for this project is now added to the Framer.cpp source code file. In the following complete listing, the new code is shown in a bold font:

```
// Framer.cpp : Defines initialization routines for the DLL.
//

#include "stdafx.h"
#include "Framer.h"

#ifdef _DEBUG
#define new DEBUG_NEW

#endif
```

```
//
//      Note!
//
//          If this DLL is dynamically linked against the MFC
//          DLLs, any functions exported from this DLL which
//          call into MFC must have the AFX_MANAGE_STATE macro
//          added at the very beginning of the function.
//
//          For example:
//
//          extern "C" BOOL PASCAL EXPORT ExportedFunction()
//          {
//              AFX_MANAGE_STATE(AfxGetStaticModuleState());
//              // normal function body here
//          }
//
//          It is very important that this macro appear in each
//          function, prior to any calls into MFC. This means
//          it must appear as the first statement within the
//          function, before any object variable declarations
//          as their constructors generate calls into the MFC
//          DLL.
//
//          Please see MFC Technical Notes 33 and 58 for more
//          details.
//
/////////////////////////////////////////////////////////////
// CFramerApp

BEGIN_MESSAGE_MAP(CFramerApp, CWinApp)
END_MESSAGE_MAP()


/////////////////////////////////////////////////////////////
// CFramerApp construction

CFramerApp::CFramerApp()
{
    // TODO: add construction code here,
    // Place all significant initialization in InitInstance
}


/////////////////////////////////////////////////////////////
```

```
// The one and only CFramerApp object

CFramerApp theApp;

__declspec( dllexport ) void WINAPI DateAndTime()
{
    AFX_MANAGE_STATE(AfxGetStaticModuleState());

    // get current date and time information
    struct tm *date_time;
    time_t timer;

    time(&timer);
    date_time=localtime(&timer);

    const CString& strtime = asctime(date_time);

    // Draw a message box to the window
    AfxMessageBox(strtime, MB_OK, 0);
}
```

As you learned while examining this listing, if this DLL is dynamically linked against the MFC DLLs, which was an option selected in the MFC DLL Wizard, certain considerations must be made. Specifically, all exported functions that call into the MFC must have the AFX_MANAGE_STATE macro added at the start of the function.

The next six lines of code, in this portion of this listing, are used to retrieve the date and time information from the system. This information is then placed in a string, *strtime*.

When a call is made to this DLL, the DLL will in turn draw a message box to the window. The message box reports the date and time that the DLL was called. The message box can be canceled by clicking the OK button.

Building the Framer.dll

Build the DLL by selecting Build | Rebuild. When the build cycle is complete, the project's debug subdirectory will contain several important files.

The Framer.dll is the dynamic link library, and Framer.lib is the associated library. Both files must be placed in specific locations.

- Copy Framer.dll to your Windows subdirectory containing system DLLs. This might be any of the following: c:\windows\system, c:\windows\system32, c:\winnt\system or c:\winnt\system32.

- Copy Framer.lib to the subdirectory of the application that will use the DLL. The subdirectory for the example in this chapter will be named c:\dlldemo.

ADVANCED
PROGRAMMING CONCEPTS

In order to test the DLL, we will have to build a standard MFC application that will, in turn, call the DLL.

An Application that Calls a DLL

In this section, you will build an application designed to take advantage of the Framer.dll dynamic link library. This application, named DLLDemo, will make a single call to the DateAndTime() function in the DLL created in the previous section.

Use the following steps to create the DLLDemo base code with the MFC Application Wizard.

1. Use the Visual C++ NET File | New menu option to bring up the New Project dialog box, as shown in Figure 28-4.

2. Select the MFC Application option and name the project DLLDemo. Click OK to start the MFC Application Wizard.

3. Follow the normal project creation steps, outlined in earlier chapters, and create an application with a single-document interface using the Document/View architecture.

4. Use Wizard defaults for all other steps and build as a shared DLL.

5. Click Finish to generate the project files.

It is now up to us to add the application-specific code to the above base code. As you have already learned, the Application Wizard generates numerous files to support each application. In this case there will be five source code files and their associated header files.

There are two files that are of interest to us. The first is DLLDemoView.h and the second is DLLDemoView.cpp.

The DLLDemoView.h Header File

The DLLDemoView.h header file is used to hold any function prototypes that we wish to import. In this example, DateAndTime() is the only function we wish to use. Here is a partial listing of this file:

```
// DLLDemoView.h : interface of the CDLLDemoView class
//
/////////////////////////////////////////////////////////////////

#pragma once

extern void WINAPI DateAndTime();
```

```
class CDLLDemoView : public CView
{
protected: // create from serialization only
    CDLLDemoView();
    DECLARE_DYNCREATE(CDLLDemoView)

// Attributes
public:
    CDLLDemoDoc* GetDocument() const;
    .
    .
    .
```

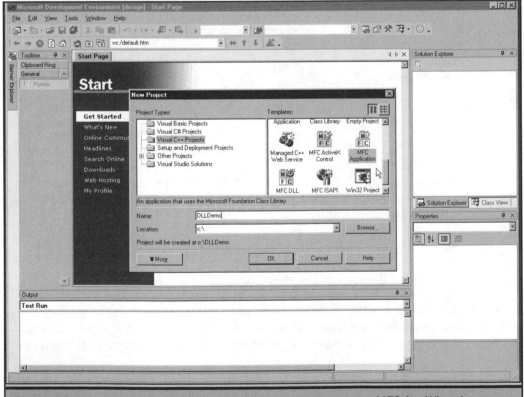

Figure 28-4.   *Use the New Project dialog box to create a new MFC AppWizard application named DLLDemo.*

The **extern** keyword alerts the compiler that this function is external to the body of the current program. During the build process, the linker will look for this function. If the linker cannot find DateAndTime() in an appropriate library, you will receive a short but sweet error message.

The DLLDemoView.cpp Source Code File

In order to handle the DLL, we'll need to modify the OnDraw() method provided in the DLLDemoView.cpp source code file. The following listing shows the modifications we have made to this method in a bold font:

```
void CDLLDemoView::OnDraw(CDC* pDC)
{
    CDLLDemoDoc* pDoc = GetDocument();
    ASSERT_VALID(pDoc);

    // TODO: add draw code for native data here

    pDC -> TextOut(280, 100, "Send text to the Window", 23);

    //Call the DLL
    DateAndTime();
}
```

Before building this project, there is one more critical step that must be taken. The DLL Frame.lib file must be identified so the linker can resolve the external functions.

This is done from the Solution Explorer pane, as shown in Figure 28-5.

Select Property Pages for the DLLDemo project as shown in the previous figure. When this option is selected, a variety of DLLDemo Property Pages will be made available to the programmer. Figure 28-6 shows that we have selected the Command Line properties under the Linker folder.

One solution to adding a DLL library resource is to simply include the path and name of that resource in the Command Line properties as shown in Figure 28-6

You can now build the application by selecting Build | Rebuild.

Run the program and you should see a screen similar to Figure 28-7.

The DLLDemo application will draw the message box on the screen anytime a WM_MOUSE message is received. This action allowed us to keep the application as simple as possible yet it demonstrates all of the steps necessary in incorporating a DLL.

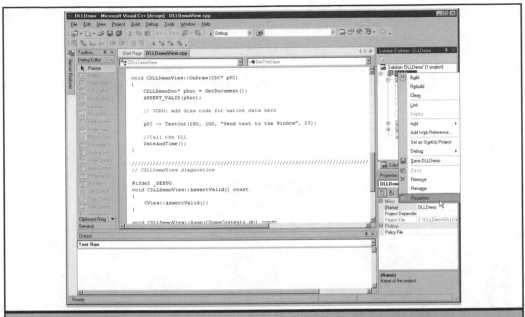

Figure 28-5. *Use the Solution Explorer pane to alter project properties.*

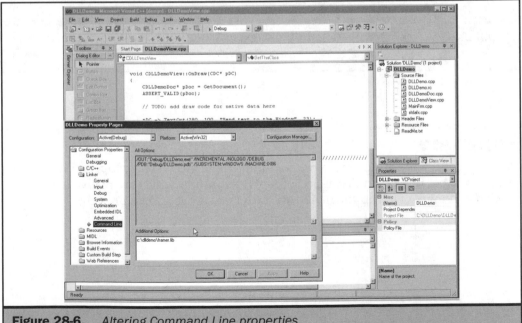

Figure 28-6. *Altering Command Line properties*

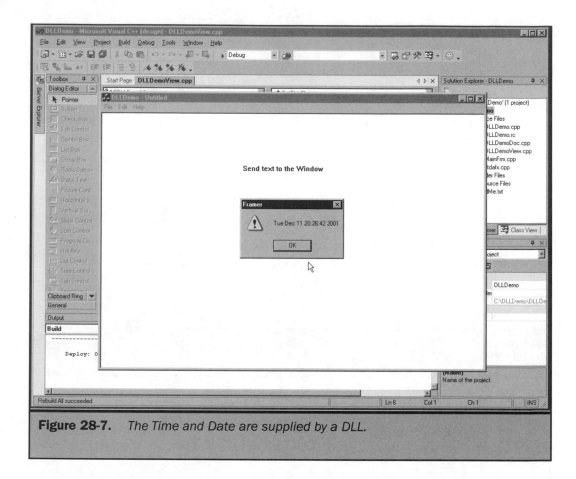

Figure 28-7. *The Time and Date are supplied by a DLL.*

Summary

DLLs are considered an advanced programming topic by most developers. We included this chapter because of our discussion of ActiveX controls, which are really small DLLs.

Can you think of a DLL you might want to create for your own project?

Chapter 29

Web Form Design

In previous chapters, you have learned a variety of C++ and C# program development techniques. However, Visual Studio.NET can take us beyond the limitations of simple applications into the realm of Web form design. In this chapter you'll learn how to design Web forms, place Web controls, set properties, and program responses. Truly interactive Web applications provide the ability to input information. This input can range from simple control interaction, to text and numeric information. In this chapter you will learn how to write programming code to gather information from the user of your Web application.

In addition to having Visual Studio.NET installed on your computer, we recommend that you also have the latest FrontPage server extensions installed and that you're operating under Windows 2000. If your system is not configured as a server or provided with server side extensions, you will not be able to correctly build the Web applications in this chapter.

Web Controls

Web applications can be designed on Web forms that are similar in appearance to the forms you have already used to develop C# applications for Windows.

In fact, the professional appearance of Visual Studio.NET Web applications comes from the standard Web forms tools provided with Visual Studio.NET. For example, the Web form designer provides these popular Web input controls, in addition to others:

- Button and ImageButton controls
- Calendar control
- CheckBox and CheckBoxList controls
- ListBox and DropDownList controls
- RadioButton and RadioButtonList controls
- TextBox controls

Additional toolkit controls can be classified as input, input/output or output controls. While other toolkit controls allow user selections and choices, the controls in our list provide a good cross section of abilities and are perhaps the most frequently used controls in Web applications. In this chapter, we'll investigate the use of several of these controls. The techniques applied to the selected controls can then be applied to almost every other control provided with the Web toolkit.

Note *If you are entering code from the pages of this book please note that several long programming lines are wrapped to the next line due to space restrictions on book pages.*

Investigating RadioButton and RadioButtonList Controls

RadioButton controls are used to present the user with a set of mutually exclusive choices. Figure 29-1 illustrates a program's interface that uses three RadioButton controls.

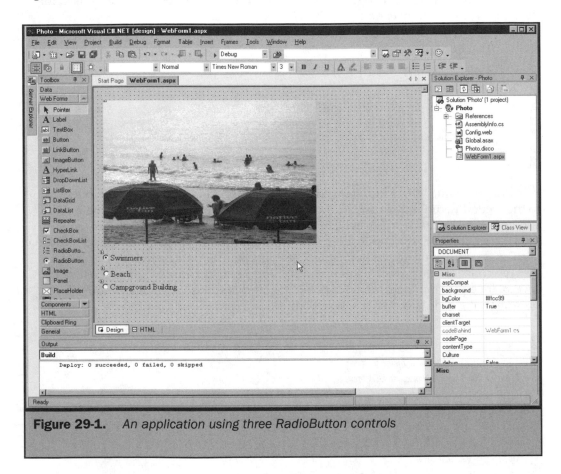

Figure 29-1.   *An application using three RadioButton controls*

This application uses an Image control and three traditional RadioButton controls. The RadioButton controls will select a picture for viewing. The first RadioButton control has its Checked property set to true at design time.

If you are creating your application to match this application, make sure you set the various control properties to match those in Figure 29-1. You can use any small photographs or JPEG images you desire.

RadioButton controls can work as a group of controls. Selecting one RadioButton control from the group effectively cancels out any other conflicting choice. For example, if a form has multiple option groups they must be physically tied to a GroupBox control.

Otherwise, all of the RadioButton controls placed directly on a form comprise a single group.

Our sample application will change picture images in the Image control in response to radioButton_CheckedChanged events. For example, the following code is used for the second RadioButton control:

```
private void RadioButton2_CheckedChanged (object sender,
    System.EventArgs e)
{
    Image1.ImageUrl = "c://beach2.jpg";
    RadioButton1.Checked = false;
    RadioButton3.Checked = false;
}
```

Now, when the "check" is changed from any other RadioButton control in the group to the second RadioButton control, the Image control's image will display the image shown. All other check marks in all of the other RadioButton controls are set to false.

The remainder of the application's code is typical of the programming code we have been examining in the previous chapters of the book. Here is a complete listing of the C# Web code for this project, named Photo. Once again, because of space constraints, several long program lines are wrapped to the next line. Also note that unique programming code is shown in a bold font:

```
using System;
using System.Collections;
using System.ComponentModel;
using System.Data;
using System.Drawing;
using System.Web;
using System.Web.SessionState;
using System.Web.UI;
using System.Web.UI.WebControls;
using System.Web.UI.HtmlControls;

namespace Photo
{
    /// <summary>
    ///     Summary description for WebForm1.
    /// </summary>
    public class WebForm1 : System.Web.UI.Page
    {
        protected System.Web.UI.WebControls.RadioButton
                RadioButton3;
```

```
protected System.Web.UI.WebControls.RadioButton
        RadioButton2;
protected System.Web.UI.WebControls.RadioButton
        RadioButton1;
protected System.Web.UI.WebControls.Image Image1;

public WebForm1()
{
    Page.Init += new System.EventHandler(Page_Init);
}

private void Page_Load(object sender, EventArgs e)
{
    // Put user code to initialize the page here
}

private void Page_Init(object sender, EventArgs e)
{
    //
    // CODEGEN: This call is required by the ASP.NET
    // Web Form Designer.
    //
    InitializeComponent();
}

#region Web Form Designer generated code
/// <summary>
///     Required method for Designer support - do
///     not modify the contents of this method with
///     the code editor.
/// </summary>
private void InitializeComponent()
{
    RadioButton1.CheckedChanged += new
        System.EventHandler
        (this.RadioButton1_CheckedChanged);
    RadioButton3.CheckedChanged += new
        System.EventHandler
        (this.RadioButton3_CheckedChanged);
    RadioButton2.CheckedChanged += new
        System.EventHandler
        (this.RadioButton2_CheckedChanged);
    this.Load += new System.EventHandler
        (this.Page_Load);
```

```
    }
    #endregion

    private void RadioButton1_CheckedChanged
        (object sender, System.EventArgs e)
    {
        Image1.ImageUrl = "c://beach1.jpg";
        RadioButton2.Checked = false;
        RadioButton3.Checked = false;
    }

    private void RadioButton2_CheckedChanged
        (object sender, System.EventArgs e)
    {
        Image1.ImageUrl = "c://beach2.jpg";
        RadioButton1.Checked = false;
        RadioButton3.Checked = false;
    }

    private void RadioButton3_CheckedChanged
        (object sender, System.EventArgs e)
    {
        Image1.ImageUrl = "c://beach3.jpg";
        RadioButton1.Checked = false;
        RadioButton2.Checked = false;
    }
  }
}
```

Figure 29-2 shows another selection being made during the program's execution.

Can you envision how this project could be expanded further to be a child's game that matches words to pictures?

Typically, Web applications use a Submit button to process form changes. However, in this application there was no need for a Submit button because each RadioButton control had its AutoPostBack property set to true at design time. Using the AutoPostBack property in this manner makes sure communications between the client and server occur automatically.

C# Web applications can take advantage of another type of RadioButton control called the RadioButtonList control. Each RadioButtonList control forms a group of multiple RadioButton controls that act together. To illustrate how RadioButtonList controls work, let's rebuild the previous example by using a single RadioButtonList control. This project will use the name RBL.

Figure 29-3 shows the layout of the initial project form while in the designer.

Figure 29-2. *Mutually exclusive RadioButton controls allow only one selection from a group.*

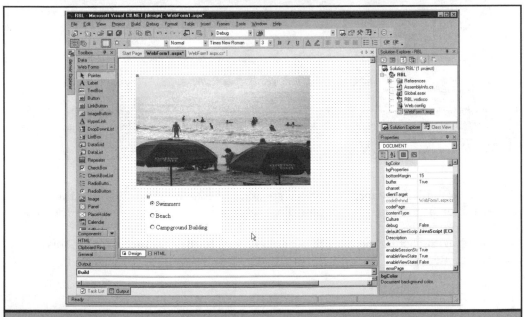

Figure 29-3. *A RadioButtonList control is used in this project.*

A single RadioButtonList control has been added to the project and stretched to the size shown in the figure. The Items property for the RadioButtonList contains information for each button displayed by the RadioButtonList control. Click on this property and you will open the ListItem Collection Editor, as shown in Figure 29-4.

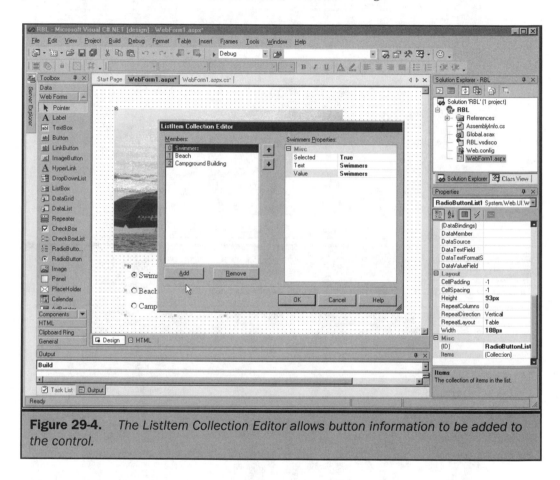

Figure 29-4.   *The ListItem Collection Editor allows button information to be added to the control.*

In this example, only three buttons were added. Note in Figure 29-4 that three other properties can be modified at this time. For each button in the control, the Selected, Text, and Value properties can be set.

The following listing includes the complete code for this example. Again, this project is named RBL:

```
using System;
using System.Collections;
using System.ComponentModel;
using System.Data;
```

```csharp
using System.Drawing;
using System.Web;
using System.Web.SessionState;
using System.Web.UI;
using System.Web.UI.WebControls;
using System.Web.UI.HtmlControls;

namespace RBL
{
    /// <summary>
    ///     Summary description for WebForm1.
    /// </summary>
    public class WebForm1 : System.Web.UI.Page
    {
        protected System.Web.UI.WebControls.Image Image1;
        protected System.Web.UI.WebControls.RadioButtonList
            RadioButtonList1;

        public WebForm1()
        {
            Page.Init += new System.EventHandler(Page_Init);
        }

        private void Page_Load(object sender, EventArgs e)
        {
            // Put user code to initialize the page here
        }

        private void Page_Init(object sender, EventArgs e)
        {
            //
            // CODEGEN: This call is required by the ASP+
            // Windows Form Designer.
            //
            InitializeComponent();
        }

        #region Web Form Designer generated code
        /// <summary>
        ///     Required method for Designer support - do
        ///     not modify the contents of this method with
        ///     the code editor.
        /// </summary>
        private void InitializeComponent()
```

```
    {
        RadioButtonList1.SelectedIndexChanged += new
            System.EventHandler
            (this.RadioButtonList1_SelectedIndexChanged);
        this.Load += new System.EventHandler
            (this.Page_Load);
    }
    #endregion

    private void RadioButtonList1_SelectedIndexChanged
        (object sender, System.EventArgs e)
    {
        if (RadioButtonList1.SelectedIndex == 0)
        {
            Image1.ImageUrl = "c://beach1.jpg";
        }
        else
            if (RadioButtonList1.SelectedIndex == 1)
        {
            Image1.ImageUrl = "c://beach2.jpg";
        }
        else
            if (RadioButtonList1.SelectedIndex == 2)
        {
            Image1.ImageUrl = "c://beach3.jpg";
        }
    }
}
}
```

The RadioButtonList control responds to a SelectedIndexChanged event. The index refers to an index provided by the ListItem Collection Editor. The first item provided for the list is held at index position 0, the second at 1, and so on.

One way to check to see if a button is selected in a RadioButtonList is to see if the index value matches a list index value. For example, in the following code the **if-else** statement was used:

```
private void RadioButtonList1_SelectedIndexChanged
    (object sender, System.EventArgs e)
{
    if (RadioButtonList1.SelectedIndex == 0)
    {
        Image1.ImageUrl = "c://beach1.jpg";
```

```
        }
        else
            .
            .
            .
```

Figure 29-5 shows this application during execution with a single button selected from the RadioButtonList control.

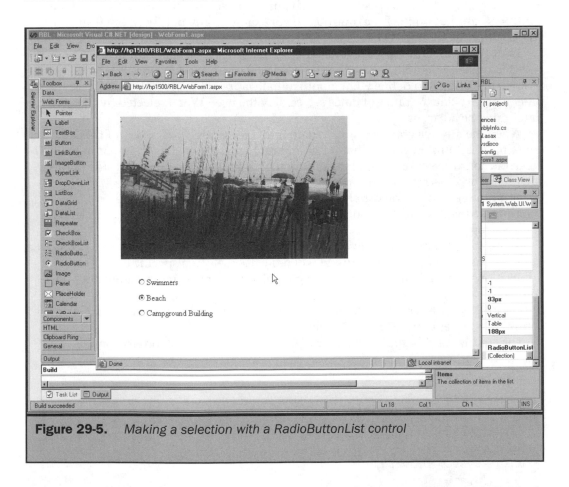

Figure 29-5.   *Making a selection with a RadioButtonList control*

The RadioButtonList control has several design advantages over the use of individual RadioButton controls: alignment, spacing, and coloring. Since individual buttons are part of a group, the alignment and spacing are automatically adjusted as you position and size the control at design time. Also, since the group of buttons function as a single group of RadioButton controls, a background color can be used to identify the collection to the user as a single group of buttons.

Investigating Calendar Controls

The Calendar control is a ASP.NET server control that can be used to display and select dates from a calendar page. The Calendar control displays a monthly calendar that can be used to view any date in any year. The control highlights the current date by default, but other dates can be selected by the user. Multiple dates can also be selected. The Calendar control can be used on a Web page to select reservation dates, determine the time of stay in days, and so on.

The Calendar control can also be used to display detailed information on a day or group of days, such as an appointment schedule, and so on. The functionality of the control is based upon the DateTime object. For example, any date between 0 and 9999 AD is supported.

The Calendar control uses several types of dates: Today's date, Visible date, and Selected date. By default, Today's date is used as the current date on the server. The Visible date is used to define what month initially appears on the calendar. The Selected date(s) gives a date or range of dates selected by the user. When selected by the user, the dates must be adjacent.

When the day selection is enabled (dates are underscored), each day of the calendar contains a LinkButton control that raises an event when clicked. In a similar manner, if week or month selection is enabled, a column of links is added to the left side of the calendar. These permit the user to select a particular week.

You can see that a wide variety of properties can be set at design time or programmed with code. Examine the Properties pane for a complete list of Calendar control properties.

In our sample application involving the use of the Calendar control, we'll print out a variety of useful information returned when the user selects a specific date. This application is named Time and uses a single Calendar control and a number of Label controls.

Figure 29-6 shows control placement while in design mode. Also note the Calendar control properties exposed in the Properties pane.

The coding for this application is straightforward, as you will observe in the following listing:

```
using System;
using System.Collections;
using System.ComponentModel;
using System.Data;
using System.Drawing;
using System.Web;
using System.Web.SessionState;
using System.Web.UI;
using System.Web.UI.WebControls;
using System.Web.UI.HtmlControls;
```

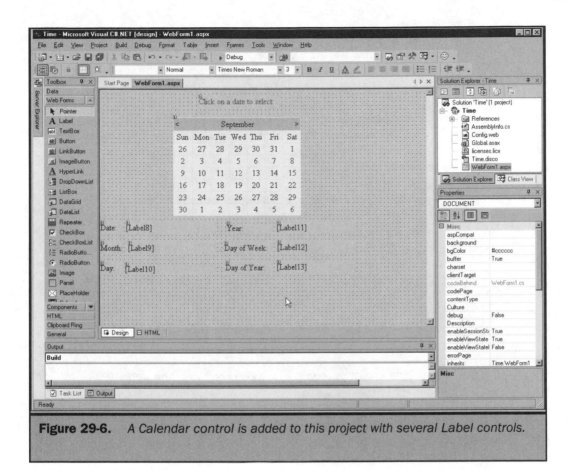

Figure 29-6. *A Calendar control is added to this project with several Label controls.*

```
namespace Time
{
/// <summary>
///     Summary description for WebForm1.
    /// </summary>
    public class WebForm1 : System.Web.UI.Page
    {
        protected System.Web.UI.WebControls.Label Label13;
        protected System.Web.UI.WebControls.Label Label12;
        protected System.Web.UI.WebControls.Label Label11;
        protected System.Web.UI.WebControls.Label Label10;
        protected System.Web.UI.WebControls.Label Label9;
        protected System.Web.UI.WebControls.Label Label8;
        protected System.Web.UI.WebControls.Label Label7;
```

```
protected System.Web.UI.WebControls.Label Label6;
protected System.Web.UI.WebControls.Label Label5;
protected System.Web.UI.WebControls.Label Label4;
protected System.Web.UI.WebControls.Label Label3;
protected System.Web.UI.WebControls.Label Label2;
protected System.Web.UI.WebControls.Label Label1;
protected System.Web.UI.WebControls.Calendar Calendar1;

public WebForm1()
{
    Page.Init += new System.EventHandler(Page_Init);
}

private void Page_Load(object sender, EventArgs e)
{
    // Put user code to initialize the page here
}

private void Page_Init(object sender, EventArgs e)
{
    //
    // CODEGEN: This call is required by the ASP.NET
    // Web Form Designer.
    //
    InitializeComponent();
}


/// <summary>
///     Required method for Designer support - do
///     not modify the contents of this method with
///     the code editor.
/// </summary>
private void InitializeComponent()
{
    Calendar1.SelectionChanged += new
        System.EventHandler
        (this.Calendar1_SelectionChanged);
    this.Load += new System.EventHandler
        (this.Page_Load);
}
```

```
        private void Calendar1_SelectionChanged (object sender,
            System.EventArgs e)
    {
        Label8.Text =
            Calendar1.SelectedDate.Date.ToString();
        Label9.Text =
            Calendar1.SelectedDate.Month.ToString();
        Label10.Text =
            Calendar1.SelectedDate.Day.ToString();
        Label11.Text =
            Calendar1.SelectedDate.Year.ToString();
        Label12.Text =
            Calendar1.SelectedDate.DayOfWeek.ToString();
        Label13.Text =
            Calendar1.SelectedDate.DayOfYear.ToString();
    }
    }
}
```

Data is gathered and processed when a SelectionChanged event is fired. This event is fired when the user selects a date from the calendar. For example, the date information can be returned with the following portion of code:

```
private void Calendar1_SelectionChanged (object sender,
    System.EventArgs e)
{
    Label8.Text = Calendar1.SelectedDate.
            Date.ToString();
    .
    .
    .
```

Figure 29-7 shows this Web project in operation.

Other interesting portions of the user's selection can be obtained individually, too. In this example we return the Month, Day, Year, Day Of Week and Day Of Year. However, it is also possible to return time information for a selected item in Hours, Minutes, Seconds, and Milliseconds.

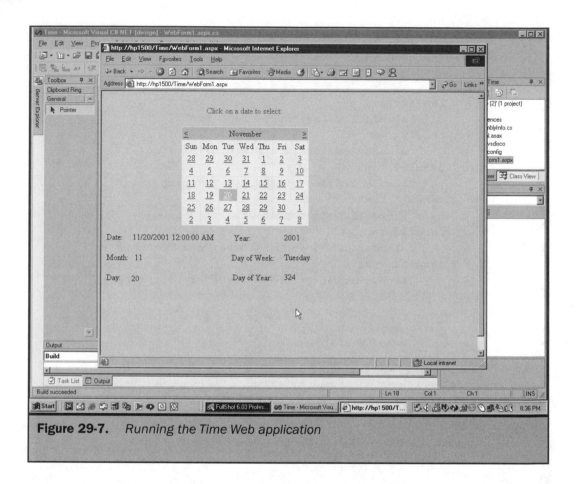

Figure 29-7.   *Running the Time Web application*

Taking Advantage of Validation Controls

Visual Studio.NET provides six unique Validation controls that can be added to Web forms. These Validation controls include the RequiredFieldValidator, CompareValidator, RangeValidator, RegularExpressionValidator, Custom Validator, and ValidationSummary controls.

The RequiredFieldValidator control is used to make sure the user has entered data (typically a TextBox control) in a required field of a form. The CompareValidator control is used to check a user-entered value against a preset value. The RangeValidator control is used to check that a user-entered value falls between a preset range of values. The RegularExpressionValidator control is used to match a user-entered value to a regular expression. The CustomValidator control is used to pass the user's input value to a customized validation routine. Finally, the ValidationSummary control is used to produce a summary of validation attempts passed by the ErrorMessage attribute of each validation control.

You will find that Validation controls are useful in ensuring that user input complies with input you expect to be entered in various Web form controls.

This section will include an example of the use of two RangeValidator controls built-in to a simple Web application named Validation.

Figure 29-8 shows the layout of the Web form, along with the insertion of two RangeValidation controls.

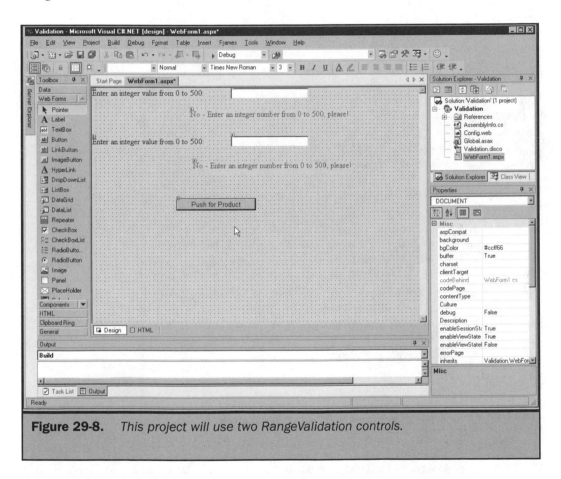

Figure 29-8.   *This project will use two RangeValidation controls.*

Examine this figure and pay particular attention to the Properties pane and the property values shown for the RangeValidator1 control. We'll be discussing these shortly.

The following listing is the complete code for the Validation example. The code that we've added is shown in a bold font:

```
using System;
using System.Collections;
using System.ComponentModel;
using System.Data;
using System.Drawing;
using System.Web;
using System.Web.SessionState;
using System.Web.UI;
using System.Web.UI.WebControls;
using System.Web.UI.HtmlControls;

namespace Validation
{
    /// <summary>
    ///     Summary description for WebForm1.
    /// </summary>
    public class WebForm1 : System.Web.UI.Page
    {
        protected System.Web.UI.WebControls.Button Button1;
        protected System.Web.UI.WebControls.RangeValidator
            RangeValidator2;
        protected System.Web.UI.WebControls.TextBox TextBox2;
        protected System.Web.UI.WebControls.Label Label2;
        protected System.Web.UI.WebControls.Label Label1;
        protected System.Web.UI.WebControls.TextBox TextBox1;
        protected System.Web.UI.WebControls.RangeValidator
            RangeValidator1;

        public WebForm1()
        {
            Page.Init += new System.EventHandler(Page_Init);
        }

        private void Page_Load(object sender, EventArgs e)
        {
            // Put user code to initialize the page here
        }

        private void Page_Init(object sender, EventArgs e)
        {
            //
```

```
        // CODEGEN: This call is required by the ASP.NET
        // Web Form Designer.
        //
        InitializeComponent();
    }

    #region Web Form Designer generated code
    /// <summary>
    ///     Required method for Designer support - do
    ///     not modify the contents of this method with
    ///     the code editor.
    /// </summary>
    private void InitializeComponent()
    {
        Button1.Click += new System.EventHandler
            (this.Button1_Click);
        this.Load += new System.EventHandler
            (this.Page_Load);
    }
    #endregion

    private void Button1_Click (object sender,
        System.EventArgs e)
    {
        Button1.Text = (int.Parse(TextBox1.Text) +
            int.Parse(TextBox2.Text)).ToString();
    }
    }
}
```

The RangeValidator controls function independently of the code we've added to the project, but we needed the project to do something!

The user is prompted to enter two integer values, each in the range 0 to 500, in two separate TextBox controls. RangeValidator controls examine each value and if a problem does not exist, the data is deemed acceptable. Information is then passed and processed by the Button_Click event to give the product of the two numbers entered by the user:

```
private void Button1_Click (object sender,
    System.EventArgs e)
{
    Button1.Text = (int.Parse(TextBox1.Text) *
                    int.Parse(TextBox2.Text)).
                    ToString();
}
```

Figure 29-9 shows the output from this application when the data complies with the range values specified.

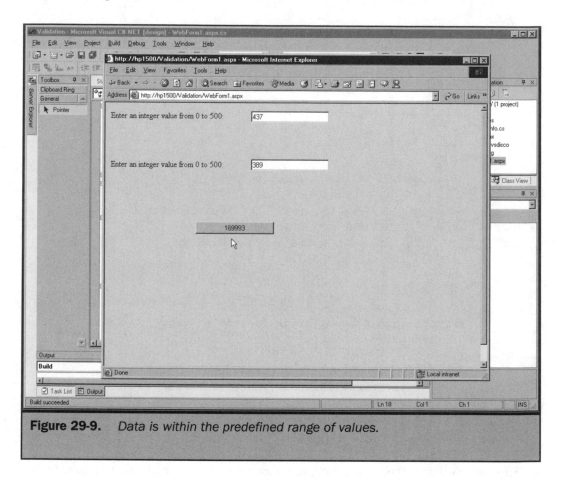

Figure 29-9.   *Data is within the predefined range of values.*

Figure 29-10 shows the RangeValidator control message when the user attempts to enter one value that exceeds the range of valid integer values.

Now, return to Figure 29-8 in order to examine the Properties pane for the first RangeValidator control. There are several important properties that must be set in order for this control to function properly.

First, the RangeValidator control must be associated with the proper TextBox control. This is done by selecting the ControlToValidate property and setting it, in this case, to TextBox1. The Text property can then be set to any message you wish to display for data that is outside of the range. Speaking of the range, the maximum value is set with the MaximumValue property and the minimum value is set with the MinimumValue property. Also, be sure to set the Type property to Integer, or the control will automatically default to String Checking.

Why not experiment with another validation control, such as RequiredFieldValidator or the CompareValidator control?

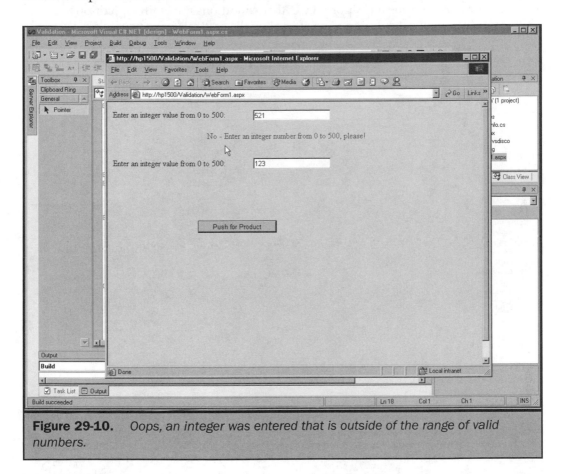

Figure 29-10.   *Oops, an integer was entered that is outside of the range of valid numbers.*

Investigating ListBox and DropDownList Controls

Programmers use ListBox controls to allow users to select single or multiple items from a list. Multiple selections are permitted when the SelectionMode property is set to Multiple. The default SelectionMode property is Single.

Programmers can also select a DropDownList control that allows the user to make single or multiple selections from a drop-down list of items. As such, the DropDownList control behaves in a manner very similar to the ListBox control.

A ListBox control, in a project named Vacation, will be used in this section to illustrate list box concepts. The Vacation application will present a ListBox control that allows the user to select a vacation destination from a short list of possible destinations. When the selection is made, it is printed in the Text field of a Label control. A small graphics icon is also displayed to the right of the ListBox control indicating acceptance of the vacation destination and giving the user an idea of the typical weather conditions for that location. For our example, the reported weather conditions are entirely fictitious.

Figure 29-11 shows the design pane after all of the controls have been placed.

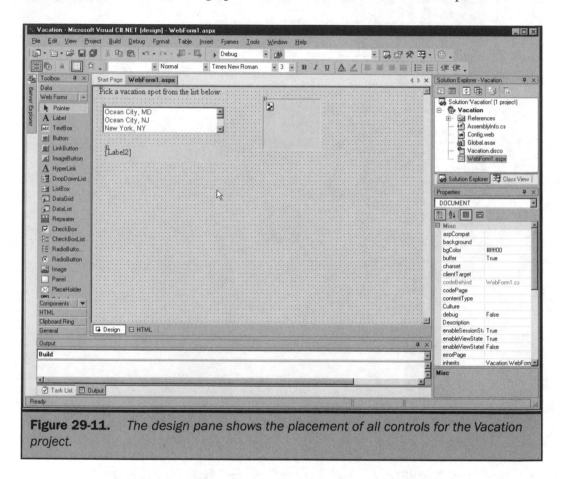

Figure 29-11.   The design pane shows the placement of all controls for the Vacation project.

Note the properties for the ListBox control shown in the Properties pane of this figure.

The following listing is the complete listing for the Vacation project. The code we added after the form was designed is shown in a bold font:

```
using System;
using System.Collections;
using System.ComponentModel;
```

```csharp
using System.Data;
using System.Drawing;
using System.Web;
using System.Web.SessionState;
using System.Web.UI;
using System.Web.UI.WebControls;
using System.Web.UI.HtmlControls;

namespace Vacation
{
    /// <summary>
    ///     Summary description for WebForm1.
    /// </summary>
    public class WebForm1 : System.Web.UI.Page
    {
        protected System.Web.UI.WebControls.Image Image1;
        protected System.Web.UI.WebControls.Label Label2;
        protected System.Web.UI.WebControls.Label Label1;
        protected System.Web.UI.WebControls.ListBox ListBox1;

        public WebForm1()
        {
            Page.Init += new System.EventHandler(Page_Init);
        }

        private void Page_Load(object sender, EventArgs e)
        {
            // Put user code to initialize the page here
        }

        private void Page_Init(object sender, EventArgs e)
        {
            //
            // CODEGEN: This call is required by the ASP.NET
            // Web Form Designer.
            //
            InitializeComponent();
        }

        #region Web Form Designer generated code
        /// <summary>
        ///     Required method for Designer support - do
        ///     not modify the contents of this method with
```

```
///     the code editor.
/// </summary>
private void InitializeComponent()
{
    ListBox1.SelectedIndexChanged += new
        System.EventHandler
        (this.ListBox1_SelectedIndexChanged);
    this.Load += new System.EventHandler
        (this.Page_Load);
}
#endregion

private void ListBox1_SelectedIndexChanged
    (object sender, System.EventArgs e)
{
    int i;

    string msg = "" ;

    for (i=0; i<ListBox1.Items.Count; i++){
        if (ListBox1.Items[i].Selected == true)
        {
            msg += "You picked: " +
                    ListBox1.Items[i].Text;
            Image1.Visible = true;

            if ((ListBox1.Items[0].Selected) ||
                (ListBox1.Items[5].Selected))
                Image1.ImageUrl = "c:\\cloud.ico";
                else if ((ListBox1.Items[1].Selected)
                    || (ListBox1.Items[6].Selected))
                    Image1.ImageUrl = "c:\\rain.ico";
                else if ((ListBox1.Items[2].Selected)
                    || (ListBox1.Items[7].Selected))
                    Image1.ImageUrl = "c:\\snow.ico";
                else if ((ListBox1.Items[3].Selected)
                    || (ListBox1.Items[8].Selected))
                    Image1.ImageUrl = "c:\\sun.ico";
                else if ((ListBox1.Items[4].Selected)
                    || (ListBox1.Items[9].Selected))
                    Image1.ImageUrl = "c:\\water.ico";
        }
```

```
            }
            Label2.Text = msg;
         }
      }
}
```

The Items property for the ListBox contains information for each item displayed by the ListBox control. Click the Items property and you will open the ListItem Collection Editor, as shown in Figure 29-12.

In this example, ten items have been added to the list. Again, note in Figure 29-12 that three other properties can be modified at this time. For each item in the list, the Selected, Text, and Value properties can be set. We'll make use of the Selected property for each item in this example.

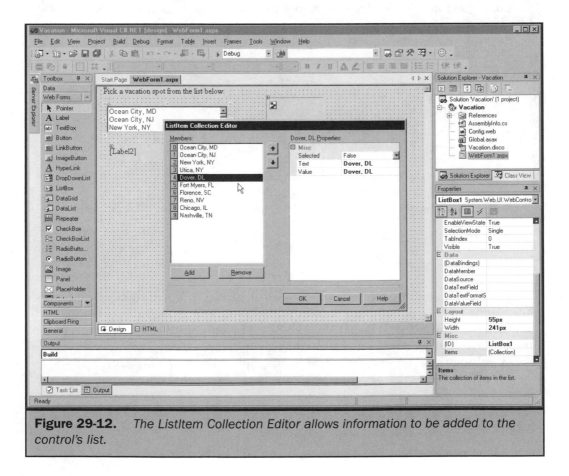

Figure 29-12. *The ListItem Collection Editor allows information to be added to the control's list.*

The following portion of code shows that the ListBox control responds to a SelectedIndexChanged event when the user makes a selection from the list:

```
private void ListBox1_SelectedIndexChanged
    (object sender, System.EventArgs e)
{
    int i;

    string msg = "" ;
        .
        .
        .
```

Next, a **for** loop is invoked to scan across all of the items in the list, checking to see which item has just been selected:

```
for (i = 0; i < ListBox1.Items.Count; i++){
    if (ListBox1.Items[i].Selected == true)
    {
        msg += "You picked: " +
                ListBox1.Items[i].Text;
        Image1.Visible = true;

        if ((ListBox1.Items[0].Selected) ||
            (ListBox1.Items[5].Selected))
            Image1.ImageUrl = "c:\\cloud.ico";
            .
            .
            .
```

When the item selected by the user has been identified (true), the Image control is made visible and one of five iconic images is displayed. The images are part of the iconic images supplied with Visual Studio.NET and were copied to the root directory of our hard drive during development. Of course, you can select any iconic image you desire for the application, even an actual photograph of the vacation destination.

Figure 29-13 shows the Web form when the user has selected one particular vacation destination.

You may to want modify this project and use it as a photographic album of your vacation snapshots.

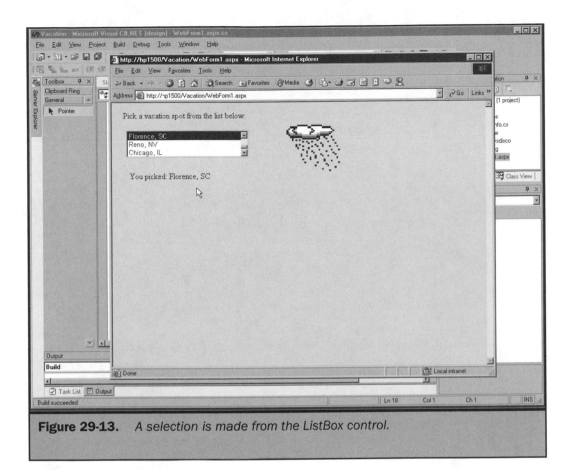

Figure 29-13.   *A selection is made from the ListBox control.*

What's Coming?

How can you reach the end of a book as large as this one and still want more? Well, you are a programmer and have an innate curiosity for solving programming problems. There are many good books on the market that will allow you to expand your knowledge into specific areas supported by Visual Studio.NET. This book has attempted to give you a solid programming foundation in C++ and a glimpse at the new world of C# as these languages apply to command-line, Windows, and Web programming. The future is yours—happy programming!

Visual C++.NET

Part VI

Appendices

Appendix A

Extended ASCII Table

Decimal	Hexadecimal	Symbol	Decimal	Hexadecimal	Symbol
0	0	(blank)	32	20	(blank)
1	1	☺	33	21	!
2	2	☻	34	22	"
3	3	♥	35	23	#
4	4	♦	36	24	$
5	5	♣	37	25	%
6	6	♠	38	26	&
7	7	✚	39	27	'
8	8	▫	40	28	(
9	9	○	41	29	)
10	A	◎	42	2A	*
11	B	♂	43	2B	+
12	C	♀	44	2C	,
13	D	♪	45	2D	-
14	E	♫	46	2E	.
15	F	☼	47	2F	/
16	10	►	48	30	0
17	11	◄	49	31	1
18	12	r	50	32	2
19	13	‼	51	33	3
20	14	∂	52	34	4
21	15	ß	53	35	5
22	16	▬	54	36	6
23	17	w	55	37	7
24	18	x	56	38	8
25	19	y	57	39	9
26	1A	→	58	3A	:
27	1B	←	59	3B	;
28	1C	∟	60	3C	<
29	1D	↔	61	3D	=
30	1E	▲	62	3E	>
31	1F	▼	63	3F	?

Decimal	Hexadecimal	Symbol	Decimal	Hexadecimal	Symbol
64	40	@	96	60	`
65	41	A	97	61	a
66	42	B	98	62	b
67	43	C	99	63	c
68	44	D	100	64	d
69	45	E	101	65	e
70	46	F	102	66	f
71	47	G	103	67	g
72	48	H	104	68	h
73	49	I	105	69	i
74	4A	J	106	6A	j
75	4B	K	107	6B	k
76	4C	L	108	6C	l
77	4D	M	109	6D	m
78	4E	N	110	6E	n
79	4F	O	111	6F	o
80	50	P	112	70	p
81	51	Q	113	71	q
82	52	R	114	72	r
83	53	S	115	73	s
84	54	T	116	74	t
85	55	U	117	75	u
86	56	V	118	76	v
87	57	W	119	77	w
88	58	X	120	78	x
89	59	Y	121	79	y
90	5A	Z	122	7A	z
91	5B	[	123	7B	{
92	5C	\	124	7C	|
93	5D	]	125	7D	}
94	5E	^	126	7E	~
95	5F	_	127	7F	Á

Decimal	Hexadecimal	Symbol	Decimal	Hexadecimal	Symbol
128	80	«	160	A0	·
129	81	¸	161	A1	Ì
130	82	È	162	A2	Û
131	83	‚	163	A3	·
132	84	‰	164	A4	Ò
133	85	‡	165	A5	—
134	86	Â	166	A6	™
135	87	Á	167	A7	∫
136	88	Í	168	A8	ø
137	89	Î	169	A9	⌐
138	8A	Ë	170	AA	¬
139	8B	Ô	171	AB	Ω
140	8C	Ó	172	AC	º
141	8D	Ï	173	AD	º
142	8E	ƒ	174	AE	´
143	8F	≈	175	AF	ª
144	90	…	176	B0	░
145	91	Ê	177	B1	▒
146	92	Δ	178	B2	▓
147	93	Ù	179	B3	│
148	94	ˆ	180	B4	┤
149	95	Ú	181	B5	╡
150	96	°	182	B6	╢
151	97	ˇ	183	B7	╖
152	98	ˇ	184	B8	╕
153	99	÷	185	B9	╣
154	9A	‹	186	BA	║
155	9B	¢	187	BB	╗
156	9C	£	188	BC	╝
157	9D	•	189	BD	╜
158	9E	Pt	190	BE	╛
159	9F	É	191	BF	┐

Decimal	Hexadecimal	Symbol	Decimal	Hexadecimal	Symbol
192	C0	└	224	E0	α
193	C1	┴	225	E1	β
194	C2	┬	226	E2	Γ
195	C3	├	227	E3	π
196	C4	─	228	E4	Σ
197	C5	┼	229	E5	σ
198	C6	╞	230	E6	μ
199	C7	╟	231	E7	τ
200	C8	╚	232	E8	ϕ
201	C9	╔	233	E9	θ
202	CA	╩	234	EA	Ω
203	CB	╦	235	EB	δ
204	CC	╠	236	EC	∞
205	CD	═	237	ED	$\varnothing$
206	CE	╬	238	EE	$\in$
207	CF	╧	239	EF	$\cap$
208	D0	╨	240	F0	$\equiv$
209	D1	╤	241	F1	$\pm$
210	D2	╥	242	F2	$\geq$
211	D3	╙	243	F3	$\leq$
212	D4	╘	244	F4	$\lceil$
213	D5	╒	245	F5	$\rfloor$
214	D6	╓	246	F6	$\div$
215	D7	╫	247	F7	$\approx$
216	D8	╪	248	F8	$\circ$
217	D9	┘	249	F9	$\bullet$
218	DA	┌	250	FA	$\bullet$
219	DB	█	251	FB	$\sqrt{}$
220	DC	▄	252	FC	ⁿ
221	DD	▌	253	FD	^{2}
222	DE	▐	254	FE	™
223	DF	▀	255	FF	(blank)

Visual C++.NET

Appendix B

DOS 10H, 21H, and 33H Interrupt Parameters

This appendix contains the most popular DOS, BIOS, and Mouse interrupts and parameters.

Screen Control with BIOS-Type 10H Interrupts

Syntax: INT 10H (when the following parameters are set to the required values).

Interface Control of the CRT

AH Value	Function	Input	Output
AH = 0	Set the mode of display	AL = 0	40×25 color text
		AL = 1	40×25 color text
		AL = 2	80×25 color text
		AL = 3	40×25 color text
		AL = 4	320×200 4-color graphics
		AL = 5	320×420 4-color graphics
		AL = 6	640×200 2-color graphics
		AL = 7	80×25 monochrome text
		AL = 13	320×200 16-color graphics
		AL = 14	640×200 16-color graphics
		AL = 15	640×350 monochrome graphics
		AL = 16	640×350 16-color graphics
		AL = 17	640×480 2-color graphics
		AL = 18	640×480 16-color graphics
		AL = 19	320×200 256-color graphics
AH = 1	Set cursor type	CH =	Bits 4–0 start of line for cursor
		CL =	Bits 4–0 end of line for cursor
AH = 2	Set cursor position	DH =	Row
		DL =	Column
		BH =	Page number of display (0 for graphics)
AH = 3	Read cursor position		DH = row
			DL = column

AH Value	Function	Input	Output
			CH = cursor mode
			CL = cursor mode
			BH = page number of display
AH = 4	Get light pen position		AH = 0, switch not down/triggered
			AH = 1, valid answers as follows:
			DH = row
			DL = column
			CH = graph line (0 to 99)
			BX = graph column (0 to 319/639)
AH = 5	Set active display page	AL =	New page value
			(0 to 7) modes 0 and 1
			(0 to 3) modes 2 and 3
AH = 6	Scroll active page up	AL =	Number of lines, 0 for entire screen
		CH =	Row, upper-left corner
		CL =	Column upper-left corner
		DH =	Row, lower-right corner
		DL =	Column, lower-right corner
		BH =	Attribute to be used
AH = 7	Scroll active page down	AL =	Number of lines, 0 for entire screen
		CH =	Row, upper-left corner
		CL =	Column, upper-left corner
		DH =	Row, lower-right corner
		DL =	Column, lower-right corner
		BH =	Attribute to be used

Handling Characters

AH Value	Function	Input	Output
AH = 8	Read attribute/ character at cursor position	BH = AL = AH =	Display page Character read Attribute of character
AH = 9	Write attribute/ character at cursor position	BH = CX = AL = BL =	Display page Count of characters to write Character to write Attribute of character
AH = 10	Write character at cursor position	BH = CX = AL =	Display page Count of characters to write Character to write

Graphics Interface

AH Value	Function	Input	Output
AH = 11	Select color palette	BH =	Palette ID (0 to 127)
		BL =	Color for above ID
			0—background (0 to 15)
			1—palette
			0—green(1), red(2), yellow(3)
			1—cyan(1), magenta(2), white(3)
AH = 12	Draw dot on screen	DX =	Row (0 to 199)
		CX =	Column (0 to 319/639)
		AL =	Color of dot
AH = 13	Read dot information	DX =	Row (0 to 199)
		CX =	Column (0 to 319/639)
		AL =	Value of dot

ASCII Teletype Output

AH Value	Function	Input	Output
AH = 14	Write to active page	AL =	Character to write
		BL =	Foreground color
AH = 15	Get video state	AL =	Current mode
		AH =	Number of screen columns
		BH =	Current display page
AH = 16	(Reserved)		
AH = 17	(Reserved)		
AH = 18	(Reserved)		
AH = 19	Write string	ES:BP =	Point to string
		CX =	Length of string
		DX =	Cursor position for start
		BH =	Page number
		AL = 0	BL = attribute (char, char, char,...char) cursor not moved
		AL = 1	BL = attribute (char, char, char,...char) cursor is moved
		AL = 2	(char, attr, char, attr...) cursor not moved
		AL = 3	(char, attr, char, attr...) cursor is moved
AH = 1A	R/W display combination code		
AH = 1B	Return functionality state information		
AH = 1C	Save/restore video state		

Specifications and Requirements for the DOS 21H Interrupt

Syntax: INT 21H (when the following parameters are set to the required values).

AH Value	Function	Input	Output
AH = 0	End of program		(similar to INT 20H)
AH = 1	Wait and display keyboard character with CTRL-BREAK check		AL = character entered
AH = 2	Display character with CTRL-BREAK check	DL =	Character to display
AH = 3	Asynchronous character input		AL = character entered
AH = 4	Asynchronous character output	DL =	Character to send
AH = 5	Character to write	DL =	Character to write
AH = 6	Input keyboard character	DL =	0FFH if character entered, 0 if none
AH = 7	Wait for keyboard character (no display)		AL = character entered
AH = 8	Wait for keyboard character (no displayó CTRL-BREAK check)		AL = character entered
AH = 9	String displayed	DS:DX	Address of string; must end with $ sentinel
AH = A	Keyboard string to buffer	DS:DX =	Address of buffer. First byte = size, second = number of characters read
AH = B	Input keyboard status		ALñno character = 0FFH character = 0
AH = C	Clear keyboard buffer and call function	AL =	1,6,7,8,0,A (function #)
AH = D	Reset default disk drive	None	None

AH Value	Function	Input	Output
AH = E	Select default disk drive		Al = number of drives DL–0 = A drive 1 = B drive, etc.
AH = F	Open file with unopened FCB	DS:DX =	Location AL = 0FFH if not found AL = 0H if found
AH = 10	Close file with FCB	DS:DX =	Location (same as AH = OFH)
AH = 11	Search directory for match of unopened FCB	 DS:DX =	AL = 0FFH if not found 00000AL = 0H if found Location DTA contains directory entry
AH = 12	Search (after AH = 11) for other files that match wildcard specifications		(Same as AH = 11H)
AH = 13	Delete file named by FCB	DS:DX =	Location (same as AH = 11H)
AH = 14	Sequential read of open file. Number of bytes in FCB (record size)	DS:DX =	Location AL = 0 transfer OK AL = 1 end of file AL = 2 overrun DTA segment AL = 3 EOF/partial read
AH = 15	Sequential write of open file. Transfer from DTA to file, with FCB update of current record	DS:DX =	Location AL = 0 transfer OK AL = 1 disk full/ROF AL = 2 overrrun DTA segment
AH = 16	Create file (length set to zero)	DS:DX =	Location (same as AH = 11H)
AH = 17	Rename file	DS:DX	Location AL = 0 rename OK AL = 0FFH no match found
AH = 18	(DOS internal use)		
AH = 19	Drive code (default)		AL–0 = A drive 1 = B drive, etc.
AH = 1A	Set Data Transfer Add	DS:DX =	Points to location

AH Value	Function	Input	Output
AH = 1B	File Allocation Table	DS:DX =	Address of FAT DX = number of units AL = record/alloc. unit CX = sector size (same as AH = 1B)
AH = 1C	Disk drive FAT information	DL =	Drive number: 0 = default, 1 = A, 2 = B
AH = 1D	(DOS internal use)		
AH = 1E	(DOS internal use)		
AH = 1F	(DOS internal use)		
AH = 20	(DOS internal use)		
AH = 21	Random read file	DS:DX =	Location of FCB (same as AH = 14H)
AH = 22	Random write file	DS:DX =	(same as AH = 21H)
AH = 23	Set file size	DS:DX =	Location of FCB AL = 0 if set AL = 0FFH if not set
AH = 24	Random record size	DS:DX =	Location of FCB
AH = 25	Set interrupt vector (change address)	DS:DX = AL =	Address of vector table Interrupt number
AH = 26	Create program segment	DX =	Segment number
AH = 27	Random block read	DS:DX =	Address of FCB AL–0 read OK 1 EOF 2 wrap around 3 partial record
AH = 28	Random block write	DS:DX =	Address of FCB AL–0 write OK 1 lack of space
AH = 29	Parse file name	DS:SI = DS:DI =	Point to command line Memory location for FCB AL = bits to set options

AH Value	Function	Input	Output
AH = 2A	Read date		CX = year (80 to 99) DH = month (1 to 12) DL = day (1 to 31)
AH = 2B	Set date		CX and DX (same as previous) AL–0 if valid 0FF if not valid
AH = 2C	Read time		CH = hours (0 to 23) CL = minutes (0 to 59)
AH = 2D	Set time		CX and DX (same as previous) AL–0 if valid 0FF if not valid
AH = 2E	Set verify state	DL = AL =	0 0 = verify off 1 = verify on
AH = 2F	Get DTA	ES:BX =	Get DTA into ES
AH = 30	Get DOS version		AL = version number AH = sub number
AH = 31	Terminate and remain resident		AL = exit code DX = memory size in paragraphs
AH = 32	(DOS internal use)		
AH = 33	CTRL-BREAK check	AL = AL =	0 = request state 1 = set the state DL = 0 for off DL = 1 for on
AH = 34	(DOS internal use)		
AH = 35	Read interrupt address	AL =	Interrupt number ES:BX point to vector address
AH = 36	Disk space available	DL =	Drive (0 = default, 1 = A, 2 = B, etc.) AX = sectors/cluster (FFFF if invalid) BX = number of free clusters CX = bytes per sector DX = total number of clusters

AH Value	Function	Input	Output
AH = 37	(DOS internal use)		
AH = 38	Country-dependent information (32-byte block)	DS:DX =	Location of memory Date/time Currency symbol Thousands separator Decimal separator
AH = 39	Make directory	DS:DX =	Address of string for directory
AH = 3A	Remove directory	DS:DX =	Address of string for directory
AH = 3B	Change directory	DS:DX =	Address of string for new directory
AH = 3C	Create a file	DS:DX = CX =	Address of string for file AX = file handle File attribute
AH = 3D	Open a file	DS:DX = AL =	Address of string for file 0 = open for reading 1 = open for writing 2 = open for both AX returns file handle
AH = 3E	Close a file handle	BX =	File handle
AH = 3F	Read a file or device	BX = CX = DS:DX =	File handle Number of bytes to read Address of buffer AX = number of bytes read
AH = 40	Write a file or device	BX = CX = DS:DX =	File handle Number of bytes to read Address of buffer AX = number of bytes written
AH = 41	Delete a file	DS:DX =	Address of file string
AH = 42	Move file pointer	BX = AL = CX:DX DX:AX	File handle Pointer's starting location Number of bytes Current file pointer
AH = 43	Set file attribute	AL = 1 CX = DS:DX =	 Attribute Address of file string
AH = 45	Duplicate file handle	BX	File handle AX = returned file handle

AH Value	Function	Input	Output
AH = 46	Force duplicate file handle	BX	File handle CX = second file handle
AH = 47	Current directory	DL = DS:SI =	Drive number (0 = default, 1 = A drive, 2 = B drive) Buffer address DS:SI returns address of string
AH = 48	Allocate memory	BX	Number of paragraphs AX = allocated blocks
AH = 49	Free allocated memory	ES	Segment of returned block
AH = 4A	Set block	ES BX	Segment block New block size
AH = 4B	Load/execute program	DS:DX	Location of ASCIIZ string (drive/path/filename) AL–0 = load and execute 3 = load/no execute
AH = 4C	Terminate (exit)	AL	Binary return code (all files closed)
AH = 4D	Retrieve return code		AX returns exit code of another program
AH = 4E	Find first matching file	DS:DX	Location of ASCIIZ string (drive/path/filename) CX = search attribute DTA completed
AH = 4F	Next matching file		(AH = 4EH called first)
AH = 50	(DOS internal use)		
AH = 51	(DOS internal use)		
AH = 52	(DOS internal use)		
AH = 53	(DOS internal use)		
AH = 54	Verify state	None	AL–0 if verify off 1 if verify on
AH = 55	(DOS internal use)		
AH = 56	Rename file	DS:DX = ES:DI =	Address of string for old information Address of string for new information

AH Value	Function	Input	Output
AH = 57	Get/set file date/time	AL	00 (return)
			01 (set)
		BX	File handle
		DX and CX	Date and time information
AH = 59	Extended error code	BX =	DOS version (3.0 = 0)
			AX = error code
			BH = class of error
			BL = suggested action
			CH = where error occurred
AH = 5A	Create temporary file		CX = file attribute
			CF = Set on error
			AX = error code
		DS:DX =	Points to string
AH = 5B	Create a new file		(same as previous)

Note *For DOS versions above 2.0, use AH = 36H for file management.*

Mouse Control Functions Accessed Through Interrupt 33H

Syntax: INT 33H (when the following parameters are set to the required values)

AH Value	Function	Input	Output
AX = 0	Install flag and reset	BX =	If AX = 0 and BX = –1
		CX =	Mouse support not available
		DX =	AX = –1, then BX = number of supported mouse buttons
AX = 1	Show pointer	BX =	Does nothing if already visible, otherwise
		CX =	increments the pointer-draw flag by 1
		DX =	Shows pointer image when pointer-draw flag = 0

AH Value	Function	Input	Output
AX = 2	Hide pointer	BX = CX = DX =	Does nothing if already hidden, otherwise decrements the pointer-draw flag Value of –1 hides image
AX = 3	Get position and button status	BX = CX = DX =	For 2- or 3-button mice, BX returns which button pressed: 0 = leftmost, 1 = rightmost, 2 = center button. Button 3 to 15 reserved. CX = x coordinate; DX = y coordinate of pointer in pixels
AX = 4	Set pointer position	CX = DX =	New horizontal position in pixels New vertical position in pixels For values that exceed screen boundaries, screen maximum and minimum are used

AX = 5	Get button press information	BX =	Button status requested, where 0 = leftmost, 1 = rightmost, 2 = center button.
			AX–bit 0 (leftmost) = 0 or 1
			    bit 1 (rightmost) = 0 or 1
			        bit 2 (center) = 0 or 1
			If 0 button up, and if 1 button down. BX = number of times button pressed since last call
			CX = horizontal coordinate of mouse
			DX = vertical coordinate of mouse

AX = 6	Get button release information	BX =	Button status requested, same format as for AX = 5 previosly described. AX, BX, CX, and DX as previously described. If 0, button up; 1 if button down

AH Value	Function	Input	Output
AX = 7	Set minimum and maximum horizontal position	CX =	Minimum virtual-screen horizontal coordinate in pixels
		DX =	Maximum virtual-screen horizontal coordinate in pixels
AX = 8	Set minimum and maximum vertical position	DX =	Maximum virtual-screen vertical coordinate in pixels
AX = 9	Set graphics pointer block	BX=	Pointer hot-spot horizontal coordinate in pixels
		CX =	Pointer hot-spot vertical coordinate in pixels
		DX =	Address of screen/pointer masks
		ES =	Segment of screen/pointer masks
AX = 10	Set text pointer	BX =	Pointer select value
		CX =	Screen mask value/hardware cursor start scan line
		DX =	Pointer mask value/ hardware cursor stop scan line BX = 0 select software text pointer BX = 1 select hardware cursor CX and DX bit map to: 0 to 7 character 8 to 10 foreground color 11 intensity 12 to 14 background color 15 blinking
AX = 11	Read mouse motion counters	BX = CX = DX =	CX = horizontal count DX = vertical count Range –32,768 to +32, 768 read in mickeys

AH Value	Function	Input	Output
AX = 12	Set user-defined subroutine	CX = DX = ES =	Call mask Offset of subroutine Segment of subroutine CX word bit map: 0 pointer position changed 1 leftmost button pressed 2 leftmost button released 3 rightmost button pressed 4 rightmost button released 5 center button pressed 6 center button released 7 to 15 reserved = 0 Following values loaded when subroutine is called: AX = condition of mask BX = button status CX = pointer horizontal coordinate DX = pointer vertical coordinate SI = last vertical mickey count read DI = last horizontal mickey count read
AX = 13	Light pen emulation on	BX = CX = DX =	Instructs mouse driver to emulate a light pen Vertical mickey/pixel ratio Ratios specify number of mickeys per 8 pixels
AX = 14	Light pen emulation off	BX = CX = DX =	Disables mouse driver light pen emulation (Same as AX = 13)
AX = 15	Set mickey/pixel ratio	CX = DX =	Horizontal mickey/pixel ratio (Same as AX = 13)

AH Value	Function	Input	Output
AX = 16	Conditional off	CX = DX = SI = DI =	Left column coordinate in pixels Upper row coordinate in pixels Right column coordinate in pixels Lower row coordinate in pixels Defines an area of the screen for updating
AX = 19	Set double speed threshold	BX = DX =	Doubles pointer motion Threshold speed in mickeys/second
AX = 20	Swap user-defined subroutine	CX = DX = ES =	Call mask Offset subroutine Segment of subroutine Sets hardware interrupts for call mask and subroutine address, returns previous values CX word call mask: 0 pointer position changed 1 leftmost button pressed 2 leftmost button released 3 rightmost button pressed 4 rightmost button released 5 center button pressed 6 center button released 7 to 12 reserved = 0 Following values loaded when subroutine is called: AX = condition of mask BX = button status CX = pointer horizontal coordinate DX = pointer vertical coordinate SI = last vertical mickey count read DI = last horizontal mickey count read

AH Value	Function	Input	Output
AX = 21	Get mouse state storage requirements	BX = CX = DX =	Gets size of buffer in bytes needed to store state of the mouse driver BX = size of buffer in bytes
AX = 22	Save mouse driver state	BX = CX = DX = ES =	Saves the mouse driver state Offset of buffer Segment of buffer
AX = 23	Restore mouse driver state	BX = CX = DX = ES =	Restores the mouse driver state from a user buffer Offset of buffer Segment of buffer

Index

G

INTERNATIONAL CONTACT INFORMATION

AUSTRALIA
McGraw-Hill Book Company Australia Pty. Ltd.
TEL +61-2-9417-9899
FAX +61-2-9417-5687
http://www.mcgraw-hill.com.au
books-it_sydney@mcgraw-hill.com

CANADA
McGraw-Hill Ryerson Ltd.
TEL +905-430-5000
FAX +905-430-5020
http://www.mcgrawhill.ca

GREECE, MIDDLE EAST,
NORTHERN AFRICA
McGraw-Hill Hellas
TEL +30-1-656-0990-3-4
FAX +30-1-654-5525

MEXICO (Also serving Latin America)
McGraw-Hill Interamericana Editores S.A. de C.V.
TEL +525-117-1583
FAX +525-117-1589
http://www.mcgraw-hill.com.mx
fernando_castellanos@mcgraw-hill.com

SINGAPORE (Serving Asia)
McGraw-Hill Book Company
TEL +65-863-1580
FAX +65-862-3354
http://www.mcgraw-hill.com.sg
mghasia@mcgraw-hill.com

SOUTH AFRICA
McGraw-Hill South Africa
TEL +27-11-622-7512
FAX +27-11-622-9045
robyn_swanepoel@mcgraw-hill.com

UNITED KINGDOM & EUROPE
(Excluding Southern Europe)
McGraw-Hill Education Europe
TEL +44-1-628-502500
FAX +44-1-628-770224
http://www.mcgraw-hill.co.uk
computing_neurope@mcgraw-hill.com

ALL OTHER INQUIRIES Contact:
Osborne/McGraw-Hill
TEL +1-510-549-6600
FAX +1-510-883-7600
http://www.osborne.com
omg_international@mcgraw-hill.com